THE ENCYCLOPÆDIA BRITANNICA
ELEVENTH EDITION

VOLUME II SLICE V

Arculf to Armour, Philip

ARCULF, a Gallican bishop and pilgrim-traveller, who visited the Levant about 680, and was the earliest Christian traveller and observer of any importance in the Nearer East after the rise of Islam. On his return he was driven by contrary winds to Britain, and so came to Iona, where he related his experiences to his host, the abbot Adamnan (679-704). This narrative, as written out by Adamnan, was presented to Aldfrith the Wise, last of the great Northumbrian kings, at York about 701, and came to the knowledge of Bede, who inserted a brief summary of the same in his *Ecclesiastical History of the English Nation*, and also drew up a separate and longer digest which obtained great popularity throughout the middle ages as a standard guide-book (the so-called *Libellus de locis sanctis*) to the Holy Places of Syria. Arculf is the first to mention the column at Jerusalem, which claimed to mark the exact centre of the Inhabited Earth, and later became one of the favourite Palestine wonders. Besides a valuable account of the principal sacred sites of Judaea, Samaria and Galilee as they existed in the 7th century, he also gives important information as to Alexandria and Constantinople, briefly describes Damascus and Tyre, the Nile and the Lipari volcanoes, and refers to the caliph Moawiya I. (A.D.661-680), whom he pictures as befriending Christians and rescuing the "sudarium" of Christ from the Jews. Arculf's record is especially useful from its plans, drawn from personal observation by the traveller himself, of the churches of the Holy Sepulchre and of Mount Sion in Jerusalem, of the Ascension on Olivet and of Jacob's well at Sichem. It is also a useful witness to the prosperity and trade of Alexandria after the Moslem conquest: it tells us how the Pharos was still lit up every night; and it gives us (from Constantinople) the first form of the story of St George which ever seems to have attracted notice in Britain.

Thirteen MSS. of the original Arculf-Adamnan narrative exist, and fully 100 of Bede's abridgment: of the former, the most important, containing all the plans, are (1) Bern, Canton Library, 582, of 9th cent.; (2) Paris, National Library, Lat. 13,048, of 9th cent.; a third MS., London, B. Mus., Cotlon, Tib. D. V., of 8th-9th cents., though damaged by fire and lacking the illustrations, is of value for the text, being the oldest of all. Among editions the first is of 1619, by Gretser; the best, that of 1877, by Tobler, in *Itinera et Descriptiones Terrae Sanctae*; we may also mention that of 1870, by Delpit, in his *Essai sur les anciens pelerinages à Jérusalem*; see also Delpit's remarks upon Arculf in the same work, pp. 260-304; Beazley, *Dawn of Modern Geography*, i. 131-40 (1897).

ARDASHIR, the modern form of the Persian royal nameARTAXERXES (*q.v.*), "he whose empire is excellent." After the three Achaemenian kings of this name, it occurs in Armenia, in the shortened form Artaxias (Armenian, Artashes or Artaxes), and among the dynasts of Persia who maintained their independence during the Parthian period (see PERSIS). One of these, (1) Artaxerxes or ARDASHIR I. (in his Greek inscriptions he calls himself Artaxares, and the same form occurs in Agathias II. 25, iv. 24), became the founder of the New-Persian or Sassanian empire. Of his reign we have only very scanty information, as the Greek and Roman authors mention only his victory over the Parthians and his wars with Rome. A trustworthy tradition about the origin of his power, from Persian sources, has been preserved by the Arabic historian Tabari (Th. Nöldeke, *Geschichte der Perser und Araber zur Zeit der Sasaniden, aus der arabischen Chronik des Tabari*, 1879). He was the second son of Pāpak (Bābek), the offspring of Sassan (Sāsān), after whom the dynasty is named. Pāpak had made himself king of the district of Istakhr (in the neighbourhood of Persepolis, which had fallen to ruins). After the death of Pāpak and his oldest son Shapur (Shāhpuhr, Sapores), Ardashir made himself king (probably A.D. 212), put his other brothers to death and began war against the neighbouring dynasts of Persis. When he had conquered a great part of Persis and Carmania, the Parthian king Artabanus IV. interfered. But he was defeated in three battles and at last killed (A.D. 236). Ardashir now considered himself sovereign of the whole empire of the Parthians and called himself "King of Kings of the Iranians." But his aspirations went farther. In Persis the traditions of the Achaemenian empire had always been alive, as the name of Ardashir himself shows, and with them the national religion of Zoroaster. Ardashir, who was a zealous worshipper of Ahuramazda and in intimate connexion with the magian priests, established the orthodox Zoroastrian creed as the official religion of his new kingdom, persecuted the infidels, and tried to restore the old Persian empire, which under the Achaemenids had extended over the whole of Asia from the Aegean Sea to the Indus. At the same time he put down the local dynasts and tried to create a strong concentrated power. His empire is thus quite different in character from the Parthian kingdom of the Arsacids, which had no national and religious basis but leant towards Hellenism, and whose organization had always been very loose. Ardashir extirpated the whole race of the Arsacids, with the exception of those princes who had found refuge in Armenia, and in many wars, in which, however, as the Persian tradition shows, he occasionally suffered heavy defeats, he succeeded in subjugating the greater part of Iran, Susiana and Babylonia. The Parthian capital Ctesiphon (*q.v.*) remained the principal residence of the Sassanian kingdom, by the side of the national metropolis

Istakhr, which was too far out of the way to become the centre of administration. Opposite to Ctesiphon, on the right bank of the Tigris, Ardashir restored Seleucia under the name of Weh-Ardashir. The attempt to conquer Mesopotamia, Armenia and Cappadocia led to a war with Rome, in which he was repelled by Alexander Severus (A.D. 233). Before his death (A.D. 241) Ardashir associated with himself on the throne his son Shapur, who successfully continued his work.

Under the tombs of Darius I. at Persepolis, on the surface of the rock, Ardashir has sculptured his image and that of the god Ahuramazda (Ormuzd or Ormazd). Both are on horseback; the god is giving the diadem to the king. Under the horse of the king lies a defeated enemy, the Parthian king Artaban; under the horse of Ormuzd, the devil Ahriman, with two snakes rising from his head. In the bilingual inscription (Greek and Pahlavi), Ardashir I. calls himself "the Mazdayasnian [*i.e.* "worshipper of Ahuramazda"] god Artaxares, king of the kings of the Arianes (Iranians), of godly origin, son of the god Pāpak the king." (See Sir R. Ker Porter, *Travels* (1821-1822), i. 548 foll.; Flandin et Coste, *Voyage en Perse*, iv. 182; F. Stolze and J.C. Andreas, *Persepolis*, pl. 116; Marcel Diculafoy, *L'Art antique de la Perse*, 1884-1889, v. pl. 14). A similar inscription and sculpture is on a rock near Gur (Firuzabad) in Persia. On his coins he has the same titles (in Pahlavi). We see that he, like his father and his successors, were worshipped as gods, probably as incarnations of a secondary deity of the Persian creed.

Like the history of the founder of the Achaemenian empire, that of Ardashir has from the beginning been overgrown with legends; like Cyrus he is the son of a shepherd, his future greatness is predicted by dreams and visions, and by the calculations of astronomers he becomes a servant at the court of King Artabanus and then flies to Persia and begins the rebellion; he fights with the great dragon, the enemy of god, &c. A Pahlavi text, which contains this legend, has been translated by Nöldeke (*Geschichte des Artachshīr i Pāpakān*, 1879). On the same tradition the account of Firdousi in the Shahnama is based; it occurs also, with some variations, in Agathias ii. 26 f. Another work, which contained religious and moral admonitions which were put into the mouth of the king, has not come down to us. On the other hand the genealogy of Ardashir has of course been connected with the Achaemenids, on whose behalf he exacts vengeance from the Parthians, and with the legendary kings of old Iran.

(2) ARDASHIR II. (379-383). Under the reign of his brother Shapur II. he had been governor (king) of Adiabene, where he persecuted the Christians. After Shapur's death, he was raised to the throne by the magnates, although more than seventy years old. Having tried to make himself independent from the court, 449and having executed some of the grandees, he was deposed after a reign of four years.

(3) ARDASHIR III. (628-630), son of Kavadh II., was raised to the throne as a boy of seven years, but was killed two years afterwards by his general, Shahrbaraz.

(ED. M.)

ARDEA, a town of the Rutuli in Latium, 3 m. from the S.W. coast, where its harbour (*Castrum Inui*) lay, at the mouth of the stream now known as Fosso dell' Incastro, and 23 m. S. of Rome by the Via Ardeatina. It was founded, according to legend, either by a son of Odysseus and Circe, or by Danae, the mother of Perseus. It was one of the oldest of the coast cities of Latium, and a place of considerable importance; according to tradition the Ardeatines and Zacynthians joined in the foundation of Saguntum in Spain. It was the capital of Turnus, the opponent of Aeneas. It was conquered by Tarquinius Superbus, and appears as a Roman possession in the treaty with Carthage of 509 B.C., though it was later one of the thirty cities of the Latin league. In 445 B.C. an unfair decision by the Romans in a frontier dispute with Aricia led, according to the Roman historians, to a rising; the town became a Latin colony 442 B.C., and shortly afterwards it appears as the place of exile of Camillus. It had the charge of the common shrine of Venus in Lavinium. It was devastated by the Samnites, was one of the 12 Latin colonies that refused in 209 B.C. to provide more soldiers, and was in 186 used as a state prison, like Alba and Setia. In imperial times the unhealthiness of the place led to its rapid decline, though it remained a colony. In the forests of the neighbourhood the imperial elephants were kept. A road, the Via Ardeatina, led to Ardea direct from Rome; the gate by which it left the Servian wall was the Porta Naevia; a large tomb behind the baths of Caracalla lay on its course. The gate by which it left the Aurelian wall has been obliterated by the bastion of Antonio da Sangallo (Ch. Hülsen in *Römische Mitteilungen*, 1894, 320).

The site of the primitive city, which later became the citadel, is occupied by the modern town; it is situated at the end of a long plateau between two valleys, and protected by perpendicular tufa cliffs some 60 ft. high on all sides except the north-east, where it joins the plateau. Here it is defended by a fine wall of *opus quadratum* of tufa, in alternate courses of headers and stretchers. Within its area are scanty remains of the podium of a temple and of buildings of the imperial period. The road entering it from the south-west is deeply cut in the rock. The area of the place was apparently twice extended, a further portion of the narrow plateau, which now bears the name of Civita Vecchia, being each time taken in and defended by a mound and ditch; the nearer and better-preserved is about ½ m. from the city and measures some 2000 ft. long, 133 ft. wide and 66 ft. high, the ditch being some 80 ft. wide. The second, ½ m. farther north-east, is smaller. In the cliffs below the plateau to the north are early rock habitations, and upon the plateau primitive Latin pottery has been found. In 1900 a group of tombs cut in the rock was examined; they are outside the farther mound and ditch, and belong, therefore, to the period after the second extension of the city.

See O. Richter, in *Annali dell' Istituto* (1884), 90; J.H. Parker in *Archaeologia*, xlix. 169 (1885); A. Pasqui, in *Notizie degli scavi*, (1900) 53.

(T. As.)

ARDEBIL, or ARDABIL, chief town of a district, or sub-province, of same name, of the province of Azerbaijan in north-western Persia, in lat. 38° 14′ N., and long. 48° 21′ E., and at an elevation of 4500 ft. It is situated on the Baluk Su (Fish river), a tributary of the Kara Su (Black river), which flows northwards to the Aras, and in a fertile plain bounded on the west by Mount Savelan, a volcanic cone with an altitude of 15,792 ft. (Russian triangulation), and on the east by the Talish mountains (9000 ft.). Ardebil has a population of about 10,000, and post and telegraph offices. Its trade, principally in the hands of Armenians, is still important, but is chiefly a transit trade between Russia and Persia by way of Astara, a port on the Caspian 30 m. north-east of Ardebil. It is surrounded by a ruinous mud wall flanked by towers; a quarter of a mile east of it stands a mud fort, 180 yds. square, constructed according to European system of fortification. Inside the city are the famous sepulchres and shrines of Shaikh Safi ud-din and his descendant Shah Ismail I. (1502-1524) the first Shiah shah of Persia and founder of the Safavi dynasty. Plans and photographs of the shrines were taken in 1897 by Dr F. Sarre of Berlin and published in 1901 (*Denkmäler Persischer Baukunst*; 65 large folio plates).

European and Chinese merchants resided at Ardebil in the middle ages, and for a long time the city was a great emporium for central Asian and Indian merchandise, which was forwarded to Europe via Tabriz, Trebizond and the Black Sea, and also by way of the Caucasus and the Volga. Since the beginning of the 16th century, when Persia fell under the sway of the Safavis, the place has been much frequented by pilgrims who come to pay their devotions at the shrine of Shaikh Safi. This shrine is a richly endowed establishment with mosques and college attached, and had a fine library containing many rare and valuable MSS. presented by Shah Abbas I. at the beginning of the 17th century, and mostly carried off by the Russians in 1828 and placed in the library at St Petersburg. The grand carpet which had covered the floor of one of the mosques for three centuries was purchased by a traveller about 1890 for 100 pounds, and was finally acquired by the South Kensington Museum for many thousands. This beautiful carpet measures 34 ft. by 17 ft. 6 in., and contains 380 hand-tied knots in the square inch, which gives over 32,500,000 knots to the whole carpet (W. Griggs, *Asian Carpet Designs*).

(A. H. S.)

ARDÈCHE, an inland department of south-eastern France, formed in 1790 from the Vivarais, a district of Languedoc. Pop. (1906) 347,140. Area, 2145 sq. m. It is bounded N.W. by the department of Loire, E. by the Rhone which divides it from Isère and Drôme, S. by Gard and W. by Lozère and Haute-Loire. The surface of Ardèche is almost entirely covered by the Cévennes mountains, the main chain, continued in the Boutières mountains, forming its western boundary. Its centre is traversed from south-east to north-west by the Coiron range which extends from the Rhone to the Mont Mézenc (5755 ft.), the highest point in the department, and the oldest of its many volcanoes. These mountains separate the southern half of the department, which comprises the basin of the Ardèche, from the northern half which is watered by numerous smaller tributaries of the Rhone, the chief of which are the Érieux and the Doux. A few rivers belong to the Atlantic side of the watershed, the chief being the Loire, which rises on the western borders of the department, and the Allier, which for a short distance separates it from Lozère. Nearly all the rivers of the department are of torrential swiftness and subject to sudden floods. The scenery through which they flow is often of great beauty and grandeur. Natural curiosities are the Pont d'Arc, over the Ardèche, and the Chaussée des Géants, near Vals. The climate in the valley of the Rhone is, in general, warm, and sometimes very hot; but westward, as the elevation increases, the cold becomes more intense and the winters longer. Some districts, especially in summer, are liable to sudden alterations in the temperature. Rye, wheat and potatoes are the chief crops cultivated. Good red and white wines are grown in the hilly region bordering the Rhone valley, the white wine of St Péray being highly esteemed. The principal fruits are the chestnut,

3

which is largely exported, the olive and the walnut. In the rearing of silk-worms, Ardèche ranks second to Gard among French departments, and great numbers of mulberry trees are grown for the purposes of this industry. The many goats and sheep of Ardèche make it one of the chief sources of supply of skins for glove-making. Mines of coal, iron, lead and zinc are worked, and the quarries furnish hydraulic lime (Le Teil) and other products. Besides flour-mills, distilleries and saw-mills, there are important silk-mills and leather-works and paper-factories. Annonay is the principal industrial town. The department exports wine, cattle, lime, mineral waters, silk, paper, &c. Hot springs are numerous, and some of them, as those of Vals, St Laurent-les-Bains, Celles and Neyrac, are largely resorted to. Ardèche is served by the Paris-Lyon-Méditerranée railway and has some 43 m. 450 of navigable waterway. The department is divided into the arrondissements of Privas, Largentière and Tournon, with 31 cantons and 342 communes. It forms the diocese of Viviers and part of the archiepiscopal province of Avignon. It is in the region of the XV. army corps, and within the circumscription of the *académie* (educational division) of Grenoble. Its court of appeal is at Nimes. Privas, the capital, Annonay, Aubenas, Largentière and Tournon are the principal towns. Bourg-St Andéol, Thines, Mélas and Cruas have interesting Romanesque churches. Mazan has remains of a Cistercian abbey founded in the 12th century to which its vast church belongs. Viviers is an old town with a church of various styles of architecture and several old houses.

ARDEE, a market-town of Co. Louth, Ireland, in the south parliamentary division, on the river Dee, 48 m. N. by W. from Dublin on a branch of the Great Northern railway. Pop. (1901) 1883. It has some trade in grain and basket-making. The town is of high antiquity, and its name (Ather-dee) is taken to signify the ford of the Dee. A form Ath-Firdia, however, is connected with the ancient story of the warrior Cuchullain of Ulster, who, while defending the ford against the men of Connaught, was forced to slay many with whom he was on friendly terms, and among them the warrior Firdia, whom he regarded with special affection. A castle of the lords of the manor was built early in the 14th century, and remains, as does another adjacent fortified building of the same period. Roger de Peppart, lord of the manor early in the 13th century, founded the present Protestant church and a house of Crutched Friars. There was also a house of Carmelite Friars, but neither of these remains. Ardee received its first recorded charter in 1377. It had a full share in the several Irish wars, being sacked by Edward Bruce (1315) and by O'Neill (1538); and it was taken by the Irish and recaptured by the English in the wars of 1641, and was occupied later by the forces of James II. and of William III. It returned two members to the Irish parliament. A large rath, or encampment, with remains of fortifications, stands to the south of the town.

ARDEN, FOREST OF, a district in the north of Warwickshire, England, the "woodland" as opposed to the "felden," or "fielden," *i.e.* open country, in the south, the river Avon separating the two. Originally it was part of a forest tract of far wider extent than that within the confines of the county, and now, though lacking the true character of a forest, it is still unusually well wooded. The undulating surface ranges for the most part from 250 to 500 ft. in elevation. Wide lands in this district were held in the time of Edward the Confessor by Alwin, whose son Thurkill of Warwick, or "of Arden," founded the family of the Warwickshire Ardens who in Queen Elizabeth's time still held several of the manors ascribed to Thurkill in *Domesday*. Shakespeare, whose mother Mary Arden claimed to be of this family, knew the district well, living as he did at Stratford; and its natural characteristics, then still unchanged, inspired his pictures of forest life in *As You Like It*. The name of the Forest of Arden, besides remaining a convenient designation of a well-marked physical area, is preserved in such place-names as Henley-in-Arden and Hampton-in-Arden.

ARDENNES, a district covering some portion of the ancient forest of Ardenne, and extending over the Belgian province of Luxemburg, part of the grand duchy, and the French department of Ardennes. Bruzen Lamartinière states in his *Dictionnaire Géographique* that the Gauls and Bretons called it by a word signifying "the forest," which was turned into Latin as *Arduenna silva*, and he thinks it quite probable that the name was really derived from the Celtic word *ardu* (dark, obscure). The Arduenna Silva was the most extensive forest of Gaul, and Caesar (*Bello Gallico*, lib. vi. cap. 29) describes it as extending from the Rhine and the confines of the Treviri as far as the limits of the Nervii. In book v. the Roman conqueror describes his campaign against Indutiomarus and the Treviri in the Ardenne forest. Strabo gave it still greater extent, treating it as covering the whole region from the Rhine to the North Sea. It is safer to give it the more reasonable dimensions of Caesar, and to accept the verdict of later commentators that it never extended west of the Scheldt. At the division of the empire of Charlemagne between the

4

three sons of Louis the Débonnaire, effected by the pact of Verdun in 843, the forest had become a district and is called therein *pagus Arduensis*. It was part of the division that fell to Lothair, and several of the charters of 843 expressly specify certain towns as being situated in this *pagus*. In the 10th century the district had become a *comitatus*, subject to the powerful count of Verdun, who changed his style to that of count of Ardenne.

The Belgian Ardennes may be said now to extend from the Meuse above Dinant on the west to the grand duchy of Luxemburg and Rhenish Prussia as far north as the Baraque de Michel on the east, and from a line drawn eastward from Dinant through Marche, Durbuy and Stavelot to the Hautes Fagnes on the north, to the French frontier roughly marked by the Semois valley in the south. Within these limits there are still some of the finest woods in Europe, which seem to have come down to us almost intact from the days of the Arduenna of Caesar. Notable among these portions of the great forest are the woods of St Hubert, the woods round La Roche, and those of the Amerois, Herbeumont, and Chiny on the Semois. In the grand duchy the forest has almost entirely disappeared, but owing to the compulsory law of replanting in Belgium this fate does not seem likely to attend the Belgian Ardennes.

In addition to being a forest the Ardennes is a plateau, and it offers to the geologist a most interesting field of investigation. The greater part of the Ardennes is occupied by a large area of Devonian beds, through which rise the Cambrian masses of Rocroi and Stavelot, and a few others of smaller size. Upon the folded slates and schists which constitute these inliers the Devonian rests with marked unconformity; but north of the ridge of Condroz Ordovician and Silurian beds make their appearance. Near Dinant carboniferous beds are infolded among the Devonian. Along the northern margin lies the intensely folded belt which constitutes the coalfield of Namur, and, beneath the overlying Mesozoic beds, is continued to the Boulonnais, Dover and beyond. The southern boundary of this belt is formed by a great thrust-plane, the *faille du midi*, along which the Devonian beds of the south have been thrust over the carboniferous beds of the coalfield.

The Ardennes are the holiday ground of the Belgian people, and much of this region is still unknown except to the few persons who by a happy chance have discovered its remoter and hitherto well-guarded charms. There is still an immense quantity of wild game to be found in the Ardennes, including red and roe deer, wild boar, &c. The shooting is preserved either by the few great landed proprietors left in the country, or by the communes, who let the right of shooting to individuals. Occasionally it is still stated in the press that wolves have been seen in the Ardennes, but this is a mere fiction. The last wolf was destroyed there in the 18th century.

ARDENNES, a department of France on the N.E. frontier, deriving its name from that of the forest, and formed in 1790 from parts of Champagne, Picardy and Hainault. Pop. (1906) 317,505. Area, 2028 sq. m. It is bounded N. and N.E. by Belgium, E. by the department of Meuse, S. by that of Marne, and W. by that of Aisne. In shape it is quadrilateral with a cape-like prolongation into Belgium on the north. The slope of the department is from north-east to south-west, though its longest river, the Meuse, entering it in the south-east, pursues a winding course of 111 m. in a north-westerly, and afterwards through deep gorges in a northerly, direction. The other principal river, the Aisne, crosses the southern border and takes a northerly, then a westerly course, separating the region known as Champagne Pouilleuse from the more elevated plateau of Argonne which forms the central zone of the department and stretches to the left bank of the Meuse. The highest points of the department are found in the wooded highlands of the Ardennes which, with an altitude varying between 980 and 1640 ft., cover the north and north-east. The climate is comparatively mild in the south-west, but becomes colder and more rainy towards the north and north-east. Agriculture is carried on to 451 most advantage in the Champagne and Argonne. Wheat and oats are the predominant cereals. Potatoes, rye, lucerne and other kinds of forage are also important crops. Pasturage is found chiefly on the banks of the Aisne and Meuse and on the plateau of Rocroi in the north. Horse-raising is carried on in the neighbourhood of Buzancy in the south, and at Bourg-Fièele in the north. Fruit-growing is confined to the west and central districts. The working of slate is very important, especially in the neighbourhood of Fumay, and quarries producing freestone, lime-stone and other minerals are found in several places. Flour-mills, saw-mills, sugar-works, distilleries and leather-works are scattered over the department, but iron-founding and various branches of metal-working which are active along the valley of the Meuse (Nouzon, &c.) are the chief industries. To these may be added wool-weaving, centred at Sedan, and minor industries such as the manufacture of basket-work, wooden shoes, &c. Coal and raw wool are prominent imports, while iron goods, cloth, timber, live-stock, alcohol and the products of the soil are exported. Various branches of the Eastern railway traverse the department. The Meuse is canalized within the department, and the Canal des Ardennes, uniting that river with the Aisne, and the lateral canal of the Aisne are together about 65 m. long. Ardennes is divided into five arrondissements: Mézières, Rocroi, Rethel, Vouziers and Sedan, with 31 cantons and 503 communes. The department forms part of the ecclesiastical province of Reims and of the circumscriptions of the appeal-court of Nancy and the VI. army corps. In educational matters, it is included in the *academic* (educational area) of Lille. Mézières, the capital, Charleville, Rocroi, Sedan and Rethel are the chief towns. Outside them its finest examples of architecture are the churches of Mouzon (13th century) and Vouziers (15th century).

ARDGLASS ("Green Height"): a small town of Co. Down, Ireland, in the east parliamentary division, at the head of a rocky bay, in a picturesque situation between two hills, 32 m. S. by E. of Belfast on a branch of the Belfast & Co. Down railway. Pop. (1901) 501. Soon after the Norman invasion it became of the first importance as a port, a fact attested by the remains of no fewer than five castles in close proximity, which give the town a picturesque aspect. There are also an ancient church crowning the eastern hill, and a curious fortified warehouse (called the New Works), dating probably from the 14th century, when a trading company was established here under a grant from Henry IV. Ardglass was a royal burgh and sent a representative to the Irish parliament. The chief industry is the herring fishery. Ships of 500 tons may enter the harbour at all times. In summer Ardglass is a frequented resort of visitors; good bathing and a golf links contribute to its attractions.

ARDITI, LUIGI (1822-1903), Italian musical composer and conductor, was born in Piedmont, and studied music at the Conservatoire in Milan, starting professionally as a violinist, and touring with Bottesini, the double-bass player, in the United States in 1847. He began composing at an early age, and in 1840 produced an overture, followed by an opera *I Briganti* in 1841, and other works. He paid frequent visits to America, conducting the opera in New York, where he produced his *La Spia* in 1856. In 1858 he became conductor of the opera at Her Majesty's theatre in London, and both in London and abroad he became famous in this capacity, having the reputation of being Madame Patti's favourite conductor. His vocal waltz *Il Bacio* was often sung by her. In 1896 he published his *Reminiscences*, and after a long and active musical life he died at Brighton on the 1st of May 1903.

ARDMORE, a township and the county-seat of Carter county, Oklahoma, U.S.A., just S. of the Arbuckle Mountains, about 120 m. S. by E. of Guthrie. Pop. (1900) 5681; (1907) 8759 (2122 being negroes, and 108 Indians); (1910) 8618. It is served by the Chicago, Rock Island & Pacific, the St Louis & San Francisco, and the Gulf, Colorado & Santa Fé railways. Ardmore is the market-town and distributing point for the surrounding agricultural region, which is the home of a large part of the Chickasaw and Choctaw nations. It is situated 890 ft. above the sea in a cotton and grain producing region, in which cattle are raised and fruit and vegetables grown; coal, oil, natural gas and rock asphalt (which is used for paving the streets of Ardmore) are found in the vicinity. Ardmore is an important cotton market, and has cotton gins, a cotton compress, machine shops, bridge works, foundries, bottling works and manufactories of cotton-seed oil, brick, concrete, flour, brooms, mattresses and dressed lumber. At Ardmore are the Saint Agnes Academy, a Catholic school for girls, and Saint Agnes College for boys, a conservatory of music, Hargrove College, and the Selvidge Commercial College. Near Ardmore is a summer school on the Chautauqua (*q.v.*) system. Ardmore was founded in 1887, and was incorporated in 1898.

ARDRES, a town of northern France in the department of Pas-de-Calais, 10½ m. by rail S.S.E. of Calaís', with which it is also connected by a canal. Pop. (1906) 1269. The "Field of the Cloth of Gold," where Henry VIII. of England and Francis I. of France met in 1520, was at Balingham in the immediate neighbourhood. The town is an important market for cattle.

ARDROSSAN, a seaport, burgh of barony, and police burgh of Ayrshire, Scotland, 32 m. from Glasgow by the Glasgow & South-Western railway, and 29½ m. by the Lanarkshire & Ayrshire branch of the Caledonian railway. Pop. (1901) 6077. The rise of Ardrossan was due to the enterprise of Hugh, 12th earl of Eglinton, who began the construction of the present town and harbour in 1806. The harbour was intended to be in connexion with a canal from Glasgow to Ardrossan, but this was only completed as far as Johnstone. Owing to the costliness of the undertaking, and the death of the earl in 1819, the works were suspended after an outlay of £100,000, but his successor completed the scheme on a reduced scale at an expense of another £100,000. The dock accommodation has since been considerably extended, and the town enjoys great prosperity. Steamers run every week-day to Arran and Belfast, and during summer there is a service also to Douglas in the Isle of Man. The exports consist principally of coal and iron from collieries and ironworks in the neighbourhood; and the imports of timber, ores and general goods. Shipbuilding thrives and the fisheries are important. The town is governed by a provost and council.

SALTCOATS (pop. 8120), a mile to the south, is a popular seaside resort, with a brisk trade, due to its proximity to Ardrossan and Stevenston; the making of salt, once a leading industry, has ceased.

Ardrossan dates from an early period. The name Arthur of Ardrossan is found in connexion with a charter dated 1226; and Sir Fergus of Ardrossan accompanied Edward Bruce in his Irish expedition in 1316, and in 1320 signed the appeal to the pope, made by the barons of Scotland, against the aggressions of England. The family of Ardrossan is now merged, by marriage, in that of the earl of Eglinton and Winton. The castle where Wallace surprised the English garrison and threw their corpses into the dungeon, grimly styled "Wallace's Larder," was finally destroyed by Cromwell, who is said to have used part of its masonry for the construction of the fort at Ayr; but its ruins still exist.

AREA, a Latin word, originally meaning a threshing-floor, namely a raised space in a field exposed on all sides to the wind; now applied in English (1) to a plot of ground on which a structure is to be erected, (2) to the court or sunk space in the front or rear of a building, (3) to the superficial space covered by a district, country, &c., or by a building or court.

ARECIBO, a city and port on the north coast of Porto Rico, at the mouth of a small stream called the Rio Grande de Arecibo, and contiguous to one of the most fertile regions of the island. Pop. (1899) 8008; of the tributary district, about 30,000; (1910) 9612. It is connected with San Juan, Mayaguezand Ponce by railway. It is a well-built and active commercial city, and has a large export trade in coffee and sugar. The harbour is an open roadstead, very dangerous to shipping in northerly winds, and the discharge and loading of cargoes is effected by means of lighters at considerable risk and expense. Arecibo was founded in 1788.

452

AREMBERG, or ARENBERG, formerly a German duchy of the Holy Roman Empire in the circle of the Rhine Palatinate, between Julich and Cologne, and now belonging to the Prussian administrative district of Coblenz. The hamlet of Aremberg is at the foot of a basalt hill 2067 ft. high, on the summit of which are the ruins of the castle which was the original seat of the family of Aremberg.

The lords of Aremberg first appear early in the 12th century, but had died out in the male line by 1279. From the marriage of the heiress Mathilda (1282-1299) with Engelbert II., count of La Marck (d. 1328), sprang two sons. The elder of these, Adolf II, (d. 1347), inherited the countship of La Marck; the second, Engelbert III. (d. 1387), the lordship of Aremberg, which he increased by his marriage with Marie de Looz, heiress of Lumain. The lordship of Aremberg remained in his family till 1547, when it passed, by his marriage with Margaret, sister of the childless Robert III., to John of Barbancon, of the great house of Ligne, who assumed the name and arms of Aremberg, and was created a count of the Empire by Charles V. He was governor of Friesland, and for a while commanded the Spanish and Catholic forces against the "beggars," falling at the battle of Heiligerlee in 1568. His son Charles (d. 1618) greatly increased the possessions of the house by his marriage with Ann of Croy, heiress of Croy and of Chimay-Aerschot, and in 1576 was made prince of the Empire by Maximilian II. His grandson, Philip Francis, was made duke in 1644 by the emperor Ferdinand III., and was succeeded by his brother Charles Eugene (d. 1681), who married Marie Henriette de Vergy de Cusance, heiress of Perwez (d. 1700). Their son, Duke Philip Charles Francis, was killed in 1691 fighting against the Turks, and was succeeded by Leopold (1754), a distinguished soldier of the War of the Spanish Succession, and patron of Rousseau and Voltaire. His son Charles (d. 1778) was an Austrian field-marshal during the Seven Years' War, and married Louise Margaret of La Marck-Lumain, heiress of the countship of Schleiden and lordship of Saffenberg. By the peace of Luneville (February 1801), the next duke, Louis Engelbert, lost the greater part of his ancestral domain, but received in compensation Meppen and Recklinghausen. On the establishment of the confederation of the Rhine, his son Prosper Louis (to whom, becoming blind, he had ceded his domains in 1803) became a member (1806), and showed great devotion to the interests of France; but in 1810 he lost his sovereignty, Napoleon incorporating Meppen with France and Recklinghausen with the grand-duchy of Berg, and indemnifying him by a rent of 240,702 francs. In 1815 he received back his possessions, which were mediatized by the congress of Vienna, Recklinghausen falling to Prussia and Meppen to Hanover. On account of the one portion he became a peer of the Westphalian estates, and by the other a member of the upper house in

7

Hanover. George IV. of England (9th May 1826) elevated the duke's Hanoverian possessions to a dukedom under the title of Aremberg Meppen. His brother Auguste Raymond, Comte de la Marck (1753-1833), became famous during the early stages of the French Revolution for his friendship with Mirabeau (*q.v.*). Duke Prosper Louis died in 1861, and was succeeded by his son Engelbert (d. 1875), who was followed in his turn by his son Engelbert (b. 1872).

The duke of Aremberg is one of the wealthiest of the great continental nobles. His feudal domain in Germany covers an area of over 1100 sq. m., besides which he has large estates in Belgium and France. The duke has residences in Brussels, where he has a famous collection of pictures, and at the château of Klemenswerth near Meppen.

ARENA (Lat. for "sand"), the central area of an amphitheatre on which the gladiatorial displays took place, its name being derived from the sand with which it was covered. The word is applied sometimes to any level open space on which spectacles take place.

ARENDAL, a seaport of Norway, in Nedenaes *amt* (county), on the south coast, 46 m. N.E. from Christiansand. Pop. (1900) 11,155. It rises picturesquely above the mouth of the river Nid, with a good harbour protected by an island from the open waters of the Skagerrack. The town itself occupies several islets, and some of the houses are supported above the water on piles. The chief exports are timber (very largely exported to Great Britain), wood-pulp, sealskins and felspar. In 1879 Arendal ranked second (after Christiania) as a ship-owning port; in 1899 it had dropped to the fifth place. In and near the town are factories for wood-pulp, paper, cotton and joinery; and at Fevig, 8 m. north-east, a shipbuilding yard and engineering works. The neighbourhood is remarkable for the number of beautiful and rare minerals found there; one of these, a variety of epidote, was formerly called Arendalite. Louis Philippe stayed here for some time during his exile.

ARENIG GROUP, in geology, the name now applied by British geologists to the lowest stage of the Ordovician System in Britain. The term was first used by Adam Sedgwick in 1847 with reference to the "Arenig Ashes and Porphyries" in the neighbourhood of Arenig Fawr, in Merioneth, North Wales.

The rock-succession in the Arenig district has been recognized by W.G. Fearnsides ("On the Geology of Arenig Fawr and Moel Llanfnant," *Q.J.G.S.* vol. lxi., 1905, pp. 608-640, with maps) as follows:—

	Caradoc	*Dicranograptus*— shales. Defrel or *Orthis*	
	Llandeilo Group	Rhyolitic ashes = Upper Massive ashes = Middle Acid andesitic ashes = Lower	Upper Ashes of Arenig.
		Daerfawr Shales.	Zone of *Didymograptus Murchisoni.*
Or dovician		Platy ashes Great Agglomerate	Lower Ashes of Arenig (Hypersthene Andesites).
	Arenig Group	Olchfa or *Bifidus*— shales	(*Didymograptus bifidus*).
		Filltirgerig or *Hirundo* Beds Erewnt or *Ogygia*— limestone	*Didymograptus Hirundo.*
		Henllan or *Calymene*—ashes Llyfnant or *Extensus* flags Basal Grit	*Didymograptus extensus.*

(unconformity)

The above succession is divisible into: (1) a lower series of gritty and calcareous sediments, the "Arenig Series," as it is now understood; (2) a middle series, mainly volcanic, with shales, the

8

"Llandeilo Series"; and (3) the shales and limestones of the Bala or Caradoc Stage. It was to the middle series (2) that Sedgwick first applied the term "Arenig."

In the typical region and in North Wales generally the Arenig series appears to be unconformable upon the Cambrian rocks; this is not the case in South Wales. The Arenig series is represented in North Wales by the Garth grit and Ty-Obry beds, by the Shelve series of the Corndon district, the Skiddaw slates of the Lake District, the Ballantrae group of Ayrshire, and by the Ribband series of slates and shales in Wicklow and Wexford. It may be mentioned here that the "Llanvirn" Series of H. Hicks was equivalent to the bifidus-shales and the Lower Llandeilo Series.

REFERENCES.—Adam Sedgwick, *Synopsis of the Classification of the British Palaeozoic Rocks* (1885); Sir A. Ramsay, "North Wales," *Geol. Survey Memoir*, vol. iii.; C. Lapworth, *Ann. Mag. Nat, Hist.* vol. vi., 1880; G.A.J. Cole and C.V. Jennings, *Q.J.G.S.*vol. xlv., 1889; C.V. Jennings and G.J. Williams, *ibid.* vol. xlvii., 1891; Messrs Crosfield and Skeat, *ibid.* vol. lii., 1896; G.L. Elles,*Geol. Mag.*, 1904; J.E. Marr and T. Roberts,*Q.J.G.S.*, 1885; H. Hicks, *ibid.* vol. xxxi., 1875. See also ORDOVICIAN.

(J. A. H.)

AREOI, or AREOITI, a secret society which originated in Tahiti and later extended its influence to other South Pacific islands. To its ranks both sexes were admitted. The society was primarily of a religious character. Members styled themselves descendants of Oro-Tetifa, the Polynesian god, and were divided into seven or more grades, each having its characteristic tattooing. Chiefs were at once qualified for the highest grade, but ordinary members attained promotion only through initiatory rites. The Areois enjoyed great privileges, and were considered as depositaries of knowledge and as mediators between God and man. They were feared, too, as ministers of the taboo and were entitled to pronounce a kind of excommunication for offences against its rules. The chief religious purpose of the society was the worship of the generative powers of nature, and the ritual and ceremonies of initiation were grossly licentious. But the 453Areois were also a social force. They aimed at communism in all things. The women members were common property; the period of cohabitation was limited to three days, and the female Areois were bound by oath at initiation to strangle at birth any child born to them. If, however, the infant was allowed to survive half an hour only, it was spared; but to have the right of keeping it the mother must find a male Areoi willing to adopt it. The Areois travelled about, devoting their whole time to feasting, dancing (the chief dance of the women being the grossly indecent *Timorodee* mentioned by Captain Cook), and debauchery, varied by elaborate realistic stage presentments of the lives and loves of gods and legendary heroes.

AREOPAGUS (Ἄρειος Πάγος), a bare, rocky hill, 370 ft. high, immediately west of the northern rim of the acropolis of Athens. The ancients interpreted the name as "Hill of Ares." Though accepted by some modern scholars, this derivation of the word is rendered improbable by the fact that Ares was not worshipped on the Areopagus. A more reasonable explanation connects the name with*Arae*, "Curses," commonly known as *Semnae*, "Awful Goddesses," whose shrine was a cave at the foot of the hill, of which they were the guardian deities (Aeschyl. Eumen. 417, 804; Schol. on Lucian, vol. iii. p. 68, ed. Jacobitz; Paus. i. 28. 6).

The Boulē, or Council, of the Areopagus (ἡ ἐν Ἀρείῳ Πάγῳ βουλή), named after the hill, is to be compared in origin and fundamental character with the council of chiefs or elders which we find among the earliest Germans, Celts, Romans, and other primitive peoples. Under the kings of Athens it must have closely resembled the Boule of elders described by Homer; and there can be no doubt that it was the chief factor in the work of transforming the kingship into an aristocracy, in which it was to be supreme. It was composed of ex-archons. Aristotle attributes to it for the period of aristocracy the appointment to all offices (*Ath. Pol.* viii. 2), the chief work of administration, and the right to fine or otherwise punish in cases, not only of violation of laws, but also of immorality (*ibid.* iii. 6; cf. Isoc. vii. 46; Androtion and Philochorus, in Müller, *Frag. Hist. Graec.* i. 387. 17, 394 60).1 This evidence is corroborated by the remnants of political power left to it in later time, after its importance had been greatly curtailed, and by the designation Boule, which in itself indicates that the body so termed was once a state council. In a passage bearing incidentally upon the early constitution of Athens, Thucydides (i. 126. 8) informs us that at the time of the Cylonian insurrection the Athenians, we may suppose in their assembly (Ἐκκλησία), commissioned the archons with absolute power to deal with the trouble at their discretion. From this passage, if we accept the Aristotelian view as to the early supremacy of the Areopagitic council, we must infer that a modification of the aristocracy in a popular direction had at that time already taken place.

9

In addition to its political functions, the council from the time of Draco, if not earlier, exercised jurisdiction in certain cases of homicide (see below, *ad fin.*). The assumption that in their criminal jurisdiction the Areopagites were called Ephetae till after the legislation of Draco (of. Philoch. 58, in Müller, *ibid.* 394) would explain the otherwise obscure circumstances that, according to Plutarch (*Sol.* 19), Draco (*q.v.*) in his laws mentioned only the Ephetae, and that Pollux (viii. 125) included the Areopagus among the localities in which sat the Ephetae.2 The same assumption would supply a reason for the notion entertained by many writers of later time that the Areopagitic council was instituted by Solon (*q.v.*)—a notion partly explained also by the desire of political thinkers to ascribe to Solon the making of a complete constitution. Conformably with the view here presented we may suppose that the name "Boule of the Areopagus" developed from the simple term "Boulē" in order to distinguish it from the new Boulē (*q.v.*), or Council of Four Hundred. The popular reforms of Solon (594 B.C.), so far as they were carried into effect, tended practically to limit the Council of the Areopagus, though constitutionally it retained all its earlier powers and functions, augmented by the right to try persons accused of conspiracy against the state (Arist. *Ath. Pol.* viii. 4). In the exercise of its duty as the protector of the laws it must have had power to inhibit in the Four Hundred, or in the Ecclesia, a measure which it judged unconstitutional or in any way prejudicial to the state, and in the levy of fines for violation of law or moral usage it remained irresponsible. As censor of the conduct of citizens it inquired into every man's source of income and punished the idle (Plut. *Sol.*22).

The tyrants (560-510 B.C.) left to the council its cognizance of murder cases (Demosth. xxiii. 66; Arist. *Ath. Pol.* xvi. 8) and probably the nominal enjoyment of all its prerogatives; but their method of filling the archonship with their own kinsmen and creatures gradually converted the Areopagites into willing supporters of tyranny. Though hostile, therefore, to the policy of Cleisthenes, their council seems to have suffered no direct abridgment of power from his reforms. After his legislation it gradually changed character and political sentiment by the annual admission of ex-archons who had held office under a popular constitution. In 487 B.C., however, the introduction of the lot as a part of the process of filling the archonship (see ARCHON) began to undermine its ability. This deterioration was necessarily slow; it could not have advanced far in 480 B.C., when on the eve of the battle of Salamis, as we are informed (Arist. *Polit.* viii. 4, p. 1304a, 17; *Ath. Pol.* xxiii. 25; Plut. *Them.* 10; Cic. *Off.* i. 22, 75), the council of the Areopagus succeeded in manning the fleet by providing pay for the seamen, thereby regaining the confidence and respect of the people. The patriotic action of the council and its attendant popularity enabled it to recover considerable administrative control, which it continued to exercise for the next eighteen years, although its deterioration in ability, becoming every year more noticeable, as well as the rapid rise of democratic ideas, prevented it from fully re-establishing the supremacy which Aristotle, with some exaggeration, attributes to it for this period. Its prestige was seriously undermined by the conduct of individual members, whose corrupt use of power was exposed and punished by Ephialtes, the democratic leader. Following up this advantage, Ephialtes (462 B.C.), and less prominently Archestratus and Pericles (*q.v.*), proposed and carried measures for the transfer of most of its functions to the Council of Five Hundred, the Ecclesia, and the popular courts of law (Arist. *Ath. Pol.* xxv. 2, xxvii. 1, xxxv. 2; Plut.*Per.* 9). Among these functions were probably jurisdiction in cases of impiety, the supervision of magistrates and the censorship of the morals of citizens, the inhibition of illegal and unconstitutional resolutions in the Five Hundred and the Ecclesia, the examination into the fitness of candidates for office, and the collection of rents from the sacred property (of. Wilamowitz-Mollendorff, *Arist. u. Ath.* ii. 186-197; Busolt, *Griech. Gesch.* (2nd ed.) iii. 269-294; G. Gilbert, *Const. Antiq. of Sparta and Athens*, Eng. trans., 154 f.). It retained jurisdiction in cases of homicide and the care of sacred olive trees. From this time to the establishment of the Thirty (462-404 B.C.) the Areopagitic council, degraded still further by the opening of the archonship to the Zeugitae (457 B.C.) and by the absolute use of the lot in filling the office, was a political nullity. The first indication of a revival of its prestige is to be traced in the action attributed to it by Lysias during the siege of Athens (404 B.C.) (in *Eratosth.* 69: πραττούσης μὲν τῆς ἐν Ἀρείῳ Πάγῳ βουλῆς σωτηρία). After the surrender of Athens and the appointment of the Thirty, the repeal of the laws of Ephialtes and Archestratus prepared the way for the rehabilitation of the council as guardian of the constitution by the restored democracy (Arist. *Ath. Pol.*xxxv. 2; decree of Tisamenus, in Andoc. i. 84; cf. Din. i. 9). Although under the new conditions the Areopagites could not hope to recover their full supremacy, they did exercise considerable political influence, especially in crises. In the time of Demosthenes, accordingly, we find them annulling the election of individuals to offices for which they were unfit (Plut. *Phoc.* 16), exercising during a crisis a disciplinary power extending to life and death over all the Athenians "in conformity with ancestral law," procuring the banishment of one, the racking of another, and the infliction of

10

capital punishment on several of the citizens. This authority seems to have been delegated to them by the assembly with reference either to individual cases or temporarily to the whole body of Athenians (Din. i. 10, 62 f.; Aeschin. iii. 252; Lye.*Leoc.* 52; Demosth. xviii. 132 f.; Plut. *Demosth.* 14). Religion, too, was their care (Pseud. Demosth. lix. 80 f.). Lycurgus (*ibid.*) even goes so far as to claim chat by their action during the crisis after Chaeroneia they had saved the state. After the period of the great orators their influence continued to grow. Demetrius of Phalerum empowered them to assist the *gynaeconomi* in supervising festivals held in private houses (*Philoch.* in Müller, *ibid.* i. 408. 143). Under Roman supremacy in addition to earlier functions they had jurisdiction in cases of forgery, tampering with the standard measures, and probably other high crimes, the supervision of buildings, and the care of religion and of education (Cic. *Fam.* xiii. i; *Att.* v. 9; Tac. *Ann.* ii. 55; Plut. *Cic.* 24;*C.I.G.* i. 123. 9; *C.I.A.* ii. 476; iii. 703, 714, 716; Acts xvii. 19). Their council acquired, too, in conjunction with the assembly, with or without the cooperation of the Five Hundred (or Six Hundred), the right to pass decrees and to represent their city in foreign relations (*C.I.A.* iii. 10, 31, 40, 41, 454, 457, 458). From the overthrow of the Thirty to the end of their history they enjoyed a high reputation for ability and integrity (Isoc. vii.; Demosth. xxiii. 65 f.; Val. Max. viii. 1.*Amb.* 2; Gell. xii. 7; Lucian, *Bis Acc.* iv. 12. 14). About A.D. 400 their council came to an end (Theodoret, *Curat.* ix. 55).

With regard to the jurisdiction of the council in cases of homicide, the procedure, so far as it may be gathered from the orators and other sources, was as follows:—accusations were brought by relatives within the circle of brothers' and sisters' children, supported by the wider kin and the phratry (Demosth. xliii. 57). On receiving the accusation the king-archon by proclamation warned the accused to keep away from temples and other places forbidden to such persons. He made three investigations of the case in the three successive months, and brought it to trial in the fourth month. As he was forbidden to hand a case over to his successor, it resulted that in the last three months of the year no accusations of homicide could be brought (Ant. vi. 42). After the examination he assigned the case to the proper court, and presided over it during the trial, which took place in the open air, that the judges and the accuser might not be polluted by being brought under the same roof with the offender (Ant. v. 11). The accuser and the accused, standing on two white stones termed "Relentlessness" (Ἀναίδεια) and "Outrage" (Ὕβρις) respectively (Paus. i. 28. 5), bound themselves to the truth by most solemn oaths (Demosth. xxiii. 68). Each was allowed two speeches, and the trial lasted three days. After the first speech the accused, unless charged with parricide, was at liberty to withdraw into exile (Poll. viii. 117). If condemned, he lost his life, and his property was confiscated. A tie vote acquitted (Aeschyl. *Eumen.* 735; Ant. v. 51; Aeschin. iii. 252). See further GREEK LAW.

AUTHORITIES.—Among other works may be mentioned E. Dugit,*Étude sur l'Areopage athenien* (Paris, 1867); E. Caillemer, "Areopagus," in Daremberg et Saglio, *Dict. d. Antiq. grecq. et rom.* (Paris, 1873) i. 395-404; A. Philippi, *Areopag und Epheten*(Berlin, 1874). The discovery of the Aristotelian "Constitution of Athens" (*Ath. Pol.*) has largely rendered obsolete all works published before 1891. See Hermann-Thumser, *Griechische Staatsaltertumer* (6th ed., Freiburg, 1892), 365-371, 387-391, 788; U. von Wilamowitz-Mollendorff, *Aristoteles und Athen* (Berlin, 1893), ii. 186-200; J.J. Terwen, *De Areopago Atheniensium Quaestiones Variae* (Utrecht, 1894); G. Gilbert, *Constitutional Antiquities of Athens and Sparta* (Eng. trans., London and New York, 1895), 114, 122, 137, 154, 282; F. Cauer, "Aischylos und der Areopag," in *Rhein. Mus.* (1895), N.F. i. 348-356; Wachsmuth and Thalheim, s.v. "Areios pagos" in Pauly-Wissowa, *Realencycl. d. kl. Altertumswiss.* (Stuttgart, 1896), ii. 627-633; G. de Sanctis,Ἀτθίς, *Storia delta Repubblica Ateniese* (Rome, 1898); L. Ziehen, "Drakontische Gesetzgebung," in *Rhein. Mus.* (1899), N.F. liv. 321-344. See also CLEISTHENES; PERICLES and ATHENS.

(G. W. B.)

1Neither Herodotus nor Thucydides tells us anything as to its powers; but their silence on this point need not surprise us, as they had no especial occasion for referring to the subject, and in general it may be said that before the 4th century B.C. writers took little interest in the constitutional history of the remote past. The statement of Thucydides (i. 126. 8) that at the time of the Cylonian insurrection the nine archons attended to a great part of the business of government does not contradict the Aristotelian view, for their administration may well have been under Areopagitic supervision (see also ARCHON); and, as is stated in the text, the supremacy of the council may have already suffered considerable limitation. *The Eumenides of Aeschylus* is a glorification of the institution, though for obvious reasons it is there represented as an essentially judicial body.

2It is possible also to explain the alleged absence of reference to the Areopagitic council in the Draconian laws by the supposition that Solon, while leaving untouched the Draconian laws concerned with the cases of homicide which came before the Ephetae, substituted a law of his own regarding wilful murder, which fell within the jurisdiction of the Areopagites. This view finds strong support in the circumstance that the copy of the Draconian laws (*C.I.A.* i. 61), made in pursuance of a decree of the people of the year 409-408 B.C., does not contain the provision for cases of premeditated homicide; cf. G. de Sanctis, Ἀτθίς, 135. The relation of the Ephetae to the court of the Areopagus is obscure; cf. Philippi,*Der Areopag und die Epheten* (Berlin, 1874); Busolt, *Griechische Geschichte* (2nd ed.), ii. 138 ff.

AREQUIPA, a coast department of southern Peru, bounded N. by the departments of Ayacucho and Cuzco, E. by Puno and Moquegua, S. and W. by Moquegua and the Pacific. It is divided into seven provinces. Area, 21,947 sq. m.; pop. (1896) 229,007. It is traversed by an important railway line from Mollendo (Islay) to Puno, on Lake Titicaca, 325 m. long, with extensions to Santa Rosa, Peru and La Paz, Bolivia. The highest point reached by this line is 14,660 ft. The department includes an arid, sand-covered region on the coast traversed by deep gorges formed by river courses, and a partly barren, mountainous region inland composed of the high Cordillera and its spurs toward the coast, between which are numerous highly fertile valleys watered by streams from the snow-clad peaks. These produce cotton, rice, sugar-cane, wheat, coffee, Indian corn, barley, potatoes and fruit. The mountainous region is rich in minerals, and there is a valuable deposit of borax near the capital, Arequipa.

AREQUIPA, a city of southern Peru, capital of the department of the same name, about 90 m. N.E. by N. of its seaport Mollendo (107 m. by rail), and near the south-west foot of the volcano Misti which rises to a height of 19,029 ft. above sea-level. The population was estimated at 35,000 in 1896. The city is provided with a tram line, and is connected with the coast at Mollendo (Islay) by a railway 107 m. long, and with Puno, on Lake Titicaca, by an extension of the same line 218 m. long. The city occupies a green, fertile valley of the Rio Chile, 7753 ft. above the sea, surrounded by an arid, barren desert. It is built on the usual rectangular plan and the streets are wide and well paved. The edifices in general are low, and are massively built with thick walls and domed ceilings to resist earthquakes, and lessen the danger from falling masonry. The material used is a soft, porous magnesian limestone, which is well adapted to the purpose in view. Arequipa is the seat of a bishopric created in 1609-1612, and possesses a comparatively modern cathedral, its predecessor having been destroyed by fire in 1849. It has several large churches, and formerly possessed five monasteries and three nunneries, which have been closed and their edifices devoted to educational and other public purposes. The religious element has always been a dominating factor in the life of the city. A university, founded in 1825, three colleges, one of them dating from colonial times, a medical school, and a public library, founded in 1821, are distinguishing features of the city, which has always taken high rank in Peru for its learning and liberalism, as well as for its political restlessness. The city's water-supply is derived from the Chile river and is considered dangerous to new arrivals because of the quantity of saline and organic matter contained. The climate is temperate and healthy, and the fertile valley (10 m. long by 5 m. wide) surrounding the city produces an abundance of cereals, fruits and vegetables common to both hot and temperate regions. Pears and strawberries grow side by side with oranges and granadillas, and are noted for their size and flavour. The trade of the city is principally in Bolivian products—mineral ores, alpaca wool, &c.—but it also receives and exports the products of the neighbouring 455Peruvian provinces, and the output of the borax deposits in the neighbourhood. Arequipa was founded by Pizarro in 1540, and has been the scene of many events of importance in the history of Peru. It was greatly damaged in the earthquakes of 1582, 1609, 1784 and 1868, particularly in the last. It was captured by the Chileans in 1883, near the close of the war between Chile and Peru.

ARES, in ancient Greek mythology, the god of war, or rather of battle, son of Zeus and Hera. (For the Roman god, identified with Ares, see <u>MARS</u>.) As contrasted with Athena, who added to her other attributes that of being the goddess of well-conducted military operations, he personifies brute strength and the wild rage of conflict. His delight is in war and bloodshed; he loves fighting for fighting's sake, and takes the side of the one or the other combatant indifferently, regardless of the justice of the cause. His quarrelsomeness was regarded as inherited from his mother, and it may have been only as an illustration of the perpetual strife between Zeus and Hera that Ares was accounted their son. According to a later tradition, he was the son of Hera (Juno) alone, who became pregnant by touching a certain flower (Ovid, *Fasti*, v. 255). All the gods, even Zeus, hate him, but his bitterest enemy is Athena, who fells him to the ground with a huge stone. Splendidly armed, he goes to battle, sometimes on foot, sometimes in the war chariot made ready by his sons Deimos and Phobos (Panic and Fear) by whom he is usually accompanied. In his train also are found Enyo, the goddess of war who delights in bloodshed and the destruction of cities; his sister, Eris, goddess of fighting and strife; and the Keres, goddesses of death, whose function it is especially to roam the battle-field, carrying off the dead to Hades. In later accounts (and even in the *Odyssey*) Ares' character is somewhat toned down; thus, in the "Homeric" hymn to Ares he is addressed as the assistant of Themis (Justice), the enemy of tyrants, and leader of the just. It is to be noted, however, that in this little poem he is to some extent confounded with the planet named after him (Ares, or Mars).

The primitive character of Ares has been much discussed. He is a god of storms; a god of light or a solar god; a chthonian god, one of the deities of the subterranean world, who could bring prosperity as well as ruin upon men, although in time his destructive qualities obscured the others. In this last aspect he was one of the chief gods of the Thracians, amongst whom his home was placed even in the time of Homer. In Scythia an old iron sword served as the symbol of the god, to which yearly sacrifices of cattle and horses were made, and in earlier times (as apparently also at Sparta) human victims, selected from prisoners of war, were offered. Thus Ares developed into the god of war, in which character he made his way into Greece. This theory may have been nothing more than an instance of the Greek tendency to assign a northern or "hyperborean" home to deities in whose character something analogous to the stormy elements of nature was found. But it appears that the Thracians and Scythians in historical times (Herodotus i. 59) worshipped chiefly a war god, and that certain Thracian settlements, formed in Greece in prehistoric times, left behind them traces of the worship of a god whom the Greeks called Ares. The story of his imprisonment for thirteen months by the Aloïdae (*Iliad*, v. 385) points to the conquest of this chthonian destroyer of the fields by the arts of peace, especially agriculture, of which the grain-fed sons of Aloeus (the thresher) are the personification.

In Homer Ares is the lover of Aphrodite, the wife of Hephaestus, who catches them together in a net and holds them up to the ridicule of the gods. In what appears to be a very early development of her character, Aphrodite also was a war goddess, known under the name of Areia; and in Thebes, the most important seat of the worship of Ares, she is his wife, and bears him Eros and Anteros, Deimos and Phobos, and Harmonia, wife of Cadmus, the founder of the city (Hesiod, *Theog.* 933). In the legend of Cadmus and his family Ares plays a prominent part. His worship was not so widely spread over Greece as that of other gods, although he was honoured here and there with festivals and sacrifices. Thus, at Sparta, under the name of Theritas, he was offered young dogs and even human beings. The Dioscuri were said to have brought his image from Colchis to Laconia, where it was set up in an old sanctuary on the road from Sparta to Therapnae. At Athens, he had a temple at the foot of the Areopagus, with a statue by Alcamenes. It was here, according to the legend, that he was tried and acquitted by a council of the gods for the murder of Halirrhothius, who had violated Alcippe, the daughter of Ares by Agraulos. The figure of Ares appears in various stories of ancient mythology. Thus, he engages in combat with Heracles on two occasions to avenge the death of his son Cycnus; once Zeus separates the combatants by a flash of lightning, but in the second encounter he is severely wounded by his adversary, who has the active support of Athena; maddened by jealousy, he changes himself into the boar which slew Adonis, the favourite of Aphrodite; and stirs up the war between the Lapithae and Centaurs. His attributes were the spear and the burning torch, symbolical of the devastation caused by war (in ancient times the hurling of a torch was the signal for the commencement of hostilities). The animals sacred to him were the dog and the vulture.

The worship of Ares being less general throughout Greece than that of the gods of peace, the number of statues of him is small; those of Ares-Mars, among the Romans, are more frequent. Previous to the 5th century B.C. he was represented as full-bearded, grim-featured and in full armour. From that time, apparently under the influence of Athenian sculptors, he was conceived as the ideal of a youthful warrior, and was for a time associated with Aphrodite and Eros. He then appears as a vigorous youth, beardless, with curly hair, broad head and stalwart shoulders, with helmet and chlamys. In the Villa Ludovisi statue (after the style of Lysippus) he appears seated, in an attitude of thought; his arms are laid aside, and Eros peeps out at his feet. In the Borghese Ares (also taken for Achilles) he is standing, his only armour being the helmet on his head. He also appears in many other groups, with Aphrodite, in marble and on engraved gems of Roman times. But before this grouping had recommended itself to the Romans, with their legend of Mars and Rhea Silvia, the Greek Ares had again become under Macedonian influence a bearded, armed and powerful god.

AUTHORITIES.—H.D. Müller, Ares (1848), H.W. Stoll, *Über die ursprungliche Bedeutung des A. und der Athene* (1881); F.A. Voigt, "Beiträge zur Mythologie des Ares und Athena" in*Leipziger Studien*, iv. 1881; W.H. Roscher, *Studien zur vergleichenden Mythologie*, i., 1873; C. Tümpel, *Ares und Aphrodite* (1880); articles in Pauly-Wissowa's *Realencyclopadie*, Roscher's *Lexikon der Mythologie*, and Daremberg and Saglio's*Dictionnaire des Antiquités* (s.v. MARS); Preller, *Griechische Mythologie*.

ARETAEUS, of Cappadocia, a Greek physician, who lived at Rome in the second half of the 2nd century A.D. We possess two treatises by him, each in four books, in the Ionic dialect: *On the Causes and Indications of Acute and Chronic Diseases, and On their Treatment.* His work was founded on that of Archigenes; like him, he belonged to the eclectic school, but did not ignore the theories of the "Pneumatics," who made the heart the seat of life and of the soul.

Editions by Kühn (1828), Ermerius (1848). English translations: Wigan (1723); Moffat (1786); Reynolds (1837); Adams (1856). See Locher, *Aretaeus aus Kappadocien* (1847).

ARETAS (Arab. Hāritha), the Greek form of a name borne by kings of the Nabataeans resident at Petra in Arabia, (i) A king in the time of Antiochus IV. Epiphanes (2 Macc. v. 8). (2) The father-in-law of Herod Antipas (Jos. *Ant.* xviii. 5. 1, 3), In 2 Cor. xi. 32 he is described as ruler of Damascus (*q.v.*) at the time of Paul's conversion. Herod Antipas had married a daughter of Aretas, but afterwards discarded her in favour of Herodias. This led to a war with Aretas in which Antipas was defeated.

An Aretas is mentioned in 1 Macc. xv. 22, but the true reading is probably Ariarathes (king of Cappadocia). See NABATAEANS.

ARÊTE (O. Fr. *areste*, Lat. *arista*, ear of corn, fish-bone or spine), a ridge or sharp edge; a French term used in Switzerland 456to denote the sharp bayonet-like edge of a mountain (such as the Matterhorn), that slopes steeply upward with two precipitous sides meeting in a long ascending ridge. Hence the word has passed into common use to denote any sharp mountain edge denuded by frost action above the snowline, where the consequent angular ridges give the characteristic "house-roof structure" of these altitudes.

ARETHAS (*c.* 860-940), Byzantine theological writer and scholar, archbishop of Caesarea in Cappadocia, was born at Patrae. He was the author of a Greek commentary on the Apocalypse, avowedly based upon that of Andrew, his predecessor in the archbishopric. In spite of its author's modest estimate, Arethas's work is by no means a slavish compilation; it contains additions from other sources, and especial care has been taken in verifying the references. His interest was not, however, confined to theological literature; he annotated the margins of his classical texts with numerous scholia (many of which are preserved), and had several MSS. copied at his own expense, amongst them the Codex Clarkianus of Plato (brought to England from the monastery of St John in Patmos), and the Dorvillian MS. of Euclid (now at Oxford).

Most divergent opinions have been held as to the time in which Arethas lived; the reasons for the dates given above will be found succinctly stated in the article "Aretas," by A. Jülicher in Pauly-Wissowa's *Realencyclopadie der klassischen Altertumswissenschaft* (1896). The text of the commentary is given in Migne, *Patrologia Graeca*, cvi.; see also O. Gebhardt and A. Harnack, *Texte und Untersuchungen zur Geschichte der altchristlichen Litt.* i. pp. 36-46 (1882), and *Vita Euthymii*(patriarch of Constantinople, d. 917), ed. C. de Boor (1888); H. Wace, *Dictionary of Christian Biography*, i.; C. Krumbacher,*Geschichte der byzantinischen Litteratur* (1897); G. Heinrici in Herzog-Hauck, *Realencyklopadie* (1897).

ARETHUSA, in Greek mythology, a nymph who gave her name to a spring in Elis and to another in the island of Ortygia near Syracuse. According to Pausanias (v. 7. 2), Alpheus, a mighty hunter, was enamoured of Arethusa, one of the retinue of Artemis; Arethusa fled to Ortygia, where she was changed into a spring; Alpheus, in the form of a river, made his way beneath the sea, and united his waters with those of the spring. In Ovid (*Metam.* v. 572 foll.), Arethusa, while bathing in the Alpheus, was seen and pursued by the river god in human form; Artemis changed her into a spring, which, flowing underground, emerged at Ortygia. In the earlier form of the legend, it is Artemis, not Arethusa, who is the object of the god's affections, and escapes by smearing her face with mire, so that he fails to recognize her (see L.R. Farnell, *Cults of the Greek States*, ii. p. 428). The probable origin of the story is the part traditionally taken in the foundation of Syracuse by the Iamidae of Olympia, who identified the spring Arethusa with their own river Alpheus, and the nymph with Artemis Alpheiaia, who was worshipped at Ortygia. The subterranean passage of the Alpheus in the upper part of its course (confirmed by modern explorers), and the freshness of the water of Arethusa in spite of its proximity to the sea, led to the belief that it was the outlet of the river. Further, according to Strabo (vi. p. 270), during the sacrifice of oxen at Olympia the waters of Arethusa were disturbed, and a cup thrown into the Alpheus would reappear in Ortygia. In Virgil (*Ecl.* x. 1) Arethusa is addressed as a divinity of poetical inspiration, like one of the Muses, who were themselves originally nymphs of springs.

For Arethusa on Syracusan coins, see B.V. Head, *Historia Numorum*, pp. 151, 155.

14

ARETINO, PIETRO (1492-1556), Italian author, was born in 1492 at Arezzo in Tuscany, from which place he took his name. He is said to have been the natural son of Luigi Bacci, a gentleman of the town. He received little education, and lived for some years poor and neglected, picking up such scraps of information as he could. When very young he was banished from Arezzo on account of a satirical sonnet which he composed against indulgences. He went to Perugia, where for some time he worked as a bookbinder, and continued to distinguish himself by his daring attacks upon religion. After some years' wandering through parts of Italy he reached Rome, where his talents, wit and impudence commended him to the papal court. This favour, however, he lost in 1523 by writing a set of obscene sonnets, to accompany an equally immoral series of drawings by the great painter, Giulio Romano. He left Rome and was received by Giovanni de' Medici, who introduced him at Milan to Francis I. of France. He gained the good graces of that monarch, and received handsome presents from him. Shortly after this Aretino attempted to regain the favour of the pope, but, having come to Rome, he composed a sonnet against a rival in some low amour, and in return was assaulted and severely wounded. He could obtain no redress from the pope, and returned to Giovanni de' Medici. On the death of the latter in December 1526, he withdrew to Venice, where he afterwards continued to reside. He spent his time here in writing comedies, sonnets, licentious dialogues, and a few devotional and religious works. He led a profligate life, and procured funds to satisfy his needs by writing sycophantish letters to all the nobles and princes with whom he was acquainted. This plan proved eminently successful, for large sums were given him, apparently from fear of his satire. So great did Aretino's pride grow, that he styled himself the "divine," and the "scourge of princes." He died in 1556, according to some accounts by falling from his chair in a fit of laughter caused by hearing some indecent story of his sisters. The reputation of Aretino in his own time rested chiefly on his satirical sonnets or burlesques; but his comedies, five in number, are now considered the best of his works. His letters, of which a great number have been printed, are also commended for their style. The dialogues and the licentious sonnets have been translated into French, under the title *Académie des Dames*.

AREZZO (anc. *Arretium*), a town and episcopal see of Tuscany, Italy, the capital of the province of Arezzo, 54 m. S.E. of Florence by rail. Pop. (1901) town, 16,780; commune, 46,926. It is an attractive town, situated on the slope of a hill 840 to 970 ft. above sea-level, in a fertile district. The walls by which it is surrounded were erected in 1320 by Guido Tarlati di Pietramala, its warlike bishop, who died in 1327, and is buried in the cathedral; they were reconstructed by Cosimo I. de Medici between 1541 and 1568, on which occasion the bronze statues of Pallas and the Chimaera, now at Florence, were discovered. The town itself is fan-shaped, the streets, which contain some fine old houses with projecting eaves and many towers, radiating from the citadel (Fortezza), which was constructed in 1502, and dismantled by the French in 1800. The cathedral, close by, is a fine specimen of Italian Gothic begun in 1277, but not completed internally until 1511, while the façade was not begun until 1880. The interior is spacious and contains some fine 14th-century sculptures, those of the high altar, which contains the tomb of St Donatus, the patron saint of Arezzo, being the best; very good stained-glass windows of the beginning of the 16th century by Guillaume de Marcillat, and some terra-cotta reliefs by Andrea della Robbia. Another fine church is S. Maria della Pieve, having a campanile and a façade of 1216, the latter with three open colonnades running for its whole length above the doors. The interior was restored to its original style in 1863-1865. The Romanesque choir and apse belong to the 11th century, the rest of the interior is contemporary with the façade. In the square behind the church is a colonnade designed by Vasari. In the cloisters of S. Bernardo, on the site of the ancient amphitheatre, is a remarkable view of medieval Rome. S. Francesco contains famous frescoes by Piero de' Franceschi, representing scenes from the legend of the Holy Cross, and others by Spinello Aretino, a pupil of Giotto. There are several other frescoes by the latter in S. Domenico. Among the Renaissance buildings the churches of S. Maria delle Grazie and the Santissima Annunziata may be noted. The collection of majolica in the municipal museum is very fine, and so is that of the Funghini family. In the middle ages Arezzo was generally on the Ghibelline side; it succumbed to Florence in 1289 at the battle of Campaldino, but at the end of the century recovered its strength under the Tarlati family. In 1336 it became subject to Florence for six years, and after intestine struggles, finally came under her rule in 1384. Among the natives of Arezzo the most famous are the Benedictine monk Guido of Arezzo, the inventor 457of the modern system of musical notation (died *c.* 1050), the poet Petrarch, Pietro Aretino, the satirist (1492-1556), and Vasari, famous for his lives of Italian painters. The town never possessed a distinct school of artists.

See C. Signorini, *Arezzo, Città y Provincia, Guida illustrata*(Arezzo,1904).

ARGALI, the Tatar name of the great wild sheep, *Ovis ammon,* of the Altai and other parts of Siberia. Standing as high as a large donkey, the argali is the finest of all the wild sheep, the horns of the rams, although of inferior length, being more massive than those of*Ovis poli* of the Pamirs. There are several local races of argali, among which *O. ammon hodgsoni* of Ladak and Tibet is one of the best known. There are likewise several nearly related central Asian species, such as *O. sairensis* and *O. littledalei.* (See SHEEP.)

ARGAO, a town on the east coast of Cebu, Philippine Islands, 36 m. S.S.W. of the town of Cebu. Pop. (1903) 35,448. Large quantities of a superior quality of cacao are produced in the vicinity, and rice and Indian corn are other important products. A limited amount of cotton is raised and woven into cloth. The language is Cebu-Visayan. Argao was founded in 1608.

ARGAUM, a village of British India in the Akola district of the Central Provinces, 32 m. north of Akola. The village is memorable for an action which took place on the 28th of November 1803 between the British army, commanded by Major-General Wellesley (afterwards duke of Wellington), and the Mahrattas under Sindhia and the raja of Berar, in which the latter were defeated with great loss. A medal struck in England in 1851 commemorates the victory.

ARGEI, the name given by the ancient Romans to a number of rush puppets (24 or 27 according to the reading of Varro, *de Ling. lat.* vii. 44, or 30 according to Dionysius i. 38) resembling men tied hand and foot, which were taken down to the ancient bridge over the Tiber (*pans sublicius*) on the 14th of May by the pontifices and magistrates, with the flaminica Dialis in mourning guise, and there thrown into the Tiber by the Vestal virgins. There were also in various parts of the four Servian regions of the city a number of *sacella Argeorum*(chapels), round which a procession seems to have gone on the 17th of March (Varro, *L.L.* v. 46-54; Jordan, *Rom. Topogr.* vol. ii. 603), and it has been conjectured that the puppets were kept in these chapels until the time came for them to be cast into the river. The Romans had no historical explanation of these curious rites, and neither the theories of their scholars nor the beliefs of the common people, who fancied that the puppets were substitutes for old men who used at one time to be sacrificed to the river, are worth serious consideration. Recently two explanations have been given: (1) that of W. Mannhardt, who by comparing numerous examples of similar customs among other European peoples arrived at the conclusion that the rite was of extreme antiquity and of dramatic rather than sacrificial character, and that its object was possibly to procure rain; (2) that of Wissowa, who refuses to date it farther back than the latter half of the 3rd century B.C., and sees in it the yearly representation of an original sacrifice of twenty-seven captive Greeks (taking Argei as a Latin form of Ἀργεῖοι) by drowning in the Tiber. This second theory is, however, not borne out by any Roman historical record.

See Wissowa's arguments in the article "Argei" in his edition of Pauly's *Realencydopadie.* For the other view see W. Mannhardt,*Antike Wald und Feldkulte,* 178 foll.; W.W. Fowler, *Roman Festivals,* pp. 111 foll.

(W. W. F.*)

ARGELANDER, FRIEDRICH WILHELM AUGUST (1799-1875), German astronomer, 'was born at Memel on the 22nd of March 1799. He studied at the university of Konigsberg, and was attracted to astronomy by F.W. Bessel, whose assistant he became (October 1, 1820). His treatise on the path of the great comet of 1811 appeared in 1822; he was, in 1823, entrusted with the direction of the observatory at Åbo; and he exchanged it for a similar charge at Helsingfors in 1832. His admirable investigation of the sun's motion in space was published in 1837; and in the same year he was appointed professor of astronomy in the university of Bonn, where he died on the 17th of February 1875. He also published *Observations Astronomicae Aboae Factae* (3 vols., 1830-1832); *DLX Stellarum Fixarum Positiones Mediae* (1835); and the first seven volumes of *Astronomische Beobachtungen auf der Sternwarte zu Benn* (1846-1869), containing his observations of northern and southern star-zones, and his great*Durchmusterung* (vols, iii,-v., 1859-1862) of 324,198 stars, from the north pole to -2° Dec. The corresponding atlas was issued in 1863. His observations (begun in 1838) and discussions of variable stars were embodied in vol. vii. of the same series.

See E. Schönfeld in *Vierteljahrsschrift der Astronomischen Gesellschaft,* x. pp. 150-178.

ARGENS, JEAN BAPTISTE DE BOYER, MARQUIS D' (1704-1771), was born at Aix in Provence on the 24th of June 1704. He entered the army at the age of fifteen, and after a dissipated and adventurous youth settled for a time at Amsterdam, where he wrote some historical compilations and began his more famous *Lettres juives*(The Hague, 6 vols., 1738-1742), *Lettres chinoises* (The Hague, 6 vols., 1730-1472), and *Lettres cabalistiques* (2nd ed., 7 vols., 1769); also the *Mémoires secrets de la république des lettres* (7 vols., 1743-1478), afterwards revised and augmented as *Histoire de l'esprit humain* (Berlin, 14 vols., 1765-1768). He was invited by Prince Frederick (afterwards Frederick the Great) to Potsdam, and received high honours at court; but Frederick was bitterly offended by his marrying a Berlin actress, Mlle Cochois. Argens returned to France in 1769, and died near Toulon on the 11th of January 1771.

ARGENSOLA, LUPERCIO LEONARDO DE (1559-1613), Spanish dramatist and poet, was baptized at Barbastro on the 14th of December 1559. He was educated at the universities of Huesca and Saragossa, becoming secretary to the duke de Villahermosa in 1585. He was appointed historiographer of Aragon in 1599, and in 1610 accompanied the count de Lemos to Naples, where he died in March 1613. His tragedies—*Filis, Isabela* and *Alejandra*—are said by Cervantes to have "filled all who heard them with admiration, delight and interest"; *Filis* is lost, and *Isabela* and *Alejandra*, which were not printed till 1772, are ponderous imitations of Seneca. Argensola's poems were published with those of his brother in 1634; they consist of excellent translations from the Latin poets, and of original satires. His "echoing sonnets"—such as *Después que al mundo el rey divino vino*—lend themselves to parody; but his diction is singularly pure.

His brother, BARTOLOMÉ LEONARDO DE ARGENSOLA (1562-1631), Spanish poet and historian, was baptized at Barbastro on the 26th of August 1562, studied at Huesca, took orders, and was presented to the rectory of Villahermosa in 1588. He was attached to the suite of the count de Lemos, viceroy of Naples, in 1610, and succeeded his brother as historiographer of Aragon in 1613. He died at Saragossa on the 4th of February 1631. His principal prose works are the *Conquista de las Islas Molucas* (1609), and a supplement to Zurita's *Anales de Aragón*, which was published in 1630. His poems (1634), like those of his elder brother, are admirably finished examples of pungent wit. His commentaries on contemporary events, and his *Alteraciones populares*, dealing with a Saragossa rising in 1591, are lost. An interesting life of this writer by Father Miguel Mir precedes a reprint of the *Conquista de las Islas Molucas*, issued at Saragossa in 1891.

ARGENSON, the name, derived from an old hamlet situated in what is now the department of Indre-et-Loire, of a French family which produced some prominent statesmen, soldiers and men of letters.

RENÉ DE VOYER, seigneur d'Argenson (1596-1651), French statesman, was born on the 21st of November 1596. He was a lawyer by profession, and became successively *avocat*, councillor at the parlement of Paris, *maître des requêtes*, and councillor of state. Cardinal Richelieu entrusted him with several missions as inspector and intendant of the forces. In 1623 he was appointed intendant of justice, police and finance in Auvergne, and in 1632 held similar office in Limousin, where he remained till 1637. After the death of Louis XIII. (1643) he retained his administrative posts, was intendant of the forces at Toulon 458(1646), commissary of the king at the estates of Languedoc (1647), and intendant of Guienne (1648), and showed great capacity in defending the authority of the crown against the rebels of the Fronde. After his wife's death he took orders (February 1651), but did not cease to take part in affairs of state. In 1651 he was appointed by Mazarin ambassador at Venice, where he died on the 14th of July 1651.

His son, MARC RENÉ DE VOYER, comte d'Argenson (1623-1700), was born at Blois on the 13th of December 1623. He also was a lawyer, being councillor at the parlement of Rouen (1642) and *maître des requêtes*. He attended his father in all his duties and succeeded him at the embassy at Venice. In 1655 he returned from his embassy, ruined, and lost favour with Mazarin, who removed him from his office of councillor of state. He then gave up public affairs and retired to his estates, where he occupied himself with good works. In September 1656 he entered the Company of the Holy Sacrament, a secret society for the diffusion of the Catholic religion. Besides writing the *Annals* of the society, he composed many pious works, which were destroyed in the fire at the Louvre in 1871. Some of his correspondence with the once famous letter-writer, Jean Louis Guez de Balzac (1597-1654), has been published. He died in May 1700, leaving two sons, Marc René (see below), and François Élie (1656-1728), who became archbishop of Bordeaux.

See Fr. Rabbe, "Compagnie du Saint-Sacrement," in the *Revue historique* (Nov. 1899); Beaucher-Filleau, *Les Annales de la compagnie du Saint-Sacrement* (Paris, 1900); R. Allier, *La Cobalt des dévots* (Paris, 1902).

MARC RENÉ DE VOYER, marquis de Paulmy and marquis d'Argenson (1652-1721), son of the preceding, was born at Venice on the 4th of November 1652. He became *avocat* in 1669, and lieutenant-general in the *sénéchaussée* of Angoulême (1679). After the death of Colbert, who disliked his family, he went to Paris and married Marguerite Lefèvre de Caomartin, a kinswoman of the comptroller-general Pontchartrain. This was the beginning of his fortunes. He became successively *maître des requêtes* (1694), member of the *conseil des prises* (prize court) (1695), *procureur-général* of the commission of inquest into false titles of nobility (1696), and finally lieutenant-general of police (1697). This last office, which had previously been filled by N.G. de la Reynie, was very important. It not only gave him the control of the police, but also the supervision of the corporations, printing press, and provisioning of Paris. All contraventions of the police regulations came under his jurisdiction, and his authority was arbitrary and absolute. Fortunately, he had, in Saint-Simon's phrase, "a nice discernment as to the degree of rigour or leniency required for every case that came before him, being ever inclined to the mildest measures, but possessed of the faculty of making the most innocent tremble before him; courageous, bold, audacious in quelling *émeutes*, and consequently the master of the people." During the twenty-one years that he exercised this office he was a party to every private and state secret; in fact, he had a share in every event of any importance in the history of Paris. He was the familiar friend of the king, who delighted in scandalous police reports; he was patronized by the duke of Orleans; he was supported by the Jesuits at court; and he was feared by all. He organized the supply of food in Paris during the severe winter of 1709, and endeavoured, but with little success, to run to earth the libellers of the government. He directed the destruction of the Jansenist monastery of Port Royal (1709), a proceeding which provoked many protests and pamphlets. Under the regency, the Chambre de Justice, assembled to inquire into the malpractices of the financiers, suspected d'Argenson and arrested his clerks, but dared not lay the blame on him. On the 28th of January 1718 he voluntarily resigned the office of lieutenant-general of police for those of keeper of the seals—in the place of the chancellor d'Aguesseau—and president of the council of finance. He was appointed by the regent to suppress the resistance of the parlements and to reorganize the finances, and was in great measure responsible for permitting John Law to apply his financial system, though he soon quarrelled with Law and intrigued to bring about his downfall. The regent threw the blame for the outcome of Law's schemes on d'Argenson, who was forced to resign his position in the council of finance (January 1720). By way of compensation he was created inspector-general of the police of the whole kingdom, but had to resign his office of keeper of the seals (June 1720). He died on the 8th of May 1721, the people of Paris throwing taunts and stones at his coffin and accusing him of having ruined the kingdom. In 1716 he had been created an honorary member of the Académie des Sciences and, in 1718, a member of the French Academy.

See the contemporary memoirs, especially those of Saint-Simon (de Boislisle's ed.), Dangeau and Math. Marais; Barbier's *Journal*; "Correspondance administrative sous Louis XIV." in *Coll. des doc. inéd. sur l'histoire de France*, edited by G.B. Depping (1850-1855); *Correspondance des contrôleurs-généraux des finances*, pub. by de Bois-lisle (1873-1900); *Correspondance de M. de Marville avec M. de Maurepas* (1896-1897); *Rapports de police de René d'Argenson*, pub. by P. Cottin (Paris, undated); P. Clément, *La police sous Louis XIV.* (1873).

RENÉ LOUIS DE VOYER DE PAULMY, marquis d'Argenson (1694-1757), eldest son of the preceding, was a lawyer, and held successively the posts of councillor at the parlement (1716), *maître des requêtes* (1718), councillor of state (1719), and intendant of justice, police and finance in Hainaut. During his five years' tenure of the last office he was mainly employed in provisioning the troops, who were suffering from the economic confusion resulting from Law's system. He returned to court in 1724 to exercise his functions as councillor of state. At that time he had the reputation of being a conscientious man, but ill adapted to intrigue, and was nicknamed "la bête." He entered into relations with the philosophers, and was won over to the ideas of reform. He was the friend of Voltaire, who had been a fellow-student of his at the Jesuit college Louis-le-grand, and frequented the Club de l'Entresol, the history of which he wrote in his memoirs. It was then that he prepared his *Considérations sur le gouvernement de la France*, which was published posthumously by his son. He was also the friend and counsellor of the minister G.L. de Chauvelin. In May 1744 he was appointed member of the council of finance, and in November of the same year the king chose him as secretary of state for foreign affairs, his brother, the comte d'Argenson (see below), being at the same time secretary of state for war. France was at that time engaged in the War of the Austrian Succession, and the government had been placed by Louis XV. virtually in the hands of the two brothers. The marquis d'Argenson endeavoured to reform the system of international relations. He dreamed of a "European Republic," and wished to establish arbitration between nations in pursuance of the ideas of his friend the abbé de Saint-Pierre. But he failed to realize any part of his projects. The generals negotiated in opposition to his instructions; his colleagues laid the blame on him; the intrigues of the courtiers passed unnoticed by him; whilst the secret diplomacy of the king neutralized his initiative. He concluded the marriage of the dauphin to the daughter of Augustus III., king of Poland, but was unable to prevent the election of the grand-duke of Tuscany as emperor in 1745. On the both of January 1747 the king thanked him for his services. He then retired into private life, eschewed the court, associated with Voltaire, Condillac and d'Alembert, and spent his declining years in working at the Academie des Inscriptions, of which he was appointed president by the king in 1747, and revising his *Mémoires*. Voltaire, in one of his letters, declared him to be "the best citizen that had ever tasted the ministry." He died on the 26th of January 1757.

He left a large number of manuscript works, of which his son, Antoine René (1722-1787), known as the marquis de Paulmy, published the *Considérations sur le gouvernement de France*(Amsterdam, 1764) and *Essais dans le gout de ceux de Montaigne (ib.*1785). The latter, which contains many useful biographical notes and portraits of his contemporaries, was republished in 1787 as *Loisirs d'un ministre d'état.* Argenson's most important work, however, is his*Mémoires*, covering in great detail the years 1725 to 1756, with an introductory part giving his recollections since the year 1696. They are, as they were intended to be, 459valuable "materials for the history of his time." There are two important editions, the first, with some letters, not elsewhere published, by the marquis d'Argenson, his great-grand-nephew (5 vols., Paris, 1857 et seq.); the second, more correct, but less complete, published by J.B. Rathery, for the Société de l'Histoire de France (9 vols., Paris, 1859 et seq.). The other works of the marquis d'Argenson, in MS., were destroyed in the fire at the Louvre library in 1871.

See Sainte-Beuve, *Causeries du lundi* (vols. xii. and xiv.); Levasseur. "Le Marquis d'Argenson" in the *Mémoires de l'Academie des Sciences Morales et Politiques* (vol. lxxxvii., 1868); and, especially, E. Zevort, *Le Marquis d'Argenson et le ministère des affaires étrangères* (Paris, 1880). See also G. de R. de Flassan, *Histoire de la diplomatie française* (2nd ed., 1811); Voltaire, *Siècle de Louis XV.*; E. Boutaric, *Correspondance secrète inédite de Louis XV.* (1866); E. Champion, "Le Marquis d'Argenson," in the *Révolution française* (vol. xxxvi., 1899); A. Alem, *D'Argenson économiste* (Paris, 1899); Arthur Ogle, *The Marquis d'Argenson* (1893).

MARC PIEERE DE VOYER DE PAULMY, comte d'Argenson (1696-1764), younger brother of the preceding, was born on the 16th of August 1696. Following the family tradition he studied law and was councillor at the parlement of Paris. He succeeded his father as lieutenant-general of police in Paris, but held the post only five months (January 26 to June 30, 1720). He then received the office of intendant of Tours, and resumed the lieutenancy of police in 1722. On the 2nd of January 1724 he was appointed councillor of state. He gained the confidence of the regent Orleans, administering his fortune and living with his son till 1737. During this period he opened his salon to the philosophers Chaulieu, la Fare and Voltaire, and collaborated in the legislative labours of the chancellor d'Aguesseau. In March 1737 d'Argenson was appointed director of the censorship of books, in which post he showed sufficiently liberal views to gain the approval of writers—a rare thing in the reign of Louis XV. He only retained this post for a year. He became president of the grand council (November 1738), intendant of the *généralité* of Paris (August 1740), was admitted to the king's council (August 1742), and in January 1743 was appointed secretary of state for war in succession to the baron de Breteuil. As minister for war he had a heavy task; the French armies engaged in the War of the Austrian Succession were disorganized, and the retreat from Prague had produced a disastrous effect. After consulting with Marshal Saxe, he began the reform of the new armies. To assist recruiting, he revived the old institution of local militias, which, however, did not come up to his expectation. In the spring of 1744 three armies were able to resume the offensive in the Netherlands, Germany and Italy, and in the following year France won the battle of Fontenoy, at which d'Argenson was present. After the peace in 1748 he occupied himself with the important work of recasting the French army on the model of the Prussian. He unified the types of cannon, grouped the grenadiers into separate regiments, and founded the École Militaire for the training of officers (1751). An edict of the 1st of November 1751 granted patents of nobility to all who had the rank of general officer. In addition to his duties as minister of war he had the supervision of the printing, postal administration and general administration of Paris. He was responsible for the arrangement of the promenade of the Champs Elysées and for the plan of the present Place de la Concorde. He was exceedingly popular, and, although the court favourites hated him, he had the support of the king. Nevertheless, after the attempt of R.F. Damiens to assassinate the king, Louis abandoned d'Argenson to the machinations of the court favourites and dismissed both him and his colleague, J.B. de Machault d'Arnouville (February 1757). D'Argenson was exiled to his estates at Les Ormes near Saumur, but he had previously found posts for his brother, the marquis d'Argenson, as minister of foreign affairs, for his son Marc René as master of the horse, and for his nephew Marc Antoine René as commissary of war. From the time of his exile he lived in the society of savants and philosophers. He had been elected member of the Académie des Inscriptions in 1749. Diderot and d'Alembert dedicated the *Encyclopedie* to him, and Voltaire, C.J.F. Hénault, and J.F. Marmontel openly visited him in his exile. After the death of Madame de Pompadour he obtained permission to return to Paris, and died a few days after his return, on the 22nd of August 1764.

MARC ANTOINE RENÉ DE VOYER, marquis de Paulmy d'Argenson (1722-1787), nephew of the preceding and son of René Louis, was born at Valenciennes on the 22nd of November 1722. Appointed councillor at the parlement (1744), and *maître des requêtes* (1747), he was associated with his father in the ministry of foreign affairs and with his uncle in the ministry of war, and, in recognition of this experience, was commissioned to inspect the troops and fortifications and sent on embassy to Switzerland (1748). In 1751 his uncle recognized him as his deputy and made over to him the reversion of the secretariate of war. He then worked on the great reform of the army, and after the dismissal of his uncle became minister of war (February 1757). But the outbreak of the Seven Years' War made this post exceedingly difficult to hold, and he resigned on the 23rd of March 1758. He was ambassador to Poland from 1762 to 1764, but failed to procure the nomination of the French candidate to that throne. From 1766 to 1770 he was ambassador at Venice. Failing to obtain the embassy at Rome, he retired at the age of forty-eight and devoted the rest of his life to indulging his tastes for history and biography. He brought together a large library, very rich in French poetry and romance, and undertook various publications with the help of his librarian. In 1775 he began his *Bibliothèque universelle des romans*, of which forty volumes appeared within three years, but subsequently handed over the publication to other editors. His great work, *Mélanges tirés d'une grande bibliothèque*, was published in 65 volumes (Paris, 1779-1788). At his death he forbade his library to be dispersed: it was bought by the comte d'Artois (afterwards Charles X.) and formed the nucleus of the present Bibliothèque de l'Arsenal at Paris (the marquis having been governor of the arsenal). He died on the 13th of August 1787.

See contemporary memoirs; also Dacier's eulogium in the *Académie des Inscriptions et Belles-Lettres* (November 1788); and Sainte-Beuve, *Causeries du lundi* (vol. xii.).

MARC RENÉ, marquis de Voyer de Paulmy d'Argenson (1721-1782), known as the marquis de Voyer, son of Marc Pierre de Voyer, the minister of war, was born in Paris on the 20th of September 1721. He served in the army of Italy and the army of Flanders in the War of the Austrian Succession, and was *mestre de camp* (proprietary colonel) of the regiment of Berry cavalry at the battle of Fontenoy (May 10, 1745), where he was promoted brigadier. He was associated with his father in his work of reorganizing the army, was made inspector of cavalry and dragoons (1749), and succeeded his father as master of the horse (1752). He introduced English horses into France. He was lieutenant-general of Upper Alsace in 1753 and governor of Vincennes in 1754, and served afterwards under Soubise in the Seven Years' War. He was wounded at Crefeld in 1758, and was promoted lieutenant-general (1759). He followed his father into exile at Les Ormes (1763), and in the last years of the reign of Louis XV. sided with the malcontents headed by Choiseul; but on the rupture with England he rejoined the service of the king (1775). He was appointed inspector of the sea-board, and put the roadstead of the island of Aix in a state of defence during the American War of Independence. He caught marsh-fever while attempting to drain the marshes of Rochefort, and died at Les Ormes on the 18th of September 1782.

MARC RENÉ MARIE DE VOYER DE PAULMY, marquis d'Argenson (1771-1842), son of the preceding, was born in Paris in September 1771. He was brought up by his father's cousin, the marquis de Paulmy, governor of the arsenal, and was made lieutenant of dragoons in 1789. Although, at the age of eighteen, he had succeeded to several estates and a large fortune, he embraced the revolutionary cause, joining the army of the North as Lafayette's aide-de-camp and remaining with it even after Lafayette's defection. Leaving France to take one of his sisters to England, he was denounced on his return as a royalist conspirator, on the charge of having in his possession portraits of the royal family. He then went to live in Touraine, married the widow of Prince Victor de Broglie, and saved her and her children from proscription. He introduced new agricultural instruments and processes on his estates, and installed machinery imported from England in his ironworks in Alsace. He was an enthusiastic adherent of Napoleon, by whom he was appointed in May 1809 prefect of Deux-Nèthes. He helped to repel the English invasion of the islands of South Beveland and Walcheren (August 1809), and afterwards directed the defence works of Antwerp, but resigned this post (March 1813) in consequence of the complaints of the inhabitants and the exacting demands of the emperor. In May 1814 he refused the prefecture of Marseilles offered to him by the Bourbons, but was elected deputy from Belfort in 1815 during the Hundred Days. On the 5th of July 1815 he took part in the declaration protesting against any tampering with the immutable rights of the nation. He was a member of the *Chambre introuvable*, where he became one of the orators of the democratic party. He was one of the founders of the journal *Le censeur européen* and of the *Club de la liberté de la presse*, and was an uncompromising opponent of reaction. Not re-elected in 1824 on account of his liberal ideas, he returned to the chamber under the Martignac ministry (1828), and resolutely persisted in his championship of the liberty of the press and of public worship. On the death of his wife he voluntarily renounced his mandate (July 1829), and hailed the revolution of 1830 with great satisfaction. On the 3rd of November 1830 he was elected to the chamber as deputy from Châtellerault, and took the oath, adding, however, the reservation "subject to the progress of the public reason." His independent attitude resulted in his defeat in the following year at the Châtellerault election, but he was returned for Strassburg. He wished the incidence of the taxes to be arranged according to social condition, and advocated a single tax proportionate to income like the English income tax. He harped incessantly on this idea in his speeches and articles (see his letters in *La Tribune* of June 20, 1832). Although he was a proprietor of ironworks he opposed the protectionist laws, which he considered injurious to the workmen. He became the mouthpiece of the advanced ideas; subsidized the opposition newspapers, especially the *National*; received into his house F.M. Buonarroti, who in 1796 had been implicated in the conspiracy of "Gracchus" Babeuf (*q.v.*); and became a member of the committee of the Society of the Rights of Man. He was even sued in the courts for a pamphlet called *Boutade d'un homme riche à sentiments populaires*, and delivered a speech to the jury in which he displayed very daring social theories. But he gradually grew discouraged and retired from public affairs, refusing even municipal office, and living in seclusion at La Grange in the forest of Guerche, where he devoted his inventive faculty to devising agricultural improvements. He subsequently returned to Paris, where he died on the 1st of August 1842.

CHARLES MARC RENÉ DE VOYER, marquis d'Argenson (1796-1862), son of the preceding, was born at Boulogne-sur-Spine on the 20th of April 1796. He concerned himself little with politics. He was, however, a member of the council-general of Vienne for six years, but was expelled from it in 1840 in consequence of his advanced ideas and his relations with the Opposition. In 1848 he was elected deputy from Vienne to the Constituent Assembly by 12,000 votes. He was an active member of the Archaeological Society of Touraine and the Society of Antiquaries of the West, and wrote learned works for these bodies. He collaborated in preparing the archives of the scientific congress at Tours in 1847; brought out two editions of the MSS. of his great-grand-uncle, the minister of foreign affairs under Louis XV., under the title *Mémoires du marquis d'Argenson*, one in 1825, and the other, in 5 vols., in 1857-1858; and published *Discours et opinions de mon père, M. Voyer d'Argenson* (2 vols., 1845). He died on the 31st of July,1862.

ARGENTAN, a town of north-western France, capital of an arrondissement in the department of Orne, 27 m. N.N.W. of Alençon on the railway from Le Mans to Caen. Pop. (1906) 5072. It is situated on the slope of a hill on the right bank of the Orne at its confluence with the Ure. The town has remains of old fortifications, among them the Tour Marguerite, and a château, now used as a law-court, dating from the 15th century. The church of St Germain (15th, 16th and 17th centuries) has several features of architectural beauty, notably the sculptured northern portal, and the central and western towers. The church of St Martin, dating from the 15th century, has good stained glass. The handsome modern town-hall contains among other institutions the tribunal of commerce, the museum and the library. Argentan is the seat of a sub-prefect, has a tribunal of first instance and a communal college. Leather-working and the manufacture of stained glass are leading industries. There are quarries of limestone in the vicinity. Argentan was a viscounty from the 11th century onwards; it was often taken and pillaged. During the Religious Wars it remained attached to the Catholic party. François Eudes de Mézeray, the historian, was born near the town, and a monument has been erected to his memory.

ARGENTEUIL, a town of northern France in the department of Seine-et-Oise, on the Seine, 5 m. N.W. of the fortifications of Paris by the railway from Paris to Mantes. Pop. (1906) 17,330. Argenteuil grew up round a monastery, which, dating from A.D. 656, was by Charlemagne changed into a nunnery; it was afterwards famous for its connexion with Héloise (see ABELARD), and on her expulsion in 1129 was again turned into a monastery. Asparagus, figs, and wine of medium quality are grown in the district; and heavy iron goods, chemical products, clocks and plaster are among the manufactures.

ARGENTINA, or the ARGENTINE REPUBLIC (officially, *Republica Argentina*), a country occupying the greater part of the southern extremity of South America. It is of wedge shape, extending from 21° 55' S. to the most southerly point of the island of Tierra del Fuego in 55° 2' 30" S., while its extremes of longitude are 53° 40' on the Brazilian frontier and 73° 17' 30" W. on the Chilean frontier. Its length from north to south is 2285 statute miles, and its greatest width about 930 m. It is the second largest political division of the continent, having an area of

1,083,596 sq. m. (Gotha measurement). It is bounded N. by Bolivia and Paraguay, E. by Paraguay, Brazil, Uruguay and the Atlantic, W. by Chile, and S. by the converging lines of the Atlantic and Chile.

Boundaries.—At different times Argentina has been engaged in disputes over boundary lines with every one of her neighbours, that with Chile being only settled in 1902. Beginning at the estuary of the Rio de la Plata, the boundary line ascends the Uruguay river, on the eastern side of the strategically important island of Martin García, to the mouth of the Pequiry, thence under the award of President Grover Cleveland in 1894 up that small river to its source and in a direct line to the source of the Santo Antonio, a small tributary of the Iguassú, thence down the Santo Antonio and Iguassú to the upper Paraná, which forms the southern boundary of Paraguay. From the confluence of the upper Paraná and Paraguay the line ascends the latter to the mouth of the Pilcomayo, which river, under the award of President R.B. Hayes in 1878, forms the boundary between Argentina and Paraguay from the Paraguay river north-west to the Bolivian frontier. In accordance with the Argentine-Bolivian treaty of 1889 the boundary line between these republics continues up the Pilcomayo to the 22nd parallel, thence west to the Tarija river, which it follows down to the Bermejo, thence up the latter to its source, and westerly through the Quiaca ravine and across to a point on the San Juan river opposite Esmoraca. From this point it ascends the San Juan south and west to the Cerro de Granadas, and thence south-west to Cerro Incahuasi and Cerro Zapalegui on the Chilean frontier. The boundary with Chile, extending across more than 32° lat., had been the cause of disputes for many years, which at times led to costly preparations for war. The debts of the two nations resulted largely from this one cause. In 1881 a treaty was signed which provided that the boundary line should follow the highest crests of the Andes forming the watershed as far south as the 52nd parallel, thence east to the 70th meridian and south-east to Cape Dungeness at the eastern entrance to the Straits of Magellan. Crossing the Straits the line should follow 461 the meridian of 68° 44′, south to Beagle Channel, and thence east to the Atlantic, giving Argentina the eastern part of the Tierra del Fuego and Staten Island. By this agreement Argentina was confirmed in the possession of the greater part of Patagonia, while Chile gained control of the Straits of Magellan, much adjacent territory on the north, the larger part of Tierra del Fuego and all the neighbouring islands south and west.

When the attempt was made to mark this boundary the commissioners were unable to agree on a line across the Puna de Atacama in the north, where parallel ranges enclosing a high arid plateau without any clearly defined drainage to the Atlantic or Pacific, gave an opportunity for conflicting claims. In the south the broken character of the Cordillera, pierced in places by large rivers flowing into the Pacific and having their upper drainage basins on the eastern side of the line of highest crests, gave rise to unforeseen and very difficult questions. Finally, under a convention of the 17th of April 1896, these conflicting claims were submitted to arbitration. In 1899 a mixed commission with Hon. W.I. Buchanan, United States minister at Buenos Aires, serving as arbitrator, reached a decision on the Atacama line north of 26° 52′ 45″ S. lat., which was a compromise though it gave the greater part of the territory to Argentina. The line starts at the intersection of the 23rd parallel with the 67th meridian and runs south-westerly and southerly to the mountain and volcano summits of Rincón, Socompa, Llullaillaco, Azufre, Aguas Blancas and Sierra Nevada, thence to the initial point of the British award. (See*Geogr. Jour.*, 1899, xiv. 322-323.) The line south of 26° 52′ 45″ S. lat. had been located by the commissioners of the two republics with the exception of four sections. These were referred to the arbitration of Queen Victoria, and, after a careful survey under the direction of Sir Thomas H. Holdich, the award was rendered by King Edward VII. in 1902. (See *Geogr. Jour.*, 1903, xxi. 45-50.) In the first section the line starts from a pillar erected in the San Francisco pass, about 26° 50′ S. lat., and follows the water-parting southward to the highest peak of the Tres Cruces mountains in 27° 0′ 45″ S. lat., 68° 49′ 5″ W. long. In the second, the line runs from 40° 2′ S. lat., 71° 40′ 36″ W. long., along the water-parting to the southern termination of the Cerro Perihueico in the valley of the Huahum river, thence across that river, 71° 40′ 36″ W. long., and along the water-parting around the upper basin of the Huahum to a junction with the line previously determined. In the third and longest section, the line starts from a pillar erected in the Perez Rosales pass, near Lake Nahuel-Huapi, and follows the water-parting southward to the highest point of Mt. Tronador, and thence in a very tortuous course along local water-partings and across the Chilean rivers Manso, Puelo, Fetaleufu, Palena, Pico and Aisen, and the lakes Buenos Aires, Pueyrredón and San Martin, to avoid the inclusion of Argentine settlements within Chilean territory, to the Cerro Fitzroy and continental water-parting north-west of Lake Viedma, between 49° and 50° S. lat. The northern half of this line does not run far from the 72nd meridian, except in 44° 30′ S. where it turns eastward nearly a degree to include the upper valley of the Frias river in Chilean territory, but south of the 49th parallel it curves westward to give Argentina sole possession of lakes Viedma and Argentino. The fourth section, which was made particularly difficult of solution by the extension inland of the Pacific coast inlets and sounds and by the Chilean colonies located there, was adjusted by running the line eastward from the point of divergence in 50° 50′ S. lat. along the Sierra Baguales, thence south and south-east to the 52nd parallel, crossing several streams and following the crests of the Cerro Cazador. The Chilean settlement of Ultima Esperanza (Last Hope), over which there had been much controversy, remains under Chilean jurisdiction.

Physical Geography.—For purposes of surface description, Argentina may be divided primarily into three great divisions—the mountainous zone and tablelands of the west, extending the full length of the republic; the great plains of the east, extending from the Pilcomayo to the Rio Negro; and the desolate, arid steppes of Patagonia. The first covers from one-third to one-fourth of the width of the country between the Bolivian frontier and the Rio Negro, and comprises the elevated Cordilleras and their plateaus, with flanking ranges and spurs toward the east. In the extreme north, extending southward from the great Bolivian highlands, there are several parallel ranges, the most prominent of which are: the Sierra de Santa Catalina, from which the detached Cachi, Gulumpaji and Famatina ranges project southward; and the Sierra de Santa Victoria, south of which are the Zenta, Aconquija, Ambato and Ancaste ranges. These minor ranges, excepting the Zenta, are separated from the Andean masses by comparatively low depressions and are usually described as distinct ranges; topographically, however, they seem to form a continuation of the ranges running southward from the Santa Victoria and forming the eastern rampart of the great central plateau of which the Puna de Atacama covers a large part. The elevated plateaus between these ranges are semi-arid and inhospitable, and are covered with extensive saline basins, which become lagoons in the wet season and morasses or dry salt-pans in the dry season. These saline basins extend down to the lower terraces of Córdoba, Mendoza and La Pampa. Flanking this great widening of the Andes on the south-east are the three short parallel ranges of Córdoba, belonging to another and older formation. North of them is the great saline depression, known as the "salinas grandes," 643 ft. above sea-level, where it is crossed by a railway; north-east is another extensive saline basin enclosing the "Mar Chiquita" (of Córdoba) and the morasses into which the waters of the Rio Saladillo disappear; and on the north are the more elevated plains, partly saline, of western Córdoba, which separate this isolated group of mountains from the Andean spurs of Rioja and San Luis. The eastern ranges parallel to the Andes are here broken into detached extensions and spurs, which soon disappear in the elevated western pampas, and the Andes contract south of Aconcagua to a single range, which descends gradually to the great plains of La Pampa and Neuquen. The lower terrace of this great mountainous region, with elevations ranging from 1000 to 1500 ft., is in reality the western margin of the great Argentine plain, and may be traced from Oran (1017 ft.) near the Bolivian frontier southward through Tucumán (1476 ft.), Frias (1129 ft.), Córdoba (1279 ft.), Rio Cuarto (1358 ft.), Paunero (1250 ft.), and thence westward and southward through still unsettled regions to the Rio Negro at the confluence of the Neuquen and Limay.

The Argentine part of the great La Plata plain extends from the Pilcomayo south to the Rio Negro, and from the lower terraces of the Andes eastward to the Uruguay and Atlantic. In the north the plain is known as the Gran Chaco, and includes the country between the Pilcomayo and Salado del Norte and an extensive depression immediately north of the latter river, believed to be the undisturbed bottom of the ancient Pampean sea. The northern part of the Gran Chaco is partly wooded and swampy, and as the slope eastward is very gentle and the rivers much obstructed by sand bars, floating trees and vegetation, large areas are regularly flooded during rainy seasons. South of the Bermejo the land is more elevated and drier, though large depressions covered with marshy lagoons are to be found, similar to those farther north. The forests here are heavier. Still farther south and south-west there are open grassy plains and large areas covered with salt-pans. The general elevation of the Chaco varies from 600 to 800 ft. above sea-level. The Argentine "mesopotamia," between the Paraná and Uruguay rivers, belongs in great measure to this same region, being partly wooded, flat and swampy in the north (Corrientes), but higher and undulating in the south (Entre Rios). The Misiones territory of the extreme north-east belongs to the older highlands of Brazil, is densely wooded, and has ranges of hills sometimes rising to a height of 1000 to 1300 ft.

The remainder of the great Argentine plain is the treeless, grassy*pampa* (Quichua for "level spaces"), apparently a dead level, but in reality rising gradually from the Atlantic westward toward the Andes. Evidence of this is to be found in the altitudes of the stations on the Buenos Aires and Pacific railway running a little north of west across the pampas to Mendoza. The average elevation of Buenos Aires is about 65 ft.; of Mercedes, 70 m. westward, 132 ft.; of Junín (160 m.), 267 ft.; and of Paunero (400 m.) it is 1250 ft., showing an average rise of about 3 ft. in a mile. The apparently uniform level of the pampas is much broken along its southern margin by the Tandil and Ventana sierras, and by ranges of hills and low mountains in the southern and western parts

23

of the territory of La Pampa. Extensive depressions also are found, some of which are subject to inundations, as along the lower Salado in Buenos Aires and along the lower courses of the Colorado and Negro. In the extreme west, which is as yet but slightly explored and settled, there is an extensive depressed area, largely saline in character, which drains into lakes and morasses, having no outlet to the ocean. The rainfall is under 6 in. annually, but the drainage from the eastern slopes of the Andes is large enough to meet the loss from evaporation and keep these inland lakes from drying up. At an early period this depressed area drained southward to the Colorado, and the bed of the old outlet can still be traced. The rivers belonging to this inland drainage system are the Vermejo, San Juan and Desaguadero, with their affluents, and their southward flow can be traced from about 28° S. lat. to the great lagoons and morasses between 36° and 37° S. lat. in the western part of La Pampa territory. Some of the principal affluents are the Vinchina and Jachal, or Zanjon, which flow into the Vermejo, the Patos, which flows into the San Juan, and the Mendoza, Tunuyan and Diamante which 462 flow into the Desaguadero, all of these being Andean snow-fed rivers. The Desaguadero also receives the outflow of the Laguna Bebedero, an intensely saline lake of western San Luis. The lower course of the Desaguadero is known as the Salado because of the brackish character of its water. Another considerable river flowing into the same great morass is the Atuel, which rises in the Andes not far south of the Diamante. (A description of the Patagonian part of Argentina will be found under PATAGONIA.)

Rivers and Lakes.—The hydrography of Argentina is of the simplest character. The three great rivers that form the La Plata system—the Paraguay, Paraná and Uruguay—have their sources in the highlands of Brazil and flow southward through a great continental depression, two of them forming eastern boundary lines, and one of them, the Paraná, flowing across the eastern part of the republic. The northern part of Argentina, therefore, drains eastward from the mountains to these rivers, except where some great inland depression gives rise to a drainage having no outlet to the sea, and except, also, in the "mesopotamia" region, where small streams flow westward into the Paraná and eastward into the Uruguay. The largest of the rivers through which Argentina drains into the Plata system are the Pilcomayo, which rises in Bolivia and flows south-east along the Argentine frontier for about 400 m.; the Bermejo, which rises on the northern frontier and flows south-east into the Paraguay; and the Salado del Norte (called Rio del Jura-mento in its upper course), which rises on the high mountain slopes of western Salta and flows south-east into the Paraná. Another river of this class is the Carcarañal, about 300 m. long, formed by the confluence of the Tercero and Cuarto, whose sources are in the Sierra de Córdoba; it flows eastward across the pampas, and discharges into the Paraná at Gaboto, about 40 m. above Rosario. Other small rivers rising in the Córdoba sierras are the Primero and Segundo, which flow into the lagoons of north-east Córdoba, and the Quinto, which flows south-easterly into the lagoons and morasses of southern Córdoba. The Luján rises near Mercedes, province of Buenos Aires, is about 150 m. long, and flows north-easterly into the Paraná delta. Many smaller streams discharge into the Paraguay and Paraná from the west, some of them wholly dependent upon the rains, and drying up during long droughts. The Argentine "mesopotamia" is well watered by a large number of small streams flowing north and west into the Paraná, and east into the Uruguay. The largest of these are the Corrientes, Feliciano and Gualeguay of the western slope, and the Aguapey and Miriñay of the eastern. None of the tributaries of the La Plata system thus far mentioned is navigable except the lower Pilcomayo and Bermejo for a few miles. These Chaco rivers are obstructed by sand bars and snags, which could be removed only by an expenditure of money unwarranted by the present population and traffic. In the southern pampa region there are many small streams, flowing into the La Plata estuary and the Atlantic; most of these are unknown by name outside the republic. The largest and only important river is the Salado del Sud, which rises in the north-west corner of the province of Buenos Aires and flows south-east for a distance of 360 m. into the bay of Samborombon. On the southern margin of the pampas are the Colorado and Negro, both large, navigable rivers flowing entirely across the republic from the Andes to the Atlantic. Many of the rivers of Argentina, as implied by their names (Salado and Saladillo), are saline or brackish in character, and are of slight use in the pastoral and agricultural industries of the country. The lakes of Argentina are exceptionally numerous, although comparatively few are large enough to merit a name on the ordinary general map. They vary from shallow, saline lagoons in the north-western plateaus, to great, picturesque, snow-fed lakes in the Andean foothills of Patagonia. The province of Buenos Aires has more than 600 lakes, the great majority small, and some brackish. The La Pampa territory also is dotted with small lakes. The Bebedero, in San Luis, and Porongos, in Córdoba, and others, are shallow, saline lakes which receive the drainage of a considerable area and have no outlet. The large saline Mar Chiquita, of Córdoba, is fed from the Sierra de Córdoba and has no outlet. In the northern part of Gorrientes there is a large area of swamps and shallow lagoons which are believed to be slowly drying up.

Harbours.—Although having a great extent of coast-line, Argentina has but few really good harbours. The two most frequented by ocean-going vessels are Buenos Aires and Ensenada (La Plata), both of which have been constructed at great expense to overcome natural disadvantages. Perhaps the best natural harbour of the republic is that of Bahia Blanca, a large bay of good depth, sheltered by islands, and 534 m. by sea south of Buenos Aires; here the government is building a naval station and port called Puerto Militar or Puerto Belgrano, and little dredging is needed to render the harbour accessible to the largest ocean-going vessels. About 100 m. south of Bahia Blanca is the sheltered bay of San Bias, which may become of commercial importance, and between the 42nd and 43rd parallels are the land-locked bays of San José and Nueva (Golfo Nuevo)—the first as yet unused; on the latter is Puerto Madryn, 838 m. from Buenos Aires, the outlet for the Welsh colony of Chubut. Other small harbours on the lower Patagonian coast are not prominent, owing to lack of population. An occasional Argentine steamer visits these ports in the interests of colonists. The beet-known among them are Puerto Deseado (Port Desire) at the mouth of the Deseado river (1253 m.), Santa Cruz, at the mouth of the Santa Cruz river (1481 m.), and Ushuaia, on Beagle Channel, Tierra del Fuego. North of Buenos Aires, on the Paraná river, is the port of Rosario, the outlet for a rich agricultural district, ranking next to the federal capital in importance. Other river ports, of less importance, are Concordia on the Uruguay river, San Nicolás and Campana on the Paraná river, Santa Fé on the Salado, a few miles from the Paraná, the city of Paraná on the Paraná river, and Gualeguay on the Gualeguay river.

Geology.—The Pampas of Argentina are generally covered by loess. The Cordillera, which bounds them on the west, is formed of folded beds, while the Sierras which rise in their midst, consist mainly of gneiss, granite and schist. In the western Sierras, which are more or less closely attached to the main chain of the Cordillera, Cambrian and Silurian fossils have been found at several places. These older beds are overlaid, especially in the western part of the country, by a sandstone series which contains thin seams of coal and many remains of plants. At Bajo de Velis, in San Luis, the plants belong to the "Glossopteris flora," which is so widely spread in South Africa, India and Australia, and the beds are correlated with the Karharbári series of India (Permian or Permo-Carboni-ferous). Elsewhere the plants generally indicate a higher horizon and are considered to correspond with the Rhaetic of Europe. Jurassic beds are known only in the Cordillera itself, and the Cretaceous beds, which occur in the west of the country, are of fresh-water origin. As far west, therefore, as the Cordillera, there is no evidence that any part of the region was ever beneath the sea in Mesozoic times, and the plant-remains indicate a land connexion with Africa. This view is supported by Neumayr's comparison of Jurassic faunas throughout the world. The Lower Tertiary consists largely of reddish sandstones resting upon the old rocks of the Cordillera and of the Sierras. Towards the east they lie at a lower level; but in the Andes they reach a height of nearly 10,000 ft., and are strongly folded, showing that the elevation of the chain was not completed until after their deposition. The marine facies of the later Tertiaries is confined to the neighbourhood of the coast, and was probably formed after the elevation of the Andes; but inland, fresh-water deposits of this period are met with, especially in Patagonia. Contemporaneous volcanic rocks are associated with the Ordovician beds and with the Rhaetic sandstones in several places. During the Tertiary period the great volcanoes of the Andes were formed, and there were smaller eruptions in the Sierras. The principal rocks are andesites, but trachytes and basalts are also common. Great masses of granite, syenite and diorite were intruded at this period, and send tongues even into the andesitic tuffs.

Silver, gold, lead and copper ores occur in many localities. They are found chiefly in the neighbourhood of the eruptive masses of the hilly regions. (See also ANDES.)1

Climate.—The great extent of Argentina in latitude—about 33°—and its range in altitude from sea-level westward to the permanently snow-covered peaks of the Andes, give it a highly diversified climate, which is further modified by prevailing winds and mountain barriers. The temperature and rainfall are governed by conditions different from those in corresponding latitudes of the northern hemisphere. Southern Patagonia and Tierra del Fuego, for instance, although they correspond in latitude to Labrador, are made habitable and an excellent sheep-grazing country by the southerly equatorial current along the continental coast. The climate, however, is colder than the corresponding latitudes of western Europe, because of the prevailing westerly winds, chilled in crossing the Andes. In the extreme north-west an elevated region, whose aridity is caused by the "blanketing" influence of the eastern Andean ranges, extends southward to Mendoza. The northern part of the republic, east of the mountains, is subject to the oscillatory movements of the south-east trade winds, which cause a division of the year into wet and dry seasons. Farther south, in Patagonia, the prevailing wind is westerly, in which case the Andes again "blanket" an extensive region and deprive it of rain, turning it into an arid desolate steppe. Below this region, where the Andean barrier is low and broken, the moist westerly winds sweep over the land freely and give it a large rainfall, good pastures and a vigorous forest growth.

25

If the republic be divided into sections by east and west lines, diversities of climate in the same latitude appear. In the extreme north a little over a degree and a half of territory lies within the torrid zone, extending from the Pilcomayo about 500 m. westward to the Chilean frontier; its eastern end is in the low, wooded plain of the Gran Chaco, where the mean annual temperature is 73° F., and the annual rainfall is 63 in.; but on the arid, elevated plateau at its western extremity the temperature falls below 57° F., and the rainfall has diminished to 2 in. The character of the soil changes from the alluvial lowlands of the Gran Chaco, covered with forests of palms and other tropical vegetation, to the sandy, saline wastes of the Puna de Atacama, almost barren of vegetation and overshadowed by permanently 463snow-crowned peaks. Between the 30th and 31st parallels, a region essentially sub-tropical in character, the temperature ranges from 66° on the eastern plains to 62-5° in Córdoba and 64° F. on the higher, arid, sun-parched tablelands of San Juan. The rainfall, which varies between 39 and 47 in. in Entre Rios, decreases to 27 in. in Córdoba and 2 in. in San Juan. The republic has a width of about 745 m. at this point, three-fourths of which is a comparatively level alluvial plain, and the remainder an arid plateau broken by mountain ranges. In the vicinity of Buenos Aires the climatic conditions vary very little from those of the pampa region; the mean annual temperature is about 63° (maximum 104°; minimum 32°), and the annual rainfall is 34 in.; snow is rarely seen. South of the pampa region, on the 40th parallel, the mean temperature varies only slightly in the 370 m. from the mouth of the Colorado to the Andes, ranging from 57° to 55°; but the rainfall increases from 8 in. on the coast to 16 in. on the east slope of the Cordillera. This section is near the northern border of the arid Patagonian steppes. In Tierra del Fuego (lat. 53° to 55°), the climatic conditions are in strong contrast to those of the north. Here the mean temperature is between 46° and 48° in summer and 36° and 38° in winter, rains are frequent, and snow falls every month in the year. The central and southern parts of the island and the neighbouring Staten Island are exceptionally rainy, the latter having 251½ rainy days in the year. The precipitation of rain, snow and hail is about 55 in.

(Click to enlarge.)

The prevailing winds through this southern region are westerly, being moist below the 52nd parallel, and dry between it and the 40th parallel. In the north and on the pampas the north wind is hot and depressing, while the south wind is cool and refreshing. The north wind usually terminates with a thunderstorm or with a *pampero*, a cold south-west wind from the Andes which blows with great violence, causes a fall in temperature of 15° to 20°, and is most frequent from June to November—the southern winter and spring. In the Andean region, a dry, hot wind from the north or north-west, called the *Zonda*, blows with great intensity, especially in September-October, and causes much discomfort and suffering. It is followed by a cold south wind which often lowers the temperature 25°. The climate of the pampas is temperate and healthy, and is admirably suited to agricultural and pastoral pursuits. Its greatest defect is the cold southerly and westerly storms, which cause great losses in cattle and sheep. The Patagonian coast-line and mountainous region are also healthy, having a dry and bracing climate. In the north, however, the hot lowlands are malarial and unsuited to north European settlement, while the dry, elevated plateaus are celebrated for their healthiness, those of Catamarca having an excellent reputation as a sanatorium for sufferers from pulmonary and bronchial diseases.

Flora.—The flora of Argentina should be studied according to natural zones corresponding to the physical divisions of the country—the rich tropical and sub-tropical regions of the north, the treeless pampas of the centre, the desert steppes of the south, and the arid plateaus of the north-west. The vegetation of each region has its distinctive character, modified here and there by elevation, irrigation from mountain streams, and by the saline character of the soil. In the extreme south, where an Arctic vegetation is found, the pastures are rich, and the forests, largely of the Antarctic beech (*Fagus antarctica*), are vigorous wherever the rainfall is heavy. The greater part of Patagonia is comparatively barren and has no arboreal growth, except in the well-watered valleys of the Andean foothills. The water-courses and depressions of the shingly steppts afford pasturage sufficient for the guanaco, and in places support a thorny vegetation of low growth and starved appearance. The Antarctic beech and Winter's bark (*Drimys Winteri*) are found at intervals along the Andes to the northern limits of this zone. The pampas, which cover so large a part of the republic, have no native trees whatever, and no woods except the scrubby growth of the delta islands of the Paraná, and a fringe of low thorn-bushes along the Atlantic coast south to Mar Chiquita and south of the Tandil sierra, which, strictly speaking, does not belong to this region. The great plains are covered with edible grasses, divided into two classes, *pasto duro* (hard grass) and *pasto blando*, or *tierno* (soft grass)—the former tall, coarse, nutritious and suitable for horses and cattle, and the latter tender grasses and herbs, including clovers, suitable for sheep and cattle. The so-called "pampas-grass" (*Gynerium argenteum*) is not found at all on the dry lands, but in the wet grounds of the south and south-west. The *pasto duro* is largely composed of the genera *Stipa* and *Melica*. In the dry, saline regions of the west and north-west, where the rainfall is slight, there are large thickets of low-growing, thorny bushes, poor in foliage. The predominating species is the chañar (*Gurliaca decorticans*), which produces an edible berry, and occurs from the Rio Negro to the northern limits of the republic. Huge cacti are also characteristic of this region. On the lower slopes of the Andes are found oak, beech, cedar, Winter's bark, pine (*Araucaria imbricata*), laurel and calden (*Prosopis algarobilla*). The provinces of Santa Fé, Córdoba and Santiago del Estero are only partially wooded; large areas of plains are intermingled with scrubby forests of algarrobo (*Prosopis*), quebracho-blanco (*Aspido-sperma quebracho*), tala (*Celtis tola, Sellowiana, acuminata*), acacias and other genera. In Tucumán and eastern Salta the same division into forests and open plains exists, but the former are of denser growth and contain walnut, cedar, laurel, tipa (*Machaerium fertile*) and quebracho-colorado (*Loxopterygium Lorentzii*). The territories of the Gran Chaco, however, are covered with a characteristic tropical vegetation, in which the palm predominates, but intermingled south of the Bermejo with heavy growths of algarrobo, quebracho-colorado, urunday (*Astronium fraxinifolium*), lapacho (*Tecoma curialis*) and palosanto (*Cuayacum officinalis*), all esteemed for hardness and fineness of grain. Other palms abound, such as the pindo (*Cocos australis*), mbocaya (*Cocos sclerocarpa*) and the yatai (*Cocos yatai*), but the predominating species north of the Bermejo is the caranday or Brazilian wax-palm (*Copernicia cerifera*), which has varied uses. The forest habit in this region is close association of species, and there are "palmares," "algarrobales," "chañarales," &c,, and among these open pasture lands, giving to a distant landscape a park-like appearance. In the "mesopotamia" region the flora is similar to that of the southern Chaco, but in the Misiones it approximates more to that of the neighbouring Brazilian highlands. Among the marvellous changes wrought in Argentina by the advent of European civilization, is the creation of a new flora by the introduction of useful trees and plants from every part of the world. Indian corn, quinoa, mandioca, possibly the potato, cotton and various fruits, including the strawberry, were already known to the aborigines, but with the conqueror came wheat, barley, oats, flax, many kinds of vegetables, apples, peaches, apricots, pears, grapes, figs, oranges and lemons, together with alfalfa and new grasses for the plains. The Australian eucalyptus is now grown in many places, and there are groves of the paradise or paraiso tree (*Melia azedarach*) on the formerly treeless pampa. The cereals of Europe are a source of increasing wealth to the nation, and alfalfa promises new prosperity for pastoral industries.

Fauna.—The Argentine fauna, like its flora, has been greatly influenced by the character and position of the pampas. Whatever it may have been in remote geological periods, it is now extremely limited both in size and numbers. Of the indigenous fauna, the tapir of the north and the guanaco of the west and south are the largest of the animals. The pampas were almost destitute of animal life before the horses and cattle of the Spanish invaders were there turned out to graze, and the puma and jaguar never came there until the herds of European cattle attracted them. The timid viscacha (*Lagostomus trichodactylus*), living in colonies, often with the burrowing owl, and digging deep under ground like the American prairie dog, was almost the only quadruped to be seen upon these immense open plains. The fox, of which several species exist, probably never ventured far into the plain, for it afforded him no shelter. Immense flocks of gulls were probably attracted to it then as now by its insect life, and its lagoons and streams teemed with aquatic birds. The occupation of this region by Europeans, and the introduction of horses, asses, cattle, sheep, goats and swine, have completely changed its aspect and character. On the Patagonian steppes there are comparatively few species of animals. Among them are the puma (*Felis concolor*), a smaller variety of the jaguar (*Felis onça*), the wolf, the fox, the Patagonian hare (*Dolichotis patagonica*) and two species of wild cat. The huge glyptodon once inhabited this region, which now possesses the smallest armadillo known, the "quir-quincho" or *Dasypus minutus*. The guanaco (*Auchenia*), which ranges from Tierra del Fuego to the Bolivian highlands, finds comparative safety in these uninhabitable solitudes, and is still numerous. The "ñandú" or American ostrich (*Rhea americana*), inhabiting the pampas and open plains of the Chaco, has in Patagonia a smaller counterpart (*Rhea Darwinii*), which is never seen north of the Rio Negro. On the arid plateaus of the north-west, the guanaco and vicuña are still to be found, though less frequently, together with a smaller species of viscacha (*Lagidium cuvieri*). The greatest development of the Argentine fauna, however, is in the warm, wooded regions of the north and north-east, where many animals are of the same species as those in the neighbouring territories of Brazil. Several species of monkeys inhabit the forests from the Paraná to the Bolivian frontier. Pumas, jaguars and one or two species of wild cat are numerous, as also the Argentine wolf and two of three species of fox. The coatí, marten, skunk and otter (*Lutra paranensis*) are widely distributed. Three species of deer are common. In the Chaco the tapir or anta (*Tapir americanus*) still finds a safe retreat, and the peccary (*Dycotyles torquatus*) ranges from Córdoba north to the Bolivian frontier. The capybara (*Hydrochoerus capybara*) is also numerous in this region. Of birds the number of species greatly exceeds that of the mammals, including the rhea of the pampas and condor of the Andes, and the tiny, brilliant-hued humming-birds of the tropical North. Vultures and hawks are well represented, but perhaps the most numerous of all are the parrots, of which there are six or seven species. The reptilians are represented in the Paraná by the jacaré (*Alligator sclerpos*), and on land by the "iguana" (*Teius teguexim, Podinema teguixin*), and some species of lizard. Serpents are numerous, but only two are described as poisonous, the cascavel (rattlesnake) and the "vibora de la cruz" (*Trigonocephalus alternatus*).2

464

Population.—In population Argentina ranks second among the republics of South America, having outstripped, during the last quarter of the 19th century, the once more populous states of Colombia and Peru. During the first half of the 19th century civil war and despotic government seriously restricted the natural growth of the country, but since the definite organization of the republic in 1860 and the settlement of disturbing political controversies, the population had increased rapidly. Climate and a fertile soil have been important elements in this growth. According to the first national census of 1869 the population was 1,830,214. The census of 1895 increased this total to 3,954,911, exclusive of wild Indians and a percentage for omissions customarily used in South American census returns. In 1904 official estimates, based on immigration and emigration returns and upon registered births and deaths, both of which are admittedly defective, showed a population increased to 5,410,028, and a small diminution in the rate of annual increase from 1895 to 1904 as compared with 1860-1895. The birth-rate is exceptionally high, largely because of the immigrant population, the greater part of which is concentrated in or near the large cities. In the rural districts of the northern provinces, the increase in population is much less than in the central provinces, the conditions of life being less favourable. According to the official returns,3 the over-sea immigration for the forty-seven years 1857-1903 aggregated 2,872,588, while the departure of emigrants during the same period was 1,066,480, showing a net addition to the population of 1,806,108. A considerable percentage of these arrivals and departures represents seasonal labourers, who come out from Europe solely for the Argentine wheat harvest and should not be classed as immigrants. Unfavourable political and economic conditions of a temporary character influence the emigration movement. During the years 1880-1889, when the country enjoyed exceptional prosperity, the arrivals numbered 1,020,907 and the departures only 175,038, but in 1890-1899, a period of financial depression following the extravagant Celman administration, the arrivals were 928,865 and the departures 532,175. Another disturbing influence has been the high protective tariffs, adopted during the closing years of the century, which increased the costs of living more rapidly than the wages for labour, and compelled thousands of immigrants to seek employment elsewhere. The influence of such legislation on unsettled immigrant labourers may be seen in the number of Italians who periodically migrate from Argentina to Brazil, and *vice versa*, seeking to better their condition. Of the immigrant arrivals for the forty-seven years given, 1,331,536 were Italians, 414,973 Spaniards, 170,293 French, 37,953 Austrians, 35,435 British, 30,699 Germans, 25,775 Swiss, 19,521 Belgians, and the others of diverse nationalities, so that Argentina is in no danger of losing her Latin character through immigration. This large influx of Europeans, however, is modifying the population by reducing the Indian and *mestizo* elements to a minority, although they are still numerous in the mesopotamian, northern and north-western provinces. The language is Spanish.

Science and Literature.—Though the university of Córdoba is the oldest but one in South America, it has made no conspicuous contribution to Argentine literature beyond the historical works of its famous rector, Gregorio Funes (1749-1830). This university was founded in 1621 and the university of Buenos Aires in 1821, but although Bonpland and some other European scientists were members of the faculty of Buenos Aires in its early years, neither there nor at Córdoba was any marked attention given to the natural sciences until President Sarmiento (official term, 1868-1874) initiated scientific instruction at the university of Córdoba under the eminent German naturalist, Dr Hermann Burmeister (1807-1892), and founded the National Observatory at Córdoba and placed it under the direction of the noted American astronomer, Benjamin Apthorp Gould (1824-1896). Both of these men made important contributions to science, and rendered an inestimable service to the country, not only through their publications but also through the interest they aroused in scientific research. A bureau of meteorology was afterwards created at Córdoba which has rendered valuable service. Dr Burmeister was afterwards placed in charge of the provincial museum of Buenos Aires, and devoted himself to the acquisition of a collection of fossil remains, now in the La Plata museum, which ranks among the best of the world. Not only has scientific study advanced at the university of Buenos Aires, but scientific research is promoting the development of the country; examples are the geographical explorations of the Andean frontier, and especially of the Patagonian Andes, by Francisco P. Moreno. In literature Argentina is still under the spell of Bohemianism and

28

dilettanteism. Exceptions are the admirable biographies of Manuel Belgrano (d. 1820) and San Martin, important contributions to the history of the country and of the war of independence, by ex-President Bartolomé Mitre (1821-1906). Buenos Aires has some excellent daily journals, but the tone of the press in general is sensational. The number of newspapers published is large, especially in Buenos Aires, where in 1902 the total, including sundry periodicals, was 183.

Political Divisions and Towns.—The chief political divisions of the republic consist of one federal district, 14 provinces and 10 territories, the last in great part dating from the settlement of the territorial controversies with Chile. For purposes of local administration the provinces are divided into departments. The names, area and population of the provinces and territories are as follows:

Administrative Divisions.	Area sq. m.	Pop. 1895.	Pop. est. for 1904.
Provinces—			
Federal Capital	72	663,854	979,235
Buenos Aires	117,778	921,168	1,312,953
Santa Fé	50,916	397,188	640,755
Entre Rios	28,784	292,019	367,006
Corrientes	32,580	239,618	299,479
Córdoba	62,160	351,223	465,464
San Luis	28,535	81,450	97,458
Santiago del Estero	39,764	161,502	186,206
Mendoza	56,502	116,136	159,780
San Juan	33,715	84,251	99,933
Rioja	34,546	69,302	82,099
Catamarca	47,531	90,161	103,082
Tucumán	8,926	215,742	263,079
Salta	62,184	118,015	136,059
Jujuy	18,977	49,713	55,430
Territories—			
Misiones	11,282	33,163	38,755
Formosa	41,402	4,829	6,094
Chaco	32,741	10,422	13,937
Pampa	56,320	25,914	52,150
Neuquen	42,345	14,517	18,022
Rio Negro	75,924	9,241	18,648
Chobut	93,	3,	9,

	,427	748	000
Santa Cruz	10	1,	1,
	9,142	058	793
Tierra del Fuego	8,	47	1,
	299	7	411
Los Andes	21	..	2,
	,989		095
Total	1,	3,	5,
	135,840	954,911	410,028
Gotha computations of 1902 with corrections for boundary changes.	1, 083,596		

The principal towns, with estimated population for 1905, are as follows: Buenos Aires (1,025,653), Rosario (129,121), La Plata (85,000), Tucumán (55,000), Córdoba (43.000), Sante Fé (33,200), Mendoza (32,000), Paraná (27,000), Salta (18,000), Corrientes (18,000), Chivilcoy (15,000), Gualeguaychú (13,300), San Nicolás (13,000), Concordia (11,700), San Juan (11,500), Río Cuarto (10,800), San Luis (10,500), Barracas al Sud (10,200).

Communications.—The development of railways in Argentina, which dates from 1857 when the construction of the Buenos Aires Western was begun, was at first slow and hesitating, but after 1880 it went forward rapidly. Official corruption and speculation have led to some unsound ventures, but in the great majority of cases the lines constructed have been beneficial and productive. The principal centres of the system are Buenos Aires, Rosario and Bahia Blanca, with La Plata as a secondary centre to the former, and from these the lines radiate westward and northward. The creation of a commercial port at Bahia Blanca and the development of the territories of La Pampa, Rio Negro and Neuquen, have given an impetus to railway construction in that region, and new lines are being extended toward the promising districts among the Andean foothills. Beginning with 6 m. in 1857, the railway mileage of the republic increased to 1563 m. in 1880, 5865 m. in 1890, 7752 m. in 1891, 10,304 m. in 1901, and 12,274 m. in 1906, with 1794 m. under construction. The greater development of railway construction between 1885 and 1891 was due, principally, to the dubious concessions of interest guarantees by the Celman administration, and also to the fever of speculation. Some of these lines resulted disastrously. The Transandine line, designed to open railway communication between Buenos Aires and Valparaiso, was so far completed early in 1909 that on the Argentine side only the summit tunnel, 2 m. 127 yds. long, remained to be finished. The piercing was completed in Nov. 1909, but in the meantime passengers were conveyed by road over the pass. The gauge is broken at Mendoza, the Buenos Aires and Pacific having a gauge of 5 ft. 6 in. and the Transandine of one metre.

Tramway lines, which date from 1870, are to be found in all important towns. Those of Buenos Aires, Rosario and La Plata are owned by public companies. According to the census returns of 1895, the total mileage was 496 m., representing a capital expenditure of $84,044,581 paper. Electric traction was first used in Buenos Aires in 1897, since when nearly all the lines of that city have been reconstructed to meet its requirements, and subways are contemplated to relieve the congested street traffic of the central districts; the companies contribute 6% of their gross receipts to the municipality, besides paying $50 per annum per square on each single track in paved streets, 5 per thousand on the value of their property, and 33% of the cost of street repaving and renewals.

The telegraph lines of Argentina are subject to the national telegraph law of 1875, the international telegraph conventions, and special conventions with Brazil and Uruguay. In 1902 the total length of wires strung was 28,125 m.; in 1906 it had been increased to 34,080 m. The national lines extend from Buenos Aires north to La Quiaca on the Bolivian frontier (1180 m.), and south to Cape Virgenes (1926 m.), at the entrance to the Straits of Magellan. Telegraphic communication with Europe is effected by cables laid along the Uruguayan and Brazilian coasts, and by the Brazilian land lines to connect with transatlantic cables from Pernambuco. Communication with the United States is effected by land lines to Valparaiso, and thence by a cable along the west coast. The service is governed by the international telegraph regulations, but is subject to local inspection and interruption in times of political disorder.

The postal and telegraph services are administered by the national government, and are under the immediate supervision of the minister of the interior. Argentina has been a member of the Postal Union since 1878. Owing to the great distances which must be covered, and also to the defective means of communication in sparsely settled districts, the costs of the postal service in Argentina are unavoidably high in relation to the receipts.

30

Shipping.—Although Argentina has an extensive coast-line, and one of the great fluvial systems of the world, the tonnage of steamers and sailing vessels flying her flag is comparatively small. In 1898 the list comprised only 1416 sailing vessels of all classes, from 10 tons up, with a total tonnage of 118,894 tons, and 222 steamships, of 36,323 tons. There has been but slight improvement since that date. There are excellent fishing grounds on the coast, but they have had no appreciable influence in developing a commerical marine. The steamships under the national flag are almost wholly engaged in the traffic between Buenos Aires and Montevideo, the river traffic, and port services.

Agriculture.—In 1878 the production of wheat was insufficient for home consumption, the amount of Indian corn grown barely covered local necessities, and the only market for live stock was in the slaughtering establishments, where the meat *Live stock, &c.* was cut into strips and cured, making the so-called "jerked beef" for the Brazilian and Cuban markets. But three years later a new economic development began. In 1881 President Roca offered for public purchase by auction the lands in the south-west of the province of Buenos Aires, the Pampa Central, and the Neuquen district, these lands having been rendered habitable after the campaign of 1878 against the Indians. The upset (reserve) price was £80 sterling per square league of 6669 acres, and, as the lands were quickly sold, an expansion of the pastoral industry immediately ensued. The demand for animals for stock-breeding purposes sent up prices, and this acted as a stimulus to other branches of trade, so that, as peace under the Roca regime seemed assured, a steady flow of immigration from Italy set in. The development of the pastoral industry of Argentina from that time to the end of the century was remarkable. In 1878 the number of cattle was 12,000,000; of sheep, 65,000,000; and of horses, 4,000,000; in 1899 the numbers were—cattle, 25,000,000; sheep, 89,000,000; and horses, about 4,500,000. Originally the cattle were nearly all of the long-horned Spanish breed and of little value for their meat, except to the saladero establishments. Gradually Durham, Shorthorn, Hereford and other stock were introduced to improve the native breeds, with results so satisfactory that now herds of three-quarters-bred cattle are to be found in all parts of the country. Holstein, Jersey and other well-known dairy breeds were imported for the new industries of butter- and cheese-making. Not only has the breed of cattle been improved, but the system of grazing has completely altered. Vast areas of land have been ploughed and sown with lucerne (alfalfa); magnificent permanent pasturage has been created where there were coarse and hard grasses in former days, and Argentina has been able to add baled hay to her list of exports. In 1889 the first shipment of Argentine cattle, consisting altogether of 1930 steers, was sent to England. The results of these first experiments were not encouraging, owing mainly to the poor class of animals, but the exporters persevered, and the business steadily grew in value and importance, until in 1898 the number of live cattle shipped was 359,296, which then decreased to 119,189 in 1901, because of the foot-and-mouth disease. In 1906 the export of live stock was prohibited for that reason. Large quantities of frozen and preserved meat are exported, profitable prices being realized. Dairy-farming is making rapid strides, and the development of sheep-farming has been remarkable. In 1878, 65,000,000 sheep yielded 230,000,000 Ib weight of wool, or an average per sheep of, about 3½ ℔ In the season of 1899-1900 the wool exports weighed 420,000,000 Ib, and averaged more than 5 ℔ per sheep. The extra weight of fleece was owing to the large importation of better breeds. The export, moreover, of live sheep and of frozen mutton to Europe has become an important factor in the trade of Argentina. In 1892 the number of live sheep shipped for foreign ports was 40,000; in 1898 the export reached a total of 577,813, which in 1901 fell off to 25,746. In 1892 the frozen mutton exported was 25,500 tons, and this had increased in 1901 to 63,013 tons.

The advance made in agricultural industry also is of very great importance. In 1872 the cultivated area was about 1,430,000 acres; in 1895, 12,083,000 acres; in 1901, 17,465,973 acres. In 1899 the wheat exports exceeded 50,000,000 bushels, and *Crops.* the Indian corn 40,000,000 bushels. The area under wheat in 1901 was 8,351,843 acres; Indian corn, 3,102,140 acres; linseed, 1,512,340 acres; alfalfa, 3,088,929 acres. The farming industry is not, however, on a satisfactory basis. No national lands in accessible districts are available for the application of a homestead law, and the farmer too often has no interest in the land beyond the growing crops, a percentage of the harvest being the rent charged by the owner of the property. This system is mischievous, since, if a few, consecutive bad seasons occur, the farmer moves to some more favoured spot; while, on the other hand, a succession of good years tends to increase rents. The principal wheat and Indian corn producing districts lie in the provinces of Santa Fé, Buenos Aires, Córdoba and Entre Rios, and the average yield of wheat throughout the country is about 12 bushels to the acre. Little attention is paid to methods of cultivation, and the farmer has no resources to help him if the cereal crops fail. In the Andean provinces of Mendoza, San Juan, Catamarca and Rioja viticulture attracts much attention, and the area in vineyards in 1901 was 109,546 acres, only 18% of which was outside the four provinces named. Wine is manufactured in large quantities, but the output is not sufficient to meet the home demand. In the provinces of Tucumán, Salta and Jujuy the main industry is sugar growing and manufacture. In 1901 the production of sugar was 151,639 tons, of which 58,000 tons were exported. The sugar manufacture, however, is a protected and bounty-fed industry, and the 51 sugar mills in operation in 1901 are a heavy tax upon consumers and taxpayers. Other products are tobacco, olives, castor-oil, peanuts, canary-seed, barley, rye, fruit and vegetables.

The pastoral and agricultural industries have been hampered by fluctuations in the value of the currency, farm products being sold at a gold value for the equivalent in paper, while labourers are paid in currency. The existing system of taxation also presses heavily upon the provinces, as may be seen from the fact that the national, provincial and municipal exactions together amount to £7 per head of population, while the total value of the exports in 1898 was only £6 in round numbers. The *guia* tax on the transport of stock from one province to another, which has been declared unconstitutional in the courts, is still enforced, and is a vexatious tax upon the stock-raiser, while the consumption, or *octroi*, tax in Buenos Aires and other cities is a heavy burden upon small producers.

Manufactures.—Manufacturing enterprise in Argentina, favoured by the protection of a high tariff, made noticeable progress in the national capital during the closing years of the last century, especially in those small industries which commanded a secure market. The principal classes of products affected are foods, wearing apparel, building materials, furniture, &c., chemical products, printing and allied trades, and sundry others, such as cigars, matches, tanning, paints, &c. In some manufactures the raw material is imported partly manufactured, such as thread for weaving. The lack of coal in Argentina greatly increases the difficulty and cost of maintaining these industries, and high prices of the products result. Electric power generated by steam is now commonly used in Buenos Aires and other large cities for driving light machinery.

Commerce.—The rapid development of the foreign trade of the republic since 1881 is due to settled internal conditions and to the 466 prime necessity to the commercial world of many Argentine products, such as beef, mutton, hides, wool, wheat and Indian corn. Efforts to hasten this development have created some serious financial and industrial crises, and have burdened the country with heavy debts and taxes. During the decade 1881-1890 great sums of European capital were invested in railways and other undertakings, encouraged by the grant of interest guarantees and by state mortgage bank loans in the form of *cedulas*, nominally secured on landed property. In 1890 the crisis came, the mortgage banks failed, credits were contracted, the value of property declined, defaults were common, imports decreased, and the losses to the country were enormous. The constant fluctuations in the value of the currency, then much depreciated, intensified the distress and complicated the situation. Recovery required years, although made easier by the sound and steady development of the pastoral and agricultural industries, which were slightly affected by the crisis; and the steadily increasing volume of exports, mainly foodstuffs and other staples, saved the situation. There have been some changes in commercial methods since 1890, the retailer, and sometimes the consumer, importing direct to save intermediate commission charges. Such transactions are made easy by the foreign banks established in all the large cities of the republic. The conversion law of 1899, which gave a fixed gold value to the currency (44 centavos gold for each 100 centavos paper), has had beneficial influence on commercial transactions, through the elimination of daily fluctuations in the value of the currency, and the commercial and financial situation has been steadily improved, notwithstanding heavy taxation and tariff restrictions. The import trade shows the largest totals in foodstuffs, wines and liquors, textiles and raw materials for their manufacture, wood and its manufactures, iron and its manufactures, paper and cardboard, glass and ceramic wares. The official valuation of imports, which is arbitrary and incorrect, was $164,569,884 gold in 1889, fell off to $67,207,780 in 1891, but gradually increased to $205,154,420 in 1905. The exports, which are almost wholly of agricultural and pastoral products, increased from $103,219,000 in 1891 to $322,843,841 in 1905.

Government.—The present constitution of Argentina dates from the 25th of September 1860. The legislative power is vested in a congress of two chambers—the senate, composed of 30 members (two from each province and two from the capital), elected by the provincial legislatures and by a special body of electors in the capital for a term of nine years; and the chamber of deputies, of 120 members (1906), elected for four years by direct vote of the people, one deputy for every 33,000 inhabitants. To the chamber of deputies exclusively belongs the initiation of all laws relating to the raising of money and the conscription of troops. It has also the exclusive right to impeach the president, vice-president, cabinet ministers, and federal judges before the senate. The executive power is exercised by the president, elected by presidential electors from each province chosen by direct vote of the people. The president and vice-president are voted for by separate tickets. The system closely resembles that followed in the

United States. The president must be a native citizen of Argentina, a Roman Catholic, not under thirty years of age, and must have an annual income of at least $2000. His term of office is six years, and neither he nor the vice-president is eligible for the next presidential term. All laws are sanctioned and promulgated by the president, who is invested with the veto power, which can be overruled only by a two-thirds vote. The president, with the advice and consent of the senate, appoints judges, diplomatic agents, governors of territories, and officers of the army and navy above the rank of colonel. All other officers and officials he appoints and promotes without the consent of the senate. The cabinet is composed of eight ministers—the heads of the government departments of the interior, foreign affairs, finance, war, marine, justice, agriculture, and public works. They are appointed by and may be removed by the president.

Justice is administered by a supreme federal court of five judges and an attorney-general, which is also a court of appeal, four courts of appeal, with three judges each, located in Buenos Aires, La Plata, Paraná and Córdoba, and by a number of inferior and local courts. Each province has also its own judicial system. Trial by jury is established by the constitution, but never practised. Civil and criminal courts are both corrupt and dilatory. In May 1899 the minister of justice stated in the chamber of deputies that the machinery of the courts in the country was antiquated, unwieldy and incapable of performing its duties; that 50,000 cases were then waiting decision in the minor courts, and 10,000 in the federal division; and that a reconstruction of the judiciary and the judicial system had become necessary. In June 1899 he sent his project for the reorganization of the legal procedure to congress, but no action was then taken beyond referring the bill to a committee for examination and report. The proceedings are, with but few exceptions, written, and the procedure is a survival of the antiquated Spanish system.

Under the constitution, the provinces retain all the powers not delegated to the federal government. Each province has its own constitution, which must be republican in form and in harmony with that of the nation. Each elects its governor, legislators and provincial functionaries of all classes, without the intervention of the federal government. Each has its own judicial system, and enacts laws relating to the administration of justice, the distribution and imposition of taxes, and all matters affecting the province. All the public acts and judicial decisions of one province have full legal effect and authority in all the others. In cases of armed resistance to a provincial government, the national government exercises the right to intervene by the appointment of an interventor, who becomes the executive head of the province until order is restored. The territories are under the direct control of the national government.

Army.—The military service of the republic was reorganized in 1901, and is compulsory for all citizens between the ages of 20 and 45. The army consists of: (1) The Line, comprising the Active and Reserve, in which all citizens 20 to 28 years of age are obliged to serve; (2) the National Guard, comprising citizens of 28 to 40 years; (3) the Territorial Guard, comprising those 40 to 45 years. Conscripts of 20 years of age have to serve two years, three months each year. The active or standing army comprises 18 battalions of infantry, 12 regiments of cavalry, 8 regiments of artillery, and 4 battalions of engineers. A military school, with 125 cadets, is maintained at San Martin, near the national capital, and a training school for non-commissioned officers in the capital itself. Compulsory attendance of young men at national guard drills is enforced for at least two months of the year, under penalty of enforced service in the Line. In 1906 the president announced that permission had been given by the German emperor for 30 Argentine officers to enter the German army each year and to serve eighteen months, and also for five officers to attend the Berlin Military Academy. The equipment of the standing army is thoroughly modern, the infantry being provided with Mauser rifles and the artillery with Krupp batteries.

Navy.—The disputes with Chile during the closing years of the 19th century led to a large increase in the navy, but in 1902 a treaty between the two countries provided for the restriction of further armaments for the next four years. The naval vessels then under construction were accordingly sold, but in 1906 both countries, influenced apparently by the action of Brazil, gave large orders in Europe for new vessels. At the time when further armaments were suspended, the effective strength of the Argentine navy consisted of 3 ironclads, 6 first-class armoured cruisers, 2 monitors (old), 4 second-class cruisers, 2 torpedo cruisers, 3 destroyers, 3 high-sea torpedo boats, 14 river torpedo boats, 1 training ship, 5 transports, and various auxiliary vessels. Two of these first-class cruisers were sold to Japan. The armament included 394 guns of all calibres, 6 of which were of 250 millimetres, 4 of 240, and 12 of 200. There are about 320 officers in active service, and the total personnel ranges from 5000 to 6000 men. The service is not popular, and it is recruited by means of conscription from the national guard, the term of service being two years. These conscripts number about 2000 a year. In addition, there is a corps of coast artillery numbering 450 men, from which garrisons are drawn for the military port, Zárate arsenal and naval prison. The government maintains a naval school at Flores, a school of mechanics in Buenos Aires, an artillery school on the cruiser "Patagonia," and a school for torpedo practice at

La Plata. The naval arsenal is situated on the "north basin" of the Buenos Aires port, and the military port at Bahia Blanca is provided 467 with a dry dock of the largest size, and extensive repair shops. There is also a dockyard and torpedo arsenal at La Plata, an artillery depot at Zárate, above Buenos Aires, and naval depots on the island of Martin Garcia and at Tigre, on the Luján river.

Education.—Primary education is free and secular, and is compulsory for children of 6 to 14 years. In the national capital and territories it is supervised by a national council of education with the assistance of local school boards; in the 14 provinces it is under provincial control. Secondary instruction is also free, but is not compulsory. It is under the control of the national government, which in 1902 maintained 10 colleges. Of these colleges four are in Buenos Aires, one in each province, and one in Concepción del Uruguay. For the instruction of teachers the republic has 28 normal schools, as follows: three in the national capital; one in Paraná, three (regional) in Corrientes, San Luis and Catamarca; 14 for female teachers in the provincial capitals; and seven for either sex in the larger towns of the provinces of Buenos Aires, Santa Fé, Córdoba and San Luis. The normal schools, maintained by the state on a secular basis, were founded by President Sarmiento, who engaged experienced teachers in the United States to direct them; their work is excellent; notably, their model primary schools. For higher and professional education there are two national universities at Buenos Aires and Córdoba, and three provincial universities, at La Plata, Santa Fé and Paraná, which comprise faculties of law, medicine and engineering, in addition to the usual courses in arts and science. To meet the needs of technical and industrial education there are a school of mines at San Juan, a school of viticulture at Mendoza, an agronomic and veterinary school at La Plata, several agricultural and pastoral schools, and commercial schools in Buenos Aires, Rosario, Bahia Blanca and Concordia. Schools of art and conservatories of music are also maintained in the large cities, where there are, besides, many private schools. Secular education has been vigorously opposed by strict churchmen, and efforts have been made to maintain separate schools under church control. The national government has founded several scholarships (some in art) for study abroad. The total school population of Argentina in 1900 (6 to 14 years) was 994,089, of which 45% attended school, and 13% of those not attending were able to read and write. The illiterate school population was about 41%, and of those of 15 years and over 54% were illiterate. Of the whole population over 6 years, 50.5% were illiterate.

Religion.—The Argentine constitution recognizes the Roman Catholic religion as that of the state, but tolerates all others. The state controls all ecclesiastical appointments, decides on the passing or rejection of all decrees of the Holy See, and provides an annual subsidy for maintenance of the churches and clergy. Churches and chapels are founded and maintained by religious orders and private gift as well. At the head of the Argentine hierarchy are one archbishop and five suffragan bishops, who have five seminaries for the education of the priesthood. From statistics of 1895 it appears that in each 1000 of population 991 are Roman Catholics, 7 Protestants, and 2 Jews, the Jews being entirely of Russian origin, sent into the republic since 1891 by the Jewish Colonization Association under the provisions of the Hirsch legacy; from 1895 to 1908 the number of Jews in Argentina increased from 6085 to about 30,000.

Finance.—The revenue of the republic is derived mainly from customs and excise, and the largest item of expenditure is the service of the public debt. Since 1891 the national budgets have been calculated in both gold and currency, and both receipts and expenditures have been carried out in this dual system. The collection of a part of the import duties in gold has served to give the government the gold it requires for certain expenditures, but it has complicated returns and accounts and increased the burden of taxation. According to a compilation of statistical returns published by Dr. Francisco Latzina in 1901, the national revenues and expenditures for the 37 years from 1864 to 1900, inclusive, reduced to a common standard, show a total deficit for that period of $408,260,795 gold, which has been met by external and internal loans, and by a continued increase in the scope and rate of taxation. The growth of the annual budget is shown by a comparison of the following years:—

	Total Revenue.	Total Expenditure.
1864	$7,005,328 gold.	$7,119,931 gold.
1880	19,594,306 "	26,919,295 "
1890	73,150,856 "	95,363,854 "
1900	62,045,458 paper.	104,501,614 paper.
	37,998,704 gold.	23,644,543 gold.

34

| 1 905 | 63,439,000 paper. 43,461,324 gold. | 105,581,680 paper. 24,865,016 gold. |

The bane of Argentine finance has been the extravagant and unscrupulous use of national credit for the promotion of schemes calculated to benefit individuals rather than the public. The large increase in military expenditures during the disputes with Chile also proved a heavy burden, and in the continued strife with Brazil for naval superiority this burden could not fail to be increased greatly. A very considerable percentage of Argentina's population of five to six millions is hopelessly poor and unprogressive, and cannot be expected to bear its share of the burden. To meet these expenditures there are a high tariff on imported merchandise, and excise and stamp taxes of a far-reaching and often vexatious character. Nothing is permitted to escape taxation, and duplicated taxes on the same thing are frequent. In Argentina these burdens bear heavily upon the labouring classes, and in years of depression they send away by thousands immigrants unable to meet the high costs of living. For the year 1900 the total expenditures of the national government, 14 provincial governments, and 16 principal cities, were estimated to have been $208,811,925 paper, which is equivalent to $91,877,247 gold, or (at $5.04 per pound stg.) to £18,229,612, 10s. The population that year was estimated to be 4,794,149, from which it is seen that the annual costs of government were no less than £3, 16s. for each man, woman, and child in the republic. About 71% of this charge was on account of national expenditures, and 29% provincial and municipal expenditures. Had the expenses of all the small towns and rural communities been included, the total would be in excess of $20 gold, or £4, *per capita*.

In 1889 the public debt of the republic amounted to about £24,000,000, but the financial difficulties which immediately followed that year, and the continuance of excessive expenditures, forced the debt up to approximately £128,000,000 during the next ten years. In the year 1905 the outstanding and authorized debt of the republic was as follows:—

External debt (July 31, 1905):

National loans	£42, 297,050
Provincial loans and others, assumed	30,3 95,916
National cedulas	11,7 63,923
Total	£84, 456,889

Consolidated Internal debt (Dec. 31, 1904):

Gold	$16,5 44,000	
Paper	79,17 4,400	
	—— ——	£10, 178,718
Total service on funded debt, 1905, $24,375,067 gold, and $15,914,335 paper		£6,2 25,669
Floating debt	£259, 170	
Treasury bills (Apr. 30, 1905)	275,2 20	
Unpaid bills, $3,332,594, paper	288,5 60	
	—— ——	£822 ,950

The paper currency forms an important part of the internal debt, and has been a fruitful source of trouble to the country. Few countries have suffered more from a depreciated currency than Argentina. During the era of so-called "prosperity" between 1881 and 1890 an enormous amount of bank notes were issued under various authorizations, especially that of the "free banking law" of 1887. During this period the bank-note circulation was increased to $161,700,000, and two mortgage banks—the National Hypothecary Bank and the Provincial Mortgage Bank (of Buenos Aires)—flooded the country with $509,000,000 of *cedulas*(hypothecary bonds). When the crash came and the national treasury was found to be without resources to meet current expenses, further issues of $110,000,000 in currency were made. The free-banking law which permitted the issue of notes by provincial banks was primarily responsible for this situation. Under the provisions of this law the provinces were authorized to borrow specie abroad and deposit the same with the national government as security for their issues. These loans aggregated £27,000,000. The Celman administration, in violation of the trust, then sold the specie and squandered the proceeds, leaving the provincial bank notes without guarantee and value. The national government has since assumed responsibility for all these provincial loans abroad. As on previous occasions, the great depreciation in the value of the currency has led to a repudiation of part of its nominal value. This depreciation reached its maximum in October 1891 ($460.82 paper for $100 gold), and remained between that figure and $264 during the next six years. To check these prejudicial fluctuations and to prevent too great a fall in the price of gold (to repeat a popular misconception), a 468conversion law was adopted on the 31st of October 1899, which provided that the outstanding circulation should be redeemed at the rate of 44 centavos gold for each 100 centavos paper, the official rate for gold being 227.27. Provisions were also made for the creation of a special conversion fund in specie to guarantee the circulation, which fund reached a total of $100,000,000 in March 1906. These measures have served to give greater stability to the value of the circulating medium, and to prevent the ruinous losses caused by a constant fluctuation in value, but the rate established prevents the further appreciation of the currency. On the 18th of January 1906 the currency in circulation amounted to $502,420,485, which is more than $95 *per capita*.

(A. J. L.)

HISTORY

The first Europeans who visited the river Plate were a party of Spanish explorers in search of a south-west passage to the East Indies. Their leader, Juan Diaz de Solis, landing incautiously in 1516 on the north coast with a few attendants to parley with a body of Charrua Indians, was suddenly attacked by them and was killed, together with a number of his followers. This untoward disaster led to the abandonment of the expedition, which forthwith returned to Spain, bringing with them the news of the discovery of a fresh-water sea. Four years later (1520) the Portuguese seaman, Ferdinand Magellan, entered the estuary in his celebrated voyage round the world, undertaken in the service of the king of Spain (Charles I., better known as the emperor Charles V.). Magellan, as soon as he had satisfied himself that there was no passage to the west, left the river without landing.

The first attempt to penetrate by way of the river Plate and its affluents inland, with a view to effecting settlements in the interior, was made in 1526 by Sebastian Cabot. This great navigator had already won renown in the service *Cabot.* of Henry VII. of England by his voyage to the coast of North America in company with his father, Giovanni Caboto or Cabot (see CABOT, JOHN). Sebastian Cabot had in 1519 deserted England for Spain, and had received from King Charles the post of pilot-major formerly held by Juan de Solis. In 1526 he was sent out in command of an expedition fitted out for the purpose of determining by astronomical observations the exact line of demarcation, under the treaty of Tordesillas, between, the colonizing spheres of Spain and Portugal, and of conveying settlers to the Moluccas. Arrived in the river Plate in 1527, rumours reached Cabot of mineral wealth and a rich and civilized empire in the far interior, and he resolved to abandon surveying for exploration. He built a fort a short distance up the river Uruguay, and despatched one of his lieutenants, Juan Alvarez Ramon, with a separate party upon an expedition up stream. This expedition was assailed by the Charruas and forced to return on foot, their leader himself being killed. Cabot, with a large following, entered the Paraná and established a settlement just above the mouth of the river Carcarañal, to which he gave the name of San Espiritù, among the Timbú Indians, with whom he formed friendly relations. He continued the ascent of the Paraná as far as the rapids of Apipé, and finding his course barred in this direction, he afterwards explored the river Paraguay, which he mounted as far as the mouth of the affluent called by the Indians Lepeti, now the river Bermejo. His party was here fiercely attacked by the Agaces or Payaguá Indians, and suffered severely. Cabot in his voyage had seen many silver ornaments in the possession of the Timbú and Guarani Indians. Some specimens of these trinkets he sent back to Spain with a report of his discoveries. The arrival of these first-fruits of the mineral wealth of the southern continent gained for the estuary of the Paraná the name which it has since borne, that of Rio de la Plata, the silver river. As Cabot was descending the stream to his settlement of San Espiritù, he encountered an expedition which had been despatched from Spain for the express purpose of exploring the river discovered by Solis, under the command of Diego Garcia. Finding that he had been forestalled, Garcia resolved to return home. Cabot himself, after an absence of more than three years, came back in 1530, and applied to Charles V. for means to open up communications with Peru by way of the river

36

Bermejo. The emperor's resources were, however, absorbed by his struggle for European supremacy with Francis I. of France, and he was obliged to leave the enterprise of South American discoveries to his wealthy nobles. Cabot's colony at San Espiritù did not long survive his departure; an attempt of the chief of the Timbús to gain possession of one of the Spanish ladies of the settlement led to a treacherous massacre of the garrison.

Two years after the return of Cabot, the news of Francisco Pizarro's marvellous conquest of Peru reached Europe (1532), and stirred many an adventurous spirit to strive to emulate his good fortune. Among these was Pedro *Mendoza.*de Mendoza, a Basque nobleman. He obtained from Charles V. a grant (*asiento*) of two hundred leagues of the coast from the boundary of the Portuguese possessions southward towards the Straits of Magellan, and the inland country which lay behind it. Mendoza undertook to conquer and settle the territory at his own charges, certain profits being reserved to the crown. In August 1534 the *adelantado*, or governor, sailed from San Lucar, at the head of the largest and wealthiest expedition that had ever left Europe for the New World. In January 1535 he entered the river Plate, where he followed the northern shore to the island of San Gabriel, and then crossing over he landed by *Buenos Aires.*a little stream, still called Riachuelo. The name of Buenos Aires was given to the country by Sancho del Campo, brother-in-law of the *adelantado*, who first stepped ashore. Here, on the 2nd of February, Mendoza laid the foundations of a settlement which in honour of the day he named Santa Maria de Buenos Aires. Mendoza, after some fierce encounters with the Indians, now proceeded up the Paraná, and built a fort, which he called Corpus Christi, near the site of Cabot's former settlement of San Espiritù. The expedition, which originally numbered 2500 men, was reduced by deaths at the hands of the Indians, by disease and privation, within a year to less than 500 men. From Corpus Christi, Mendoza sent out various bodies to explore the interior in the direction of Peru, but without much success, and at length, thoroughly discouraged and broken in health, he abandoned his enterprise, and returned to Spain in 1537.

A portion of one of the expeditions he despatched, under Juan de Ayolas, pushing up the Paraguay, is said to have reached the south-east districts of Peru, but while returning laden with booty, was attacked by the Payaguá Indians, and every man*Asunción*perished. The other portion, which had stayed behind as a reserve under Domingos Iralá, had better fortunes. Finding their comrades did not return, Iralá and his companions determined to descend the river, and on their downward journey opposite the mouth of the river Pilcomayo, finding a suitable site for colonizing, they founded (1536) what proved to be the first permanent Spanish settlement in the interior of South America, the future city of Asunción (15th August 1536).

In the meantime the colony at Buenos Aires had been dragging on a miserable existence, and after terrible sufferings from famine and from the ceaseless attacks of the Indians, the remaining settlers abandoned the place and made their way up *Iralá*the river first to Corpus Christi, then to Asunción. Here, by the emperor's orders, the assembled Spaniards proceeded to the election of a captain-general, and their choice fell almost unanimously on Domingos Martinez de Iralá, who was proclaimed captain-general of the Rio de la Plata (August 1538). In 1542 the settlement of Buenos Aires was re-established by an expedition sent for the purpose from Spain, under a tried *adelantado*, Cabeza de Vaca. This able leader, eager to reach Asunción as quickly as possible, sent on his ships to the river Plate, but himself with a small following marched overland from Santa Catherina on the coast of Brazil to join Iralá. His doings at Asunción belong, however, not to the history of Argentina, but of Paraguay. Suffice it to say that differences with Iralá eventually led to his arrest, and to his being sent back to Spain to answer to the charges brought against him for maladministration. The second settlement made by his expedition at Buenos Aires was even less successful and 469long-lived than the first. Exposed to the incessant attacks of the savages, the piace was a second time abandoned, February 1543.

Forty years were now to elapse before any further efforts were made by the Spaniards to colonize any part of the territory of the river Plate and lower Paraná. In 1573 Juan de Garay, at the head of an expedition despatched *Juan de Garay.*from Asunción, founded the city of Santa Fé near the abandoned settlements of San Espiritù and Corpus Christi. Seven years later (1580), when the new colony had been firmly established, Juan de Garay proceeded southwards, and made the third attempt to build a city on the site of Buenos Aires; and despite the determined hostility of the Querendi Indians he succeeded in finally gaining a complete mastery over them. In a desperate battle, the natives were defeated with great slaughter, and the territory surrounding the town was divided into ranches, in which the conquered natives had to labour. The new town received from Garay the name of *Ciudad de la Santissima Trinidad*, while its port retained the old appellation of Santa Maria de Buenos Aires. It was endowed by its founder with a *cabildo* (corporation) and full Spanish municipal privileges. Garay, when on his way to Santa Fé, was unfortunately murdered by a party of Indians, Minuas (Mimas), three years later, while incautiously sleeping on the river bank near the ruins of San Espiritù. The new settlement, however, continued to prosper, and the cattle and horses brought from Europe multiplied and spread over the plains of the Pampas.

In the meantime the Spaniards had penetrated into the interior of what is now the Argentine Republic, and established themselves on the eastern slopes of the Andes. In 1553 an expedition from Peru made their way through the mountain region and founded the city of Santiago del Estero, that of Tucumán in 1565, and that of Córdoba in 1573. Another expedition from Chile, under Garcia Hurtado de Mendoza, crossed the Cordillera in 1559, and having defeated the Araucanian Indians, made a settlement which from the name of the leader was called Mendoza. In 1620 Buenos Aires was separated from the authority of the government established at Asunción, and was made the seat of a government extending over Mendoza, Santa Fé, Entre Rios and Corrientes, but at the same time remained like the government of Paraguay at Asunción, and that of the province of Tucumán, which had Córdoba as its capital, subject to the authority of the viceroyalty of Peru.

Thus at the opening of the 17th century, after many adventurous efforts, and the expenditure of many lives and much treasure, the Spaniards found themselves securely established on the river Plate, and had planted a *Evils of Spanish colonial system.* number of centres of trade and colonization in the interior. Unfortunately, in no part of the Spanish oversea possessions did the restrictive legislation of the home government operate more harshly or disadvantageously to the interests of the colony; it was a more effective hindrance to the development of its resources and the spread of civilization over the country, than the hostility of the Indians. Cabot had urged the feasibility of opening an easier channel for trade with the interior of Peru through the river Plate and its tributaries, than that by way of the West Indies and Panama; and now that his views were able to be realized, the interests of the merchants of Seville and of Lima, who had secured a monopoly of the trade by the route of the isthmus, were allowed to destroy the threatened rivalry of that by the river Plate. Never in the history of colonization has a mother country pursued so relentlessly a policy more selfish and short-sighted. Spanish legislation was not satisfied with endeavouring to exclude all European nations except Spain from trading with the West Indies, but it sought to limit all commerce to one particular route, and it forbade any trade being transacted by way of the river Plate, thus enacting the most flagrant injustice towards the people it had encouraged to settle in the latter country. The strongest protests were raised, but the utmost they could effect was that, in 1618, permission was granted to export from Buenos Aires two shiploads of produce a year. But the Spanish government was not content with the prohibition of sea-borne commerce. To prevent internal trade with Peru a custom-house was set up at Córdoba to levy a duty of 50% on everything in transit to and from the river Plate. In 1665 the relaxation of this system was brought about by the continual remonstrances of the people, *Asiento question.* but for more than a century afterwards (until 1776) the policy of exclusion was enforced. This naturally led to a contraband trade of considerable dimensions. The English, after the treaty of Utrecht (1715) held the contract (*asiento*) for supplying the Spanish-American colonies with negro slaves. Among other places the slave ships regularly visited Buenos Aires, and despite the efforts of the Spanish authorities, contrived both to smuggle in and carry away a quantity of goods. This illicit commerce went on steadily till 1739, when it led to an outbreak of war between England and Spain, which put an end to the *asiento*. The Portuguese were even worse offenders, for in 1680 they made a settlement on the north of the river Plate, right opposite to Buenos Aires, named Colonia, which with one or two short intervals, remained in their hands till 1777. From this port foreign merchandise found its way duty free into the Spanish provinces of Buenos Aires, Tucumán and Paraguay, and even into the interior of Peru. The continual encroachments of the Portuguese at length led the Spanish government to take the important step of making Buenos Aires the seat of a viceroyalty with jurisdiction over the territories of the present republics of Bolivia, Paraguay, Uruguay and the Argentine Confederation (1776). At the same time all this country was opened to Spanish trade even with Peru, and the development of its resources, so long thwarted, was allowed comparatively free play. Pedro de Zeballos, the first viceroy, took with him from Spain a large military force with which he finally expelled the Portuguese from the banks of the river Plate.

The wars of the French Revolution, in which Spain was allied with France against Great Britain, interrupted the growing prosperity of Buenos Aires. On the 17th of June 1806 General William Beresford landed with a body of *Effects of French war.* troops from a British fleet under the command of Sir Home Popham, and obtained possession of Buenos Aires. But a French officer, Jacques de Liniers, gathered together a large force with which he enclosed the British within the walls, and finally, on the 12th of August, by a successful assault, forced Beresford and his troops to surrender. In July 1807 another British force of eight thousand men under General Whitelock endeavoured to regain possession of Buenos Aires, but strenuous preparations had been made for resistance, and after fierce street fighting the invading army, after suffering severe losses, was compelled to capitulate. The colonists, who had achieved their two great successes without any aid from the home government, were naturally elated, and began to feel a new sense of self-reliance and confidence in their own resources. The successful defence of Buenos Aires accentuated the growing feeling of dissatisfaction with the Spanish connexion, which was soon to lead to open insurrection. The establishment of the Napoleonic dynasty at Madrid was the actual cause which brought about the disturbances which were to end in separation. Liniers was viceroy on the arrival of the news of the crowning of Joseph Bonaparte as king of Spain, but as a Frenchman he was distrusted and was deposed by the adherents of Ferdinand VII. The central junta at Seville, acting in the name of Ferdinand, appointed Balthasar de Cisneros to be viceroy in his place. He entered upon the duties of his office on the 19th of July 1809, and at first he gained popularity by acceding to the urgent appeals of the people and throwing open the trade of the country to all nations. But his measures speedily gave dissatisfaction to the Argentine or Creole party, who had chafed under the disabilities of Spanish rule, and who now felt themselves no longer bound by ties of loyalty to a country which was in the possession of the French armies.

On the 25th of May 1810 a great armed assembly met at Buenos Aires and a provisional junta was formed to supersede the authority of the viceroy and carry on the government. The acts of the new government ran in the name of Ferdinand VII., *Struggle for independence.* 470 but the step taken was a revolutionary one, and the 25th of May has ever since been regarded as the birthday of Argentine independence. The most prominent leader of the junta was its secretary Mariano Moreno (1778-1811), who with a number of other active supporters of the patriot cause succeeded in raising a considerable force of Buenos Aireans to maintain, arms in hand, their nationalist and anti-Spanish doctrines. An attempt of the Spanish party to make Balthasar de Cisneros president of the junta failed, and the ex-viceroy retired to Montevideo. A sanguinary struggle between the party of independence and the adherents of Spain spread over the whole country, and was carried on with varying fortune. Foremost among the leaders of the revolutionary armies were Manuel Belgrano, and after March 1812 General José de San Martin, an officer who had gained experience against the French in the Peninsular War. A state of disorder, almost of anarchy, reigned in the provinces, but on the 25th of March 1816 a congress of deputies was assembled at Tucumán, who named Don Martin Pueyrredón supreme director, and on the 9th of July the separation of the united provinces of the Rio de la Plata was formally proclaimed, and comparative order was re-established in the country; Buenos Aires was declared the seat of the government. The jealousy of the provinces, however, against the capital led to a series of disturbances, and for many years continual civil war devastated every part of the country. Bolivia, Paraguay and Uruguay rose in armed revolt, and finally established themselves as separate republics, whilst the city of Buenos Aires itself was torn with faction and the scene of many a sanguinary fight.

From 1816, however, the independence of the Argentine Republic was assured, and success attended the South Americans in their contest with the royal armies. The combined forces of Buenos Aires and Chile defeated the Spaniards *Republic established.* at Chacabuco in 1817, and at Maipú in 1818; and from Chile the victorious general José de San Martin led his troops into Peru, where on the 9th of July 1821, he made a triumphal entry into Lima, which had been the chief stronghold of the Spanish power, having from the time of its foundation by Pizarro been the seat of government of a viceroyalty which at one time extended to the river Plate. A general congress was assembled at Buenos Aires on the 1st of March 1822, of representatives from all the liberated provinces, and a general amnesty was decreed, though the war was not over until the 9th of December 1824, when the republican forces gained the final, victory of Ayacucho, in the Peruvian border-land. The Spanish government did not, however, formally acknowledge the independence of the country until the year 1842. On the 23rd of January 1825, a national constitution for the federal states, which formed the Argentine Republic, was decreed; and on the 2nd of February of the same year Sir Woodbine Parish, acting under the instructions of George Canning, signed a commercial treaty in Buenos Aires, by which the British government acknowledged the independence of the country. It had already been recognized by the United States of America two years previously.

In 1826 Bernardo Rivadavia was elected president of the confederation. His policy was to establish a strong central government, and he became the head of a party known as Unitarians in contradistinction to their opponents, *Unitarians and Federalists.* who were styled Federalists, their aim being to maintain to the utmost the local autonomy of the various provinces. Under the government of Rivadavia the people of Buenos Aires became involved, practically single-handed, in a war with Brazil in defence of the Banda Oriental, which had been seized by the imperial forces (see URUGUAY). The Brazilians were defeated, notably at Ituzaingo, and in 1827 the war issued in the independence of Uruguay. Rivadavia's term of office was likewise memorable for the constitution of the 24th of December 1826, passed by the constituent congress of all the provinces, by which the bonds which united the confederated states of the Argentine Republic were strengthened. This project of closer union met, however, with much opposition both at Buenos Aires and the provinces. Rivadavia resigned, and Vicente Lopez, a Federalist, was elected to succeed him, but was speedily displaced by Manuel Dorrego (1827), another representative of the same party. The carrying out of Federalist principles led, however, to the formation in the republic of a number of quasi-independent military states, and Dorrego only ruled in Buenos Aires. After the conclusion of the peace with Brazil, the Unitarians placed themselves under the leadership of General Juan de Lavalle, the victor of Ituzaingo. Lavalle, at the head of a division of troops, drove Dorrego from Buenos Aires, pursued him into the interior, and captured him. He was shot (December 9, 1828), by the order of Lavalle, and during the year 1828 the country was given up to the horrors of civil war.

On the death of Dorrego, a remarkable man, Juan Manuel de Rosas, became the Federalist chief. In 1829 he defeated Lavalle, made himself master of Buenos Aires, and in the course of the next three years made his authority recognized *Rosas dictator.*after much fighting throughout the provinces. The Unitarians were relentlessly hunted down and a veritable reign of terror ensued. Rosas gradually concentrated all power in his own hands, and was hailed by the populace as a saviour of the state. In 1835, with the title of governor and captain-general, he acquired dictatorial powers, and all public authority passed into his hands. This dictatorship of Rosas continued until 1852. In every department of administration and of government he was supreme. He was exceedingly jealous of foreign interference, and quarrelled with France on questions connected with the rights of foreign residents. Buenos Aires was in 1838 blockaded by a French fleet; but Rosas stood firm. A formidable revolt took place in 1839 under General Lavalle, who had returned to the country accompanied by a number of banished Unitarians. In 1840 he invaded Buenos Aires at the head of troops raised chiefly in the province of Entre Rios; but he was defeated at Santa Fé, then at Luján, and finally was captured in Jujuy and shot, 1841. The rule of Rosas was now one of tyranny and almost incessant bloodshed in Buenos Aires, while his partisans, foremost amongst whom was General Ignacio Oribe, endeavoured to exterminate the Unitarians throughout the provinces. The scene of slaughter was extended to the Banda Oriental by the attempt of Oribe, with the support of Rosas, and of Justo José de Urquiza, governor of Entre Rios, to establish himself as president of that republic (see URUGUAY), where the existing government was hostile to Rosas and sheltered all political refugees from the country under his despotic rule. The siege of Montevideo led to a joint intervention of England and France. Buenos Aires was blockaded by the combined English and French fleets, September 1845, which landed a force to open the passage up the Paraná to Paraguay, which had been declared closed to foreigners by Rosas. A convention was signed in 1849, which secured the free navigation of the Paraná and the independence of the Banda Oriental. The downfall of Rosas was at last brought about by the instrumentality of Justo José de Urquiza, who as governor of Entre Rios, had for many years been one of his strongest supporters. The breach between the two men which led to open collision took place in 1846. The first efforts of Urquiza to rouse the country against the oppressor were unsuccessful, but in 1851 he concluded an alliance with Brazil, to which Uruguay afterwards adhered. A large army of twenty-four thousand men was collected at Montevideo, and on the 8th of January 1852 the allied forces crossed the Paraná and the road to Buenos Aires lay open before them. Rosas met the allies at the head of a body of troops fully equal in numbers to their own, but was crushingly routed, February 3rd, at Monte Caseros, about 10 m. from the capital. The dictator fled for refuge to the British legation, from whence he was conveyed on board H.B.M.S. "Locust," which carried him into exile.

A provisional government was formed under Urquiza, and the Brazilian and Uruguayan troops withdrew. He summoned all the provincial governors at San Nicolás in the province of Buenos Aires, and on the 31st of May they proclaimed *Urquiza president.*a new constitution, with Urquiza as provisional director of the Argentine nation. A constituent congress, in which each province had equal representation, was duly elected, and in order to provide against the predominance of Buenos Aires, it was determined that Sante Fé should be the place of session. But this did not suit the *porteños*, as the people of Buenos Aires were called, and the province refused to take any part in the congressional proceedings. But Urquiza *Buenos Aires and the provinces.*was a man of different temperament from Rosas, and when he found that Buenos Aires refused to submit to his authority, he declined to use force. The congress had (May 1, 1853) appointed Urquiza president of the confederation, and he established the seat of government at Paraná. The province of Buenos Aires was recognized as an independent state, and under the enlightened administration of Doctor Obligado made rapid strides in commercial prosperity. The two sections of the Argentine nation contrived to exist as separate governments without an open breach of the peace until 1859, when the long-continued tension led to the outbreak of hostilities. The army of the *porteños*, commanded by Colonel Bartolomé Mitre, was defeated at Cepeda by the confederate forces under Urquiza, and Buenos Aires agreed to re-enter the confederation (November 11, 1859). Urquiza at this juncture resigned the presidency, and Doctor Santiago Derqui was elected president of the fourteen provinces with the seat of government at Paraná; while Urquiza became once more governor of Entre Rios, and Mitre was appointed governor of Buenos Aires.

The struggle for supremacy between Buenos Aires and the provinces had, however, to be fought out, and hostilities once more broke out in 1861. The armies of the opposing parties, under Generals Mitre and Urquiza respectively, *Mitre president.* met at Pavón in the province of Santa Fé (September 17). The battle ended in the disastrous defeat of the provincial forces; General Mitre used his victory in a spirit of moderation and sincere patriotism. He was elected president of the Argentine confederation and did his utmost to settle the questions which had led to so many civil wars, on a permanent and sound basis. The constitution of 1853 was maintained, but Buenos Aires became the seat of federal government without ceasing to be a provincial capital. Causes of friction still remained, but they did not develop into open quarrels, for Mitre was content to leave Urquiza in his province of Entre Rios, and the other administrators (*caudillos*) in their several governments, a large measure of autonomy, trusting that the position and growing commercial importance of Buenos Aires would inevitably tend to make the federal capital the real centre of power of the republic. In 1865 the Argentines were forced into war with Paraguay through the overbearing attitude of the president Francisco Solano Lopez. The dictator of Paraguay had quarrelled with Brazil for its intervention in the internal affairs of Uruguay, *Paraguay war.* and he demanded free passage for his troops across the Argentine province of Corrientes. This Mitre refused, and alliance was formed between Argentina, Brazil and Uruguay, for joint action against Lopez. General Mitre became commander-in-chief of the combined armies for the invasion of Paraguay and was absent for several years in the field. The struggle was severe and attended by heavy losses, and it was not until 1870 that the Paraguayans were conquered, Lopez killed, and peace concluded (see PARAGUAY). Meanwhile, disturbances had broken out in the interior of Argentina (1867), which compelled Mitre to relinquish his command in Paraguay, and to call back a large part of the Argentine forces to suppress the insurrection. The rebels had hoped for assistance from Urquiza, but the powerful governor of Entre Rios maintained the peace in his province, which under his firm and beneficent rule had greatly prospered, and the revolutionary movement was quickly subdued.

In 1868 the term of General Mitre came to an end, and Doctor Domingo Faustino Sarmiento, a native of San Juan, was quietly elected to succeed him. His conduct of affairs was broad-minded and upright, and was characterized *Sarmiento president.* by earnest efforts to promote education and to develop the resources of the country. His period of office was marked by the rapid advance of Buenos Aires in population and prosperity, and by an expansion of trade that was unfortunately accompanied by financial extravagance. The war with Paraguay left a legacy of disputes concerning boundaries which almost led to war between the two victorious allies, Argentina and Brazil, but by the exertions of Mitre, who was sent at the close of 1872 as special envoy to Rio, a settlement was arrived at and friendly relations restored. The month of April 1870 saw an insurrection in Entre Rios headed by the *caudillo*, Lopez Jordan. Urquiza was assassinated, and the provincial legislature, through fear, at once proclaimed Lopez Jordan governor. The federal government refused to acknowledge the new governor, and troops were despatched by Sarmiento against Entre Rios. The contest lasted with varying success for more than a year, but finally Lopez Jordan was completely defeated and driven into exile.

The presidential election of 1874 resolved itself, as so often before, into a struggle between the provincials and the *porteños* (Buenos Aires). The candidate of the former, Dr Nicolas Avellaneda, triumphed over General Mitre, *Avellaneda president.* not without suspicions of tampering with the returns; and the unsuccessful party appealed to arms. The new president, however, who was installed in office on the 12th of October, took active steps to suppress the revolution, which never assumed a really serious character. The government troops gained two decisive victories over the insurgents under Generals Mitre and Arredondo, and they were compelled to surrender at discretion. But though peace was for a time restored, the old causes of soreness and dissension remained unappeased, and as the time for the next presidential election began to draw near, it became more and more evident that a critical struggle was at hand, and that the people of Buenos Aires, supported by the province of Corrientes, were determined to bring to an issue the question as to what position Buenos Aires was to hold for the future with regard to the remaining provinces of the confederation. It was evident that the president intended to use all the influence which the party in power could exercise, to secure the return of General Julio Roca, who had distinguished himself in 1878 by a successful campaign against the warlike Indian tribes bordering on the Andes. The *porteños* on their part were determined to resist this policy to the utmost. Mass meetings were held, and a committee was appointed for the purpose

41

of considering what action should be taken to defeat the ambitious designs of the provincials. *The Tiro Nacional.* Under the direction of this committee, the association known as the "Tiro Nacional" was formed, with the avowed object of training the able-bodied citizens of Buenos Aires in military exercises and creating a volunteer army, ready for service if called upon, to withstand by force the pretensions of their opponents. The establishment of the Tiro Nacional was enthusiastically received by all classes in Buenos Aires, the men turning out regularly to drill, and the women aiding the movement by collecting subscriptions for the purpose of armament and other necessaries. On the 13th of February 1880, the minister of war, Dr Carlos Pellegrini, summoned the principal officers connected with the Tiro Nacional, General Bartolomé Mitre, his brother Emilio, Colonel Julio Campos, Colonel Hilario Lagos and others, and warned them that as officers of the national army they owed obedience to the national government, and would be severely punished if concerned in any revolutionary outbreak against the constituted authorities. The reply to this threat was the immediate resignation of their commissions by all the officers connected with the Tiro Nacional. Two days later, the national government occupied, with a strong force of infantry and artillery, the parade ground at Palermo used by the Buenos Aires volunteers for drill purposes. A great meeting of citizens was then called and marched through the streets. President Avellaneda was frightened at the results of his action, and to avoid a collision ordered the troops to be withdrawn. Negotiations were now opened by the government with the provincial authorities for the disarmament of the city and province of Buenos Aires, but they led to nothing. Matters became still further strained on account of the outrages committed by the national troops, and such was the bitterness of feeling developed between the two factions, that an appeal to arms became inevitable.

In the month of June 1880, President Avellaneda and his ministers left Buenos Aires, and this act was considered by the *porteño* leaders equivalent to a declaration of war. The national government and the twelve provinces *Appeal to Arms.* forming the Córdoba League, were ranged on one side; the city and province of Buenos Aires and the province of Corrientes on the other. The national troops were well armed with Remington rifles, provided with abundant ammunition, equipped with artillery and supported by the fleet. In the city and province of Buenos Aires, plenty of volunteers offered their services, and an army of some twenty-five thousand men was quickly raised, but they were armed with old-fashioned weapons and there was only a limited supply of ammunition. Feverish attempts were made to remedy the lack of warlike stores, but difficulty was experienced on account of the fleet blockading the entrance to the river. After several skirmishes, the national army commanded by General Roca, containing many troops seasoned in Indian campaigns, assaulted the *porteños* posted *Fall of Buenos Aires.* before Buenos Aires, and after two days' hard fighting (20th and 21st July) forced its way into the town. On 23rd July the surrender of the city was demanded and obtained. The terms of the surrender were that all the leaders of the revolution should be removed from positions of authority, all government employees implicated in the movement dismissed, and the force in the province and city of Buenos Aires at once disarmed and disbanded. The power of Buenos Aires was thus completely broken and at the mercy of the Córdoba League. The *porteños* were no longer in a position to nominate a candidate in opposition to General Julio Roca, who was duly elected. He assumed office in October 1880.

Hitherto General Roca had been regarded only in his capacity as a soldier, and not from the point of view of an administrator. In the campaigns against the Indians in the south-west of the province of Buenos Aires and the valley of *Roca president.* the Rio Negro he had gained much prestige; the victory over Buenos Aires added to his fame, and secured his authority in the outlying provincial centres. One of the first notable acts of the Roca administration was to declare the city of Buenos Aires the property of the national government. This separation of the city from the province, and its federalization had been one of the chief aims of the Córdoba League, and was the natural consequence of the crushing defeat inflicted on the *porteños*. As a sequel to this step, in 1884 the town of La Plata was declared to be the capital of the province of Buenos Aires, and the provincial administration was moved to that place. This federalization of the capital has proved to be a most important factor in binding together the different parts of the confederation, and in promoting the evolution of an Argentine nation out of a loosely cemented union of a number of semi-independent states.

Considering the circumstances in which General Roca assumed office, it must be admitted that he showed great moderation and used the practically absolute power that he possessed to establish a strong central government, and to initiate a national policy, which aimed at furthering the prosperity and development of the whole country. He was able by the influence he exerted to keep down the internal dissensions and insurrectionary outbreaks which had so greatly impeded for many years the development of the vast natural resources of the republic. With this object he had promoted the extension of railways so as to link the provinces with the great port of Buenos

42

Aires, and to provide at the same time facilities for the rapid despatch of military forces to disturbed districts. Unfortunately the last two years of Roca's term of office were marked by two grave errors, which subsequently caused widespread suffering and distress throughout the country. The first of these mistakes was a measure making (January 1885) the currency inconvertible for a period of two years. This act, which was only decided upon after much hesitation, had a most deleterious effect upon the national credit. The second was the nomination of Dr Miguel Juarez Celman for the presidential term commencing in October 1886. The nomination was brought about by the Córdoba clique, and Roca lacked the moral courage to oppose the decision of this group, though he was well aware that Celman, who was his brother-in-law, was neither intellectually nor morally fitted for the post.

No sooner had President Juarez Celman come into power towards the close of 1886, than the respectable portion of the community began to feel alarmed at the methods practised by the new president in his conduct of *Celman president.* public affairs. At first it was hoped that the influence of General Roca would serve to check any serious extravagance on the part of Celman. This hope, however, was doomed to disappointment, and before many months had elapsed it was clear that the president would listen to no prudent counsels from Roca or from any one else. The men of the old Córdoba League became dominant in all branches of the government, and carpet-bagging politicians occupied every official post. In their hurry to obtain wealth, this crowd of office-mongers from the provinces lent themselves to all kinds of bribery and corruption. The public credit was pledged at home and abroad to fill the pockets of the adventurers, and the wildest excesses were committed under the guise of administrative acts. What followed in the second and third years of the Celman administration can only adequately be described as a debauchery of the national honour, of the national resources, of the rights of Argentines as citizens of the republic. Buenos Aires was still prostrate under the crushing blow of the misfortunes of 1880, and lacked strength and power of organization necessary to raise any effective protest against the proceedings of Celman and his friends when the true character of these proceedings was first understood. The conduct of public affairs, however, at length became so scandalous, that action on the part of the more sober-minded and conservative sections was seen to be absolutely imperative if the country was to be saved from speedy and certain ruin. In 1889 the association of the "Union Civica" *The Union Civica.* was founded, and the organization undertaken by Dr Leandro Alem, Dr Aristobulo del Valle, Dr Bernardo Irigoyen, Dr Vicente Lopez, Dr Lucio Lopez, Dr Oscar Lilliedale and other leading citizens. The untiring energy and zeal of Leandro Alem fitted him for being the chief organizer of a movement into which he threw himself heart and soul. Mass meetings were held in Buenos Aires, and it fell specially to the lot of Dr del Valle, who was an able orator as well as a sincere patriot, to expose the irresponsible and corrupt character of the administration, and the terrible dangers that threatened the republic through its reckless extravagance and financial improvidence. Subsidiary clubs affiliated to the central administration were formed throughout the length and breadth of the country, and millions of leaflets and pamphlets were distributed broadcast to explain the importance of the movement. President Celman underrated the strength of the new opposition, and relied upon his armed forces promptly to suppress any signs of open hostility. No change was made in official methods, and the condition of affairs drifted from bad to worse, until the temper of the people, so long and so sorely tried, showed plainly that the situation had become insufferable. The Union Civica then decided to make a bold bid for freedom by attempting forcibly to eject Celman and his clique from office.

On the night of the 26th of July 1890 the Union Civica called its members to arms. It was joined by some regiments of the regular army and received the support of the fleet. Barricades were thrown up in the principal streets, and the surrounding houses were occupied by the insurgents. Two days of desultory street fighting ensued, during which the fleet began to bombard the city, but was compelled to desist by the interference of foreign men-of-war, on the ground that the bombardment was causing unnecessary damage to the life and property of non-combatants. A suspension of hostilities then took place, and negotiations were opened between the contending parties. Celman, acting upon the advice of General Roca, who recognized the strength of public opinion in the outbreak, placed his resignation in the hands of congress on the 31st of July. A scene of 473 intense enthusiasm followed, and Buenos Aires was *en fête* for the following three days. The vice-president of the confederation, Carlos Pellegrini, who had been minister of war under presidents Avellaneda and Roca and had had much administrative experience, succeeded without opposition to the vacant post.

Much satisfaction was shown in Europe at the fall of President Celman, for investors had suffered heavily by the way in which the resources of Argentina had been dissipated by a corrupt government, and hopes were entertained *Pellegrini president.* that the uprising of public opinion against his financial methods signified a more honest conduct of the national affairs in the future.

43

Great expectations were entertained of the ability of President Pellegrini to establish a sound administration, and he succeeded in forming a ministry which gave general satisfaction throughout the country. General Roca was induced to undertake the duties of minister of the interior, and his influence in the provinces was sufficient to check any attempts to stir up disturbances at Córdoba or elsewhere. The most onerous post of all, that of minister of finance, was confided to Dr Vicente Lopez, who, though he was not of marked financial ability, was at least a man of untiring industry and of a personal integrity that was above suspicion. But the economic and financial situation was one of almost hopeless embarrassment and confusion, and Pellegrini proved himself incapable of grappling with it. Instead of facing the difficulties, the president preferred to put off the day of reckoning by flooding the country with inconvertible notes, with the result that the financial crisis became more and more aggravated. Through the rapid depreciation of Argentine credit, the great firm of Baring Brothers, the financial agents of the government in London, became so heavily involved that they were forced into liquidation, November 1890. The consequences of this catastrophe were felt far and wide, and in the spring of 1891 both the Banco Nacional and the Banco de la provincia de Buenos Aires were unable to meet their obligations. Amidst this sea of financial troubles the government drifted helplessly on, without showing any inclination or capacity to initiate a strong policy of reform in the methods of administration which had done so much to ruin the country.

It is little wonder that, in these circumstances, the choice of a successor to Pellegrini, whose term of office expired in 1892, should have been felt to possess peculiar importance. General Bartolomé Mitre was proposed by the *porteños* as their candidate. He had been absent from Argentina on a journey to Europe, and on his return in April 1891, a popular reception was given to him at which 50,000 persons attended. A petition was presented to him begging him to be a candidate for the presidency, and with some reluctance the veteran leader gave his consent. His partisans, however, found themselves confronted by a compact provincial party, who proposed to put forward the other strong man of the republic, General Roca, to oppose him. But the two generals were equally averse to a contest *à outrance*, which could only end in civil war. They met accordingly at a conference known as *El Acuerdo*, and it was arranged that both should withdraw, and that a non-party candidate should be selected who should receive the support of them both. The choice fell upon Dr Saenz Peña, a judge of the supreme court, and a man universally respected, who had never taken any part in political life. This compact aroused the bitter enmity of Dr Leandro Alem, who did his utmost to stir up the Union Civica to a campaign against the neutral candidate. Finding that the more conservative section of the union would not follow him, Alem formed a new association to which he gave the name of Union Civica Radical. Such was his energy, that soon a network of branches of the Union Civica Radical was organized throughout the republic, and Dr Bernardo Irigoyen was put forward as a rival candidate to Dr Saenz Peña. But Alem was not content with constitutional opposition to the Acuerdo, and his movement soon assumed the character of a revolutionary propaganda against the national government. His violence gave Pellegrini the opportunity of taking active steps to preserve the peace. In April 1892 Alem and his chief colleagues were arrested and sent into exile.

In the following month (May), the presidential elections were held; Dr Saenz Peña was declared duly elected, and Dr José Uriburu, the minister in Chile, was chosen as vice-president.

The idea of Dr Saenz Peña was to conduct the government on common sense and non-partisan lines, in fact to translate into practical politics the principles which underlay the compromise of the Acuerdo. He was a straightforward *Saenz Peña president.*and honourable man, who tried his best to do his duty in a position that had been forced upon him, and was in no sense of the word his own seeking. No sooner, however, was he installed in office than difficulties began to crop up on all sides, and he quickly discovered that to attempt to govern without the aid of a majority in congress was practically impossible. He had had no experience of political life, and he refused to create the support he needed by using his presidential prerogative to build up a political majority. Obstruction met his well-meant efforts to promote the general good, and before twelve months of the presidential term had run public affairs were at a deadlock. Dr Alem, who had been permitted to return from exile, was not slow to profit by the occasion. Embittered by his treatment in 1892, he openly preached the advisability of an armed rising to overthrow the existing administration. Public opinion had been outraged by the immunity with which the governors of certain provinces, and more particularly Dr Julio Costa, the governor of the province of Buenos Aires, had been allowed to maintain local forces, by the aid of which they exacted the payment of illegal taxes and exercised other acts of injustice and oppression. A number of officers of the army and navy agreed to lend assistance to a revolutionary outbreak, and towards the end of July 1893 matters came to a head. The population of Buenos Aires assembled in armed bodies with the avowed intention of ejecting the governor from office, and electing in his stead a man who would give them a just administration. The president was for some time in doubt whether he had any right to intervene in provincial affairs, but eventually troops were despatched to La Plata. There was no serious fighting. Negotiations were soon opened which quickly led to the resignation of Costa, and the return of the insurgents to their homes. While these disturbances were taking place in the province of Buenos Aires, another revolutionary rising was in progress in Santa Fé. Here the efforts of Dr Alem succeeded in supplying a large body of rebels with arms and ammunition, and he was able, by a bold attack, to seize the town of Rosario and there establish the revolutionary headquarters. This capture so alarmed the national government that a force was sent under the command of Roca to put down the insurrection. The revolt speedily collapsed before this redoubtable commander, and Alem and the other leaders surrendered. They were sentenced to banishment in Staten Island at the pleasure of the federal government.

But the suppression of disorder did not relieve the tension between the congress and the executive. During the whole of the 1894 session, the attitude of senators and deputies alike was one of pronounced hostility to the president. All his acts were opposed, legislation was at a standstill and every effort was made to force Dr Saenz Peña to resign. But although he experienced the utmost difficulty in forming a cabinet, the president was obstinate in his determination to retain office without identifying himself with any party. A definite issue was therefore sought by the congress on which to join battle, and it arose out of the death sentences which had been pronounced on certain naval and military officers who had been implicated in the Santa Fé outbreak. The president had made up his mind that the sentence must be carried out; the congress by a great majority were resolved not to permit the death penalty to be inflicted. It was a one-sided struggle, for without the consent of the congress the president could not raise any money for supplies, and congress refused to vote the budget. But heavy expenses had been incurred in putting down revolutionary movements in various parts of the provinces, and war with Chile 474was threatened upon the question of a dispute concerning the boundaries between the two republics. In January 1895 a special session of congress was summoned to take into consideration the financial proposals of the government, which included an increase in the naval and military estimates. Congress, however, had now got their opportunity, and they used the time of national stress to bring increased pressure to bear upon the president. On the 21st of January Dr Saenz Peña at last perceived that his position was untenable, and he handed in his resignation. It was accepted at once by the chambers, and the vice-president, Dr José Uriburu, became president of the republic for the three years and nine months of Peña's term which remained unexpired.

Uriburu was neither a politician nor a statesman, but had spent the greater portion of his life abroad in the diplomatic service. His knowledge of foreign affairs was, however, peculiarly useful at a juncture when boundary questions *Uriburu President.*were the subjects that chiefly attracted public attention. After disputes with Brazil, extending over fifteen years, about the territory of "Misiones," the matter had been submitted to the arbitration of the president of the United States. In March 1895 President Cleveland gave his decision, which was wholly favourable to the contention of Brazil. The Argentine government, though disappointed at the result, accepted the award loyally. The boundary dispute with Chile, to which reference has already been made, was of a more serious character. The dispute was of old standing. Already in 1884 a protocol had been signed between the contending parties, by which it was agreed that the frontier should follow the line where "the highest peaks of the Andine ranges divide the watershed." This definition unfortunately ignored the fact that the Andes do not run from north to south in one continuous line, but are separated into cordilleras with valleys between them, and covering in their total breadth a considerable extent of country. Difference of opinion, therefore, arose as to the interpretation of the protocol, the Argentines insisting that the boundary should run from highest peak to highest peak, the Chileans that it should follow the highest points of the watershed. The quarrel at length became acute, and on both sides the populace clamoured from time to time for an appeal to arms, and the resources of both countries were squandered in military and naval preparations for a struggle. Nevertheless despite these obstacles, President Uriburu did something during his term of office to relieve the nation's financial difficulties. In 1896 a bill was passed by congress, which authorized the state by the issue of national bonds to assume the provincial external indebtedness. This proof of the desire of the Argentine government to meet honestly all its obligations did much to restore its credit abroad. Uriburu found in 1897 the financial position so far improved that he was able to resume cash payments on the entire foreign debt.

In 1898 there was another presidential election. Public opinion, excited by the prospect of a war with Chile, naturally supported the candidature of General Roca, and he was elected without opposition (12th October 1898). *Roca President.*The first question which he had to handle was the Chilean boundary dispute. During the last months of President Uriburu's

45

administration, matters had reached a climax, especially in connexion with the delimitation in a district known as the Puña de Atacama. In August an ultimatum was received from Chile demanding arbitration. After some hesitation, on the advice of Roca the Argentines agreed to the demand, and peace was maintained. The principle of arbitration being accepted, the conditions were quickly arranged. The question of the Puña de Atacama was referred to a tribunal composed of the United States minister to Argentina and of one Argentine and one Chilean delegate; that of the southern frontier in Patagonia to the British crown. One of the first steps of President Roca, after his accession to office, was to arrange a meeting with the president of Chile at the Straits of Magellan. At their conference all difficulties were discussed and settled, and an undertaking was given on both sides to put a stop to warlike preparations. The decision of the representative of the United States was given in April 1899. Although the Chileans professed dissatisfaction, no active opposition was raised, and the terms were duly ratified. In his message to congress, on the 1st of May 1899, General Roca spoke strongly of the immediate necessity of a reform in the methods of administering justice, the expediency of a revision of the electoral law, and the imperative need of a reconstruction of the department of public instruction. The administration of justice, he declared, had fallen to so low an ebb as to be practically non-existent. By the powerful influence of the president, government measures were sanctioned by the legislature dealing with the abuses which had been condemned. On the 31st of August of the same year a series of proposals upon the currency question was submitted to congress by the president, whose real object was to counteract the too rapid appreciation of the inconvertible paper money. The official value of the dollar was fixed at 44 cents gold for all government purposes. The violent fluctuations in the value of the paper dollar, which caused so much damage to trade and industry, were thus checked. In October 1900 Dr Manuel Campos Salles, president of Brazil, paid a visit to Buenos Aires, and was received with great demonstrations of friendliness. The aggressive attitude of Chile towards Bolivia was causing considerable anxiety, and Argentina and Brazil wished to show that they were united in opposing a policy which aimed at acquiring an extension of territory by force of arms. The feeling of enmity between Chile and Argentina was indeed anything but extinct. The delay of the arbitration tribunal in London in giving its decision in the matter of the disputed boundary in Patagonia led to a crop of wild rumours being disseminated, and to a revival of animosity between the two peoples. In December 1901 warlike preparations were being carried on in both states, and the outbreak of active hostilities appeared to be imminent. At the critical moment the British government, urged to move in the matter by the British residents in both countries, who feared that war would mean the financial ruin of both Chile and Argentina, used its utmost influence both at Santiago and Buenos Aires to allay the misunderstandings; and negotiations were set on foot which ended in a treaty for the cessation of further armaments being signed, June 1902. The award of King Edward VII. upon the delimitation of the boundary was given a few months later, and was received without controversy and ratified by both governments.

To the calm resourcefulness and level-headedness of President Roca at a very difficult and critical juncture must be largely ascribed the preservation of peace, and the permanent removal of a dispute that had aroused so much irritation. His term *Quintana and Alcorta Presidents.* of office came to an end in 1904, when Dr Manuel Quintana was elected president and Dr José Figueroa Alcorta vice-president, both having Roca's support. Dr Quintana at the time of his election was sixty-four years of age. He proved a hard-working progressive president, who did much for the development of communications and the opening up of the interior of the country. He died amidst general regret in March 1906, and was succeeded by Dr Alcorta for the remaining years of his term.

(G. E.)

AUTHORITIES.—C.E. Akers, *Argentine, Patagonian and Chilian Sketches* (London, 1893), and *A History of South America 1854-1904* (New York, 1905); Theodore Child, *The Spanish-American Republics* (London, 1891); Sir T.H. Holdich, *The Countries of the King's Award* (London, 1904); W.H. Hudson, *The Naturalist in La Plata* (London, 1892), and *Idle Days in Patagonia* (London, 1893); A.H. Keane and C.R. Markham, *Central and South America*, in Stanford's "Compendium of Geography and Travel" (London, 1901); G. E. Church, "Argentine Geography and the Ancient Pampean Sea" (*Geogr. Journal*, xii. p. 386); "South America: an Outline of its Physical Geography" (*Geogr. Journal*, xvii. p. 333); Dr Karl Kärger, *Landwirtschaft und Kolonisation im spanischen Amerika* (2 vols., Leipzig, 1901); F.P. Moreno, "Explorations in Patagonia" (*Geogr. Journal*, xiv. pp. 241, 354); Carlos Lix Klett, *Estudios sobre producción, comercio, finanzas e intereses generales de la Republica Argentina* (2 vols., Buenos Aires, 1900); G. Carrasco, *El crecimiento de la población de la Republica Argentina comparado con el de las principales naciones 1890-1903* (Buenos Aires, 1904); C.M. Urien and C. Colombo, *Geografia Argentina* (Buenos Aires, 1905); E. von Rosen, *Archaeological Researches on the Frontier of Argentina and Bolivia 1901-1902* (Stockholm, 1904); Arturo B. Carranza,*Constitución*

Nacional y Constituciones Provinciales Vigentes(Buenos Aires, 1898); Angelo de Gubernatis, *L'Argentina*(Firenze, 1898); Meliton Gonzales, *El Gran Chaco Argentino*(Buenos Aires, 1890); John Grant & Sons, *The Argentine Year Book* (Buenos Aires, 1902 et seq.); Francis Latzina, *Diccionario Geografico Argentino* (Buenos Aires, 1891); *Géographie de la République Argentine* (Buenos Aires, 1890); *L'Agriculture et l'Elevage dans la République Argentine* (Paris, 1889); Bartolomé Mitre, *Historia de San Martin y de la Emancipatión Sud-Americana, según nuevos documentos* (3 vols., Buenos Aires, 1887); *Historia de Belgrano y de la Independencia Argentina* (3 vols., Buenos Aires, 1883); Felipe Soldan, *Diccionario Geografico Estadistico Nacional Argentino* (Buenos Aires, 1885); Thomas A. Turner, *Argentina and the Argentines* (New York and London, 1892); Estanislao S. Zeballos, *Descripción Amena de la Republica Argentina* (3 vols., Buenos Aires, 1881); *Anuario de la Direción General de Estadistica 1898* (Buenos Aires, 1899); Charles Wiener, *La République Argentine* (Paris, 1899); *Segundo Censo República Argentina* (3 vols., Buenos Aires, 1898); *Handbook of the Argentine Republic* (Bureau of the American Republics, Washington, 1892-1903).

(A. J. L.)

1For the geology of Argentina, see Stelzner, *Beiträge zur geologie der argentinischen Republik* (Cassel and Berlin, 1885); Brackebusch,*Mapa geológico del Interiore de la República Argentina* (Gotha, 1892); Valentin, *Bosquejo geólogico de la Argentina* (Buenos Aires, 1897); Hauthal, "Beiträge zur Geologie der argentinischen Provinz Buenos Aires," *Peterm. Mitt.* vol. 1., 1904, pp. 83-92, 112-117, pl. vi.

2Interesting details of the Argentine fauna may be found in Darwin's *Voyage of the Beagle*; W.H. Hudson's *Idle Days in Patagonia*, and *Naturalist in the La Plata*; G. Pelleschi's *Eight Months on the Gran Chaco*; R. Napp's *Argentine Republic*; and de Moussy's *Confédération argentine*.

3There are two distinct statistical offices compiling immigration returns and their totals do not agree, owing in part to the traffic between Buenos Aires and Montevideo. Another report gives the arrivals in 1904 as 125,567 and the departures 38,923. Of the arrivals 67,598 were Italians and 39,851 Spaniards. The total for the years 1859-1904 was 3,166,073 and the departures 1,239,064, showing a net gain of 1,927,009.

ARGENTINE, a former city of Wyandotte county, Kansas, U.S.A., since 1910 a part of Kansas City, on the S. bank of the Kansas river, just above its mouth. Pop. (1890) 4732; (1900) 5878, of whom 623 were foreign-born and 603 of negro descent; (1905, state census) 6053. It is served by the Atchison, Topeka & Santa Fé railway, which maintains here yards and machine shops. The streets of the city run irregularly up the steep face of the river bluffs. Its chief industrial establishment is that of the United Zinc and Chemical Company, which has here one of the largest plants of its kind in the country. There are large grain interests. The site was platted in 1880, and the city was first incorporated in 1882 and again, as a city of the second class, in 1889.

ARGENTITE, a mineral which belongs to the galena group, and is cubic silver sulphide (Ag2S). It is occasionally found as uneven cubes and octahedra, but more often as dendritic or earthy masses, with a blackish lead-grey colour and metallic lustre. The cubic cleavage, which is so prominent a feature in galena, is here present only in traces. The mineral is perfectly sectile and has a shining streak; hardness 2.5, specific gravity 7.3. It occurs in mineral veins, and when found in large masses, as in Mexico and in the Comstock lode in Nevada, it forms an important ore of silver. The mineral was mentioned so long ago as 1529 by G. Agricola, but the name argentite (from the Lat. *argentum,* "silver") was not used till 1845 and is due to W. von Haidinger. Old names for the species are Glaserz, silver-glance and vitreous silver. A cupriferous variety, from Jalpa in Tabasco, Mexico, is known as jalpaite. Acanthite is a supposed dimorphous form, crystallizing in the orthorhombic system, but it is probable that the crystals are really distorted crystals of argentite.

(L. J. S.)

ARGENTON, a town of western France, in the department of Indre, on the Creuse, 19 m. S.S.W. of Châteauroux on the Orléans railway. Pop. (1906) 5638. The river is crossed by two bridges, and its banks are bordered by picturesque old houses. There are numerous tanneries, and the manufacture of boots and shoes and linen goods is carried on. The site of the ancient *Argentomagus* lies a little to the north.

ARGHANDAB, a river of Afghanistan, about 250 m. in length. It rises in the Hazara country north-west of Ghazni, and flowing south-west falls into the Helmund 20 m. below Girishk. Very little is known about its upper course. It is said to be shallow, and to run nearly dry in height of summer; but when its depth exceeds 3 ft. its great rapidity makes it a serious obstacle to travellers. In its lower course it is much used for irrigation, and the valley is cultivated and populous; yet the water is said to be somewhat brackish. It is doubtful whether the ancient Arachotus is to be identified with the Arghandab or with its chief confluent the Tarnak, which joins it on the left about 30 m. S.W. of Kandahar. The two rivers run nearly parallel, inclosing the backbone of the Ghilzai plateau. The Tarnak is much the shorter (length about 200 m.) and less copious. The ruins at Ulân Robât, supposed to represent the city Arachosia, are in its basin; and the lake known as Ab-i-Istâda, the most probable representative of Lake Arachotus, is near the head of the Tarnak, though not communicating with it. The Tarnak is dammed for irrigation at intervals, and in the hot season almost exhausted. There is a good deal of cultivation along the river, but few villages. The high road from Kabul to Kandahar passes this way (another reason for supposing the Tarnak to be Arachotus), and the people live off the road to avoid the onerous duties of hospitality.

ARGHOUL, ARGHOOL, or ARGHUL (in the Egyptian hieroglyphs, AS or AS-IT),[1] an ancient and modern Egyptian and Arab wood-wind instrument, with cylindrical bore and single reed mouthpiece of the clarinet type. The arghoul consists of two reed pipes of unequal lengths bound together by means of waxed thread, so that the two mouthpieces lie side by side, and can be taken by the performer into his mouth at the same time. The mouthpiece consists of a reed having a small tongue detached by means of a longitudinal slit which forms the beating reed, as in the clarinet mouthpiece. The shorter pipe has six holes on which the melody is played; the three upper holes being covered by the fingers of the right hand, and the lower by those of the left hand. The longer pipe has no lateral holes; it is a drone pipe with one note only, which, however, can be varied by the addition of extra lengths of reed. In the illustration all three lengths are shown in use. An arghoul belonging to the collection of the Conservatoire Royal at Brussels, described by Victor Mahillon in his catalogue[2] (No. 113), gives the following scale:—

(From Edward William Lane's *An Account of the Manners and Customs of the Modern Egyptians*.)

Modern Arghoul, 3 ft. 2½ in. long.

The total length of the shorter pipe, including the mouthpiece, is 0.435 m.; of the longer pipe, without additional joints, 0.555 m. An Egyptian arghoul,[3] presented by the khedive to the Victoria and Albert Museum, measures 4 ft. 8½ in.

For further information see Victor Loret, *L'Egypte au temps des Pharaons* (Paris, 1889), 8vo, pp. 139, 143, 144; G.A. Villoteau, *Description historique technique et littéraire des instruments de musique des orientaux* (*Description de l'Egypte*, Paris, 1823, tome xiii, pp. 456-473).

(K. S.)

1 See Victor Loret. "Les Flûtes égyptiennes antiques," *Journal Asiatique*, 8ème série, tome xiv., Paris, 1889, pp. 129, 130 and 132.

2 *Catalogue descriptif et analytique du musée du Conservatoire Royal de Bruxelles* (Ghent, 1880), p. 141.

3 *A Descriptive Catalogue of the Musical Instruments in the South Kensington Museum*, by Carl Engel (London, 1874), p. 143.

ARGOL, the commercial name of crude tartar (*q.v.*). It is a semi-crystalline deposit which forms on wine vats, and is generally grey or red in colour.

ARGON (from the Gr. ἀ-, privative, and ἔργον, work; hence meaning "inert"), a gaseous constituent of atmospheric air. For more than a hundred years before 1894 it had been supposed that the composition of the atmosphere was thoroughly known. Beyond variable quantities of moisture and traces of carbonic acid, hydrogen, ammonia, &c., the only constituents recognized were nitrogen and oxygen. The analysis of air was conducted by determining the amount of oxygen present and assuming the remainder to be nitrogen. Since the time of Henry Cavendish no one seemed even to have asked the question whether the residue was, in truth, all capable of conversion into nitric acid.

The manner in which this condition of complacent ignorance came to be disturbed is instructive. Observations undertaken mainly in the interest of Prout's law, and extending over many years, had been conducted to determine afresh the densities of the principal gases— hydrogen, oxygen and nitrogen. In the latter case, the first preparations were according to the convenient method devised by Vernon Harcourt, in which air charged with ammonia is passed over red-hot copper. Under the influence of the heat the atmospheric oxygen, unites with the hydrogen of the ammonia, and when the excess of the latter is removed with sulphuric acid, the gas properly desiccated should be pure nitrogen, derived in part from the ammonia, but principally from the air. A few concordant determinations of density having been effected, the question was at first regarded as disposed of, until the thought occurred that it might be desirable to try also the more usual method of preparation in which the oxygen is removed by actual oxidation of copper without the aid of ammonia. Determinations made thus were equally concordant among themselves, but the resulting density was about 1/1000 part greater than that found by Harcourt's method (Rayleigh, *Nature*, vol. xlvi. p. 512, 1892). Subsequently when *oxygen* was substituted for air in the first method, so that all (instead of about one-seventh part) of the nitrogen was derived from ammonia, the difference rose to ½%. Further experiment only brought out more clearly the diversity of the gases hitherto assumed to be identical. Whatever were the means employed to rid air of accompanying oxygen, a uniform value of the density was arrived at, and this value was ½% greater than that appertaining to nitrogen extracted from compounds such as nitrous oxide, ammonia and ammonium nitrite. No impurity, consisting of any known substance, could be discovered capable of explaining an excessive weight in the one case, or a deficiency in the other. Storage for eight months did not disturb the density of the chemically extracted gas, nor had the silent electric discharge any influence upon either quality. ("On an Anomaly encountered in determining the Density of Nitrogen Gas," *Proc. Roy. Soc.*, April 1894.)

At this stage it became clear that the complication depended upon some hitherto unknown body, and probability inclined to the existence of a gas in the atmosphere heavier than nitrogen, and remaining unacted upon during the removal of the oxygen—a conclusion afterwards fully established by Lord Rayleigh and Sir William Ramsay. The question which now pressed was as to the character of the evidence for the universally accepted view that the so-called nitrogen of the atmosphere was all of one kind, that the nitrogen of the air was the same as the nitrogen of nitre. Reference to Cavendish showed that he had already raised this question in the most distinct manner, and indeed, to a certain extent, resolved it. In his memoir of 1785 he writes:—

"As far as the experiments hitherto published extend, we scarcely know more of the phlogisticated part of our atmosphere than that it is not diminished by lime-water, caustic alkalies, or nitrous air; that it is unfit to support fire or maintain life in animals; and that its specific gravity is not much less than that of common air; so that, though the nitrous acid, by being united to phlogiston, is converted into air possessed of these properties, and consequently, though it was reasonable to suppose, that part at least of the phlogisticated air of the atmosphere consists of this acid united to phlogiston, yet it may fairly be doubted whether the whole is of this kind, or whether there are not in reality many different substances confounded together by us under the name of phlogisticated air. I therefore made an experiment to determine whether the whole of a given portion of the phlogisticated air of the atmosphere could be reduced to nitrous acid, or whether there was not a part of a different nature to the rest which would refuse to undergo that change. The foregoing experiments indeed, in some measure, decided this point, as much the greatest part of air let up into the tube lost its elasticity; yet, as some remained unabsorbed, it did not appear for certain whether that was of the same nature as the rest or not. For this purpose I diminished a similar mixture of dephlogisticated [oxygen] and common air, in the same manner as before [by sparks over alkali], till it was reduced to a small part of its original bulk. I then, in order to decompound as much as I could of the phlogisticated air [nitrogen] which remained in the tube, added some dephlogisticated air to it and continued the spark until no further diminution took place. Having by these means condensed as much as I could of the phlogisticated air, I let up some solution of liver of sulphur to absorb the dephlogisticated air; after which only a small bubble of air remained unabsorbed, which certainly was not more than 1/120 of the bulk of the dephlogisticated air let up into the tube; so that, if there be any part of the dephlogisticated air of our atmosphere which differs from the rest, and cannot be reduced to nitrous acid, we may safely conclude that it is not more than 1/120 part of the whole."

Although, as was natural, Cavendish was satisfied with his result, and does not decide whether the small residue was genuine, it is probable that his residue was really of a different kind from the main bulk of the "phlogisticated air," and contained the gas afterwards named argon.

49

FIG. 1.

The announcement to the British Association in 1894 by Rayleigh and Ramsay of a new gas in the atmosphere was received with a good deal of scepticism. Some doubted the discovery of a new gas altogether, while others denied that it was present in the atmosphere. Yet there was nothing inconsistent with any previously ascertained fact in the asserted presence of 1% of a non-oxidizable gas about half as heavy again as nitrogen. The nearest approach to a difficulty lay in the behaviour of liquid air, from which it was supposed, as the event proved erroneously, that such a constituent would separate itself in the solid form. The evidence of the existence of a new gas (named Argon on account of its chemical inertness), and a statement of many of its properties, were communicated to the Royal Society (see *Phil. Trans.* clxxxvi. p. 187) by the discoverers in January 1895. The isolation of the new substance by removal of nitrogen from air was effected by two distinct methods. Of these the first is merely a development of that of Cavendish. The gases were contained in a test-tube A (fig. 1) standing over a large quantity of weak alkali B, and the current was conveyed in wires insulated by U-shaped glass tubes CC passing through the liquid and round the mouth of the test-tube. The inner platinum ends DD of the wire may be sealed into the glass insulating tubes, but reliance should not be placed upon these sealings. In order to secure tightness in spite of cracks, mercury was placed in the bends. With a battery of five Grove cells and a Ruhmkorff coil of medium size, a somewhat short spark, or arc, of about 5 mm. was found to be more favourable than a longer one. When the mixed gases were in the right proportion, the rate of absorption was about 30 c.c. per hour, about thirty times as fast as Cavendish could work with the electrical machine of his day. Where it is available, an alternating electric current is much superior to a battery and break. This combination, introduced by W. Spottiswoode, allows the absorption in the apparatus of fig. 1 to be raised to about 80 c.c. per hour, and the method is very convenient for the purification of small quantities of argon and for determinations of the amount present in various samples of gas, *e.g.* in the gases expelled from solution in water. A convenient adjunct to this apparatus is a small voltameter, with the aid of which oxygen or hydrogen can be introduced at pleasure. The gradual elimination of the nitrogen is tested at a moment's notice with a miniature spectroscope. For this purpose a small Leyden jar is connected as usual to the secondary terminals, and if necessary the force of the discharge is moderated by the insertion of resistance in the primary circuit. When with a fairly wide slit the yellow line is no longer visible, the residual nitrogen may be considered to have fallen below 2 or 3%. During this stage the oxygen should be in considerable excess. When the yellow line of nitrogen has disappeared, and no further contraction seems to be in progress, the oxygen maybe removed by cautious introduction of hydrogen. The spectrum may now be further examined with a more powerful instrument. The most conspicuous group in the argon spectrum at atmospheric pressure is that first recorded by A. Schuster (fig. 2). Water vapour and excess of oxygen in moderation do not interfere seriously with its visibility. It is of interest to note that the argon spectrum may be fully developed by operating upon a miniature scale, starting with only 5 c.c. of air (*Phil. Mag.* vol. i. p. 103, 1901).

The development of Cavendish's method upon a large scale involves arrangements different from what would at first be expected. The transformer working from a public supply should give about 6000 volts on open circuit, although when the electric flame is established the voltage on the platinums is only from 1600 to 2000. No sufficient advantage is attained by raising the pressure of the gases above atmosphere, but a capacious vessel is necessary. This may consist of a glass sphere of 50 litres' capacity, into the neck of which, presented downwards, the necessary tubes are fitted. The whole of the interior surface is washed with a fountain of alkali, kept in circulation by means of a small centrifugal pump. In this apparatus, and with about one horse-power utilized at the transformer, the absorption of gas is 21 litres per hour ("The Oxidation of Nitrogen Gas," *Trans. Chem. Soc.*, 1897).

In one experiment, specially undertaken for the sake of measurement, the total air employed was 9250 c.c., and the oxygen consumed, manipulated with the aid of partially de-aërated water, amounted to 10,820 c.c. The oxygen contained in the air would be 1942 c.c.; so that the quantities of atmospheric nitrogen and of total oxygen which enter into combination would be 7308 c.c. and 12,762 c.c. respectively. This corresponds to N + 1.75 O, the oxygen being decidedly in excess of the proportion required to form nitrous acid. The argon ultimately found was 75.0 c.c., or a little more than 1% of the atmospheric nitrogen used. A subsequent determination over mercury by A.M. Kellas (*Proc. Roy. Soc.* lix. p. 66, 1895) gave 1.186 c.c. as the amount of argon present in 100 c.c. of mixed atmospheric nitrogen and argon. In the earlier stages of the inquiry, when it was important to meet the doubts which had been expressed as to the presence of the new gas in the atmosphere, blank experiments were executed in which air was replaced by nitrogen from ammonium nitrite. The residual argon, derived doubtless from the water used to manipulate the gases, was but a small fraction of what would have been obtained from a corresponding quantity of air.

F

IG. 2.

The other method by which nitrogen may be absorbed on a considerable scale is by the aid of magnesium. The metal in the form of thin turnings is charged into hard glass or iron tubes heated to a full red in a combustion furnace. Into this air, previously deprived of oxygen by red-hot copper and thoroughly dried, is led in a continuous stream. At this temperature the nitrogen combines with the magnesium, and thus the argon is concentrated. A still more potent absorption is afforded by calcium prepared *in situ* by heating a mixture of magnesium dust with thoroughly dehydrated quick-lime. The density of argon, prepared and purified by magnesium, was found by Sir William Ramsay to be 19.941 on the O = 16 scale. The volume actually weighed was 163 c.c. Subsequently large-scale operations with the same apparatus as had been used for the principal gases gave an almost identical result (19.940) for argon prepared with oxygen.

Argon is soluble in water at 12° C. to about 4.0%, that is, it is about 2½ times more soluble than nitrogen. We should thus expect to find it in increased proportion in the dissolved gases of rain-water. Experiment has confirmed this anticipation. The weight of a mixture of argon and nitrogen prepared from the dissolved gases showed an excess of 24 mg. over the weight of true nitrogen, the corresponding excess for the atmospheric mixture being only 11 mg. Argon is contained in the gases liberated by many thermal springs, but not in special quantity. The gas collected from the King's Spring at Bath gave only ½%, *i.e.* half the atmospheric proportion.

The most remarkable physical property of argon relates to the constant known as the ratio of specific heats. When a gas is warmed one degree, the heat which must be supplied depends upon whether the operation is conducted at a constant volume or at a constant pressure, being greater in the latter case. The ratio of specific heats of the principal gases is 1.4, which, according to the kinetic theory, is an indication that an important fraction of the energy absorbed is devoted to rotation or vibration. If, as for Boscovitch points, the whole energy is translatory, the ratio of specific heats must be 1.67. This is precisely the number found from the velocity of sound in argon as determined by Kundt's method, and it leaves no room for any sensible energy of rotatory or vibrational motion. The same value had previously been found for mercury vapour by Kundt and Warburg, and had been regarded as confirmatory of the monatomic character attributed on chemical grounds to the mercury molecule. It may be added that helium has the same character as argon in respect of specific heats (Ramsay, *Proc. Roy. Soc.* l. p. 86, 1895).

The refractivity of argon is .961 of that of air. This low refractivity is noteworthy as strongly antagonistic to the view at one time favoured by eminent chemists that argon was a condensed form of nitrogen represented by N3. The viscosity of argon is 1.21, referred to air, somewhat higher than for oxygen, which stands at the head of the list of the principal gases ("On some Physical Properties of Argon and Helium," *Proc. Roy. Soc.* vol. lix. p. 198, 1896).

The spectrum shows remarkable peculiarities. According to circumstances, the colour of the light obtained from a Plücker vacuum tube changes "from red to a rich steel blue," to use the words of Crookes, who first described the phenomenon. A third spectrum is distinguished by J.M. Eder and Edward Valenta. The red spectrum is obtained at moderately low pressures (5 mm.) by the use of a Ruhmkorff coil without a jar or air-gap. The red lines at 7056 and 6965 (Crookes) are characteristic. The blue spectrum is best seen at a somewhat lower pressure (1 mm. to 2.5 mm.), and usually requires a Leyden jar to be connected to the secondary terminals. In some conditions very small causes effect a transition from the one spectrum to the other. The course of electrical events attending the operation of a Ruhmkorff coil being extremely complicated, special interest attaches to some experiments conducted by John Trowbridge and T.W. Richards, in which the source of power was a secondary battery of 5000 cells. At a pressure of 1 mm. the red glow of argon was readily obtained with a voltage of 2000, but not with much less. After the discharge was once started, the difference of potentials at the terminals of the tube varied from 630 volts upwards.

The introduction of a capacity between the terminals of the Geissler tube, for example two plates of metal 1600 sq. cm. in area separated by a glass plate 1 cm. thick, made no difference in the red glow so long as the connexions were good and the condenser was quiet. As soon as a spark-gap was introduced, or the condenser began to emit the humming sound peculiar to it, the beautiful blue glow so characteristic of argon immediately appeared. (*Phil. Mag.* xliii. p. 77, 1897.)

The behaviour of argon at low temperatures was investigated by K.S. Olszewski (*Phil. Trans.*, 1895, p. 253). The following results are extracted from the table given by him:—

Name.	Critical Temperature, Cent.	Critical Pressure, Atmos.	Boiling Point Cent.	Freezing Point Cent.
Nitrogen	−146.0	35.0	−194.4	−214.0
Argon	−121.0	50.6	−187.0	−189.6
Oxygen	−118.8	50.8	−182.7	?

The smallness of the interval between the boiling and freezing points is noteworthy.

From the manner of its preparation it was clear at an early stage that argon would not combine with magnesium or calcium at a red heat, nor under the influence of the electric discharge with oxygen, hydrogen or nitrogen. Numerous other, attempts to induce combination also failed. Nor does it appear that any well-defined compound of argon has yet been prepared. It was found, however, by M.P.E. Berthelot that under the influence of the silent electric discharge, a mixture of benzene vapour and argon underwent contraction, with formation of a gummy product from which the argon could be recovered.

The facts detailed in the original memoir led to the conclusion that argon was an element or a mixture of elements, but the question between these alternatives was left open. The behaviour on liquefaction, however, seemed to prove that in the latter case either the proportion of the subordinate constituents was small, or else that the various constituents were but little contrasted. An attempt, somewhat later, by Ramsay and J. Norman Collie to separate argon by diffusion into two parts, which should have different densities or refractivities, led to no distinct effect. More recently Ramsay and M.W. Travers have obtained evidence of the existence in the atmosphere of three new gases, besides helium, to which have been assigned the names of neon, krypton and xenon. These gases agree with argon in respect of the ratio of the specific heats and in being non-oxidizable under the electric spark. As originally defined, argon included small proportions of these gases, but it is now preferable to limit the name to the principal constituent and to regard the newer gases as "companions of argon." The physical constants associated with the name will scarcely be changed, since the proportion of the "companions" is so small. Sir William Ramsay considers that probably the volume of all of them taken together does not exceed 1/400th part of that of the argon. The physical properties of these gases are given in the following table (*Proc. Roy. Soc.* lxvii. p. 331, 1900):—

	Helium.	Neon.	Argon.	Krypton.	Xenon.
Refractivities (air = 1)	.1238	.2345	.968	1.449	2.364
Densities (O = 16)	1.98	9.97	19.96	40.88	64
Boiling points at 760 mm.	c. 6°1 abs.	?	86.9° abs.	121.3° abs.	163.9° abs.
Critical temperatures	?	below 68° abs.	155.6° abs.	210.5° abs.	287.7° abs.
Critical pressures	?	?	40.2 metres.	41.24 metres.	43.5 metres.
Weight of 1 c.c. of liquid	?	?	1.212 gm.	2.155 gm.	3.52 gm.

The glow obtained in vacuum tubes is highly characteristic, whether as seen directly or as analysed by the spectroscope.

Now that liquid air is available in many laboratories, it forms an advantageous starting-point in the preparation of argon. Being less volatile than nitrogen, argon accumulates relatively as liquid air evaporates. That the proportion of oxygen increases at the same time is little or no drawback. The following analyses (Rayleigh, *Phil. Mag.*, June 1903) of the *vapour* arising from liquid air at various stages of the evaporation will give an idea of the course of events:—

Percentage of Oxygen.	Percentage of Argon.	Argon as a Percentage of the Nitrogen and Argon.
30	1.3	1.9
43	2.0	3.5
64	2.0	5.6
75	2.1	8.4
90	2.0	20.0

(R.)

1 Sir James Dewar, *Compt. Rend.* (1904), 139, 261 and 241.

ARGONAUTS (Ἀργοναῦται, the sailors of the "Argo"), in Greek legend a band of heroes who took part in the Argonautic expedition under the command of Jason, to fetch the golden fleece. This task had been imposed on Jason by his uncle Pelias (*q.v.*), who had usurped the throne of Iolcus in Thessaly, which rightfully belonged to Jason's father Aeson. The story of the fleece was as follows. Jason's uncle Athamas had two children, Phrixus and Helle, by his wife Nephele, the cloud goddess. But after a time he became enamoured of Ino, the daughter of Cadmus, and neglected Nephele, who disappeared in anger. Ino, who hated the children of Nephele, persuaded Athamas, by means of a false oracle, to offer Phrixus as a sacrifice, as the only means of alleviating a famine which she herself had caused by ordering the grain to be secretly roasted before it was sown. But before the sacrifice the shade of Nephele appeared to Phrixus, bringing a ram with a golden fleece on which he and his sister Helle endeavoured to escape over the sea. Helle fell off and was drowned in the strait, which after her was called the Hellespont. Phrixus, however, reached the other side in safety, and proceeding by land to Aea in Colchis on the farther shore of the Euxine Sea, sacrificed the ram, and hung up its fleece in the grove of Ares, where it was guarded by a sleepless dragon.

Jason, having undertaken the quest of the fleece, called upon the noblest heroes of Greece to take part in the expedition. According to the original story, the crew consisted of the chief members of Jason's own race, the Minyae. But when the legend became common property, other and better-known heroes were added to their number—Orpheus, Castor and Polydeuces (Pollux), Zetes and Calais, the winged sons of Boreas, Meleager, Theseus, Heracles. The crew was supposed to consist of fifty, agreeing in number with the fifty oars of the "Argo," so called from its builder Argos, the son of Phrixus, or from ἀργός (swift). It was a larger vessel than had ever been seen before, built of pine-wood that never rotted from Mount Pelion. The goddess Athena herself superintended its construction, and inserted in the prow a piece of oak from Dodona, which was endowed with the power of speaking and delivering oracles. The outward course of the "Argo" was the same as that of the Greek traders, whose settlements as early as the 6th century B.C. dotted the southern shores of the Euxine. The first landing-place was the island of Lemnos, which was occupied only by women, who had put to death their fathers, husbands and brothers. Here the Argonauts remained some months, until they were persuaded by Heracles to leave. It is known from Herodotus (iv. 145) that the Minyae had formed settlements at Lemnos at a very early date. Proceeding up the Hellespont, they sailed to the country of the Doliones, by whose king, Cyzicus, they were hospitably received. After their departure, being driven back to the same place by a storm, they were attacked by the Doliones, who did not recognize them, and in a battle which took place Cyzicus was killed by Jason. After Cyzicus had been duly mourned and buried, the Argonauts proceeded along the coast of Mysia, where occurred the incident of Heracles and Hylas (*q.v.*). On reaching the country of the Bebryces, they again landed to get water, and were challenged by the king, Amycus, to match him with a boxer. Polydeuces came forward, and in the end overpowered his adversary, and bound him to a tree, or according to others, slew him. At the entrance to the Euxine, at Salmydessus on the coast of Thrace, they met Phineus, the blind and aged king whose food was being constantly polluted by the Harpies. He knew the course to Colchis, and offered to tell it, if the Argonauts would free him from the Harpies. This was done by the winged sons of Boreas, and Phineus now told them their course, and that the way to pass through the Symplegades or Cyanean rocks—two cliffs which moved on their bases and crushed whatever sought to pass—was first to fly a pigeon through, and when the cliffs, having closed on the pigeon, began to retire to each side, to row the "Argo" swiftly through. His advice was successfully followed, and the "Argo" made the passage unscathed, except for trifling damage to the stern. From that time the rocks became fixed and never closed again. The next halting-places were the country of the Maryandini, where the helmsman Tiphys died, and the land of the Amazons on the banks of the Thermodon. At the island of Aretias they drove away the Stymphalian birds, who used their feathers of brass as arrows. Here they found and took on board the four sons of Phrixus who, after their father's death, had been sent by Aeetes, king of Colchis, to fetch the treasures of Orchomenus, but had been driven by a storm upon the island. Passing near Mount Caucasus, they heard the groans of Prometheus and the flapping of the wings of the eagle which gnawed his liver. They now reached their goal, the river Phasis, and the following morning Jason repaired to the palace of Aeetes, and demanded the golden fleece. Aeetes required of Jason that he should first yoke to a plough his bulls, given him by Hephaestus, which snorted fire and had hoofs of brass, and with them plough the field of Ares. That done, the field was to be sown with the dragons' teeth brought by Phrixus, from which armed men were to spring. Successful so far by means of the mixture which Medea, daughter of Aeetes, had given him as proof against fire and sword, Jason was next allowed to approach the dragon which watched the fleece; Medea soothed the monster with another mixture, and Jason became master of the fleece. Then the voyage homeward began, Medea accompanying Jason, and Aeetes pursuing them. To delay him and obtain escape, Medea dismembered her young brother Absyrtus, whom she had taken with her, and cast his limbs about in the sea for his father to pick up. Her plan succeeded, and while Aeetes was burying the remains of his son at Tomi, Jason and Medea escaped. In another account Absyrtus had grown to manhood then, and met his death in an encounter with Jason, in pursuit of whom he had been sent. Of the homeward course various accounts are given. In the oldest (Pindar) the "Argo" sailed along the river Phasis into the eastern Oceanus, round Asia to the south coast of Libya, thence to the mythical lake Tritonis, after being carried twelve days over land through Libya, and thence again to Iolcus. Hecataeus of Miletus (Schol. Apollon. Rhod. iv. 259) suggested that from the Oceanus it may have sailed into the Nile, and so to the Mediterranean. Others, like Sophocles, described the return voyage as differing from the outward course only in taking the northern instead of the southern shore of the Euxine. Some (pseudo-Orpheus) supposed that the Argonauts had sailed up the river Tanaïs, passed into another river, and by it reached the North Sea, returning to the Mediterranean by the Pillars of Hercules. Again, others (Apollonius Rhodius) laid down the course as up the Danube (Ister), from it into the Adriatic by a supposed mouth of that river, and on to Corcyra, where a storm overtook them. Next they sailed up the Eridanus into the Rhodanus, passing through the country of the Celts and Ligurians to the Stoechades, then to the island of Aethalia (Elba), finally reaching the Tyrrhenian Sea and the island of Circe, who absolved them from the murder of Absyrtus. Then they passed safely through Scylla and Charybdis, past the Sirens, through the Planctae, over the island of the Sun, Trinacria and on to Corcyra again, the land of the Phaeacians, where Jason and Medea held their nuptials. They had sighted the coast of Peloponnesus when a storm overtook them and drove them to the coast of Libya, where they were saved from a quicksand by the local nymphs. The "Argo" was now carried twelve days and twelve nights to the Hesperides, and thence to lake Tritonis (where the seer Mopsus died), whence Triton conducted them to the Mediterranean. At Crete the brazen Talos, who would not permit them to land, was killed by the Dioscuri. At Anaphe, one of the Sporades, they were saved from a storm by Apollo. Finally, they reached Iolcus, and the "Argo" was placed in a groove sacred to Poseidon on the isthmus of Corinth. Jason's death, it is said, was afterwards caused by part of the stern giving way and falling upon him.

The story of the expedition of the Argonauts is very old. Homer was acquainted with it and speaks of the "Argo" as well known to all men; the wanderings of Odysseus may have been partly founded on its voyage. Pindar, in the fourth Pythian ode, gives the oldest detailed account of it. In Greek, there are also extant the *Argonautica* of Apollonius Rhodius and the pseudo-Orpheus (4th century A.D.), and the account in Apollodorus (i. 9), based on the best extant authorities; in Latin, the imitation of Apollonius (a free translation or adaptation of whose *Argonautica* was made by Terentius Varro Atacinus in the time of Cicero) by Valerius Flaccus. In ancient times the expedition was regarded as a historical fact, an incident in the opening up of the Euxine to Greek commerce and colonization. Its object was the acquisition of gold, which was caught by the inhabitants of Colchis in fleeces as it was washed down the rivers. Suidas says that the fleece was a book written on parchment, which taught how to make gold by chemical processes. The rationalists explained the ram on which Phrixus crossed the sea as the name or ornament of the ship on which he escaped. Several interpretations of the legend have been put forward by modern scholars. According to C.O. Müller, it had its origin in the worship of Zeus Laphystius; the fleece is the pledge of reconciliation; Jason is a propitiating god of health, Medea a goddess akin to Hera; Aeetes is connected with the Colchian sun-worship. Forchhammer saw in it an old nature symbolism; Jason, the god of healing and fruitfulness, brought the fleece—the fertilizing rain-cloud—to the western land that was parched by the heat of the sun. Others treat it as a solar myth; the ram is the light of the sun, the flight of Phrixus and the death of Helle signify its setting, the recovery of the fleece its rising again.

There are numerous treatises on the subject: F. Vater, *Der Argonautenzug* (1845); J. Stender, *De Argonautarum Expeditione*(1874); D. Kennerknecht, *De Argonautarum Fabula* (1886); M. Groeger, *De Argonautarum Fabularum Historia* (1889); see also Grote, *History of Greece*, part i. ch. 13; Preller, *Griechische Mythologie*; articles in Pauly-Wissowa's *Realencyclopädie*, Roscher's *Lexikon der Mythologie*, and Daremberg and Saglio's*Dictionnaire des Antiquités*.

ARGONNE, a rocky forest-clad plateau in the north-east of France, extending along the borders of Lorraine and Champagne, and forming part of the departments of Ardennes, Meuse and Marne. The Argonne stretches from S.S.E. to N.N.W., a distance of 63 m. with an average breadth of 19 m., and an average height of 1150 ft. It forms the connecting-link between the plateaus of Haute Marne and the Ardennes, and is bounded E. by the Meuse and W. by the Ante and the Aisne, which rises in its southern plateau. The valleys of the Aire and other rivers traverse it longitudinally, a fact to which its importance as a bulwark of north-eastern France is largely due. Of the numerous forests which clothe both slopes of the plateau, the chief is that of Argonne, which extends for 25 m. between the Aire and the Aisne.

For Dumouriez's Argonne campaign in 1792, see FRENCH REVOLUTIONARY WARS.

ARGOS, the name of several ancient Greek cities or districts, but specially appropriated in historic times to the chief town in eastern Peloponnese, whence the peninsula of Argolis derives its name. The Argeia, or territory of Argos proper, consisted of a shelving plain at the head of the Gulf of Argolis, enclosed between the eastern wall of the Arcadian plateau and the central highlands of Argolis. The waters of this valley (Inachus, Charadrus, Erasinus), when properly regulated, favoured the growth of excellent crops, and the capital standing only 3 m. from the sea was well placed for Levantine trade. Hence Argos was perhaps the earliest town of importance in Greece; the legends indicate its high antiquity and its early intercourse with foreign countries (Egypt, Lycia, &c.). Though eclipsed in the Homeric age, when it appears as the seat of Diomedes, by the later foundation of Mycenae, it regained its predominance after the invasion of the Dorians (*q.v.*), who seem to have occupied this site in considerable force. In accordance with the tradition which assigned the portion to the eldest-born of the Heracleid conquerors, Argos was for some centuries the leading power in Peloponnesus. There is good evidence that its sway extended originally over the entire Argolis peninsula, the land east of Parnon, Cythera, Aegina and Sicyon. Under King Pheidon the Argive empire embraced all eastern Peloponnesus, and its influence spread even to the western districts.

This supremacy was first challenged about the 8th century by Sparta. Though organized on similar lines, with a citizen population divided into three Dorian tribes (and one containing other elements), with a class of Perioeci (neighbouring dependents) and of serfs, the Argives had no more constant foe than their Lacedaemonian kinsmen. In a protracted struggle for the possession of the eastern seaboard of Laconia in spite of the victory at Hysiae (apparently in 669), they were gradually driven back, until by 550 they had lost the whole coast strip of Cynuria. A later attempt to retrieve this loss resulted in a crushing defeat near Tiryns at the hands of King Cleomenes I. (probably in 495), which so weakened the Argives that they had to open the franchise to their Perioeci. By this time they 480had also lost control over the other cities of Argolis, which they never succeeded in recovering. Partly in consequence of its defeat, partly out of jealousy against Sparta, Argos took no part in the war against Xerxes. Indeed on this, as on later occasions, its relations with Persia seem to have been friendly. About 470 the conflict with Sparta was renewed in concert with the Arcadians, but all that the Argives could achieve was to destroy their revolted dependencies of Mycenae and Tiryns (468 or 464). In 461 they contracted an alliance with Athens, thus renewing a connexion established by Peisistratus (*q.v.*). In spite of this league Argos made no headway against Sparta, and in 451 consented to a truce. A more important result of Athenian intervention was the substitution of the democratic government for the oligarchy which had succeeded the early monarchy; at any rate forty years later we find that Argos possessed complete democratic institutions.

During the early Peloponnesian War Argos remained neutral; after the break-up of the Spartan confederacy consequent upon the peace of Nicias the alliance of this state, with its unimpaired resources and flourishing commerce, was courted on all sides. By throwing in her lot with the Peloponnesian democracies and Athens, Argos seriously endangered Sparta's supremacy, but the defeat of Mantineia (418) and a successful rising of the Argive oligarchs spoilt this chance. The speedily restored democracy put little heart into the conflict, and beyond sending mercenary detachments, lent Athens no further help in the war (see PELOPONNESIAN WAR).

At the outset of the 4th century, Argos, with a population and resources equalling those of Athens, took a prominent part in the Corinthian League against Sparta. In 394 the Argives helped to garrison Corinth, and the latter state seems for a while to have been annexed by them. But the peace of Antalcidas (*q.v.*) dissolved this connexion, and barred Argive pretensions to control all Argolis. After the battle of Leuctra Argos experienced a political crisis; the oligarchs attempted a revolution, but were put down by their opponents with such vindictiveness that 1200 of them are said to have been executed (370). The democracy consistently supported the victorious Thebans against Sparta, figuring with a large contingent on the decisive field of Mantineia (362). When pressed in turn by their old foes the Argives were among the first to call in Philip of Macedon, who reinstated them in Cynuria after becoming master of Greece. In the Lamian War Argos was induced to side with the patriots against Macedonia; after its capture by Cassander from Polyperchon (317) it fell in 303 into the hands of Demetrius Poliorcetes. In 272 the Argives joined Sparta in resisting the ambition of King Pyrrhus of Epirus, whose death ensued in an unsuccessful night attack upon the city. They passed instead into the power of Antigonus Gonatas of Macedonia, who maintained his control by means of tyrants. After several unavailing attempts Aratus (*q.v.*) contrived to win Argos for the Achaean League (229), in which it remained save during a brief occupation by the Spartans Cleomenes III. (*q.v.*) and Nabis (224 and 196).

The Roman conquest of Achaea enhanced the prosperity of Argos by removing the trade competition of Corinth. Under the Empire, Argos was the headquarters of the Achaean synod, and continued to be a resort of Roman merchants. Though plundered by the Goths inA.D. 267 and 395 it retained some of its commerce and culture in Byzantine days. The town was captured by the Franks in 1210; after 1246 it was held in fief by the rulers of Athens. In later centuries it became the scene of frequent conflicts between the Venetians and the Turks, and on two occasions (1397 and 1500) its population was massacred by the latter. Repeopled with Albanian settlers, Argos was chosen as seat of the Greek national assembly in the wars of independence. Its citadel was courageously defended by the patriots (1822); in 1825 the city was burnt to the ground by Ibrahim Pasha. The present town of 10,000 inhabitants is a purely agricultural settlement. The Argive plain, though not yet sufficiently reclaimed, yields good crops of corn, rice and tobacco.

In the early days of Greece the Argives enjoyed high repute for their musical talent. Their school of bronze sculpture, whose first famous exponent was Ageladas (Hagelaidas), the reputed master of Pheidias, reached its climax towards the end of the 5th century in the atelier of Polyclitus (*q.v.*) and his pupils. To this period also belongs the new Heraeum (see below), one of the most splendid temples of Greece.

Remains of the early city are still visible on the Larissa acropolis, which towers 900 ft. high to the north-west of the town. A few courses of the ancient ramparts appear under the double enceinte of the surviving medieval fortress. An aqueduct of Greek times is represented by some fragments on the south-western edge. In the slope above the town was hewn a theatre equalling that of Athens in size. The Aspis or smaller citadel to the north-east has revealed traces of an early Mycenaean settlement; the Deiras or ridge connecting the two heights contains a prehistoric cemetery.

AUTHORITIES.—Herodotus, Thucydides, Xenophon; Plutarch,*Pyrrhus*, 30-34; Strabo pp. 373-374; Pausanias ii. 15-24; W.M. Leake, *Travels in the Morea* (London, 1835), ii. chs. 19-22; E. Curtius, *Peloponnesos* (Gotha, 1851), ii. 350-364; H.F. Tozer,*Geography of Greece* (London, 1873), pp. 292-294; J.K. Kophiniotis, Ἱστορία τοῦ Ἄργους (Athens, 1892-1893); W. Vollgraff in *Bulletin de Correspondance Hellénique* (1904, pp. 364-399; 1906, pp. 1-45; 1907, pp. 139-184).

(M. O. B. C.)

The Argive Heraeum.—Since 1892 investigation has added considerably to our knowledge concerning the Argive Heraeum or Heraion, the temple of Hera, which stood, according to Pausanias, "on one of the lower slopes of Euboea." The term Euboea did not designate the eminence upon which the Heraeum is placed, or the mountain-top behind the Heraeum only, but, as Pausanias distinctly indicates, the group of foothills of the hilly district adjoining the mountain. When once we admit that this designated not only the mountain, which is 1730 ft. high, but also the hilly district adjoining it, the general scale of distance for this site grows larger. The territory of the Heraeum was divided into three parts, namely Euboea, Acraea and Prosymna. Pausanias tells us that the Heraeum is 15 stadia from Mycenae. Strabo, on the other hand, says that the Heraeum was 40 stadia from Argos and 10 from Mycenae. Both authors underestimate the distance from Mycenae, which is about 25 stadia, or a little more than 3 m., while the distance from Argos is 45 stadia, or a little more than 5 m. The distance from the Heraeum to the ancient Midea is slightly greater than to Mycenae, while that from the Heraeum to Tiryns is about 6 m. The Argive Heraeum was the most important centre of Hera and Juno worship in the ancient world; it always remained the chief sanctuary of the Argive district, and was in all probability the earliest site of civilized life in the country inhabited by the Argive people. In fact, whereas the site of Hissarlik, the ancient Troy, is not in Greece proper, but in Asia Minor, and can thus not furnish the most direct evidence for the earliest Hellenic civilization as such; and whereas Tiryns, Mycenae, and the city of Argos, each represent only one definite period in the successive stages of civilization, the Argive Heraeum, holding the central site of early civilization in Greece proper, not only retained its importance during the three periods marked by the supremacy of Tiryns, Mycenae and the city of Argos, but in all probability antedated them as a centre of civilized Argive life. These conditions alone account for the extreme archaeological importance of this ancient sanctuary.

According to tradition the Heraeum was founded by Phoroneus at least thirteen generations before Agamemnon and the Achaeans ruled. It is highly probable that before it became important merely as a temple, it was the fortified centre uniting the Argive people dwelling in the plain, the citadel which was superseded in this function by Tiryns. There is ample evidence to show that it was the chief sanctuary during the Tirynthian period. When Mycenae was built under the Perseïds it was still the chief sanctuary for that centre, which superseded Tiryns in its dominance over the district, and which this temple clearly antedated in construction. According to the *Dictys Cretensis*, it was at this Heraeum that Agamemnon assembled the leaders 481before setting out for Troy. In the period of Dorian supremacy, in spite of the new cults which were introduced by these people, the Heraeum maintained its supreme importance: it was here that the tablets recording the succession of priestesses were kept which served as a chronological standard for the Argive people, and even far beyond their borders; and it was here that Pheidon deposited the ὀβελίσκοι when he introduced coinage into Greece.

We learn from Strabo that the Heraeum was the joint sanctuary for Mycenae and Argos. But in the 5th century the city of Argos vanquished the Mycenaeans, and from that time onwards the city of Argos becomes the political centre of the district, while the Heraeum remains the religious centre. And when in the year 423 B.C., through the negligence of the priestess Chryseis, the old temple was burnt down, the Argives erected a splendid new temple, built by Eupolemos, in which was placed the great gold and ivory statue of Hera, by the sculptor Polyclitus, the contemporary and rival of Pheidias, which was one of the most perfect works of sculpture in antiquity. Pausanias describes the temple and its contents (ii. 17), and in his time he still saw the ruins of the older burnt temple above the temple of Eupolemos.

PLAN OF THE HERAEUM (*surveyed and drawn by Edward L. Tilton*).

I. Old Temple.	V. 5th-Century Temple.	IX. Roman Building.
II. Stoa.	VI. South Stoa.	X. Lower Stoa.
III. Stoa.	VII. West Building.	XI. Phylakeion.
IV. East Building.	VIII. North-West Building.	A, B, C, D, E, F, Cisterns.

All these facts have been verified and illustrated by the excavations of the American Archaeological Institute and School of Athens, which were carried on from 1892 to 1895. In 1854 A.R. Rhangabé made tentative excavations on this site, digging a trench along the north and east sides of the second temple. Of these excavations no trace was to be seen when those of 1892 were begun. The excavations have shown that the sanctuary, instead of consisting of but one temple with the ruins of the older one above it, contained at least eleven separate buildings, occupying an area of about 975 ft. by 325.

On the uppermost terrace, defined by the great Cyclopean supporting wall, exactly as described by Pausanias, the excavations revealed a layer of ashes and charred wood, below which were found numerous objects of earliest date, together with some remains of the walls resting on a polygonal platform—all forming part of the earliest temple. Immediately adjoining the Cyclopean wall and below it were found traces of small houses of the rudest, earliest masonry which are pre-Mycenaean, if not pre-Cyclopean.

57

We then descend to the second terrace, in the centre of which the substructure of the great second temple was revealed, together with so much of the walls, as well as the several architectural members forming the superstructure, that it has been possible for E.L. Tilton to design a complete restoration of the temple. On the northern side of this terrace, between the second temple and the Cyclopean supporting wall, a long stoa or colonnade runs from east to west abutting at the west end in structures which evidently contained a well-house and waterworks; while at the eastern end of this stoa a number of chambers were erected against the hill, in front of which were placed statues and inscriptions, the bases for which are still extant. At the eastern-most end of this second terrace a large hall with three rows of columns in the interior, with a porch and entrance at the west end facing the temple, is built upon elaborate supporting walls of good masonry.

Below the second terrace at the south-west end a large and complicated building, with an open courtyard surrounded on three sides by a colonnade and with chambers opening out towards the north, may have served as a gymnasium or a sanatorium. It is of good early Greek architecture, earlier than the second temple. A curious, ruder building to the north of this and to the west of the second terrace is probably of much earlier date, perhaps of the Mycenaean period, and may have served as propylaea.

Immediately below the second temple at the foot of the elevation on which this temple stands, towards the south, and thus facing the city of Argos, a splendid stoa or colonnade, to which large flights of steps lead, was erected about the time of the building of the second temple. It is a part of the great plan to give worthy access to the temple from the city of Argos. To the east of this large flights of steps lead up to the temple proper.

At the western extremity of the whole site, immediately beside the river-bed, we again have a huge stoa running round two sides of a square, which was no doubt connected with the functions of this sanctuary as a health resort, especially for women, the goddess 482Hera presiding over and protecting married life and child-birth. Finally, immediately to the north of this western stoa there is an extensive house of Roman times also connected with baths.

While the buildings give archaeological evidence for every period of Greek life and history from the pre-Mycenaean period down to Roman times, the topography itself shows that the Heraeum must have been constructed before Mycenae and without any regard to it. The foothills which it occupies form the western boundary to the Argive plain as it stretches down towards the sea in the Gulf of Nauplia. While it was thus probably chosen as the earliest site for a citadel facing the sea, its second period points towards Tiryns and Midea. It could not have been built as the sanctuary of Mycenae, which was placed farther up towards the north-west in the hills, and could not be seen from the Heraeum, its inhabitants again not being able to see their sanctuary. The west building, the traces of bridges and roads, show that at one time it did hold some relation to Mycenae; but this was long after its foundation or the building of the huge Cyclopean supporting wall which is coeval with the walls of Tiryns, these again being earlier than those of Mycenae. There are, moreover, traces of still more primitive walls, built of rude small stones placed one upon the other without mortar, which are in character earlier than those of Tiryns, and have their parallel in the lowest layers of Hissarlik.

Bearing out the evidence of tradition as well as architecture, the numerous finds of individual objects in terra-cotta figurines, vases, bronzes, engraved stones, &c., point to organized civilized life on this site many generations before Mycenae was built, *a fortiori* before the life as depicted by Homer flourished—nay, before, as tradition has it, under Proetus the walls of Tiryns were erected. We are aided in forming some estimate of the chronological sequence preceding the Mycenaean age, as suggested by the finds of the Heraeum, in the new distribution which Dörpfeld has been led to make of the chronological stratification of Hissarlik. For the layer, which he now assigns to the Mycenaean period, is the sixth stratum from below. Now, as some of the remains at the Heraeum correspond to the two lowest layers of Hissarlik, the evidence of the Argive temple leads us far beyond the date assigned to the Mycenaean age, and at least into the second millennium B.C. (see also AEGEAN CIVILIZATION). As to its chronological relation to the Cretan sites—Cnossus, Phaestus, &c., and the "Minoan" civilization as determined by Dr A. Evans, see the discussion under CRETE.

This sanctuary still holds a position of central importance as illustrating the art of the highest period in Greek history, namely, the art of the 5th century B.C. under the great sculptor Polyclitus. Though the excavations in the second temple have clearly revealed the outlines of the base upon which the great gold and ivory statue of Hera stood, it is needless to say that no trace of the statue itself has been found. From Pausanias we learn that "the image of Hera is seated and is of colossal size: it is made of gold and ivory, and is the work of Polyclitus." Based on the computations made by the architect of the American excavations, E.L. Tilton, on the ground of the height of the nave, the total height of the image, including the base and the top of the throne, would be about 26 ft., the seated figure of the goddess herself about 18 ft. It is probable that the face, neck, arms and feet were of ivory, while the rest of the figure was draped in gold. Like the Olympian Zeus of Pheidias, Hera was seated on an elaborately decorated throne, holding in her left hand the sceptre, surmounted in her case by the cuckoo (as that of Zeus had an eagle), and in her right, instead of an elaborate figure of Victory (such as the Athena Parthenos and the Olympian Zeus held), simply a pomegranate. The crown was adorned with figures of Graces and the Seasons. A Roman imperial coin of Antoninus Pius shows us on a reduced scale the general composition of the figure; while contemporary Argive coins of the 5th century give a fairly adequate rendering of the head. A further attempt has been made to identify the head in a beautiful marble bust in the British Museum hitherto known as Bacchus (Waldstein, *Journal of Hellenic Studies*, vol. xxi., 1901, pp. 30 seq.)

We also learn from Pausanias that the temple was decorated with "sculptures over the columns, representing some the birth of Zeus and the battle of the gods and giants, others the Trojan War and the taking of Ilium." It was formerly supposed that the phrase "over the columns" pointed to the existence of sculptured metopes, but no pedimental groups. Finds made in the excavations, however, have shown that the temple also had pedimental groups. Besides numerous fragments of nude and draped figures belonging to pedimental statues, a well-preserved and very beautiful head of a female divinity, probably Hera, as well as a draped female torso of excellent workmanship, both belonging to the pediments, have been discovered. Of the metopes also a great number of fragments have been found, together with two almost complete metopes, the one containing the torso of a nude warrior in perfect preservation, as well as ten well-preserved heads. These statues bear the same relation to the sculptor Polyclitus which the Parthenon marbles hold to Pheidias; and the excavations have thus yielded most important material for the illustration of the Argive art of Polyclitus in the 5th century B.C.

See Waldstein, *The Argive Heraeum* (vol. i., Boston and New York, 1902; vol. ii., the Vases by J.C. Hoppin, the Bronzes by H.F. de Cosa, 1905); *Excavations of the American School of Athens at the Heraion of Argos* (1892); and numerous reports and articles in the *American Archaeological Journal* since 1892.

(C. W.*)

ARGOSTOLI (anc. *Cephallenia*), the capital of Cephalonia (one of the Ionian islands), and the seat of a bishop of the Greek church. Pop. about 10,000. It possesses an excellent harbour, a quay a mile in length, and a fine bridge. Shipbuilding and silk-spinning are carried on. Near at hand are the ruins of Cranii, which afford fine examples of Greek military architecture; and at the west side of the harbour there is a curious stream, flowing *from* the sea, and employed to drive mills before losing itself in caverns inland.

See Sir C. Fellows's *Journal of an Excursion in Asia Minor* in 1838, and Wiebel's *Die Insel Kephalonia und die Meermühlen von Argostoli* (Hamburg, 1873).

ARGOSY (a corruption, by transposition of letters, of the name of the seaport Ragusa), the term originally for a carrack or merchant ship from Ragusa and other Adriatic ports, now used poetically of any vessel carrying rich merchandise. In English writings of the 16th century the seaport named is variously spelt Ragusa, Aragouse or Aragosa, and ships coming thence were named Ragusyes, Arguzes and Argosies; the last form surviving and passing into literature. The incorrect derivation from Jason's ship, the "Argo," is of modern origin.

ARGUIN, an island (identified by some writers with Hanno's Cerne), off the west coast of Africa, a little south of Cape Blanco, in 20° 25′ N., 16° 37′ W. It is some 4 m. long by 2½ broad, produces gum-arabic, and is the seat of a lucrative turtle-fishery. Off the island, which was discovered by the Portuguese in the 15th century, are extensive and very dangerous reefs. Arguin was occupied in turn by Portuguese, Dutch, English and French; and to France it now belongs. The aridity of the soil and the bad anchorage prevent a permanent settlement. The fishery is mostly carried on by inhabitants of the Canary Isles. In July 1816 the French frigate "Medusa," which carried officers on their way to Senegal to take possession of that country for France, was wrecked off Arguin, 350 lives being lost.

ARGUMENT, a word meaning "proof," "evidence," corresponding in English to the Latin word *argumentum*, from which it is derived; the originating Latin verb *arguere*, to make clear, from which comes the English "argue," is from a root meaning bright, appearing in Greek ἀργής, white. From its primary sense are derived such applications of the word as a chain of reasoning, a fact or reason given to support a proposition, a discussion of the evidence or reasons for or against some theory or proposition and the like. More particularly "argument" means a synopsis of the contents of a book, the outline of a novel, play, &c. In logic it is used for the middle term in a syllogism, and for many species of fallacies, such as the *argumentum ad hominem, ad baculum*, &c. (see FALLACY). In mathematics the term has received special meanings; in mathematical tables the "argument" is the quantity upon which the other quantities in the table are made to depend; in the theory of complex variables, *e.g.* such as a + ib where i = √−1, the "argument" (or "amplitude") is the angle θ given by tan θ = b/a. In astronomy, the term is used in connexion with the Ptolemaic theory to denote the angular distance on the epicycle of a planet from the true apogee of the epicycle; and the "equation to the argument" is the angle subtended at the earth by the distance of a planet from the centre of the epicycle.

ARGUS, in ancient Greek mythology, the son of Inachus, Agenor or Arestor, or, according to others, an earth-born hero (autochthon). He was called Panoptes (all-seeing), from having eyes all over his body. After performing several feats of valour, he was appointed by Hera to watch the cow into which Io had been transformed. While doing this he was slain by Hermes, who stoned him to death, or put him to sleep by playing on the flute and then cut off his head. His eyes were transferred by Hera to the tail of the peacock. Argus with his countless eyes originally denoted the starry heavens (Apollodorus ii. 1; Aeschylus, *P. V.* 569; Ovid, *Metam.* i. 264).

Another ARGUS, the old dog of Odysseus, who recognized his master on his return to Ithaca, figures in one of the best-known incidents in Homer's *Odyssey* (xvii. 291-326).

ARGYLL, EARLS AND DUKES OF. The rise of this family of Scottish peers, originally the Campbells of Lochow, and first ennobled as Barons Campbell, is referred to in the article ARGYLLSHIRE.

ARCHIBALD CAMPBELL, 5th earl of Argyll (1530-1573), was the elder son of Archibald, 4th earl of Argyll (d. 1558), and a grandson of Colin, the 3rd earl (d. 1530). His great-grandfather was the 2nd earl, Archibald, who was killed at Flodden in 1513, and this nobleman's father was Colin, Lord Campbell (d. 1493), the founder of the greatness of the Campbell family, who was created earl of Argyll in 1457. With Lord James Stuart, afterwards the regent Murray, the 5th earl of Argyll became an adherent of John Knox about 1556, and like his father was one of the most influential members of the party of religious reform, signing what was probably the first "godly band" in December 1557. As one of the "lords of the congregation" he was one of James Stuart's principal lieutenants during the warfare between the reformers and the regent, Mary of Lorraine; and later with Murray he advised and supported Mary queen of Scots, who regarded him with great favour. It was about this time that William Cecil, afterwards Lord Burghley, referred to Argyll as "a goodly gentleman universally honoured of all Scotland." Owing to his friendship with Mary, Argyll was separated from the party of Knox, but he forsook the queen when she determined to marry Lord Darnley; he was, however, again on Mary's side after Queen Elizabeth's refusal to aid Murray in 1565. Argyll was probably an accomplice in the murder of Rizzio; he was certainly a consenting party to that of Darnley, and then separating himself from Murray he commanded Mary's soldiers after her escape from Lochleven, and by his want of courage and resolution was partly responsible for her defeat at Langside in May 1568. Soon afterwards he made his peace with Murray, but it is possible that he was accessory to the regent's murder in 1570. After this event Argyll became lord high chancellor of Scotland, and he died on the 12th of September 1573. His first wife was an illegitimate daughter of James V., and he was thus half-brother-in-law to Mary and to Murray. His relations with her were not harmonious; he was accused of adultery, and in 1568 he performed a public penance at Stirling.

He left no children, and on his death his half-brother Colin (d. 1584) became 6th earl of Argyll. This nobleman, whose life was partly spent in feuds with the regent Morton, died in October 1584. He was succeeded as 7th earl by his young son Archibald (1576-1638), who became a Roman Catholic, fought for Philip III. of Spain in Flanders, whither he had gone to avoid his creditors, and, having entrusted the care of his estates to his son, died in London.

ARCHIBALD CAMPBELL, 1st marquess and 8th earl of Argyll (1607-1661), eldest son of Archibald, 7th earl, by his first wife, Lady Anne Douglas, daughter of William, 1st earl of Morton, was born in 1607 and educated at St Andrews University, where he matriculated on the 15th of January 1622. He had early in life, as Lord Lorne, been entrusted with the possession of the Argyll estates when his father renounced Protestantism and took service with Philip of Spain; and he exercised over his clan an authority almost absolute, disposing of a force of 20,000 retainers, and being, according to Baillie, "by far the most powerful subject in the kingdom." On the outbreak of the religious dispute between the king and Scotland in 1637 his support was eagerly desired by Charles I. He had been made a privy councillor in 1628, and in 1638 the king summoned him, together with Traquair and Roxburgh, to London; but he refused to be won over, openly and courageously warned Charles against his despotic ecclesiastical policy, and showed great hostility towards Laud. In consequence a secret commission was given to the earl of Antrim to invade Argyllshire and stir up the Macdonalds against the Campbells, a wild and foolish project which completely miscarried. Argyll, who inherited the title by the death of his father in 1638, had originally no preference for Presbyterianism, but now definitely took the side of the Covenanters in defence of the national religion and liberties. He continued to attend the meetings of the Assembly after its dissolution by the marquess of Hamilton, when Episcopacy was abolished. In 1639 he sent a statement to Laud, and subsequently to the king, defending the Assembly's action; and raising a body of troops he seized Hamilton's castle of Brodick in Arran. After the pacification of Berwick he carried a motion, in opposition to Montrose, by which the estates secured to themselves the election of the lords of the articles, who had formerly been nominated by the king, a fundamental change in the Scottish constitution, whereby the management of public affairs was entrusted to a representative body and withdrawn from the control of the crown. An attempt by the king to deprive him of his office as justiciary of Argyll and Tarbet failed, and on the prorogation of the parliament by Charles, in May 1640, Argyll moved that it should continue its sittings and that the government and safety of the kingdom should be secured by a committee of the estates, of which, though not a member, he was himself the guiding spirit. In June he was entrusted with a "commission of fire and sword" against the royalists in Atholl and Angus, which, after succeeding in entrapping the earl of Atholl, he carried out with completeness and some cruelty. It was on this occasion that took place the burning of "the bonnie house of Airlie." By this time the personal rivalry and difference in opinion between Montrose and Argyll had led to an open breach. The former arranged that on the occasion of Charles's approaching visit to Scotland, Argyll should be accused of high treason in the parliament. The plot, however, was disclosed, and Montrose with others was imprisoned. Accordingly when the king arrived he found himself deprived of every remnant of influence and authority. It only remained for Charles to make a series of concessions. He transferred the control over judicial and political appointments to the parliament, created Argyll a marquess (1641) with a pension of £1000 a year, and returned home, having in Clarendon's words "made a perfect deed of gift of that kingdom." Meanwhile the king's policy of peace and concession had, as usual, been rudely and treacherously interrupted by a resort to force, an unsuccessful attempt, known as the "incident," being made to kidnap Argyll, Hamilton and Lanark. Argyll was mainly instrumental at this crisis in keeping the national party faithful to what was to him evidently the common cause, and in accomplishing the alliance with the Long Parliament in 1643. In January 1644 he accompanied the Scottish army into England as a member of the committee of both kingdoms and in command of a troop of horse, but was soon in March compelled to return to suppress royalist movements in the north and to defend his own territories. He compelled Huntly to retreat in April, and in July advanced to meet the Irish troops now landed in Argyllshire, which were acting in conjunction with Montrose, who had put himself at the 484head of the royalist forces in Scotland. A campaign followed in the north in which neither general succeeded in obtaining any advantage over the other, or even in engaging battle. Argyll then returned to Edinburgh, threw up his commission, and retired to Inveraray Castle. Thither Montrose unexpectedly followed him in December, compelled him to flee to Roseneath, and devastated his territories. On the 2nd of February 1645, when following Montrose northwards, Argyll was surprised by him at Inverlochy and witnessed from his barge on the lake, to which he had retired owing to a dislocated arm, a fearful slaughter of his troops, which included 1500 of the Campbells. He arrived at Edinburgh on the 12th of February and was again present at Montrose's further great victory on the 15th of August at Kilsyth, whence he escaped to Newcastle. Argyll was at last delivered from his formidable antagonist by Montrose's final defeat at Philiphaugh on the 12th of September. In 1646 he was sent to negotiate with the king at Newcastle after his surrender to the Scottish army, when he endeavoured to moderate the demands of the parliament and at the same time to persuade the king to accept them. On the 7th of July 1646 he was appointed a member of the Assembly of Divines.

Up to this point the statesmanship of Argyll had been highly successful. The national liberties and religion of Scotland had been defended and guaranteed, and the power of the king in Scotland reduced to a mere shadow. In addition, these privileges had been still further secured by the alliance with the English opposition, and by the subsequent triumph of the parliament and Presbyterianism in the neighbouring kingdom. The sovereign himself, after vainly contending in arms, was a prisoner in their midst. But Argyll's influence could not survive the rupture of the alliance between the two nations on which his whole policy was constructed. He opposed in vain the secret treaty now concluded between the king and the Scots against the parliament, and while Hamilton marched into England and was defeated by Cromwell at Preston, Argyll, after a narrow escape from a surprise at Stirling, joined the Whiggamores, a body of Covenanters at Edinburgh;

and, supported by London, Leven and Leslie, he established a new government, which welcomed Cromwell on his arrival there on the 4th of October. This alliance, however, was at once destroyed by the execution of Charles I., which excited universal horror in Scotland. In the series of tangled incidents which followed, Argyll lost control of the national policy. He describes himself at this period as "a distracted man ... in a distracted time" whose "remedies ... had the quite contrary operation." He supported the invitation from the Covenanters to Charles II. to land in Scotland, gazed upon the captured Montrose, bound on a cart on his way to execution at Edinburgh, and subsequently, when Charles II. came to Scotland, having signed the Covenant and repudiated Montrose, Argyll remained at the head of the administration. After the defeat of Dunbar, Charles retained his support by the promise of a dukedom and the Garter, and an attempt was made by Argyll to marry the king to his daughter. On the 1st of January 1651 he placed the crown on Charles's head at Scone. But his power had now passed to the Hamilton party. He strongly opposed, but was unable to prevent, the expedition into England, and in the subsequent reduction of Scotland, after having held out in Inveraray Castle for nearly a year, was at last surprised in August 1652 and submitted to the Commonwealth. His ruin was then complete. His policy had failed, his power had vanished. In his estate he was hopelessly in debt, and on terms of such violent hostility with his eldest son as to be obliged to demand a garrison in his house for his protection. During his visit to Monk at Dalkeith in 1654 to complain of this, he was subjected to much personal insult from his creditors, and on visiting London in September 1655 to obtain money due to him from the Scottish parliament, he was arrested for debt, though soon liberated. In Richard Cromwell's parliament of 1659 Argyll sat as member for Aberdeenshire. At the Restoration he presented himself at Whitehall, but was at once arrested by order of Charles and placed in the Tower (1660), being sent to Edinburgh to stand his trial for high treason. He was acquitted of complicity in the death of Charles I., and his escape from the whole charge seemed imminent, but the arrival of a packet of letters written by Argyll to Monk showed conclusively his collaboration with Cromwell's government, particularly in the suppression of Glencairn's royalist rising in 1652. He was immediately sentenced to death, his execution by beheading taking place on the 27th of May 1661, before even the death warrant had been signed by the king. His head was placed on the same spike upon the west end of the Tolbooth on which that of Montrose had previously been exposed, and his body was buried at the Holy Loch, where the head was also deposited in 1664. A monument was erected to his memory in St Giles's church in Edinburgh in 1895.

While imprisoned in the Tower he wrote *Instructions to a Son*(1661; reprinted in 1689 and 1743). Some of his speeches, including the one delivered on the scaffold, were published and are printed in the*Harleian Miscellany*. He married Lady Margaret Douglas, daughter of William, 2nd earl of Morton, and had two sons and four daughters.

See also the *Life and Times of Archibald Marquis of Argyll*(1903), by John Willcock, who prints for the first time the six incriminating letters to Monk; *Eng. Hist. Review*, xviii. 369 and 624; *Scottish History Society*, vol. xvii. (1894); *Charles II. and Scotland in 1650*, ed. by S.R. Gardiner, and vol. xviii. (1895);*History of Scotland*, by A. Lang, vol. iii. (1904).

ARCHIBALD CAMPBELL, 9th earl of Argyll (1629-1685), eldest son of the 8th earl, studied abroad, and at the age of thirteen was appointed captain in the Scottish regiment serving in France under his uncle the earl of Irvine. He returned home at the close of 1649, and was made captain of Charles II.'s life guards on the king's arrival in Scotland in 1650. He declared himself a royalist in opposition to his father, with the view, as some said, of securing the family estates in any event. He fought at Dunbar on the 3rd of September 1650, and after the battle of Worcester joined Glencairn in the Highlands. Bitter disputes arose, and on the 2nd of January 1654 Lorne, quitting his troops, fled to avoid arrest. In 1653 he submitted to Monk. He appears, however, to have maintained communications with Charles, and on his refusal to take the oath renouncing allegiance to the Stuarts in 1657 he was imprisoned, remaining in confinement probably till a short time before the Restoration. He was then well received at court by Charles II. After the execution of his father, he endeavoured to obtain the restitution of his forfeited estates and title, but having incautiously attacked certain members of the government in letters which were made public, he was indicted at Edinburgh on the capital charge of "leasing-making" and was sentenced to death on the 26th of August. He remained a prisoner in Edinburgh Castle till the 4th of June 1663, when the sentence was cancelled and he was re-created earl and restored to his estates. He disapproved of the severities practised upon the Covenanters in the west, and in 1671 pleaded for milder methods. His staunch Protestantism rendered him exceedingly obnoxious to James, duke of York, who in 1680 arrived as high commissioner in Scotland and at once expressed his jealousy of Argyll's immense territorial influence. Argyll moved the re-enactment of "all the acts against popery" omitted on James's account, and opposed the exemption of the royal family from the test, though allowing it in the case of James. In signing the test himself, in its final form both ambiguous and self-contradictory, he made the reservation "so far as consistent with itself and the Protestant faith," and declined to engage himself not to promote any alteration of advantage in church or state. On his refusal to record his oath in writing and to sign it, he was dismissed from the Scottish privy council, and on the 9th of November 1681 was accused of treason, a charge which Halifax declared openly in England "they would not hang a dog upon." A trial followed, a scandalous exhibition of illegality and injustice, at the close of which Argyll was sentenced to death and to the forfeiture of his estates. Shortly afterwards, through the instrumentality of his step-daughter, Sophia Lindsay, he succeeded in making his escape, and after some adventures retired to Holland. His subsequent movements are uncertain, but he appears to have 485again visited London, and was in correspondence with the Rye House plotters and proposing to head a rebellion in Scotland in 1683. In 1685 he joined the conspiracy in Holland to set Monmouth on the throne instead of James II., arriving in Orkney on the 6th of May and making his way to his own country. But his clansmen refused to join him, and whatever small chances of success remained were destroyed by constant and paralysing disputes. His ships and ammunition were captured, and after some aimless wanderings he found himself deserted, with but one companion, Major Fullerton. On the 18th of June he was taken prisoner at Inchinnan and arrived at Edinburgh on the 20th, where he was paraded through the streets and put in irons in the castle. James ordered his summary execution on the 29th, and it was carried out by beheading on the following day, on the old charge of 1681. His head was exposed on the west side of the Tollbooth, where his father's and Montrose's had also been exhibited, his body finding its final place of burial at Inveraray.

By his first wife, Lady Mary Stewart, daughter of the 4th earl of Moray (Murray), he had four sons and three daughters.

See *Argyll Papers* (1834); *Letters from Archibald, 9th Earl of Argyle, to the Duke of Lauderdale* (1829); *Hist. MSS. Comm.* vi. Rep. 606; *Life of Mr Donald Cargile*, by P. Walker, pp. 45 et seq.;*The 3rd Part of the Protestant Plot ... and a Brief Account of the Case of the Earl of Argyle* (1682); Sir George MacKenzie's *Hist. of Scotland*, p. 70; and J. Willcock, *A Scots Earl in Covenanting Times* (1908).

ARCHIBALD CAMPBELL, 1st duke of Argyll (? 1651-1703), was the eldest son of the 9th earl. He tried to get his father's attainder reversed by seeking the king's favour, but being unsuccessful he went over to the Hague and joined William of Orange as an active promoter of the revolution of 1688. In spite of the attainder, he was admitted in 1689 to the convention of the Scottish estates as earl of Argyll, and he was deputed, with Sir James Montgomery and Sir John Dalrymple, to present the crown to William III. in its name, and to tender him the coronation oath. In 1690 an act was passed restoring his title and estates, and it was in connexion with the refusal of the Macdonalds of Glencoe to join in the submission to him that he organized the terrible massacre which has made his name notorious. In 1696 he was made a lord of the treasury, and his political services were rewarded in 1701 by his being created duke of Argyll. He had two sons by his wife Elizabeth, daughter of Sir Lionel Talmash, John (the 2nd duke) and Archibald (the 3rd duke.)

JOHN CAMPBELL, 2nd duke of Argyll and duke of Greenwich (1678-1743), was born on the 10th of October 1678. He entered the army in 1694, and in 1701 was promoted to the command of a regiment. On the death of his father in 1703, he was appointed a member of the privy council, and at the same time colonel of the Scotch horse guards, and one of the extraordinary lords of session. In return for his services in promoting the Union, he was created (1705) a peer of England, by the titles of baron of Chatham and earl of Greenwich, and in 1710 was made a knight of the Garter. He first distinguished himself in a military capacity at the battle of Oudenarde (1708), where he served as a brigadier-general; and was afterwards present under the duke of Marlborough at the sieges of Lille, Ghent, Bruges and Tournay, and did remarkable service at the battle of Malplaquet in 1709. He was very popular with the troops, and his rivalry with Marlborough on this account is thought to have been the cause of the enmity shown by Argyll afterwards to his old commander. In 1711 he was sent to take command in Spain; but being seized with a violent fever at Barcelona, and disappointed of supplies from home, he returned to England. Having a seat in the House of Lords, and being gifted with an extraordinary power of oratory, he censured the measures of the ministry with such freedom that all his places were disposed of to other noblemen; but at the accession of George I. he recovered his influence. On the breaking out of the rebellion in 1715 he was appointed commander-in-chief of the forces in North Britain, and was principally instrumental in effecting the total extinction of the rebellion in Scotland without much bloodshed. He arrived in London early in March 1716, and at first stood high in the favour of the king, but in a few months was strippee of his offices. This disgrace, however, did not deter him from the discharge of his parliamentary duties; he supported the bill for the impeachment of Bishop Atterbury, and lent his aid to his countrymen by opposing the bill for punishing the city of Edinburgh for the Porteous riot. In the beginning of the year 1719 he was again admitted into favour, appointed lord steward of the household, and, in April following, created duke of Greenwich; he held various offices in succession, and in 1735 was made a field marshall. He continued in the administration till after the accession of George II., when, in April 1740, a violent speech against the government led again to his dismissal from office. He was soon restored on a change of the ministry, but disapproving the measures of the new administration, and apparently disappointed at not being given the command of the army, he shortly resigned all his posts, and spent the rest of his life in privacy and retirement. He died on the 4th of October 1743. A monument by Roubillac was erected to his memory in Westminster Abbey. He was twice married, and by his second wife, Jane Warburton, had five daughters; his Scottish titles passed to his brother, but his English titles became extinct, and though his eldest daughter was created baroness of Greenwich in 1767 this title also became extinct on her death in 1794.

ARCHIBALD CAMPBELL, 3rd duke of Argyll (1682-1761), was born at Ham House in Surrey, in June 1682. On his father being created a duke, he joined the army, and served for a short time under the duke of Marlborough. In 1705 he was appointed treasurer of Scotland, and in the following year was one of the commissioners for treating of the Union; on the consummation of which, having been raised to the peerage of Scotland as earl of Islay, he was chosen one of the sixteen peers for Scotland in the first parliament of Great Britain. In 1711 he was called to the privy council, and commanded the royal army at the battle of Sheriffmuir in 1715. he was appointed keeper of the privy seal in 1721, and was afterwards entrusted with the principal management of Scottish affairs to an extent which caused him to be called "king of Scotland." In 1733 he was made keeper of the great seal, an office which he held till his death. He succeeded to the dukedom in 1743. Both as earl of Islay and as duke of Argyll he was prominently connected (with Duncan Forbes of Culloden) with the movement for consolidating Scottish loyalty by the formation of locally recruited highland regiments. The duke was eminent not only for his political abilities, but also for his literary accomplishments, and he collected one of the most valuable private libraries in Great Britain. He died suddenly on the 15th of April 1761. He was married but had no legitimate issue, and his English property was left to a Mrs Williams, by whom he had a son, William Campbell.

The succession now passed to the descendants of the younger son of the 9th earl, the Campbells of Mamore; the 4th duke died in 1770, and was succeeded by his son JOHN, the 5th duke (1723-1806) He was a soldier who had fought at Dettingen and Culloden, and became colonel of the 42nd regiment (Black Watch), and eventually a field marshall. He sat in the House of Commons for Glasgow from 1744 to 1761, when on his father's succession to the dukedom he became legally disqualified, as courtesy marquess of Lorne, for a Scottish constituency; he could sit, however, for an English one, and was returned for Dover, which he represented till 1766, when he was created an English peer as Baron Sundridge, the title by which till 1892 the dukes of Argyll sat in the House of Lords. The 5th duke was an active landlord, and was the first president of the Highland and Agricultural Society. In 1759 he had married the widowed duchess of Hamilton (the beautiful Elizabeth Gunning), by whom he had two sons and two daughters. The eldest of his sons, GEORGE (d. 1841), became 6th duke, and on his death was succeeded as 7th duke by his brother JOHN (1777-1847), who from 1799-1822 sat in parliament as member for Argyllshire. He was thrice married, and by his second wife, Joan Glassell (d. 1828), had two sons, the eldest of whom (b. 1821) died 486in 1837, and two daughters, the second of whom died in infancy.

GEORGE JOHN DOUGLAS CAMPBELL, 8th duke (1823-1900), the second son of the 7th duke, was born on the 30th of April 1823, and succeeded his father in April 1847. He had already obtained notice as a writer of pamphlets on the disruption of the Church of Scotland, which he strove to avert, and he rapidly became prominent on the Liberal side in parliamentary politics. He was a frequent and eloquent speaker in the House of Lords, and sat as lord privy seal (1852) and postmaster-general (1855) in the cabinets of Lord Aberdeen and Lord Palmerston. In Mr Gladstone's cabinet of 1868 he was secretary of state for India, and somewhat infelicitously signalized his term of office by his refusal, against the advice of the Indian government, to promise the amir of Afghanistan support against Russian aggression, a course which threw that ruler into the arms of Russia and was followed by the second Afghan War. His eminence alike as a great Scottish noble, and as a British statesman, was accentuated in 1871 when his son, the marquess of Lorne, married Princess Louise, the fourth daughter of Queen Victoria; but in the political world few memorable acts on his part call for record except his resignation of the office of lord privy seal, which he held in Mr Gladstone's administration of 1880, from his inability to assent to the Irish land legislation of 1881. He opposed the Home Rule Bill with equal vigour, though Mr Gladstone subsequently stated that, among all the old colleagues who dissented from his course, the duke was the only one whose personal relations with him remained entirely unchanged. Detached from party, the duke took an independent position, and for many years spoke his mind with great freedom in letters to *The Times* on public questions, especially such as concerned the rights or interests of landowners. He was no less active on scientific questions in their relation to religion, which he earnestly strove to reconcile with the progress of discovery. With this aim he published *The Reign of Law* (1866), *Primeval Man* (1869), *The Unity of Nature* (1884), *The Unseen Foundations of Society* (1893), and other essays. He also wrote on the Eastern question, with especial reference to India, the history and antiquities of Iona, patronage in the Church of Scotland, and many other subjects. The duke (to whose Scottish title was added a dukedom of the United Kingdom in 1892) died on the 24th of April 1900. He was thrice married: first (1844) to a daughter of the second duke of Sutherland (d. 1878); secondly (1881) to a daughter of Bishop Claughton of St Albans (d. 1894); and thirdly (1895) to Ina Erskine M'Neill. Few men of the duke's era displayed more versatility of intellect, and he was remarkable among the men of his time for his lofty eloquence.

He was succeeded as 9th duke by his eldest son JOHN DOUGLAS SUTHERLAND CAMPBELL (1845- emsp;), whose marriage in 1871 to H.R.H. Princess Louise gave him a special prominence in English public life. He was governor-general of Canada from 1878 to 1883; member of parliament for South Manchester, in the Unionist interest, 1895 to 1900; and he also became known as a writer both in prose and verse. In 1907 he published his reminiscences, *Pages from the Past*.

See the *Autobiography and Memoirs* of the 8th duke, edited by his widow (1906), which is full of interesting historical and personal detail.

(P. C. Y.; H. CH.)

1 The date of 1598, previously accepted, is shown by Willcock to be incorrect.

ARGYLLSHIRE, a county on the west coast of Scotland, the second largest in the country, embracing a large tract of country on the mainland and a number of the Hebrides or Western Isles. The mainland portion is bounded N. by Inverness-shire; E. by Perth and Dumbarton, Loch Long and the Firth of Clyde; S. by the North Channel (Irish Sea); and W. by the Atlantic. Its area is 1,990,471 acres or 3110 sq. m. The principal districts are Ardnamurchan on the Atlantic, Ardnamurchan Point being the most westerly headland of Scotland; Morven or Morvern, bounded by Loch Sunart, the Sound of Mull and Loch Linnhe; Appin, on Loch Linnhe, with piers at Ballachulish and Port Appin; Benderloch, lying between Loch Creran and Loch Etive; Lorne, surrounding Loch Etive and giving the title of marquess to the Campbells; Argyll, in the middle of the shire, containing Inveraray Castle and furnishing the titles of earl and duke to the Campbells; Cowall, between Loch Fyne and the Firth of Clyde, in which lie Dunoon and other favourite holiday resorts; Knapdale between the Sound of Jura and Loch Fyne; and Kintyre or Cantyre, a long narrow peninsula (which, at the isthmus of Tarbert, is little more than 1 m. wide), the southernmost point of which is known as the Mull, the nearest part of Scotland to the coast of Ireland, only 13 m. distant.

There are no navigable rivers. The two principal mountain streams are the Orchy and Awe. The Orchy flows from Loch Tulla through Glen Orchy, and falls into the north-eastern end of Loch Awe; and the Awe drains the loch at its north-western extremity, discharging into Loch Etive. Among other streams are the Add, Aray, Coe or Cona, Creran, Douglas, Eachaig, Etive, Euchar, Feochan, Finart, Fyne, Kinglass, Nell, Ruel, Shiel, Shira, Strae and Uisge-Dhu. The county is remarkable for the numerous sea-lochs which deeply indent the coast, the principal being Loch Long (with its branches Loch Goil and the Holy Loch), Loch Striven (Rothesay's "weather glass"), Loch Riddon, Loch Fyne (with Loch Gilp and Loch Gair), Lochs Tarbert, Killispurt, Swin, Crinan, Craignish, Melfort, Feochan, Etive, Linnhe (with its branches Loch Creran, Loch Leven and Loch Eil) and Sunart. There are also a large number of inland lakes, the total area of which is about 25,000 acres. Of these the principal are Lochs Awe, Avich, Eck, Lydoch and Shiel. The principal islands are Mull, Islay, Jura, Colonsay, Lismore, Tyree, Coll, Gigha, Luing and Kerrera. Besides these there are the two small but interesting islands of Staffa and Iona. The mountains are so many as to give the shire a markedly rugged character. Some of them are among the loftiest in the kingdom, as Ben Cruachan with its summit of twin pyramids (3689 ft.), Ben More, in Mull (3172), Ben Ima (3318), Buachaille Etive (3345), Ben Bui (3106), Ben Lui (or Loy), on the confines of the shires of Perth and Argyll (3708), Ben Starav near the head of Loch Etive (3541), and Ben Arthur, called from its shape "The Cobbler" (2891), on the borders of Dumbartonshire. There are many picturesque glens, of which the best-known are Glen Aray, Glen Croe, Glen Etive, Glendaruel, Glen Lochy ("the wearisome glen"—some 10 m. of bare hills and boulders—between Tyndrum and Dalmally), Glen Strae, Hell's Glen (off Lech

Goil) and Glencoe, the scene of the massacre in 1692. The waterfalls of Cruachan are beautiful; and those of Connel, which are more in the nature of rapids, caused by the rush of the ebbing tide over the rocky bar at the narrowing mouth of Loch Etive, have been made celebrated by Ossian, who called them "the Falls of Lora." In several of the glens, as Glen Aray, small falls may be seen, enhanced in beauty when the rivers are in flood. Pre-eminently Argyll is the shire of the sportsman. The lovely Western Isles provide endless enjoyment for the yachtsman; the lochs and rivers abound with salmon and trout; the deer forests and grouse moors are second to none in Scotland.

Geology.—The mainland portion of the county consists chiefly of the metamorphic rocks of the Eastern Highlands, nearly all the subdivisions of that series (see SCOTLAND: *Geology*) being represented. They form parallel belts of varying width trending north-east and south-west. The slates and phyllites referred to the lowest group occur along the shore at Dunoon, and are followed by the Beinn Bheula grits and albite schists, forming nearly all the highest ground in Cowall between Loch Fyne and the Firth of Clyde and the greater part of Kintyre. The green beds, Glensluan mica-schists and Loch Tay limestones are developed in Glendaruel, and have been traced north-east to Glen Fyne and at intervals south-west to Campbeltown. The next prominent zone is that of the Ardrishaig phyllites, with quartzites in the lower portion and soft phyllites in the upper part, which cover a belt from 3 to 6 m. across, stretching from Glen Shira by Inveraray and Ardrishaig to south Knapdale.

Next in order come the Easdale slates, phyllites with thin dark limestone, the main limestone of Loch Awe and the pebbly quartzite (Schiehallion), which are repeated by innumerable folds and spread northwards to Loch Linnhe and westwards to Jura and Islay. The slates of this horizon have been largely quarried at Easdale and Ballachulish, and this main limestone is typically developed near Loch Awe, near Kilmartin, on the islands of Lismore and Shuna, and in Islay between Bridgend and Portaskaig. The quartzites of this series form the highest hills in the south of Islay, occupy nearly the whole of Jura, and are continued in the mainland, where, by 487 means of the rapid isoclinal folding, they form lenticular masses. In Islay and at various localities on the mainland a conglomerate occurs at or near the base of the quartzites, which contains fragments of the underlying rocks and boulders of granite not now found in place in that region.

On the mainland, on the north side of the compound synclinal folding of Loch Awe, the Ardrishaig phyllites reappear at Craignish near Kilmartin, and the quartzites of this group are supposed to come to the surface again in Glencoe, not far from the outcrop of the Schiehallion quartzite.

The metamorphic rocks are associated with bands of epidiorite which have shared in the folding and metamorphism of the region. These are largely developed near Loch Awe, in Knapdale, and on the south-east coast of Islay. They have been usually regarded as intrusive, but south of Tayvallich on the mainland, lavas and tuffs, which have escaped deformation, occur in the Easdale slates and the pebbly limestone.

The Lower Old Red Sandstone, chiefly composed of volcanic rocks—lavas and tuffs—rests unconformably on the metamorphic series. These rocks cover a wide area in Lorne between Loch Melfort, Oban and the Pass of Brander, and they reappear in the lofty mountains on both sides of Glencoe. Representatives of this formation are found in Kintyre, south of Campbeltown, where the sediments prevail. The intrusive igneous rocks belonging to this period are widely distributed and form conspicuous features. The plutonic masses are represented by the granite of Ben Cruachan, by the diorite of Gleann Domhainn, and by the kentallenite (a basic rock related to the monxonites), near Ballachulish. Throughout the Lorne volcanic plateau there are numerous dykes of porphyrite which likewise traverse the schists and part of the Ben Cruachan granite. Sheets of quartz-porphyry, lamprophyre and diorite are also represented, the first of these types being quarried at Crarae on the north shore of Loch Fyne.

The Upper Old Red Sandstone forms isolated patches resting unconformably on all older rocks, on the west coast of Kintyre, and between Campbeltown and Southend. In the district of Campbeltown these red sandstones and cornstones are followed by the volcanic rocks of the Calciferous Sandstone series, which lie to the south of the depression at Machrihanish, and are succeeded by the lower limestones and coals of the Carboniferous Limestone series.

On the north and south shores of the promontory of Ardnamurchan there are small patches of Jurassic strata ranging from the Lower Lias to the Oxford Clay, and in Morvern on the shores of Loch Aline representatives of the Upper Greensand are covered by the basaltic lavas of Tertiary age. The acid and basic plutonic rocks (gabbros and granophyres) of Tertiary time occur in Ardnamurchan. A striking geological feature of the county is the number of dolerite and basalt dykes trending in a north-west direction, which are referred to the same period of intrusion.

There is, however, another group of dolerite dykes running east and west near Dunoon and elsewhere, which are cut by the former and are probably of older date.

Lead veins occur at Strontian which have yielded a number of minerals, including sphalerite, fluorite, strontianite, harmotone, brewsterite and pilolite. Near Inveraray, nickeliferous ore has been obtained at two localities.

Climate.—The rainfall is very abundant. At Oban, the average annual amount is 64.18 in.; in Glen Fyne, 104.11 in.; at the bridge of Orchy, 113.62 in., and at Upper Glencoe 127.65. The prevailing winds, as observed near Crinan, are south-west and south-east, and next in frequency are the north-west and north-east. The average yearly temperature is 48° F.

Agriculture.—Argyllshire was formerly partly covered with natural forests, remains of which, consisting chiefly of oak, ash, pine and birch, are still visible in the mosses; but, owing to the clearance of the ground for the introduction of sheep, and to past neglect of planting, the county is now remarkable for its lack of wood, except in the neighbourhood of Inveraray, where there are extensive and flourishing plantations, and a few other places. Replanting, however, has been carried on. Most of the county is unfitted for agriculture; but many districts afford fine pasturage for mountain sheep; and some of the valleys, such as Glendaruel, are very fertile. The chief crop is oats; there is a little barley, but no wheat. The shire is one of those where the crofting system exists, but it is by no means universal. It is predominant in Tyree and the western district of the mainland, but elsewhere farms of moderate size are the rule. The cattle, though small, are equal to any other breed in the kingdom, and are marketed in large numbers in the south. Dairy farming is carried on to some extent in the southern parts of Kintyre, where there is a large proportion of arable land. In the higher tracts sheep have taken the place of cattle with excellent results. The black-faced is the species most generally reared.

Industries.—Whisky is manufactured at Campbeltown, in Islay, at Oban, Ardrishaig and elsewhere. Gunpowder is made at Kames (Kyles of Bute), Melfort and Furnace. Coarse woollens are made for home use; but fishing is the most important industry, Loch Fyne being famous for its herrings. The season lasts from June to January, but white fishing is carried on at one or other of the ports all the year round. Slate and granite quarrying and some coal-mining are the only other industries of any consequence.

Communications.—Owing partly to the paucity of trading industries and partly to the fact that, owing to its greatly indented coast-line, no place in the shire is more than 12 m. from the sea, the railway mileage in the county is very small. The Tyndrum to Oban section of the Caledonian railway company's system is within the county limits; a small portion of the track of the North British railway company's line to Mallaig skirts the extreme west of the shire, and the Caledonian line from Oban to Ballachulish serves the northern coast districts of the Argyllshire mainland. In connexion with this last route mention should be made of the cantilever bridge crossing the Falls of Lora with a span of 500 ft. at a height of 125 ft. above the water-way. The chief means of communication is by steamers, which maintain regular intercourse between Glasgow and various parts of the coast. In order to avoid the circuitous passage round the Mull of Kintyre the Crinan Canal, across the isthmus from Ardrishaig to Loch Crinan, a distance of 9 m., was constructed in 1793-1801, at a cost of £142,000. It has 15 locks, an average depth of 10 ft., a surface width of 66 ft., and bottom width of 30 ft., is navigable by vessels of 200 tons, and runs through a district of remarkable beauty. Another canal unites Campbeltown with Dalavaddy. In summer the mails for the islands and the great bulk of the tourist traffic by the MacBrayne fleet is conveyed through the Crinan Canal, transhipment being effected at Ardrishaig and Crinan. Throughout the year goods traffic between the Clyde and elsewhere and the West Highland ports is conveyed by deep-sea steamers round the Mull. Before the advent of railways the shire contained many famous coaching routes, but now coaches only run during the tourist season, either in connexion with train and steamer, or in districts still not served by either.

Population and Government.—Owing to emigration, chiefly to Canada, the population has declined, almost without a break, since 1831, when it was 100,973, to 74,085 in 1891 and 73,642 in 1901, in which year there were 24 persons to the sq. m. In 1901 the number of Gaelic-speaking persons was 34,224, of whom 3313 spoke Gaelic only. The chief towns are Campbeltown (population in 1901, 8286), Dunoon (6779) and Oban (5427), with Ardrishaig (1285), Ballachulish (1143), Lochgilphead (1313) and Tarbert (1697). The county returns a member to parliament. Inveraray, Campbeltown and Oban belong to the Ayr district group of parliamentary burghs. Argyllshire is a sheriffdom, and there are resident sheriffs-substitute at Inveraray, Campbeltown and Oban; courts are held also at Tobermory, Lochgilphead, Bowmore in Islay, and Dunoon. Both Presbyterian bodies are strongly represented; there are Roman Catholic and (Anglican) Episcopal bishops of Argyll and the Isles, and there is a Roman Catholic pro-cathedral at Oban. Campbeltown, Dunoon and Oban have secondary schools, Tarbert public school has a secondary department, and several other schools earn grants for giving higher education. Part of the "residue" grant is spent by the county council on classes of navigation and other subjects in various schools, short courses in agriculture for farmers, and in providing bursaries.

History.—The early history of Argyll (Airergaidheal) is very obscure. At the close of the 5th century Fergus, son of Erc, a descendant of Conor II., *airdrigh* or high king of Ireland, came over with a band of Irish Scots and established himself in Argyll and Kintyre. Nothing more is known till, in the days of Conall I., the descendant of Fergus in the fourth generation, St Columba 488appears. Conall died in 574, and Columba was mainly instrumental in establishing his first cousin, Aidan, founder of the Dalriad kingdom and ancestor of the royal house of Scotland, in power. In the 8th century Argyll, with the Western Islands and Man, fell under the power of the Norsemen until, in the 12th century, Somerled (or Somhairle), a descendant of Colla-Uais, *airdrigh* of Ireland (327-331), succeeded in ousting them and established his authority, not only as thane of Argyll, but also in Kintyre and the Western Islands. Somerled died in 1164 and his descendants maintained themselves in Argyll and the islands, between the conflicting claims of the kings of Scotland, Norway and Man, until the end of the 15th century.

Up to 1222 Argyll had formed an independent Celtic princedom; but in that year it was reduced by Alexander II., the Scottish king, to a sheriffdom, and was henceforth regarded as an integral part of Scotland. Among the various clans in Argyll, the Campbells of Loch Awe, a branch of the clan McArthur, now began to come to the fore, though the mainland was still chiefly in the possession of the MacDougals. The position of the lords of the house of Somerled was now curious, since they were feudatories of the king of Norway for the isles and of the king of Scotland for Argyll. Their policy in the wars between the two powers was a masterly neutrality. Thus, during the expedition of Alexander II. to the Western Isles in 1249, Ewan (Eoghan), lord of Argyll, refused to fight against the Norwegians; in 1263 the same Ewan refused to join Haakon of Norway in attacking Alexander III. Forty years later the clansmen of Argyll, mainly MacDougals, were warring on the side of Edward of England against Robert Bruce, by whom they were badly beaten on Loch Awe in 1309. The clansmen of the house of Somerled in the isles, on the other hand, the MacDonalds, remained loyal to Scotland in spite of the persuasions of John of Argyll, appointed admiral of Edward II.'s western fleet; and, under their chief Angus Og, they contributed much to the victory of Bannockburn. The alliance of John, earl of Ross and lord of the Isles, with Edward IV. of England in 1461 led to the breaking of the power of the house of Somerled, and in 1478 John was forced to resign Ross to the crown and, two years later, his lordships of Knapdale and Kintyre as well. In Argyll itself the Campbells had already made the first step to supremacy through the marriage of Colin, grandson of Sir Duncan Campbell of Lochow, first Lord Campbell, with Isabel Stewart, eldest of the three co-heiresses of John, third lord of Lorne. He acquired the greater part of the lands of the other sisters by purchase, and the lordship of Lorne from Walter their uncle, the heir in tail male, by an exchange for lands in Perthshire. In 1457 he was created, by James II., earl of Argyll. He died on the 10th of May 1493. From him dates the greatness of the house of the earls and dukes of Argyll (*q.v.*), whose history belongs to that of Scotland. The house of Somerled survives in two main branches—that of Macdonald of the Isles, Alexander Macdonald (d. 1795) having been raised to the peerage in 1776, and that of the Macdonnells, earls of Antrim in Ireland. The principal clans in Argyll, besides those already mentioned, were the Macleans, the Stewarts of Appin, the Macquarries and the Macdonalds of Glencoe, and the Macfarlanes of Glencroe. The Campbells are still very numerous in the county.

Argyllshire men have made few contributions to English literature. For long the natives spoke Gaelic only and their bards sang in Gaelic (see CELT: *Literature:* Scottish). Near Inistrynich on the north-eastern shore of Loch Awe stands the monumental cairn erected in honour of Duncan Ban McIntyre (1724-1812), the most popular of modern Gaelic bards. But the romantic beauty of the country has made it a favourite setting for the themes of many poets and story-tellers, from "Ossian" and Sir Walter Scott to Robert Louis Stevenson, while not a few men distinguished in affairs or in learning have been natives of the county.

The antiquities comprise monoliths, circles of standing stones, crannogs and cairns. In almost all the burying-grounds—as at Campbeltown, Keil, Soroby, Kilchousland, Kilmun—there are specimens of sculptured crosses and slabs. Besides the famous ecclesiastical remains at Iona (*q.v.*), there are ruins of a Cistercian priory in Oronsay, and of a church founded in the 12th century by Somerled, thane of Argyll, at Saddell. Among castles may be mentioned Dunstaffnage, Ardtornish, Skipness, Kilchurn (beloved of painters), Ardchonnel, Dunolly, Stalker, Dunderaw and Carrick.

AUTHORITIES.—The (Eighth) Duke of Argyll, *Commercial Principles Applied to the Hire of Land* (London, 1877); *Crofts and Farms in the Hebrides* (Edinburgh, 1883); *Iona* (Edinburgh, 1889); *Scotland as it Was and Is* (Edinburgh, 1887), *House of Argyll* (Glasgow, 1871); A. Brown, *Memorials of Argyllshire*(Greenock, 1889); Harvie-Brown and Buckley, *Vertebrate Fauna of*

Argyll and the Inner Hebrides (Edinburgh, 1892); D. Clerk, "On the Agriculture of the County of Argyll" (*Trans. of H. and A. Soc.*, 1878); T. Gray, *Week at Oban* (Edinburgh, 1881); Stewart,*Collection of Views of Campbeltown*. For antiquities see *The Sculptured Stones of Scotland*, vol. ii., published by the Spalding Club, and Capt. T.P. White's *Archaeological Sketches in Kintyre*and *Proc. Antiq. Soc. of Scotland*, vols. iv., v., viii.

ARGYRODITE, a mineral which is of interest as being that in which the element germanium was discovered by C. Winkler in 1886. It is a silver sulpho-germanate, Ag_8GeS_6, and crystallizes in the cubic system. The crystals have the form of the octahedron or rhombic dodecahedron, and are frequently twinned. The botryoidal crusts of small indistinct crystals first found in a silver mine at Freiberg in Saxony were originally thought to be monoclinic, but were afterwards proved to be identical with the more distinctly developed crystals recently found in Bolivia. The colour is iron-black with a purplish tinge, and the lustre metallic. There is no cleavage; hardness 2½, specific gravity 6.2. It is of interest to note that the Freiberg mineral was long ago imperfectly described by A. Breithaupt under the name*Plusinglanz*, and that the Bolivian crystals were incorrectly described in 1849 as crystallized brongniardite. The name argyrodite is from the Greek ἀργυρώδης, rich in silver.

Isomorphous with argyrodite is the corresponding tin compound Ag_8SnS_6, also found in Bolivia as cubic crystals, and known by the name canfieldite. Other Bolivian crystals are intermediate in composition between argyrodite and canfieldite.

(L. J. S.)

ARGYROKASTRO, or ARGYROCASTRON (Turkish, *Ergeri*; Albanian *Ergir Castri*), a town of southern Albania, Turkey, in the vilayet of Iannina. Pop. (1900) about 11,000. Argyrokastro is finely situated 1060 ft. above sea-level, on the eastern slopes of the Acroceraunian mountains, and near the left bank of the river Dhrynos, a left-hand tributary of the Viossa. It is the capital of a sanjak bearing the same name, and was formerly important as the headquarters of the local Moslem aristocracy, partly owing to the mountainous and easily defensible nature of the district. It contains the ruins of an imposing castellated fort. A fine kind of snuff, known as *fuli*, is manufactured here. Argyrokastro has been variously identified with the ancient Hadrianopolis and Antigonea. In the 18th century it is said to have contained 20,000 inhabitants, but it was almost depopulated by plague in 1814. Albanian Moslems constitute the greater part of the population.

ARGYROPULUS, or ARGYROPULO, **JOHN** (*c.* 1416-1486), Greek humanist, one of the earliest promoters of the revival of learning in the West, was born in Constantinople, and became a teacher there, Constantine Lascaris being his pupil. He then appears to have crossed over to Italy, and taught in Padua in 1434, being subsequently made rector of the university. About 1441 he returned to Constantinople, but after its capture by the Turks, again took refuge in Italy. About 1456 he was invited to Florence by Cosimo de' Medici, and was there appointed professor of Greek in the university. In 1471, on the outbreak of the plague, he removed to Rome, where he continued to act as a teacher of Greek till his death. Among his scholars were Angelus Politianus and Johann Reuchlin. His principal works were translations of the following portions of Aristotle,— *Categoriae, De Interpretatione, Analytica Posteriora, Physica, De Caelo, De Anima, Metaphysica, Ethica Nicomachea, Politica*; 489and an *Expositio Ethicorum Aristotelis*. Several of his writings exist still in manuscript.

See Humphrey Hody, *De Graecis Illustribus*, 1742, and Smith's*Dictionary of Greek and Roman Biography, s.v. Joannes*.

ARIA (Ital. for "air"), a musical term, equivalent to the English "air," signifying a melody apart from the harmony, but especially a musical composition for a single voice or instrument, with an accompaniment of other voices or instruments.

The aria originally developed from the expansion of a single vocal melody, generally on the lines of what is known as binary form (seeSONATA and SONATA FORMS). Accordingly, while the germs of aria form may be traceable in the highest developments of folk-song, the aria as a definite art-form could not exist before the middle of the 17th century; because up to that time the whole organization of music was based upon polyphonic principles which left no room for the development of melody for melody's sake. When at the beginning of the 17th century the Monodists (see HARMONY and MONTEVERDE) inaugurated a new era and showed in their first experiments the enormous possibilities latent in their new art of accompanying single voices by instruments, it was natural that for many years the mere suggestiveness and variety of their experiments should suffice to retain the attention of contemporary listeners, without any real artistic coherence in the works as wholes. But, even at the outset, mere novelty of harmony, however poignant its emotional expression, was felt by the profounder spirits of the new art to be an untrustworthy guide to progress. And Monteverde's famous lament of the deserted Ariadne is one of many early examples that appeal to an elementary sense of form by making the last phrase identical with the first. As instrumental music grew, and the modern sense of key became strong and consistent, composers felt themselves more and more able to appeal to that sense of harmonically consistent melody which has asserted itself in folk-music before the history of harmonic music may be said to have begun. The technique of solo singers grew as rapidly as that of solo players, and composers soon found their chief musical interest in doing justice to both. In Sir Hubert Parry's work, *The Music of the 17th Century (Oxford History of Music*, vol. iii.), will be found numerous illustrations of the early development of aria forms, from their first indications in Monteverde's instinctive struggles after coherence, to their complete maturity in the works of Alessandro Scarlatti.

By Scarlatti's time it was thoroughly established that the binary form of melody was that which could best be expanded into a form which should do justice both to singers and to the players who accompanied them. Thus the aria became on a small scale the prototype of the Concerto; and under that heading will accordingly be found all that need be said as to the relation between the instrumental *ritornello* and the material of the voice part in an aria.

So far we have spoken only of the main body of the aria; but the addition of a middle section with a *da Capo*, which constitutes the universal 18th-century *da Capo* form of aria, adds a very simple new principle to the essential scheme without really modifying it. A typical aria of the Scarlatti or Handelian type is a very large melody in binary form, delivered by the voice, which expands it with florid perorations before each cadence (and sometimes also with florid preludes); while relief is given to the voice, further spaciousness to the form, and justice done to the accompaniment, by the addition of an instrumental ritornello containing the gist of the melody not only at the beginning and end, but also in suitable shorter forms at the principal intermediate cadences in foreign keys. A smaller scheme of the same kind in a new group of related keys, but generally without much new material, is then appended as a middle section after which follows the main section *da Capo*. The result is generally a piece of music of considerable length, in a form which cannot fail to be effective and coherent; and there is little cause for wonder in the extent to which it dominated 18th-century music. It was not, however, invariable. In the *Cavatina* we find a form too small for the *da Capo*; and in the oratorios of Handel and the choral works of Bach we find a majority of arias in a larger form which evades the possibility of exact repetition.

The aria forms are profoundly influenced by the difference between the Sonata style and the style of Bach and Handel. But the scale of the form is inevitably small, and in any opera an aria is hardly possible except in a situation which is a tableau rather than an action. Consequently there is no such difference between the form of the classical operatic aria of Mozart and that of the Handelian type as there is between sonata music and suite music. The scale, however, has become too large for the *da Capo*, which was in any case too rigid to survive in music designed to intensify a dramatic situation instead of to distract attention from it. The necessary change of style was so successfully achieved that, until Wagner succeeded in devising music that moved absolutely *pari passu* with his drama, the aria remained as the central formal principle in dramatic music; and few things in artistic evolution are more interesting than the extent to which Mozart's predecessor, the great dramatic reformer Gluck, profited by the essential resources of his pet aversion, the aria style, when he had not only purged it of what had become the stereotyped ideas of ritornellos and vocal flourishes, but animated it by the new sense of dramatic climax to which the sonata style appealed.

In modern opera the aria is almost always out of place, and the forms in which definite melodies nowadays appear are rather those of the song in its limited sense as that of a poem in formal stanzas all set to the same music. In other words, a song in a modern opera tends to be something which would be sung even if the drama had to be performed as a play without music; whereas a classical aria would in non-musical drama be a soliloquy. This can be shown by works at such opposite poles of musical and dramatic technique as Bizet's *Carmen* and the later works of Wagner. In *Carmen* the librettist has so managed that, if his work were performed as a play, almost the whole of it would have to be sung; and the one exception of musical importance is the developed soliloquy of Micaëla in the third act, which, although treated in no old-fashioned or commonplace spirit by the composer, is the one thing in the opera which sounds "operatic."

In the later works of Wagner those passages in which we can successfully detach complete melodies from their context have, one and all, dramatically the aspect of songs and not of soliloquies. Siegmund sings the song of Spring to his sister-bride; Mime teaches Siegfried lessons of gratitude in nursery rhymes; and the whole story of the *Meistersinger* is a series of opportunities for song-singing.

70

The distinctions and gradations between aria and song are of great aesthetic importance, but their history would carry us too far. The distinction is obviously of the same importance as that between dramatic and lyric poetry. Beethoven's *Adelaïde* is a famous example of what is called a song when it is really entirely in aria style; while the operas of Mozart and Weber naturally contain in appropriate situations many numbers which really are songs. The composers themselves generally give appropriate names. Thus Mozart, in *Figaro*, calls "Non so piu cosa son" an aria, because of its free style, though Cherubino actually sings it as a song he has just invented; while "Voi che sapete," being more purely lyric, is called *Canzona*.

The term *aria form* is applied, generally most inaccurately, to all kinds of slow cantabile instrumental music of which the general design can be traced to the operatic aria. Mozart, for example, is very fond of slow movements in large binary form without development, and this is constantly called aria-form, though the term ought certainly to be restricted to such examples as have some traits of the aria style, such as the first slow movement in the great serenade in B flat. At all events, until writers on music have agreed to give the term some more accurate use, it is as well to avoid it and its cognate version, *Lied-form*, altogether in speaking of instrumental music.

The *air* or *aria* in a suite is a short binary movement in a flowing rhythm in common or duple time and by no means of the broadly tunelike quality which its name would seem to imply.

(D. F. T.)

490

ARIADNE (in Greek mythology), was the daughter of Minos, king of Crete, and Pasiphae, the daughter of Helios the Sun-god. When Theseus landed on the island to slay the Minotaur (*q.v.*), Ariadne fell in love with him, and gave him a clue of thread to guide him through the mazes of the labyrinth. After he had slain the monster, Theseus carried her off, but, according to Homer (*Odyssey*, xi. 322) she was slain by Artemis at the request of Dionysus in the island of Dia near Cnossus, before she could reach Athens with Theseus. In the later legend, she was abandoned, while asleep on the island of Naxos, by Theseus, who had fallen a victim to the charms of Aegle (Plutarch,*Theseus*, 20; Diodorus, iv. 60, 61). Her abandonment and awakening are celebrated in the beautiful *Epithalamium* of Catullus. On Naxos she is discovered by Dionysus on his return from India, who is enchanted with her beauty, and marries her when she awakes. She receives a crown as a bridal gift, which is placed amongst the stars, while she herself is honoured as a goddess (Ovid, *Metam.* viii. 152,*Fasti*, iii. 459).

The name probably means "very holy" = ἀρι-αγνη; another (Cretan) form Ἀριδήλα (= φανερά)indicates the return to a "bright" season of nature. Ariadne is the personification of spring. In keeping with this, her festivals at Naxos present a double character; the one, full of mourning and sadness, represents her death or abandonment by Theseus, the other, full of joy and revelry, celebrates her awakening from sleep and marriage with Dionysus. Thus nature sleeps and dies during winter, to awake in springtime to a life of renewed luxuriance. With this may be compared the festivals of Adonis and Osiris and the myth of Persephone. Theseus himself was said to have founded a festival at Athens in honour of Ariadne and Dionysus after his return from Crete. The story of Dionysus and Ariadne was a favourite subject for reliefs and wall-paintings. Most commonly Ariadne is represented asleep on the shore at Naxos, while Dionysus, attended by satyrs and bacchanals, gazes admiringly upon her; sometimes they are seated side by side under a spreading vine. The scene where she is holding the clue to Theseus occurs on a very early vase in the British Museum. There is a statue of the sleeping Ariadne in the Vatican Museum.

Kanter, *De Ariadne* (1879); Pallat, *De Fabula Ariadnea* (1891).

ARIANO DI PUGLIA, a town and episcopal see, which, despite its name, now belongs to Campania, Italy, in the province of Avellino, 1509 ft. above sea-level, on the railway between Benevento and Foggia, 24 m. E. of the former by rail. Pop. (1901) town, 8384; commune, 17,653. It lies in the centre of a fertile district, but has no buildings of importance, as it has often been devastated by earthquakes. A considerable part of the population still dwells in caves. It has been supposed to occupy the site of Aequum Tuticum, an ancient Samnite town, which became a post-station on the Via Traiana1 in Roman times; but this should probably be sought at S. Eleuterio 5½ m. north. It was a military position of some importance in the middle ages. Thirteen miles south-south-east is the Sorgente Mefita, identical with the pools of Ampsanctus (*q.v.*).

(T. As.)

71

1This has generally been supposed to be the place referred to by Horace (*Sat.* i. 5. 87), as one which the metre would not allow him to mention by name; but H.-Nissen (*Halische Landeskunde*, Berlin, 1902, ii. 845) proposes Ausculum instead.

ARIAS MONTANO, BENITO (1527-1598), Spanish Orientalist and editor of the Antwerp Polyglot, was born at Fregenal de la Sierra, in Estremadura, in 1527. After studying at the universities of Seville and Alcala, he took orders about the year 1559 and in 1562 he was appointed consulting theologian to the council of Trent. He retired to Peña de Aracena in 1564, wrote his commentary on the minor prophets (1571), and was sent to Antwerp by Philip II. to edit the polyglot Bible projected by Christopher Plantin. The work appeared in 8 volumes folio, between 1568 and 1573. León de Castro, a professor at Salamanca, thereon brought charges of heresy against Arias Montano, who was finally acquitted after a visit to Rome in 1575-1576. He was appointed royal chaplain, but withdrew to Peña de Aracena from 1579 to 1583; he resigned the chaplaincy in 1584, and went into complete seclusion at Santiago de la Espada in Seville, where he died in 1598.

He is the subject of an *Elogio histórico* by Tomás Gonzalez Carvajal in the *Memorias de la Real Academia de la Historia*(Madrid, 1832), vol. vii.

ARICA (SAN MARCOS DE ARICA), a town and port of the Chilean-governed province of Tacna, situated in 18° 28′ 08″ S. lat. and 70° 20′ 46″ W. long. It is the port for Tacna, the capital of the province, 38 m. distant, with which it is connected by rail, and is the outlet for a large and productive mining district. Arica at one time had a population of 30,000 and enjoyed much prosperity, but through civil war, earthquakes and conquest, its population had dwindled to 2853 in 1895 and 2824 in 1902. The great earthquake of 1868, followed by a tidal wave, nearly destroyed the town and shipping. Arica was captured, looted and burned by the Chileans in 1880, and in accordance with the terms of the treaty of Ancon (1883) should have been returned to Peru in 1894, but this was not done. Late in 1906 the town again suffered severely from an earthquake.

ARICIA (mod. *Ariccia*), an ancient city of Latium, on the Via Appia, 16 m. S.E. of Rome. The old town, or at any rate its acropolis, now occupied by the modern town, lay high (1350 ft. above sea-level) above the circular Valle Aricciana, which is probably an extinct volcanic crater; some remains of its fortifications, consisting of a mound of earth supported on each side by a wall of rectangular blocks of peperino stone, have been discovered (D. Marchetti, in *Notizie degli scavi*, 1892, 52). The lower town was situated on the north edge of the valley, close to the Via Appia, which descended into the valley from the modern Albano, and re-ascended partly upon very fine substructions of *opus quadratum*, some 200 yds. in length, to the modern Genzano. Remains of the walls of the lower town, of the *cella* of a temple built of blocks of peperino, and also of later buildings in brickwork and *opus reticulatum*, connected with the post-station (Aricia being the first important station out of Rome, cf. Horace, *Sat.* i. 5. 1, *Egressum magna me excepit Aricia Roma hospitio modico*) on the highroad, may still be seen (cf. T. Ashby in *Mélanges de l'école française de Rome*, 1903, 399). Aricia was one of the oldest cities of Latium, and appears as a serious opponent of Rome at the end of the period of the kings and beginning of the republic. In 338 B.C. it was conquered by C. Maenius and became a *civitas sine suffragio*, but was soon given full rights. Even in the imperial period its chief magistrate was styled *dictator*, and its council *senatus*, and it preserved its own calendar of festivals. Its vegetables and wine were famous, and the district is still fertile.

(T. As.)

ARICINI, the ancient inhabitants of Aricia (*q.v.*), the form of the name ranking them with the Sidicini, Marrucini (*q.v.*), &c., as one of the communities belonging probably to the earlier or Volscian stratum of population on the west side of Italy, who were absorbed by the Sabine or Latin immigrants. Special interest attaches to this trace of their earlier origin, because of the famous cult of Diana Nemorensis, whose temple in the forest close by Aricia, beside the *lacus Nemorensis*, was served by "the priest who slew the slayer, and shall himself be slain"; that is to say, the priest, who was called *rex Nemorensis*, held office only so long as he could defend himself from any stronger rival. This cult, which is unique in Italy, is picturesquely described in the opening chapter of J.G. Frazer's *Golden Bough* (2nd ed., 1900) where full references will be found. Of these references the most important are, perhaps, Strabo v. 3. 12; Ovid, *Fasti*, iii. 263-272; and Suetonius, *Calig*. 35, whose wording indicates that the old-world custom was dying out in the 1st century A.D. It is a reasonable conjecture that this extraordinary relic of barbarism was characteristic of the earlier stratum of the population who presumably called themselves *Arici*.

On the anthropological aspect of the cult, see also A.B. Cook,*Class. Rev.* xvi., 1902, p. 365, where the whole evidence is very fully collected; and Frazer's *Studies in the Early History of Kingship* (1907), where he accepts Cook's criticism of his own earlier theory.

(R. S. C.)

ARIÈGE, an inland department of southern France, bounded S. by Spain, W. and N. by the department of Haute-Garonne, N.E. and E. by Aude, and S.E. by Pyrénées-Orientales. It 491embraces the old countship of Foix, and a portion of Languedoc and Gascony. Area, 1893 sq. m. Pop. (1906) 205,684. Ariège is for the most part mountainous. Its southern border is occupied by the snow-clad peaks of the eastern Pyrenees, the highest of which within the department is the Pic de Montcalm (10,512 ft.). Communication with Spain is afforded by a large number of *ports* or *cols*, which are, however, for the most part difficult paths, and only practicable for a few months in the year. Farther to the north two lesser ranges running parallel to the main chain traverse the centre of the department from south-east to north-west. The more southerly, the Montagne de Tabe, contains, at its south-eastern end, several heights between 7200 and 9200 ft., while the Montagues de Plantaurel to the north of Foix are of lesser altitude. These latter divide the fertile alluvial plains of the north from the mountains of the centre and south. The department is intersected by torrents belonging to the Garonne basin—the Salat, the Arize, which, near Mas d'Azil, flows through a subterranean gallery, the Ariège and the Hers. The climate is mild in the south, but naturally very severe among the mountains. Generally speaking, the arable land, which is chiefly occupied by small holdings, is confined to the lowlands. Wheat, maize and potatoes are the chief crops. Good vineyards and market gardens are found in the neighbourhood of Pamiers in the north. Flax and hemp are also cultivated. The mountains afford excellent pasture, and a considerable number of cattle, sheep and swine are reared. Poultry- and bee-farming flourish. Forests cover more than one-third of the department and harbour wild boars and even bears. Game, birds of prey and fish are plentiful. There is abundance of minerals, including lead, copper, manganese and especially iron. Grindstones, building-stone, talc, gypsum, marble and phosphates are also produced. Warm mineral springs of note are found at Ax, Aulus and Ussat. Pamiers and St Girons are the most important industrial towns. Iron founding and forging, which have their chief centre at Pamiers are principal industries. Flour-milling, paper-making and cloth-weaving may also be mentioned. Ariège is served by the Southern railway. It forms the diocese of Pamiers and belongs to the ecclesiastical province of Toulouse. It is within the circumscriptions of the académie (educational division) and of the court of appeal of Toulouse and of the XVII. army corps. Its capital is Foix; it comprises the arrondissements of Foix, St Girons and Pamiers, with 20 cantons and 338 communes. Foix, Pamiers, St Girons and St Lizier-de-Cousérans are the more noteworthy towns. Mention may also be made of Mirepoix, once the seat of a bishopric, and possessing a cathedral (15th and 16th centuries) with a remarkable Gothic spire.

ARIES ("The Ram"), in astronomy, the first sign of the zodiac (*q.v.*), denoted by the sign ♈, in imitation of a ram's head. The name is probably to be associated with the fact that when the sun is in this part of the heavens (in spring) sheep bring forth their young; this finds a parallel in *Aquarius*, when there is much rain. It is also a constellation, mentioned by Eudoxus (4th century B.C.) and Aratus (3rd century B.C.); Ptolemy catalogued eighteen stars, Tycho Brahe twenty-one, and Hevelius twenty-seven. According to a Greek myth, Nephele, mother of Phrixus and Helle, gave her son a ram with a golden fleece. To avoid the evil designs of Hera, their stepmother, Phrixus and Helle fled on the back of the ram, and reaching the sea, attempted to cross. Helle fell from the ram and was drowned (hence the *Hellespont*); Phrixus, having arrived in Colchis and been kindly received by the king, Aeetes, sacrificed the ram to Zeus, to whom he also dedicated the fleece, which was afterwards carried away by Jason. Zeus placed the ram in the heavens as the constellation.

ARIKARA, or ARICARA (from *ariki*, horn), a uibe of North American Indians of Caddoan stock. They are now settled with the Hidatsas and the Mandans on the Fort Berthold Reservation, North Dakota. They originally lived in the Platte Valley, Nebraska, with the Pawnees, to whom they are related. They number about 400.
See *Handbook of American Indians*, ed. F.W. Hodge (Washington 1907)

ARIMASPI, an ancient people in the extreme N.E. of Scythia (*q.v.*), probably the eastern Altai. All accounts of them go back to a poem by Aristeas of Proconnesus, from whom Herodotus (iii. 116, iv. 27) drew his information. They were supposed to be one-eyed (hence their Scythian name), and to steal gold from the griffins that guarded it. In art they are usually represented as richly dressed Asiatics, picturesquely grouped with their griffin foes; the subject is often described by poets from Aeschylus to Milton. They are so nearly mythical that it is impossible to insist on the usual identification with the ancestors of the Huns. Their gold was probably real, as gold still comes from the Altai.

ARIMINUM (mod. *Rimini*), a city of Aemilia, on the N.E. coast of Italy, 69 m. S.E. of Bononia. It was founded by the Umbrians, but in 268 B.C. became a Roman colony with Latin rights. It was reached from Rome by the Via Flaminia, constructed in 220 B.C., and from that time onwards was the bulwark of the Roman power in Cisalpine Gaul, to which province it even gave its name. Its harbour was of some importance, but is now silted up, the sea having receded. The remains of its moles were destroyed in 1807-1809. Ariminum became a place of considerable traffic owing to the construction of the Via Aemilia (187 B.C.) and the Via Popilia (132 B.C.), and is frequently mentioned by ancient authors. In 90 B.C. it acquired Roman citizenship, but in 82B.C. having been held by the partisans of Marius, it was plundered by those of Sulla (who probably made the Rubicon the frontier of Italy instead of the Aesis), and a military colony settled there. Caesar occupied it in 49 B.C. after his crossing of the Rubicon. It was one of the eighteen richest cities of Italy which the triumviri selected as a reward for their troops. In 27 B.C. Augustus planted new colonists there, and divided the city into seven *vici* after the model of Rome, from which the names of the *vici* were borrowed. He also restored the Via Flaminia (*Mon. Ancyr.* c. 20) from Rome to Ariminum. At the entrance to the latter the senate erected, in his honour, a triumphal arch which is still extant—a fine simple monument with a single opening. At the other end of the *decumanus maximus* or main street (3000 Roman ft. in length) is a fine bridge over the Ariminus (mod. Marecchia) begun by Augustus and completed by Tiberius in A.D. 20. It has five wide arches, the central one having a span of 35 ft., and is well preserved. Both it and the arch are built of Istrian stone. The present Piazza Giulio Cesare marks the site of the ancient forum. The remains of the amphitheatre are scanty; many of its stones have gone to build the city wall, which must, therefore, at the earliest belong to the end of the classical period. In A.D. 1 Augustus's grandson Gaius Caesar had all the streets of Ariminum paved. In A.D. 69 the town was attacked by the partisans of Vespasian, and was frequently besieged in the Gothic wars. It was one of the five seaports which remained Byzantine until the time of Pippin. (See RIMINI.)

See A. Tonini, *Storia della Città di Rimini* (Rimini, 1848-1862).

(T. AS.)

ARIOBARZANES, the name of three ancient kings or satraps of Pontus, and of three kings of Cappadocia and a Persian satrap.

Of the Pontic rulers two are most famous, (1) The son of Mithradates I., who revolted against Artaxerxes in 362 B.C. and may be regarded as the founder of the kingdom of Pontus (*q.v.*). According to Demosthenes he and his three sons received from the Athenians the honour of citizenship. (2) The son of Mithradates III., who reigned c. 266-240 B.C., and was one of those who enlisted the help of the invading Gauls (see GALATIA).

Of the Cappadocian rulers the best-known one ("Philo-Romaeus" on the coins) reigned nominally from 93 to 63 B.C., but was three times expelled by Mithradates the Great and as often reinstated by Roman generals. Soon after the third occasion he formally abdicated in favour of his son Ariobarzanes "Philopator," of whom we gather only that he was murdered some time before 51. His son Ariobarzanes, called "Eusebes" and "Philo-Romaeus," earned the gratitude of Cicero during his proconsulate in Cilicia, and fought for Pompey in the civil wars, but was afterwards received with honour by Julius Caesar, who subsequently reinstated him when expelled by Pharnaces of Pontus. In 42 B.C. Brutus and Cassius declared him a traitor, invaded his territory and put him to death.

The Persian satrap of this name unsuccessfully opposed Alexander the Great on his way to Persepolis (331 B.C.).

ARION, of Methymna, in Lesbos, a semi-legendary poet and musician, friend of Periander, tyrant of Corinth. He flourished about 625 B.C. Several of the ancients ascribe to him the invention of the dithyramb and of dithyrambic poetry; it is probable, however, that his real service was confined to the organization of that verse, and the conversion of it from a mere drunken song, used in the Dionysiac revels, to a measured antistrophic hymn, sung by a trained body of performers. The name Cycleus given to his father indicates the connexion of the son with the "cyclic" or circular chorus which was the origin of tragedy. According to Suidas he composed a number of songs and proems; none of these is extant; the fragment of a hymn to Poseidon attributed to him (Aelian, *Hist. An.* xii. 45) is spurious and was probably written in Attica in the time of Euripides. Nothing is known of the life of Arion, with the exception of the

74

beautiful story first told by Herodotus (i. 23) and elaborated and embellished by subsequent writers. According to Herodotus, Arion being desirous of exhibiting his skill in foreign countries left Corinth, and travelled through Sicily and parts of Italy, where he gained great fame and amassed a large sum of money. At Taras (Tarentum) he embarked for his homeward voyage in a Corinthian vessel. The sight of his treasure roused the cupidity of the sailors, who resolved to possess themselves of it by putting him to death. In answer to his entreaties that they would spare his life, they insisted that he should either die by his own hand on shipboard or cast himself into the sea. Arion chose the latter, and as a last favour begged permission to sing a parting song. The sailors, desirous of hearing so famous a musician, consented, and the poet, standing on the deck of the ship, in full minstrel's attire, sang a dirge accompanied by his lyre. He then threw himself overboard; but instead of perishing, he was miraculously borne up in safety by a dolphin, supposed to have been charmed by the music. Thus he was conveyed to Taenarum, whence he proceeded to Corinth, arriving before the ship from Tarentum. Immediately on his arrival Arion related his story to Periander, who was at first incredulous, but eventually learned the truth by a stratagem. Summoning the sailors, he demanded what had become of the poet. They affirmed that he had remained behind at Tarentum; upon which they were suddenly confronted by Arion himself, arrayed in the same garments in which he had leapt overboard. The sailors confessed their guilt and were punished. Arion's lyre and the dolphin were translated to the stars. Herodotus and Pausanias (iii. 25. 7) both refer to a brass figure at Taenarum which was supposed to represent Arion seated on the dolphin's back. But this story is only one of several in which the dolphin appears as saving the lives of favoured heroes. For instance, it is curious that Taras, the mythical founder of Tarentum, is said to have been conveyed in this manner from Taenarum to Tarentum. On Tarentine coins a man and dolphin appear, and hence it may be thought that the monument at Taenarum represented Taras and not Arion. At the same time the connexion of Apollo with the celebrated dolphin must not be forgotten. Under this form the god appeared when he founded the celebrated oracle at Delphi, the name of which commemorates the circumstance. He was also the god of music, the special preserver of poets, and to him the lyre was sacred.

Among the numerous modern versions of the story, particular mention may be made of the pretty ballad by A.W. Schlegel; see also Lehrs, *Populare Aufsatze aus dem Alterthum* (1844-1846); Clement, *Arion* (1898).

ARIOSTO, LODOVICO (1474-1533) Italian poet, was born at Reggio, in Lombardy, on the 8th of September 1474. His father was Niccolo Ariosto, commander of the citadel of Reggio. He showed a strong inclination to poetry from his earliest years, but was obliged by his father to study the law—a pursuit in which he lost five of the best years of his life. Allowed at last to follow his inclination, he applied himself to the study of the classics under Gregorio da Spoleto. But after a short time, during which he read the best Latin authors, he was deprived of his teacher by Gregorio's removal to France as tutor of Francesco Sforza. Ariosto thus lost the opportunity of learning Greek, as he intended. His father dying soon after, he was compelled to forego his literary occupations to undertake the management of the family, whose affairs were embarrassed, and to provide for his nine brothers and sisters, one of whom was a cripple. He wrote, however, about this time some comedies in prose and a few lyrical pieces. Some of these attracted the notice of the cardinal Ippolito d'Este, who took the young poet under his patronage and appointed him one of the gentlemen of his household. This prince usurped the character of a patron of literature, whilst the only reward which the poet received for having dedicated to him the *Orlando Furioso*, was the question, "Where did you find so many stories, Master Ludovic?" The poet himself tells us that the cardinal was ungrateful; deplores the time which he spent under his yoke; and adds, that if he received some niggardly pension, it was not to reward him for his poetry, which the prelate despised, but to make some just compensation for the poet's running like a messenger, with the risk of his life, at his eminence's pleasure. Nor was even this miserable pittance regularly paid during the period that the poet enjoyed it. The cardinal went to Hungary in 1518, and wished Ariosto to accompany him. The poet excused himself, pleading ill health, his love of study, the care of his private affairs and the age of his mother, whom it would have been disgraceful to leave. His excuses were not received, and even an interview was denied him. Ariosto then boldly said, that if his eminence thought to have bought a slave by assigning him the scanty pension of 75 crowns a year, he was mistaken and might withdraw his boon—which it seems the cardinal did.

The cardinal's brother, Alphonso, duke of Ferrara, now took the poet under his patronage. This was but an act of simple justice, Ariosto having already distinguished himself as a diplomatist, chiefly on the occasion of two visits to Rome as ambassador to Pope Julius II. The fatigue of one of these hurried journeys brought on a complaint from which he never recovered; and on his second mission he was nearly killed by order of the violent pope, who happened at the time to be much incensed against the duke of Ferrara. On account of the war, his salary of only 84 crowns a year was suspended, and it was withdrawn altogether after the peace; in consequence of which Ariosto asked the duke either to provide for him, or to allow him to seek employment elsewhere. A province, situated on the wildest heights of the Apennines, being then without a governor, Ariosto received the appointment, which he held for three years. The office was no sinecure. The province was distracted by factions and banditti, the governor had not the requisite means to enforce his authority and the duke did little to support his minister. Yet it is said that Ariosto's government satisfied both the sovereign and the people confided to his care; and a story is added of his having, when walking out alone, fallen in with a party of banditti, whose chief, on discovering that his captive was the author of *Orlando Furioso*, humbly apologized for not having immediately shown him the respect which was due to his rank. Although he had little reason to be satisfied with his office, he refused an embassy to Pope Clement VII. offered to him by the secretary of the duke, and spent the remainder of his life at Ferrara, writing comedies, superintending their performance as well as the construction of a theatre, and correcting his *Orlando Furioso*, of which the complete edition was published only a year before his death. He died of consumption on the 6th of June 1533.

That Ariosto was honoured and respected by the first men of his age is a fact; that most of the princes of Italy showed him great partiality is equally true; but it is not less so that their patronage was limited to kind words. It is not known that he ever received any substantial mark of their love for literature; he lived and died poor. He proudly wrote on the entrance of a house built by himself,

493

"Parva, sed apta mihi, sed nulli obnoxia,
sed non
Sordida, parta meo sed tamen aere
domus;"

which serves to show the incorrectness of the assertion of flatterers, followed by Tiraboschi, that the duke of Ferrara built that house for him. The only one who seems to have given anything to Ariosto as a reward for his poetical talent was the marquess del Vasto, who assigned him an annuity of 100 crowns on the revenues of Casteleone in Lombardy; but it was only paid, if ever, from the end of 1531. That he was crowned as poet by Charles V. seems untrue, although a diploma may have been issued to that effect by the emperor.

The character of Ariosto seems to have been fully and justly delineated by Gabriele, his brother:—

"Ornabat pietas et grata modestia
Vatem,
Sancta fides, dictique memor,
munitaque recto
Justitia, et nullo patientia victa labore,
Et constans virtus animi, et clementia
mitis,
Ambitione procul pulsa, fastusque
tumore."

His satires, in which we see him before us such as he was, show that there was no flattery in this portrait. In these compositions we are struck with the noble independence of the poet. He loved liberty with a most jealous fondness. His disposition was changeable withal, as he himself very frankly confesses in his Latin verses, as well as in the satires.

"Hoc olim ingenio vitales hausimus auras,
Multa cito ut placeant, displicitura brevi.
Non in amore modo mens haec, sed in
omnibus impar
Ipsa sibi longa non retinenda mora."

Hence he never would bind himself, either by going into orders, or by marrying, till towards the end of his life, when he espoused Alessandra, widow of Tito Strozzi. He had no issue by his wife, but he left two natural sons by different mothers.

His Latin poems do not perhaps deserve to be noticed: in the age of Flaminio, Vida, Fracastoro and Sannazaro, better things were due from a poet like Ariosto. His lyrical compositions show the poet, although they do not seem worthy of his powers. His comedies, of which he wrote four, besides one which he left unfinished, are avowedly imitated from Plautus and Terence; and although native critics may admire in them the elegance of the diction, the liveliness of the dialogue and the novelty of some scenes, few will feel interest either in the subject or in the characters, and it is hard to approve the immoral passages by which they are disfigured, however grateful these might be to the audiences and patrons of theatrical representations in Ariosto's own day.

Of all the works of Ariosto, the most solid monument of his fame is the *Orlando Furioso*, the extraordinary merits of which have cast into oblivion the numberless romance poems which inundated Italy during the 15th, 16th and 17th centuries.

The popularity which an earlier poem on the same theme, *Orlando Innamorato*, by Boiardo, enjoyed in Ariosto's time, cannot be well conceived, now that the enthusiasm of the crusades, and the interest which was attached to a war against the Moslems, have passed away. Boiardo wrote and read his poem at the court of Ferrara, but died before he was able to finish it. Many poets undertook the difficult task of its completion; but it was reserved for Ariosto both to finish and to surpass, his original. Boiardo did not, perhaps, yield to Ariosto either in vigour or in richness of imagination, but he lived in a less refined age, and died before he was able to recast or even finish the poetical romance which he had written under the impulse of his exuberant fancy. Ariosto, on the other hand, united to a powerful imagination an elegant and cultivated taste. He began to write his great poem about 1503, and after having consulted the first men of the age of Leo X., he published it in 1516, in only 40 cantos (extended afterwards to 46); and up to the moment of his death never ceased to correct and improve both the subject and the style. It is in this latter quality that he excels, and for which he had assigned him the name of *Divino Lodovico*. Even when he jests, he never compromises his dignity; and in pathetic description or narrative he excites the reader's deepest feelings. In his machinery he displays a vivacity of fancy with which no other poet can vie; but he never lets his fancy carry him so far as to omit to employ, with an art peculiar to himself, those simple and natural pencil-strokes which, by imparting to the most extraordinary feats a colour of reality, satisfy the reason without disenchanting the imagination. The death of Zerbino, the complaints of Isabella, the effects of discord among the Saracens, the flight of Astolfo to the moon, the passion which causes Orlando's madness, teem with beauties of every variety. The supposition that the poem is not connected throughout is wholly unfounded; there is a connexion which, with a little attention, will become evident. The love of Ruggero and Bradamante forms the main subject of the *Furioso*; every part of it, except some episodes, depend upon this subject; and the poem ends with their marriage.

The first complete edition of the *Orlando Furioso* was published at Ferrara in 1532, as noted above. The edition of Morali (Milan, 1818) follows the text of the 1532 edition with great correctness. Of editions published in England, those of Baskerville (Birmingham, 1773) and Panizzi (London, 1834) are the most important. The indifferent translations into English of Sir John Harrington (1591) and John Hoole (1783) have been superseded by the spirited rendering of W. Stewart Rose (1823). See also E. Gardner, *Ariosto: the Prince of Court Poets* (1906).

ARISTAENETUS, Greek epistolographer, flourished in the 5th or 6th century A.D. He was formerly identified with Aristaenetus of Nicaea (the friend of Symmachus), who perished in an earthquake at Nicomedia, A.D. 358, but internal evidence points to a much later date. Under his name two books of love stories, in the form of letters, are extant; the subjects are borrowed from the erotic elegies of such Alexandrian writers as Callimachus, and the language is a patchwork of phrases from Plato, Lucian, Alciphron and others. The stories are feeble and insipid, and full of strange and improbable incidents.

Text: Boissonade (1822); Hercher, *Epistolographi Graeci*(1873). English translations: Boyer (1701); Thomas Brown (1715); R.B. Sheridan and Halked (1771 and later).

ARISTAEUS, a divinity whose worship was widely spread throughout ancient Greece, but concerning whom the myths are somewhat obscure. The account most generally received connects him specially with Thessaly. Apollo carried off from Mount Pelion the nymph Cyrene, daughter or granddaughter of the river-god Peneus, and conveyed her to Libya, where she gave birth to Aristaeus. From this circumstance the town of Cyrene took its name. The child was at first handed over to the care of the Hours, or the nymph Melissa and the centaur Cheiron. He afterwards left Libya and went to Thebes, where he received instruction from the Muses in the arts of healing and prophecy, and married Autonoe, daughter of Cadmus, by whom he had several children, among others, the unfortunate Actaeon. He is said to have visited Ceos, where, by erecting a temple to Zeus Icmaeus (the giver of moisture), he freed the inhabitants from a terrible drought. The islanders worshipped him, and occasionally identified him with Zeus, calling him Zeus Aristaeus. After travelling through many of the Aegean islands, through Sicily, Sardinia and Magna Graecia, everywhere conferring benefits and receiving divine honours, Aristaeus reached Thrace, where he was initiated into the mysteries of Dionysus, and finally disappeared near Mount Haemus. While in Thrace he is said to have caused the death of Eurydice, who was bitten by a snake while fleeing from him. Aristaeus was essentially a benevolent deity; he was worshipped as the first who introduced the cultivation of bees (Virgil, *Georg.* iv. 315-558), and of the vine and olive; he was the protector of herdsmen and hunters; he warded off the evil effects of the dog-star; he possessed the arts of healing and prophecy. He was often identified with Zeus, Apollo and Dionysus. In ancient sculptures and coins he is represented as a young man, habited like a shepherd, and sometimes carrying a sheep on his shoulders. Coins of Ceos exhibit the head of Aristaeus and Sirius in the form of a dog crowned with rays.

Pindar, *Pythia*, ix. 5-65; Apollonius Rhodius, schol. on ii. 498, 500; Diodorus, iv. 81.

ARISTAGORAS (d. 497 B.C.), brother-in-law and cousin of Histiaeus, tyrant of Miletus. While Histiaeus was practically a prisoner at the court of Darius, he acted as regent in Miletus. 494In 500 B.C. he persuaded the Persians to join him in an attack upon Naxos, but he quarrelled with Megabates, the Persian commander, who warned the inhabitants of the island, and the expedition failed. Finding himself the object of Persian suspicion, Aristagoras, instigated by a message from Histiaeus, raised the standard of revolt in Miletus, though it seems likely that this step had been under consideration for some time (seeIONIA). After the complete failure of the Ionian revolt he emigrated to Myrcinus in Thrace. Here he fell in battle (497), while attacking Ennea Hodoi (afterwards Amphipolis) on the Strymon, which belonged to the Edonians, a Thracian tribe. The aid given to him by Athens and Eretria, and the burning of Sardis, were the immediate cause of the invasion of Greece by Darius.

See Herodotus v. 30-51, 97-126; Thucydides iv. 102; Diodorus xii. 68; for a more favourable view see G.B. Grundy, *Great Persian War* (London, 1901).

ARISTANDER, of Telmessus in Lycia, was the favourite soothsayer of Alexander the Great, who consulted him on all occasions. After the death of the monarch, when his body had lain unburied for thirty days, Aristander procured its burial by foretelling that the country in which it was interred would be the most prosperous in the world. He is frequently mentioned by the historians who wrote about Alexander, and was probably the author of a work on prodigies, which is referred to by Pliny (*Nat. Hist.* xvii. 38) and Lucian.

Philopatris, 21; Arrian, *Anabasis,* ii. 26, iii. 2, iv. 4; Plutarch,*Alexander;* Curtius iv. 2, 6, 15, vii. 7.

ARISTARCHUS, of Samos, Greek astronomer, flourished about 250 B.C. He is famous as having been the first to maintain that the earth moves round the sun. On this account he was accused of impiety by the Stoic Cleanthes, just as Galileo, in later years, was attacked by the theologians. His only extant work is a short treatise (with a commentary by Pappus) *On the Magnitudes and Distances of the Sun and Moon.* His method of estimating the relative lunar and solar distances is geometrically correct, though the instrumental means at his command rendered his data erroneous. Although the heliocentric system is not mentioned in the treatise, a quotation in the *Arenarius* of Archimedes from a work of Aristarchus proves that he anticipated the great discovery of Copernicus. Further, Copernicus could not have known of Aristarchus's doctrine, since Archimedes's work was not published till after Copernicus's death. Aristarchus is also said to have invented two sun-dials, one hemispherical, the so-called *scaphion,* the other plane.

Editio princeps by Wallis (1688); Fortia d'Urban (1810); Nizze (1856). See Bergk-Hinrichs, *Aristarchus van Samos* (1883); Tannery, *Aristarque de Samos;* also ASTRONOMY.

ARISTARCHUS, of Samothrace (*c.* 220-143 B.C.), Greek grammarian and critic, flourished about 155. He settled early in Alexandria, where he studied under Aristophanes of Byzantium, whom he succeeded as librarian of the museum. On the accession of the tyrant Ptolemy Physcon (his former pupil), he found his life in danger and withdrew to Cyprus, where he died from dropsy, hastened, it is said, by voluntary starvation, at the age of 72. Aristarchus founded a school of philologists, called after him "Aristarcheans," which long flourished in Alexandria and afterwards at Rome. He is said to have written 800 commentaries alone, without reckoning special treatises. He edited Hesiod, Pindar, Aeschylus, Sophocles and other authors; but his chief fame rests on his critical and exegetical edition of Homer, practically the foundation of our present recension. In the time of Augustus, two Aristarcheans, Didymus and Aristonicus, undertook the revision of his work, and the extracts from these two writers in the Venetian scholia to the *Iliad* give an idea of Aristarchus's Homeric labours. To obtain a thoroughly correct text, he marked with an obelus the lines he considered spurious; other signs were used by him to indicate notes, varieties of reading, repetitions and interpolations. He arranged the *Iliad* and the *Odyssey* in twenty-four books as we now have them. As a commentator his principle was that the author should explain himself, without recourse to allegorical interpretation; in grammar, he laid chief stress on analogy and uniformity of usage and construction. His views were opposed by Crates of Mallus, who wrote a treatise Ἀνωμαλίας, especially directed against them.

See Lehrs, *De Aristarchi Stud. Homericis* (3rd ed., 1882); Ludwich, *Aristarchs homerische Textcritik* (1884); especially Sandys, *Hist. of Class. Schol.* (ed. 1906), vol. i. with authorities; also HOMER.

ARISTEAS, a somewhat mythical personage in ancient Greece, said to have lived in the time of Cyrus and Croesus, or, according to some, ca. 690 B.C. We are chiefly indebted to Herodotus (iv. 13-15) for our knowledge of him and his poem *Arimaspeia*. He belonged to a noble family of Proconnesus, an island colony from Miletus in the Propontis, and was supposed to be inspired by Apollo. He travelled through the countries north and east of the Euxine, and visited the Hyperboreans, Issedonians and Arimaspians, who fought against the gold-guarding griffins. An important historical fact which seems to be indicated in his poem is the rush of barbarian hordes towards Europe under pressure from their neighbours. Twelve lines of the poem are preserved in Tzetzes and Longinus. Wonderful stories are told of Aristeas. At Proconnesus, he fell dead in a shop; simultaneously a traveller declared he had spoken with him near Cyzicus; his body vanished; six years afterwards, he returned. Again disappearing, 240 years later he was at Metapontum, and commanded the inhabitants to raise a statue to himself and an altar to Apollo, whom he had accompanied in the form of a raven, at the founding of the city. According to Suidas, Aristeas also wrote a prose theogony. The genuineness of his works is disputed by Dionysius of Halicarnassus.

See Tournier, *De Aristea Proconneso* (1863); Macan, *Hdt.* iv. 14 note.

ARISTEAS, the pseudonymous author of a famous *Letter* in which is described, in legendary form, the origin of the Greek translation of the Old Testament known as the Septuagint (*q.v.*). Aristeas represents himself as a Gentile Greek, but was really an Alexandrian Jew who lived under one of the later Ptolemies. Though the *Letter* is unauthentic, it is now recognized as a useful source of information concerning both Egyptian and Palestinian affairs in the 2nd and possibly in the 3rd century B.C.

An English translation, based on a critical Greek text, was published by H. St J. Thackeray in the *Jewish Quarterly Review*, vol. xv. There are two modern editions of the Greek, one by the last named (in Swete's *Introduction to the Old Testament in Greek*, Cambridge, 1900), the other by P. Wendland (Leipzig, 1900).

ARISTIDES [Ἀριστείδης] (*c.* 530-468 B.C.), Athenian statesman, called "the Just," was the son of Lysimachus, and a member of a family of moderate fortune. Of his early life we are told merely that he became a follower of the statesman Cleisthenes and sided with the aristocratic party in Athenian politics. He first comes into notice as strategus in command of his native tribe Antiochis at Marathon, and it was no doubt in consequence of the distinction which he then achieved that he was elected chief archon for the ensuing year (489-488). In pursuance of his conservative policy which aimed at maintaining Athens as a land power, he was one of the chief opponents of the naval policy of Themistocles (*q.v.*). The conflict between the two leaders ended in the ostracism of Aristides, at a date variously given between 485 and 482. It is said that, on this occasion, a voter, who did not know him, came up to him, and giving him his sherd, desired him to write upon it the name of Aristides. The latter asked if Aristides had wronged him. "No," was the reply, "and I do not even know him, but it irritates me to hear him everywhere called *the just.*"

Early in 480 Aristides profited by the decree recalling the post-Marathonian exiles to help in the defence of Athens against the Persian invaders, and was elected strategus for the year 480-479. In the campaign of Salamis he rendered loyal support to Themistocles, and crowned the victory by landing Athenian infantry on the island of Psyttaleia and annihilating the Persian garrison stationed there (see SALAMIS). In 479 he was re-elected strategus, and invested with special powers as commander of the Athenian contingent at Plataea; he is also said to have judiciously suppressed a conspiracy among some oligarchic malcontents in the army, and to have played a prominent part 495in arranging for the celebration of the victory. In 478 or 477 Aristides was in command of the Athenian squadron off Byzantium, and so far won the confidence of the Ionian allies that, after revolting from the Spartan admiral Pausanias, they offered him the chief command and left him with absolute discretion in fixing the contributions of the newly formed confederacy (see DELIAN LEAGUE). His assessment was universally accepted as equitable, and continued as the basis of taxation for the greater part of the league's duration; it was probably from this that he won the title of "the Just." Aristides soon left the command of the fleet to his friend Cimon (*q.v.*), but continued to hold a predominant position in Athens. At first he seems to have remained on good terms with Themistocles, whom he is said to have helped in outwitting the Spartans over the rebuilding of the walls of Athens. But in spite of statements in which ancient authors have represented Aristides as a democratic reformer, it is certain that the period following the Persian wars during which he shaped Athenian policy was one of conservative reaction. (For the theory based on Plutarch, *Aristid.* 22, that Aristides after Plataea threw open the archonship to all the citizens, see ARCHON.)

He is said by some authorities to have died at Athens, by others on a journey to the Euxine sea. The date of his death is given by Nepos as 468; at any rate he lived to witness the ostracism of Themistocles, towards whom he always displayed a generous conduct, but had died before the rise of Pericles. His estate seems to have suffered severely from the Persian invasions, for apparently he did not leave enough money to defray the expenses of his burial, and it is known that his descendants even in the 4th century received state pensions. (See ATHENS; THEMISTOCLES.)

AUTHORITIES.—Herodotus viii. 79-81, 95; ix. 28; "Constitution of Athens" (*Ath. Pol.*), 22-24, 41; Plutarch, *Aristides*; Cornelius Nepos, *Vita Aristidis*. See also E. Meyer, *Geschichte des Altertums* (Stuttgart, 1901), iii. pp. 481, 492. In the absence of positive information the 4th-century writers (on whom Plutarch and Nepos mainly rely) seized upon his surname of "Just," and wove round it a number of anecdotes more picturesque than historical. Herodotus is practically our only trustworthy authority.

(M. O. B. C.)

ARISTIDES, of Miletus, generally regarded as the father of Greek prose romance, flourished 150-100 B.C. He wrote six books of erotic *Milesian Tales* (Μιλησιακὰ), which enjoyed great popularity, and were subsequently translated into Latin by Cornelius Sisenna (119-67B.C.). They are lost, with the exception of a few fragments, but the story of the Ephesian matron in Petronius gives an idea of their nature. They have been compared with the old French *fabliaux* and the tales of Boccaccio.

Plutarch, *Crassus*, 32; Ovid, *Tristia*, ii. 413, 443; Müller, *Fragmenta Historicorum Graecorum*, iv.

ARISTIDES, of Thebes, a Greek painter of the 4th century B.C. He is said to have excelled in expression. For example, a picture of his representing a dying mother's fear lest her infant should suck death from her breast was much celebrated. He also painted one of Alexander's battles. One of his pictures is said to have been bought by King Attalus for 100 talents (more than £20,000).

ARISTIDES, AELIUS, surnamed THEODORUS, Greek rhetorician and sophist, son of Eudaemon, a priest of Zeus, was born at Hadriani in Mysia, A.D. 117 (or 129). He studied under Herodes Atticus of Athens, Polemon of Smyrna, and Alexander of Cotyaeum, in whose honour he composed a funeral oration still extant. In the practice of his calling he travelled through Greece, Italy, Egypt and Asia, and in many places the inhabitants erected statues to him in recognition of his talents. In 156 he was attacked by an illness which lasted thirteen years, the nature of which has caused considerable speculation. However, it in no way interfered with his studies; in fact, they were prescribed as part of his cure. Aristides' favourite place of residence was Smyrna. In 178, when it was destroyed by an earthquake, he wrote an account of the disaster to Aurelius, which deeply affected the emperor and induced him to rebuild the city. The grateful inhabitants set up a statue in honour of Aristides, and styled him the "builder" of Smyrna. He refused all honours from them except that of priest of Asclepius, which office he held till his death, about 189. The extant works of Aristides consist of two small rhetorical treatises and fifty-five declamations, some not really speeches at all. The treatises are on *political* and *simple speech*, in which he takes Demosthenes and Xenophon as models for illustration; some critics attribute these to a later compiler (Spengel, *Rhetores Graeci*). The six *Sacred Discourses* have attracted some attention. They give a full account of his protracted illness, including a mass of superstitious details of visions, dreams and wonderful cures, which the god Asclepius ordered him to record. These cures, from his account, offer similarities to the effects produced by hypnotism. The speeches proper are epideictic or show speeches—on certain gods, panegyrics of the emperor and individual cities (Smyrna, Rome); justificatory—the attack on Plato's *Gorgias* in defence of rhetoric and the four statesmen, Thucydides, Miltiades, Pericles, Cimon; symbouleutic or political, the subjects being taken from the past history of free Greece—the Sicilian expedition, peace negotiations with Sparta, the political situation after the battle of Leuctra. The *Panathenaicus* and *Encomium of Rome* were actually delivered, the former imitated from Isocrates. The *Leptinea*—the genuineness of which is disputed—contrast unfavourably with the speech of Demosthenes. Aristides' works were highly esteemed by his contemporaries; they were

80

much used for school instruction, and distinguished rhetoricians wrote commentaries upon them. His style, formed on the best models, is generally clear and correct, though sometimes obscured by rhetorical ornamentation; his subjects being mainly fictitious, the cause possessed no living interest, and his attention was concentrated on form and diction.

Editio princeps (52 declamations only) (1517); Dindorf (1829); Keil (1899); Sandys, *Hist. of Class. Schol.* i. 312 (ed. 1906).

ARISTIDES, QUINTILIANUS, the author of an ancient treatise on music, who lived probably in the third century A.D. According to Meibomius, in whose collection (*Antiq. Musicae Auc. Septem*, 1652) this work is printed, it contains everything on music that is to be found in antiquity. (See Pauly-Wissowa, *Realencyc.* ii. 894.)

ARISTIDES, APOLOGY OF. Until 1878 our knowledge of the early Christian writer Aristides was confined to the statement of Eusebius that he was an Athenian philosopher, who presented an apology "concerning the faith" to the emperor Hadrian. In that year, however, the Mechitharists of S. Lazzaro at Venice published a fragment in Armenian1 from the beginning of the apology; and in 1889 Dr Rendel Harris found the whole of it in a Syriac version on Mount Sinai. While his edition was passing through the press, it was observed by the present writer that all the while the work had been in our hands in Greek, though in a slightly abbreviated form, as it had been imbedded as a speech in a religious novel written about the 6th century, and entitled "The Life of Barlaam and Josaphat." The discovery of the Syriac version reopened the question of the date of the work. For although its title there corresponds to that given by the Armenian fragment and by Eusebius, it begins with a formal inscription to "the emperor Titus Hadrianus Antoninus Augustus Pius"; and Dr R. Harris is followed by Harnack and others in supposing that it was only through a careless reading of this inscription that the work was supposed to have been addressed to Hadrian. If this be the case, it must be placed somewhere in the long reign of Antoninus Pius (138-161). There are, however, no internal grounds for rejecting the thrice-attested dedication to Hadrian his predecessor, and the picture of primitive Christian life which is here found points to the earlier rather than to the later date. It is possible that the Apology was read to Hadrian in person when he visited Athens, and that the Syriac inscription was prefixed by a scribe on the analogy of Justin's Apology, a mistake being made in the amplification of Hadrian's name.

The Apology opens thus: "I, O king, by the providence of God came into the world; and having beheld the heaven, and the earth, and the sea, the sun and moon, and all besides, I 496marvelled at their orderly disposition; and seeing the world and all things in it, that it is moved by compulsion, I understood that He that moveth and governeth it is God. For whatsoever moveth is stronger than that which is moved, and whatsoever governeth is stronger than that which is governed." Having briefly spoken of the divine nature in the terms of Greek philosophy, Aristides proceeds to ask which of all the races of men have at all partaken of the truth about God. Here we have the first attempt at a systematic comparison of ancient religions. For the purpose of his inquiry he adopts an obvious threefold division into idolaters, Jews and Christians. Idolaters, or, as he more gently terms them in addressing the emperor, "those who worship what among you are said to be gods," he subdivides into the three great world-civilizations—Chaldeans, Greeks and Egyptians. He chooses this order so as to work up to a climax of error and absurdity in heathen worship. The direct nature-worship of the Chaldeans is shown to be false because its objects are works of the Creator, fashioned for the use of men. They obey fixed laws and have no power over themselves. "The Greeks have erred worse than the Chaldeans ... calling those gods who are no gods, according to their evil lusts, in order that having these as advocates of their wickedness they may commit adultery, and plunder and kill, and do the worst of deeds." The gods of Olympus are challenged one by one, and shown to be either vile or helpless, or both at once. A heaven of quarrelling divinities cannot inspire a reasonable worship. These gods are not even respectable; how can they be adorable? "The Egyptians have erred worse than all the nations; for they were not content with the worships of the Chaldeans and Greeks, but introduced, moreover, as gods even brute beasts of the dry land and of the waters, and plants and herbs.... Though they see their gods eaten by others and by men, and burned, and slain, and rotting, they do not understand concerning them that they are no gods."

Throughout the whole of the argument there is strong common-sense and a stern severity unrelieved by conscious humour. Aristides is engaged in a real contest; he strikes hard blows, and gives no quarter. He cannot see, as Justin and Clement see, a striving after truth, a feeling after God, in the older religions, or even in the philosophies of Greece. He has no patience with attempts to find a deeper meaning in the stories of the gods. "Do they say that one nature underlies these diverse forms? Then why does god hate god, or god kill god? Do they say that the histories are mythical? Then the gods themselves are myths, and nothing more."

The Jews are briefly treated. After a reference to their descent from Abraham and their sojourn in Egypt, Aristides praises them for their worship of the one God, the Almighty Creator; but blames them as worshipping angels, and observing "sabbaths and new moons, and the unleavened bread, and the great fast, and circumcision, and cleanness of meats." He then proceeds to the description of the Christians. He begins with a statement which, when purged of glosses by a comparison of the three forms in which it survives, reads thus: "Now the Christians reckon their race from the Lord Jesus Christ; and He is confessed to be the Son of God Most High. Having by the Holy Spirit come down from heaven, and having been born of a Hebrew virgin, He took flesh and appeared unto men, to call them back from their error of many gods; and having completed His wonderful dispensation, He was pierced by the Jews, and after three days He revived and went up to heaven. And the glory of His coming thou canst learn, O king, from that which is called among them the evangelic scripture, if thou wilt read it. He bad twelve disciples, who after His ascent into heaven went forth into the provinces of the world and taught His greatness; whence they who at this day believe their preaching are called Christians." This passage contains striking correspondences with the second section of the Apostles' Creed. The attribution of the Crucifixion to the Jews appears in several 2nd-century documents; Justin actually uses the words "He was pierced by you" in his dialogue with Trypho the Jew.

"These are they," he proceeds, "who beyond all the nations of the earth have found the truth: for they know God as Creator and Maker of all things, and they worship no other god beside Him; for they have His commandments graven on their hearts, and these they keep in expectation of the world to come.... Whatsoever they would not should be done unto them, they do not to another.... He that hath supplieth him that hath not without grudging: if they see a stranger they bring him under their roof, and rejoice over him, as over a brother indeed, for they call not one another brethren after the flesh, but after the spirit. They are ready for Christ's sake to give up their own lives; for His commandments they securely keep, living holily and righteously, according as the Lord their God hath commanded them, giving thanks to Him at all hours, over all their food and drink, and the rest of their good things." This simple description is fuller in the Syriac, but the additional details must be accepted with caution: for while it is likely that the monk who appropriated the Greek may have cut it down to meet the exigencies of his romance, it is the habit of certain Syriac translators to elaborate their originals. After asserting that "this is the way of truth," and again referring for further information to "the writings of the Christians," he says: "And truly this is a new race, and there is something divine mingled with it." At the close we have a passage which is found only in the Syriac, but which is shown by internal evidence to contain original elements: "The Greeks, because they practise foul things ... turn the ridicule of their foulness upon the Christians." This is an allusion to the charges of Thyestean banquets and other immoralities, which the early apologists constantly rebut. "But the Christians offer up prayers for them, that they may turn from their error; and when one of them turns, he is ashamed before the Christians of the deeds that were done by him, and he confesses to God saying: 'In ignorance I did these things'; and he cleanses his heart, and his sins are forgiven him, because he did them in ignorance in former time, when he was blaspheming the true knowledge of the Christians."

These last words point to the use in the composition of this Apology of a lost apocryphal work of very early date, *The Preaching of Peter*. This book is known to us chiefly by quotations in Clement of Alexandria: it was widely circulated, and at one time claimed a place within the Canon. It was used by the Gnostic Heracleon and probably by the unknown writer of the epistle to Diognetus. From the fragments which survive we see that it contained: (1) a description of the nature of God, which closely corresponds with Arist. i., followed by (2) a warning not to worship according to the Greeks, with an exposure of various forms of idolatry; (3) a warning not to worship according to the Jews—although they alone think they know the true God—for they worship angels and are superstitious about moons and sabbaths, and feasts, comp. Arist. xiv.; (4) a description of the Christians as being "a third race," and worshipping God in "a new way" through Christ; (5) a proof of Christianity from Jewish prophecy; (6) a promise of forgiveness to Jews and Gentiles who should turn to Christ, because they had sinned "in ignorance" in the former time. Now all these points, except the proof from Jewish prophecy, are taken up and worked out by Aristides with a frequent use of the actual language of *The Preaching of Peter*. A criterion is thus given us for the reconstruction of the Apology, where the Greek which we have has been abbreviated, and we are enabled to claim with certainty some passages of the Syriac which might otherwise be suspected as interpolations.

The style of the Apology is exceedingly simple. It is curiously misdescribed by Jerome, who never can have seen it, as "Apologeticum pro Christianis contextum philosophorum sententiis." Its merits are its recognition of the helplessness of the old heathenism to satisfy human aspiration after the divine, and the impressive simplicity with which it presents the unfailing argument of the lives of Christians.

The student may consult *The Apology of Aristides*, Syriac text and translation (J.R. Harris), with an appendix containing the Greek text, *Texts and Studies*, i. 1 (1891), and a critical discussion by R. Seeberg in Zahn's *Forschungen*, v. 2 (1893); also, brief [497]discussions by A. Harnack, *Altchristl. Litteratur*, i. 96 ff.,*Chronologie*, i. 271 ff., where references to other writers may be found. The *Epistola ad omnes philosophos* and the *Homily on the Penitent Thief*, ascribed by Armenian tradition to Aristides, are really of 5th-century origin. Trans. of *Apology* by W.S. Walford (1909).

(J. A. R.)

1 *Codex Venet. ann.*, 981, and *Codex Etchmiaz.* of the 11th century.

ARISTIPPUS (*c*. 435-356 B.C.), Greek philosopher, the founder of the Cyrenaic school, was the son of Aritadas, a merchant of Cyrene. At an early age he came to Athens, and was induced to remain by the fame of Socrates, whose pupil he became. Subsequently he travelled through a number of Grecian cities, and finally settled in Cyrene, where he founded his school. His philosophy was eminently practical (see CYRENAICS). Starting from the two Socratic principles of virtue and happiness, he emphasized the second, and made pleasure the criterion of life. That he held to be good which gives the maximum of pleasure. In pursuance of this he indulged in all forms of external luxury. At the same time he remained thoroughly master of himself and had the self-control to refrain or to enjoy. Diogenes Laertius (ii. 65), quoting Phanias the peripatetic, says that he received money for his teaching, and Aristotle (*Met*. ii. 2) expressly calls him a sophist. Diogenes further states that he wrote several treatises, but none have survived. The five letters attributed to him are undoubtedly spurious. His daughter Arete, and her son Aristippus (μητροδίδακτος, "pupil of his mother"), carried on the school after his death. A cosmopolitan on principle, and a convinced disbeliever in the ethics of his day, he comes very near to modern empiricism and especially to the modern Hedonist school.

ARISTO or ARISTON, of Chios (*c*. 250 B.C.), a Stoic philosopher and pupil of Zeno. He differed from Zeno on many points, and approximated more closely to the Cynic school. He was eloquent (hence his nickname "the Siren") but controversial in tone. He despised logic, and rejected the philosophy of nature as beyond the powers of man. Ethics alone he considered worthy of study, and in that only general and theoretical questions. He rejected Zeno's doctrine of desirable things, intermediate between virtue and vice. There is only one virtue—a clear, intelligent, healthy state of mind (*hygeia*). Aristo is frequently confounded with another philosopher of the same name, Ariston of Iulis, in Ceos, who, about 230 B.C., succeeded Lyco as scholarch of the Peripatetics. (See STOICS.)

ARISTO, of Pella, a Jewish Christian writer of the middle of the 2nd century, who like Hegesippus (*q.v.*) represents a school of thought more liberal than that of the Pharisaic and Essene Ebionites to which the decline of Jewish Christianity mainly led. Aristo is cited by Eusebius (*Hist. Eccl.* iv. 6. 3) for a decree of Hadrian respecting the Jews, but he is best known as the writer of a *Dialogue* (between Papiscus, an Alexandrian Jew, and Jason, who represents the author) on the witness of prophecy to Jesus Christ, which was approvingly defended by Origen against the reproaches of Celsus. The little book was perhaps used by Justin Martyr in his own *Dialogue with Trypho*, and probably also by Tertullian and Cyprian, but it has not been preserved.

The literature is cited in G. Krüger's *Early Christian Literature*, pp. 104 f.

ARISTOBULUS, of Cassandreia, Greek historian, accompanied Alexander the Great on his campaigns, of which he wrote an account, mainly geographical and ethnological. His work was largely used by Arrian.

Müller, *Historicorum Graecorum Fragmenta*; Schöne, *De Rerum Alexandri Magni Scriptoribus* (1870).

ARISTOBULUS, of Paneas (*c*. 160 B.C.), a Jewish philosopher of the Peripatetic school. Gercke places him in the time of Ptolemy X. Philometor (end of 2nd century), Anatolius in that of Ptolemy II. Philadelphus, but the middle of the 2nd century is more probable. He was among the earliest of the Jewish-Alexandrian philosophers whose aim was to reconcile and identify Greek philosophical conceptions with the Jewish religion. Only a few fragments of his work, apparently entitled *Commentaries on the Writings of Moses*, are quoted by Clement, Eusebius and other theological writers, but they suffice to show its object. He endeavoured to prove that early Greek philosophers had borrowed largely from certain parts of Scripture, and quoted from Linus, Orpheus, Musaeus and others, passages which strongly resemble the Mosaic writings. These passages, however, were obvious forgeries. It is suggested that the name Aristobulus was taken from 2 Macc. i. 10. The hypothesis (Schlatter, *Das neugefundene hebräische Stück des Sirach*) that it was from Aristobulus that the philosophy of *Ecclesiasticus* was derived is not generally accepted.

See E. Schürer, *History of the Jewish People* (Eng. trans., 1890-1891), ii. 237 seq.; article ALEXANDRIAN SCHOOL: *Philosophy*; and *s.v.* "Aristobulus" in *Jewish Encyclopedia* (Paul Wendland).

ARISTOCRACY (Gr. ἄριστος, best; κρατία, government), etymologically, the "rule of the best," a form of government variously defined and appreciated at different times and by different authorities. In Greek political philosophy, aristocracy is the government of those who most nearly attain to the ideal of human perfection. Thus Plato in the *Republic* advocates the rule of the "philosopher-king" who, in the social scheme, is analogous to Reason in the intellectual, and alone is qualified to control the active principles, *i.e.* the fighting population and the artisans or workers. Aristocracy is thus the government by those who are superior both morally and intellectually, and, therefore, govern directly in the interests of the governed, as a good doctor works for the good of his patient. Aristotle classified good governments under three heads— monarchy, aristocracy and commonwealth πολιτεία, to which he opposed the three perverted forms—tyranny or absolutism, oligarchy and democracy or mob-rule. The distinction between aristocracy and oligarchy, which are both necessarily the rule of the few, is that whereas the few ἄριστοι will govern unselfishly, the oligarchs, being the few wealthy ("plutocracy" in modern terminology), will allow their personal interests to predominate. While Plato's aristocracy might be the rule of the wise and benevolent despot, Aristotle's is necessarily the rule of the few.

Historically aristocracy develops from primitive monarchy by the gradual progressive limitation of the regal authority. This process is effected primarily by the nobles who have hitherto formed the council of the king (an excellent example will be found in Athenian politics, see ARCHON), whose triple prerogative— religious, military and judicial—is vested, *e.g.*, in a magistracy of three. These are either members of the royal house or the heads of noble families, and are elected for life or periodically by their peers, *i.e.* by the old royal council (cf. the Areopagus at Athens, the Senate at Rome), now the sovereign power. In practice this council depends primarily on a birth qualification, and thus has always been more or less inferior to the Aristotelian ideal; it is, by definition, an "oligarchy" of birth, and is recruited from the noble families, generally by the addition of emeritus magistrates. From the earliest times, therefore, the word "aristocracy" became practically synonymous with "oligarchy," and as such it is now generally used in opposition to democracy (which similarly took the place of Aristotle's πολιτεία), in which the ultimate sovereignty resides in the whole citizen body.

The aristocracy of which we know most in ancient Greece was that of Athens prior to the reforms of Cleisthenes, but all the Greek city-states passed through a period of aristocratic or oligarchic government. Rome, between the regal and the imperial periods, was always more or less under the aristocratic government of the senate, in spite of the gradual growth of democratic institutions (the Lat. *optimates* is the equivalent of ἄριστοι). There is, however, one feature which distinguishes these aristocracies from those of modern states, namely, that they were all slave-owning. The original relation of the slave-population, which in many cases outnumbered the free citizens, cannot always be discovered. But in some cases we know that the slaves were the original inhabitants who had been overcome by an influx of racially different invaders (cf. Sparta with its Helots); in others they were captives taken in war. Hence even the most democratic states of antiquity were so far aristocratic that the larger proportion of the inhabitants had no voice in the government. In the second place this relation gave rise to a philosophic doctrine, held even by Aristotle, that there were peoples who were inferior by nature and adapted to submission (Φύσει δοῦλοι); such people had no "virtue" in the technical civic sense, and were properly occupied in performing the menial functions of society, under the control of the ἄριστοι. Thus, combined with the criteria of descent, civic status and the ownership of the land, there was the further idea of intellectual and social superiority. These qualifications were naturally, in course of time, shared by an increasingly large number of the lower class who broke down the barriers of wealth and education. From this stage the transition is easy to the aristocracy of wealth, such as we find at Carthage and later at Venice, in periods when the importance of commerce was paramount and mercantile pursuits had cast off the stigma of inferiority (in Gr. βαναυσία).

It is important at this stage to distinguish between aristocracy and the feudal governments of medieval Europe. In these it is true that certain power was exercised by a small number of families, at the expense of the majority. But under this system each noble governed in a particular area and within strict limitations imposed by his sovereign; no sovereign authority was vested in the nobles collectively.

Under the conditions of the present day the distinction of aristocracy, democracy and monarchy cannot be rigidly maintained from a purely governmental point of view. In no case does the sovereign power in a state reside any longer in an aristocracy, and the word has acquired a social rather than a political sense as practically equivalent to "nobility," though the distinction is sometimes drawn between the "aristocracy of birth" and the "aristocracy of wealth." Modern history, however, furnishes many examples of government in the hands of an aristocracy. Such were the aristocratic republics of Venice, Genoa and the Dutch Netherlands, and those of the free imperial cities in Germany. Such, too, in practice though not in theory, was the government of Great Britain from the Revolution of 1689 to the Reform Bill of 1832. The French nobles of the *Ancien Régime*, denounced as "aristocrats" by the Revolutionists, had no share as such in government, but enjoyed exceptional privileges (*e.g.* exemption from taxation). This privileged position is still enjoyed by the heads of the German mediatized families of the "High Nobility." In Great Britain, on the other hand, though the aristocratic principle is still represented in the constitution by the House of Lords, the "aristocracy" generally, apart from the peers, has no special privileges.

ARISTODEMUS (8th century B.C.), semi-legendary ruler of Messenia in the time of the first Messenian War. Tradition relates that, after some six years' fighting, the Messenians were forced to retire to the fortified summit of Ithome. The Delphic oracle bade them sacrifice a virgin of the house of Aepytus. Aristodemus offered his own daughter, and when her lover, hoping to save her life, declared that she was no longer a maiden, he slew her with his own hand to prove the assertion false. In the thirteenth year of the war, Euphaes, the Messenian king, died. As he left no children, popular election was resorted to, and Aristodemus was chosen as his successor, though the national soothsayers objected to him as the murderer of his daughter. As a ruler he was mild and conciliatory. He was victorious in the pitched battle fought at the foot of Ithome in the fifth year of his reign, a battle in which the Messenians, reinforced by the entire Arcadian levy and picked contingents from Argos and Sicyon, defeated the combined Spartan and Corinthian forces. Shortly afterwards, however, led by unfavourable omens to despair of final success, he killed himself on his daughter's tomb. Though little is known of his life and the chronology is uncertain, yet Aristodemus may fairly be regarded as a historical character. His reign is dated 731-724 B.C. by Pausanias, and this may be taken as approximately correct, though Duncker (*History of Greece*, Eng. trans., ii. p. 69) inclines to place it eight years later.

Pausanias iv. 9-13 is practically our only authority. He followed as his chief source the prose history of Myron of Priene, an untrustworthy writer, probably of the 2nd century B.C.; hence a good deal of his story must be regarded as fanciful, though we cannot distinguish accurately between the true and the fictitious.

(M. N. T.)

ARISTOLOCHIA (Gr. ἄριστος, best, λοχεία, child-birth, in allusion to its repute in promoting child-birth), a genus of shrubs or herbs of the natural order Aristolochiaceae, often with climbing stems, found chiefly in the tropics. The flower forms a tube inflated at the base. *A. Clematitis*, birthwort, is a central and southern European species, found sometimes in England apparently wild on ruins and similar places, but not a native. *A. Sipho*, Dutchman's pipe, or pipe vine, is a climber, native in the woods of the Atlantic United States, and grown in Europe as a garden plant. The flower is bent like a pipe.

A member of the same order is the *asarabacca* (*Asarum europaeum*), a small creeping herb with kidney-shaped leaves and small purplish bell-shaped flowers. It is a native of the woods of Europe and north temperate Asia, and occurs wild in some English counties. It was formerly grown for medicinal purposes, the underground stem having cathartic and emetic properties. An allied species, *A. canadense*, is the Canadian snake-root, a native of Canada and the Atlantic United States.

ARISTOMENES, of Andania, the semi-legendary hero of the second Messenian war. He was a member of the Aepytid family, the son of Nicomedes (or, according to another version, of Pyrrhus) and Nicoteleia, and took a prominent part in stirring up the revolt against Sparta and securing the co-operation of Argos and Arcadia. He showed such heroism in the first encounter, at Derae, that the crown was offered him, but he would accept only the title of commander-in-chief. His daring is illustrated by the story that he came by night to the temple of Athene "of the Brazen House" at Sparta, and there set up his shield with the inscription, "Dedicated to the goddess by Aristomenes from the Spartans." His prowess contributed largely to the Messenian victory over the Spartan and Corinthian forces at "The Boar's Barrow" in the plain of Stenyclarus, but in the following year the treachery of the Arcadian king Aristocrates caused the Messenians to suffer a crushing defeat at "The Great Trench." Aristomenes and the survivors retired to the mountain stronghold of Eira, where they defied the Spartans for eleven years. On one of his raids he and fifty of his companions were captured and thrown into the Caeadas, the chasm on Mt. Taygetus into which criminals were cast. Aristomenes alone was saved, and soon reappeared at Eira: legend told how he was upheld in his fall by an eagle and escaped by grasping the tail of a fox, which led him to the hole by which it had entered. On another occasion he was captured during a truce by some Cretan auxiliaries of the Spartans, and was released only by the devotion of a Messenian girl who afterwards became his daughter-in-law. At length Eira was betrayed to the Spartans (668 B.C. according to Pausanias), and after a heroic resistance Aristomenes and his followers had to evacuate Messenia and seek a temporary refuge with their Arcadian allies. A desperate plan to seize Sparta itself was foiled by Aristocrates, who paid with his life for his treachery. Aristomenes retired to Ialysus in Rhodes, where Damagetus, his son-in-law, was king, and died there while planning a journey to Sardis and Ecbatana to seek aid from the Lydian and Median sovereigns (Pausanias iv. 14-24). Another tradition represents him as captured and slain by the Spartans during the war (Pliny, *Nat. Hist.* xi. 187; Val. Maximus i. 8, 15; Steph. Byzant. s.v. Ἀνδανία). Though there seems to be no conclusive reason for doubting the existence of Aristomenes, his history, as related by Pausanias, following mainly the *Messeniaca* of the Cretan epic poet Rhianus (about 230 B.C.), is evidently largely interwoven with fictions. These probably arose after the foundation of Messene in 369 B.C.Aristomenes' statue was set up in the stadium there: his bones were fetched from Rhodes and placed in a tomb surmounted by a column (Paus. iv. 32. 3, 6); and more than five centuries later we still find heroic honours paid to him, and his exploits a popular subject of song (*ib.* iv. 14. 7; 16. 6).

For further details see Pausanias iv.; Polyaenus ii. 31; G. Grote,*History of Greece*, pt. ii. chap. vii.; M. Duncker, *History of Greece*, Eng. trans., book iv. chap, viii.; A. Holm, *History of Greece*, Eng. trans., vol. i. chap. xvi.

(M. N. T.)

ARISTONICUS, of Alexandria, Greek grammarian, lived during the reigns of Augustus and Tiberius. He taught at Rome and wrote commentaries and grammatical treatises. His chief work was Περὶ Σημείων Ὁμήρου, in which he gave an account of the "critical marks" inserted by Aristarchus in the margin of his recension of the text of the *Iliad* and *Odyssey*. Important fragments are preserved in the scholia of the Venetian Codex A of the *Iliad*.

Friedländer, *Aristonici* Περὶ Σημείων Ἰλιάδος *reliquiae*(1853); Carnuth, *Aristonici* Περὶ Σημείων Ὀδυσσείας *reliquiae*(1869).

ARISTOPHANES (*c.* 448-385 B.C.1), the great comic dramatist and poet of Athens. His birth-year is uncertain. He is known to have been about the same age as Eupolis, and is said to have been "almost a boy" when his first comedy (*The Banqueters*) was brought out in 427B.C. His father Philippus was a landowner in Aegina. Aristophanes was an Athenian citizen of the tribe Pandionis, and the deme Cydathene. The stories which made him a native of Camirus in Rhodes, or of the Egyptian Naucratis, had probably no other foundation than an indictment for usurpation of civic rights (ξενίας γραφή) which appears to have been more than once laid against him by Cleon. His three sons— Philippus, Araros and Nicostratus—were all comic poets. Philippus, the eldest, was a rival of Eubulus, who began to exhibit in 376 B.C. Araros brought out two of his father's latest comedies—the *Cocalus* and the *Aeolosicon*, and in 375 began to exhibit works of his own. Nicostratus, the youngest, is assigned by Athenaeus to the Middle Comedy, but belongs, as is shown by some of the names and characters of his pieces, to the New Comedy also.

Although tragedy and comedy had their common origin in the festivals of Dionysus, the regular establishment of tragedy at Athens preceded by half a century that of comedy. The Old Comedy may be said to have lasted about eighty years (470-390 B.C.), and to have flourished about fifty-six (460-404 B.C.). Of the forty poets who are named as having illustrated it the chief were Cratinus, Eupolis and Aristophanes. The Middle Comedy covers a period of about seventy years (390-320 B.C.), its chief poets being Antiphanes, Alexis, Theopompus and Strattis. The New Comedy was in vigour for about seventy years (320-250 B.C.), having for its foremost representatives Menander, Philemon and Diphilus. The Old Comedy was possible only for a thorough democracy. Its essence was a satirical censorship, unsparing in personalities, of public and of private life—of morality, of statesmanship, of education, of literature, of social usage—in a word, of everything which had an interest for the city or which could amuse the citizens. Preserving all the freedom of banter and of riotous fun to which its origin gave it an historical right, it aimed at associating with this a strong practical purpose—the expression of a democratic public opinion in such a form that no misconduct or folly could altogether disregard it. That licentiousness, that grossness of allusion which too often disfigures it, was, it should be remembered, exacted by the sentiment of the Dionysiac festivals, as much as a decorous cheerfulness is expected at the holiday times of other worships. This was the popular element. Without this the entertainment would have been found flat and unseasonable. But for a comic poet of the higher calibre the consciousness of a recognized power which he could exert, and the desire to use this power for the good of the city, must always have been the uppermost feelings. At Athens the poet of the Old Comedy had an influence analogous, perhaps, rather to that of the journalist than to that of the modern dramatist. But the established type of Dionysiac comedy gave him an instrument such as no public satirist has ever wielded. When Molière wished to brand hypocrisy he could only make his Tartuffe the central figure of a regular drama, developed by a regular process to a just catastrophe. He had no choice between touching too lightly and using sustained force to make a profound impression. The Athenian dramatist of the Old Comedy worked under no such limitations of form. The wildest flights of extravagance were permitted to him. Nothing bound him to a dangerous emphasis or a wearisome insistence. He could deal the keenest thrust, or make the most earnest appeal, and at the next moment—if his instinct told him that it was time to change the subject—vary the serious strain by burlesque. He had, in short, an incomparable scope for trenchant satire directed by sure tact.

Aristophanes is for us the representative of the Old Comedy. But his genius, while it includes, also transcends the genius of the Old Comedy. He can denounce the frauds of a Cleon, he can vindicate the duty of Athens to herself and to her allies, with a stinging scorn and a force of patriotic indignation which makes the poet almost forgotten in the citizen. He can banter Euripides with an ingenuity of light mockery which makes it seem for the time as if the leading Aristophanic trait was the art of seeing all things from their prosaic side. Yet it is neither in the denunciation nor in the mockery that he is most individual. His truest and highest faculty is revealed by those wonderful bits of lyric writing in which he soars above everything that can move laughter or tears, and makes the clear air thrill with the notes of a song as free, as musical and as wild as that of the nightingale invoked by his own chorus in the *Birds*. The speech of Dikaios Logos in the *Clouds*, the praises of country life in the *Peace*, the serenade in the *Ecclesiazusae*, the songs of the Spartan and Athenian maidens in the *Lysistrata*, above all, perhaps, the chorus in the *Frogs*, the beautiful chant of the Initiated,—these passages, and such as these, are the true glories of Aristophanes. They are the strains, not of an artist, but of one who warbles for pure gladness of heart in some place made bright by the presence of a god. Nothing else in Greek poetry has quite this wild sweetness of the woods. Of modern poets Shakespeare alone, perhaps, has it in combination with a like richness and fertility of fancy.

Fifty-four2 comedies were ascribed to Aristophanes. Forty-three of these are allowed as genuine by Bergk. Eleven only are extant. These eleven form a running commentary on the outer and the inner life of Athens during thirty-six years. They may be ranged under three periods. The first, extending to 420 B.C., includes those plays in which Aristophanes uses an absolutely unrestrained freedom of political satire. The second ends with the year 405. Its productions are distinguished from those of the earlier time by a certain degree of reticence and caution. The third period, down to 388 B.C., comprises two plays in which the transition to the character of the Middle Comedy is well marked, not merely by disuse of the parabasis, but by general self-restraint.

I. *First Period*, (1) 425 B.C. *The Acharnians*.—Since the defeat in Boeotia the peace party at Athens had gained ground, and in this play Aristophanes seeks to strengthen their hands. Dicaeopolis, an honest countryman, is determined to make peace with Sparta on his own account, not deterred by the angry men of Acharnae, who crave vengeance for the devastation of their vineyards. He sends to Sparta for samples of peace; and he is so much pleased with the flavour of the Thirty Years' sample that he at once concludes a treaty for himself and his family. All the blessings of life descend on him; while Lamachus, the leader of the war party, is smarting from cold, snow and wounds.

(2) 424 B.C. *The Knights*.—Three years before, in his *Babylonians*, Aristophanes had assailed Cleon as the typical demagogue. In this play he continues the attack. The Demos, or State, is represented by an old man who has put himself and his household into the hands of a rascally Paphlagonian steward. Nicias and Demosthenes, slaves of Demos, contrive that the

Paphlagonian shall be supplanted in their master's favour by a sausage-seller. No sooner has Demos been thus rescued than his youthfulness and his good sense return together.

(3) 423 B.C. *The Clouds* (the first edition; a second edition was brought out in 422 B.C.).— This play would be correctly described as an attack on the new spirit of intellectual inquiry and culture rather than on a school or class. Two classes of thinkers or teachers are, however, specially satirized under the general name of "Sophist" (v. 331)—1. The Physical Philosophers— indicated by allusions to the doctrines of Anaxagoras, Heraclitus and Diogenes of Apollonia. 2. The professed teachers of rhetoric, belles lettres, &c., such as Protagoras and Prodicus. Socrates is taken as the type of the entire tendency. A youth named Pheidippides—obviously meant for Alcibiades—is sent by his father to Socrates to be cured of his dissolute propensities. Under the discipline of Socrates the youth becomes accomplished in dishonesty and impiety. The conclusion of the play shows the indignant father preparing to burn up the philosopher and his hall of contemplation.

(4) 422 B.C. *The Wasps*.—This comedy, which suggested *Les Plaideurs* to Racine, is a satire on the Athenian love of litigation. The strength of demagogy, while it lay chiefly in the ecclesia, lay partly also in the paid dicasteries. From this point of view the *Wasps* may be regarded as supplementing the *Knights*. Philocleon (admirer of Cleon), an old man, has a passion for lawsuits—a passion which his son, Bdelycleon (detester of Cleon) fails to check, until he hits upon the device of turning the house into a law-court, and paying his father for absence from the public suits. The house-dog steals a Sicilian cheese; the old man is enabled to gratify his taste by trying the case, and, by an oversight, acquits the defendant. In the second half of the play a change comes over the dream of Philocleon; from litigation he turns to literature and music, and is congratulated by the chorus on his happy conversion.

(5) 421 B.C.3 *The Peace*.—In its advocacy of peace with Sparta, this play, acted at the Great Dionysia shortly before the conclusion of the treaty, continues the purpose of the *Acharnians*. Trygaeus, a distressed Athenian, soars to the sky on a beetle's back. There he finds the gods engaged in pounding the Greek states in a mortar. In order to stop this, he frees the goddess Peace from a well in which she is imprisoned. The pestle and mortar are laid aside by the gods, and Trygaeus marries one of the handmaids of Peace.

II. *Second Period*. (6) 414 B.C. *The Birds*.—Peisthetaerus, an enterprising Athenian, and his friend Euelpides persuade the birds to build a city—"Cloud-Cuckoo-borough"—in mid-air, so as to cut off the gods from men. The plan succeeds; the gods send envoys to treat with the birds; and Peisthetaerus marries Basileia, daughter of Zeus. Some have found in the *Birds* a complete historical allegory of the Sicilian expedition; others, a general satire on the prevalence at Athens of headstrong caprice over law and order; others, merely an aspiration towards a new and purified Athens—a dream to which the poet had turned from his hope for a revival of the Athens of the past. In another view, the piece is mainly a protest against the religious fanaticism which the incident of the Hermae had called forth.

(7) 411 B.C. *The Lysistrata*.—This play was brought out during the earlier stages of those intrigues which led to the revolution of the Four Hundred. It appeared shortly before Peisander had arrived in Athens from the camp at Samos for the purpose of organizing the oligarchic policy. The *Lysistrata* expresses the popular desire for peace at any cost. As the men can do nothing, the women take the question into their own hands, occupy the citadel, and bring the citizens to surrender.

(8) 411 B.C. *The Thesmophoriazusae* (Priestesses of Demeter).— This came out three months later than the *Lysistrata*, during the reign of terror established by the oligarchic conspirators, but before their blow had been struck. The political meaning of the play lies in the absence of political allusion. Fear silences even comedy. Only women and Euripides are satirized. Euripides is accused and condemned at the female festival of the Thesmophoria.

(9) 405 B.C. *The Frogs*.—This piece was brought out just when Athens had made her last effort in the Peloponnesian War, eight months before the battle of Aegospotami, and about fifteen months before the taking of Athens by Lysander. It may be considered as an attempt to distract men's minds from public affairs. It is a literary criticism. Aeschylus and Euripides were both lately dead. Athens is beggared of poets; and Dionysus goes down to Hades to bring back a poet. Aeschylus and Euripides contend in the under-world for the throne of tragedy; and the victory is at last awarded to Aeschylus.

III. *Third Period*.4 (10) 393 B.C.4 *The Ecclesiazusae* (women in parliament).—The women, disguised as men, steal into the ecclesia, and succeed in decreeing a new constitution. At this time the demagogue Agyrrhius led the assembly; and the play is, in fact, a satire on the general demoralization of public life.

(11) 388 B.C. *The Plutus* (Wealth).—The first edition of the play had appeared in 408 B.C., being a symbolical representation of the fact that the victories won by Alcibiades in the

Hellespont had brought back the god of wealth to the treasure-chamber of the Parthenon. In its extant form the *Plutus* is simply a moral allegory. Chremylus, a worthy but poor man, falls in with a blind and aged wanderer, who proves to be the god of wealth. Asclepius restores eyesight to Plutus; whereupon all the just are made rich and all the unjust are reduced to poverty.

Among the lost plays, the following are the chief of which anything is known:—

1. *The Banqueters* Δαιταλεῖς, 427 B.C.—A satire on young Athens. A father has two sons; one is brought up in the good old school, another in the tricky subtleties of the new; and the contrast of results is the chief theme.

2. *The Babylonians*, 426 B.C.—Under this name the subject-allies of Athens are represented as "Babylonians"-barbarian slaves, employed to grind in the mill. The oppression of the allies by the demagogues—a topic often touched elsewhere—was, then, the main subject of the piece, in which Aristophanes is said to have attacked especially the system of appointing to offices by lot. The comedy is memorable as opening that Aristophanic war upon Cleon which was continued in the *Knights* and the *Wasps*.

The Merchantmen, The Farmers, The Preliminary Contest(Proagon), and possibly the *Old Age (Geras)*, belonged to the First Period. The *Geras* is assigned by Süvern to 422 B.C., and is supposed to have been a picture of dotage similar to that in the*Knights*. A comedy called *The Islands* is conjectured to have dealt with the sufferings imposed by the war on the insular tributaries. The *Triphales* was probably a satire on Alcibiades; the *Storks*, on the tragic poet Patrocles.

In the *Aeolosicon*—produced by his son Araros in 387 B.C.—Aristophanes probably parodied the *Aeolus* of Euripides. The*Cocalus* is thought to have been a parody of the legend, according to which a Sicilian king of that name slew Minos.

A sympathetic reader of Aristophanes can hardly fail to perceive that, while his political and intellectual tendencies are well marked, his opinions, in so far as they colour his comedies, are too indefinite to reward, or indeed to tolerate, analysis. Aristophanes was a natural conservative. His ideal was the Athens of the Persian wars. He disapproved the policy which had made Athenian empire irksome to the allies and formidable to Greece; he detested the vulgarity and the violence of mob-rule; he clave to the old worship of the gods; he regarded the new ideas of education as a tissue of imposture and impiety. How far he was from clearness or precision of view in regard to the intellectual revolution which was going forward, appears from the *Clouds*, in which thinkers and literary workers who had absolutely nothing in common are treated with sweeping ridicule as prophets of a common heresy. Aristophanes is one of the men for whom opinion is mainly a matter of feeling, not of reason. His imaginative susceptibility gave him a warm and loyal love for the traditional glories of Athens, however dim the past to which they belonged; a horror of what was ugly or ignoble in the present; a keen perception of what was offensive or absurd in pretension. The broad preferences and dislikes thus generated were enough not only to point the moral of comedy, but to make him, in many cases, a really useful censor for the city. The service which he could render in this way was, however, only negative. He could hardly be, in any positive sense, a political or a moral teacher for Athens. His rooted antipathy to intellectual progress, while it affords easy and wide scope for his wit, must after all, lower his intellectual rank. The great minds are not the enemies of ideas. But as a mocker—to use the word which seems most closely to describe him on this side—he is incomparable for the union of subtlety with riot of the comic 501imagination. As a poet, he is immortal. And, among Athenian poets, he has it for his distinctive characteristic that he is inspired less by that Greek genius which never allows fancy to escape from the control of defining, though spiritualizing, reason, than by such ethereal rapture of the unfettered fancy as lifts Shakespeare or Shelley above it,—

"Pouring his full heart
In profuse strains of
unpremeditated art."

BIBLIOGRAPHY.—Editio princeps (Aldine, Venice, 1498), by Marcus Musurus (not including the *Lysistrata* and*Thesmophoriazusae*); S. Bergler (ed. P. Burmann, 1760); Invernizi-Beck-Dindorf (1794-1834); I. Bekker (1829); H.A. Holden (expurgated text, 1868), with *Onomasticon* (new ed., 1902); F.H.M. Blaydes (1880-1893), and critical edition (1886); J. van Leeuwen (1893 foll.); F.W. Hall and E.M. Geldart (text, 1900-1901), with the fragment (from the Oxyrhynchus papyri) of a dialogue between two women concerning a leathern phallus, perhaps from Aristophanes. There is a complete edition of the valuable scholia by F. Dübner (1842, Didot series),—with the anonymous biographies of the poet; of the Ravenna MS. by A. Martin (1883), and W.G. Rutherford (1896-1905). Among English translations mention may be made of those of V.J. Hickie (prose, in Bohn's *Classical Library*); (verse) J. Hookham Frere, five plays; T.

Mitchell, four plays; and, above all, B.B. Rogers, a brilliant work of exceptional merit. There is a concordance to the plays and fragments by H. Dunbar (1883). On Aristophanes generally see H. Müller-Strübing, *Aristophanes und die historische Kritik* (1873); the article by G. Kaibel in Pauly-Wissowa's *Realencyclopadie*, ii. 1 (1896); A. Couat, *Aristophane et l'ancienne comédie attique*(1889); E. Deschanel, *Études sur Aristophane* (3rd ed., 1892); G. Dantu, *Opinions et critiques d'Aristophane sur le mouvement politique et intellectuel à Athènes* (Paris, 1907). For the numerous editions and translations of separate plays in English and other languages see the introductions to Blaydes's edition, and, for the literature, the introduction to W.J.M. Starkie's edition of the *Wasps*(1897); W. Engelmann, *Scriptores Graeci* (1880); and "Bericht über die Literatur der griechischen Komödie aus den Jahren 1892-1901" in C. Bursian's *Jahresbericht über die Fortschritte der classischen Altertumswissenschaft*, cxvi. (1904).

(R. C. J.)

1The dates in the text, as given by Jebb, are retained. According to R.G. Kent, *Classical Review* (April 1905, April 1906), Aristophanes was born in 465, and died in 375 B.C.
2Or "fourty-four" (reading μδ´ for νδ´ in Suidas).
3See E. Curtius, *Hist. of Greece*, iii (Eng. trans. p. 275).
4The date is uncertain; others give 392 and 389.

ARISTOPHANES, of Byzantium, Greek critic and grammarian, was born about 257 B.C. He removed early to Alexandria, where he studied under Zenodotus and Callimachus. At the age of sixty he was appointed chief librarian of the museum. He died about 185-180 B.C.Aristophanes chiefly devoted himself to the poets, especially Homer, who had already been edited by his master Zenodotus. He also edited Hesiod, the chief lyric, tragic and comic poets, arranged Plato's dialogues in trilogies, and abridged Aristotle's *Nature of Animals*. His arguments to the plays of Aristophanes and the tragedians are in great part preserved. His works on Athenian courtesans, masks and proverbs were the results of his study of Attic comedy. He further commented on the Πίνακες of Callimachus, a sort of history of Greek literature. As a lexicographer, Aristophanes compiled collections of foreign and unusual words and expressions, and special lists (words denoting relationship, modes of address). As a grammarian, he founded a scientific school, and in his *Analogy*systematically explained the various forms. He introduced critical signs—except the obelus; punctuation prosodiacal, and accentual marks were probably already in use. The foundation of the so-called Alexandrian "canon" was also due to his impulse (*Sandys, Hist. Class. Schol.*, ed. 1906, i. 129 f.).

Nauck, *Aristophanis Byzantii Grammatici Fragmenta* (1848).

ARISTOTLE (384-322 B.C.), the great Greek philosopher, was born at Stagira, on the Strymonic Gulf, and hence called "the Stagirite." Dionysius of Halicarnassus, in his *Epistle on Demosthenes and Aristotle* (chap. 5), gives the following sketch of his life:—Aristotle (Ἀριστοτέλης) was the son of Nicomachus, who traced back his descent and his art to Machaon, son of Aesculapius; his mother being Phaestis, a descendant of one of those who carried the colony from Chalcis to Stagira. He was born in the 99th Olympiad in the archonship at Athens of Diotrephes (384-383), three years before Demosthenes. In the archonship of Polyzelus (367-366), after the death of his father, in his eighteenth year, he came to Athens, and having joined Plato spent twenty years with him. On the death of Plato (May 347) in the archonship of Theophilus (348-347) he departed to Hermias, tyrant of Atarneus, and, after three years' stay, during the archonship of Eubulus (345-344) he moved to Mitylene, whence he went to Philip of Macedon in the archonship of Pythodotus (343-342), and spent eight years with him as tutor of Alexander. After the death of Philip (336), in the archonship of Euaenetus (335-334), he returned to Athens and kept a school in the Lyceum for twelve years. In the thirteenth, after the death of Alexander (June 323) in the archonship of Cephisodorus (323-322), having departed to Chalcis, he died of disease (322), after a life of three-and-sixty years.

I. ARISTOTLE'S LIFE

This account is practically repeated by Diogenes Laertius in his *Life of Aristotle*, on the authority of the *Chronicles* of Apollodorus, who lived in the 2nd century B.C. Starting then from this tradition, near enough to the time, we can confidently divide Aristotle's career into four periods: his youth under his parents till his eighteenth year; his philosophical education under Plato at Athens till his thirty-eighth year; his travels in the Greek world till his fiftieth year; and his philosophical teaching in the Lyceum till his departure to Chalcis and his death in his sixty-third year. But when we descend from generals to particulars, we become less certain, and must here content ourselves with few details.

Aristotle from the first profited by having a father who, being physician to Amyntas II., king of Macedon, and one of the Asclepiads who, according to Galen, practised their sons in dissection, both prepared the way for his son's influence at the Macedonian court, and gave him a bias to medicine and biology, which certainly led to his belief in nature and natural science, and perhaps induced him to practise medicine, as he did, according to his enemies, Timaeus and Epicurus, when he first went to Athens. At Athens in his second period for some twenty years he acquired the further advantage of balancing natural science by metaphysics and morals in the course of reading Plato's writings and of hearing Plato's unwritten dogmas (cf.ἐν τοῖς λεγομένοις ἀγράφοις δόγμασιν, Ar. *Physics*, iv. 2, 209 b 15, Berlin ed.). He was an earnest, appreciative, independent student. The master is said to have called his pupil the intellect of the school and his house a reader's. He is also said to have complained that his pupil spurned him as colts do their mothers. Aristotle, however, always revered Plato's memory (*Nic. Ethics*, i. 6), and even in criticizing his master counted himself enough of a Platonist to cite Plato's doctrines as what "we say" (cf. φαμέν, *Metaphysics*, i. 9, 990 b 16). At the same time, he must have learnt much from other contemporaries at Athens, especially from astronomers such as Eudoxus and Callippus, and from orators such as Isocrates and Demosthenes. He also attacked Isocrates, according to Cicero, and perhaps even set up a rival school of rhetoric. At any rate he had pupils of his own, such as Eudemus of Cyprus, Theodectes and Hermias, books of his own, especially dialogues, and even to some extent his own philosophy, while he was still a pupil of Plato.

Well grounded in his boyhood, and thoroughly educated in his manhood, Aristotle, after Plato's death, had the further advantage of travel in his third period, when he was in his prime. The appointment of Plato's nephew, Speusippus, to succeed his uncle in the Academy induced Aristotle and Xenocrates to leave Athens together and repair to the court of Hermias. Aristotle admired Hermias, and married his friend's sister or niece, Pythias, by whom he had his daughter Pythias. After the tragic death of Hermias, he retired for a time to Mitylene, and in 343-342 was summoned to Macedon by Philip to teach Alexander, who was then a boy of thirteen. According to Cicero (*De Oratore*, iii. 41), Philip wished his son, then a boy of thirteen, to receive from Aristotle "agendi praecepta et eloquendi." Aristotle is said to have written on monarchy and on colonies for Alexander; and the pupil is said to have slept with his master's edition of Homer under his pillow, and to have respected him, until from hatred of Aristotle's tactless relative, Callisthenes, who was done to death in 328, he turned at last against Aristotle himself. Aristotle had power to teach, and Alexander to learn. Still we must not exaggerate the result. Dionysius must have spoken too strongly 502when he says that Aristotle was tutor of Alexander for eight years; for in 340, when Philip went to war with Byzantium, Alexander became regent at home, at the age of sixteen. From this date Aristotle probably spent much time at his paternal house in his native city at Stagira as a patriotic citizen. Philip had sacked it in 348: Aristotle induced him or his son to restore it, made for it a new constitution, and in return was celebrated in a festival after his death. All these vicissitudes made him a man of the world, drew him out of the philosophical circle at Athens, and gave him leisure to develop his philosophy. Besides Alexander he had other pupils: Callisthenes, Cassander, Marsyas, Phanias, and Theophrastus of Eresus, who is said to have had land at Stagira. He also continued the writings begun in his second period; and the Macedonian kings have the glory of having assisted the Stagirite philosopher with the means of conducting his researches in the *History of Animals*.

At last, in his fourth period, after the accession of Alexander, Aristotle at fifty returned to Athens and became the head of his own school in the Lyceum, a gymnasium near the temple of Apollo Lyceius in the suburbs. The master and his scholars were called Peripatetics (οἱ ἐκ τοῦ περιπάτου), certainly from meeting, like other philosophical schools, in a walk (περίπατος), and perhaps also, on the authority of Hermippus of Smyrna, from walking and talking there, like Protagoras and his followers as described in Plato's*Protagoras* (314 E, 315 C). Indeed, according to Ammonius, Plato too had talked as he walked in the Academy; and all his followers were called Peripatetics, until, while the pupils of Xenocrates took the name "Academics," those of Aristotle retained the general name. Aristotle also formed his Peripatetic school into a kind of college with common meals under a president (ἄρχων) changing every ten days; while the philosopher himself delivered lectures, in which his practice, as his pupil Aristoxenus tells us (*Harmonics* ii, *init.*), was, avoiding the generalities of Plato, to prepare his audience by explaining the subject of investigation and its nature. But Aristotle was an author as well as a lecturer; for the hypothesis that the Aristotelian writings are notes of his lectures taken down by his pupils is contradicted by the tradition of their learning while walking, and disproved by the impossibility of taking down such complicated discourses from dictation. Moreover, it is clear that Aristotle addressed himself to readers as well as hearers, as in concluding his whole theory of syllogisms he says, "There would remain for all of you or for our hearers (πάντων ὑμῶν ἢ τῶν) a duty of according to the defects of the investigation consideration, to its discoveries much gratitude" (*Sophisticai Elenchi*, 34,184 b 6). In short, Aristotle was at once a student, a reader, a lecturer, a writer and a book collector. He was, says Strabo (608), the first we knew who collected books and taught the kings in Egypt the arrangement of a library. In his library no doubt were books of others, but also his own. There we must figure to ourselves the philosopher, constantly referring to his autograph rolls; entering references and cross-references; correcting, rewriting, collecting and arranging them according to their subjects; showing as well as reading them to his pupils; with little thought of publication, but with his whole soul concentrated on being and truth.

On his first visit to Athens, during which occurred the fatal battle of Mantineia (362 B.C.), Aristotle had seen the confusion of Greece becoming the opportunity of Macedon under Philip; and on his second visit he was supported at Athens by the complete domination of Macedon under Alexander. Having witnessed the unjust exactions of a democracy at Athens, the dwindling population of an oligarchy at Sparta, and the oppressive selfishness of new tyrannies throughout the Greek world, he condemned the actual constitutions of the Greek states as deviations (παρεκβάσεις) directed merely to the good of the government; and he contemplated a right constitution (ὀρθὴ πολιτεία), which might be either a commonwealth, an aristocracy or a monarchy, directed to the general good; but he preferred the monarchy of one man, pre-eminent in virtue above the rest, as the best of all governments (*Nicomachean Ethics*, viii. 10; *Politics*, Γ 14-18). Moreover, by adding (*Politics*, H 7, 1327 b 29-33) that the Greek race could govern the world by obtaining one constitution (μιᾶς τυγχάνον πολιτείας), he indicated some leaning to a universal monarchy under such a king as Alexander. On the whole, however, he adhered to the Greek city-state (πόλις), partly perhaps out of patriotism to his own Stagira. Averse at all events to the Athenian democracy, leaning towards Macedonian monarchy, and resting on Macedonian power, he maintained himself in his school at Athens, so long as he was supported by the friendship of Antipater, the Macedonian regent in Alexander's absence. But on Alexander's sudden death in 323, when Athens in the Lamian war tried to reassert her freedom against Antipater, Aristotle found himself in danger. He was accused of impiety on the absurd charge of deifying the tyrant Hermias; and, remembering the fate of Socrates, he retired to Chalcis in Euboea. There, away from his school, in 322 he died. (A tomb has been found in our time inscribed with the name of Biote, daughter of Aristotle. But is this *our* Aristotle?)

Such is our scanty knowledge of Aristotle's life, which seems to have been prosperous by inheritance and position, and happy by work and philosophy. His will, which was quoted by Hermippus, and, as afterwards quoted by Diogenes Laertius, has come down to us, though perhaps not complete, supplies some further details, as follows:—Antipater is to be executor with others. Nicanor is to marry Pythias, Aristotle's daughter, and to take charge of Nicomachus his son. Theophrastus is to be one of the executors if he will and can, and if Nicanor should die to act instead, if he will, in reference to Pythias. The executors and Nicanor are to take charge of Herpyllis, "because," in the words of the testator, "she has been good to me," and to allow her to reside either in the lodging by the garden at Chalcis or in the paternal house at Stagira. They are to provide for the slaves, who in some cases are to be freed. They are to see after the dedication of four images by Gryllion of Nicanor, Proxenus, Nicanor's mother and Arimnestus. They are to dedicate an image of Aristotle's mother, and to see that the bones of his wife Pythias are, as she ordered, taken up and buried with him. On this will we may remark that Proxenus is said to have been Aristotle's guardian after the death of his father, and to have been the father of Nicanor; that Herpyllis of Stagira was the mother of Nicomachus by Aristotle; and that Arimnestus was the brother of Aristotle, who also had a sister, Arimneste. Every clause breathes the philosopher's humanity.

II. DEVELOPMENT FROM PLATONISM

Turning now from the man to the philosopher as we know him best in his extant writings (see *Aristoteles*, ed. Bekker, Berlin, 1831, the pages of which we use for our quotations), we find, instead of the general dialogues of Plato, special didactic treatises, and a fundamental difference of philosophy, so great as to have divided philosophers into opposite camps, and made Coleridge say that everybody is born either a Platonist or an Aristotelian. Platonism is the doctrine that the individuals we call things only become, but a thing is always one universal form beyond many individuals, *e.g.* one good beyond seeming goods; and that without supernatural forms, which are models of individuals, there is nothing, no being, no knowing, no good. Aristotelianism is the contrary doctrine: a thing is always a separate individual, a *substance* (οὐσία), natural such as earth or supernatural such as God; and without these individual substances, which have attributes and universals belonging to them, there is nothing, to be, to know, to be good. Philosophic differences are best felt by their practical effects: philosophically, Platonism is a philosophy of universal forms, Aristotelianism a philosophy of individual substances: practically, Plato makes us

92

think first of the supernatural and the kingdom of heaven, Aristotle of the natural and the whole world.

So diametrical a difference could not have arisen at once. For, though Aristotle was different from Plato, and brought with him from Stagira a Greek and Ionic but colonial origin, a medical descent and tendency, and a matter-of-fact worldly kind of character, nevertheless on coming to Athens as pupil of Plato he must have begun with his master's philosophy. What then in 503more detail was the philosophy which the pupil learnt from the master? When Aristotle at the age of eighteen came to Athens, Plato, at the age of sixty-two, had probably written all his dialogues except the *Laws*; and in the course of the remaining twenty years of his life and teaching, he expounded "the so-called unwritten dogmas" in his lectures on the Good. There was therefore a written Platonism for Aristotle to read, and an unwritten Platonism which he actually heard.

To begin with the written philosophy of the Dialogues. Individual so-called things neither are nor are not, but become: the real thing is always one universal form beyond the many individuals, *e.g.* the one beautiful beyond all beautiful individuals; and each form (ἰδέα) is a model which causes individuals by participation to become like, but not the same as, itself. Above all forms stands the form of the good, which is the cause of all other forms being, and through them of all individuals becoming. The creator, or the divine intellect, with a view to the form of the good, and taking all forms as models, creates in a receptacle (ὑποδοχή, Plato, *Timaeus*, 49 A) individual impressions which are called things but really change and become without attaining the permanence of being. Knowledge resides not in sense but in reason, which, on the suggestion of sensations of changing individuals, apprehends, or (to be precise) is reminded of, real universal forms, and, by first ascending from less to more general until it arrives at the form of good and then descending from this unconditional principle to the less general, becomes science and philosophy, using as its method the dialectic which gives and receives questions and answers between man and man. Happiness in this world consists proximately in virtue as a harmony between the three parts, rational, spirited and appetitive, of our souls, and ultimately in living according to the form of the good; but there is a far higher happiness, when the immortal soul, divesting itself of body and passions and senses, rises from earth to heaven and contemplates pure forms by pure reason. Such in brief is the Platonism of the written dialogues; where the main doctrine of forms is confessedly advanced never as a dogma but always as a hypothesis, in which there are difficulties, but without which Plato can explain neither being, nor truth nor goodness, because throughout he denies the being of individual things. In the unwritten lectures of his old age, he developed this formal into a mathematical metaphysics. In order to explain the unity and variety of the world, the one universal form and the many individuals, and how the one good is the main cause of everything, he placed as it were at the back of his own doctrine of forms a Pythagorean mathematical philosophy. He supposed that the one and the two, which is indeterminate, and is the great and little, are opposite principles or causes. Identifying the form of the good with the one, he supposed that the one, by combining with the indeterminate two, causes a plurality of forms, which like every combination of one and two are numbers but peculiar in being incommensurate with one another, so that each form is not a mathematical number (μαθηματικὸς ἀριθμός), but a formal number (εἰδητικὸς ἀριθμός). Further he supposed that in its turn each form, or formal number, is a limited one which, by combining again with the indeterminate two, causes a plurality of individuals. Hence finally he concluded that the good as the one combining with the indeterminate two is directly the cause of all forms as formal numbers, and indirectly through them all of the multitude of individuals in the world.

Aristotle knew Plato, was present at his lectures on the Good, wrote a report of them (περὶ τἀγαθοῦ), and described this latter philosophy of Plato in his *Metaphysics*. Modern critics, who were not present and knew neither, often accuse Aristotle of misrepresenting Plato. But Heracleides and Hestiacus, Speusippus and Xenocrates were also present and wrote similar reports. What is more, both Speusippus and Xenocrates founded their own philosophies on this very Pythagoreanism of Plato. Speusippus as president of the Academy from 347 to 339 taught that the one and the many are principles, while abolishing forms and reducing the good from cause to effect. Xenocrates as president from 339 onwards taught that the one and many are principles, only without distinguishing mathematical from formal numbers. Aristotle's critics hardly realize that for the rest of his life he had to live and to struggle with a formal and a mathematical Platonism, which exaggerated first universals and attributes and afterwards the quantitative attributes, one and many, into substantial things and real causes.

Aristotle had no sympathy with the unwritten dogmas of Plato. But with the written dialogues of Plato he always continued to agree almost as much as he disagreed. Like Plato, he believed in real universals, real essences, real causes; he believed in the unity of the universal, and in the immateriality of essences; he believed in the good, and that there is a good of the universe;

he believed that God is a living being, eternal and best, who is a supernatural cause of the motions and changes of the natural world, and that essences and matter are also necessary causes; he believed in the divine intelligence and in the immortality of our intelligent souls; he believed in knowledge going from sense to reason, that science requires ascent to principles and is descent from principles, and that dialectic is useful to science; he believed in happiness involving virtue, and in moral virtue being a control of passions by reason, while the highest happiness is speculative wisdom. All these inspiring metaphysical and moral doctrines the pupil accepted from his master's dialogues, and throughout his life adhered to the general spirit of realism without materialism pervading the Platonic philosophy. But what he refused to believe with Plato was that reality is not here, but only above; and what he maintained against Plato was that it is both, and that universals and forms, one and many, the good, are real but not separate realities. This deep metaphysical divergence was the prime cause of the transition from Platonism to Aristotelianism.

Fragmenta Aristotelis.—Aristotle's originality soon asserted itself in early writings, of which fragments have come down to us, and have been collected by Rose (see the Berlin edition of Aristotle's works, or more readily in the Teubner series, which we shall use for our quotations). Many, no doubt, are spurious; but some are genuine, and a few perhaps cited in Aristotle's extant works. Some are dialogues, others didactic works. A special interest attaches to the dialogues written after the manner of Plato but with Aristotle as principal interlocutor; and some of these, *e.g.* the περὶ ποιητῶν and the *Eudemus*, seem to have been published. It is not always certain which were dialogues, which didactic like Aristotle's later works; but by comparing those which were certainly dialogues with their companions in the list of Aristotle's books as given by Diogenes Laertius, we may conclude with Bernays that the books occurring first in that list were dialogues. Hence we may perhaps accept as genuine the following:—

1. Dialogues:—

περὶ δικαιοσύνης: On justice.

περὶ ποιητῶν: On poets (perhaps cited in *Poetics*, 15, 1454 b 18, ἐν τοῖς ἐκδεδομένοις λόγοις).

περὶ φιλοσοφίας: On philosophy (perhaps cited in *Physics*, ii. 2, 194 a 35-36).

περὶ πολιτικοῦ: A politician.

περὶ ῥητορικῆς ἢ Γρύλλος: On rhetoric.

προτρεπτικός: An exhortation to philosophy (probably in dialogue, because it is the model of Cicero's dialogue *Hortensius*).

Εὔδημος ἢ περὶ Ψυχῆς: On soul (perhaps cited in *De Anima*, i. 4, 407 b 29, καὶ τοῖς ἐν κοινῷ γενομένοις λόγοις).

2. Didactic writings:—

(1) Metaphysical:—

περὶ τἀγαθοῦ: On the good (probably not a dialogue but a report of Plato's lectures).

περὶ ἰδεῶν: On forms.

(2) Political:—

περὶ βασιλείας: On monarchy.

Ἀλέξανδρος ἢ ὑπὲρ ἀποίκων: On colonies.

(3) Rhetorical:—

τέχνης τῆς Θεοδέκτου συναγωγή: The *Theodectea* (cited in the Preface to the *Rhetoric to Alexander* (chap. i.)), and as τὰ Θεοδέκτεια in the *Rhetoric* (iii. 9, 1410 b 2).

τεχνῶν συναγωγή: A historical collection of arts of rhetoric.

Difficult as it is to determine when Aristotle wrote all these various works, some of them indicate their dates. Gryllus, celebrated in the dialogue on rhetoric, was Xenophon's son who fell at Mantineia in 362; and Eudemus of Cyprus, lamented in the dialogue on soul, died in Sicily in 352. These then were probably written before Plato died in 347; and so probably were most of the dialogues, precisely because they were imitations of the dialogues of Plato. Among the didactic writings, the περὶ τἀγαθοῦ would probably belong to the same time, because it was Aristotle's report of Plato's lectures. On the other hand, the two political works, if written for Alexander, would be after 343-342 when Philip made Aristotle his tutor. So probably were the rhetorical works, especially the *Theodectea*; since both politics and oratory were the subjects which the father wanted the tutor to teach his son, and, when Alexander came to Phaselis, he is said by Plutarch (*Alexander*, 17) to have decorated the statue of Theodectes in honour of his association with the man through Aristotle and philosophy. On the whole, then, it seems as if Aristotle began with dialogues during his second period under Plato, but gradually came to prefer writing didactic works, especially in the third period after Plato's death, and in connexion with Alexander.

94

These early writings show clearly how Aristotle came to depart from Plato. In the first place as regards style, though the Stagirite pupil Aristotle could never rival his Attic master in literary form, yet he did a signal service to philosophy in gradually passing from the vague generalities of the dialogue to the scientific precision of the didactic treatise. The philosophy of Plato is dialogue trying to become science; that of Aristotle science retaining traces of dialectic. Secondly as regards subject-matter, even in his early writings Aristotle tends to widen the scope of philosophic inquiry, so as not only to embrace metaphysics and politics, but also to encourage rhetoric and poetics, which Plato tended to discourage or limit. Thirdly as regards doctrines, the surpassing interest of these early writings is that they show the pupil partly agreeing, partly disagreeing, with his master. The*Eudemus* and *Protrepticus* are with Plato; the dialogues *on Philosophy*and the treatise *on Forms* are against Plato.

The *Eudemus*, on the soul (*Fragmenta*, 37 seq.), must have been in style and thought the most Platonic of all the Aristotelian writings. Plato's theory of the soul and its immortality was not the ordinary Greek view derived from Homer, who regarded the body as the self, the soul as a shade having a future state but an obscure existence, and stamped that view on the hearts of his countrymen, and affected Aristotle himself. After Homer there had come to Greece the new view that the soul is more real than the body, that it is imprisoned in the carcase as a prison-house, that it is capable of enjoying a happier life freed from the body, and that it can transmigrate from body to body. This strange, exotic, ascetic view was adopted by some philosophers, and especially by the Pythagoreans, and so transmitted to Plato. Aristotle in the*Eudemus*, written about 352, when he was thirty-two, also believed in it. Accordingly, the soul of Eudemus, when it left his body, is said to be returning home: the soul is made subject to the casting of lots, and in coming from the other world to this it is supposed to forget its former visions: but its disembodied life is regarded as its natural life in a better world. The *Eudemus* also contained a celebrated passage, preserved by Plutarch (*Consolat. ad Apoll..*27;*Fragm.* 44). Here we can read the young Aristotle, writing in the form of the dialogue like Plato, avoiding hiatus like Isocrates, and justifying the praises accorded to his style by Cicero, Quintilian and Dionysius. It shows how nearly the pupil could imitate his master's dialogues, and still more how exactly he at first embraced his master's doctrines. It makes Silenus, captured by Midas, say that the best of all things is not to have been born, and the next best, having been born, to die as soon as possible. Nothing could be more like Plato's *Phaedo*, or more unlike Aristotle's later work*on the Soul*, which entirely rejects transmigration and allows the next life to sink into the background.

Hardly less Platonic is the *Protrepticus* (*Fragm.* 50 seq.), an exhortation to philosophy which, according to Zeno the Stoic, was studied by his master Crates. It is an exhortation, whose point is that the chief good is philosophy, the contemplation of the universe by divine and immortal intellect. This is indeed a doctrine of Platonic ethics from which Aristotle in his later days never swerved. But in the *Protrepticus* he goes on to say that seeming goods, such as strength, size, beauty, honours, opinions, are mere illusion (σκιαγραφία), worthless and ridiculous, as we should know if we had Lyncean eyes to compare them with the vision of the eternal. This indifference to goods of body and estate is quite Platonic, but is very different from Aristotle's later ethical doctrine that such goods, though not the essence, are nevertheless necessary conditions of happiness. Finally, in the spirit of Plato's*Phaedo* and the dialogue *Eudemus*, the *Protrepticus* holds that the soul is bound to the sentient members of the body as prisoners in Etruria are bound face to face with corpses; whereas the later view of the *De Anima* is that the soul is the vital principle of the body and the body the necessary organ of the soul.

Thus we find that at first, under the influence of his master, Aristotle held somewhat ascetic views on soul and body and on goods of body and estate, entirely opposed both in psychology and in ethics to the moderate doctrines of his later writings. This perhaps is one reason why Cicero, who had Aristotle's early writings, saw no difference between the Academy and the Peripatetics (*Acad. Post*, i. 4, 17-18).

On the other hand, the dialogue *on Philosophy* (περὶ φιλοσοφίας, *Fragm.* 1 seq.) strikingly exhibits the origin of Aristotle's divergence from Platonism, and that too in Plato's lifetime. The young son of a doctor from the colonies proved too fond of this world to stomach his Athenian master's philosophy of the supernatural. Accordingly in this dialogue he attacked Plato's fundamental position, both in its written and in its unwritten presentment, as a hypothesis both of forms and of formal numbers. First, he attacked the hypothesis of forms (τὴν τῶν ἰδεῶν ὑπόθεσιν, *Fragm.* 8), exclaiming in his dialogues, according to Proclus, that he could not sympathize with the dogma even if it should be thought that he was opposing it out of contentiousness; while Plutarch says that his attacks on the forms by means of his exoteric dialogues were thought by some persons more contentious than philosophical, as presuming to disdain Plato's philosophy: so far was he, says Plutarch, from following it. Secondly, in the same dialogue (*Fragm.* 9), according to Syrianus, he disagreed with the hypothesis of formal numbers (τοῖς εἰδητικοῖς ἀριθμοῖς). If, wrote Aristotle, the forms are another sort of number, not mathematical, there would be no understanding of it. Lastly, in the same dialogue (*Fragm.* 18 seq.) he revealed his emphasis on nature by contending that the universe is uncreate and indestructible. According to Plato, God caused the natural world to become: according to Aristotle it is eternal. This eternity of the world became one of his characteristic doctrines, and subsequently enabled him to explain how essences can be eternal without being separate from this world which is also eternal (cf. *Metaph.* Z 8). Thus early did Aristotle begin, even in Plato's lifetime, to oppose Plato's hypothesis of supernatural forms, and advance his own hypothesis of the eternity of the world.

He made another attack on Platonism in the didactic work περὶ ἰδεῶν, (*Fragm.* 185 seq.), contending that the Platonic arguments prove not forms (ἰδέαι) but only things common (τὰ κοινά). Here, according to Alexander the commentator, he first brought against Plato the argument of "the third man" (ὁ τρίτος ἄνθρωπος); that, if there is the form, one man beyond many men, there will be a third man predicated of both man and men, and a fourth predicated of all three, and so on to infinity (*Fragm.* 188). Here, too, he examined the hypothesis of Eudoxus that things are caused by mixture of forms, a hypothesis which formed a kind of transition to his own later views, but failed to satisfy him on account of its difficulties. Lastly, in the didactic work περὶ τἀγαθοῦ (*Fragm.* 27 seq.), containing his report of Plato's lectures on the Good, he was dealing with the same mathematical metaphysics which in his dialogue *on Philosophy* he criticized for converting forms into formal numbers. Aristoxenus, at the beginning of the second book of the *Harmonics*, gives a graphic account of the astonishment caused by these lectures of Plato, and of their effect on the lectures of Aristotle. In contending, as Aristotle's pupil, that a teacher should begin by proposing his subject, he tells us how Aristotle used to relate that most of Plato's hearers came expecting to get something about human goods and happiness, but that when the discourses turned out to be all about mathematics, with the conclusion that good is one, it appeared to them a paradox, which some despised and others condemned. The reason, he adds, was that they were not informed by Plato beforehand; and for this very reason, Aristotle, as he told Aristoxenus himself, used to prepare his hearers by informing them of the nature of the subject. From this rare personal reminiscence we see at a glance that the mind of Plato and the mind of Aristotle were so different, that their philosophies must diverge; the one towards the supernatural, the abstract, the discursive, and the other towards the natural, the substantial, the scientific.

Aristotle then even in the second period of his life, while Plato was still alive, began to differ from him in metaphysics. He rejected the Platonic hypothesis of forms, and affirmed that they are not separate but common, without however as yet having advanced to a constructive metaphysics of his own; while at the same time, after having at first adopted his master's dialectical treatment of metaphysical problems, he soon passed from dialogues to didactic works, which had the result of separating metaphysics from dialectic. The all-important consequence of this first departure from Platonism was that Aristotle became and remained primarily a metaphysician. After Plato's death, coming to his third period he made a further departure from Platonism in his didactic works on politics and rhetoric, written in connexion with Alexander and Theodectes. Those on politics (*Fragm.* 646-648) were designed to instruct Alexander on monarchy and on colonization; and in them Aristotle agreed with Plato in assigning a moral object to the state, but departed from him by saying that a king need not be a philosopher, as Plato had said in the *Republic*, but does need to listen to philosophers. Still more marked was his departure from Plato as regards rhetoric. Plato in the *Gorgias*, (501A) had contended that rhetoric is not an art but an empirical practice (τριβὴ καὶ ἐμπειρία); Aristotle in the *Gryllus* (*Fragm.*68-69), written in his second period, took according to Quintilian a similar view. But in his third period, in the *Theodectea* (*Fragm.*125 seq.), rhetoric is treated as an art, and is laid out somewhat in the manner of his later *Art of Rhetoric*; while he also showed his interest in the subject by writing a history of other arts of rhetoric called τεχνῶν συναγωγή (*Fragm.* 136 seq.). Further, in treating rhetoric as an art in the *Theodectea* he was forced into a conclusion, which carried him far beyond Plato's rigid notions of proof and of passion: he concluded that it is the work of an orator to use persuasion, and to arouse the passions (τὸ τὰ πάθη διαγεῖραι), *e.g.* anger and pity (*ib.* 133-134). Nor could he treat poetry as he is said to have done without the same result.

On the whole then, in his early dialectical and didactic writings, of which mere fragments remain, Aristotle had already diverged from Plato, and first of all in metaphysics. During his master's life, in the second period of his own life, he protested against the Platonic hypothesis of forms, formal numbers and the one as the good, and tended to separate metaphysics from dialectic by beginning to pass from dialogues to didactic works. After his master's death, in the third period of his own life, and during his connexion with Alexander, but before the final construction of his philosophy into a system, he was tending to write more and more in the didactic style; to separate from dialectic, not only metaphysics, but also politics, rhetoric and poetry; to admit by the side of philosophy the arts of persuasive language; to think it part of their legitimate work to rouse the passions; and in all these ways to depart from the ascetic rigidity of the philosophy of Plato, so as to prepare for the tolerant spirit of his own, and especially for his ethical doctrine that virtue consists not in suppressing but in moderating almost all human passions. In both periods, too, as we shall find in the sequel, he was already occupied in composing some of the extant writings which were afterwards to form parts of his final philosophical system. But as yet he had given no sign of system, and—what is surprising—no trace of logic. Aristotle was primarily a metaphysician against Plato; a metaphysician before he was a logician; a metaphysician who made what he called primary philosophy (πρώτη φιλοσοφία) the starting-point of his philosophical development, and ultimately of his philosophical system.

III. COMPOSITION OF HIS EXTANT WORKS

The system which was taught by Aristotle at Athens in the fourth period of his life, and which is now known as the Aristotelian philosophy, is contained not in fragments but in extant books. It will be best then to give at once a list of these extant works, following the traditional order in which they have long been arranged, and marking with a dagger (†) those which are now usually considered not to be genuine, though not always with sufficient reason.

A. LOGICAL

1. Κατηγορίαι: *Categoriae*: On simple expressions signifying different kinds of things and capable of predication [probably an early work of Aristotle, accepting species and genera as "secondary substances" in deference to Plato's teaching].

2. περὶ Ἑρμηνείας: *De interpretatione*: On language as expression of mind, and especially on the enunciation or assertion (ἀπόφανσις, ἀποφαντικὸς λόγος) [rejected by Andronicus according to Alexander; but probably an early work of Aristotle, based on Plato's analysis of the sentence into noun and verb].

3. Ἀναλυτικὰ πρότερα: *Analytica Priora*, On syllogism, with a view to demonstration.

4. Ἀναλυτικὰ ὕστερα: *Analytica Posteriora*: On demonstration, or demonstrative or scientific syllogism (ἀπόδειξις, ἀποδεικτικὸς ἢ ἐπιστημονικὸς συλλογισμός).

5. Τοπικά: *Topica*: On dialectical syllogism (διαλεκτικὸς συλλογισμός), so called from consisting mainly of commonplaces (τόποι. *loci*), or general sources of argument.

6. Σοφιστικοὶ ἔλεγχοι: *Sophistici Elenchi*: On sophistic (σοφιστικὸς) or eristic syllogism (ἐριστικὸς συλλογισμός), so called from the fallacies used by sophists in refutation (ἔλεγχος) of their opponents.

[Numbers 1-6 were afterwards grouped together as the*Organon*.]

B. PHYSICAL

1. Φυσικὴ ἀκρόασις: *Physica Auscultatio*: On Nature as cause of change, and the general principles of natural science.

2. περὶ οὐρανοῦ: *De coelo*: On astronomy, &c.

3. περὶ γενέσεως καὶ φθορᾶς: *De generatione et corruptione*: On generation and destruction in general.

4. Μετεωρολογικά: *Meteorologica*: On sublunary changes.

5. † περὶ κόσμου: *De mundo*: On the universe. [Supposed by Zeller to belong to the latter half of the 1st century B.C.]

6. περὶ ψυχῆς: *De anima*: On soul, conjoined with organic body.

7. περὶ αἰσθήσεως καὶ αἰσθητῶν: *De sensu et sensili*: On sense and objects of sense.

8. περὶ μνήμης καὶ ἀναμνήσεως: *De memoria et reminiscentia*: On memory and recollection.

9. περὶ ὕπνου καὶ ἐγρηγόρσεως: *De somno et vigilia*: On sleep and waking.

10. περὶ ἐνυπνίων: *De insomniis*: On dreams.

11. περὶ τῆς καθ᾽ ὕπνον μαντικῆς or περὶ μαντικῆς τῆς ἐν τοῖς ὕπνοις: *De divinatione per somnum*. On prophecy in sleep.

12. περὶ μακροβιότητος καὶ βραχυβιότητος: *De longitudine et brevitate vitae*: On length and shortness of life.

13. περὶ νεότητος καὶ γήρως καὶ περὶ ζωῆςκαὶ θανάτου:*De juventute et senectute et de vita et morte*: On youth and age, and on life and death.

14. περὶ ἀναπνοῆς: *De respiratione*: On respiration. [Numbers 7-14 are grouped together as Parva naturalia.]

15. † περὶ πνεύματος: *De spiritu*: On innate spirit (*spiritus vitalis*).

16. περὶ τὰ ζῷα ἱστορίαι: *Historia animalium*: Description of facts about animals, *i.e.* their organs. &c.

17. περὶ ζῴων μορίων. *De partibus animalium*: Philosophy of the causes of the facts about animals, *i.e.* their functions.

18. † περὶ ζῴων κινήσεως: *De animalium motione*: On the motion of animals. [Ascribed to the school of Theophrastus and Strato by Zeller.]

19. περὶ ζῴων πορείας: *De animalium incessu*: On the going of animals.

20. περὶ ζῴων γενέσεως: *De animalium generatione*: On the generation of animals.

21. † περὶ χρωμάτων: *De coloribus*: On colours. [Ascribed to the school of Theophrastus and Strato by Zeller.]

22. † πεςὶ ἀκουστῶν: *De audibilibus*. [Ascribed to the school of Theophrastus and Strato by Zeller.]

23. † Φυσιογνωμονικά: *Physiognomonica*: On physiognomy, and the sympathy of body and soul.

24. † περὶ φυτῶν: *De plantis*: On plants. [Not Aristotle's work on this subject.]

25. † περὶ θαυμασίων ἀκουσμάτων: *De mirabilibus ausculationibus*: On phenomena chiefly connected with natural history.

26. † Μηχανικά: *Quaestiones mechanicae*: Mechanical questions.

C. MISCELLANEOUS

1. † Προβλήματα: *Problemata*: Problems on various subjects [gradually collected by the Peripatetics from partly Aristotelian materials, according to Zeller].

2. † περὶ ἀτόμων γραμμῶν: *De insecabilibus lineis*: On indivisible lines. [Ascribed to Theophrastus, or his time, by Zeller.]

3. † ἀνέμων θέσεις καὶ προσηγορίαι: *Ventorum situs et appellationes*: A fragment on the winds.

4. † περὶ Ξενοφάνους, περὶ Ζήνωνος, περὶ Γοργίου: *De Xenophane, Zenone et Gorgia*: On Xenophanes, Zeno and Gorgias.

D. PRIMARY PHILOSOPHY OR THEOLOGY OR WISDOM

τὰ μετὰ τὰ φυσικά: *Metaphysica*: On being as being and its properties, its causes and principles, and on God as the motive motor of the world.

E. PRACTICAL

1. Ἠθικὰ Νικομάχεια: *Ethica Nicomachea*: On the good of the individual.

2. † Ἠθικὰ μεγάλα: *Magna Moralia*: On the same subject. [According to Zeller, an abstract of the *Nicomachean* and the *Eudemian Ethics*, tending to follow the latter, but possibly an early draft of the *Nicomachean Ethics*.]

3. † Ἠθικὰ Εὐδήμια or πρὸς Εὔδημον: *Ethica ad Eudemum*: On the same subject. [Usually supposed to be written by Eudemus, but possibly an early draft of the *Nicomachean Ethics*.]

4. † περὶ ἀρετῶν καὶ κακιῶν: *De virtutibus et vitiis*: On virtues and vices. [An eclectic work of the 1st century B.C., half Academic and half Peripatetic, according to Zeller.]

5. Πολιτικά: *De re publica*: Politics, on the good of the state.

6. † Οἰκονομικά: *De cura rei familiaris*: Economics, on the good of the family. [The first book a work of the school of Theophrastus or Eudemus, the second later Peripatetic, according to Zeller.]

506

F. ART

1. τέχνη Ῥητορική: *Ars rhetorica*: On the art of oratory.

2. † Ῥητορικὴ πρὸς: Ἀλέξανδρον: *Rhetorica ad Alexandrum*: On the same subject. [Ascribed to Anaximenes of Lampsacus (fl. 365, Diodorus xv. 76) by Petrus Victorius, and Spengel, but possibly an earlier rhetoric by Aristotle.]

3. περὶ Ποιητικῆς: *De poetica*: On the art of poetry [fragmentary].

G. HISTORICAL

Ἀθηναίων πολιτεία *De republica Atheniensium*: On the Constitution of Athens. [One of the Πολιτεῖαι, said to have been 158 at least, the genuineness of which is attested by the defence which Polybius (xii.) makes of Aristotle's history of the Epizephyrian Locrians against Timaeus, Aristotle's contemporary and critic. Hitherto, only fragments have come down to us (cf.*Fragm.* 381-603). The present treatise, without however its beginning and end, written on a papyrus discovered in Egypt and now in the British Museum, was first edited by F.G. Kenyon 1890-1891.] (See the article CONSTITUTION OF ATHENS.)

The Difficulty.—The genuineness of the Aristotelian works, as Leibnitz truly said (*De Stilo Phil. Nizolii*, xxx.), is ascertained by the conspicuous harmony of their theories, and by their uniform method of swift subtlety. Nevertheless difficulties lurk beneath their general unity of thought and style. In style they are not quite the same: now they are brief and now diffuse:

sometimes they are carelessly written, sometimes so carefully as to avoid hiatus, *e.g.* the *Metaphysics* A, and parts of the *De Coelo* and *Parva Naturalia*, which in this respect resemble the fragment quoted by Plutarch from the early dialogue*Eudemus* (*Fragm.* 44). They also appear to contain displacements, interpolations, prefaces such as that to the *Meteorologica*, and appendices such as that to the *Sophistical Elenchi*, which may have been added. An Aristotelian work often goes on continuously at first, and then becomes disappointing by suddenly introducing discussions which break the connexion or are even inconsistent with the beginning; as in the *Posterior Analytics*, which, after developing a theory of demonstration from necessary principles, suddenly makes the admission, which is also the main theory of science in the*Metaphysics*, that demonstration is about either the necessary or the contingent, from principles either necessary or contingent, only not accidental. At times order is followed by disorder, as in the *Politics*. Again, there are repetitions and double versions, *e.g.* those of the*Physics*, vii., and those of the *De Anima*, ii., discovered by Torstrik; or two discussions of the same subject, *e.g.* of pleasure in the*Nicomachean Ethics*, vii. and x.; or several treatises on the same subject very like one another, viz. the *Nicomachean Ethics*, the*Eudemian Ethics* and the *Magna Moralia*; or, strangest of all, a consecutive treatise and other discourses amalgamated, *e.g.* in the*Metaphysics*, where a systematic theory of being running through several books (B, Γ, E, Z, H, Θ) is preceded, interrupted and followed by other discussions of the subject. Further, there are frequently several titles of the same work or of different parts of it. Sometimes diagrams (διαγραφαί or ὑπογραφαί) are mentioned, and sometimes given (*e.g.* in *De Interp.* 13, 22 a 22; *Nicomachean Ethics*, ii. 7; *Eudemian Ethics*, ii. 3), but sometimes only implied (*e.g.*in *Hist. An.* i. 17, 497 a 32; iii. 1, 510 a 30; iv. 1, 525 a 9). The different works are more or less connected by a system of references, which give rise to difficulties, especially when they are cross-references: for example, the *Analytics* and *Topics* quote one another: so do the *Physics* and the *Metaphysics*; the *De Vita* and *De Respiratione* and the *De Partibus Animalium*; this latter treatise and the *De Animalium Incessu*; the *De Interpretatione* and the *De Anima*. A late work may quote an earlier; but how, it may be asked, can the earlier reciprocally quote the later?

Besides these difficulties in and between the works there are others beyond them. On the one hand, there is the curious story given partly by Strabo (608-609) and partly in Plutarch's *Sulla* (c. 26), that Aristotle's successor Theophrastus left the books of both to their joint pupil, Neleus of Scepsis, where they were hidden in a cellar, till in Sulla's time they were sold to Apellicon, who made new copies, transferred after Apellicon's death by Sulla to Rome, and there edited and published by Tyrannio and Andronicus. On the other hand, there are the curious and puzzling catalogues of Aristotelian books, one given by Diogenes Laertius, another by an anonymous commentator (perhaps Hesychius of Miletus) quoted in the notes of Gilles Ménage on Diogenes Laertius, and known as "Anonymus Menagii," and a third copied by two Arabian writers from Ptolemy, perhaps King Ptolemy Philadelphus, son of the founder of the library at Alexandria. (See Rose, *Fragm.* pp. 1-22.) But the extraordinary thing is that, without exactly agreeing among themselves, the catalogues give titles which do not agree well with the Aristotelian works as we have them. A title in some cases suits a given work or a part of it; but in other cases there are no titles for works which exist, or titles for works which do not exist.

These difficulties are complicated by various hypotheses concerning the composition of the Aristotelian works. Zeller supposes that, though Aristotle may have made preparations for his philosophical system beforehand, still the properly didactic treatises composing it almost all belong to the last period of his life, *i.e.* from 335-334 to 322; and from the references of one work to another Zeller has further suggested a chronological order of composition during this period of twelve years, beginning with the treatises on Logic and Physics, and ending with that on Metaphysics. There is a further hypothesis that the Aristotelian works were not originally treatises, but notes of lectures either for or by his pupils. This easily passes into the further and still more sceptical hypothesis that the works, as we have them, under Aristotle's name, are rather the works of the Peripatetic school, from Aristotle, Theophrastus and Eudemus downwards. "We cannot assert with certainty," says R. Shute in his *History of the Aristotelian Writings* (p. 176), "that we have even got throughout a treatise in the exact words of Aristotle, though we may be pretty clear that we have a fair representation of his thought. The unity of style observable may belong quite as much to the school and the method as to the individual." This sceptical conclusion, the contrary of that drawn by Leibnitz from the harmony of thought and style pervading the works, shows us that the Homeric question has been followed by the Aristotelian question.

The Solution.—Such hypotheses attend to Aristotle's philosophy to the neglect of his life. He was really, as we have seen, a prolific writer from the time when he was a young man under Plato's guidance at Athens; beginning with dialogues in the manner of his master, but afterwards preferring to write didactic works during the prime of his own life between thirty-eight and fifty

(347-335-334), and with the further advantage of leisure at Atarneus and Mitylene, in Macedonia and at home in Stagira. When at fifty he returned to Athens, as head of the Peripatetic school, he no doubt wrote much of his extant philosophy during the twelve remaining years of his life (335-322). But he was then a busy teacher, was growing old, and suffered from a disease in the stomach for a considerable time before it proved fatal at the age of sixty-three. It is therefore improbable that he could between fifty and sixty-three have written almost the whole of the many books on many subjects constituting that grand philosophical system which is one of the most wonderful works of man. It is far more probable that he was previously composing them at his leisure and in the vigour of manhood, precisely as his contemporary Demosthenes composed all his great speeches except the *De Corona* before he was fifty.

Turning to Aristotle's own works, we immediately light upon a surprise: Aristotle began his extant scientific works during Plato's lifetime. By a curious coincidence, in two different works he mentions two different events as contemporary with the time of writing, one in 357 and the other in 356. In the *Politics* (E 10, 1312 b 10), he mentions as now (νῦν) Dion's expedition to Sicily which occurred in 357. In the *Meteorologica* (iii. 1, 371 a 30), he mentions as now (νῦν) the burning of the temple at Ephesus, which occurred in 356. To save his hypothesis of late composition, Zeller resorts to the vagueness of the word "now" (νῦν). But Aristotle is graphically describing isolated events, and could hardly speak of events of 357 and 356 as happening "now" in or near 335. Moreover, these two works contain further proofs that they were both begun earlier than this 507date. The *Politics* (B 10) mentions as having happened lately (νεωστί) the expedition of Phalaecus to Crete, which occurred towards the end of the Sacred War in 346. The *Meteorologica* (Γ 7) mentions the comet of 341. It is true that the *Politics* also mentions much later events, *e.g.* the assassination of Philip which took place in 336 (E 10, 1311 b 1-3). Indeed, the whole truth about this great work is that it remained unfinished at Aristotle's death. But what of that? The logical conclusion is that Aristotle began writing it as early as 357, and continued writing it in 346, in 336, and so on till he died. Similarly, he began the *Meteorologica* as early as 356 and was still writing it in 341. Both books were commenced some years before Plato's death: both were works of many years: both were destined to form parts of the Aristotelian system of philosophy. It follows that Aristotle, from early manhood, not only wrote dialogues and didactic works, surviving only in fragments, but also began some of the philosophical works which are still parts of his extant writings. He continued these and no doubt began others during the prime of his life. Having thus slowly matured his separate writings, he was the better able to combine them more and more into a system, in his last years. No doubt, however, he went on writing and rewriting well into the last period of his life; for example, the recently discovered Ἀθηναίων πολιτεία mentions on the one hand (c. 54) the archonship of Cephisophon (329-328), on the other hand (c. 46) triremes and quadriremes but without quinqueremes, which first appeared at Athens in 325-324; and as it mentions nothing later it probably received its final touches between 320 and 324. But it may have been begun long before, and received additions and changes. However early Aristotle began a book, so long as he kept the manuscript, he could always change it. Finally he died without completing some of his works, such as the *Politics*, and notably that work of his whole philosophic career and foundation of his whole philosophy—the *Metaphysics*—which, projected in his early criticism of Plato's philosophy of universal forms, gradually developed into his positive philosophy of individual substances, but remained unfinished after all.

On the whole, then, Aristotle was writing his extant works very gradually for some thirty-five years (357-322), like Herodotus (iv. 30) contemplated additions, continued writing them more or less together, not so much successively as simultaneously, and had not finished writing at his death.

There is a curious characteristic connected with this gradual composition. An Aristotelian treatise frequently has the appearance of being a collection of smaller discourses (λόγοι), as, *e.g.*, K.L. Michelet has remarked.

This is obvious enough in the *Metaphysics*: it has two openings (Books A and α); then comes a nearly consecutive theory of being (B, Γ, E, Z, H, Θ), but interrupted by a philosophical lexicon Δ; afterwards follows a theory of unity (I); then a summary of previous books and of doctrines from the *Physics* (K); next a new beginning about being, and, what is wanted to complete the system, a theory of God in relation to the world (Λ); finally a criticism of mathematical metaphysics (M, N), in which the argument against Plato (A 9) is repeated almost word for word (M 4-5). The *Metaphysics* is clearly a compilation formed from essays or discourses; and it illustrates another characteristic of Aristotle's gradual method of composition. It refers back to passages "in the first discourses" (ἐν τοῖς πρώτοις λόγοις) —an expression not uncommon in Aristotelian writings. Sometimes the reference is to the beginning of the whole treatise; *e.g. Met.* B 2, 997 b 3-5, referring back to A 6 and 9 about Platonic forms. Sometimes, on

100

the other hand, the reference only goes back to a previous part of a given topic, *e.g. Met.* Θ 1, 1045 b 27-32, referring back to Z 1, or at the earliest to Γ 2. On either alternative, however, "the first discourses" mentioned may have originally been a separate discourse; for Book Γ begins quite fresh with the definition of the science of being, long afterwards called "Metaphysics," and Book Z begins Aristotle's fundamental doctrine of substance.

Another indication of a treatise having arisen out of separate discourses is its consisting of different parts imperfectly connected. Thus the *Nicomachean Ethics* begins by identifying the good with happiness (εὐδαιμονία), and happiness with virtuous action. But when it comes to the moral virtues (Book iii. 6), a new motive of the "honourable" (τοῦ καλοῦ ἕνεκα) is suddenly introduced without preparation, where one would expect the original motive of happiness. Then at the end of the moral virtues justice is treated at inordinate length, and in a different manner from the others, which are regarded as means between two vices, whereas justice appears as a mean only because it is of the middle between too much and too little. Later, the discussion on friendship (Books viii.-ix.) is again inordinate in length, and it stands alone. Lastly, pleasure, after having been first defined (Book vii.) as an activity, is treated over again (Book x.) as an end beyond activity, with a warning against confusing activity and pleasure. The probability is that the *Nicomachean Ethics* is a collection of separate discourses worked up into a tolerably systematic treatise; and the interesting point is that these discourses correspond to separate titles in the list of Diogenes Laertius (περὶ καλοῦ, περὶ δικαίων, περὶ φιλίας, περὶ ἡδονῆς, and περὶ ἡδονῶν). The same list also refers to tentative notes (ὑπομνήματα ἐπιχειρηματικά), and the commentators speak of ethical notes (ἠθικὰ ὑπομνήματα). Indeed, they sometimes divide Aristotle's works into notes (ὑπομνηματικά) and compilations (συνταγματικά). How can it be doubted that in the gradual composition of his works Aristotle began with notes (ὑπομνήματα) and discourses (λόγοι), and proceeded to treatises (πραγματεῖαι)? He would even be drawn into this process by his writing materials, which were papyrus rolls of some magnitude; he would tend to write discourses on separate rolls, and then fasten them together in a bundle into a treatise.

If then Aristotle was for some thirty-five years gradually and simultaneously composing manuscript discourses into treatises and treatises into a system, he was pursuing a process which solves beforehand the very difficulties which have since been found in his writings. He could very easily write in different styles at different times, now avoiding hiatus and now not, sometimes writing diffusely and sometimes briefly, partly polishing and partly leaving in the rough, according to the subject, his own state of health or humour, his age, and the degree to which he had developed a given topic; and all this even in the same manuscript as well as in different manuscripts, so that a difference of style between different parts of a work or between different works, explicable by one being earlier than another, does not prove either to be not genuine. As he might write, so might he think differently in his long career. To put one extreme case, about the soul he could think at first in the *Eudemus* like Plato that it is imprisoned in the body, and long afterwards in the *De Anima* like himself that it is the immateriate essence of the material bodily organism. Again, he might be inconsistent; now, for example, calling a universal a substance in deference to Plato, and now denying that a universal can be a substance in consequence of his own doctrine that every substance is an individual; and so as to contradict himself in the same treatise, though not in the same breath or at the same moment of thinking. Again, in developing his discourses into larger treatises he might fall into dislocations; although it must be remembered that these are often inventions of critics who do not understand the argument, as when they make out that the treatment of reciprocal justice in the *Ethics* (v. 5-6) needs rearrangement through their not noticing that, according to Aristotle, reciprocal justice, being the fairness of a commercial bargain, is not part of absolute or political justice, but is part of analogical or economical justice. Or he might make repetitions, as in the same book, where he twice applies the principle, that so far as the agent does the patient suffers, first to the corrective justice of the law court (*Eth.* v. 4) in order to prove that in a wrong the injurer gains as much as the injured loses, and immediately afterwards to the reciprocal justice of commerce (*ib.* 5) in order to prove that in a bargain a house must be exchanged for as many shoes as equal it in value. Or he might himself, without double versions, repeat the same argument with a different shade of meaning; as when in the *Nic. Ethics* (vii. 4) he first argues that incontinence 508 about such natural pleasures as that of gain is only modified incontinence, a sign (as *causa cognoscendi*) of which is that it is not so bad as incontinence about carnal pleasures, and then argues that, because (as *causa essendi*) it is only modified incontinence, therefore it is not so bad. Or he might return again and again to the same point with a difference: there is a good instance in his conclusion that the speculative life is the highest happiness; which he first infers because it is the life of man's highest and divine faculty, intelligence (1176 b-1178 a 8), then after an interval infers a second time because our speculative life is an imitation of that of God (1178 b 7-32), and finally after another interval infers a third time, because it will make man most dear to God (1179 a 22-32). Or, extending himself as it were still more, he might write two drafts, or double versions of his own, on the same subject; *e.g. Physics*, vii. and *De Anima*, ii. Or he might, going still further, in his long literary career write two or more treatises on the same subject, different and even more or less inconsistent with each other, as we shall find in the sequel. Finally, having a great number of discourses and treatises, containing all those small blemishes, around him in his library, and determined to collect, consolidate and connect them into a philosophical system, he would naturally be often taking them down from their places to consult and compare one with another, and as naturally enter in them references one to the other, and cross-references between one another. Thus he would enter in the *Metaphysics* a reference to the *Physics*, and in the *Physics* a reference to the *Metaphysics*, precisely because both were manuscripts in his library. For the same purpose of connexion he would be tempted to add a preface to a book like the *Meteorologica*. In order to refer back to the *Physics*, the *De Coelo*, and the *De Generatione*, this work begins by stating that the first causes of all nature and all natural motion, the stars ordered according to celestial motion and the bodily elements with their transmutations, and generation and corruption have all been discussed; and by adding that there remains to complete this investigation, what previous investigators called meteorology. To suppose this preface, presupposing many sciences, to have been written in 356, when the *Meteorologica* had been already commenced, would be absurd; but equally absurd would it be to reject that date on account of the preface, which even a modern author often writes long after his book. Nor is it at all absurd to suppose that, long after he began the *Meteorologica*, Aristotle himself added the preface in the process of gathering his general treatises on natural science into a system. So he might afterwards add the preface to the *De Interpretatione*, in order to connect it with the *De Anima*, though written afterwards, in order to connect his treatises on mind and on its expression. So also he might add the appendix to the *Sophistical Elenchi*, long after he had written that book, and perhaps, to judge from its being a general claim to have discovered the syllogism, when the founder of logic had more or less realized that he had written a number of connected treatises on reasoning.

The Question of Publication.—There is still another point which would facilitate Aristotle's gradual composition of discourses into treatises and treatises into a system; there was no occasion for him to publish his manuscripts beyond his school. Printing has accustomed us to publication, and misled us into applying to ancient times the modern method of bringing out one book after another at definite dates by the same author. But Greek authors contemplated works rather than books. Some of the greatest authors were not even writers: Homer, Aesop, Thales, Socrates. Some who were writers were driven to publish by the occasion; and after the orders of government, which were occasionally published to be obeyed, occasional poems, such as the poems of Solon, the odes of Pindar and the plays of the dramatists, which all had a political significance, were probably the first writings to be published or, rather, recited and acted, from written copies. With them came philosophical poems, such as those of Xenophanes and Empedocles; the epical history of Herodotus; the dramatic philosophy of Plato. On a larger scale speeches written by orators to be delivered by litigants were published and encouraged publication; and, as the Attic orators were his contemporaries, publication had become pretty common in the time of Aristotle, who speaks of many bundles (δέσμας) of judicial speeches by Isocrates being hawked about by the booksellers (*Fragm.* 140).

No doubt then Aristotle's library contained published copies of the works of other authors, as well as the autographs of his own. It does not follow that his own works went beyond his library and his school. Publication to the world is designed for readers, who at all times have demanded popular literature rather than serious philosophy such as that of Aristotle. Accordingly it becomes a difficult question, how far Aristotle's works were published in his lifetime. In answering it we must be careful to exclude any evidence which refers to Aristotle as a man, not as a writer, or refers to him as a writer but does not prove publication while he was alive.

Beginning then with his early writings, which are now lost, the dialogues *On Poetry* and the *Eudemus* were probably the published discourses to which Aristotle himself refers (*Poetics*, 15; *De Anima*, i. 4); and the dialogue *Protrepticus* was known to the Cynic Crates, pupil of Diogenes and master of Zeno (*Fragm.* 50), but not necessarily in Aristotle's lifetime, as Crates was still alive in 307. Again, Aristotle's early rhetorical instructions and perhaps writings, as well as his opinion that a collection of proverbs is not worth while, must have been known outside Aristotle's rhetorical school to the orator Cephisodorus, pupil of Isocrates and master of Demosthenes, for him to be able to write in his *Replies to Aristotle* (ἐν ταῖς πρὸς Ἀριστοτέλην ἀντιγραφαῖς) an admired defence of Isocrates (Dionys. H. *De Isoc.* 18). But this early dialectic and rhetoric, being popular, would tend to be published. History comes nearer to philosophy; and Aristotle's *Constitutions* were known to his enemy Timaeus, who attacked him for disparaging the descent of the Locrians of Italy, according to Polybius (xii.), who defended Aristotle. But as

Timaeus brought his history down to 264 B.C. (Polyb. i. 5), and therefore might have got his information after Aristotle's death, we cannot be sure that any of the *Constitutions* were published in the author's lifetime. We are equally at a loss to prove that Aristotle published his philosophy. He had, like all the great, many enemies, personal and philosophical; but in his lifetime they attacked the man, not his philosophy. In the Megarian school, first Eubulides quarrelled with him and calumniated him (Diog. Laert. ii. 109) in his lifetime; but the attack was on his life, not on his writings: afterwards Stilpo wrote a dialogue (Ἀριστοτέλης]), which may have been a criticism of the Aristotelian philosophy from the Megarian point of view; but he outlived Aristotle thirty years. In the absence of any confirmation, "the current philosophemata" (τὰ ἐγκύκλια φιλοσοφήματα), mentioned in the *De Coela* (i. 9, 279 a 30), are sometimes supposed to be Aristotle's published philosophy, to which he is referring his readers. But the example there given, that the divine is unchangeable, is precisely such a religious commonplace as might easily be a current philosopheme of Aristotle's day, not of Aristotle; and this interpretation suits the parallel passage in the *Nic. Ethics* (i. 5, 1096 a 3) where opinions about the happiness of political life are said to have been sufficiently treated "even in current discussions" (καὶ ἐν τοῖς ἐγκυκλίοις).

There is therefore no contemporary proof that Aristotle published any part of his mature philosophical system in his lifetime. It is true that a book of Andronicus, as reported by Aulus Gellius (xx. 5), contained a correspondence between Alexander and Aristotle in which the pupil complained that his master had published his "acroatic discourses" (τοὺς ἀκροατικοὺς τῶν λόγων). But ancient letters are proverbially forgeries, and in the three hundred years which elapsed between the supposed correspondence and the time of Andronicus there was plenty of time for the forgery of these letters. But even if the correspondence is genuine, "acroatic discourses" must be taken to mean what Alexander would mean by them in the time of Aristotle, and not what they had come to mean by the time of Andronicus. Alexander meant those discourses which Aristotle, when he was his tutor, intended for the ears of himself and his fellow-pupils; such as the early political works on *Monarchy* and on *Colonies*, and the early rhetorical works, the *Theodectea*, the *Collection of Arts*, 509and possibly the *Rhetoric to Alexander*, in the preface to which the writer actually says to Alexander: "You wrote to me that nobody else should receive this book." These few early works may have been published, and contrary to the wishes of Alexander, without affecting Aristotle's later system. But even so, Alexander's complaint would not justify writers three centuries later in taking Alexander to have referred to mature scientific writings, which were not addressed, and not much known, to him, the conqueror of Asia; although by the times of Andronicus and Aulus Gellius, Aristotle's scientific writings were all called acroatic, or acroamatic, or sometimes esoteric, in distinction from exoteric—a distinction altogether unknown to Aristotle, and therefore to Alexander. In the absence of any contemporary evidence, we cannot believe that Aristotle in his lifetime published any, much less all, of his scientific books. The conclusion then is that Aristotle on the one hand to some extent published his early dialectical and rhetorical writings, because they were popular, though now they are lost, but on the other hand did not publish any of the extant historical and philosophical works which belong to his mature system, because they were best adapted to his philosophical pupils in the Peripatetic school. The object of the philosopher was not the applause of the public but the truth of things. Now this conclusion has an important bearing on the composition of Aristotle's writings and on the difficulties which have been found in them. If he had like a modern author brought out each of his extant philosophical works on a definite day of publication, he would not have been able to change them without a second edition, which in the case of serious writings so little in demand would not be worth while. But as he did not publish them, but kept the unpublished manuscripts together in his library and used them in his school, he was able to do with them as he pleased down to the very end of his life, and so gradually to consolidate his many works into one system.

While Aristotle did not publish his philosophical works to the world, he freely communicated them to the Peripatetic school. They are not mere lectures; but he used them for lectures: he allowed his pupils to read them in his library, and probably to take copies from them. He also used diagrams, which are sometimes incorporated in his works, but sometimes are only mentioned, and were no doubt used for purposes of teaching. He also availed himself of his pupils' co-operation, as we may judge from his description in the *Ethics* (x. 7) of the speculative philosopher who, though he is self-sufficing, is better having co-operators (συνεργοὺς ἔχων). From an early time he had a tendency to address his writings to his friends. For example, he addressed the *Theodectea* to his pupil Theodectes; and even in ancient times a doubt arose whether it was a work of the master or the pupil. It was certainly by Aristotle, because it contained the triple grammatical division of words into noun, verb and conjunction, which the history of grammar recognized as his discovery. But we may explain the share of Theodectes by supposing that he had a hand in the work (cf. Dionys. H. *De Comp. Verb.* 2; Quintilian i. 4. 18). Similarly in astronomy, Aristotle used the assistance of Eudoxus and Callippus. Indeed, throughout his writings he shows a constant wish to avail himself of what is true in the opinions of others, whether they are philosophers, or poets or ordinary people expressing their thoughts in sayings and proverbs. With one of his pupils in particular, Theophrastus, who was born about 370 and therefore was some fifteen years younger than himself, he had a long and intimate connexion; and the work of the pupil bears so close a resemblance to that of his master, that, even when he questions Aristotle's opinions (as he often does), he seems to be writing in an Aristotelian atmosphere; while he shows the same acuteness in raising difficulties, and has caught something of the same encyclopaedic genius. Another pupil, Eudemus of Rhodes, wrote and thought so like his master as to induce Simplicius to call him the most genuine of Aristotle's companions (ὁ γνησιώτατος τῶν Ἀριστοτέλους ἑταίρων). It is probable that this extraordinary resemblance is due to the pupils having actually assisted their master; and this supposition enables us to surmount a difficulty we feel in reading Aristotle's works. How otherwise, we wonder, could one man writing alone and with so few predecessors compose the first systematic treatises on the psychology of the mental powers and on the logic of reasoning, the first natural history of animals, and the first civil history of one hundred and fifty-eight constitutions, in addition to authoritative treatises on metaphysics, biology, ethics, politics, rhetoric and poetry; in all penetrating to the very essence of the subject, and, what is most wonderful, describing more facts than any other man has ever done on so many subjects?

The Uncompleted Works.—Such then was the method of composition by which Aristotle began in early manhood to write his philosophical works, continued them gradually and simultaneously, combined shorter discourses into longer treatises, compared and connected them, kept them together in his library without publishing them, communicated them to his school, used the co-operation of his best pupils, and finally succeeded in combining many mature writings into one harmonious system. Nevertheless, being a man, he did not quite succeed. He left some unfinished; such as the *Categories*, in which the main part on categories is not finished, while the last part, afterwards called postpredicaments, is probably not his, the *Politics*and the *Poetics*. He left others imperfectly arranged, and some of the most important, the *Metaphysics*, the *Politics* and the logical writings. Of the imperfect arrangement of the *Metaphysics* we have already spoken; and we shall speak of that of his logical writings when we come to the order of his whole system. At present the *Politics* will supply us with a conspicuous example of the imperfect arrangement of some, as well as of the gradual composition of all, of Aristotle's extant writings.

The *Politics* was begun as early as 357, yet not finished in 322. It betrays its origin from separate discourses. First comes a general theory of constitutions, right and wrong (Books A, B, Γ); and this part is afterwards referred to as "the first discourses" (ἐν τοῖς πρώτοις λόγοις). Then follows the treatment of oligarchy, democracy, commonwealth and tyranny, and of the various powers of government (Δ), and independent investigation of revolution, and of the means of preserving states (E), and a further treatment of democracy and oligarchy, and of the different offices of the state (Z), and finally a return to the discussion of the right form of constitution (H, Θ). But Δ and Z are a group interrupted by E, and H and Θ are another group unconnected with the previous group and with E, and are also distinguished in style by avoiding hiatus. Further, the group (Δ, Z) and the group (H, Θ) are both unfinished. Finally the group (Δ, Z), the book (E) and the group (H, Θ) though unconnected with one another, are all connected though imperfectly with "the first discourses" (A, B, Γ). This complicated arrangement may be represented in the following diagram:—

The simplest explanation is that Aristotle began by writing separate discourses, four at least, on political subjects; that he continued to write them and perhaps tried to combine them: but that in the end he failed and left the *Politics* unfinished and in disorder. But modern commentators, possessed by the fallacy that Aristotle like a modern author must from the first have comtemplated a whole treatise in a regular order for definite publication, lose themselves in vain disputes as to whether to go by the traditional order of books indicated by their letters and known to have existed as early as the abstract (given in Stobaeus, *Ecl.* ii. 7) ascribed to Didymus (1st century A.D.), or to put the group H, Θ, as more connected with A, B, Γ, before the group Δ, Z, and this group before the book H. It is agreed, says Zeller, that the traditional order contradicts the original plan. But what right have we to say that Aristotle had an original plan?

The incomplete state in which Aristotle left the *Metaphysics*, the*Politics* and his logical works, brings us to the hard question how much he did, and how much his Peripatetic followers did 510to his writings after his death. To answer it we should have to go far beyond Aristotle. But two corollaries follow from our present investigation of his extant writings; the first, that it was the long continuance of the Peripatetic school which gradually caused the publication, and in some cases the forgery, of the separate writings; and the second, that his Peripatetic successors arranged and edited some of Aristotle's writings, and gradually arrived by the time of Andronicus, the eleventh from Aristotle, at an order of the whole body of writings forming the system. Now, it is probable that the arrangement of the works which we are considering was done by the Peripatetic successors of Aristotle. There is nothing indeed in the *Metaphysics* to show whether he left it in isolated treatises or in its present disorder; and nothing in the*Politics*. On the other hand, in the case of logic, it is certain that he did not combine his works on the subject into one whole, but that the Peripatetics afterwards put them together as organic, and made them the parts of logic as an organon, as they are treated by Andronicus. Perhaps something similar occurred to the *Metaphysics*, as Alexander imputed its redaction to Eudemus, and the majority of ancient commentators attributed its second opening (Book α) to Pasicles, nephew of Eudemus. Again, it is not unlikely that the *Politics* was arranged in the traditional order of books by Theophrastus, and that this is the meaning of the curious title occurring in the list of Aristotle's works as given by Diogenes Laertius, πολιτικῆς ἀκροάσεως ὡς ἡ Θεοφράστου α΄β΄γ΄δ΄ε΄ς΄ζ΄η΄, which agrees with the *Politics* in having eight books. Although, however, we may concede that such great works as the *Metaphysics*, the *Politics* and the logical writings did not receive their present form from Aristotle himself, that concession does not deprive Aristotle of the authorship, but only of the arrangement of those works. On the contrary, Theophrastus and Eudemus, his immediate followers, both wrote works presupposing Aristotle's *Metaphysics* and his logical works, and Dicaearchus, their contemporary, used his *Politics* for his own *Tripoliticus*. It was Aristotle himself then who wrote these works, whether he arranged them or not; and if he wrote the incomplete works, then *a fortiori* he wrote the completed works except those which are proved spurious, and practically consummated the Aristotelian system, which, as Leibnitz said, by its unity of thought and style evinces its own genuineness and individuality. We must not exaggerate the school and underrate the individual, especially such an individual. What he mainly wanted was the time, the leisure and the labour, which we have supposed to have been given to the gradual composition of the extant Aristotelian writings. Aristotle, asked where dwell the Muses, answered, "In the souls of those who love work."

IV. EARLIER AND LATER WRITINGS

Aristotle's quotations of his other books and of historical facts only inform us at best of the dates of isolated passages, and cannot decide the dates and sequences of whole philosophical books which occupied him for many years. Is there then any way of discriminating between early and late works? There is the evidence of the influences under which the books were written. This evidence applies to the whole Aristotelian literature including the fragments. As to the fragments, we are safe in saying that the early dialogues in the manner of Plato were written under the influence of Plato, and that the subsequent didactic writings connected with Alexander were written more under the influence of Philip and Alexander. Turning to the extant writings, we find that some are more under the influence of Plato, while others are more original and Aristotelian. Also some writings are more rudimentary than others on the same subject; and some have the appearance of being first drafts of others. By these differences we can do something to distinguish between earlier and later philosophical works; and also vindicate as genuine some works, which have been considered spurious because they do not agree in style or in matter with his most mature philosophy. In thirty-five years of literary composition, Aristotle had plenty of time to change, because any man can differ from himself at different times.

On these principles, we regard as early genuine philosophical works of Aristotle, (1) the *Categories*, (2) the *De Interpretatione*;(3) the*Eudemian Ethics* and *Magna Moralia*; (4) the *Rhetoric to Alexander*.

1. The Categories (κατηγορίαι).—This short discourse turns on Aristotle's fundamental doctrine of individual substances, without which there is nothing. He arrives at it from a classification of categories, by which he here means "things stated in no combination" (τὰ κατὰ μηδεμίαν συμπλοκὴν λεγόμενα) or what we should call "names," capable of becoming predicates (κατηγορούμενα κατηγορίαι). "Every name," says he (chap. 4), "signifies either substance or something quantitative, or qualitative, or relative, or somewhere, or sometimes, or that it is in a position, or in a condition, or active or passive." He immediately adds that, by the combination of these names with one another, affirmation or negation arises. The categories then are names signifying things capable of becoming predicates in a proposition. Next he proceeds to substances (οὐσίαι), which he divides into primary (πρῶται) and secondary (δεύτεραι). "Substance", says he (chap. 5), "which is properly, primarily and especially so called, is that which

is neither a predicate of a subject nor inherent in a subject; for example, a particular man, or a particular horse. Secondary substances so called are the species in which are the primarily called substances, and the genera of these species: for example, a particular man is in a species, man, the genus of which is animal: these then are called secondary substances, man and animal." Having made these subdivisions of substance, he thereupon reduces secondary substances and all the rest of the categories to belongings of individual or primary substances. "All other things", says he, "are either predicates of primary substances as subjects" (καθ᾿ ὑποκειμένων τῶν πρώτων οὐσιῶν) "or inherent in them as subjects" (ἐν ὑποκειμέναις αὐταῖς). He explains that species and genus are predicates of, and that other categories (e.g. the quality of colour) are inherent in, some individual substance such as a particular man. Then follows his conclusion: "without primary substances it is impossible for anything to be" (μὴ οὐσῶν οὖν τῶν πρώτων οὐσιῶν τῶν ἄλλων τι εἶναι. Cat. 5, 2 b 5-6).

Things are individual substances, without which there is nothing—this is the fundamental point of Aristotelianism, as against Platonism, of which the fundamental point is that things are universal forms without which there becomes nothing. The world, according to Aristotle, consists of substances, each of which is a separate individual, this man, this horse, this animal, this plant, this earth, this water, this air, this fire; in the heavens that moon, that sun, those stars; above all, God. On the other hand, a universal species or genus of substances is a predicate which, as well as everything else in all the other categories, always belongs to some individual substance or other as subject, and has no separate being. In full, then, a substance is a separate individual, having universals, and things in all other categories, inseparably belonging to it. The individual substance Socrates, for example, is a man and an animal (οὐσία), tall, (ποσόν), white (ποιόν), a husband (πρός τι), in the market (ποῦ), yesterday (πότε), sitting (κεῖσθαι), armed (ἔχειν), talking (ποιεῖν), listening (πάσχειν). Aristotelianism is this philosophy of substantial things.

The doctrine that all things are substances which are separate individuals, stated in the *Categories*, is expanded in the *Metaphysics*. Both works arrive at it from the classification of categories, which is the same in both; except that in the former the categories are treated rather as a logical classification of names signifying things, in the latter rather as a metaphysical classification of things. In neither, however, are they a grammatical classification of words by their structure; and in neither are they a psychological classification of notions or general conceptions (νοήματα), such as they afterwards became in Kant's *Critique* and the post-Kantian idealism. Moreover, even in the *Categories* as names signifying distinct things they imply distinct things; and hence the *Categories*, as well as the *Metaphysics*, draws the metaphysical conclusion that individual substances are the things without which there is nothing else, and thereby lays the positive foundation of the philosophy running through all the extant Aristotelian writings.

Again, according to both works, an individual substance is a 511 subject, a universal its predicate; and they have in common the Aristotelian metaphysics, which differs greatly from the modern logic of subject and predicate. Subject (ὑποκείμενον) originally meant a real thing which is the basis of something, and was used by Aristotle both for a thing to which something belongs and for a name of which another is asserted: accordingly "predicate" (κατηγορούμενον) came with him to mean something really belonging (ὑπάρχον) to a substance as real subject, as well as a name capable of being asserted of a name as a nominal subject. In other words, to him subject meant real as well as nominal subject, and predicate meant real as well as nominal predicate; whereas modern logic has gradually reduced both to the nominal terms of a proposition. Accordingly, when he said that a substance is a subject, he meant a real subject; and when he said that a universal species or genus is a predicate, he meant that it is a real predicate belonging to a real subject, which is always some individual substance of the kind. It follows that Aristotelianism in the *Categories* and in the *Metaphysics* is a realism both of individuals and of universals; of individual substances as real subjects, and of universals as real predicates.

Lastly, the two works agree in reducing the *Categories* to substance and its belongings (ὑπάρχοντα). According to both, it is always some substance, such as Socrates, which is quantitative, qualitative, relative, somewhere, some time, placed, conditioned, active, passive; so that all things in all other categories are attributes which are belongings of substances. There are therefore two kinds of belongings, universals and attributes; and in both cases belonging in the sense of having no being but the being of the substance.

In brief then the common ground of the *Categories* and the *Metaphysics* is the fundamental position that all things are substances having belonging to them universals and attributes, which have no separate being as Plato falsely supposed.

This essential agreement suffices to show that the *Categories* and the *Metaphysics* are the result of one mind. Nevertheless, there is a deep difference between them in detail, which may be expressed by saying that the *Categories* is nearer to Platonism. We have seen how anxious Aristotle was to be considered one of the Platonists, how reluctant he was to depart from Plato's hypothesis of forms, and how, in denying the separability, he retained the Platonic belief in the reality and even in the unity of the universal. We have now to see that, in writing the *Categories*, on the one hand he carried his differences from his master further than he had done in his early criticisms by insisting that individual substances are not only real, but are the very things which sustain the universal; but on the other hand, he clung to further relics of the Platonic theory, and it is those which differentiate the *Categories* and the *Metaphysics*.

In the first place, in the *Categories* the belonging of things in other categories to individual substances in the first category is not so well developed. A distinction (chap. 2) is drawn between things which are predicates of a subject (καθ᾽ ὑποκείμενον) and things which inhere in a subject (ἐν ὑποκειμένῳ); and, while universals are called predicates of a subject, things in a subordinate category, *i.e.* attributes such as colour (χρῶμα) in the qualitative, are said to inhere in a subject. It is true that the work gives only a negative definition of the inherent, namely, that it does not inhere as a part and cannot exist apart from that in which it inheres (1 a 24-25), and it admits that what is inherent may sometimes also be a predicate (chap. 5, 2 a 27-34). The commentators explain this to mean that an attribute as individual is inherent, as universal is a predicate. But even so the *Categories* concludes that everything is either a predicate of, or inherent in, a substance; and the view that this colour belongs to this substance only in the sense of being in it, not of it, leaves the impression that, like a Platonic form, it is an entity rather in than of an individual substance, though even in the *Categories* Aristotle is careful to deny its separability. The hypothesis of inherence gives an inadequate account of the dependence of an attribute on a substance, and is a kind of half-way house between separation and predication.

On the other hand, in the *Metaphysics*, the distinction between inherence and predication disappears; and what is more, the relation of an attribute to a substance is regarded as so close that an attribute is merely the substance modified. "The thing itself and the thing affected," says Aristotle, "are in a way the same; *e.g.* Socrates and Socrates musical" (*Met.* Δ 29, 1024 b 30-31). Consequently, all attributes, as well as universals, belong as predicates of individual substances as subjects, according to the *Metaphysics*, and also according to the most authoritative works of Aristotle, such as the *Posterior Analytics*, where (cf. i. 4, 22) an attribute (συμβεβηκός) is said to be only by being the substance possessing it, and any separation of an attribute from a substance is held to be entirely a work of human abstraction (ἀφαίρεσις). At this point, Plato and Aristotle have become very far apart: to the master beauty appears to be an independent thing, and really separate, to the pupil at his best only something beautiful, an attribute which is only mentally separable from an individual substance. The first difference then between the *Categories* and the *Metaphysics* is in the nature of an attribute; and the theory of inherence in the *Categories* is nearer to Plato and more rudimentary than the theory of predication in the *Metaphysics*. The second difference is still nearer to Plato and more rudimentary, and is in the nature of substance. For though both works rest on the reality of individual substances, the *Categories* (chap. 5) admits that universal species and genera can be called substances, whereas the *Metaphysics* (Z 13) denies that a universal can be a substance at all.

It is evident that in the category of substance, as Aristotle perceived, substance is predicate of substance, *e.g.* Socrates (οὐσία) is a man (οὐσία), and an animal (οὐσία). The question then arises, what sort of substance can be predicate; and in the *Categories* Aristotle gave an answer, which would have been impossible, if he had not, under Plato's influence, accepted both the unity and the substantiality of the universal. What he said in consequence was that the substance in the predicate is not an individual substance, *e.g.* this man or this animal, because such a primary substance is not a predicate; but that the species man or the genus animal is the substance which is the predicate of Socrates the subject (*Cat.* 5, 3 a 36 seq.). Finding then that substances are real predicates, and supposing that in that case they must be species or genera, he could not avoid the conclusion that some substances are species or genera, which were therefore called by him "secondary substances," and by his Latin followers *substantiae universales*. It is true that this conclusion gave him some misgivings, because he recognized that it is a characteristic of a substance to signify an individual (τόδε τι), which a species or a genus does not signify (*ib.* 5, 3 b 10-21). Nevertheless, in the *Categories*, he did not venture to deny that in the category of substance a universal species (*e.g.* man), or genus (*e.g.* animal), is itself a substance. On the other hand, in the *Metaphysics* (Z 13), he distinctly denies that any universal can be a substance, on the ground that a substance is a subject, whereas a universal is a predicate and a belonging of a subject, from which it follows as he says that no universal is a substance, and no substance universal. Here again the *Categories* forms a kind of transition from Platonism to the *Metaphysics* which is the reverse: to call universals "secondary substances" is half way between Plato's calling them the only substances and Aristotle's denial in the *Metaphysics* that they are substances at all.

What conclusion are we to draw from these differences between the *Categories* and the *Metaphysics*? The only logical conclusion is that the *Categories*, being nearer to Plato on the nature of attributes, and still nearer on the relation of universals to substances, is earlier than the *Metaphysics*. There are difficulties no doubt in drawing this conclusion; because the *Metaphysics*, though it denies that universals can be substances, and does not allow species and genera to be called "secondary substances," nevertheless falls itself into calling a universal essence (τὸ τί ἦν εἶναι) a substance—and that too in the very book where it is proved that no universal can be a substance. But this lapse only shows how powerful a dominion Plato exercised over Aristotle's soul to the last; for it arises out of the pupil still accepting from his master the unity of the universal though now applying it, not to classes, but to essences. The argument about essences in the *Metaphysics* is as follows:—Since a separate individual, *e.g.* Socrates, is a substance, and he is essentially a rational animal, then his essence, being what he is, is a substance; for we cannot affirm that Socrates is a substance and then deny that this rational animal is a substance (*Met.* Z 3). Now, according to the unity of a universal asserted by Plato and accepted by Aristotle, the universal essence of species, being one and the same for all individuals of the kind, is the same as the essence of each individual: *e.g.* the rational animal in the human species and in Socrates is one and the same; "for the essence is indivisible" (ἄτομον γὰρ τὸ εἶδος, *Met.* Z 8, 1034 *a* 8). It follows that we must call this selfsame essence, at once individual and universal, substance—a conclusion, however, which Aristotle never drew in so many words, though he continued always to call essence substance, and definition a knowledge of substance.

There is therefore a history of Aristotle's metaphysical views, corresponding to his gradual method of composition. It is as follows:—

(1) Negative rejection of Plato's hypothesis of forms and formal numbers, and reduction of forms to the common in the early dialogue περὶ φιλοσοφίας and in the early work περὶ ἰδεῶν.

(2) Positive assertion of the doctrine that things are individual substances in the *Categories*, but with the admission that attributes sometimes inhere in substance without being predicates of it, and that universal species and genera are "secondary substances."

(3) Expansion of the doctrine that things are individual substances in the *Metaphysics*, coupled with the reduction of all attributes to predicates, and the direct denial of universal substances; but nevertheless calling the universal essence of a species of substances substance, because the individual essence of an individual substance really is that substance, and the universal essence of the whole species is supposed to be indivisible and therefore identical with the individual essence of any individual of the species.

2. The *De Interpretatione*.—Another example of Aristotle's gradual desertion of Plato is exhibited by the *De Interpretatione* as compared with the *Prior Analytics*, and it shows another gradual history in Aristotle's philosophy, namely, the development of subject, predicate and copula, in his logic.

The short discourse on the expression of thought by language (περὶ Ἑρμηνείας, *De Interpretatione*) is based on the Platonic division of the sentence (λόγος) into noun and verb (ὄνομα and ῥῆμα.) Its point is to separate the enunciative sentence, or that in which there is truth or falsity, from other sentences; and then, dismissing the rest to rhetoric or poetry (where we should say grammar), to discuss the enunciative sentence (ἀποφαντικὸς λόγος), or enunciation (ἀπόφανσίς), or what we should call the proposition (*De Int.* chap. 4). Here Aristotle, starting from the previous grammar of sentences in general, proceeded, for the first time in philosophical literature, to disengage the logic of the proposition, or that sentence which can alone be true or false, whereby it alone enters into reasoning. But in spite of this great logical achievement, he continued throughout the discourse to accept Plato's grammatical analysis of all sentences into noun and verb, which indeed applies to the proposition as a sentence but does not give its particular elements. The first part of the work confines itself strictly to noun and verb, or the form of proposition called *secundi adjacentis*. Afterwards (chap. 10) proceeding to the opposition of propositions, he adds the form called *tertii adjacentis*, in a passage which is the first appearance, or rather adumbration, of the verb of being as a copula. In the form *secundi adjacentis* we only get oppositions, such as the following:—

man is—man is not
not-man   is—not-
man is not

In the form *tertii adjacentis* the oppositions, becoming more complex, are doubled, as follows:—

> man is just—man is not just
> man is non-just—man is not non-just
> not-man is just—not-man is not just
> not-man is non-just—not-man is not

non-just.

The words introducing this form (ὅταν δὲ τὸ ἔστι τρίτον προσκατηγορῆται, chap. 10, 19 b 19), which are the origin of the phrase *tertii adjacentis*, disengage the verb of being (ἔστι) partially but not entirely, because they still treat it as an extra part of the predicate, and not as a distinct copula. Nor does the work get further than the analysis of some propositions into noun and verb with "is" added to the predicated verb; an analysis, however, which was a great logical discovery and led Aristotle further to the remark that "is" does not mean "exists"; *e.g.* "Homer is a poet" does not mean "Homer exists" (*De Int.* chap. 11).

How then did Aristotle get further in the logical analysis of the proposition? Not in the *De Interpretatione*, but in the *Prior Analytics*. The first adumbration was forced upon him in the former work by his theory of opposition; the complete appearance in the latter work by his theory of syllogism. In analysing the syllogism, he first says that a premiss is an affirmative or negative sentence, and then that a term is that into which a premiss is dissolved, *i.e.* predicate and subject, combined or divided by being and not being (*Pr. An.* i. 1). Here, for the first time in logical literature, subject and predicate suddenly appear as terms, or extremes, with the verb of being (τὸ εἶναι) or not being (τὸ μὴ εἶναι) completely disengaged from both, but connecting them as a copula. Why here? Because the crossing of terms in a syllogism requires it. In the syllogism "Every man is mortal and Socrates is a man," if in the minor premiss the copula "is" were not disengaged from the predicate "man," there would not be one middle term "man" in the two premisses. It is not necessary in every proposition, but it is necessary in the arrangement of a syllogism, to extricate the terms of its propositions from the copula; *e.g.* mortal—man—Socrates.

This important difference between the *De Interpretatione* and the *Prior Analytics* can only be explained by supposing that the former is the earlier treatise. It is nearer to Plato's analysis of the sentence, and no logician would have gone back to it, after the Prior Analytics. It is not spurious, as some have supposed, nor later than the *De Anima*, as Zeller thought, but Aristotle in an earlier frame of mind.

Moreover we can make a history of Aristotle's thought and gradual composition thus:

(1) Earlier acceptance in the *De Interpretatione* of Plato's grammatical analysis of the sentence into noun and verb (*secundi adjacentis*) but gradually disengaging the proposition, and afterwards introducing the verb of being as a third thing added (*tertium adjacens*) to the predicated verb, for the purpose of opposition.

(2) Later logical analysis in the *Prior Analytics* of the proposition as premiss into subject, predicate and copula, for the purpose of syllogism; but without insisting that the original form is illogical.

3. The *Eudemian Ethics* and *Magna Moralia* in relation to the *Nicomachean Ethics*.—Under the name of Aristotle, three treatises on the good of man have come down to us, Ἠθικὰ Νικομάχεια (πρὸς Νικόμαχον, Porphyry), Ἠθικὰ Εὐδήμια (πρὸς Εὔδημον, Porphyry), and Ἠθικὰ μεγάλα; so like one another that there seems no tenable hypothesis except that they are the manuscript writings of one man. Nevertheless, the most usual hypothesis is that, while the *Nicomachean Ethics* (E.N.) was written by Aristotle to Nicomachus, the *Eudemian* (E.E.) was written, not to, but by, Eudemus, and the *Magna Moralia* (M.M.) was written by some early disciple before the introduction of Stoic and Academic elements into the Peripatetic school. The question is further complicated by the fact that three Nicomachean books (E.N. v.-vii.) and three Eudemian (E.E. Δ-Z) are common to the two treatises, and by the consequent question whether, on the hypothesis of different authorship, the common books, as we may style them, were written for the *Nicomachean* by Aristotle, or for the *Eudemian Ethics* by Eudemus, or some by one and some by the other author. Against the "Chorizontes," who have advanced various hypotheses on all these points without convincing one another, it may be objected that they have not considered Aristotle's method of gradual and simultaneous composition of manuscripts within the Peripatetic school. We have to remember the traces of his separate discourses, and his own double versions; and that, as in ancient times Simplicius, who had two versions of the *Physics*, Book vii., suggested that both were early versions of Book viii. on the same subject, so in modern times Torstrik, having discovered that there were two versions of the *De Anima*, Book ii., suggested that both were by Aristotle. Above all, we must consider our present point that Platonic influence is a sign of earliness in an Aristotelian work; and generally, the same man may both think and write differently at different times, especially if, like Aristotle, he has been a prolific author.

These considerations make it probable that the author of all three treatises was Aristotle himself; while the analysis of the treatises favours the hypothesis that he wrote the *Eudemian Ethics* and the *Magna Moralia* more or less together as the rudimentary first drafts of the mature *Nicomachean Ethics*.

As the Platonic philosophy was primarily moral, and its metaphysics a theory of the moral order of the universe, Aristotle from the first must have mastered the Platonic ethics. At first he adopted the somewhat ascetic views of his master about soul and body, and about goods of body and estate; but before Plato's death he had rejected the hypothesis of forms, formal numbers and the form of the good identified with the one, by which Plato tried to explain moral phenomena; while his studies and teaching on rhetoric and poetry soon began to make him take a more tolerant view than Plato did of men's passions. Throughout his whole subsequent life, however, he retained the fundamental doctrine, which he had learnt from Plato, and Plato from Socrates, that virtue is essential to happiness. Twice over this tenet, which makes Socrates, Plato and Aristotle one ethical school, inspired Aristotle to attempt poetry: first, in the Elegy to Eudemus of Cyprus, in which, referring to either Socrates or Plato, he praises the man who first showed clearly that a good and happy man are the same (*Fragm.* 673); and secondly, in the Hymn in memory of Hermias, beginning "Virtue, difficult to the human race, noblest pursuit in life" (*ib.* 675). Moreover, the successors of Plato in the Academy, Speusippus and Xenocrates, showed the same belief in the essentiality of virtue. The question which divided them was what the good is. Speusippus took the ascetic view that the good is a perfect condition of neutrality between two contrary evils, pain and pleasure. Xenocrates took the tolerant view that it is the possession of appropriate 513 virtue and noble actions, requiring as conditions bodily and external goods. Aristotle was opposed to Speusippus, and nearly agreed with Xenocrates. According to him, the good is activity of soul in accordance with virtue in a mature life, requiring as conditions bodily and external goods of fortune; and virtue is a mean state of the passions. It is probable that when, after Plato's death and the accession of Speusippus in 347, Aristotle with Xenocrates left Athens to visit his former pupil Hermias, the three discussed this moderate system of Ethics in which the two philosophers nearly agreed. At any rate, it was adopted in each of the three moral treatises which pass under the name of Aristotle.

The three treatises are in very close agreement throughout, and in the following details. The good of Ethics is human good; and human good is happiness, not the universal good or form of the good to which Plato subordinated human happiness. Happiness is activity of soul according to virtue in a mature life: it requires other goods only as conditions. The soul is partly irrational, partly rational; and therefore there are two kinds of virtue. Moral virtue, which is that of the irrational desires so far as they are obedient to reason, is a purposive habit in the mean. The motive of the moral virtues is the honourable (τὸ καλόν, *honestum*). As the rational is either deliberative or scientific, either practical or speculative intellect, there are two virtues of the intellect—prudence of the deliberative or practical, and wisdom of the scientific or speculative, intellect. The right reason by which moral virtue is determined is prudence, which is determined in its turn by wisdom. Pleasure is a psychical state, and is not a generation in the body supplying a defect and establishing a natural condition, but an activity of a natural condition of the soul. It should be specially noted that this doctrine like the rest is common to the three treatises: in Book vii. of the *Nicomachean*, which is Z of the *Eudemian*, pleasure is defined as ἐνέργεια τῆς κατὰ φύσιν ἕξεως ἀνεμπόδιστος (chap. 12, 1153 a 14-15); and in the *Magna Moralia* as ἡ κίνησις αὐτοῦ καὶ ἡ ἐνέργεια (ii. 7, 1204 b 28; cf. 1205 b 20-28). It is plain from the context that in the former definition "the natural condition" (ἡ κατὰ φύσιν ἕξις) refers to the soul which, while the body is regenerated, remains unimpaired (cf. 1152 b 35 seq., 1154 b 15 seq.); and in the latter definition the thing (αὐτοῦ), whose "motion, that is activity" is spoken of, is the part of the soul with which we feel pleased.

Down then to their common definition of pleasure as activity the three treatises present a harmonious system of morals, consistently with one another, and with the general philosophy of Aristotle. In particular, the theory that pleasure is activity (ἐνέργεια) is the theory of two of his most authoritative works. In the *De Anima* (iii. 7, 431 a 10-12), being pleased and pained are defined by him as acting τὸ (ἐνεργεῖν) by a sensitive mean in relation to good or evil as such. In the *Metaphysics* (Λ 7, 1072 b 16), in discussing the occupation of God, he says "his pleasure is activity," or "his activity is pleasure," according to a difference of readings which makes no difference to the identification of pleasure and activity (ἐνέργεια). As then we find this identification of pleasure with activity in the *Metaphysics* and in the *De Anima*, as well as in the *Nicomachean Ethics*, the *Eudemian Ethics* and the *Magna Moralia*, the only logical conclusion, from which there is no escape, is that, so far as the treatment of pleasure goes, any Aristotelian treatise which defines it as activity is genuine. There is no reason for doubting that

110

the *Nicomachean Ethics* to the end of Book vii., the *Eudemian Ethics* to the end of Book Z, and the *Magna Moralia* as far as Book ii. chap. 7, were all three written by Aristotle.

Why then doubt at all? It is because the *Nicomachean Ethics* contains a second discourse on pleasure (x. 1-5), in which the author, while agreeing with the previous treatment of the subject that pleasure is not a bodily generation, even when accompanied by it, but something psychical, nevertheless defines it (x. 4, 1174 b 31-33) not as an activity, but as a supervening end (ἐπιγιγνόμενόν τι τέλος) perfecting an activity (τελειοῖ τὴν ἐνέργειαν). He allows indeed that activity and pleasure are very closely related; that a pleasure of sense or thought perfects an act of sensation or of thinking, depends on it, and is so inseparably conjoined with it as to raise a doubt whether pleasure is end of life or life end of pleasure, and even whether the activity is the same as the pleasure. But he disposes of this doubt in a very emphatic and significant manner. "Pleasure," says he, "does not seem to be thinking or perceiving; for it is absurd: but on account of not being separated from them, it appears to some persons to be the same." Now it is not likely that Aristotle either, after having so often identified pleasure with activity, would say that the identification is absurd though it appears true to some persons, of whom he would in that case be one, or, having once disengaged the pleasure of perceiving and thinking from the acts of perceiving and thinking, would go backwards and confuse them. It is more likely that Aristotle identified pleasure with activity in the *De Anima*, the *Metaphysics* and the three moral treatises, as we have seen; but that afterwards some subsequent Peripatetic, considering that the pleasure of perceiving or thinking is not the same as perceiving or thinking, declared the previous identification of pleasure with activity absurd. At any rate, if we are to choose, it is the identification that is Aristotle's, and the distinction not Aristotle's. Moreover, the distinction between activity and pleasure in the tenth book is really fatal to the consistency of the whole *Nicomachean Ethics*, which started in the first book with the identification of happiness and virtuous activity. For if the pleasure of virtuous activity is a supervening end beyond the activity, it becomes a supervening end beyond the happiness of virtuous activity, which thus ceases to be the final end. Nevertheless, the distinction between activity and pleasure is true. Some unknown Peripatetic detected a flaw in the *Nicomachean Ethics* when he said that pleasure is a supervening end beyond activity, and, if he had gone on to add that happiness is also a supervening end beyond the virtuous activities which are necessary to produce it, he would have destroyed the foundation of his own founder's Ethics.

It is further remarkable that the *Nicomachean Ethics* proceeds to a different conclusion. After the intrusion of this second discourse on pleasure, it goes on (*E.N.* x. 6-fin.) to the famous theory that the highest happiness is the speculative life of intellect or wisdom as divine, but that happiness as human also includes the practical life of combining prudence and moral virtue; and that, while both lives need external goods as necessaries, the practical life also requires them as instruments of moral action. The treatise concludes with the means of making men virtuous; contending that virtue requires habituation, habituation law, law legislative art, and legislative art politics: Ethics thus passes into Politics. The *Eudemian Ethics* proceeds to its conclusion (*E.E.* H 13-15) differently, with the consideration of (1) good fortune (εὐτυχία), and (2) gentlemanliness (καλοκἀγαθία). Good fortune it divides into two kinds, both irrational; one divine, according to impulse, and more continuous; the other contrary to impulse and not continuous. Gentlemanliness it regards as perfect virtue, containing all particular virtues, and all goods for the sake of the honourable. Finally, it concludes with the limit (ὅρος) of goods. First it finds the limit of goods of fortune in that desire and possession of them which will conduce to the contemplation of God, whereas that which prevents the service and contemplation of God is bad. Then it adds that the best limit of the soul is as little as possible to perceive the other part of the soul (*i.e.* desire). Finally, the treatise concludes with saying that the limit of gentlemanliness has thus been stated, meaning that its limit is the service and contemplation of God and the control of desire by reason. The *Magna Moralia* (*M.M.* ii. 8-10) on these points is unlike the *Nicomachean*, and like the *Eudemian Ethics* in discussing good fortune and gentlemanliness, but it discusses them in a more worldly way. On good fortune (ii. 8), after recognizing the necessity of external goods to happiness, it denies that fortune is due to divine grace, and simply defines it as irrational nature (ἄλογος φύσις). Gentlemanliness (ii. 9) it regards as perfect virtue, and defines the gentleman as the man to whom really good things are good and really honourable things honourable. It then adds (ii. 10) that acting according to right reason is when the irrational part of the soul does not hinder the rational part of intellect from doing its work. Thereupon it proceeds to a discourse on friendship, which in the *Nicomachean* and *Eudemian Ethics* is discussed in an earlier position, but breaks off unfinished.

On the whole, the three moral treatises proceed on very similar lines down to the common identification of pleasure with activity, and then diverge. From this point the *Eudemian*

Ethics and the *Magna Moralia* become more like one another than like the *Nicomachean Ethics*. They also become less like one another than before: for the treatment of good fortune, gentlemanliness, and their limit is more theological in the *Eudemian Ethics* than in the *Magna Moralia*.

How are the resemblances and differences of the three to be explained? By Aristotle's gradual method of composition. All three are great works, contributing to the origin of the independent science of Ethics. But the *Eudemian Ethics* and the *Magna Moralia* are more rudimentary than the *Nicomachean Ethics*, which as it were seems to absorb them except in the conclusion. They are, in short, neither independent works, nor mere commentaries, but Aristotle's first drafts of his Ethics.

In the *Ethics to Eudemus*, as Porphyry properly called the *Eudemian Ethics*, Aristotle in the first four books successively investigates happiness, virtue, the voluntary and the particular moral virtues, in the same order and in the same letter and spirit as in his *Ethics to Nicomachus*. But the investigations are never so good. They are all such rudiments as Aristotle might well polish into the more developed expositions in the first four books of the *Nicomachean Ethics*. On the other hand, nobody would have gone back afterwards on his masterly treatment of happiness, in the first book, or of virtue in the second, or of the voluntary in the third, or of the particular virtues in the third and fourth, to write the sketchy accounts of the *Eudemian Ethics*.

Again, these sketches are rough preparations for the subsequent books common to the two treatises. It is true, as Dr Henry Jackson has pointed out, though with some exaggeration, that the Eudemian agrees in detail rather better than the Nicomachean treatment of the voluntary with the subsequent discussion of injury (*E.E.* Δ = *E.N.* v. 8); and, as Th. H. Fritzsche remarks, the distinction between politics, and economics, and prudence in the *Eudemian Ethics* (A 8) is a closer anticipation of the subsequent triple distinction of ⁵¹⁴practical science (*E.E.* E = *E.N.* vi 8). On the other hand, there are still more fundamental points in which the first three books of the *Eudemian Ethics* are a very inadequate preparation for the common books. Notably its treatment of prudence (φρόνησις) is a chaos. At first, prudence appears as the operation of the philosophical life and connected with the speculative philosophy of Anaxagoras (*E.E.* A 1-5): then it is brought into connexion with the practical philosophy of Socrates (*ib.* 5) and co-ordinated with politics and economics (*ib.* 8); then it is intruded into the diagram of moral virtues as a mean between villainy (πανουργία) and simplicity ((εὐήθεια) (*E.E.* B 33, 1221 a 12); finally, a distinction between virtue by nature and virtue with prudence (μετὰ φρονήσεως) is promised (*E.E.* T 7, 1234 a 4). In addition to all this confusion of speculative and practical knowledge, prudence is absent when it ought to be present; *e.g.* from the division of virtues into moral and intellectual (*E.E.* D 1, 1220 a 4-13), and from the definition of moral virtue (*ib.* 5, 10), while, in a passage (B 11) anticipating the subsequent discussion of the relation between prudence and moral virtue (*E.E.* E = *E.N.*vi. 12-13), it is stated that in purpose the end is made right by moral virtue, the means by another power, reason, without this right reason being stated to be prudence. After this, it can never be said that the earlier books of the *Eudemian Ethics* are so good a preparation as those of the *Nicomachean Ethics* for the distinction between prudence (φρόνησις) and wisdom (σοφία), which is the main point of the common books, and one of Aristotle's main points against Plato's philosophy.

Curiously enough, although little is made of it, this distinction, absent from the earlier books, is present in the final book II of the *Eudemian Ethics* (cf. 1246 b 4 seq., 1248 a 35, 1249 b 14); and probably therefore this part was a separate discourse. Meanwhile, however, the truth about the *Eudemian Ethics* in general is that it was an earlier rudimentary sketch written by Aristotle, when he was still struggling, without quite succeeding, to get over Plato's view that there is one philosophical knowledge of universal good, by which not only the dialectician and mathematician must explain the being and becoming of the world, but also the individual and the statesman guide the life of man. Indeed, the final proof that the *Eudemian Ethics* is earlier than the *Nicomachean* is the very fact that it is more under Platonic influence. In the first place, the reason why the account of prudence begins by confusing the speculative with the practical is that the *Eudemian Ethics* starts from Plato's *Philebus*, where, without differentiating speculative and practical knowledge, Plato asks how far good is prudence (φρόνησις), how far pleasure (ἡδονή); and in the *Eudemian Ethics* Aristotle asks the same question, adding virtue (ἀρετή) in order to correct the Socratic confusion of virtue with prudence. Secondly, the *Eudemian Ethics*, while not agreeing with Plato's *Republic* that the just can be happy by justice alone, does not assign to the external goods of good fortune (εὐτυχία) the prominence accorded to them in the *Nicomachean Ethics* as the necessary conditions of all virtue, and the instruments of moral virtue. Thirdly, the emphasis of the *Eudemian Ethics* on the perfect virtue of gentlemanliness (καλοκἀγαθία) is a decidedly old-fashioned trait, which descended to Aristotle from the Greek notion of a

112

gentleman who does his duty to his state (cf. Herodotus i. 30, Thucydides iv. 40) and to his God (Xenophon, *Symp.* iv. 49) through Plato, who in the *Gorgias* (470 E) says that the gentleman is happy, and in the *Republic* (489 E) imputes to him the love of truth essential to philosophy. Moreover, when Plato goes on (*ib.*505 B) to identify the form of good, without which nothing is good, with the gentlemanly thing (καλὸν καὶ ἀγαθόν), without which any possession is worthless, he inspired into the author of the *Eudemian Ethics* the very limit (ὅρος) of good fortune and gentlemanliness with which it concludes, only without Plato's elevation of the good into the form of the good. In the *Nicomachean Ethics* the old notion, we gladly see, survives (cf. i. 8): virtuous actions are gentlemanly actions, and happiness accordingly is being at our best and noblest and pleasantest (ἄριστον καὶ κάλλιστον καὶ ἥδιστον). But gentlemanliness is no longer called perfect virtue, as in the *Eudemian Ethics*: its place has been taken by justice, which is perfect virtue to one's neighbour, by prudence which unites all the moral virtues, and by wisdom which is the highest virtue. Accordingly, in the end the old ideal of gentlemanliness is displaced by the new ideal of the speculative and practical life.

Lastly, the *Eudemian Ethics* derives from Platonism a strong theological bias, especially in its conclusion (H 14-15). The opposition of divine good fortune according to impulse to that which is contrary to impulse reminds us of Plato's point in the*Phaedrus* that there is a divine as well as a diseased madness. The determination of the limit of good fortune and of gentlemanliness by looking to the ruler, God, who governs as the end for which prudence gives its orders, and the conclusion that the best limit is the most conducive to the service and contemplation of God, presents the Deity and man's relation to him as a final and objective standard more definitely in the *Eudemian* than in the*Nicomachean Ethics*, which only goes so far as to say that man's highest end is the speculative wisdom which is divine, like God, dearest to God.

Because, then, it is very like, but more rudimentary and more Platonic, we conclude that the *Eudemian* is an earlier draft of the*Nicomachean Ethics*, written by Aristotle when he was still in process of transition from Plato's ethics to his own.

The *Magna Moralia* contains similar evidence of being earlier than the *Nicomachean Ethics*. It treats the same subjects, but always in a more rudimentary manner; and its remarks are always such as would precede rather than follow the masterly expositions of the *Nicomachean Ethics*. This inferiority applies also to its treatment not only of the early part (i. 1-33 corresponding to E.N.i.-iv.), but also of the middle part (i. 34-11. 7 corresponding to*E.N.* v.-vii. = *E.E.* Δ-Z). In dealing with justice, it does not make it clear, as the *Nicomachean Ethics* (Book v.) does, that even universal justice is virtue towards another (*M.M.* i. 34, 1193 b 1-15), and it omits altogether the division into distributive and corrective justice. In dealing with what the *Nicomachean Ethics*(Book vi.) calls intellectual virtues, but the *Magna Moralia* (i. 5, 35) virtues of the rational part of the soul, and right reason, it distinguishes (i. 35, 1196 b 34-36) science, prudence, intelligence, wisdom, apprehension (ὑπόληψις), in a rough manner very inferior to the classification of science, art, prudence, intelligence, wisdom, all of which are coordinate states of attaining truth, in the*Nicomachean Ethics* (vi. 3). It distinguishes prudence (φρόνησις) and wisdom (σοφία) as the respective virtues of deliberative and scientific reason; and on the whole its account of prudence (cf.*M.M.* i. 5) is more consistent than that of the *Eudemian Ethics*. In these points it is a better preparation for the *Nicomachean Ethics*. But it falls into the confusion of first saying that praise is for moral virtues, and not for virtues of the reason, whether prudence or wisdom (*M.M.* i. 5, 1185 b 8-12), and afterwards arguing that prudence is a virtue, precisely because it is praised (i. 35, 1197 a 16-18). In dealing with continence and incontinence, the same doubts and solutions occur as in the *Nicomachean Ethics* (Book vii. = *E.E.* Z), but sometimes confusing doubts and solutions together, instead of first proposing all the doubts and then supplying the solutions as in the *Nicomachean Ethics*. Such rudimentary and imperfect sketches would be quite excusable in a first draft, but inexcusable and incredible after the *Nicomachean Ethics* had been written.

It has another characteristic which points to its being an early work of Aristotle, when he was still under the influence of Plato's style; namely its approximation to dialogue. It asks direct questions (*e.g.* διὰ τί; *M.M.* i. 1 repeatedly, 12; ii. 6, 7), incorporates direct statements of others (*e.g.* φησί, i. 12, 13; ii. 3, 6, 7), alternates direct objections and answers (i. 34), and introduces conversations between the author and others, expressed interrogatively, indicatively and even imperatively (ἀλλ᾽ ἐρεῖ μοι, τὰ ποῖα διασάφησον ὑγιεινά ἐστιν. i. 35, 1196 b 10; cf. ii. 10, 1208 a 20-22). The whole treatise inclines to run into dialogue. It is also Platonic, like the *Endemian Ethics*, in making little of external goods in the account of good fortune (ii. 8), and in emphasizing the perfect virtue of gentlemanliness (ii. 9). Indeed, in some respects it is more like the *Eudemian*, though in the main more like the *Nicomachean Ethics*. In the first book, it has the Eudemian distinction between prudence, virtue and pleasure (i. 3, 1184 b 5-6); but does not make so much of it as the distinction between prudence and wisdom blurred in the *Eudemian* but defined in

113

the *Nicomachean Ethics*. In the second book, it runs parallel to the *Eudemian Ethics* in placing good fortune and gentlemanliness (ii. 8-9), where the *Nicomachean Ethics* places the speculative and the practical life; but it omits the theological element by denying that good fortune is divine grace, and by submitting gentlemanliness to no standard but that of right reason, when the irrational part of the soul does not hinder the rational part, or intellect (νοῦς), from doing its work.

Because, then, the *Magna Moralia* is very like the *Nicomachean Ethics*, but more rudimentary, nearer to the Platonic dialogues in style and. to a less degree in matter, and also like the *Eudemian Ethics*, we conclude that it is also like that treatise in having been written as an earlier draft of the *Nicomachean Ethics* by Aristotle himself.

The hypothesis that the *Eudemian Ethics*, and by consequence the *Magna Moralia*, are later than Aristotle has arisen from a simple misconception, continued in a Scholium attributed to Aspasius, who lived in the 2nd century A.D. Nicomachean means "addressed to Nicomachus," and Eudemian "addressed to Eudemus"; but, as Cicero thought that the *Nicomachean Ethics* was written by Nicomachus, so the author of the Scholium thought that the *Eudemian Ethics*, at least so far as the first account of pleasure goes, was written by Eudemus. He only thought so, however, because Aristotle could not have written both accounts of pleasure; and, taking for granted that Aristotle had written the second account of pleasure in the *Nicomachean Ethics* (Book x.), he concluded that the first account (Book vii.) was not the work of Aristotle, but of Eudemus (*Comm. in Ar.* (Berlin) xix. p. 151). We have seen reason to reverse this argument: Aristotle did write the first account in Book vii., because it contains his usual theory; and, if we must choose, he did not write the second account in Book x. In this way, too, we get a historical development of the theory of pleasure: Plato and Speusippus said it is generation (cf. Plato's *Philebus*): Aristotle said it is psychical activity sometimes requiring bodily generation, sometimes not (*E.N.* vii. = *E.E.Z*): Aristotle, or some Aristotelian, afterwards said that it is a supervening end completing an activity (*E.N.* x.). Secondly, some modern commentators, starting from the false conclusion that the definition of pleasure as activity (*E.N.* vii. = *E.E.Z*) is by Eudemus, and supposing without proof that he was also author of 515 the first three books of the *Eudemian Ethics*, have further asserted that these are a better introduction than the first four books of the *Nicomachean Ethics* to the books common to both treatises (*E.N.* Books v.-vii. =*E.E.* Books Δ-Z), and have concluded that Eudemus wrote these common books. But we have seen that Aristotle wrote the first three books of the *Eudemian* as an earlier draft of the *Nicomachean Ethics*; so that, even so far as they form a better introduction, this will not prove the common books to be by Eudemus. Again, those first three books are a better introduction only in details; whereas in regard to the all-important subject of prudence as distinct from wisdom, they are so bad an introduction that the common book which discusses that subject at large (*E.N.* Book vi. = *E.E.* Book E) must be rather founded on the first four books of Aristotle's *Nicomachean Ethics*. Further, as Aristotle wrote both the first three Eudemian and the first four Nicomachean books, there is no reason why sometimes one, sometimes the other, should not be the best introduction to the common books by the same author. Finally, the common books are so integral a part of the Aristotelian system of philosophy that they cannot be disengaged from it: the book on justice (*E.N.* v.) quotes and is quoted in the *Politics* (cf. 1130 b 28, 1280 a 16, 1261 a 30); the book on intellectual virtues (*E.N.* vi.) quotes (vi. 3) the *Posterior Analytics*, i. 2, and is quoted in the *Metaphysics* (A 1); and we have seen that the book (*E.N.* vii.) which defines pleasure as activity is simply stating an Aristotelian commonplace. Thirdly, in order to prove that the *Eudemian Ethics* was by Eudemus, it is said that in its first part it contemplates that there must be a limit (ὅρος) for virtue as a mean (*E.E.* B 5, 1222 b 7-8), in its middle part it criticizes the *Nicomackean Ethics* for not being clear about this limit (*E.E.* E 1), and in the end it alone assigns this limit, in the service and contemplation of God (*E.E.* H 15, 1249 b 16 seq.). This argument is subtle, but over-subtle. The *Eudemian* and the *Nicomachean* treatments of this subject do not really differ. In the *Nicomachean* as in the *Eudemian Ethics* the limit above moral virtue is right reason, or prudence, which is right reason on such matters; and above prudence wisdom, for which prudence gives its orders; while wisdom is the intelligence and science of the most venerable objects, of the most divine, and of God. After this agreement, there is a shade of difference. While the *Eudemian Ethics* in a more theological vein emphasizes God, the object of wisdom as the end for which prudence gives its orders, the Nicomachean Ethics in a more humanizing spirit emphasizes wisdom itself, the speculative activity, as that end, and afterwards as the highest happiness, because activity of the divine power of intellect, because an imitation of the activity of God, because most dear to God. This is too fine a distinction to found a difference of authorship. Beneath it, and behind the curious hesitation which in dealing with mysteries Aristotle shows between the divine and the human, his three moral treatises agree that wisdom is a science of things divine, which the *Nicomachean Ethics* (vi. 7) defines as science and intelligence of the most venerable things, the *Magna Moralia* (i. 35) regards as that which is concerned with the eternal and the divine, and the *Eudemian Ethics* (H 15) elevates into the service and contemplation of God.

Aristotle then wrote three moral treatises, which agree in the fundamental doctrines that happiness requires external fortune, but is activity of soul according to virtue, rising from morality through prudence to wisdom, or that science of the divine which constitutes the theology of his *Metaphysics*. Surely, the harmony of these three moral gospels proves that Aristotle wrote them, and wrote the *Eudemian Ethics* and the *Magna Moralia* as preludes to the Nicomachean Ethics. When did he begin? We do not know; but there is a pathetic suggestiveness in a passage in the *Magna Moralia* (i. 35), where he says, "Clever even a bad man is called; as Mentor was thought clever, but prudent he was not." Mentor was the treacherous contriver of the death of Hermias (345-344 B.C.). Was this passage written when Aristotle was mourning for his friend?

4. *The Rhetoric to Alexander.*—This is one of a series of works emanating from Aristotle's early studies in rhetoric, beginning with the *Gryllus*, continuing in the *Theodectea* and the *Collection of Arts*, all of which are lost except some fragments; while among the extant Aristotelian writings as they stand we still possess the *Rhetoric to Alexander* (Ῥητορικὴ πρὸς Ἀλέξανδρον) and the *Rhetoric* (Τέχνη Ῥητορική). But the *Rhetoric to Alexander* was considered spurious by Erasmus, for the inadequate reasons that it has a preface and is not mentioned in the list of Diogenes Laertius, and was assigned by Petrus Victorius, in his preface to the *Rhetoric*, to Anaximenes. It remained for Spengel to entitle the work *Anaximenis Ars Rhetorica* in his edition of 1847, and thus substitute for the name of the philosopher Aristotle that of the sophist Anaximenes on his title-page. We have therefore to ask, first who was the author, and secondly what is the relation of the *Rhetoric to Alexander* to the *Rhetoric*, which nowadays alone passes for genuine.

After a dedicatory epistle to Alexander (chap. 1) the opening of the treatise itself (chap. 2) is as follows:—"There are three genera of political speeches; one deliberative, one declamatory, one forensic: their species are seven; hortative, dissuasive, laudatory, vituperative, accusatory, defensive, critical." This brief sentence is enough to prove the work genuine, because it was Aristotle who first distinguished the three genera (cf. *Rhet.* i. 3; Quintilian iii. 4, 1. 7, 1), by separating the declamatory (ἐπιδεικτικόν) from the deliberative (δημηγορικόν, συμβουλευτικόν) and judicial (δικανικόν); whereas his rival Isocrates had considered that laudation and vituperation, which Aristotle elevated into species of declamation, run through every kind (Quintilian iv. 4), and Anaximenes recognized only the deliberative and the judicial (Dionys. H. *de Isaeo*, 19). In order, however, to impute the whole work to Anaximenes, Spengel took one of the most inexcusable steps ever taken in the history of scholarship. Without any manuscript authority he altered the very first words "three genera" (τρία γένη) into "two genera" (δύο γένη), and omitted the words "one declamatory" (τὸ δὲ ἐπιδεικτικόν). Quintilian (iii. 4) imputes to Anaximenes two genera, deliberative and judicial, and seven species, "hortandi, dehortandi, laudandi, vituperandi, accusandi, defendendi, exquirendi, quod ἐξεταστικὸν dicit." But the author of this rhetoric most certainly recognized three genera (τρία γένη), since, besides the deliberative and judicial, the declamatory genus constantly appears in the work (chaps. 2 *init.*, 4, 7, 18, 36, cf. οὐκ ἀγῶνος ἀλλ᾽ ἐπιδείξεως ἕνεκα 1440 *b* 13); and, if the terms for it are not always the same, this is just what one would expect in a new discovery. Moreover, he could recognize seven species in the *Rhetoric to Alexander*, though he recognized only six in the *Rhetoric*, provided the two works were not written at the same time; and as a matter of fact even in the *Rhetoric to Alexander* the seventh or critical species (ἐξεταστικόν) is in process of disappearing (cf. chap. 37). As then Anaximenes did not, but Aristotle did, recognize three genera, and as Aristotle could as well as Anaximenes recognize seven species, the evidence is overwhelming that the *Rhetoric to Alexander* is the work not of Anaximenes, but of Aristotle; on the condition that its date is not that of Aristotle's confessedly genuine *Rhetoric*.

There is a second and even stronger evidence that the *Rhetoric to Alexander* is a genuine work of Aristotle. It divides (chap. 8) evidences (πίστεις) into two kinds (1) evidence from arguments, actions and men (αἱ μὲν ἐξ αὐτῶν τῶν λόγων καὶ τῶν πράξεων καὶ τῶν ἀνθρώπων); (2) adventitious evidences (αἱ δ᾽ ἐπίθετοι τοῖς λεγομένοις καὶ τοῖς πραττομένοις). The former are immediately enumerated as probabilities (εἰκότα), examples (παραδείγματα), proofs (τεκμήρια), considerations (ἐνθυμήματα), maxims (γνῶμαι), signs (σημεῖα), refutations (ἔλεγχοι); the latter as opinion of the speaker (δόξα τοῦ λεγοντος), witnesses (μαρτυρίαι), tortures (βάσανοι), oaths (ὅρκοι). It is confessed by Spengel himself that these two kinds of evidences are the two kinds recognized in Aristotle's *Rhetoric* as (1) artificial (ἐντέχνοι πίστεις) and (2) inartificial (ἄτεχνοι πίστεις). Now, from the outset of his *Rhetoric* Aristotle himself claims to be the first to distinguish between artificial evidences from arguments and other evidences which he regards as mere additions; and he complains that the composers of arts of speaking had neglected the former for the latter. In particular, rhetoricians appeared to him to have neglected argument in comparison with passion. No doubt, rational evidences had appeared in books of rhetoric, as we see from Plato's *Phaedrus*, 266-267,where we find proofs, probabilities, refutation and maxim, but mixed up with other evidences. The point of Aristotle was to draw a line between rational and other evidences, to insist on the former, and in fact to found a logic of rhetoric. But if in the *Rhetoric to Alexander*, not he, but Anaximenes, had already performed this great achievement, Aristotle would have been the meanest of mankind; for the logic of rhetoric would have been really the work of Anaximenes the sophist, but falsely claimed by Aristotle the philosopher. As we cannot without a tittle of evidence accept such a consequence, 516we conclude that Aristotle formulated the distinction between argumentative and adventitious, artificial and inartificial evidences, both in the *Rhetoric to Alexander* and in the *Rhetoric*; and that the former as well as the latter is a genuine work of Aristotle, the founder of the logic of rhetoric.

What is the relation between these two genuine Rhetorics? The last event mentioned in the *Rhetoric to Alexander* occurred in 340, the last in the *Rhetoric* is the common peace (κοινὴ εἰρήνη) made between Alexander and the Greeks in 336 (*Rhet.* ii. 23, 1399 b 12). The former treatise (chap. 9), under the head of examples (παραδείγματα), gives historical examples of the unexpected in war for the years 403, 371, 358, concluding with the year 340, in which the Corinthians, coming with nine triremes to the assistance of the Syracusans, defeated the Carthaginians who were blockading Syracuse with 150 ships. Spengel, indeed, tries to bring the latest date in the book down to 330; but it is by absurdly supposing that the author could not have got the commonplace, "one ought to criticize not bitterly but gently," except from Demosthenes, *De Corona* (§ 265). We may take it then that the last date in the *Rhetoric to Alexander* is 340; and by a curious coincidence 340 was the year when, on Philip's marching against Byzantium, Alexander was left behind as regent and keeper of the seal, and distinguished himself so greatly that Philip was only too glad that the Macedonians called Alexander king (Plutarch,*Alexander*, 9). It is possible then that Aristotle may have written the dedication to Alexander about 340 and treated him as if he were king in the dedicatory epistle. At the same time, as such prefaces are often forgeries, not prejudicing the body of the treatise, it does not really matter whether Aristotle actually dedicated his work to Alexander in that epistle about that year or not. If he did, then the *Rhetoric to Alexander* in 340 was at least four years prior to the *Rhetoric*, which was as late as 336. If he did not, the question still remains, what is the internal relation between these two genuine Rhetorics? It will turn out most important.

The relation between the two Rhetorics turns on their treatment of rational, argumentative, artificial evidences. Each of them, the probability (chap. 8), the example (chap. 9), the proof (chap. 10), the consideration (chap. 11), the maxim (chap. 12), the sign (chap. 13), the refutation (chap. 14), though very like what it is in the*Rhetoric*, receives in the *Rhetoric to Alexander* a definition slightly different from the definition in the *Rhetoric*, which it must be remembered is also the definition in the *Prior Analytics*. Strange as this point is, it is still stranger that not one of these internal evidences is brought into relation with induction and deduction. Example (παράδειγμα) is not called rhetorical induction, and consideration (ἐνθύμημα) is not called rhetorical syllogism, as they are in the *Rhetoric*, and in the *Analytics*. Induction (ἐπαγωγή) and syllogism (συλλογισμός), the general forms of inference, do not occur in the *Rhetoric to Alexander*. In fact, this interesting treatise contains a rudimentary treatment of rational evidences in rhetoric and is therefore earlier than the *Rhetoric*, which exhibits a developed analysis of these rational evidences as special logical forms. Together, the earlier and the later *Rhetoric*show us the logic of rhetoric in the making, going on about 340, the last date of the *Rhetoric to Alexander*, and more developed in or after 336 B.C., the last date of the *Rhetoric*.

Nor is this all: the earlier *Rhetoric to Alexander* and the later*Rhetoric* show us logic itself in the making. We have already said that Aristotle was primarily a metaphysician. He gradually became a logician out of his previous studies: out of metaphysics, for with him being is always the basis of thinking, and common principles, such as that of contradiction, are axioms of things before axioms of thought, while categories are primarily things signified by names; out of the mathematics of the Pythagoreans and the Platonists, which taught him the nature of demonstration; out of the physics, of which he imbibed the first draughts from his father, which taught him induction from sense and the modification of strict demonstration to suit facts; out of the dialectic between man and man which provided him with beautiful examples of inference in the Socratic dialogues of Xenophon and Plato; out of the rhetoric addressed to large audiences, which with dialectic called his attention to probable inferences; out of the grammar taught with rhetoric and poetics which led him to the logic of the proposition. We cannot write a history of the varied origin of logic, beyond putting the rudimentary logic of the proposition in the *De Interpretatione* before the less rudimentary theory of categories as significant names capable of becoming predicates in the*Categories*, and before the maturer analysis of the syllogism in the *Analytics*. But at any rate the process was gradual; and Aristotle was advanced in metaphysics, mathematics, physics, dialectics, rhetoric and poetics, before he became the founder of logic.

V. ORDER OF THE PHILOSOPHICAL WRITINGS

Some of Aristotle's philosophical writings then are earlier than others; because they show more Platonic influence, and are more rudimentary; *e.g.* the *Categories* earlier than some parts of the *Metaphysics*, because under the influence of Platonic forms it talks of inherent attributes, and allows secondary substances which are universal; the *De Interpretatione* earlier than the *Analytics*, because in it the Platonic analysis of the sentence into noun and verb is retained for the proposition; the *Eudemian Ethics* and the *Magna Moralia* earlier than the *Nicomachean Ethics*, because they are rudimentary sketches of it, and the one written rather in the theological spirit, the other rather in the dialectical style, of Plato; and the *Rhetoric to Alexander* earlier than the *Rhetoric*, because it contains a rudimentary theory of the rational evidences afterwards developed into a logic of rhetoric in the *Rhetoric* and *Analytics*.

It is tempting to think that we can carry out the chronological order of the philosophical writings in detail. But in the gradual process of composition, by which a work once begun was kept going with the rest, although a work such as the *Politics* (begun in 357) was begun early, and some works more rudimentary came earlier than others, the general body of writings was so kept together in Aristotle's library, and so simultaneously elaborated and consolidated into a system that it soon becomes impossible to put one before another.

Zeller, indeed, has attempted an exact order of succession:—

1. The logical treatises.
2. The *Physics, De Coelo, De Generatione et Corruptione, Meteorologica*.
3. *Historia Animalium, De Anima, Parva Naturalia, De Partibus Animalium, De Animalium Incessu, De Generatione Animalium*.
4. *Ethics* and *Politics*.
5. *Poetics* and *Rhetoric*.
6. *Metaphysics* (unfinished).

But Zeller does not give enough weight either to the evidence of early composition contained in the *Politics* and *Meteorology*, or to the evidence of subsequent contemporaneous composition contained in the cross-references, *e.g.* between the *Physics* and the *Metaphysics*. On the other hand he gives too much weight to the references from one book to another, which Aristotle could have entered into his manuscripts at any time before his death. Moreover, the arrangement sometimes breaks down: for example, though on the whole the logical books are quoted without quoting the rest, the *De Interpretatione* (chap. 1) quotes the *De Anima*, and therefore is falsely taken by Zeller against its own internal evidence to be subsequent to it and consequently to the other logical books. Again, the *Meteorologica* (iii. 2, 372 b 9) quotes the *De Sensu* (c. 3), and therefore, on Zeller's arguments, ought to follow one of the *Parva Naturalia*. Lastly, though the *Metaphysics* often quotes the *Physics*, and is therefore regarded as being subsequent, it is itself quoted in the *Physics* (i. 8, 191 b 29), and therefore ought to be regarded as antecedent. Zeller tries to get over this difficulty of cross-reference by detaching *Metaphysics*, Book Δ, from the rest and placing it before the *Physics*. But this violent and arbitrary remedy is only partial. The truth is that the *Metaphysics* both precedes and follows the *Physics*, because it had been all along occupying Aristotle ever since he began to differ from Plato's metaphysical views and indeed forms a kind of presupposed basis of his whole system. So generally, the references backwards and forwards, and the cross-references, are really evidences that Aristotle mainly wrote his works not successively but simultaneously, and entered references as and when he pleased, because he had not published them.

There are two kinds of quotations in Aristotle's extant works, the quotation of another book, and the quotation of a historical fact. While the former is useless to determine the sequence of books written simultaneously, the latter is insufficient to determine a complete chronological order. When Aristotle, *e.g.* in the *Politics*, quotes an event as now (νῦν), he was writing about it at that time; and when he quotes another event as lately (νεωστί) he was writing about it shortly after that time; but he might have been writing the rest of the *Politics* both before and after either event. When he quotes the last event mentioned in the book, *e.g.* in the *Rhetoric* (ii. 23, 1399 b 12) the "common peace" of Greece under Alexander in 336, he was writing as late as that date, but he might also have been writing the *Rhetoric* both before it and after it. When he quotes what persons used to say in the past, *e.g.* Plato and Speusippus in the *Ethics*, Eudoxus and Callippus in the *Metaphysics*, he was writing these passages after the deaths of these persons; but he might have been also writing the *Ethics* and the *Metaphysics* both beforehand and afterwards. Lastly, when he is silent about a historical fact, the argument from silence is evidence only when he could not have failed to mention it; as, for example, in the *Constitution of Athens*, when he could not have failed to mention quinqueremes and other facts after 325-324. But this is in a historical work; whereas the argument from silence about historical facts in a philosophical work can seldom apply.

The chronological order therefore is not sufficiently detailed to be the real order of Aristotelian writings. Secondly, the traditional order, which for nearly 2000 years has descended from the edition of Andronicus to the Berlin edition, is satisfactory in details, but unsatisfactory in system. It gives too much weight to Aristotle's logic, and too little to his metaphysics, on account of two prejudices of the commentators which led them to place both logic and physics before metaphysics. Aristotle rightly used all the sciences of his day, and especially his own physics, as a basis of his metaphysics. For example, at the very outset he refers to the *Physics* (ii. 2) for his use of the four causes, material, efficient, formal and final, in the *Metaphysics* (A 2). This and other applications of the science of nature to the science of all being induced the commentators to adopt this order, and entitle the science of being the *Sequel to the Physics* (τὰ μετὰ τὰ φυσικά). But Aristotle knew nothing of this title, the first known use of which was by Nicolaus Damascenus, a younger contemporary of Andronicus, the editor of the Aristotelian writings, and Andronicus was probably the originator of the title, and of the order. On the other hand, Aristotle entitles the science of all being "Primary Philosophy" (πρώτη φιλοσοφία), and the science of physical being "Secondary Philosophy" (δεύτερα φιλοσοφία), which suggests that his order is from Metaphysics to Physics, the reverse of his editor's order from Physics to Metaphysics. Thus the traditional order puts Physics before Metaphysics without Aristotle's authority. With some more show of authority it puts Logic before Metaphysics. Aristotle, on introducing the principle of contradiction (*Met.* Γ 3), which belongs to Metaphysics as an axiom of being, says that those who attempt to discuss the question of accepting this axiom, do so on account of their ignorance of *Analytics*, which they ought to know beforehand (προεπισταμένους). He means that the logical analysis of demonstration in the *Analytics* would teach them beforehand that there cannot be demonstration, though there must be induction, of an axiom, or any other principle; whereas, if they are not logically prepared for metaphysics, they will expect a demonstration of the axiom, as Heraclitus, the Heraclitean Cratylus and the Sophist Protagoras actually did,—and in vain. Acting on this hint, not Aristotle but the Peripatetics inferred that all logic is an instrument (ὄργανον) of all sciences; and by the time of Andronicus, who was one of them and sometimes called "the eleventh from Aristotle," the order, Logic-Physics-Metaphysics, had become established pretty much as we have it now. It is, however, not the real order for studying the philosophy of Aristotle, because there is more Metaphysics in his Physics than Physics in his Metaphysics, and more Metaphysics in his Logic than Logic in his Metaphysics. The commentators themselves were doubtful about the order: Boethus proposed to begin with Physics, and some of the Platonists with Ethics or Mathematics, while Andronicus preferred to put Logic first as Organon (*Scholia*, 25 b 34 seq.). None of the parties to the dispute had the authority of Aristotle. What do we find in his works? Primary philosophy, Metaphysics, the science of being, is the solid foundation of all parts of his philosophical system; not only in the *Physics*, but also in the *De Coelo* (i. 8, 277 b 10), in the *De Generatione* (i. 3, 318 a 6; ii. 10, 336 b 29), in the *De Anima* (i. 1, 403 a 28, cf. b 16), in the *De Partibus Animalium* (i. 1, 641 a 35), in the *Nicomachean Ethics* (i. 6, 1096 b 30), in the *De Interpretatione* (5, 17 a 14); and in short throughout his extant works. The reason is that Aristotle was primarily a metaphysician half for and half against Plato, occupied himself with metaphysics all his philosophical life, made the science of things the universal basis of all sciences without destroying their independence, and so gradually brought round philosophy from universal forms to individual substances. The traditional order of the Aristotelian writings, still continued in the Berlin edition, beginning with the logical writings on page 1, proceeding to the physical writings on page 184, and postponing the Metaphysics to page 980, is not the real order of Aristotle's philosophy.

The real order of Aristotle's philosophy is that of Aristotle's mind, revealed in his writings, and by the general view of thinking, science, philosophy and all learning therein contained. He classified thinking (*Met.* E 1) and science (*Topics*, vi. 6) by the three operations of speculation (θεωρία), practice (πρᾶξις) and production (ποίησις), and made the following subdivisions:—

I. Speculative: about things; subdivided (*Met.* E 1; *De An.* i. 1) into:—

i. Primary Philosophy, Theology, also called Wisdom, about things as things.

ii. Mathematical Philosophy, about quantitative things in the abstract.

iii. Physical Philosophy, about things as changing, and therefore about natural substances or bodies, composed of matter and essence.

II. Practical or Political Philosophy, or philosophy of things human (cf. *E.N.* x. 9-fin.): about human good; subdivided (*E.N.* vi. 8, cf. *E.E.* A 8, 1218 b 13) into:—

i. Ethics, about the good of the individual.

ii. Economics, about the good of the family.

iii. Politics, about the general good of the state.

III. Productive, or Art (τέχνη): about works produced; subdivided (*Met.* A. 1, 981 b 17-20) into:—

    i. Necessary (πρὸς τάναγκαῖα), *e.g.* medicine.

    ii. Fine (πρὸβ διαγωγήν), *e.g.* poetry.

Aristotle calls all these investigations sciences (ἐπιστῆμαι): but he also uses the term "sciences" in a narrower sense in consequence of a classification of their objects, which pervades his writings, into things necessary and things contingent, as follows.—

(A) The necessary (τὸ μὴ ἐνδεχόμενον ἄλλως ἔχειν), what must be; subdivided into:—

(1) Absolutely (ἁπλῶς), *e.g.* the mathematical.

(2) Hypothetically (ἐξ ὑποθέσεως), *e.g.* matter necessary as means to an end.

(B) The contingent (τὸ ἐνδεχόμενον ἄλλως ἔχειν), what may be; subdivided into:—

(1) The usual (τὸ ὡς ἐπὶ τὸ πολύ) or natural (τὸ φυσικόν),*e.g.* a man grows grey.

(2) The accidental (τὸ κατὰ συμβεβηκός), *e.g.* a man sits or not.

Now, according to Aristotle, science in the narrow sense is concerned only with the absolutely necessary (*E.N.* iii. 3), and in the classification would stop at mathematics, which we still call exact science: in the wide sense, on the other hand, it extends to the whole of the necessary and to the usual contingent, but excludes the accidental (*Met.* E 2), and would in the classification include not only metaphysics and mathematics, but also physics, ethics, economics, politics, necessary and fine art; or in short all speculative, practical and productive thinking of a systematic kind. Hence the *Posterior Analytics*, which is Aristotle's authoritative logic of science, is of peculiar interest because, after beginning by defining science as investigating necessary objects from necessary principles (i. 4), it proceeds to say that it is either of the necessary or of the usual though not of the accidental (i. 29), and to admit that its principles are some necessary and some contingent (i. 32, 88 b 7). Philosophy (φιλοςοφία) also is used by him in a similar manner. Though occasionally he means by it primary philosophy (*Met.* Γ 2-3, K 3), more frequently he extends it to all three speculative philosophies (E 1, 1026 a 18, τρεῖς ἂν εἶεν φιλοσοφίαι θεωρητικαί, μαθηματική, φυσική, θεολογική), and to all three practical philosophies, as we see from the constant use of the phrase "political philosopher" in the *Ethics*; and in short applies it to all sciences except productive science or art. With him, as with the Greeks generally, the problems of philosophy are the nature and origin of being and of good: it is not as with too many of us a mere science of mind.

Aristotle's view of thinking in science and philosophy is essentially comprehensive; but it is not so wide as to become indefinite. According to him, science at its widest selects a special subject, *e.g.*number in arithmetic, magnitude in geometry, stars in astronomy, a man's good in ethics; concentrates itself on the causes and appropriate principles of its subject, especially the definition of the subject and its species by their essences or formal causes; and after an inductive intelligence of those principles proceeds by a deductive demonstration from definitions to consequences: philosophy is simply a desire of this definite knowledge of causes and effects. Beyond philosophy, not beyond science, there is art; and beyond philosophy and science there is history, the description of facts preparatory to philosophy, the investigation of causes (cf. *Pr. An.* i. 30); and this may be natural history, preparatory to natural philosophy, as in the *History of Animals*preparatory to the *De Partibus Animalium*, or what we call civil history, preparatory to political philosophy, as in the 158 Constitutions more or less preparatory to the *Politics*.

Wide as is all his knowledge of facts and causes, it does not appear to Aristotle to be the whole of learning and the show of it. Beyond knowledge lies opinion, beyond discovery disputation, beyond philosophy and science dialectic between man and man, which was much practised by the Greeks in the dialogues of Socrates, Plato, the Megarians and Aristotle himself in his early manhood. With Plato, who thought that the interrogation of 518man is the best instrument of truth, dialectic was exaggerated into a universal science of everything that is. Aristotle, on the other hand, learnt to distinguish dialectic (διαλεκτική) from science (ἐπιστήμη); in that it has no definite subject, else it would not ask questions (*Post. An.* i. 11, 77 a 31-33); in that for appropriate principles it substitutes the probabilities of authority (τὰ ἔνδοξα) which are the opinions of all, or of the majority, or of the wise (*Top.* i. 1, 100 b 21-23); and in that it is not like science a deduction from true and primary principles of a definite subject to true consequences, but a deduction from opinion to opinion, which may be true or false. Sophistry appeared to him to be like it, except that it is a fallacious deduction either from merely apparent probabilities in its matter or itself merely apparently syllogistic in its form (cf. *Topics*, i. 1). Moreover, he compared dialectic and sophistry, on account of their generality, with primary philosophy in the*Metaphysics* (Γ 2, 1004 b 17-26); to the effect that all three concern themselves with all things, but that about everything metaphysics is scientific, dialectic tentative, sophistry

119

apparent, not real. He means that a sophist like Protagoras will teach superficially anything as wisdom for money; and that even a dialectician like Plato will write a dialogue, such as the *Republic*, nominally about justice, but really about all things from the generality of the form of good, instead of from appropriate moral principles; but that a primary philosopher selects as a definite subject all things as such without interfering with the special sciences of different things each in its kind (*Met.* Γ 1), and investigates the axioms or common principles of things as things (*ib*.3), without pretending, like Plato, to deduce from any common principle the special principles of each science (*Post. An.* i. 9, 32). Aristotle at once maintains the primacy of metaphysics and vindicates the independence of the special sciences. He is at the same time the only Greek philosopher who clearly discriminated discovery and disputation, science and dialectic, the knowledge of a definite subject from its appropriate principles and the discussion of anything whatever from opinions and authority. On one side he places science and philosophy, on the other dialectic and sophistry.

Such is the great mind of Aristotle manifested in the large map of learning, by which we have now to determine the order of his extant philosophical writings, with a view to studying them in their real order, which is neither chronological nor traditional, but philosophical and scientific. Turning over the pages of the Berlin edition, but passing over works which are perhaps spurious, we should put first and foremost speculative philosophy, and therein the primary philosophy of his *Metaphysics* (980 a 21-1093 b 29); then the secondary philosophy of his *Physics*, followed by his other physical works, general and biological, including among the latter the *Historia Animalium* as preparatory to the *De Partibus Animalium*, and the *De Anima* and *Parva Naturalia*, which he called "physical" but we call "psychological" (184 a 10-967 b 27); next, the practical philosophy of the *Ethics*, including the *Eudemian Ethics* and the *Magna Moralia* as earlier and the *Nicomachean Ethics* as later (1094-1249 b 25), and of the *Politics* (1252-1342), with the addition of the newly discovered*Athenian Constitution* as ancillary to it; finally, the productive science, or art, of the *Rhetoric*, including the earlier *Rhetoric to Alexander* and the later *Rhetorical Art*, and of the *Poetics*, which was unfinished (1354-end). This is the real order of Aristotle's system, based on his own theory and classification of sciences.

But what has become of Logic, with which the traditional order of Andronicus begins Aristotle's works (1-148 b 8)? So far from coming first, Logic comes nowhere in his classification of science. Aristotle was the founder of Logic; because, though others, and especially Plato, had made occasional remarks about reason (λόγος), Aristotle was the first to conceive it as a definite subject of investigation. As he says at the end of the *Sophistical Elenchi* on the syllogism, he had no predecessor, but took pains and laboured a long time in investigating it. Nobody, not even Plato, had discovered that the process of deduction is a combination of premisses (συλλογισμός) to produce a new conclusion. Aristotle, who made this great discovery, must have had great difficulty in developing the new investigation of reasoning processes out of dialectic, rhetoric, poetics, grammar, metaphysics, mathematics, physics and ethics; and in disengaging it from other kinds of learning. He got so far as gradually to write short discourses and long treatises, which we, not he, now arrange in the order of the*Categories* or names; the *De Interpretatione* on propositions; the*Analytics, Prior* on syllogism, *Posterior* on scientific syllogism; the*Topics* on dialectical syllogism; the *Sophistici Elenchi* on eristical or sophistical syllogism; and, except that he had hardly a logic of induction, he covered the ground. But after all this original research he got no further. First, he did not combine all these works into a system. He may have laid out the sequence of syllogisms from the *Analytics*onwards; but how about the *Categories* and the *De Interpretatione*? Secondly, he made no division of logic. In the *Categories* he distinguished names and propositions for the sake of the classification of names; in the *De Interpretatione* he distinguished nouns and verbs from sentences with a view to the enunciative sentence: in the*Analytics* he analysed the syllogism into premisses and premisses into terms and copula, for the purpose of syllogism. But he never called any of these a division of all logic. Thirdly, he had no one name for logic. In the *Posterior Analytics* (i. 22, 84 a 7-8) he distinguishes two modes of investigation, analytically (ἀναλυτικῶς) and logically (λογικῶς). But "analytical" means scientific inference from appropriate principles, and "logical" means dialectical inference from general considerations; and the former gives its name to the *Analytics*, the latter suits the *Topics*, while neither analytic nor logic is a name for all the works afterwards called logic. Fourthly, and consequently, he gave no place to any science embracing the whole of those works in his classification of science, but merely threw out the hint that we should know analytics before questioning the acceptance of the axioms of being (*Met.* Γ 3).

It is a commentator's blunder to suppose that the founder of logic elaborated it into a system, and then applied it to the sciences. He really left the Peripatetics to combine his scattered discourses and treatises into a system, to call it logic, and logic *Organon*, and to put it first as the instrument of sciences; and it was the Stoics who first called logic a science, and assigned it the first place in their triple classification of science into logic, physics, ethics. Would Aristotle have consented? Would he not rather have given the first place to primary philosophy?

Dialectic was distinguished from science by Aristotle. Is logic, then, according to him, not science but dialectic? The word logically (λογικῶς) means the same as dialectically (διαλεκτικῶς). But the general discussion of opinions, signified by both words, is only a subordinate part of Aristotle's profound investigation of the whole process of reasoning. The *Analytics*, the most important part, so far from being dialectic or logic in that narrow sense, is called by him not logic but analytic science (ἀναλυτικὴ ἐπιστήμη, *Rhet.* i. 4, 1359 b 10; cf, 1356 b 9, 1357 a 30, b 25); and in the *Metaphysics* he evidently refers to it as "the science which considers demonstration and science," which he distinguishes from the three speculative sciences, mathematics, physics and primary philosophy (Met. K 1, 1059 b 9-21). The *Analytics* then, which from the beginning claims to deal with science, is a science of sciences, without however forming any part of the classification. On the other hand, it does not follow that Aristotle would have regarded the *Topics*, which he calls "the investigation" and "the investigation of dialectic" (ἡ πραγματεία,*Top*, i. 1, ἡ πραγματεία ἡ περὶ τὴν διαλεκτικήν, Pr. *An.* i. 30, 46 a 30), or the *De Interpretatione*, which he calls "the present theory" (τῆς νῦν θεωρίας, *De Int.* 6, 17 a 7), as science. In fact, as to the *Categories* as well as the *De Interpretatione*, we are at a complete loss. But about the *Topics* we may venture to make the suggestion that, as in describing consciousness Aristotle says we perceive that we perceive, and understand that we understand, and as he calls *Analytics* a science of sciences, so he might have called the *Topics* a dialectical investigation of dialectic. Now, this suggestion derives support from his own description of the allied art of Rhetoric. "Rhetoric is counterpart to dialectic" is the first sentence of the *Rhetoric*; and the reason is that both are concerned with common objects of no definite science. Afterwards dialectic and rhetoric are said to differ from other arts in taking either side of a question (i. 1, 1355 a 33-35); rhetoric, since its artificial evidences involve characters, passions and reasoning, is called a kind of offshoot of dialectic and morals, and a copy of dialectic, because neither is a science of anything definite, but both faculties (δυνάμεις) of providing arguments (i. 2, 1356 a 33); and, since rhetorical arguments are examples and enthymemes analysed in the *Analytics*, rhetoric is finally regarded as a compound of analytic science and of 519morals, while it is like dialectical and sophistic arguments (i. 4, 1359 b 2-17).

As then Aristotle himself regarded rhetoric as partly science and partly dialectic, perhaps he would have said that his works on reasoning are some science and others not, and that, while the investigation of syllogism with a view to scientific syllogism in the *Analytics* is analytic science, the investigation of dialectical syllogism, in the *Topics*, with its abuse, eristical syllogism, in the *Sophistici Elenchi*, is dialectic. At any rate, these miscellaneous works on reasoning have no right to stand first in Aristotle's writings under any one name, logic or *Organon*. As he neither put them together, nor on any one definite plan, we are left to convenience; and the most convenient place is with the psychology of the *De Anima*.

As for dialectic itself, it would have been represented by Aristotle's early dialogues, had they not been lost except a few fragments. But none of his extant writings is so much dialectic, like a Platonic dialogue. They contain however many relics of dialectic. The *Rhetoric* is declared by him to be partly dialectic. The *Topics* is at least an investigation of dialectic, which has had an immense influence on the method of argument. The *Magna Moralia* almost runs into dialogue. Besides, all the extant works, though apparently didactic, are full of dialectical matter in the way of opinions (λεγόμενα), difficulties and doubts (ἀπορήματα, ἀπορίαι), solutions (λύσεις), and of dialectical style in the way of conversational expressions. It is probable also that the "extraneous discourses" (οἱ ἐξωτερικοὶ λόγοι) sometimes mentioned in them here mean dialectical discussions of a subject from opinions extraneous to its nature, as opposed to scientific deduction from its appropriate principles. From the eight passages, which refer to the extraneous discourses, we find (1) that Platonic forms were made by them matters of common talk (τεθρύληται, *Met.* M 1, 1076a 28); (2) that time was made by them matter of doubts, which in this case are Aristotle's own doubts (*Phys.* iv. 10, 217 b 31-218 a 30); (3) that the discussions of Platonic forms in them and in philosophical discourses were different (*E.E.* i. 8, 1217 b 22); (4) that the ordinary distinction between goods of mind, body and estate is one which we make (διαιρούμεθα) in them (*E.E.* ii. 1, 1218 b 34); (5) that in them appeared the division of soul into irrational and rational, used by Aristotle (*E.N.* i. 13, 1102 a 26), and attributed to Plato; (6) that the distinction between action and production accepted by Aristotle appeared in them (*E.N.* vi. 4, 1140 a 3); (7) that a distinction between certain kinds of rule is one which we make often (διοριζόμεθα ... πολλάκις) in them (*Pol.*16, 1278 b 31); (8) that a discussion about the best life, used by Aristotle, was made in them (*Pol.* H 1, 1323 a 22). On the whole, the interpretation which best suits all the passages is that extraneous discourses mean any extra-scientific dialectical discussions, oral or written, occurring in dialogues by Plato, or by Aristotle, or by anybody else, or in ordinary conversation, on any subject under the sun.

Among all the eight passages mentioned above, the most valuable is that from the *Eudemian Ethics* (A 8), which discriminates extraneous discourses and philosophical (καὶ ἐν τοῖς ἐξωτερικοῖς λόγοις καὶ ἐν τοῖς κατὰ φιλοσοφίαν, 1217 b 22-23); and it is preceded (A 6, 1216 b 35-37 a 17), by a similar distinction between foreign discourses (ἀλλοτρίοι λόγοι) and discourses appropriate to the thing (οἰκεῖοι λόγοι τοῦ πράγματος), which marks even better the opposition intended between dialectic and philosophy. Now, as in all eight passages Aristotle speaks, somewhat disparagingly, of "even (καὶ) extraneous discourses," and as these include his own early dialogues, they must be taken to mean that though he might quote them, he no longer wished to be judged by his early views, and therefore drew a strong line of demarcation between his early dialogues and the mature treatises of his later philosophical system. Now, both were in the hands of his readers in the time of Andronicus. Therefore his contemporary, Cicero, who knew the early dialogues on *Philosophy*, the *Eudemus* and the *Protrepticus*, and also among the mature scientific writings the *Topics, Rhetoric,Politics, Physics* and *De Coelo*, to some extent, was justified by Aristotle's example and precept in drawing the line between two kinds of books, one written popularly, called exoteric, the other more accurately (Cic. *De Finibus*, v. 5). But there was no doubt a tendency to extend the term "exoteric" from the dialectical to the more popular of the scientific writings of Aristotle, to make a new distinction between exoteric and acroamatic or esoteric, and even to make out that Aristotle was in the habit of teaching both exoterically and acroamatically day by day as head of the Peripatetic school at Athens. Aulus Gellius in the 2nd century A.D.supplies the best proof of this growth of tradition in his *Noctes Atticae* (xx. 5). He says that Aristotle (1) divided his*commentationes* and arts taught to his pupils into ἐξωτερικά and ἀκροατικά; (2) taught the latter in the morning walk (ἑωθινὸν περίπατον), the former in the evening walk (δειλινὸν περίπατον); (3) divided his books in the same manner; (4) defended himself against Alexander's letter, complaining that it was not right to his pupils to have published his acroamatic works, by replying in a letter that they were published and not published, because they are intelligible only to those who heard them. Gellius then quotes this correspondence, also given by Plutarch, and quotes it *ex Andronici philosophi libro*. The answer to the first three points is that Aristotle did not make any distinction between exoteric and acroamatic, and was not likely to have any longer taught his exoteric dialogues when he was teaching his mature philosophy at Athens, but may have alternated the teaching of the latter between the more abstruse and the more popular parts which had gradually come to be called "exoteric." As regards the last point, the authority of Andronicus proves that he at all events did not exaggerate his own share in publishing Aristotle's works; but it does not prove either that this correspondence between Alexander and Aristotle took place, or that Aristotle called his philosophical writings acroamatic, or that he had published them wholesale to the world.

The literary career of Aristotle falls into three periods, (1) The early period; when he was writing and publishing exoteric dialogues, but also tending to write didactic works, and beginning his scientific writings, *e.g.* the *Politics* in 357, the *Meteorologica* in 356. (2) The immature period; when he was continuing his didactic and scientific works, and composing first drafts, *e.g.* the *Categories*, the *Eudemian Ethics*, the *Magna Moralia*, the *Rhetoric to Alexander*. (3) The mature period; when he was finishing his scientific works, completing his system, and not publishing it but teaching it in the Peripatetic school; when he would teach not his early dialogues, nor his immature writings and first drafts, but mature works, *e.g.* the *Metaphysics*, the*Nicomachean Ethics*, the *Rhetoric*; and above all teach his whole system as far as possible in the real order of his classification of science.

VI. THE ARISTOTELIAN PHILOSOPHY

We have now (1) sketched the life of Aristotle as a reader and a writer from early manhood; (2) have watched him as a Platonist, partly imitating but gradually emancipating himself from his master to form a philosophy of his own; (3) have traced the gradual composition of his writings from Plato's time onwards; (4) have distinguished earlier, more Platonic and rudimentary, from later, more independent and mature, writings; (5) have founded the real order of his writings, not on chronology, nor on tradition, but on his classification of science and learning. It remains to answer the final question:—What is the Aristotelian philosophy, which its author gradually formed with so much labour? Here we have only room for its spirit, which we shall try to give as if he were himself speaking to us, as head of the Peripatetic school at Athens, and holding no longer the early views of his dialogues, or the immature views of such treatises as the *Categories*, but only his mature views, such as he expresses in the *Metaphysics*. Aristotle was primarily a metaphysician, a philosopher of things, who uses the objective method of proceeding from being to thinking. We shall begin therefore with that

122

primary philosophy which is the real basis of his philosophy, and proceed in the order of his classification of science to give his chief doctrines on:—

(1) Speculative philosophy, metaphysical and physical, including his psychology, and with it his logic.

(2) Practical philosophy, ethics and politics.

(3) Productive science, or art.

Things are substances (οὐσίαι), each of which is a separate individual (χωριστόν, τόδε τι, καθ᾽ ἕκαστον) and is variously affected as quantified, qualified, related, active, passive and so forth, in categories of things which are attributes (συμβεβηκότα), different from the category of substance, but real only as predicates belonging to some substance, and are in fact only the substance itself affected (αὐτὸ πεπονθός). The essence of each substance, being what it is (τὸ τί ἐστι, τὸ τί ἦν εἶναι), is that substance; *e.g.* this rational animal, Socrates. Substances are so similar that the individuals of a species are even the same in essence or substance, *e.g.* Callias and Socrates differ in matter but are the same in essence, as rational animals. The universal (τὸ καθόλου) is real only as one predicate belonging to many individual substances: it is therefore not a substance. There are then no separate universal forms, as Plato supposed. There are attributes and universals, real as belonging to individual substances, whose being is their being. The mind, especially in mathematics, abstracts numbers, motions, relations, causes, essences, ends, kinds; and it over-abstracts things mentally separate into things really separate. But reality consists only of individual substances, numerous, moving, related, active as efficient causes, passive as material causes, essences as formal causes, ends as final causes, and in classes which are real 520universals only as real predicates of individual substances. Such is Aristotle's realism of individuals and universals, contained in his primary philosophy, as expressed in the*Metaphysics*, especially in Book Z, his authoritative pronouncement on being and substance.

The individual substances, of which the universe is composed, fall into three great irreducible kinds: nature, God, man.

I. Nature.—The obvious substances are natural substances or bodies (φυσικαὶ οὐσίαι, σώματα), *e.g.* animals, plants, water, earth, moon, sun, stars. Each natural substance is a compound (σύνθετον, συνθέτη οὐσία) of essence and matter; its essence (εἶδος, μορφή, τὸ τί ἐστι, τὸ τί ἦν εἶναι) being its actual substance, its matter (ὕλη) not; its essence being determinate, its matter not; its essence being immaterial, its matter conjoined with the essence; its essence being one in all individuals of a species, its matter different in each individual; its essence being cause of uniformity, its matter cause of accident. At the same time, matter is not nothing, but something, which, though not substance, is potentially substance; and it is either proximate to the substance, or primary; proximate, as a substance which is potentially different, *e.g.* wood potentially a table; primary, as an indeterminate something which is a substratum capable of becoming natural substances, of which it is always one; and it is primarily the matter of earth, water, air, fire, the four simple bodies (ἁπλᾶ σώματα) with natural rectilineal motions in the terrestrial world (*De Gen. et Cor.* ii. I seq.); while aether (αἰθήρ) is a fifth simple body, with natural circular motion, being the element of the stars (τὸ τῶν ἄστρων στοιχεῖον) in the celestial world. Each natural substance is a formal cause, as being what it is; a material cause, as having passive power to be changed; an efficient cause, as having active power to change, by communicating the selfsame essence into different matter so as to produce therein a homogeneous effect in the same species; and a final cause, as an end to be realized. Moreover, though each natural substance is corruptible (φθαρτόν), species is eternal (ἀΐδιον), because there was always some individual of it to continue its original essence (expressed by the imperfect tense in τὸ τί ἦν εἶναι), which is ungenerated and incorruptible; the natural world therefore is eternal; and nature is for ever aiming at an eternal propagation, by efficient acting on matter, of essence as end. For even nature does nothing in vain, but aims at final causes, which she uniformly realizes, except so far as matter by its spontaneity (ἀπὸ τοῦ αὐτομάτου) causes accidental effects; and the ends of nature are no form of good, nor even the good of man, but the essences of natural substances themselves, and, above them all, the good God Himself. Such is Aristotle's natural realism, pervading his metaphysical and physical writings.

II. *God.*—Nature is but one kind of being (ἓν γάρ τι γένος τοῦ ὄντος ἡ φύσις, *Met.* Γ 3, 1005 a 34). Above all natural substances, the objects of natural science, there stands a supernatural substance, the object of metaphysics as theology. Nature's boundary is the outer sphere of the fixed stars, which is eternally moved day after day in a uniform circle round the earth. Now, an actual cause is required for an actual effect. Therefore, there must be a prime mover of that prime movable, and equally eternal and uniform. That prime mover is God, who is not the creator, but the mover directly of the heavens, and indirectly through the planets of sublunary substances. But God is no mechanical mover. He moves as motive (κινεῖ δὲ ὡς ἐρώμενον,*Met.* Λ 7, 1072 b 3); He is the efficient only as the final cause of nature. For God is a living being, eternal, very good (ζῷον ἀΐδιον ἄριστον, *ib.* 1072 b 29). While nature aims at Him as design, as an end, a motive, a final cause, God's occupation (διαγωγή) is intelligence (νόησις); and since essence, not indeed in all being, but in being understood, becomes identical with intelligence, God in understanding essence is understanding Himself; and in short, God's intelligence is at once intelligence of Himself, of essence and of intelligence,—καὶ ἔστιν ἡ νόησις νοήσεως νόησις (*Met.* Λ 7, 1074 b 34). But at the same time the essence of good exists not only in God and God's intelligence on the one hand, but also on the other hand on a declining scale in nature, as both in a general and in his army; but rather in God, and more in some parts of nature than in others. Thus even God is a substance, a separate individual, whose differentiating essence is to be a living being, eternal and very good; He is however the only substance whose essence is entirely without matter and unconjoined with matter; and therefore He is a substance, not because He has or is a substratum beneath attributes, but wholly because He is a separate individual, different both from nature and men, yet the final good of the whole universe. Such is Aristotle's theological realism without materialism and the origin of all spiritualistic realism, contained in his *Metaphysics* (Λ 6-end).

III. *Man.*—There is a third kind of substance, combining something both of the natural and of the divine: we men are that privileged species. Each man is a substance, like any other, only because he is a separate individual. Like any natural substance, he is composed of matter and immateriate essence. But natural substances are inorganic and organic; and a man is an organic substance composed of an organic body (ὀργανικὸν σῶμα) as matter, and a soul (ψυχή) as essence, which is the primary actuality of an organic body capable of life (ζωή). Still a man is not the only organism; and every organism has a soul, whose immediate organ is the spirit (πνεῦμα), a body which—analogous to a body diviner than the four so-called elements, namely the aether, the element of the stars—gives to the organism its non-terrestrial vital heat, whether it be a plant or an animal. In an ascending scale, a plant is an organism with a nutritive soul; an animal is a higher organism with a nutritive, sensitive, orectic and locomotive soul; a man is the highest organism with a nutritive, sensitive, orectic, locomotive and rational soul. What differentiates man from other natural and organic substances, and approximates him to a supernatural substance, God, is reason (λόγος), or intellect (νοῦς). Now, though only one of the powers of the soul, intellect alone of these powers has no bodily organ; it alone is immortal: it alone is divine. While the soul is propagated, like any other essence, by the efficient, which is the seed, to the matter, which is the germ, of the embryo man, intellect alone enters from without (θύραθεν), and is alone divine (θεῖον, not θεός), because its activity communicates with no bodily activity (*De Gen.* II. 3, 736-737). A man then is a third kind of substance, like a natural substance in bodily matter, like a supernatural substance in divine reason or intellect. Such is Aristotle's dual, or rather triple, realism, continued in his *De Anima* and other biological writings, especially *De Generatione Animalium*, ii.

There are three points about a man's life which both connect him with, and distinguish him from, God. God's occupation is speculative; man's is speculation, practice and production.

I. *Speculation* (θεωρία).—Since things are individuals, and there is nothing, and nothing universal, beyond them, there are two kinds of knowledge (γνῶσις), sense (αἴσθησις) of individuals, intellect (νοῦς) of universals. Both powers know by being passively receptive of essence propagated by an efficient cause; but, while in sense the efficient cause is an external object (ἔξωθεν), in intelligence it is active intellect (νοῦς τῷ ποιεῖν) propagating its essence in passive intellect (νοῦς παθητικός). Nevertheless, without sense there is no knowledge. Sense receives from the external world an essence, *e.g.* of white, which is really universal as well as individual, but apprehends it only as individual, *e.g.* this white substance: intellect thereupon discovers the universal essence but only in the individuals of sense. This intellectual discovery requires sensation and retention of sensation; so that sense (αἴσθησις) receives impressions, imagination (φαντασία) retains them as images, intellect (νοῦς) generalizes the universal, and, when it is intelligence of essence, is always true.

This is the origin of knowledge, psychologically regarded (in the *De Anima*). Logically regarded, the origin of all teaching and learning of an intellectual kind is a process of induction (ἐπαγωγή) from particulars to universal, and of syllogism (συλλογισμός) from universal to further particulars; induction, whenever it starts from sense, becomes the origin of scientific knowledge (ἐπιστήμη); while there is also a third process of example (παράδειγμα) from particular to particular, which produces only persuasion. In acquiring scientific knowledge, syllogism cannot start from universals without induction, nor induction acquire universals without sense. At the same time, there are three species of syllogism, scientific, dialectical and eristical or sophistical; and in consequence there are different ways of acquiring premisses. In

124

order to acquire the knowledge of the true and primary principles of scientific knowledge, and especially the 521intelligence of the universal essence of the subject, which is always true, the process of knowledge consists of (1) sense (αἴσθησις), which receives the essence as individual, (2) memory (μνήμη), which is a retention of sensible impression, (3) experience (ἐμπειρία), which consists of a number of similar memories, (4) induction (ἐπαγωγή), which infers the universal as a fact (τὸ ὅτι), (5) intellect (νοῦς), which apprehends the principle (ἀρχή); because it is a true apprehension that the universal induced is the very essence and formal cause of the subject: thereupon, scientific syllogism (ἐπιστημονικὸς συλλογισμός), making the definition (ὁρισμος) of this essence the middle term (τὸ μέσον), becomes a demonstration (ὁρισμος) of the consequences which follow from the essence in the conclusion. Such then is science. In order to acquire the probabilities (τὰ ἔνδοξα) of opinion (δόξα), which are the premisses of dialectical syllogism, the process is still induction, as in science, but dialectical induction by interrogation from the opinions of the answerers until the universal is conceded: thereupon the dialectical syllogism (διαλεκτικὸς συλλογισμός) deduces consequent opinions in the conclusion. Nor does the process of acquiring the premisses of eristical syllogism, which is fallacious either in its premisses or in its process, differ, except that, when the premisses are fallacious, the dialectical interrogations must be such as to cause this fallacy. Hence, as science and dialectic are different, so scientific induction and syllogism must be distinguished from dialectical induction and syllogism. Dialectic is useful, for exercise, for conversation and for philosophical sciences, where by being critical it has a road to principles. But it is by a different process of sense, memory, experience, induction, intelligence, syllogism, that science becomes knowledge of real causes, of real effects, and especially of real essences from which follow real consequences, not beyond, but belonging to real substances. So can we men, not, as Plato thought, by having in our souls universal principles innate but forgotten, but by acquiring universal principles from sense, which is the origin of knowledge, arrive at judgments which are true, and true because they agree with the things which we know by sense, by inference and by science. Such is Aristotle's psychological and logical realism, contained in the *De Anima* and logical treatises.

2. *Practice* (πρᾶξις).—In this natural world of real substances, human good is not an imitation of a supernatural universal form of the good, but is human happiness; and this good is the same both of the individual as a part and of the state as a whole. Ethics then is a kind of Politics. But in Ethics a man's individual good is his own happiness; and his happiness is no mere state, but an activity of soul according to virtue in a mature life, requiring as conditions moderate bodily and external goods of fortune; his virtue is (1) moral virtue, which is acquired by habituation, and is a purposive habit of performing actions in the mean determined by right reason or prudence; requiring him, not to exclude, but to moderate his desires; and (2) intellectual virtue, which is either prudence of practical, or wisdom of speculative intellect; and his happiness is a kind of ascending scale of virtuous activities, in which moral virtue is limited by prudence, and prudence by wisdom; so that the speculative life of wisdom is the happiest and most divine, and the practical life of prudence and moral virtue secondary and human. Good fortune in moderation is also required as a condition of his happiness. Must we then, on account of misfortunes, look with Solon at the end, and call no man happy till he is dead? Or is this altogether absurd for us who say that happiness is an activity? Virtuous activities determine happiness, and a virtuous man is happy in this life, in spite of misfortunes unless they be too great; while after death he will not feel the misfortunes of the living so much as to change his happiness. Still, for perfect happiness a man should prefer the speculative life of divine intellect, and immortalize (ἀθανατίζειν) as far as possible. For intellect is what mainly makes a man what he is, and is divine and immortal.

To turn from Ethics to Politics, the good of the individual on a small scale becomes on a large scale the good of the citizen and the state, whose end should be no far-off form of good, and no mere guarantee of rights, but the happiness of virtuous action, the life according to virtue, which is the general good of the citizen. Hence, the citizen of the best state is he who has the power and the purpose to be governed and govern for the sake of the life according to virtue.

A right government is one which aims at the general good, whereas any government which aims at its own good is a deviation. Hence governments are to be arranged from best to worst in the following order:—

I. Right governments (ὀρθαὶ πολιτεῖαι), aiming at the general good:—
i. Monarchy, of one excelling in virtue:
ii. Aristocracy, of a class excelling in virtue:
iii. Commonwealth, of the majority excelling in virtue.
II. Deviations (παρεκβάσεις), aiming at the good of the government:—
i. Democracy, aiming at the good of the majority:

ii. Oligarchy, aiming at the good of the few:

iii. Tyranny, aiming at the good of one.

Such is Aristotle's practical philosophy, contained in his matured*Nicomachean Ethics*, and his unfinished *Politics*.

3. *Production* (ποίησις).—Production differs from practice in being an activity (ἐνέργεια; *e.g.* building) which is always a means to a work (ἔργον; *e.g.* a house) beyond itself. Productive science, or art, is an intellectual habit of true reasoning from appropriate principles, acquired from experiences, and applied to the production of the work which is the end of the art. All the arts are therefore at once rational and productive. They are either for necessity (*e.g.* medicine) or for occupation (*e.g.* poetry), the former being inferior to the latter. Rhetoric is a faculty on any subject of investigating what may be persuasive (πιθανόν), which is the work of no other art; its means are artificial and inartificial evidences (πίστεις), and, among artificial evidences, especially the logical arguments of example and enthymeme. Poetry is the art of producing representations; (1) in words, rhythm and harmony (ἁρμονία, "harmony" in the original sense); (2) of men like ourselves, or better as in tragedy, or worse as in comedy; (3) by means of narrative as in epic, or by action as in the drama. The cause of poetry is man's instinct of representation and his love of representations caused by the pleasure of learning. Comedy is representation of men inferior in being ludicrous: epic is like tragedy a representation of superior men, but by means of narrative and unlimited in time: tragedy is a representation of an action superior and complete, in a day if possible, by means of action, and accomplishing by pity and fear the purgation of such passions (*Poetics*, 1449 b 24). Music is a part of moral education; and for this end we should use the most moral harmonies. But music has also other ends and uses, and on the whole four; namely amusement, virtue, occupation and purgation of the affections; for some men are liable more than others to pity and fear and enthusiasm, but from sacred melodies we see them, when they have heard those which act orgiastically on the soul, becoming settled by a kind of medicine and purgation (κάθαρσις), and being relieved with pleasure. Finally, art is not morality, because its end is always a work of art, not virtuous action: on the other hand, art is subordinate to morality, because all the ends of art are but means to the end of life, and therefore a work of art which offends against morality is opposed to the happiness and the good of man. Such is Aristotle's productive science or art, contained in his *Rhetoric* and *Poetics*, compared with his *Ethics* and *Politics*.

Aristotle, even in this sketch of his system, shows himself to be the philosopher of facts, who can best of all men bear criticism; and indeed it must be confessed that he retained many errors of Platonism and laid himself open to the following objections. Two substances, being individuals, *e.g.* Socrates and Callias, are in no way the same, but only similar, even in essence, *e.g.* Socrates is one rational animal, Callias another. A universal, *e.g.* the species man, is not predicate of many individuals (ἓν κατὰ πολλῶν, *Post. An.* i. II), but a whole number of similar individuals, *e.g.* all men; and not a whole species, but only an individual, is a predicate of such individual, *e.g.* Socrates is a man, not all men, and one white thing, not all white things. Consequently, a species or genus is not a substance, as Aristotle says it is in the *Categories* (inconsistently with his own doctrine of substances), but a whole number of substances, *e.g.* all men, all animals. Similarly, the universal essence of a species is not one and the same as each individual essence, but is the whole number of similar individual essences of the similar individuals of the species, *e.g.* all rational animals. Consequently, the universal essence of a species of substances is not one and the same eternal essence in all the individuals of a species but only similar, and is not substance as Aristotle calls it in the *Metaphysics*, inconsistently with his own doctrine of substance, but is a whole number of similar substances, *e.g.*all rational animals which are what all men are. Hence again, the natural world of species and essences is not eternal, but only endures as long as there are individual substances. Hence, moreover, a natural substance or body as an efficient cause or force causes an effect on another, not by propagating one eternal essence of a species into the matter of the other, but so far as we really understand force, by their reciprocally preventing one another from occupying the same place at the same moment on account of the mutual resistance of any two bodies. The essence of a natural substance, *e.g.* wood, is not immateriate, but is the whole body as what it is. The matter of a natural substance is not a primary matter which is one indeterminate substratum of all natural substances, but is only one body as able to be changed by a force which is another substance able to change it, *e.g.* a seed becoming wood, wood becoming coal, &c. A natural substance or body, therefore, is not a heterogeneous compound of essence and matter, but is essence as what it is, matter as able passively to be changed, force as able actively to change. The simple bodies which are the matter of the rest are not terrestrial earth, water, air, fire, 522and a different celestial aether, but whatever elementary bodies natural science, starting anew from mechanics and chemistry, may determine to be the matter of all other bodies whatever. Nature does not aim at God as end, but God, thinking and willing ends, produces and acts on nature. Soul is not an immateriate essence of an organic body capable, but an immateriate conscious substance within an organic body. Sensation is not the reception of the selfsame essence of an external body, but one's perception of one's sentient organism as affected, and especially of its organs resisting one another, *e.g.* one's lips, hands, &c., preventing one another from occupying the same place at the same moment within one's organism. Intelligence does not differ from sense by having no bodily organ, but the nervous system is the bodily organ of both. Intelligence is not active intellect propagating universal essence in passive intellect, but only logical inference starting from sense, and both requiring nervous body and conscious soul. It is not always a true apprehension of essence, but often, especially in physical matter, such as sound or heat or light, takes superficial effects to be the essence of the thing. Aristotle did not altogether solve the question, What is, and scarcely solved at all the question, How do we know the external world?

We might continue to object. But at bottom there remains the fundamental position of Aristotelianism, that all things are substances, individuals separate though related; that some things are attributes, real only as being some individual substance somehow affected, or, as we should say, modified or determined; and that without individual substances there is nothing, and nothing universal apart from individuals. There remains too the consequence that there are different substances, separate from but related to one another; and these substances of three irreducible kinds, natural, supernatural, human. Aristotelianism has to be considered against the philosophy which preceded it and against the philosophy which has since followed it. Platonism preceded it, and was the metaphysical doctrine that all things are supernatural—forms, gods, souls. Idealism has since followed it, and is the metaphysical doctrine that all things are mind and states of mind. Aristotelianism intervenes between ancient Platonism and modern Idealism, and is the metaphysical doctrine that all things are substances, natural and supernatural and human. It is a philosophy of substantial things, standing as a *via media* between a philosophy of the supernatural and a philosophy of mind. There are three alternatives, which may be put as questions which every thinker must ask himself. Are the things which surround me in what I call the environment,—the men, the animals, the plants, the ground, the stones, the water, the air, the moon, the sun, the stars and God—are they shadows, unsubstantial things, as formerly Platonism made all things to be except the supernatural world of forms, gods and souls? Or are they, as modern Idealism says, mind and states of mind? Or are they really substances separate from, though related to, myself, who am also a substance? The Aristotelian answer is—"Yes, all things are substances, but not all supernatural, nor all mental; for some are natural substances, or bodies"; and by that answer Aristotelianism stands or falls.

LITERATURE.—The Aristotelian philosophy is to be studied first in Aristotle's works, which are the best commentaries on one another; the best complete edition is the Berlin edition (1831-1870), by Bekker and Brandis, in which also are the fragments collected by V. Rose, the scholia collected by Brandis, and the index compiled by Bonitz. After reading the remains of the Peripatetic school, the Greek commentators should be further studied in this edition. The Latin commentators, the Arabians and the schoolmen show how Aristotle has been the chief author of modern culture; while the vindication of modern independence comes out in its critics, the greatest of whom were Roger and Francis Bacon. Since the modern discovery of the science of motion by Galileo which changed natural science, and the modern revolution of philosophy by Descartes which changed metaphysics, the study of Aristotle has become less universal; but it did not die out, and received a fresh stimulus especially from Julius Pacius, who going back through G. Zabarella to the Arabians, and himself gifted with great logical powers, always deserves study in his editions of the *Organon* and the *Physics* and in his *Doctrinae Peripateticae*. In more recent times, as part of the growing conviction of the essentiality of everything Greek, Aristotle has received marked attention. In France there are the works of Cousin (1835), Félix Ravaisson, who wrote on the *Metaphysics* (1837-1846), and Barthélemy St Hilaire, who translated the *Organon* and other works (1844 seq.). In Germany there has been a host of commentaries, among which we may mention the *Organon* edited (1844-1846) by F. Th. Waitz (not so well as by Pacius), the *De Anima* edited (1833) by F.A. Trendelenburg and later by A. Torstrik, the *Historia Animalium* by H. Aubert and F. Wimmer (1868), the *Ethics* by K.L. Michelet (1827), the *Metaphysics* by A. Schwegler (1847) and (best of all) by H. Bonitz (1848), who is the most faithful of all commentators, because to great industry and acumen he adds the rare gift of confessing when he does not understand, and when he does not know what Aristotle might have thought. With Aristotle's works before one, with the *Index Aristotelicus*, and the edition and translation of the *Metaphysics* by Bonitz on one side, and Zeller's *Die Philosophie der Griechen*, ii. 2, "Aristoteles" (trans. by Costelloe and Muirhead), on the other side, one can go a considerable way towards understanding the foundations of Aristotelianism.

In England scholars tend to take up certain parts of Aristotle's philosophy. Grote indeed intended to write a general account of Aristotle like that of Plato; but his *Aristotle* went little further than the logical writings. From Cambridge we have J.W. Blakesley's *Life of Aristotle*, E.M. Cope's *Rhetoric*, Dr Henry Jackson's *Nicomachean Ethics*, v., S.H. Butcher's *Poetics*, Hicks's *De Anima*, J.E. Sandys's *Athenian Constitution*, Jebb's *Rhetoric* (ed. Sandys). Oxford in particular, since the beginning of the 19th century, has kept alive the study of Aristotle. E. Cardwell in his edition of the *Nicomachean Ethics* (1828) had the wisdom to found his text on the Laurentian Manuscript (Kb); E. Poste wrote translations of the *Posterior Analytics* and *Sophistici Elenchi*; R. Congreve edited the *Politics*; A. Grant edited the *Nicomachean Ethics*; E. Wallace translated and annotated the *De Anima*; B. Jowett translated the *Politics*; W.L. Newman has edited the *Politics* in four volumes; Dr Ogle has translated the *De Partibus Animalium*, with notes; R. Shute wrote a *History of the Aristotelian Writings*; Professor J.A. Stewart has written *Notes on the Nicomachean Ethics*; Professor J. Burnet has issued an annotated edition of the *Nicomachean Ethics*, and W.D. Ross has translated the *Metaphysics*. All these are, or were, Oxford men; and it remains to mention two others: I. Bywater, who as an Aristotelian scholar has done much for the improvement of Bekker's text, especially of the *Nicomachean Ethics* and the *Poetics*; and F.G. Kenyon, who has the proud distinction of having been the first modern editor of the Ἀθηναίων πολιτεία.

(T. CA.)

ARISTOXENUS, of Tarentum (4th century B.C.), a Greek peripatetic philosopher, and writer on music and rhythm. He was taught first by his father Spintharus, a pupil of Socrates, and later by the Pythagoreans, Lamprus of Erythrae and Xenophilus, from whom he learned the theory of music. Finally he studied under Aristotle at Athens, and was deeply annoyed, it is said, when Theophrastus was appointed head of the school on Aristotle's death. His writings, said to have numbered four hundred and fifty-three, were in the style of Aristotle, and dealt with philosophy, ethics and music. The empirical tendency of his thought is shown in his theory that the soul is related to the body as harmony to the parts of a musical instrument. We have no evidence as to the method by which he deduced this theory (cf. T. Gomperz, *Greek Thinkers*, Eng. trans. 1905, vol. iii. p. 43). In music he held that the notes of the scale are to be judged, not as the Pythagoreans held, by mathematical ratio, but by the ear. The only work of his that has come down to us is the three books of the *Elements of Harmony* (ῥυθμικὰ στοιχεῖα), an incomplete musical treatise. Grenfell and Hunt's *Oxyrhynchus Papyri* (vol. i., 1898) contains a five-column fragment of a treatise on metre, probably this treatise of Aristoxenus.

The best edition is by Paul Marquard, with German translation and full commentary, *Die harmonischen Fragmente des Aristoxenus* (Berlin, 1868). The fragments are also given in C W Müller, *Frag. Hist. Graec.*, ii. 269 sqq.; and R. Westphal, *Melik und Rhythmik d. klass. Hellenenthums* (2nd vol. edited by F. Saran, Leipzig, 1893). Eng. trans. by H.S. Macran (Oxford, 1902). See also W.L. Mahne, *Diatribe de Aristoxeno* (Amsterdam, 1793); B. Brill, *Aristoxenus' rhythmische und metrische Messungen* (1871); R. Westphal, *Griechische Rhythmik und Harmonik* (Leipzig, 1867); L. Laloy, *Aristoxène de Tarente et la musique de l'antiquité* (Paris, 1904); See PERIPATETICS, PYTHAGORAS (*Music*) and art. "Greek Music" in Grove's *Dict. of Music* (1904). For the Oxyrhynchus fragment see *Classical Review* (January 1898), and C. van Jan in Bursian's *Jahresbericht*, civ. (1901).

ARISUGAWA, the name of one of the royal families of Japan, going back to the seventh son of the mikado Go-Yozei (d. 1638). After the revolution of 1868, when the mikado Mutsu-hito was restored, his uncle, Prince Taruhito Arisugawa (1835-1895), became commander-in-chief, and in 1875 president of the senate. After his suppression of the Satsuma rebellion he was made a field-marshal, and he was chief of the staff in the war with China (1894-95). His younger brother, Prince Takehito Arisugawa (b. 1862), was from 1879 to 1882 in the British navy, serving in the Channel Squadron, and studied at the Naval College, Greenwich. In the Chino-Japanese War of 1894-95 he was in command of a cruiser, and subsequently became admiral-superintendent at Yokosuka. Prince Arisugawa represented Japan in England together with Marquis Ito at the Diamond Jubilee (1897), and in 1905 was again received there as the king's guest.

ARITHMETIC (Gr. ἀριθμητική, sc. τέχνη, the art of counting, from ἀριθμός, number), the art of dealing with numerical quantities in their numerical relations.

1. Arithmetic is usually divided into *Abstract Arithmetic* and *Concrete Arithmetic*, the former dealing with numbers and the latter with concrete objects. This distinction, however, might be misleading. In stating that the sum of 11d. and 9d. is 1s. 8d. we do not mean that nine pennies when added to eleven pennies produce a shilling and eight pennies. The sum of money

corresponding to 11d. may in fact be made up of coins in several different ways, so that the symbol "11d." cannot be taken as denoting any definite concrete objects. The arithmetical fact is that 11 and 9 may be regrouped as 12 and 8, and the statement "11d. + 9d. = 1s. 8d." is only an arithmetical statement in so far as each of the three expressions denotes a numerical quantity (§ 11).

2. The various stages in the study of arithmetic may be arranged in different ways, and the arrangement adopted must be influenced by the purpose in view. There are three main purposes, the practical, the educational, and the scientific; *i.e.* the subject may be studied with a view to technical skill in dealing with the arithmetical problems that arise in actual life, or for the sake of its general influence on mental development, or as an elementary stage in mathematical study.

3. The practical aspect is an important one. The daily activities of the great mass of the adult population, in countries where commodities are sold at definite prices for definite quantities, include calculations which have often to be performed rapidly, on data orally given, and leading in general to results which can only be approximate; and almost every branch of manufacture or commerce has its own range of applications of arithmetic. Arithmetic as a school subject has been largely regarded from this point of view.

4. From the educational point of view, the value of arithmetic has usually been regarded as consisting in the stress it lays on accuracy. This aspect of the matter, however, belongs mainly to the period when arithmetic was studied almost entirely for commercial purposes; and even then accuracy was not found always to harmonize with actuality. The development of physical science has tended to emphasize an exactly opposite aspect, viz. the impossibility, outside a certain limited range of subjects, of ever obtaining absolute accuracy, and the consequent importance of not wasting time in attempting to obtain results beyond a certain degree of approximation.

5. As a branch of mathematics, arithmetic may be treated logically, psychologically, or historically. All these aspects are of importance to the teacher: the logical, in order that he may know the end which he seeks to attain; the psychological, that he may know how best to attain this end; and the historical, for the light that history throws on psychology,

The logical arrangement of the subject is not the best for elementary study. The division into abstract and concrete, for instance, is logical, if the former is taken as relating to number and the latter to numerical quantity (§ 11). But the result of a rigid application of this principle would be that the calculation of the cost of 3 ℔ of tea at 2s. a ℔ would be deferred until after the study of logarithms. The psychological treatment recognizes the fact that the concrete precedes the abstract and that the abstract is based on the concrete; and it also recognizes the futility of attempting a strictly continuous development of the subject.

On the other hand, logical analysis is necessary if the subject is to be understood. As an illustration, we may take the elementary processes of addition, subtraction, multiplication and division. These are still called in text-books the "four simple rules"; but this name ignores certain essential differences. (i) If we consider that we are dealing with numerical quantities, we must recognize the fact that, while addition and subtraction might in the first instance be limited to such quantities, multiplication and division necessarily introduce the idea of pure number. (ii) If on the other hand we regard ourselves as dealing with pure number throughout, then, as multiplication is continued addition, we ought to include in our classification involution as continued multiplication. Or we might say that, since multiplication is a form of addition, and division a form of subtraction, there are really only two fundamental processes, viz. addition and subtraction. (iii) The inclusion of the four processes under one general head fails to indicate the essential difference between addition and multiplication, as direct processes, on the one hand, and subtraction and division, as inverse processes, on the other (§ 59).

6. The present article deals mainly with the principles of the subject, for which a logical arrangement is on the whole the more convenient. It is not suggested that this is the proper order to be adopted by the teacher.

I. NUMBER

7. *Ordinal and Cardinal Numbers.*—One of the primary distinctions in the use of number is between ordinal and cardinal numbers, or rather between the ordinal and the cardinal aspects of number. The usual statement is that *one, two, three,* ... are cardinal numbers, and *first, second, third,* ... are ordinal numbers. This, however, is an incomplete statement; the words one, two, three, ... and the corresponding symbols 1, 2, 3, ... or I, II, III, ... are used sometimes as ordinals, *i.e.* to denote the place of an individual in a series, and sometimes as cardinals, *i.e.* to denote the total number since the commencement of the series.

On the whole, the ordinal use is perhaps the more common. Thus "100" on a page of a book does not mean that the page is 100 times the page numbered 1, but merely that it is the page after 99. Even in commercial transactions, in dealing with sums of money, the statement of an amount often has reference to the last item added rather than to a total; and geometrical measurements are practically ordinal (§ 26).

For ordinal purposes we use, as symbols, not only figures, such as 1, 2, 3, ... but also letters, as a, b, c, ... Thus the pages of a book may be numbered 1, 2, 3, ... and the chapters I, II, III, ... but the sheets are lettered A, B, C, ... Figures and letters may even be used in combination; thus 16 may be followed by 16a and 16b, and these by 17, and in such a case the ordinal 100 does not correspond with the total (cardinal) number up to this point.

Arithmetic is supposed to deal with cardinal, not with ordinal numbers; but it will be found that actual numeration, beyond about three or four, is based on the ordinal aspect of number, and that a scientific treatment of the subject usually requires a return to this fundamental basis.

One difference between the treatment of ordinal and of cardinal numbers may be noted. Where a number is expressed in terms of various denominations, a cardinal number usually begins with the largest denomination, and an ordinal number with the smallest. Thus we speak of one thousand eight hundred and seventy-six, and represent it by MDCCCLXXVI or 1876; but we should speak of the third day of August 1876, and represent it by 3. 8. 1876. It might appear as if the writing of 1876 was an exception to this rule; but in reality 1876, when used in this way, is partly cardinal and partly ordinal, the first three figures being cardinal and the last ordinal. To make the year completely ordinal, we should have to describe it as the 6th year of the 8th decade of the 8th century of the 2nd millennium; *i.e.* we should represent the date by 3. 8. 6. 8. 9. 2, the total number of years, months and days completed being 1875. 7. 2.

524

In using an ordinal we direct our attention to a term of a series, while in using a cardinal we direct our attention to the interval between two terms. The total number in the series is the sum of the two cardinal numbers obtained by counting up to any interval from the beginning and from the end respectively; but if we take the ordinal numbers from the beginning and from the end we count one term twice over. Hence, if there are 365 days in a year, the 100th day from the beginning is the 266th, not the 265th, from the end.

8. *Meaning of Names of Numbers.*—What do we mean by any particular number, *e.g.* by *seven*, or by *two hundred and fifty-three*? We can define *two* as *one and one*, and *three* as *one and one and one*; but we obviously cannot continue this method for ever. For the definition of large numbers we may employ either of two methods, which will be called the *grouping* method and the *counting* method.

(i) *Method of Grouping.*—The first method consists in defining the first few numbers, and forming larger numbers by groups or aggregates, formed partly by multiplication and partly by addition. Thus, on the denary system (§16) we can give independent definitions to the numbers up to ten, and then regard (*e.g.*) fifty-three as a composite number made up of five tens and three ones. Or, on the quinary-binary system, we need only give independent definitions to the numbers up to five; the numbers *six, seven,* ... can then be regarded as *five and one, five and two,* ..., a fresh series being started when we get to *five and five* or *ten*. The grouping method introduces multiplication into the definition of large numbers; but this, from the teacher's point of view, is not now such a serious objection as it was in the days when children were introduced to millions and billions before they had any idea of elementary arithmetical processes.

(ii) *Method of Counting.*—The second method consists in taking a series of names or symbols for the first few numbers, and then repeating these according to a regular system for successive numbers, so that each number is defined by reference to the number immediately preceding it in the series. Thus *two* still means *one and one*, but *three* means *two and one*, not *one and one and one*. Similarly *two hundred and fifty-three* does not mean two hundreds, five tens and three ones, but *one* more than *two hundred and fifty-two*; and the number which is called one hundred is not defined as ten tens, but as one more than ninety-nine.

9. *Concrete and Abstract Numbers.*—Number is concrete or abstract according as it does or does not relate to particular objects. On the whole, the grouping method refers mainly to concrete numbers and the counting method to abstract numbers. If we sort objects into groups of ten, and find that there are five groups of ten with three over, we regard the five and the three as names for the actual sets of groups or of individuals. The three, for instance, are regarded as a whole when we name them *three*. If, however, we count these three as one, two, three, then the number of times we count is an abstract number. Thus number in the abstract is the number of times that the act of counting is performed in any particular case. This, however, is a description, not a definition, and we still want a definition for "number" in the phrase "number of times."

10. *Definition of "Number."*—Suppose we fix on a certain sequence of names "one," "two," "three," ..., or symbols such as 1, 2, 3, ...; this sequence being always the same. If we take a set of concrete objects, and name them in succession "one," "two," "three," ..., naming each once and once only, we shall not get beyond a certain name, *e.g.* "six." Then, in saying that the number of

objects is six, what we mean is that the name of the last object named is six. We therefore only require a definite law for the formation of the successive names or symbols. The symbols 1, 2, ... 9, 10, ..., for instance, are formed according to a definite law; and in giving 253 as the *number* of a set of objects we mean that if we attach to them the symbols 1, 2, 3, ... in succession, according to this law, the symbol attached to the last object will be 253. If we say that this act of attaching a symbol has been performed 253 times, then 253 is an *abstract* (or *pure*) *number*.

Underlying this definition is a certain assumption, viz. that if we take the objects in a different order, the last symbol attached will still be 253. This, in an elementary treatment of the subject, must be regarded as axiomatic; but it is really a simple case of mathematical induction. (See ALGEBRA.) If we take two objects A and B, it is obvious that whether we take them as A, B, or as B, A, we shall in each case get the sequence 1, 2. Suppose this were true for, say, eight objects, marked 1 to 8. Then, if we introduce another object anywhere in the series, all those coming after it will be displaced so that each will have the mark formerly attached to the next following; and the last will therefore be 9 instead of 8. This is true, whatever the arrangement of the original objects may be, and wherever the new one is introduced; and therefore, if the theorem is true for 8, it is true for 9. But it is true for 2; therefore it is true for 3; therefore for 4, and so on.

11. *Numerical Quantities.*—If the term *number* is confined to number in the abstract, then number in the concrete may be described as *numerical quantity.* Thus £3 denotes £1 taken 3 times. The £1 is termed the *unit.* A numerical quantity, therefore, represents a certain unit, taken a certain number of times. If we take £3 twice, we get £6; and if we take 3s. twice, we get 6s., *i.e.* 6 times 1s. Thus arithmetical processes deal with numerical quantities by dealing with numbers, provided the unit is the same throughout. If we retain the unit, the arithmetic is concrete; if we ignore it, the arithmetic is abstract. But in the latter case it must always be understood that there is some unit concerned, and the results have no meaning until the unit is reintroduced.

II. NOTATION, NUMERATION AND NUMBER-IDEATION

12. *Terms used.*—The representation of numbers by spoken sounds is called *numeration*; their representation by written signs is called *notation*. The systems adopted for numeration and for notation do not always agree with one another; nor do they always correspond with the idea which the numbers subjectively present. This latter presentation may, in the absence of any accepted term, be called *number-ideation*; this word covering not only the perception or recognition of particular numbers, but also the formation of a number-concept.

13. *Notation of Numbers.*—The system which is now almost universally in use amongst civilized nations for representing cardinal numbers is the Hindu, sometimes incorrectly called the Arabic, system. The essential features which distinguish this from other systems are (1) the limitation of the number of different symbols, only ten being used, however large the number to be represented may be; (2) the use of the *zero* to indicate the absence of number; and (3) the principle of local value, by which a symbol in effect represents different numbers, according to its position. The symbols denoting a number are called its *digits*.

A brief account of the development of the system will be found under NUMERAL. Here we are concerned with the principle, the explanation of which is different according as we proceed on the grouping or the counting system.

(i) On the grouping system we may in the first instance consider that we have separate symbols for numbers from "one" to "nine," but that when we reach ten objects we put them in a group and denote this group by the symbol used for "one," but printed in a different type or written of a different size or (in teaching) of a different colour. Similarly when we get to ten tens we denote them by a new representation of the figure denoting one. Thus we may have:

ones

tens

hund

reds,

&c.

c.   c.

On this principle 24 would represent twenty-four, **24** two hundred and forty, and **24** two hundred and four. To prevent confusion the *zero* or "nought" is introduced, so that the successive figures, beginning from the right, may represent ones, tens, hundreds, ... We then have, *e.g.*, **240** to denote two hundreds and four tens; and we may now adopt a uniform type for all the figures, writing this 240.

(ii) On the counting system we may consider that we have a series of objects (represented in the adjoining diagram by dots), and that we attach to these objects in succession the symbols 1, 2, 3, 4, 5, 6, 7, 8, 9, 0, repeating this series indefinitely. There is as yet no distinction between the first object marked 1 and the second object marked 1. We can, however, attach to the 0's the same symbols, 1, 2, ... 0 in succession, in a separate column, repeating the series indefinitely; then do the same with every 0 of this new series; and so on. Any particular object is then defined completely by the combination of the symbols last written down in each series; and this combination of symbols can equally be used to denote the number of objects up to and including the last one (§ 10).

In writing down a number in excess of 1000 it is (except where the number represents a particular year) usual in England and America to group the figures in sets of three, starting from the right, and to mark off the sets by commas. On the continent of Europe the figures are taken in sets of three, but are merely spaced, the comma being used at the end of a number to denote the commencement of a decimal.

The zero, called "nought," is of course a different thing from the letter O of the alphabet, but there may be a historical connexion between them (§ 79). It is perhaps interesting to note that the latter-day telephone operator calls 1907 "nineteen O seven" instead of "nineteen nought seven."

14. *Direction of the Number-Series.*—There is no settled convention as to the direction in which the series of symbols denoting the successive numbers one, two, three, ... is to be written.

(i) If the numbers were written down in succession, they would naturally proceed from left to right, thus:—1, 2, 3, ... This system, however, would require that in passing to "double figures" the figure denoting tens should be written either above or below the figure denoting ones, *e.g.*

$$
\begin{array}{ccc}
 & 1 & \\
1, 2, & 0, 1, 2, \text{... or } 1, 2, & 0, \\
\text{... 8, 9,} & \text{... , 8, 9,} & 1, 2, \text{...} \\
 & & 1
\end{array}
$$

The placing of the tens-figure to the left of the ones-figure will not seem natural unless the number-series runs either up or down.

(ii) In writing down any particular number, the successive powers of ten are written from right to left, *e.g.* 5,462,198 is

$$6) \quad 5) \quad 4) \quad 3) \quad 2) \quad 1) \quad 0)$$

the small figures in brackets indicating the successive powers. On the other hand, in writing decimals, the sequence (of negative powers) is from left to right.

(iii) In making out lists, schedules, mathematical tables (*e.g.* a multiplication-table), statistical tables, &c., the numbers are written vertically downwards. In the case of lists and schedules the numbers are only ordinals; but in the case of mathematical or statistical tables they are usually regarded as cardinals, though, when they represent values of a continuous quantity, they must be regarded as ordinals (§§ 26, 93).

(iv) In graphic representation measurements are usually made upwards; the adoption of this direction resting on certain deeply rooted ideas (§ 23).

This question of direction is of importance in reference to the development of useful number-forms (§ 23); and the existence of the two methods mentioned under (iii) and (iv) above produces confusion in comparing numerical tabulation with graphical representation. It is generally accepted that the horizontal direction of increase, where a horizontal direction is necessary, should be from left to right; but uniformity as regards vertical direction could only be attained either by printing mathematical tables upwards or by taking "downwards," instead of "upwards," as the "positive" direction for graphical purposes. The downwards direction will be taken in this article as the normal one for succession of numbers (*e.g.* in multiplication), and, where the arrangement is horizontal, it is to be understood that this is for convenience of printing. It should be noticed that, in writing the components of a number 253 as 200, 50 and 3, each component beneath the next larger one, we are really adopting the downwards principle, since the figures which make up 253 will on this principle be successively 2, 5 and 3 (§ 13 (ii)).

2
00
5

132

0

3

—

—

2

53

=

===

15. *Roman Numerals.*—Although the Roman numerals are no longer in use for representing cardinal numbers, except in certain special cases (*e.g.* clock-faces, milestones and chemists' prescriptions), they are still used for ordinals.

The system differs completely from the Hindu system. There are no single symbols for two, three, &c.; but numbers are represented by combinations of symbols for one, five, ten, fifty, one hundred, five hundred, &c., the numbers which have single symbols, viz. I, V, X, L, C, D, M, proceeding by multiples of five and two alternately. Thus 1878 is MDCCCLXXVIII, *i.e.* thousand five-hundred hundred hundred hundred fifty ten ten five one one one.

The system is therefore essentially a cardinal and grouping one, *i.e.*it represents a number as the sum of sets of other numbers. It is therefore remarkable that it should now only be used for ordinal purposes, while the Hindu system, which is ordinal in its nature, since a single series is constantly repeated, is used almost exclusively for cardinal numbers. This fact seems to illustrate the truth that the counting principle is the fundamental one, to which the interpretation of grouped numbers must ultimately be referred.

The normal process of writing the larger numbers on the left is in certain cases modified in the Roman system by writing a number in front of a larger one to denote subtraction. Thus *four*, originally written IIII, was later written IV. This may have been due to one or both of two causes; a primitive tendency to refer numbers, in numeration, to the nearest large number (§ 24 (iv)), and the difficulty of perceiving the number of a group of objects beyond about three (§ 22). Similarly IX, XL and XC were written for nine, forty and ninety respectively. These, however, were later developments.

16. *Scales of Notation.*—In the Hindu system the numbering proceeds by tens, tens of tens, &c.; thus the figure in the fifth place, counting from the right, denotes the product of the corresponding number by four tens in succession. The notation is then said to be in the *scale* of which ten is the *base*, or in the *denary scale*. The Roman system, except for the use of symbols for five, fifty, &c., is also in the denary scale, though expressed in a different way. The introduction of these other symbols produces a compound scale, which may be called a *quinary-binary*, or, less correctly, a *quinary-denary* scale.

The figures used in the Hindu notation might be used to express numbers in any other scale than the denary, provided new symbols were introduced if the base of the scale exceeded ten. Thus 1878 in the quinary-binary scale would be 1131213, and 1828 would be 1130213; the meaning of these is seen at once by comparison with MDCCCLXXVIII and MDCCCXXVIII. Similarly the number which in the denary scale is 215 would in the quaternary scale (base 4) be 3113, being equal to $3 \cdot 4 \cdot 4 \cdot 4 + 1 \cdot 4 \cdot 4 + 1 \cdot 4 + 3$.

The use of the denary scale in notation is due to its use in numeration (§ 18); this again being due (as exemplified by the use of the word *digit*) to the primitive use of the fingers for counting. If mankind had had six fingers on each hand and six toes on each foot, we should be using a *duodenary scale* (base twelve), which would have been far more convenient.

17. *Notation of Numerical Quantities.*—Over a large part of the civilized world the introduction of the metric system (§ 118) has caused the notation of all numerical quantities to be in the denary scale. In Great Britain and her colonies, however, and in the United States, other systems of notation still survive, though there is none which is consistently in one scale, other than the denary. The method is to form quantities into groups, and these again into larger groups; but the number of groups making one of the next largest groups varies as we proceed along the scale. The successive groups or units thus formed are called *denominations*. Thus twelve pennies make a shilling, and twenty shillings a pound, while the penny is itself divided into four farthings (or 526two halfpennies). There are, therefore, four denominations, the bases for conversion of one denomination into the next being successively four (or two), twelve and twenty. Within each denomination, however, the denary notation is employed exclusively,*e.g.* "twelve shillings" is denoted by 12s.

The diversity of scales appears to be due mainly to four causes: (i) the tendency to group into scores (§ 20); (ii) the tendency to subdivide into twelve; (iii) the tendency to subdivide into two or four, with repetitions, making subdivision into sixteen or sixty-four; and (iv) the independent adoption of different units for measuring the same kind of magnitude.

Where there is a division into sixteen parts, a binary scale may be formed by dividing into groups of two, four or eight. Thus the weights ordinarily in use for measuring from ¼ oz. up to 2 ℔ give the basis for a binary scale up to not more than eight figures, only 0 and 1 being used. The points of the compass might similarly be expressed by numbers in a binary scale; but the numbers would be ordinal, and the expressions would be analogous to those of decimals rather than to those of whole numbers.

In order to apply arithmetical processes to a quantity expressed in two or more denominations, we must first express it in terms of a single denomination by means of a varying scale of notation. Thus £254, 13S. 6d. may be written   each of the numbers in brackets indicating the number of units in one denomination that go to form a unit in the next higher denomination. To express the quantity in terms of £, it ought to be written   this would mean £254 (136/12)/20 or £(254 + 13/20 + 6/20·12), and therefore there would involve a fractional number.

A quantity expressed in two or more denominations is usually called a *compound number* or *compound quantity*. The former term is obviously incorrect, since a quantity is not a number; and the latter is not very suggestive. For agreement with the terminology of fractional numbers (§ 62) we shall describe such a quantity as a *mixed quantity*. The letters or symbols descriptive of each denomination are visually placed after or (in actual calculations) above the figures denoting the numbers of the corresponding units; but in a few cases, *e.g.* in the case of £, the symbol is placed before the figures. There would be great convenience in a general adoption of this latter method; the combination of the two methods in such an expression as £123, 16s. 4½d. is especially awkward.

18. *Numeration.*—The names of numbers are almost wholly based on the denary scale; thus eighteen means eight and ten, and twenty-four means twice ten and four. The words *eleven* and *twelve* have been supposed to suggest etymologically a denary basis (see, however, NUMERAL).

Two exceptions, however, may be noted.

(i) The use of *dozen, gross* (= dozen dozen), and *great gross* (= dozen gross) indicates an attempt at a duodenary basis. But the system has never spread; and the word "dozen" itself is based on the denary scale.

(ii) The *score* (twenty) has been used as a basis, but to an even more limited extent. There is no essential difference, however, between this and the denary basis. As the latter is due to finger-reckoning, so the use of the fingers and the toes produced a vigesimal scale. Examples of this are given in § 20; it is worthy of notice that the vigesimal (or, rather, quinary-quaternary) system was used by the Mayas of Yucatan, and also, in a more perfect form, by the Nahuatl (Aztecs) of Mexico.

The number ten having been taken as the basis of numeration, there are various methods that might consistently be adopted for naming large numbers.

(i) We might merely name the figures contained in the number. This method is often adopted in practical life, even as regards mixed quantities; thus £57,593, 16s. 4d. would be read as *five seven, five nine three, sixteen and four pence.*

(ii) The word *ten* might be introduced, *e.g.* 593 would be *five ten ten ninety* (= nine ten) *and three.*

(iii) Names might be given to the successive powers of ten, up to the point to which numeration of ones is likely to go. Partial applications of this method are found in many languages.

(iv) A compromise between the last two methods would be to have names for the series of numbers, beginning with ten, each of which is the "square" of the preceding one. This would in effect be analysing numbers into components of the form a. 10b where a is less than 10, and the index b is expressed in the binary scale, *e.g.* 7,000,000 would be 7·104·102, and 700,000 would be 7·104·101.

The British method is a mixture of the last two, but with an index-scale which is partly ternary and partly binary. There are separate names for ten, ten times ten (= *hundred*), and ten times ten times ten (=*thousand*); but the next single name is *million*, representing a thousand times a thousand. The next name is *billion*, which in Great Britain properly means a million million, and in the United States (as in France) a thousand million.

19. *Discrepancies between Numeration and Notation.*—Although numeration and notation are both ostensibly on the denary system, they are not always exactly parallel. The following are a few of the discrepancies.

(i) A set of written symbols is sometimes read in more than one way, while on the other hand two different sets of symbols (at any rate if denoting numerical quantities) may be read in the same way. Thus 1820 might be read as *one thousand eight hundred and twenty* if it represented a number of men, but it would be read as *eighteen hundred and twenty* if it represented a year of the Christian era; while 1s. 6d. and 18d. might both be read as *eighteenpence*. As regards the first of these two examples, however, it would be more correct to write 1,820 for the former of the two meanings (cf. § 13).

(ii) The symbols 11 and 12 are read as *eleven* and *twelve*, not (except in elementary teaching) as *ten-one* and *ten-two*.

(iii) The names of the numbers next following these, up to 19 inclusive, only faintly suggest a *ten*. This difficulty is not always recognized by teachers, who forget that they themselves had to be told that *eighteen* means *eight-and-ten*.

(iv) Even beyond twenty, up to a hundred, the word *ten* is not used in numeration, *e.g.* we say *thirty-four*, not *three ten four*.

(v) The rule that the greater number comes first is not universally observed in numeration. It is not observed, for instance, in the names of numbers from 13 to 19; nor was it in the names from which *eleven* and *twelve* are derived. Beyond twenty it is usually, but not always, observed; we sometimes instead of *twenty-four* say *four and twenty*. (This latter is the universal system in German, up to 100, and for any portion of 100 in numbers beyond 100.)

20. *Other Methods of Numeration and Notation.*—It is only possible here to make a brief mention of systems other than those now ordinarily in use.

(i) *Vigesimal Scale.*—The system of counting by twenties instead of by tens has existed in many countries; and, though there is no corresponding notation, it still exhibits itself in the names of numbers. This is the case, for instance, in the Celtic languages; and the Breton or Gaulish names have affected the Latin system, so that the French names for some numbers are on the vigesimal system. This system also appears in the Danish numerals. In English the use of the word *score* to represent twenty—*e.g.* in "threescore and ten" for seventy—is superimposed on the denary system, and has never formed an essential part of the language. The word, like *dozen* and *couple*, is still in use, but rather in a vague than in a precise sense.

(ii) *Roman System.*—The Roman notation has been explained above (§ 15). Though convenient for exhibiting the composition of any particular number, it was inconvenient for purposes of calculation; and in fact calculation was entirely (or almost entirely) performed by means of the abacus (*q.v.*). The numeration was in the denary scale, so that it did not agree absolutely with the notation. The principle of subtraction from a higher number, which appeared in notation, also appeared in numeration, but not for exactly the same numbers or in exactly the same way; thus XVIII was two-from-twenty, and the next number was one-from-twenty, but it was written XIX, not IXX.

527

(iii) *Other Systems of Antiquity.*—The Egyptian notation was purely denary, the only separate signs being those for 1, 10, 100, &c. The ordinary notation of the Babylonians was denary, but they also used a sexagesimal scale, *i.e.* a scale whose base was 60. The Hebrews had a notation containing separate signs (the letters of the alphabet) for numbers from 1 to 10, then for multiples of 10 up to 100, and then for multiples of 100 up to 400, and later up to 1000.

The earliest Greek system of notation was similar to the Roman, except that the symbols for 50, 500, &c., were more complicated. Later, a system similar to the Hebrew was adopted, and extended by reproducing the first nine symbols of the series, preceded by accents, to denote multiplication by 1000.

On the island of Ceylon there still exists, or existed till recently, a system which combines some of the characteristics of the later Greek (or Semitic) and the modern European notation; and it is conjectured that this was the original Hindu system.

For a further account of the above systems see NUMERAL, and the authorities quoted at the end of the present article.

21. *The Number-Concept.*—It is probable that very few people have any definite mental presentation of individual numbers (*i.e.* numbers proceeding by differences of *one*) beyond 100, or at any rate beyond 144. Larger numbers are grasped by forming numbers into groups or by treating some large number as a unit. A person would appreciate the difference between 93,000,000 m. and 94,000,000 m. as the distance of the centre of the sun from the centre of the earth at a particular moment; but he certainly would not appreciate the relative difference between 93,000,000 m. and 93,000,001 m. In order to get an idea of 93,000,000, he must take a million as his unit. Similarly, in the metric system he cannot mentally compare two units, one of which is 1000 times the other. The metre and the kilometre, for instance, or the metre and the millimetre, are not directly comparable; but the metre can be conceived as containing 100 centimetres.

135

On the other hand, it would seem that, for most educated people, sixteen and seventeen or twenty-six and twenty-seven, and even eighty-six and eighty-seven, are single numbers, just as six and seven are, and are not made up of groups of tens and ones. In other words, the denary scale, though adopted in notation and in numeration, does not arise in the corresponding mental concept until we get beyond 100.

Again, in the use of decimals, it is unusual to give less than two figures. Thus 3.142 or 3.14 would be quite intelligible; but 3.1 does not convey such a good idea to most people as either 31/10 or 3.10, *i.e.*as an expression denoting a fraction or a percentage.

There appears therefore to be a tendency to use some larger number than ten as a basis for grouping into new units or for subdivision into parts. The Babylonians adopted 60 for both these purposes, thus giving us the sexagesimal division of angles and of time.

This view is supported, not only by the intelligibility of percentages to ordinary persons, but also by the tendency, noted above (§ 19), to group years into centuries, and to avoid the use of thousands. Thus 1876 is not 1 thousand, 8 hundred, 7 tens and 6, but 18 hundred and 76, each of the numbers 18 and 76 being named as if it were a single number. It is also in accordance with what is so far known about number-forms (§ 23).

If there is this tendency to adopt 100 as a basis instead of 10, the teaching of decimals might sometimes be simplified by proceeding from percentages to percentages of percentages, *i.e.* by commencing with *centesimals* instead of with *decimals*.

22. *Perception of Number.*—In using material objects as a basis for developing the number-concept, it must be remembered that it is only when there are a few objects that their number can be perceived without either counting or the performance of some arithmetical process such as addition. If four coins are laid on a table, close together, they can (by most adults) be seen to be four, without counting; but seven coins have to be separated mentally into two groups, the numbers of which are added, or one group has to be seen and the remaining objects counted, before the number is known to be seven.

The actual limit of the number that can be "seen"—*i.e.* seen without counting or adding—depends for any individual on the shape and arrangement of the objects, but under similar conditions it is not the same for all individuals. It has been suggested that as many as six objects can be seen at once; but this is probably only the case with few people, and with them only when the objects have a certain geometrical arrangement. The limit for most adults, under favourable conditions, is about four. Under certain conditions it is less; thus IIII, the old Roman notation for *four*, is difficult to distinguish from III, and this may have been the main reason for replacing it by IV (§ 15).

In the case of young children the limit is probably two. That this was also the limit in the case of primitive races, and that the classification of things was into one, two and many, before any definite process of counting (*e.g.* by the fingers) came to be adopted, is clear from the use of the "dual number" in language, and from the way in which the names for three and four are often based on those for one and two. With the individual, as with the race, the limit of the number that can be seen gradually increases up to four or five.

The statement that a number of objects can be seen to be three or four is not to be taken as implying that there is a simultaneous perception of all the objects. The attention may be directed in succession to the different objects, so that the perception is rhythmical; the distinctive rhythm thus aiding the perception of the particular number.

In consequence of this limitation of the power of perception of number, it is practically impossible to use a pure denary scale in elementary number-teaching. If a quinary-binary system (such as would naturally fit in with counting on the fingers) is not adopted, teachers unconsciously resort to a binary-quinary system. This is commonly done where cubes are used; thus seven is represented by three pairs of cubes, with a single cube at the top.

23. *Visualization of the Series.*—A striking fact, in reference to ideas of number, is the existence of number-forms, *i.e.* of definite arrangements, on an imagined plane or in space, of the mental representations of the successive numbers from 1 onwards. The proportion of persons in whom number-forms exist has been variously estimated; but there is reason to believe that the forms arise at a very early stage of childhood, and that they did at some time exist in many individuals who have afterwards forgotten them. Those persons who possess them are also apt to make spatial arrangements of days of the week or the month, months of the year, the letters of the alphabet, &c.; and it is practically certain that only children would make such arrangements of letters of the alphabet. The forms seem to result from a general tendency to visualization as an aid to memory; the letter-forms may in the first instance be quite as frequent as the number-forms, but they vanish in early childhood, being of no practical value, while the number-forms continue as an aid to arithmetical work.

The forms are varied, and have few points in common; but the following tendencies are indicated.

(i) In the majority of cases the numbers lie on a continuous (but possibly zigzag) line.

(ii) There is nearly always (at any rate in English cases) a break in direction at 12. From 1 to 12 the numbers sometimes lie in the circumference of a circle, an arrangement obviously suggested by a clock-face; in these cases the series usually mounts upwards from 12. In a large number of cases, however, the direction is steadily upwards from 1 to 12, then changing. In some cases the initial direction is from right to left or from left to right; but there are very few in which it is downwards.

(iii) The multiples of 10 are usually strongly marked; but special stress is also laid on other important numbers, *e.g.* the multiples of 12.

(iv) The series sometimes goes up to very high numbers, but sometimes stops at 100, or even earlier. It is not stated, in most cases, whether all the numbers within the limits of the series have definite positions, or whether there are only certain numbers which form an essential part of the figure, while others only 528 exist potentially. Probably the latter is almost universally the case.

These forms are developed spontaneously, without suggestion from outside. The possibility of replacing them by a standard form, which could be utilized for performing arithmetical operations, is worthy of consideration; some of the difficulties in the way of standardization have already been indicated (§ 14). The general tendency to prefer an upward direction is important; and our current phraseology suggests that this is the direction which increase is naturally regarded as taking. Thus we speak of counting *up* to a certain number; and similarly mathematicians speak of *high* and *ascending* powers, while engineers speak of high pressure, high speed, high power, &c. This tendency is probably aided by the use of bricks or cubes in elementary number-teaching.

24. *Primitive Ideas of Number.*—The names of numbers give an idea of the way in which the idea of number has developed. Where civilization is at all advanced, there are usually certain names, the origin of which cannot be traced; but, as we go farther back, these become fewer, and the names are found to be composed on certain systems. The systems are varied, and it is impossible to lay down any absolute laws, but the following seem to be the main conclusions.

(i) Amongst some of the lowest tribes, as (with a few exceptions) amongst animals, the only differentiation is between one and many, or between one, two and many, or between one, two, three and many. As it becomes necessary to use higher but still small numbers, they are formed by combinations of one and two, or perhaps of three with one or two. Thus many of the Australasian and South American tribes use only one and two; seven, for instance, would be two two one.

(ii) Beyond ten, and in many cases beyond five, the names have reference to the use of the fingers, and sometimes of the toes, for counting; and the scale may be quinary, denary or vigesimal, according as one hand, the pair of hands, or the hands and feet, are taken as the new unit. *Five* may be signified by the word for hand; and either *ten* or *twenty* by the word for *man*. Or the words signifying these numbers may have reference to the completion of some act of counting. Between five and ten; or beyond ten, the names may be due to combinations, *e.g.* 16 may be 10 + 5 + 1; or they may be the actual names of the fingers last counted.

(iii) There are a few, but only a few, cases in which the number 6 or 8 is named as twice 3 or twice 4; and there are also a few cases in which 7, 8 and 9 are named as 6 + 1, 6 + 2 and 6 + 3. In the large majority of cases the numbers 6, 7, 8 and 9 are 5 + 1, 5 + 2, 5 + 3 and 5 + 4, being named either directly from their composition in this way or as the fingers on the second hand.

(iv) There is a certain tendency to name 4, 9, 14 and 19 as being one short of 5, 10, 15 and 20 respectively; the principle being thus the same as that of the Roman IV, IX, &c. It is possible that at an early stage the number of the fingers on one hand or on the two hands together was only thought of vaguely as a large number in comparison with 2 or 3, and that the number did not attain definiteness until it was linked up with the smaller by insertion of the intermediate ones; and the linking up might take place in both directions.

(v) In a few cases the names of certain small numbers are the names of objects which present these numbers in some conspicuous way. Thus the word used by the Abipones to denote 5 was the name of a certain hide of five colours. It has been suggested that names of this kind may have been the origin of the numeral words of different races; but it is improbable that direct visual perception would lead to a name for a number unless a name based on a process of counting had previously been given to it.

25. *Growth of the Number-Concept.*—The general principle that the development of the individual follows the development of the race holds good to a certain extent in the case of the number-concept, but it is modified by the existence of language dealing with concepts which are beyond the reach of the child, and also, of course, by the direct attempts at instruction. One

result is the formation of a number-series as a mere succession of names without any corresponding ideas of number; the series not being necessarily correct.

When numbering begins, the names of the successive numbers are attached to the individual objects; thus the numbers are originally ordinal, not cardinal.

The conception of number as cardinal, *i.e.* as something belonging to a group of objects as a whole, is a comparatively late one, and does not arise until the idea of a whole consisting of its parts has been formed. This is the *quantitative* aspect of number.

The development from the name-series to the quantitative conception is aided by the numbering of material objects and the performance of elementary processes of comparison, addition, &c., with them. It may also be aided, to a certain extent, by the tendency to find rhythms in sequences of sounds. This tendency is common in adults as well as in children; the strokes of a clock may, for instance, be grouped into fours, and thus eleven is represented as two fours and three. Finger-counting is of course natural to children, and leads to grouping into fives, and ultimately to an understanding of the denary system of notation.

FIG. 1.

26. *Representation of Geometrical Magnitude by Number.*—The application of arithmetical methods to geometrical measurement presents some difficulty. In reality there is a transition from a cardinal to an ordinal system, but to an ordinal system which does not agree with the original ordinal system from which the cardinal system was derived. To see this, we may represent ordinal numbers by the ordinary numerals 1, 2, 3, ... and cardinal numbers by the Roman I, II, III, ... Then in the earliest stage each object counted is indivisible; either we are counting it as a whole, or we are not counting it at all. The symbols 1, 2, 3, ... then refer to the individual objects, as in fig. 1; this is the primary ordinal stage. Figs. 2 and 3 represent the cardinal stage; fig. 2 showing how the I, II, III, ... denote the successively larger groups of objects, while fig. 3 shows how the name II of the whole is determined by the name 2 of the last one counted.

F   F
IG. 2.   IG. 3.

When now we pass to geometrical measurement, each "one" is a thing which is itself divisible, and it cannot be said that at any moment we are counting it; it is only when one is completed that we can count it. The names 1, 2, 3, ... for the individual objects cease to have an intelligible meaning, and measurement is effected by the cardinal numbers I, II, III, ..., as in fig. 4. These cardinal numbers have now, however, come to denote individual points in the line of measurement,*i.e.* the points of separation of the individual units of length. The point III in fig. 4 does not include the point II in the same way that the number III includes the number II in fig. 2, and the points must therefore be denoted by the ordinal numbers 1, 2, 3, ... as in fig. 5, the zero 0 falling into its natural place immediately before the commencement of the first unit.

F   F
IG. 4.   IG. 5.

Thus, while arithmetical numbering refers to units, geometrical numbering does not refer to units but to the intervals between units.

III. ARITHMETIC OF INTEGRAL NUMBERS

(i.) *Preliminary*

27. *Equality and Identity.*—There is a certain difference between the use of words referring to equality and identity in arithmetic and in algebra respectively; what is an *equality* in the former becoming an*identity* in the latter. Thus the statement that 4 times 3 is equal to 3 times 4, or, in abbreviated form, $4 \times 3 = 3 \times 4$ (§ 28), is a statement not of identity but of equality; *i.e.* 4×3 and 3×4 mean different things, but the operations which they denote produce the same result. But in algebra $a \times b = b \times a$ is called an identity, in the sense that it is true whatever a and b may

be; while n × X = A is called an equation, as being true, when n and A are given, for one value only of X. Similarly the numbers represented by 6/12 and ½ are not identical, but are equal.

28. *Symbols of Operation.*—The failure to observe the distinction between an identity and an equality often leads to loose reasoning; and in order to prevent this it is important that definite meanings should be attached to all symbols of operation, and especially to those which represent elementary operations. The symbols − and ÷ mean respectively that the first quantity mentioned is to be reduced or divided by the second; but there is some vagueness about + and ×. In the present article a + b will mean that a is taken first, and b added to it; but a × b will mean that b is taken first, and is then multiplied by a. In the case of numbers the × may be replaced by a dot; thus 4·3 means 4 times 3. When it is necessary to write the multiplicand before the multiplier, the symbol × will be used, so that b × a will mean the same as a × b.

29. *Axioms.*—There are certain statements that are sometimes regarded as axiomatic; *e.g.* that if equals are added to equals the results are equal, or that if A is greater than B then A + X is greater than B + X. Such statements, however, are capable of logical proof, and are generalizations of results obtained empirically at an elementary stage; they therefore belong more properly to the laws of arithmetic (§ 58).

(ii.) *Sums and Differences.*

30. *Addition and Subtraction.*—*Addition* is the process of expressing (in numeration or notation) a whole, the parts of which have already been expressed; while, if a whole has been expressed and also a part or parts, *subtraction* is the process of expressing the remainder.

Except with very small numbers, addition and subtraction, on the grouping system, involve analysis and rearrangement. Thus the sum of 8 and 7 cannot be expressed as ones; we can either form the whole, and regroup it as 10 and 5, or we can split up the 7 into 2 and 5, and add the 2 to the 8 to form 10, thus getting 8 + 7 = 8 + (2 + 5) = (8 + 2) + 5 = 10 + 5 = 15. For larger numbers the rearrangement is more extensive; thus 24 + 31 = (20 + 4) + (30 + 1) = (20 + 30) + (4 + 1) = 50 + 5 = 55, the process being still more complicated when the ones together make more than ten. Similarly we cannot subtract 8 from 15, if 15 means 1 ten + 5 ones; we must either write 15 − 8 = (10 + 5) − 8 = (10 − 8) + 5 = 2 + 5 = 7, or else resolve the 15 into an inexpressible number of ones, and then subtract 8 of them, leaving 7.

Numerical quantities, to be added or subtracted, must be in the same denomination; we cannot, for instance, add 55 shillings and 100 pence, any more than we can add 3 yards and 2 metres.

31. *Relative Position in the Series.*—The above method of dealing with addition and subtraction is synthetic, and is appropriate to the grouping method of dealing with number. We commence with processes, and see what they lead to; and thus get an idea of sums and differences. If we adopted the counting method, we should proceed in a different way, our method being analytic.

One number is less or greater than another, according as the symbol (or ordinal) of the former comes earlier or later than that of the latter in the number-series. Thus (writing ordinals in light type, and cardinals in heavy type) 9 comes after 4, and therefore **9** is greater than **4**. To find how much greater, we compare two series, in one of which we go up to 9, while in the other we stop at 4 and then recommence our counting. The series are shown below, the numbers being placed horizontally for convenience of printing, instead of vertically (§ 14):—

This exhibits **9** as the sum of **4** and **5**; it being understood that the sum of **4** and **5** means that we add **5** to **4**. That this gives the same result as adding **4** to **5** may be seen by reckoning the series backwards.

It is convenient to introduce the zero; thus

indicates that after getting to 4 we make a fresh start from 4 as our zero.

To subtract, we may proceed in either of two ways. The subtraction of **4** from **9** may mean either "What has to be added to **4** in order to make up a total of **9**," or "To what has **4** to be added in order to make up a total of **9**." For the former meaning we count forwards, till we get to 4, and then make a new count, parallel with the continuation of the old series, and see at what number we arrive when we get to 9. This corresponds to the concrete method, in which we have **9** objects, take away **4** of them, and recount the remainder. The alternative method is to retrace the steps of addition, *i.e.* to count backwards, treating 9 of one (the standard) series as corresponding with 4 of the other, and finding which number of the former corresponds with 0 of the latter. This is a more advanced method, which leads easily to the idea of negative quantities, if the subtraction is such that we have to go behind the 0 of the standard series.

32. *Mixed Quantities.*—The application of the above principles, and of similar principles with regard to multiplication and division, to numerical quantities expressed in any of the diverse British denominations, presents no theoretical difficulty if the successive denominations are regarded as constituting a varying scale of notation (§17). Thus the expression 2 ft. 3 in. implies that in counting inches we use 0 to eleven instead of 0 to 9 as our first repeating series, so that we put down 1 for the next denomination when we get to twelve instead of when we get to ten. Similarly 3 yds. 2 ft. means

y

ds.

f

t.

The practical difficulty, of course, is that the addition of two numbers produces different results according to the scale in which we are for the moment proceeding; thus the sum of 9 and 8 is 17, 15, 13 or 11 according as we are dealing with shillings, pence, pounds (avoirdupois) or ounces. The difficulty may be minimized by using the notation explained in § 17.

(iii.) *Multiples, Submultiples and Quotients.*

33. *Multiplication* and *Division* are the names given to certain numerical processes which have to be performed in order to find the result of certain arithmetical operations. Each process may arise out of either of two distinct operations; but the terminology is based on the processes, not on the operations to which they belong, and the latter are not always clearly understood.

34. *Repetition and Subdivision.*—*Multiplication* occurs when a certain number or numerical quantity is treated as a *unit* (§ 11), and is taken a certain *number* of times. It therefore arises in one or other of two ways, according as the unit or the number exists first in consciousness. If pennies are arranged in groups of five, the total amounts arranged are successively once 5d., twice 5d., three times 5d., ... ; which are written 1 × 5d., 2 × 5d., 3 × 5d., ... (§ 28). This process is *repetition*, and the quantities 1 × 5d., 2 × 5d., 3 × 5d., ... are the successive *multiples* of 5d. If, on the other hand, we have a sum of 5s., and treat a shilling as being equivalent to twelve pence, the 5s. is equivalent to 5 × 12d.; here the multiplication arises out of a *subdivision* of the original unit 1s. into 12d.

Although multiplication may arise in either of these two ways, the actual process in each case is performed by commencing with the unit and taking it the necessary number of times. In the above case of subdivision, for instance, each of the 5 shillings is separately converted into pence, so that we do in fact find in succession once 12d., twice 12d., ; i e we find the multiples of 12d. up to 5 times.

The result of the multiplication is called the *product* of the unit by the number of times it is taken.

35. *Diagram of Multiplication.*—The process of multiplication is performed in order to obtain such results as the following:—

If 1 boy receives 7 apples,
then 3 boys receive 21 apples;

or

If 1s. is equivalent to 12d.,
then 5s. is equivalent to 60d.

The essential portions of these statements, from the arithmetical point of view, may be exhibited in the form of the diagrams A and B:—

or more briefly, as in C or C' and D or D':—

the general arrangement of the diagram being as shown in E or E':—

Multiplication is therefore equivalent to completion of the diagram by entry of the product.

36. *Multiple-Tables.*—The diagram C or D of § 35 is part of a complete table giving the successive multiples of the particular unit. If we take several different units, and write down their successive multiples in parallel columns, preceded by the number-series, we obtain a *multiple-table* such as the following:—

				1		3		1	
				s.	5d.	yds. 2 ft.	7359		..

				2		7		3
			8	s. 10d.	yds. 1 ft.	4718	..	
				4		11		5
			7	s. 3d.	yds. 0 ft.	2077	..	
				5		14		6
			6	s. 8d.	yds. 2 ft.	9436	..	
				7		16		8
		0	5	s. 1d.	yds. 1 ft.	6795	..	
			.		.		.	..
			.		.		.	..
			.		.		.	..
			.		.		.	..

It is to be considered that each column may extend downwards indefinitely.

37. *Successive Multiplication.*—In multiplication by repetition the unit is itself usually a multiple of some other unit, *i.e.* it is a product which is taken as a new unit. When this new unit has been multiplied by a number, we can again take the product as a unit for the purpose of another multiplication; and so on indefinitely. Similarly where multiplication has arisen out of the subdivision of a unit into smaller units, we can again subdivide these smaller units. Thus we get successive multiplication; but it represents quite different operations according as it is due to repetition, in the sense of § 34, or to subdivision, and these operations will be exhibited by different diagrams. Of the two diagrams below, A exhibits the successive multiplication of £3 by 20, 12 and 4, and B the successive reduction of £3 to shillings, pence and farthings. The principle on which the diagrams are constructed is obvious from § 35. It should be noticed that in multiplying £3 by 20 we find the value of 20 ·3, but that in reducing £3 to shillings, since each £ becomes 20s., we find the value of 3 ·20.

38. *Submultiples.*—The relation of a unit to its successive multiples as shown in a multiple-table is expressed by saying that it is a submultiple of the multiples, the successive submultiples being *one-half, one-third, one-fourth,* ... Thus, in the diagram of § 36, 1s. 5d. is one-half of 2s. 10d., one-third of 4s. 3d., one-fourth of 5s. 8d., ...; these being written "½ of 2s. 10d.," "⅓ of 4s. 3d.," "¼ of 5s. 8d.,"...

The relation of submultiple is the converse of that of multiple; thus if a is 1/5 of b, then b is 5 times a. The determination of a submultiple is therefore equivalent to completion of the diagram E or E′ of § 35 by entry of the unit, when the number of times it is taken, and the product, are given. The operation is the converse of repetition; it is usually called *partition*, as representing division into a number of equal shares.

39. *Quotients.*—The converse of subdivision is the formation of units into groups, each constituting a larger unit; the number of the groups so formed out of a definite number of the original units is called a *quotient.* The determination of a quotient is equivalent to completion of the diagram by entry of the number when the unit and the product are given. There is no satisfactory name for the operation, as distinguished from partition; it is sometimes called measuring, but this implies an equality in the original units, which is not an essential feature of the operation.

40. *Division.*—From the commutative law for multiplication, which shows that 3 × 4d. = 4 × 3d. = 12d., it follows that the number of pence in one-fourth of 12d. is equal to the quotient when 12 pence are formed into units of 4d., each of these numbers being said to be obtained by *dividing* 12 by 4. The term *division* is therefore used in text-books to describe the two processes described in §§ 38 and 39; the product mentioned in § 34 is the *dividend,* the number or the unit, whichever is given, is called the *divisor,* and the unit or number which is to be found is called the *quotient.* The symbol ÷ is used to denote both kinds of division; thus A ÷ n denotes the unit, n of which make up A, and A ÷ B denotes the number of times that B has to be taken to make up A. In the present article this confusion is avoided by writing the former as 1/n of A.

Methods of division are considered later (§§ 106-108).

41. *Diagrams of Division.*—Since we write from left to right or downwards, it may be convenient for division to interchange the rows or the columns of the multiplication-diagram. Thus the uncompleted diagram for partition is F or G, while for measuring it is usually H; the

vacant compartment being for the unit in F or G, and for the number in H. In some cases it may be convenient in measuring to show both the units, as in K.

42. *Successive Division* may be performed as the converse of successive multiplication. The diagrams A and B below are the converse (with a slight alteration) of the corresponding diagrams 531 in § 37; A representing the determination of 1/20 of 1/12 of 1/4 of 2880 farthings, and B the conversion of 2880 farthings into £.

(iv.) Properties of Numbers.
(A) Properties not depending on the Scale of Notation.

43. *Powers, Roots and Logarithms.*—The standard series 1, 2, 3, ... is obtained by successive additions of 1 to the number last found. If instead of commencing with 1 and making successive additions of 1 we commence with any number such as 3 and make successive multiplications by 3, we get a series 3, 9, 27, ... as shown below the line in the margin. The first member of the series is 3; the second is the product of two numbers, each equal to 3; the third is the product of three numbers, each equal to 3; and so on. These are written 31 (or 3), 32, 33, 34, ... where np denotes the product of p numbers, each equal to n. If we write np = N, then, if any two of the three numbers n, p, N are known, the third is determinate. If we know n and p, p is called the *index*, and n, n2, ... np are called the *first power, second power,* ... *pth power* of n, the series itself being called the *power-series*. The *second power* and *third power* are usually called the *square* and *cube* respectively. If we know p and N, n is called the *pth root* of N, so that n is the *second* (or *square*) *root* of n2, the *third* (or *cube*) *root* of n3, the *fourth root* of n4, ... If we know n and N, then p is the *logarithm* of N to *base* n.

1

= 30   0

3
= 31   1
9
= 32   2
2
7 = 33   3
8
1 = 34   4
.
.
.

The calculation of powers (*i.e.* of N when n and p are given) is *involution*; the calculation of roots (*i.e.* of n when p and N are given) is *evolution*; the calculation of logarithms (*i.e.* of p when n and N are given) has no special name.

Involution is a direct process, consisting of successive multiplications; the other two are inverse processes. The calculation of a logarithm can be performed by successive divisions; evolution requires special methods.

The above definitions of logarithms, &c., relate to cases in which n and p are whole numbers, and are generalized later.

44. *Law of Indices.*—If we multiply np by nq, we multiply the product of p n's by the product of q n's, and the result is therefore np + q. Similarly, if we divide np by nq, where q is less than p, the result is np − q. Thus multiplication and division in the power-series correspond to addition and subtraction in the index-series, and vice versa.

If we divide np by np, the quotient is of course 1. This should be written n0. Thus we may make the power-series commence with 1, if we make the index-series commence with 0. The added terms are shown above the line in the diagram in § 43.

45. *Factors, Primes and Prime Factors.*—If we take the successive multiples of 2, 3, ... as in § 36, and place each multiple opposite the same number in the original series, we get an arrangement as in the adjoining diagram. If any number N occurs in the vertical series commencing with a number n (other than 1) then n is said to be a *factor* of N. Thus 2, 3 and 6 are factors of 6; and 2, 3, 4, 6 and 12 are factors of 12.

.   .   .   .

```
        .     .        .        .
   .        .     .        .     .
   .     .        .     .        .
   .     .        .     .
   .     .        .
   .     .     .        .     .

0  0  .     .  0     .  .  .

1  .     .     .     .  .  .

2  2  2  2     .  2     .  .
```

A number (other than 1) which has no factor except itself is called a *prime number*, or, more briefly, a *prime*. Thus 2, 3, 5, 7 and 11 are primes, for each of these occurs twice only in the table. A number (other than 1) which is not a prime number is called a *composite* number.

If a number is a factor of another number, it is a factor of any multiple of that number. Hence, if a number has factors, one at least of these must be a prime. Thus 12 has 6 for a factor; but 6 is not a prime, one of its factors being 2; and therefore 2 must also be a factor of 12. Dividing 12 by 2, we get a submultiple 6, which again has a prime 2 as a factor. Thus any number which is not itself a prime is the product of several factors, each of which is a prime, *e.g.* 12 is the product of 2, 2 and 3. These are called *prime factors*.

The following are the most important properties of numbers in reference to factors:—

(i) If a number is a factor of another number, it is a factor of any multiple of that number.

(ii) If a number is a factor of two numbers, it is a factor of their sum or (if they are unequal) of their difference. (The words in brackets are inserted to avoid the difficulty, at this stage, of saying that every number is a factor of 0, though it is of course true that $0 \cdot n = 0$, whatever n may be.)

(iii) A number can be resolved into prime factors in one way only, no account being taken of their relative order. Thus $12 = 2 \times 2 \times 3 = 2 \times 3 \times 2 = 3 \times 2 \times 2$, but this is regarded as one way only. If any prime occurs more than once, it is usual to write the number of times of occurrence as an index; thus $144 = 2 \times 2 \times 2 \times 2 \times 3 \times 3 = 2^4 \cdot 3^2$.

The number 1 is usually included amongst the primes; but, if this is done, the last paragraph requires modification, since 144 could be expressed as $1 \cdot 2^4 \cdot 3^2$, or as $1^2 \cdot 2^4 \cdot 3^2$, or as $1^p \cdot 2^4 \cdot 3^2$, where p might be anything.

If two numbers have no factor in common (except 1) each is said to be *prime to* the other.

The multiples of 2 (including $1 \cdot 2$) are called *even* numbers; other numbers are *odd* numbers.

46. *Greatest Common Divisor.*—If we resolve two numbers into their prime factors, we can find their *Greatest Common Divisor* or *Highest Common Factor* (written G.C.D. or G.C.F. or H.C.F.), *i.e.* the greatest number which is a factor of both. Thus $144 = 2^4 \cdot 3^2$, and $756 = 2^2 \cdot 3^3 \cdot 7$, and therefore the G.C.D. of 144 and 756 is $2^2 \cdot 3^2 = 36$. If we require the G.C.D. of two numbers, and cannot resolve them into their prime factors, we use a process described in the text-books. The process depends on (ii) of § 45, in the extended form that, if x is a factor of a and b, it is a factor of $pa - qb$, where p and q are any integers.

The G.C.D. of three or more numbers is found in the same way.

47. *Least Common Multiple.*—The *Least Common Multiple*, or L.C.M., of two numbers, is the least number of which they are both factors. Thus, since $144 = 2^4 \cdot 3^2$, and $756 = 2^2 \cdot 3^3 \cdot 7$, the L.C.M. of 144 and 756 is $2^4 \cdot 3^3 \cdot 7$. It is clear, from comparison with the last paragraph, that the product of the G.C.D. and the L.C.M. of two numbers is equal to the product of the numbers

themselves. This gives a rule for finding the L.C.M. of two numbers. But we cannot apply it to finding the L.C.M. of three or more numbers; if we cannot resolve the numbers into their prime factors, we must find the L.C.M. of the first two, then the L.C.M. of this and the next number, and so on.

(B) Properties depending on the Scale of Notation.

48. *Tests of Divisibility.*—The following are the principal rules for testing whether particular numbers are factors of a given number. The number is divisible—

(i) by 10 if it ends in 0;

(ii) by 5 if it ends in 0 or 5;

(iii) by 2 if the last digit is even;

(iv) by 4 if the number made up of the last two digits is divisible by 4;

(v) by 8 if the number made up of the last three digits is divisible by 8;

(vi) by 9 if the sum of the digits is divisible by 9;

(vii) by 3 if the sum of the digits is divisible by 3;

(viii) by 11 if the difference between the sum of the 1st, 3rd, 5th, ... digits and the sum of the 2nd, 4th, 6th, ... is zero or divisible by 11.

(ix) To find whether a number is divisible by 7, 11 or 13, arrange the number in groups of three figures, beginning from the end, treat each group as a separate number, and then find the difference between the sum of the 1st, 3rd, ... of these numbers and the sum of the 2nd, 4th, ... Then, if this difference is zero or is divisible by 7, 11 or 13, the original number is also so divisible; and conversely. For example, 31521 gives $521 - 31 = 490$, and therefore is divisible by 7, but not by 11 or 13.

49. *Casting out Nines* is a process based on (vi) of the last paragraph. The remainder when a number is divided by 9 is equal to the remainder when the sum of its digits is divided by 9. Also, if the remainders when two numbers are divided by 9 are respectively a and b, the remainder when their product is divided by 9 is the same as the remainder when a·b is divided by 9. This gives a rule for testing multiplication, which is found in most text-books. It is doubtful, however, whether such a rule, giving a test which is necessarily incomplete, is of much educational value.

(v.) *Relative Magnitude.*

50. *Fractions.*—A *fraction* of a quantity is a submultiple, or a multiple of a submultiple, of that quantity. Thus, since $3 \times 1s. 5d. = 4s. 3d.$, 1s. 5d. may be denoted by 1/3 of 4s. 3d.; and any multiple of 1s. 5d., denoted by n × 1s. 5d., may also be denoted by n/3 of 4s. 3d. We therefore use "n/a of A" to mean that we find a quantity X such that $a \times X = A$, and then multiply X by n.

It must be noted (i) that this is a definition of "n/a of," not a definition of "n/a," and (ii) that it is not necessary that n should be less than a.

51. *Subdivision of Submultiple.*—By 5/7 of A we mean 5 times the unit, 7 times which is A. If we regard this unit as being 4 times a lesser unit, then A is 7·4 times this lesser unit, and 5/7 of A is 5·4 times the lesser unit. Hence 5/7 of A is equal to 5·4/7·4 of A; and, conversely, 5·4/7·4 of A is equal to 5/7 of A. Similarly each of these is equal to 5·3/7·3 of A. Hence the value of a fraction is not altered by substituting for the numerator and denominator the corresponding numbers in any other column of a multiple-table (§ 36). If we write 5·4/7·4 in the form 4·5/4·7 we may say that the value of a fraction is not altered by multiplying or dividing the numerator and denominator by any number.

52. *Fraction of a Fraction.*—To find 11/4 of 5/7 of A we must convert 5/7 of A into 4 times some unit. This is done by the preceding paragraph. For 5/7 of $A = 5·4/7·4$ of $A = 4·5/7·4$ of A; *i.e.* it is 4 times a unit which is itself 5 times another unit, 7·4 times, which is A. Hence, taking the former unit 11 times instead of 4 times,

11/4 of 5/7 $$\text{of A} = \frac{11·5}{7·4} \text{ of A}$$

A fraction of a fraction is sometimes called a *compound fraction.*

53. *Comparison, Addition and Subtraction of Fractions.*—The quantities ¾ of A and 5/7 of A are expressed in terms of different units. To compare them, or to add or subtract them, we must express them in terms of the same unit. Thus, taking 1/28 of A as the unit, we have (§ 51)

¾ of A = 21/28 of A; 5/7 of A = 20/28 of A.

Hence the former is greater than the latter; their sum is 41/28 of A; and their difference is 1/28 of A.

Thus the fractions must be reduced to a *common denominator.* This denominator must, if the fractions are in their lowest terms (§ 54), be a multiple of each of the denominators; it is usually most convenient that it should be their L.C.M. (§ 47).

144

54. *Fraction in its Lowest Terms*.—A fraction is said to be *in its lowest terms* when its numerator and denominator have no common factor; or to be reduced to its lowest terms when it is replaced by such a fraction. Thus 8/22 of A is said to be reduced to its lowest terms when it is replaced by 4/11 of A. It is important always to bear in mind that 4/11of A is not the *same* as 8/22 of A, though it is *equal* to it.

55. *Diagram of Fractional Relation*.—To find 10/24 of 14s. we have to take 10 of the units, 24 of which make up 14s. Hence the required amount will, in the multiple-table of § 36, be opposite 10 in the column in which the amount opposite 24 is 14s.; the quantity at the head of this column, representing the unit, will be found to be 7d. The elements of the multiple-table with which we are concerned are shown in the diagram in the margin. This diagram serves equally for the two statements that (i) 10/24 of 14s. is 5s. 10d., (ii)24/10 of 5s. 10d. is 14s. The two statements are in fact merely different aspects of a single relation, considered in the next section.

56. *Ratio*.—If we omit the two upper compartments of the diagram in the last section, we obtain the diagram A. This diagram exhibits a relation between the two amounts 5s. 10d. and 14s. on the one hand, and the numbers 10 and 24 of the standard series on the other, which is expressed by saying that 5s. 10d. is to 14s. in the *ratio* of 10 to 24, or that 14s. is to 5s. 10d. in the ratio of 24 to 10. If we had taken 1s. 2d. instead of 7d. as the unit for the second column, we should have obtained the diagram B. Thus we must regard the ratio of a to b as being the same as the ratio of c to d, if the fractions a/b and c/d are equal. For this reason the ratio of a to b is sometimes written a/b, but the more correct method is to write it a:b.

If two quantities or numbers P and Q are to each other in the ratio of p to q, it is clear from the diagram that p times $Q = q$ times P, so that $Q = q/p$ of P.

57. *Proportion*.—If from any two columns in the table of § 36 we remove the numbers or quantities in any two rows, we get a diagram such as that here shown. The pair of compartments on either side may, as here, contain numerical quantities, or may contain numbers. But the two pairs of compartments will correspond to a single pair of numbers, *e.g.*2 and 6, in the standard series, so that, denoting them by M, N and P, Q respectively, M will be to N in the same ratio that P is to Q. This is expressed by saying that M is to N as P to Q, the relation being written M:N :: P:Q; the four quantities are then said to be *in proportion* or to be *proportionals*.

This is the most general expression of the relative magnitude of two quantities; *i.e.* the relation expressed by proportion includes the relations expressed by multiple, submultiple, fraction and ratio.

If M and N are respectively m and n times a unit, and P and Q are respectively p and q times a unit, then the quantities are in proportion if mq = np; and conversely.

IV. LAWS OF ARITHMETIC

58. *Laws of Arithmetic*.—The arithmetical processes which we have considered in reference to positive integral numbers are subject to the following laws:—

(i) *Equalities and Inequalities*.—The following are sometimes called*Axioms* (§ 29), but their truth should be proved, even if at an early stage it is assumed. The symbols ">" and "<" mean respectively "is greater than" and "is less than." The numbers represented by a, b, c, x and m are all supposed to be positive.

533

(a) If a = b, and b = c. then a = c;
(b) If a = b, then a + x = b + x, and a − x = b − x;
(c) If a > b, then a + x > b + x, and a − x > b − x;
(d) If a < b, then a + b < b + x, and a − x < b − x;

(e) If a = b, then ma = mb, and a ÷ m = b ÷ m;

(f) If a > b, then ma > mb, and a ÷ m > b ÷ m;

(g) If a < b, then ma < mb, and a ÷ m < b ÷ m.

(ii) *Associative Law for Additions and Subtractions.*—This law includes the *rule of signs*, that a − (b − c) = a − b + c; and it states that, subject to this, successive operations of addition or subtraction may be grouped in sets in any way; *e.g.* a − b + c + d + e − f = a − (b − c) + (d + e − f).

(iii) *Commutative Law for Additions and Subtractions*, that additions and subtractions may be performed in any order; *e.g.* a − b + c + d = a + c − b + d = a − b + c − b.

(iv) *Associative Law for Multiplications and Divisions.*—This law includes a rule, similar to the rule of signs, to the effect that a ÷ (b ÷ c) = a ÷ b × c; and it states that, subject to this, successive operations of multiplication or division may be grouped in sets in any way; *e.g.* a ÷ b × c × d × e ÷ f = a ÷ (b ÷ c) × (d × e ÷ f).

(v) *Commutative Law for Multiplications and Divisions*, that multiplications and divisions may be performed in any order: *e.g.* a ÷ b× c × d = a × c ÷ b × d = a × d × c ÷ b.

(vi) *Distributive Law*, that multiplications and divisions may be distributed over additions and subtractions, *e.g.* that m(a + b − c) = m·a + m·b − m·c, or that (a + b − c) ÷ n = (a ÷ n) + (b ÷ n) + (c ÷ n).

In the case of (ii), (iii) and (vi), the letters a, b, c, ... may denote either numbers or numerical quantities, while m and n denote numbers; in the case of (iv) and (v) the letters denote numbers only.

59. *Results of Inverse Operations.*—Addition, multiplication and involution are direct processes; and, if we start with positive integers, we continue with positive integers throughout. But, in attempting the inverse processes of subtraction, division, and either evolution or determination of index, the data may be such that a process cannot be performed. We can, however, denote the result of the process by a symbol, and deal with this symbol according to the laws of arithmetic. In this way we arrive at (i) negative numbers, (ii) fractional numbers, (iii) surds, (iv) logarithms (in the ordinary sense of the word).

60. *Simple Formulae.*—The following are some simple formulae which follow from the laws stated in § 58.

(i) (a + b + c + ...)(p + q + r + ...) = (ap + aq + ar + ...) + (bp + bq + br + ...) + (cp + cq + cr + ...) + ...; *i.e.* the product of two or more numbers, each of which consists of two or more parts, is the sum of the products of each part of the one with each part of the other.

(ii) (a + b)(a − b) = a2 − b2; *i.e.* the product of the sum and the difference of two numbers is equal to the difference of their squares.

(in) (a + b)2 = a2 + 2ab + b2.

V. NEGATIVE NUMBERS

61. *Negative Numbers* may be regarded as resulting from the commutative law for addition and subtraction. According to this law, 10 + 3 + 6 − 7 = 10 + 3 − 7 + 6 = 3 + 6 − 7 + 10 = &c. But, if we write the expression as 3 − 7 + 6 + 10, this means that we must first subtract 7 from 3. This cannot be done; but the result of the subtraction, if it could be done, is something which, when 6 is added to it, becomes 3 − 7 + 6 = 3 + 6 − 7 = 2. The result of 3 − 7 is the same as that of 0 − 4; and we may write it "−4," and call it a *negative number*, if by this we mean something possessing the property that −4 + 4 = 0.

This, of course, is unintelligible on the grouping system of treating number; on the counting system it merely means that we count backwards from 0, just as we might count inches backwards from a point marked 0 on a scale. It should be remembered that the counting is performed with something as unit. If this unit is A, then what we are really considering is −4A; and this means, not that A is multiplied by −4, but that A is multiplied by 4, and the product is taken negatively. It would therefore be better, in some ways, to retain the unit throughout, and to describe −4A as a *negative quantity*, in order to avoid confusion with the "negative numbers" with which operations are performed in formal algebra.

The positive quantity or number obtained from a negative quantity or number by omitting the "−" is called its *numerical value*.

VI. FRACTIONAL AND DECIMAL NUMBERS

62. *Fractional Numbers.*—According to the definition in § 50 the quantity denoted by 3⁄6 of A is made up of a number, 3, and a unit, which is one-sixth of A. Similarly p/n of A, q/n of A, r/n of A, ... mean quantities which are respectively p times, q times r times, ... the unit, n of which make up A. Thus any arithmetical processes which can be applied to the numbers p, q, r, ... can be applied to p/n, q/n, r/n, ... , the denominator n remaining unaltered.

146

If we denote the unit 1/n of A by X, then A is n times X, and p/n of n times X is p times X; *i.e.* p/n of n times is p times.

Hence, so long as the denominator remains unaltered, we can deal with p/n, q/n, r/n, ... exactly as if they were numbers, any operations being performed on the numerators. The expressions p/n, q/n, r/n, ... are then *fractional numbers*, their relation to ordinary or *integral* numbers being that p/n times n times is equal to p times.

This relation is of exactly the same kind as the relation of the successive digits in numbers expressed in a scale of notation whose base is n. Hence we can treat the fractional numbers which have any one denominator as constituting a number-series, as shown in the adjoining diagram. The result of taking 13 sixths of A is then seen to be the same as the result of taking twice A and one-sixth of A, so that we may regard 13/6 as being equal to 2 1/6. A fractional number is called a *proper fraction* or an *improper fraction* according as the numerator is or is not less than the denominator; and an expression such as 2 1/6 is called a mixed number. An improper fraction is therefore equal either to an integer or to a mixed number. It will be seen from § 17 that a mixed number corresponds with what is there called a *mixed quantity*. Thus £3, 17s. is a mixed quantity, being expressed in pounds and shillings; to express it in terms of pounds only we must write it £3 17/20.

63. *Fractional Numbers with different Denominators.*—If we divided the unit into halves, and these new units into thirds, we should get sixths of the original unit, as shown in A; while, if we divided the unit into thirds, and these new units into halves, we should again get sixths, but as shown in B. The series of halves in the one case, and of thirds in the other, are entirely different series of fractional numbers, but we can compare them by putting each in its proper position in relation to the series of sixths. Thus 3/2 is equal to 9/6, and 5/3 is equal to 10/6, and conversely; in other words, any fractional number is equivalent to the fractional number obtained by multiplying or dividing the numerator and denominator by any integer. We can thus find fractional numbers equivalent to the sum or difference of any two fractional numbers. The process is the same as that of finding the sum or difference of 3 sixpences and 5 fourpences; we cannot subtract 3 sixpenny-bits from 5 fourpenny-bits, but we can express each as an equivalent number of 534 pence, and then perform the subtraction. Generally, to find the sum or difference of two or more fractional numbers, we must replace them by other fractional numbers having the same denominator; it is usually most convenient to take as this denominator the L.C.M. of the original fractional numbers (cf. § 53).

64. *Complex Fractions.*—A fraction (or fractional number), the numerator or denominator of which is a fractional number, is called a *complex* fraction (or fractional number), to distinguish it from a *simple* fraction, which is a fraction having integers for numerator and denominator. Thus 5 2/3 / 11 1/3 of A means that we take a unit X such that 11 1/3 times X is equal to A, and then take 5 2/3 times X. To simplify this, we take a new unit Y, which is 1/3 of X. Then A is 34 times Y, and 5 2/3 / 11 1/3 of A is 17 times Y, *i.e.* it is 1/2 of A.

65. *Multiplication of Fractional Numbers.*—To multiply 8/3 by 5/7 is to take 5/7 times 8/3. It has already been explained (§ 62) that 5/7 times is an operation such that 5/7 times 7 times is equal to 5 times. Hence we must express 8/3, which itself means 8/3 times, as being 7 times something. This is done by multiplying both numerator and denominator by 7; *i.e.* 8/3 is equal to 7·8/7·3, which is the same thing as 7 times 8/7·3. Hence 5/7 times 8/3 = 5/7 times 7 times 8/7·3 = 5 times 8/7·3 = 5·8/7·3. The rule for multiplying a fractional number by a fractional number is therefore the same as the rule for finding a fraction of a fraction.

66. *Division of Fractional Numbers.*—To divide 8/3 by 5/7 is to find a number (*i.e.* a fractional number) x such that 5/7 times x is equal to 8/3. But 7/5 times 5/7 times x is, by the last section, equal to x. Hence x is equal to 7/5 times 8/3. Thus to divide by a fractional number we must multiply by the number obtained by interchanging the numerator and the denominator, *i.e.* by the *reciprocal* of the original number.

If we divide 1 by 5/7 we obtain, by this rule, 7/5. Thus the reciprocal of a number may be defined as the number obtained by dividing 1 by it. This definition applies whether the original number is integral or fractional.

147

By means of the present and the preceding sections the rule given in § 63 can be extended to the statement that a fractional number is equal to the number obtained by multiplying its numerator and its denominator by any fractional number.

67. *Negative Fractional Numbers.*—We can obtain negative fractional numbers in the same way that we obtain negative integral numbers; thus $-5/7$ or $-5/7$A means that $5/7$ or $5/7$A is taken negatively.

68. *Genesis of Fractional Numbers.*—A fractional number may be regarded as the result of a measuring division (§ 39) which cannot be performed exactly. Thus we cannot divide 3 in. by 11 in. exactly, *i.e.* we cannot express 3 in. as an integral multiple of 11 in.; but, by extending the meaning of "times" as in § 62, we can say that 3 in. is $3/11$ times 11 in., and therefore call $3/11$ the quotient when 3 in. is divided by 11 in. Hence, if p and n are numbers, p/n is sometimes regarded as denoting the result of dividing p by n, whether p and n are integral or fractional (mixed numbers being included in fractional).

The idea and properties of a fractional number having been explained, we may now call it, for brevity, a *fraction*. Thus "$2/3$ of A" no longer means two of the units, three of which make up A; it means that A is multiplied by the fraction $2/3$, *i.e.* it means the same thing as "$2/3$ times A."

69. *Percentage.*—In order to deal, by way of comparison or addition or subtraction, with fractions which have different denominators, it is necessary to reduce them to a common denominator. To avoid this difficulty, in practical life, it is usual to confine our operations to fractions which have a certain standard denominator. Thus (§ 79) the Romans reckoned in twelfths, and the Babylonians in sixtieths; the former method supplied a basis for division by 2, 3, 4, 6 or 12, and the latter for division by 2, 3, 4, 5, 6, 10, 12, 15, 20, 30, or 60. The modern method is to deal with fractions which have 100 as denominator; such fractions are called *percentages*. They only apply accurately to divisions by 2, 4, 5, 10, 20, 25 or 50; but they have the convenience of fitting in with the denary scale of notation, and they can be extended to other divisions by using a mixed number as numerator. One-fortieth, for instance, can be expressed as $2\frac{1}{2}/100$, which is called $2\frac{1}{2}$ *per cent.*, and usually written $2\frac{1}{2}\%$. Similarly $3\frac{1}{3}\%$ is equal to one-thirtieth.

If the numerator is a multiple of 5, the fraction represents twentieths. This is convenient, *e.g.* for expressing *rates in the pound*; thus 15% denotes the process of taking 3s. for every £1, *i.e.* a rate of 3s. in the £.

In applications to money "per cent." sometimes means "per £100." Thus "£3, 17s. 6d. per cent." is really the complex fraction

$$
\dfrac{\dfrac{1}{76/12}}{\dfrac{0}{10}} \quad 0
$$

70. *Decimal Notation of Percentage.*—An integral percentage, *i.e.* a simple fraction with 100 for denominator, can be expressed by writing the two figures of the numerator (or, if there is only one figure, this figure preceded by 0) with a dot or "point" before them; thus .76 means 76%, or $76/100$. If there is an integral number to be taken as well as a percentage, this number is written in front of the point; thus $23.76 \times$ A means 23 times A, with 76% of A. We might therefore denote 76% by 0.76.

If as our unit we take $X = 1/100$ of A $= 1\%$ of A, the above quantity might equally be written $2376 X = 2376/100$ of A; *i.e.* $23.76 \times$ A is equal to 2376% of A.

71. *Approximate Expression by Percentage.*—When a fraction cannot be expressed by an integral percentage, it can be so expressed approximately, by taking the *nearest* integer to the numerator of an equal fraction having 100 for its denominator. Thus $1/7 = 142/7 / 100$, so that $1/7$ is approximately equal to 14%; and $2/7 = (284/7)/100$, which is approximately equal to 29%. The difference between this approximate percentage and the true value is less than $\frac{1}{2}\%$, *i.e.* is less than $1/200$.

If the numerator of the fraction consists of an integer and $\frac{1}{2}$—*e.g.* in the case of $3/8 = (37\frac{1}{2})/100$—it is uncertain whether we should take the next lowest or the next highest integer. It is best in such cases to retain the $\frac{1}{2}$; thus we can write $3/8 = 37\frac{1}{2}\% = .37\frac{1}{2}$.

72. *Addition and Subtraction of Percentages.*—The sum or difference of two percentages is expressed by the sum or difference of the numbers expressing the two percentages.

73. *Percentage of a Percentage.*—Since 37% of 1 is expressed by 0.37, 37% of 1% (*i.e.* of 0.01) might similarly be expressed by 0.00.37. The second point, however, is omitted, so that we write it 0.0037 or .0037, this expression meaning $37/100$ of $1/100 = 37/10000$.

148

On the same principle, since 37% of 45% is equal to 37/100 of 45/100 =1665/10000 = 16/100 + (65/100 of 1/100), we can express it by .1665; and 3% of 2% can be expressed by .0006. Hence, to find a percentage of a percentage, we multiply the two numbers, put 0's in front if necessary to make up four figures (not counting fractions), and prefix the point.

74. *Decimal Fractions.*—The percentage-notation can be extended to any fraction which has any power of 10 for its denominator. Thus153/1000 can be written .153 and 15300/100000 can be written .15300. These two fractions are equal to each other, and also to .1530. A fraction written in this way is called a *decimal fraction*, or we might define a decimal fraction as a fraction having a power of 10 for its denominator, there being a special notation for writing such fractions.

A mixed number, the fractional part of which is a decimal fraction, is expressed by writing the integral part in front of the point, which is called the *decimal point*. Thus 271530/10000} can be written 27.1530. This number, expressed in terms of the fraction 1/10000 or .0001, would be 271530. Hence the successive figures after the decimal point have the same relation to each other and to the figures before the point as if the point did not exist. The point merely indicates the *denomination* in which the number is expressed: the above number, expressed in terms 535of 1/10, would be 271.530, but expressed in terms of 100 it would be .271530.

Fractions other than decimal fractions are usually called *vulgar fractions*.

75. *Decimal Numbers.*—Instead of regarding the .153 in 27.153 as meaning 153/1000, we may regard the different figures in the expression as denoting numbers in the successive orders of submultiples of 1 on a denary scale. Thus, on the grouping system, 27.153 will mean $2 \cdot 10 + 7 + 1/10 + 5/10^2 + 3/10^3$, while on the counting system it will mean the result of counting through the tens to 2, then through the ones to 7, then through tenths to 1, and so on. A number made up in this way may be called a *decimal number*, or, more briefly, a *decimal*. It will be seen that the definition includes integral numbers.

76. *Sums and Differences of Decimals.*—To add or subtract decimals, we must reduce them to the same denomination, *i.e.* if one has more figures after the decimal point than the other, we must add sufficient 0's to the latter to make the numbers of figures equal. Thus, to add 5.413 to 3.8, we must write the latter as 3.800. Or we may treat the former as the sum of 5.4 and .013, and recombine the .013 with the sum of 3.8 and 5.4.

77. *Product of Decimals.*—To multiply two decimals exactly, we multiply them as if the point were absent, and then insert it so that the number of figures after the point in the product shall be equal to the sum of the numbers of figures after the points in the original decimals.

In actual practice, however, decimals only represent approximations, and the process has to be modified (§ 111).

78. *Division by Decimal.*—To divide one decimal by another, we must reduce them to the same denomination, as explained in § 76, and then omit the decimal points. Thus 5.413 ÷ 3.8 = 5413/1000 ÷ 3800/1000 = 5413 ÷ 3800.

79. *Historical Development of Fractions and Decimals.*—The fractions used in ancient times were mainly of two kinds: unit-fractions, *i.e.* fractions representing aliquot parts (§ 103), and fractions with a definite denominator.

The Egyptians as a rule used only unit-fractions, other fractions being expressed as the sum of unit-fractions. The only known exception was the use of 2/3 as a single fraction. Except in the case of2/3 and ½, the fraction was expressed by the denominator, with a special symbol above it.

The Babylonians expressed numbers less than 1 by the numerator of a fraction with denominator 60; the numerator only being written. The choice of 60 appears to have been connected with the reckoning of the year as 360 days; it is perpetuated in the present subdivision of angles.

The Greeks originally used unit-fractions, like the Egyptians; later they introduced the sexagesimal fractions of the Babylonians, extending the system to four or more successive subdivisions of the unit representing a degree. They also, but apparently still later and only occasionally, used fractions of the modern kind. In the sexagesimal system the numerators of the successive fractions (the denominators of which were the successive powers of 60) were followed by ', ", "', "", the denominator not being written. This notation survives in reference to the minute (') and second (") of angular measurement, and has been extended, by analogy, to the foot (') and inch ("). Since ξ represented 60, and o was the next letter, the latter appears to have been used to denote absence of one of the fractions; but it is not clear that our present sign for zero was actually derived from this. In the case of fractions of the more general kind, the numerator was written first with ', and then the denominator, followed by ", was written twice. A different method was used by Diophantus, accents being omitted, and the denominator being written above and to the right of the numerator.

149

The Romans commonly used fractions with denominator 12; these were described as *unciae* (ounces), being twelfths of the *as* (pound).

The modern system of placing the numerator above the denominator is due to the Hindus; but the dividing line is a later invention. Various systems were tried before the present notation came to be generally accepted. Under one system, for instance, the continued sum 4/5 + 1/(7 × 5) + 3/(8 × 7 × 5) would be denoted by (3 1 4)/(8 7 5); this is somewhat similar in principle to a decimal notation, but with digits taken in the reverse order.

Hindu treatises on arithmetic show the use of fractions, containing a power of 10 as denominator, as early as the beginning of the 6th century A.D. There was, however, no development in the direction of decimals in the modern sense, and the Arabs, by whom the Hindu notation of integers was brought to Europe, mainly used the sexagesimal division in the ' " ''' notation. Even where the decimal notation would seem to arise naturally, as in the case of approximate extraction of a square root, the portion which might have been expressed as a decimal was converted into sexagesimal fractions. It was not until A.D. 1585 that a decimal notation was published by Simon Stevinus of Bruges. It is worthy of notice that the invention of this notation appears to have been due to practical needs, being required for the purpose of computation of compound interest. The present decimal notation, which is a development of that of Stevinus, was first used in 1617 by H. Briggs, the computer of logarithms.

80. *Fractions of Concrete Quantities.*—The British systems of coinage, weights, lengths, &c., afford many examples of the use of fractions. These may be divided into three classes, as follows:—

(i) The fraction of a concrete quantity may itself not exist as a concrete quantity, but be represented by a token. Thus, if we take a shilling as a unit, we may divide it into 12 or 48 smaller units; but corresponding coins are not really portions of a shilling, but objects which help us in counting. Similarly we may take the farthing as a unit, and invent smaller units, represented either by tokens or by no material objects at all. Ten marks, for instance, might be taken as equivalent to a farthing; but 13 marks are not equivalent to anything except one farthing and three out of the ten acts of counting required to arrive at another farthing.

(ii) In the second class of cases the fraction of the unit quantity is a quantity of the same kind, but cannot be determined with absolute exactness. Weights come in this class. The ounce, for instance, is one-sixteenth of the pound, but it is impossible to find 16 objects such that their weights shall be exactly equal and that the sum of their weights shall be exactly equal to the weight of the standard pound.

(iii) Finally, there are the cases of linear measurement, where it is theoretically possible to find, by geometrical methods, an exact submultiple of a given unit, but both the unit and the submultiple are not really concrete objects, but are spatial relations embodied in objects.

Of these three classes, the first is the least abstract and the last the most abstract. The first only involves number and counting. The second involves the idea of *equality* as a necessary characteristic of the units or subunits that are used. The third involves also the idea of *continuity* and therefore of unlimited subdivision. In weighing an object with ounce-weights the fact that it weighs more than 1 ℔ 3 oz. but less than 1 ℔ 4 oz. does not of itself suggest the necessity or possibility of subdivision of the ounce for purposes of greater accuracy. But in measuring a distance we may find that it is "between" two distances differing by a unit of the lowest denomination used, and a subdivision of this unit follows naturally.

VII. Approximation

81. *Approximate Character of Numbers.*—The numbers (integral or decimal) by which we represent the results of arithmetical operations are often only approximately correct. All numbers, for instance, which represent physical measurements, are limited in their accuracy not only by our powers of measurement but also by the accuracy of the measure we use as our unit. Also most fractions cannot be expressed exactly as decimals; and this is also the case for surds and logarithms, as well as for the numbers expressing certain ratios which arise out of geometrical relations. Even where numbers are supposed to be exact, calculations based on them can often only be approximate. We might, for instance, calculate the exact cost of 3 ℔ 5 oz. of meat at 9½ d. a ℔, but there are no coins in which we could pay this exact amount.

When the result of any arithmetical operation or operations is represented approximately but not exactly by a number, the excess (positive or negative) of this number over the number which would express the result exactly is called the *error*.

82. *Degree of Accuracy.*—There are three principal ways of expressing the degree of accuracy of any number, *i.e.* the extent to which it is equal to the number it is intended to represent.

(i) A number can be *correct to* so many *places of decimals*. This means (cf. § 71) that the number differs from the true value by less than one-half of the unit represented by 1 in the last place of decimals. For instance, .143 represents 1/7 correct to 3 places of decimals, since it differs from it by less than .0005. The final figure, in a case like this, is said to be *corrected*.

This method is not good for comparative purposes. Thus .143 and 14.286 represent respectively 1/7 and 100/7 to the same number of places of decimals, but the latter is obviously more exact than the former.

(ii) A number can be correct to so many *significant figures*. The significant figures of a number are those which commence with the first figure other than zero in the number; thus the significant figures of 13.027 and of .00013027 are the same.

This is the usual method; but the relative accuracy of two numbers expressed to the same number of significant figures depends to a certain extent on the magnitude of the first figure. Thus .14286 and .85714 represent 1/7 and 6/7 correct to 5 significant figures; but the latter is relatively more accurate than the former. For the former shows only that 1/7 lies between .142855 and .142865, or, as it is better expressed, between .142855½ and .142865½; but the latter shows that 6/7 lies between .857135½ and .857145½, and therefore that 1/7 lies between .142857/12 and .142859/12.

In either of the above cases, and generally in any case where a number is known to be within a certain limit on each side of the stated value, the *limit of error* is expressed by the sign ±. Thus the former of the above two statements would give 1/7 = .14286 ± .000005. It should be observed that the numerical value of the error is to be subtracted from or added to the stated value according as the error is positive or negative.

(iii) The limit of error can be expressed as a fraction of the number as stated. Thus 1/7 = .143 ± .0005 can be written 1/7 = 143(1 ± 1/286).

83. *Accuracy after Arithmetical Operations.*—If the numbers which are the subject of operations are not all exact, the accuracy of the result requires special investigation in each case.

Additions and subtractions are simple. If, for instance, the values of a and b, correct to two places of decimals, are 3.58 and 1.34, then 2.24, as the value of a − b, is not necessarily correct to two places. The limit of error of each being ±.005, the limit of error of their sum or difference is ±.01.

For multiplication we make use of the formula (§ 60 (i)) (a' ± α)(b' ± β) = a'b' + αβ ± (a'β + b'α). If a' and b' are the stated values, and ±α and ±β the respective limits of error, we ought strictly to take a'b' + αβ as the product, with a limit of error ±(a'β + b'α). In practice, however, both αβ and a certain portion of a'b' are small in comparison with a'β and b'α, and we therefore replace a'b' + αβ by an approximate value, and increase the limit of error so as to cover the further error thus introduced. In the case of the two numbers given in the last paragraph, the product lies between 3.575 × 1.335 = 4.772625 and 3.585 × 1.345 = 4.821825. We might take the product as (3.58 × 1.34) + (.005)2 = 4.797225, the limits of error being ±.005(3.58 + 1.34) = ±.0246; but it is more convenient to write it in such a form as 4.797 ± .025 or 4.80 ± .03.

If the number of decimal places to which a result is to be accurate is determined beforehand, it is usually not necessary in the actual working to go to more than two or three places beyond this. At the close of the work the extra figures are dropped, the last figure which remains being corrected (§ 82 (i)) if necessary.

VIII. SURDS AND LOGARITHMS

84. *Roots and Surds.*—The pth root of a number (§ 43) may, if the number is an integer, be found by expressing it in terms of its prime factors; or, if it is not an integer, by expressing it as a fraction in its lowest terms, and finding the pth roots of the numerator and of the denominator separately. Thus to find the cube root of 1728, we write it in the form 26} ·33, and find that its cube root is 22 ·3 = 12; or, to find the cube root of 1.728, we write it as 1728/1000 = 216/125 = 23 ·33/53, and find that the cube root is 2 ·3/5 = 1.2. Similarly the cube root of 2197 is 13. But we cannot find any number whose cube is 2000.

It is, however, possible to find a number whose cube shall approximate as closely as we please to 2000. Thus the cubes of 12.5 and of 12.6 are respectively 1953.125 and 2000.376, so that the number whose cube differs as little as possible from 2000 is somewhere between 12.5 and 12.6. Again the cube of 12.59 is 1995.616979, so that the number lies between 12.59 and 12.60. We may therefore consider that there is some number x whose cube is 2000, and we can find this number to any degree of accuracy that we please.

A number of this kind is called a *surd*; the surd which is the pth root of N is written p√N, but if the index is 2 it is usually omitted, so that the square root of N is written √N.

85. *Surd as a Power.*—We have seen (§§ 43, 44) that, if we take the successive powers of a number N, commencing with 1, they may be written N0, N1, N2, N3, ..., the series of indices being the standard series; and we have also seen (§ 44) that multiplication of any two of these numbers corresponds to addition of their indices. Hence we may insert in the power-series numbers with fractional indices, provided that the multiplication of these numbers follows the

same law. The number denoted by N1/3 will therefore be such that N1/3 × N1/3 × N1/3= N1/3 + 1/3 + 1/3 = N; *i.e.* it will be the cube root of N. By analogy with the notation of fractional numbers, N2/3 will be N1/3 + 1/3 = N1/3 × N1/3; and, generally, Np/q will mean the product of p numbers, the product of q of which is equal to N. Thus N2/6 will not mean the *same* as N1/3, but will mean the square of N1/6; but this will be *equal* to N1/3, *i.e.*(6√N)2 = 3√N.

86. *Multiplication and Division of Surds.*—To add or subtract fractional numbers, we must reduce them to a common denominator; and similarly, to multiply or divide surds, we must express them as power-numbers with the same index. Thus 3√2 × √5 = 21/3 × 51/2 = 22/6 × 53/6 = 41/6 × 1251/6 = 5001/6 = 6√500.

87. *Antilogarithms.*—If we take a fixed number, *e.g.* 2, as base, and take as indices the successive decimal numbers to any particular number of places of decimals, we get a series of *antilogarithms* of the indices to this base. Thus, if we go to two places of decimals, we have as the integral series the numbers 1, 2, 4, 8, ... which are the values of 20, 21, 22, ... and we insert within this series the successive powers of x, where x is such that x100 = 2. We thus get the numbers 2.01, 2.02, 2.03, ..., which are the antilogarithms of .01, .02, .03, ... to base 2; the first antilogarithm being 2.00 = 1, which is thus the antilogarithm of 0 to this (or any other) base. The series is formed by successive multiplication, and any antilogarithm to a larger number of decimal places is formed from it in the same way by multiplication. If, for instance, we have found 2.31, then the value of 2.316 is found from it by multiplying by the 6th power of the 1000th root of 2.

For practical purposes the number taken as base is 10; the convenience of this being that the increase of the index by an integer means multiplication by the corresponding power of 10, *i.e.* it means a shifting of the decimal point. In the same way, by dividing by powers of 10 we may get negative indices.

88. *Logarithms.*—If N is the antilogarithm of p to the base a, *i.e.* if N = ap, then p is called the logarithm of N to the base a, and is written loga N. As the table of antilogarithms is formed by successive multiplications, so the logarithm of any given 537number is in theory found by successive divisions. Thus, to find the logarithm of a number to base 2, the number being greater than 1, we first divide repeatedly by 2 until we get a number between 1 and 2; then divide repeatedly by10√2 until we get a number between 1 and 10√2; then divide repeatedly by 100√2; and so on. If, for instance, we find that the number is approximately equal to 23 × (10√2)5 × (100√2)7 × (1000√2)4, it may be written 23.574, and its logarithm to base 2 is 3.574.

For a further explanation of logarithms, and for an explanation of the treatment of cases in which an antilogarithm is less than 1, seeLOGARITHM.

For practical purposes logarithms are usually calculated to base 10, so that log10 10 = 1, log10 100 = 2, &c.

IX. UNITS

89. *Change of Denomination* of a numerical quantity is usually called *reduction*, so that this term covers, *e.g.*, the expression of £153, 7s. 4d. as shillings and pence and also the expression of 3067s. 4d. as £, s. and d.

The usual statement is that to express £153, 7s. as shillings we multiply 153 by 20 and add 7. This, as already explained (§ 37), is incorrect. £153 denotes 153 units, each of which is £1 or 20s.; and therefore we must multiply 20s. by 153 and add 7s., *i.e.* multiply 20 by 153 (the unit being now 1s.) and add 7. This is the expression of the process on the grouping method. On the counting method we have a scale with every 20th shilling marked as a £; there are 153 of these 20's, and 7 over.

The simplest case, in which the quantity can be expressed as an integral number of the largest units involved, has already been considered (§§ 37, 42). The same method can be applied in other cases by regarding a quantity expressed in several denominations as a fractional number of units of the largest denomination mentioned; thus 7s. 4d. is to be taken as meaning 74⁄12s., but £0, 7s. 4d. as £0[(74⁄12) / 20] (§ 17). The reduction of £153, 7s. 4d. to pence, and of 36808d. to £, s. d., on this principle, is shown in diagrams A and B above.

For reduction of pounds to shillings, or shillings to pounds, we must consider that we have a multiple-table (§ 36) in which the multiples of £1 and of 20s. are arranged in parallel columns; and similarly for shillings and pence.

90. *Change of Unit.*—The statement "£153 = 3060s." is not a statement of *equality* of the same kind as the statement "153 × 20 = 3060," but only a statement of *equivalence* for certain purposes; in other words, it does not convey an absolute truth. It is therefore of interest to see whether we cannot replace it by an absolute truth.

To do this, consider what the ordinary processes of multiplication and division mean in reference to concrete objects. If we want to give, to 5 boys, 4 apples each, we are said to multiply 4 apples by 5. We cannot multiply 4 apples by 5 boys, for then we should get 20 "boy-apples," an expression which has no meaning. Or, again, to distribute 20 apples amongst 5 boys, we are not regarded as dividing 20 apples by 5 boys, but as dividing 20 apples by the number 5. The multiplication or division here involves the omission of the unit "boy," and the operation is incomplete. The complete operation, in each case, is as follows.

(i) In the case of multiplication we commence with the conception of the number "5" and the unit "boy"; and we then convert this unit into 4 apples, and thus obtain the result, 20 apples. The conversion of the unit may be represented as multiplication by a factor (4 apples)/(1 boy), so that the operation is (4 apples)/(1 boy) × (5 boys) = 5 × (4 apples)/(1 boy) × (1 boy) = 5 × 4 apples = 20 apples. Similarly, to convert £153 into shillings we must multiply it by a factor 20s./£1, so that we get

$$\frac{0s.}{1} \times £153 \qquad \frac{0s.}{1} \times £1 = 153 \times 20s. =$$
$$= 153 \times \qquad\qquad\qquad 3060s.$$

Hence we can only regard £153 as being equal to 3060s. if we regard this converting factor as unity.

(ii) In the case of partition we can express the complete operation if we extend the meaning of division so as to enable us to divide 20 apples by 5 boys. We thus get (20 apples)/(5 boys) = (4 apples)/(1 boy), which means that the distribution can be effected by distributing at the rate of 4 apples per boy. The converting factor mentioned under (i) therefore represents a *rate*; and partition, applied to concrete cases, leads to a rate.

In reference to the use of the sign × with the converting factor, it should be observed that "(7 ℔)/(4 ℔) ×" symbolizes the replacing of so many times 4 ℔ by the same number of times 7 ℔, while "7/4 ×" symbolizes the replacing of 4 times something by 7 times that something.

X. ARITHMETICAL REASONING

91. *Correspondence of Series of Numbers.*—In §§ 33-42 we have dealt with the parallelism of the original number-series with a series consisting of the corresponding multiples of some unit, whether a number or a numerical quantity; and the relations arising out of multiplication, division, &c., have been exhibited by diagrams comprising pairs of corresponding terms of the two series. This, however, is only a particular case of the correspondence of two series. In considering addition, for instance, we have introduced two parallel series, each being the original number-series, but the two being placed in different positions. If we add 1, 2, 3, ... to 6, we obtain a series 7, 8, 9, ..., the terms of which correspond with those of the original series 1, 2, 3,...

Again, in §§ 61-75 and 84-88 we have considered various kinds of numbers other than those in the original number-series. In general, these have involved two of the original numbers, *e.g.* 53 involves 5 and 3, and log2 8 involves 2 and 8. In some cases, however, *e.g.* in the case of negative numbers and reciprocals, only one is involved; and there might be three or more, as in the case of a number expressed by (a + b)n. If all but one of these constituent elements are settled beforehand, *e.g.* if we take the numbers 5, 52, 53, ..., or the numbers3√1, 3√2, 3√3, ... or log10 1.001, log10 1.002, log10 1.003 ... we obtain a series in which each term corresponds with a term of the original number-series.

This correspondence is usually shown by *tabulation, i.e.* by the formation of a table in which the original series is shown in one column, and each term of the second series is placed in a second column opposite the corresponding term of the first series, each column being headed by a description of its contents. It is sometimes convenient to begin the first series with 0, and even to give the series of negative numbers; in most cases, however, these latter are regarded as belonging to a different series, and they need not be considered here. The diagrams, A, B, C are simple forms of tables; A giving a sum-series, B a multiple-series, and C a series of square roots, calculated approximately.

92. *Correspondence of Numerical Quantities.*—Again, in § 89, we have considered cases of multiple-tables of numerical quantities, where each quantity in one series is *equivalent* to the corresponding quantity in the other series. We might extend this principle to cases in which the terms of two series, whether of numbers or 538of numerical quantities, merely *correspond* with each other, the correspondence being the result of some relation. The volume of a cube, for

instance, bears a certain relation to the length of an edge of the cube. This relation is not one of proportion; but it may nevertheless be expressed by tabulation, as shown at D.

93. *Interpolation.*—In most cases the quantity in the second column may be regarded as increasing or decreasing continuously as the number in the first column increases, and it has intermediate values corresponding to intermediate (*i.e.* fractional or decimal) numbers not shown in the table. The table in such cases is not, and cannot be, complete, even up to the number to which it goes. For instance, a cube whose edge is 1½ in. has a definite volume, viz. 33/8 cub. in. The determination of any such intermediate value is performed by *Interpolation* (*q.v.*).

In treating a fractional number, or the corresponding value of the quantity in the second column, as intermediate, we are in effect regarding the numbers 1, 2, 3, ..., and the corresponding numbers in the second column, as denoting points between which other numbers lie, *i.e.* we are regarding the numbers as *ordinal*, not cardinal. The transition is similar to that which arises in the case of geometrical measurement (§ 26), and it is an essential feature of all reasoning with regard to continuous quantity, such as we have to deal with in real life.

94. *Nature of Arithmetical Reasoning.*—The simplest form of arithmetical reasoning consists in the determination of the term in one series corresponding to a given term in another series, when the relation between the two series is given; and it implies, though it does not necessarily involve, the establishment of each series as a whole by determination of its unit. A method involving the determination of the unit is called a *unitary* method. When the unit is not determined, the reasoning is algebraical rather than arithmetical. If, for instance, three terms of a proportion are given, the fourth can be obtained by the relation given at the end of § 57, this relation being then called the *Rule of Three*; but this is equivalent to the use of an algebraical formula.

More complicated forms of arithmetical reasoning involve the use of series, each term in which corresponds to particular terms in two or more series jointly; and cases of this kind are usually dealt with by special methods, or by means of algebraical formulae. The old-fashioned problems about the amount of work done by particular numbers of men, women and boys, are of this kind, and really involve the solution of simultaneous equations. They are not suitable for elementary purposes, as the arithmetical relations involved are complicated and difficult to grasp.

XI. METHODS OF CALCULATION
(1.) *Exact Calculation.*

95. *Working from Left.*—It is desirable, wherever possible, to perform operations on numbers or numerical quantities from the left, rather than from the right. There are several reasons for this. In the first place, an operation then corresponds more closely, at an elementary stage, with the concrete process which it represents. If, for instance, we had one sum of £3, 15s. 9d. and another of £2, 6s. 5d., we should add them by putting the coins of each denomination together and commencing the addition with the £. In the second place, this method fixes the attention at once on the larger, and therefore more important, parts of the quantities concerned, and thus prevents arithmetical processes from becoming too abstract in character. In the third place, it is a better preparation for dealing with approximate calculations. Finally, experience shows that certain operations in which the result is written down at once—*e.g.* addition or subtraction of two numbers or quantities, and multiplication by some small numbers—are with a little practice performed more quickly and more accurately from left to right.

96. *Addition.*—There is no difference in principle between addition (or subtraction) of numbers and addition (or subtraction) of numerical quantities. In each case the grouping system involves rearrangement, which implies the commutative law, while the counting system requires the expression of a quantity in different denominations to be regarded as a notation in a varying scale (§§ 17, 32). We need therefore consider numerical quantities only, our results being applicable to numbers by regarding the digits as representing multiples of units in different denominations.

When the result of addition in one denomination can be partly expressed in another denomination, the process is technically called *carrying*. The name is a bad one, since it does not correspond with any ordinary meaning of the verb. It would be better described as *exchanging*, by analogy with the "changing" of subtraction. When, *e.g.*, we find that the sum of 17s. and 18s. is 35s., we take out 20 of the 35 shillings, and exchange them for £1.

154

To add from the left, we have to look ahead to see whether the next addition will require an exchange. Thus, in adding £3, 17s. 0d. to £2, 18s. 0d., we write down the sum of £3 and £2 as £6, not as £5, and the sum of 17s. and 18s. as 15s., not as 35s.

When three or more numbers or quantities are added together, the result should always be checked by adding both upwards and downwards. It is also useful to look out for pairs of numbers or quantities which make 1 of the next denomination, *e.g.* 7 and 3, or 8d. and 4d.

97. *Subtraction.*—To subtract £3, 5s. 4d. from £9, 7s. 8d., on the grouping system, we split up each quantity into its denominations, perform the subtractions independently, and then regroup the results as the "remainder" £6, 2s. 4d. On the counting system we can count either forwards or backwards, and we can work either from the left or from the right. If we count forwards we find that to convert £3, 5s. 4d. into £9, 7s. 8d. we must successively add £6, 2s. and 4d. if we work from the left, or 4d., 2s. and £6 if we work from the right. The intermediate values obtained by the successive additions are different according as we work from the left or from the right, being £9, 5s. 4d. and £9, 7s. 4d. in the one case, and £3, 5s. 8d. and £3, 7s. 8d. in the other. If we count backwards, the intermediate values are £3, 7s. 8d. and £3, 5s. 8d. in the one case, and £9, 7s. 4d. and £9, 5s. 4d. in the other.

The determination of each element in the remainder involves reference to an addition-table. Thus to subtract 5s. from 7s. we refer to an addition-table giving the sum of any two quantities, each of which is one of the series 0s., 1s., ... 19s.

Subtraction by counting forward is called *complementary addition.*

To subtract £3, 5s. 8d. from £9, 10s. 4d., on the grouping system, we must *change* 1s. out of the 10s. into 12d., so that we subtract £3, 5s. 8d. from £9, 9s. 16d. On the counting system it will be found that, in determining the number of shillings in the remainder, we subtract 5s. from 9s. if we count forwards, working from the left, or backwards, working from the right; while, if we count backwards, working from the left, or forwards, working from the right, the subtraction is of 6s. from 10s. In the first two cases the successive values (in direct or reverse order) are £3, 5s. 8d., £9, 5s. 8d., £9, 9s. 8d. and £9, 10s. 4d.; while in the last two cases they are £9, 10s. 4d., £3, 10s. 4d., £3, 6s. 4d. and £3, 5s. 8d.

In subtracting from the left, we look ahead to see whether a 1 in any denomination must be reserved for changing; thus in subtracting 274 from 637 we should put down 2 from 6 as 3, not as 4, and 7 from 3 as 6.

98. *Multiplication-Table.*—For multiplication and division we use a *multiplication-table*, which is a multiple-table, arranged as explained in § 36, and giving the successive multiples, up to 9 times or further, of the numbers from 1 (or better, from 0) to 10, 12 or 20. The column (vertical) headed 3 will give the multiples of 3, while the row (horizontal) commencing with 3 will give the values of 3 × 1, 3 × 2, ... To multiply by 3 we use the row. To divide by 3, in the sense of partition, we also use the row; but to divide by 3 as a unit we use the column.

99. *Multiplication by a Small Number.*—The idea of a large 539multiple of a small number is simpler than that of a small multiple of a large number, but the calculation of the latter is easier. It is therefore convenient, in finding the product of two numbers, to take the smaller as the multiplier.

To find 3 times 427, we apply the distributive law (§ 58 (vi)) that 3·427 = 3(400 + 20 + 7) = 3·400 + 3·20 + 3·7. This, if we regard 3·427 as 427 + 427 + 427, is a direct consequence of the commutative law for addition (§ 58 (iii)), which enables us to add separately the hundreds, the tens and the ones. To find 3·400, we treat 100 as the unit (as in addition), so that 3·400 = 3·4·100 = 12·100 = 1200; and similarly for 3·20. These are examples of the associative law for multiplication (§ 58 (iv)).

100. *Special Cases.*—The following are some special rules:—

(i) To multiply by 5, multiply by 10 and divide by 2. (And conversely, to divide by 5, we multiply by 2 and divide by 10.)

(ii) In multiplying by 2, from the left, add 1 if the next figure of the multiplicand is 5, 6, 7, 8 or 9.

(iii) In multiplying by 3, from the left, add 1 when the next figures are not less than 33 ... 334 and not greater than 66 ... 666, and 2 when they are 66 ... 667 and upwards.

(iv) To multiply by 7, 8, 9, 11 or 12, treat the multiplier as 10 − 3, 10 − 2, 10 − 1, 10 + 1 or 10 + 2; and similarly for 13, 17, 18, 19, &c.

(v) To multiply by 4 or 6, we can either multiply from the left by 2 and then by 2 or 3, or multiply from the right by 4 or 6; or we can treat the multiplier as 5 − 1 or 5 + 1.

101. *Multiplication by a Large Number.*—When both the numbers are large, we split up one of them, preferably the multiplier, into separate portions. Thus 231·4273 = (200 + 30 + 1)·4273 = 200·4273 + 30·4273 + 1·4273. This gives the *partial products*, the sum of which is the complete products. The process is shown fully in A below,—

and more concisely in B. To multiply 4273 by 200, we use the commutative law, which gives 200·4273 = 2 × 100 × 4273 = 2 × 4273 × 100 = 8546 × 100 = 854600; and similarly for 30·4273. In B the terminal 0's of the partial products are omitted. It is usually convenient to make out a preliminary table of multiples up to 10 times; the table being checked at 5 times (§ 100) and at 10 times.

The main difficulty is in the correct placing of the curtailed partial products. The first step is to regard the product of two numbers as containing as many digits as the two numbers put together. The table of multiples will them be as in C. The next step is to arrange the multiplier and the multiplicand above the partial products. For elementary work the multiplicand may come immediately after the multiplier, as in D; the last figure of each partial product then comes immediately under the corresponding figure of the multiplier. A better method, which leads up to the multiplication of decimals and of approximate values of numbers, is to place the first figure of the multipler under the first figure of the multiplicand, as in E; the first figure of each partial product will then come under the corresponding figure of the multiplier.

102. *Contracted Multiplication.*—The partial products are sometimes omitted; the process saves time in writing, but is not easy. The principle is that, *e.g.*(a ·102 + b ·10 + c)(p ·102 + q10 + r) = ap ·104 + (aq + bp) ·103 + (ar + bq + cp) ·102 + (br + cq) ·10 + cr. Hence the digits are multiplied in pairs, and grouped according to the power of 10 which each product contains. A method of performing the process is shown here for the case of 162 ·427. The principle is that 162 ·427 = 100 ·427 + 60 ·427 + 2 ·427 = 1 ·42700 + 6 ·4270 + 2 ·427; but, instead of writing down the separate products, we (in effect) write 42700, 4270, and 427 in separate rows, with the multipliers 1, 6, 2 in the margin, and then multiply each number in each column by the corresponding multiplier in the margin, making allowance for any figures to be "carried." Thus the second figure (from the right) is given by 1 + 2 ·2 + 6 ·7 = 47, the 1 being carried.

103. *Aliquot Parts.*—For multiplication by a proper fraction or a decimal, it is sometimes convenient, especially when we are dealing with mixed quantities, to convert the multiplier into the sum or difference of a number of fractions, each of which has 1 as its numerator. Such fractions are called *aliquot parts* (from Lat. *aliquot*, some, several). This can usually be done in a good many ways. Thus5/6 = 1 − 1/6, and also = ½ + 1/3; and 15% = .15 = 1/10 + 1/20 = 1/6 − 1/60 =1/8 + 1/40. The fractions should generally be chosen so that each part of the product may be obtained from an earlier part by a comparatively simple division. Thus ½ + 1/20 − 1/60 is a simpler expression for 8/15 than ½ + 1/30.

The process may sometimes by applied two or three times in succession; thus 8/15 = 4/5 ·2/3 = (1 − 1/5)(1 − 1/3), and 33/40 = ¾ ·11/10 = (1 − ¼)(1 + 1/10).

104. *Practice.*—The above is a particular case of the method called*practice*, but the nomenclature of the method is confusing. There are two kinds of practice, *simple practice* and *compound practice*, but the latter is the simpler of the two. To find the cost of 2 ℔ 8 oz. of butter at 1s. 2d. a ℔, we multiply 1s. 2d. by 28/16 = 2½. This straightforward process is called "compound" practice. "Simple" practice involves an application of the commutative law. To find the cost of n articles at £a, bs, cd. each, we express £a, bs, cd. in the form £(a + f), where f is a fraction (or the sum of several fractions); we then say that the cost, being n × £(a + f), is equal to (a + f) × £n, and apply the method of compound practice, *i.e.* the method of aliquot parts.

105. *Multiplication of a Mixed Number.*—When a mixed quantity or a mixed number has to be multiplied by a large number, it is sometimes convenient to express the former in terms of one only of its denominations. Thus, to multiply £7, 13s. 6d. by 469, we may express the former in any of the ways £7.675, 307/40 of £1, 153½s., 153.5s., 307 sixpences, or 1842 pence. Expression in £ and decimals of £1 is usually recommended, but it depends on circumstances whether some other method may not be simpler.

A sum of money cannot be expressed exactly as a decimal of £1 unless it is a multiple of ¾d. A rule for approximate conversion is that 1s. = .05 of £1, and that 2½d.= .01 of £1. For accurate conversion we write .1£ for each 2s., and .001£ for each farthing beyond 2s., their number being first increased by one twenty-fourth.

156

106. *Division.* Of the two kinds of division, although the idea of partition is perhaps the more elementary, the process of measuring is the easier to perform, since it is equivalent to a series of subtractions. Starting from the dividend, we in theory keep on subtracting the unit, and count the number of subtractions that have to be performed until nothing is left. In actual practice, of course, we subtract large multiples at a time. Thus, to divide 987063 by 427, we reverse the procedure of § 101, but with intermediate stages. We first construct the multiple-table C, and then subtract successively 200 times, 30 times and 1 times; these numbers being the *partial quotients.* The theory of the process is shown fully in F. Treating x as the unknown quotient corresponding to the original dividend, 540 we obtain successive dividends corresponding to quotients x − 200, x − 230 and x − 231. The original dividend is written as 0987063, since its initial figures are greater than those of the divisor; if the dividend had commenced with (*e.g.*) 3 ... it would not have been necessary to insert the initial 0. At each stage of the division the number of digits in the reduced dividend is decreased by one. The final dividend being 0000, we have x − 231 = 0, and therefore x = 231.

107. *Methods of Division.*—What are described as different methods of division (by a single divisor) are mainly different methods of writing the successive figures occurring in the process. In *long division* the divisor is put on the left of the dividend, and the quotient on the right; and each partial product, with the remainder after its subtraction, is shown in full. In *short division* the divisor and the quotient are placed respectively on the left of and below the dividend, and the partial products and remainders are not shown at all. The *Austrian* method (sometimes called in Great Britain the *Italian* method) differs from these in two respects. The first, and most important, is that the quotient is placed above the dividend. The second, which is not essential to the method, is that the remainders are shown, but not the partial products; the remainders being obtained by working from the right, and using complementary addition. It is doubtful whether the brevity of this latter process really compensates for its greater difficulty.

The advantage of the Austrian arrangement of the quotient lies in the indication it gives of the true value of each partial quotient. A modification of the method, corresponding with D of § 101, is shown in G; the fact that the partial product 08546 is followed by two blank spaces shows that the figure 2 represents a partial quotient 200. An alternative arrangement, corresponding to E of § 101, and suited for more advanced work, is shown in H.

108. *Division with Remainder.*—It has so far been assumed that the division can be performed exactly, *i.e.* without leaving an ultimate remainder. Where this is not the case, difficulties are apt to arise, which are mainly due to failure to distinguish between the two kinds of division. If we say that the division of 41d. by 12 gives quotient 3d. with remainder 5d., we are speaking loosely; for in fact we only distribute 36d. out of the 41d., the other 5d. remaining undistributed. It can only be distributed by a subdivision of the unit; *i.e.* the true result of the division is 35/12d. On the other hand, we can quite well express the result of dividing 41d. by 1s (= 12d.) as 3 with 5d. (not "5") over, for this is only stating that 41d. = 3s. 5d.; though the result might be more exactly expressed as 35/12s.

Division with a remainder has thus a certain air of unreality, which is accentuated when the division is performed by means of factors (§ 42). If we have to divide 935 by 240, taking 12 and 20 as factors, the result will depend on the fact that, in the notation of § 17, In incomplete partition the quotient is 3, and the remainders 11 and 17 are in effect disregarded; if, after finding the quotient 3, we want to know what remainder would be produced by a direct division, the simplest method is to multiply 3 by 240 and subtract the result from 935. In complete partition the successive quotients are 7711/12 and 3[(1711/12)/20] = 3215/240. Division in the sense of measuring leads to such a result as 935d. = £3, 17s. 11d.; we may, if we please, express the 17s. 11d. as 215d., but there is no particular reason why we should do so.

109. *Division by a Mixed Number.*—To divide by a mixed number, when the quotient is seen to be large, it usually saves time to express the divisor as either a simple fraction or a decimal of a unit of one of the denominations. Exact division by a mixed number is not often required in real life; where approximate division is required (*e.g.* in determining the rate of a "dividend"), approximate expression of the divisor in terms of the largest unit is sufficient.

110. *Calculation of Square Root.*—The calculation of the square root of a number depends on the formula (iii) of § 60. To find the square root of N, we first find some number whose square is less than N, and subtract a2 from N. If the complete square root is a + b, the remainder after subtracting a2 is (2a + b)b. We therefore guess b by dividing the remainder by 2a, and form the product (2a + b)b. If this is equal to the remainder, we have found the square root. If it exceeds the square root, we must alter the value of b, so as to get a product which does not exceed the remainder. If the product is less than the remainder, we get a new remainder, which is N − (a +

b)2; we then assume the full square root to be c, so that the new remainder is equal to (2a + 2b + c)c, and try to find c in the same way as we tried to find b.

An analogous method of finding cube root, based on the formula for (a + b)3, used to be given in text-books, but it is of no practical use. To find a root other than a square root we can use logarithms, as explained in § 113.

111. *Multiplication.*—When we have to multiply two numbers, and the product is only required, or can only be approximately correct, to a certain number of significant figures, we need only work to two or three more figures (§ 83), and then correct the final figure in the result by means of the superfluous figures.

A common method is to reverse the digits in one of the numbers; but this is only appropriate to the old-fashioned method of writing down products from the right. A better method is to ignore the positions of the decimal points, and multiply the numbers as if they were decimals between .1 and 1.0. The method E of § 101 being adopted, the multiplicand and the multiplier are written with a space after as many digits (of each) as will be required in the product (on the principle explained in § 101); and the multiplication is performed from the left, two extra figures being kept in. Thus, to multiply 27.343 by 3.1415927 to one decimal place, we require 2 + 1 + 1 = 4 figures in the product. The result is 085.9 = 85.9, the position of the decimal point being determined by counting the figures before the decimal points in the original numbers.

112. *Division.*—In the same way, in performing approximate division, we can at a certain stage begin to abbreviate the divisor, taking off one figure (but with correction of the final figure of the partial product) at each stage. Thus, to divide 85.9 by 3.1415927 to two places of decimals, we in effect divide .0859 by .31415927 to four places of decimals. In the work, as here shown, a 0 is inserted in front of the 859, on the principle explained in § 106. The result of the division is 27.34.

113. *Logarithms.*—Multiplication, division, involution and evolution, when the results cannot be exact, are usually most simply performed, at any rate to a first approximation, by means of a table of logarithms. Thus, to find the square root of 2, we have log √2 = log (21/2) = ½ log 2. We take out log 2 from the table, halve it, and then find from the table the number of which this is the logarithm. (See LOGARITHM.) The *slide-rule* (see CALCULATING MACHINES) is a simple apparatus for the mechanical application of the methods of logarithms.

When a first approximation has been obtained in this way, further approximations can be obtained in various ways. Thus, having found √2 = 1.414 approximately, we write √2 = 1.414 + θ, whence 2 = (1.414)2 + (2.818)θ + θ2. Since θ2 is less than ¼ of 541(.001)2, we can obtain three more figures approximately by dividing 2 − (1.414)2 by 2.818.

114. *Binomial Theorem.*—More generally, if we have obtained a as an approximate value for the pth root of N, the binomial theorem gives as an approximate formula p√N = a + θ, where N = ap + pap − 1θ.

115. *Series.*—A number can often be expressed by a series of terms, such that by taking successive terms we obtain successively closer approximations. A decimal is of course a series of this kind, *e.g.* 3.14159 ... means 3 + 1/10 + 4/102 + 1/103 + 5/104 + 9/105 + ... A series of aliquot parts is another kind, *e.g.* 3.1416 is a little less than 3 + 1/7 − 1/800.

Recurring Decimals are a particular kind of series, which arise from the expression of a fraction as a decimal. If the denominator of the fraction, when it is in its lowest terms, contains any other prime factors than 2 and 5, it cannot be expressed exactly as a decimal; but after a certain point a definite series of figures will constantly recur. The interest of these series is, however, mainly theoretical.

116. *Continued Products.*—Instead of being expressed as the sum of a series of terms, a number may be expressed as the product of a series of factors, which become successively more and more nearly equal to 1. For example,

$$3.1416 = 3 \times 10472/10000 = 3 \times 1309/1250 = 3 \times 22/21 \times 2499/2500 = 3(1 + 1/21)(1 - 1/2500).$$

Hence, to multiply by 3.1416, we can multiply by 31⁄7, and subtract1⁄2500 (= .0004) of the result; or, to divide by 3.1416, we can divide by 3, then subtract 1⁄22 of the result, and then add 1⁄2499 of the new result.

117. *Continued Fractions.*—The theory of *continued fractions(q.v.)* gives a method of expressing a number, in certain cases, as a continued product. A continued fraction, of the kind we are considering, is an expression of the form   where b, c, d, ... are integers, and a is an integer or zero. The expression is usually written, for compactness, a + 1/b+ 1/c+ 1/d+ &c. The numbers a, b, c, d, ... are called the *quotients.*

Any exact fraction can be expressed as a continued fraction, and there are methods for expressing as continued fractions certain other numbers, *e.g.* square roots, whose values cannot be expressed exactly as fractions.

The successive values, a/1, (ab + 1)/b, ..., obtained by taking account of the successive quotients, are called *convergents, i.e.*convergents to the true value. The following are the main properties of the convergents.

(i) If we precede the series of convergents by 0⁄1 and 1⁄0, then the numerator (or denominator) of each term of the series 0⁄1, 1⁄0, a/1, (ab + 1)/b ..., after the first two, is found by multiplying the numerator (or denominator) of the last preceding term by the corresponding quotient and adding the numerator (or denominator) of the term before that. If a is zero, we may regard 1/b as the first convergent, and precede the series by 1⁄0 and 0⁄1.

(ii) Each convergent is a fraction in its lowest terms.

(iii) The convergents are alternately less and greater than the true value.

(iv) Each convergent is nearer to the true value than any other fraction whose denominator is less than that of the convergent.

(v) The difference of two successive convergents is the reciprocal of the product of their denominators; *e.g.* (ab + 1)/b − a/1 = 1/(1·b), and (abc + c + a)/(bc + 1) − (ab + 1)/b = −1/b(bc + 1).

It follows from these last three properties that if the successive convergents are p1/1, p2/q2, p3/q3, ... the number can be expressed in the form p1(1 + 1/p1q2) (1 − 1/p2q3) (1 + 1/p3q4) ..., and that if we go up to the factor 1 ± 1/(pnqn + 1) the product of these factors differs from the true value of the number by less than ±{1/(qnqn + 1).

In certain cases two or more factors can be combined so as to produce an expression of the form 1 ± 1/k, where k is an integer. For instance, 3.1415927 = 3(1 + 1/3.7) (1 − 1/22.106) (1 + 1/333.113) ...; but the last two of these factors may be combined as (1 − 1/22.113). Hence 3.1415927 = 3⁄1 · 22/21 · 2485/2486 ...

XII. APPLICATIONS
(i.) *Systems of Measures.*[1]

118. *Metric System.*—The metric system was adopted in France at the end of the 18th century. The system is decimal throughout. The principal units of length, weight and volume are the *metre, gramme*(or *gram*) and *litre.* Other units are derived from these by multiplication or division by powers of 10, the names being denoted by prefixes. The prefixes for multiplication by 10, 102, 103 and 104 are*deca-, hecto-, kilo-* and *myria-,* and those for division by 10, 102 and 103 are *deci-, centi-* and *milli-*; the former being derived from Greek, and the latter from Latin. Thus *kilogramme* means 1000 grammes, and*centimetre* means 1⁄100 of a metre. There are also certain special units, such as the *hectare,* which is equal to a square hectometre, and the*micron,* which is 1⁄1000 of a millimetre.

The metre and the gramme are defined by standard measures preserved at Paris. The litre is equal to a cubic decimetre. The gramme was intended to be equal to the weight of a cubic centimetre of pure water at a certain temperature, but the equality is only approximate.

The metric system is now in use in the greater part of the civilized world, but some of the measures retain the names of old disused measures. In Germany, for instance, the *Pfund* is ½ kilogramme, and is approximately equal to 11⁄10 ℔ English.

119. *British Systems.*—The British systems have various origins, and are still subject to variations caused by local usage or by the usage of particular businesses. The following tables are given as illustrations of the arrangement adopted elsewhere in this article; the entries in any column denote multiples or submultiples of the unit stated at the head of the column, and the entries in any row give the expression of one unit in term of the other units.

LENGTH

Inch.	Foot.	Yard.	Chain.	Furlong.	Mile.
1	/12	/36	1 /792	1 /7920	1 /63360

159

1/2		/3	1/66	1/660	1/5280
3/6			1/22	1/220	1/1760
7/92	6	2	1/0	1/10	1/80
7/920	60	20	1/0	1	1/8
6/3360	280	760	80	8	1

WEIGHT (AVOIRDUPOIS)

Ounce.	Pound.	Stone.	Quarter.	Hundred-weight.	Ton.
1	1/16	1/224	1/448	1/1792	1/33840
16	1	1/14	1/28	1/112	1/2240
224	14	1	½	1/8	1/160
448	28	2	1	¼	1/80
1792	112	8	4	1	1/20
33840	2240	160	80	20	1

(Also 7000 grains = 1 ℔ avoirdupois.)

120. *Change of System.*—It is sometimes necessary, when a quantity is expressed in one system, to express it in another. [542] The following are the ratios of some of the units; each unit is expressed approximately as a decimal of the other, and their ratio is shown as a continued product (§ 116), a few of the corresponding convergents to the continued fraction (§ 117) being added in brackets. It must be remembered that the number expressing any quantity in terms of a unit is *inversely proportional* to the magnitude of the unit, i.e., the number of new units is to be found by multiplying the number of old units by the ratio of the old unit to the new unit.

Yard, Metre $= \dfrac{9144}{10000} = \dfrac{10000}{10935} = \dfrac{22}{12} \cdot \dfrac{884}{385} \cdot \dfrac{8225}{8224} \ldots \left(\dfrac{11}{32},\ \dfrac{32}{35} = \dfrac{8}{7} \cdot \dfrac{4}{5},\ \dfrac{235}{257}\right).$

Inch, Centimetre $= \dfrac{25400}{10000} = \dfrac{10000}{3937} = \dfrac{2}{5} \cdot \dfrac{66}{65} \cdot \dfrac{1651}{1650} \ldots \left(\dfrac{5}{2},\ \dfrac{33}{13},\ \dfrac{127}{50}\right).$

Mile, Kilometre $= \dfrac{16093}{10000} = \dfrac{10000}{6214} = \dfrac{8}{5} \cdot \dfrac{185}{184} \cdot \dfrac{2369}{2368} \ldots \left(\dfrac{8}{5},\ \dfrac{37}{23},\ \dfrac{103}{64}\right).$

Square Yard, Square Metre $= \dfrac{8361}{10000} = \dfrac{10000}{11960} = \dfrac{5}{6} \cdot \dfrac{306}{305} \cdot \dfrac{15250}{15249} \ldots \left(\dfrac{5}{6},\ \dfrac{51}{61},\ \dfrac{250}{299}\right).$

Acre, Hectare $= \dfrac{4047}{10000} = \dfrac{10000}{24711} = \dfrac{2}{5} \cdot \dfrac{85}{84} \cdot \dfrac{5320}{5321} \ldots \left(\dfrac{2}{5},\ \dfrac{17}{42},\ \dfrac{380}{939}\right).$

Quart $= \dfrac{11365}{10000} = \dfrac{10000}{8799} = \dfrac{8}{7} \cdot \dfrac{175}{176} \cdot \dfrac{8976}{8975} \ldots \left(\dfrac{8}{7},\ \dfrac{25}{22},\ \dfrac{408}{359}\right).$

160

Lit
re
Po
und   = 45   = 10   = $1/2 \cdot 10/11 \cdot 484/485 \cdot 29391/29392$ ...
Kil   36/10000   000/22046   (1/2, 5/11, 44/97, 303/668).
ogramme

(ii.) Special Applications.

121. *Commercial Arithmetic.*—This term covers practically all dealings with money which involve the application of the principle of proportion. A simple class of cases is that which deals with equivalence of sums of money in different currencies; these cases really come under § 120. In other cases we are concerned with a proportion stated as a *numerical percentage*, or as a *money percentage*(*i.e.* a sum of money per £100), or as a *rate* in the £ or the shilling. The following are some examples. Percentage: *Brokerage, commission, discount, dividend, interest, investment, profit and loss.* Rate in the £:*Discount, dividend, rates, taxes.* Rate in the shilling: *Discount.*

Text-books on arithmetic usually contain explanations of the chief commercial transactions in which arithmetical calculations arise; it will be sufficient in the present article to deal with interest and discount, and to give some notes on percentages and rates in the £. *Insurance*and *Annuities* are matters of general importance, which are dealt with elsewhere under their own headings.

122. *Percentages and Rates in the £.*—In dealing with percentages and rates it is important to notice whether the sum which is expressed as a percentage of a rate on another sum is a part of or an addition to that sum, or whether they are independent of one another. Income tax, for instance, is calculated on income, and is in the nature of a deduction from the income; but local rates are calculated in proportion to certain other payments, actual or potential, and could without absurdity exceed 20s. in the £.

It is also important to note that if the increase or decrease of an amount A by a certain percentage produces B, it will require a different percentage to decrease or increase B to A. Thus, if B is 20% less than A, A is 25% greater than B.

123. *Interest* is usually calculated yearly or half-yearly, at a certain rate per cent. on the principal. In legal documents the rate is sometimes expressed as a certain sum of money "per centum per annum"; here "centum" must be taken to mean "£100."

Simple interest arises where unpaid interest accumulates as a debt not itself bearing interest; but, if this debt bears interest, the total, *i.e.*interest and interest on interest, is called *compound interest.* If 100r is the rate per cent. per annum, the simple interest on £A for n years is £nrA, and the compound interest (supposing interest payable yearly) is $£[(1 + r)n - 1]A$. If n is large, the compound interest is most easily calculated by means of logarithms.

124. *Discount* is of various kinds. Tradesmen allow discount for ready money, this being usually at so much in the shilling or £. Discount may be allowed twice in succession off quoted prices; in such cases the second discount is off the reduced price, and therefore it is not correct to add the two rates of discount together. Thus a discount of 20%, followed by a further discount of 25%, gives a total discount of 40%, not 45%, off the original amount. When an amount will fall due at some future date, the *present value* of the debt is found by deducting discount at some rate per cent. for the intervening period, in the same way as interest to be added is calculated. This discount, of course, is not equal to the interest which the present value would produce at that rate of interest, but is rather greater, so that the present value as calculated in this way is less than the theoretical present value.

125. Applications to *Physics* are numerous, but are usually only of special interest. A case of general interest is the measurement of*temperature.* The graduation of a thermometer is determined by the freezing-point and the boiling-point of water, the interval between these being divided into a certain number of degrees, representing equal increases of temperature. On the Fahrenheit scale the points are respectively 32° and 212°; on the Centigrade scale they are 0ⁿ and 100°; and on the Réaumur they are 0° and 80°. From these data a temperature as measured on one scale can be expressed on either of the other two scales.

126. *Averages* occur in statistics, economics, &c. An average is found by adding together several measurements of the same kind and dividing by the number of measurements. In calculating an average it should be observed that the addition of any numerical quantity (positive or negative) to each of the measurements produces the addition of the same quantity to the average, so that the calculation may often be simplified by taking some particular measurement as a new zero from which to measure.

AUTHORITIES.—For the history of the subject, see W.W.R. Ball,*Short History of Mathematics* (1901), and F. Cajori, *History of Elementary Mathematics* (1896); or more detailed information in M. Cantor, *Vorlesungen über Geschichte der Mathematik* (1894-1901). L.C. Conant, *The Number-Concept* (1896), gives a very full account of systems of numeration. For the latter, and for systems of notation, reference may also be made to Peacock's article "Arithmetic" in the *Encyclopaedia Metropolitana*, which contains a detailed account of the Greek system. F. Galton, *Inquiries into Human Faculty* (1883), contains the first account of number-forms; for further examples and references see D.E. Phillips, "Genesis of Number-Forms," *American Journal of Psychology*, vol. viii. (1897). There are very few works dealing adequately but simply with the principles of arithmetic. Homersham Cox, *Principles of Arithmetic* (1885), is brief and lucid, but is out of print. *The Psychology of Number*, by J.A. McLellan and J. Dewey (1895), contains valuable suggestions (some of which have been utilized in the present article), but it deals only with number as the measure of quantity, and requires to be read critically. This work contains references to Grube's system, which has been much discussed in America: for a brief explanation, see L. Seeley, *The Grube Method of Teaching Arithmetic* (1890). On the teaching of arithmetic, and of elementary mathematics generally, see J.W.A. Young, *The Teaching of Mathematics in the Elementary and the Secondary School* (1907); D.E. Smith, *The Teaching of Elementary Mathematics* (1900), also contains an interesting general sketch; W.P. Turnbull, *The Teaching of Arithmetic* (1903), is more elaborate. E.M. Langley, *A Treatise on Computation* (1895), has notes on approximate and abbreviated calculation. Text-books on arithmetic in general and on particular applications are numerous, and any list would soon be out of date. Recent English works have been influenced by the brief *Report on the Teaching of Elementary Mathematics*, issued by the Mathematical Association (1905); but this is critical rather than constructive. The Association has also issued a *Report on the Teaching of Mathematics in Preparatory Schools* (1907). In the United States of America the *Report of the Committee of Ten* on secondary school studies (1893) and the *Report of the Committee of Fifteen* on elementary education (1893-1894), both issued by the United States Bureau of Education, have attracted a good deal of attention. Sir O. Lodge, *Easy Mathematics, chiefly Arithmetic* (1905), treats the subject broadly in its practical aspects. The student who is interested in elementary teaching should consult the annual bibliographies in the *Pedagogical Seminary*; an article by D.E. Phillips in vol. v. (October 1897) contains references to works dealing with the psychological aspect of number. For an account of German methods, see W. King, *Report on Teaching of Arithmetic and Mathematics in the Higher Schools of Germany* (1903).

(W. F. SH.)

1See also WEIGHTS AND MEASURES.

ARIUS (Ἄρειος), a name celebrated in ecclesiastical history, not so much on account of the personality of its bearer as of the "Arian" controversy which he provoked. Our knowledge of Arius is scanty, and nothing certain is known of his birth or of his early training. Epiphanius of Salamis, in his well-known treatise against eighty heresies (*Haer.* lxix. 3), calls him a Libyan by birth, and if the statement of Sozomen, a church historian of the 5th century, is to be trusted, he was, as a member of the Alexandrian church, connected with the Meletian schism (see 543 MELETIUS OF LYCOPOLIS), and on this account excommunicated by Peter of Alexandria, who had ordained him deacon. After the death of Peter (November 25, 311), he was received into communion by Peter's successor, Achillas, elevated to the presbytery, and put in charge of one of the great city churches, Baucalis, where he continued to discharge his duties with apparent faithfulness and industry after the accession of Alexander. This bishop also held him in high repute. Theodoret (*Hist. Eccl.* i. 2) indeed does not hesitate to say that Arius was chagrined because Alexander, instead of himself, had been appointed to the see of Alexandria, and that the beginning of his heretical attitude is, in consequence, to be attributed to discontent and envy. But this must be rejected, for it is a common explanation of heretical movements with the early church historians, and there is no evidence for it in the original sources. However, Arius was ambitious. Epiphanius, using older documents, describes him as a man inflamed with his own opinionativeness, of a soft and smooth address, calculated to persuade and attract, especially women: "in no time he had drawn away seven hundred virgins from the church to his party." When the controversy broke out, Arius was an old man.

The real causes of the controversy lay in differences as to dogma. Arius had received his theological education in the school of the presbyter Lucian of Antioch, a learned man, and distinguished especially as a biblical scholar. The latter was a follower of Paul of Samosata, bishop of Antioch, who had been excommunicated in 269, but his theology differed from that of his master in a fundamental point. Paul, starting with the conviction that the One God cannot appear substantially (οὐσιωδῶς) on earth, and, consequently, that he cannot have become a person in Jesus Christ, had taught that God had filled the man Jesus with his Logos (σοφία) or Power (δύναμις). Lucian, on the other hand, persisted in holding that the Logos became a person

162

in Christ. But since he shared the above-mentioned belief of his master, nothing remained for him but to see in the Logos a second essence, created by God before the world, which came down to earth and took upon itself a human body. In this body the Logos filled the place of the intellectual or spiritual principle. Lucian's Christ, then, was not "perfect man," for that which constituted in him the personal element was a divine essence; nor was he "perfect God," for the divine essence having become a person was other than the One God, and of a nature foreign to him. It is this idea which Arius took up and interpreted unintelligently. His doctrinal position is explained in his letters to his patron Eusebius, bishop of the imperial city of Nicomedia, and to Alexander of Alexandria, and in the fragments of the poem in which he set forth his dogmas, which bears the enigmatic title of "Thalia" (θάλεια), used in Homer, in the sense of "a goodly banquet," most unjustly ridiculed by Athanasius as an imitation of the licentious style of the drinking-songs of the Egyptian Sotades (270B.C.). From these writings it can even nowadays be seen clearly that the principal object which he had in view was firmly to establish the unity and simplicity of the eternal God. However far the Son may surpass other created beings, he remains himself a created being, to whom the Father before all time gave an existence formed out of not being (ἐξ οὐκ ὄντων); hence the name of *Exoukontians* sometimes given to Arius's followers. On the other hand, Arius affirmed of the Son that he was "perfect God, only-begotten" (πλήρης θεὸς μονογενής); that through him God made the worlds (αἰῶνες, ages); that he was the product or offspring of the Father, and yet not as one among things made (γέννημα ἀλλ' οὐχ ὡς ἓν τῶν γεγενημένων). In his eyes it was blasphemy when he heard that Alexander proclaimed in public that "as God is eternal, so is his Son,—when the Father, then the Son,—the Son is present in God without birth (ἀγεννήτως), ever-begotten (ἀειγενής), an unbegotten-begotten (ἀγεννητογενής)." He detected in his bishop Gnosticism, Manichaeism and Sabellianism, and was convinced that he himself was the champion of pure doctrine against heresy. He was quite unconscious that his own monotheism was hardly to be distinguished from that of the pagan philosophers, and that his Christ was a demi-god.

For years the controversy may have been fermenting in the college of presbyters at Alexandria. Sozomen relates that Alexander only interfered after being charged with remissness in leaving Arius so long to disturb the faith of the church. According to the general supposition, the negotiations which led to the excommunication of Arius and his followers among the presbyters and deacons took place in 318 or 319, but there are good reasons for assigning the outbreak of the controversy to the time following the overthrow of Licinius by Constantine, *i.e.* to the year 323. In any case, from this time events followed one another to a speedy conclusion. Arius was not without adherents, even outside Alexandria. Those bishops who, like him, had passed through the school of Lucian were not inclined to let him fall without a struggle, as they recognized in the views of their fellow-student their own doctrine, only set forth in a somewhat radical fashion. In addressing to Eusebius of Nicomedia a request for his help, Arius ended with the words: "Be mindful of our adversity, thou faithful comrade of Lucian's school (συλλουκιανιστής)"; and Eusebius entered the lists energetically on his behalf. But Alexander too was active; by means of a circular letter he published abroad the excommunication of his presbyter, and the controversy excited more and more general interest.

It reached even the ears of Constantine. Now sole emperor, he saw in the one Catholic church the best means of counteracting the movement in his vast empire towards disintegration; and he at once realized how dangerous dogmatic squabbles might prove to its unity. His letter, preserved by the imperial biographer, Eusebius of Caesarea, is a state document inspired by a wisely conciliatory policy; it made out both parties to be equally in the right and in the wrong, at the same time giving them both to understand that such questions, the meaning of which would be grasped only by the few, had better not be brought into public discussion; it was advisable to come to an agreement where the difference of opinion was not fundamental. This well-meaning attempt at reconciliation, betraying as it did no very deep understanding of the question, came to nothing. No course was left for the emperor except to obtain a general decision. This took, place at the fist oecumenical council, which was convened in Nicaea (*q.v.*) in 325. After various turns in the controversy, it was finally decided, against Arius, that the Son was "of the same substance" (ὁμοούσιος) with the Father, and all thought of his being created or even subordinate had to be excluded. Constantine accepted the decision of the council and resolved to uphold it. Arius and the two bishops of Marmarica Ptolemais, who refused to subscribe the creed, were excommunicated and banished to Illyria, and even Eusebius of Nicomedia, who accepted the creed, but not its anathemas, was exiled to Gaul. Alexander returned to his see triumphant, but died soon after, and was succeeded by Athanasius (*q.v.*), his deacon, with whose indomitable fortitude and strange vicissitudes the further course of the controversy is bound up.

It only remains for us here to sketch what is known of the future career of Arius and the Arians. Although defeated at the council of Nicaea, the Arians were by no means subdued. Constantine, while strongly disposed at first to enforce the Nicene decrees, was gradually won to a more conciliatory policy by the influence especially of Eusebius of Caesarea and Eusebius of Nicomedia, the latter of whom returned from exile in 328 and won the ear of the emperor, whom he baptized on his death-bed. In 330 even Arius was recalled from banishment. Athanasius, on the other hand, was banished to Trèves in 335. During his absence Arius returned to Alexandria, but even now the people are said to have raised a fierce riot against the heretic. In 336 the emperor was forced to summon him to Constantinople. Bishop Alexander reluctantly assented to receive him once more into the bosom of the church, but before the act of admission was completed, Arius was suddenly taken ill while walking in the streets, and died in a few moments. His death seems to have exercised no influence worth speaking of on the course of events. His theological radicalism had in any case never found many convinced adherents. It was mainly the opposition to the Homoousios, as a formula 544open to heretical misinterpretation, and not borne out by Holy Writ, which kept together the large party known as Semiarians, who under the leadership of the two Eusebiuses carried on the strife against the Nicenes and especially Athanasius. Under the sons of Constantine Christian bishops in numberless synods cursed one another turn by turn. In the western half of the empire Arianism found no foothold, and even the despotic will of Constantius, sole emperor after 351, succeeded only for the moment in subduing the bishops exiled for the sake of their belief. In the east, on the other hand, the Semiarians had for long the upper hand. They soon split up into different groups, according as they came to stand nearer to or farther from the original position of Arius. The actual centre was formed by the *Homoii*, who only spoke generally of a likeness ὁμοιότης of the Son to the Father; to the left of them were the *Anomoii*, who, with Arius, held the Son to be unlike ἀνόμοιοςthe Father; to the right, the *Homoiousians* who, taking as their catchword "likeness of nature" ὁμοιότης κατ᾽ οὐσίαν, thought that they could preserve the religious content of the Nicene formula without having to adopt the formula itself. Since this party in the course of years came more and more into sympathy with the representatives of the Nicene party, the *Homoousians*, and notably with Athanasius, the much-disputed formula became more and more popular, till the council summoned in 381 at Constantinople, under the auspices of Theodosius the Great, recognized the Nicene doctrine as the only orthodox one. Arianism, which had lifted up its head again under the emperor Valens, was thereby thrust out of the state church. It lived to flourish anew among the Germanic tribes at the time of the great migrations. Goths, Vandals, Suebi, Burgundians and Langobardi embraced it; here too as a distinctive national type of Christianity it perished before the growth of medieval Catholicism, and the name of Arian ceased to represent a definite form of Christian doctrine within the church, or a definite party outside it.

The best account of the proceedings, both political and theological, may be found in the following books:—H.M. Gwatkin, *Studies of Arianism* (2nd edit., Cambridge, 1900); A. Harnack, *History of Dogma* (Eng. trans., 1894-1899); J.F. Bethune-Baker, *An Introduction to the Early History of Christian Doctrine* (London, 1903); W. Bright, *The Age of the Fathers*(London, 1903). Cardinal Newman's celebrated *Arians of the Fourth Century* is interesting more from the controversial than from the historical point of view. See also Paavo Snellman, *Der Anfang des arianischen Streites* (Helsingfors, 1904); Sigismund Rogala, *Die Anfange des arianischen Streites* (Paderborn, 1907).

(G. K.)

ARIZONA (from the Spanish-Indian *Arizonac*, of unknown meaning,—possibly "few springs,"—the name of an 18th-century mining camp in the Santa Cruz valley, just S. of the present border of Arizona), a state on the S.W. border of the United States of America, lying between 31° 20' and 37° N. lat. and 109° 2' and 114° 45' W. long. It is bounded N. by Utah, E. by New Mexico, S. by Mexico and W. by California and Nevada, the Colorado river separating it from California and in part from Nevada. On the W. is the Great Basin. Arizona itself is mostly included in the great arid mountainous uplift of the Rocky Mountain region, and partly within the desert plain region of the Gulf of California, or Open Basin region. The whole state lies on the south-western exposure of a great roof whose crest, along the continental divide in western New Mexico, pitches southward. Its altitudes vary from 12,800 ft. to less than 100 ft. above the sea. Of its total area of 113,956 sq. m. (water surface, 116 sq. m.), approximately 39,000 lie below 3000 ft., 27,000 from 3000 to 5000 ft., and 47,000 above 5000 ft.

Physical Features.—Three characteristic physiographic regions are distinctly marked: first the great Colorado Plateau, some 45,000 sq. m. in area, embracing all the region N. and E. of a line drawn from the Grand Wash Cliffs in the N.W. corner of the state to its E. border near Clifton;

next a broad zone of compacted mountain ranges with a southern limit of similar trend; and lastly a region of desert plains, occupying somewhat more than the S.W. quarter of the state. The plateau region has an average elevation of 6000-8000 ft. eastward, but it is much broken down in the west. The plateau is not a plain. It is dominated by high mountains, gashed by superb canyons of rivers, scarred with dry gullies and washes, the beds of intermittent streams, varied with great shallow basins, sunken deserts, dreary levels, bold buttes, picturesque mesas, forests and rare verdant bits of valley. In the N.W. there is a giddy drop into the tremendous cut of the Grand Canyon (*q.v.*) of the Colorado river. The surface in general is rolling, with a gentle slope northward, and drains through the Little Colorado (or Colorado Chiquito), Rio Puerco and other streams into the Grand Canyon. Along the Colorado is the Painted Desert, remarkable for the bright colours—red, brown, blue, purple, yellow and white—of its sandstones, shales and clays. Within the desert is a petrified forest, the most remarkable in the United States. The trees are of mesozoic time, though mostly washed down to the foot of the mesas in which they were once embedded, and lying now amid deposits of a later age. Blocks and logs of agate, chalcedony, jasper, opal and other silicate deposits lie in hundreds over an area of 60 sq. m. The forest is now protected as a national reserve against vandalism and commercialism. Everywhere are evidences of water and wind erosion, of desiccation and differential weathering. This is the history of the mesas, which are the most characteristic scenic feature of the highlands. The marks of volcanic action, particularly lava-flows, are also abundant and widely scattered.

Separating the plateau from the mountain region is an abrupt transition slope, often deeply eroded, crossing the entire state as has been indicated. In localities the slope is a true escarpment falling 150 and even 250 ft. per mile. In the Aubrey Cliffs and along the Mogollon mesa, which for about 200 m. parts the waters of the Gila and the Little Colorado, it often has an elevation of 1000 to 2000 ft., and the ascent is impracticable through long distances to the most daring climber. It is not of course everywhere so remarkable, or even distinct, and especially after its trend turns southward W. of Clifton, it is much broken down and obscured by erosion and lava deposits. The mountain region has a width of 70 to 150 m., and is filled with short parallel ranges trending parallel to the plateau escarpment. Many of the mountains are extinct volcanoes. In the San Francisco mountains, in the north central part of the state, three peaks rise to from 10,000 to 12,794 ft.; three others are above 9000 ft.; all are eruptive cones, and among the lesser summits are old cinder cones. The S.E. corner of Arizona is a region of greatly eroded ranges and gentle aggraded valleys. This mountain zone has an average elevation of not less than 4000 ft., while in places its crests are 5000 ft. above the plains below. The line dividing the two regions runs roughly from Nogales on the Mexican border, past Tucson, Florence and Phoenix to Needles (California), on the W. boundary. These plains, the third or desert region of the state, have their mountains also, but they are lower, and they are not compacted; the plains near the mountain region slope toward the Gulf of California across wide valleys separated by isolated ranges, then across broad desert stretches traversed by rocky ridges, and finally there is no obstruction to the slope at all. Small parts of the desert along the Mexican boundary are shifting sand.

(Click to enlarge.)

Climate.—As may be inferred from the physical description, Arizona has a wide variety of local climates. In general it is characterized by wonderfully clear air and extraordinarily low humidity. The scanty rainfall is distributed from July to April, with marked excess from July to September and a lesser maximum in December. May and June are very dry. Often during a month, sometimes for several months, no rain falls over the greatest part of Arizona. Very little rain comes from the Pacific or the Gulf of California, the mountains and desert, as well as the adverse winds, making it impossible. Rain and snow fall usually from clouds blown from the Gulf of Mexico and not wholly dried in Texas. The mountainous areas are the only ones of adequate precipitation; the northern slope of the Colorado Plateau is almost destitute of water; the region of least precipitation is the "desert" region. The mean annual rainfall varies from amounts of 2 to 5.5 in. at various points in the lower gulf valley, and on the western border to amounts of 25 to 54530 in. in the mountains. The highest recorded maximum in Arizona is 35 in. The proportion of perfectly clear days in the year varies at different points from a half to two-thirds; of the rest not more than half are without brilliant sunshine part of the day. Local thunderstorms and cloud-bursts are a characteristic phenomenon, inundating limited areas and transforming dried-up streams into muddy torrents carrying boulders and débris. Often in the plateau country the dry under-air absorbs the rain as it falls; and rarely in the Hopi Country do flooded gullies "run through" to the Little Colorado. The country of the cliff-dwellers in the N.E. is desert-like. Only points high in altitude catch much rain. Mountain snows feed the Gila, the Little Colorado, and the Colorado rivers. The Colorado, apart from the Gila, draws little water from Arizona. The mountain zone W. of Prescott drains into the Colorado, and to the S. and E. into the Gila; and the latter is by far the heavier drainage in volume. The floods come in May and June, and during the wet season the rivers, all with steep beds in their upper courses, wash along detritus that lower down narrows, and on smaller streams almost chokes, their courses. These gradients enable the inconstant streams tributary to the Colorado to carve their canyons, some of which are in themselves very remarkable, though insignificant beside the Grand Canyon. Many streams that are turned in spring or by summer cloud-bursts into torrents are normally mere water films or dry gulches. Even the Gila is dry in its bed part of the year at its mouth near Yuma. From the Gila to the southern boundary the parched land gives no water to the sea, and the international boundary runs in part through a true desert. In the hot season there is almost no surface water. Artesian wells are used in places, as in the stock country of the Baboquivari valley.

The temperature of Arizona is somewhat higher than that of points of equal latitude on the Atlantic and Gulf of Mexico coasts. In the mountains on the plateau it ranges from that of the temperate zone to that of regions of perpetual snow; S. of the mountains it ranges from temperate heats in the foothills to semi-tropic heat in the lower valleys of the Gila and Colorado. The average annual temperature over the region N. of 34′ N. is about 55°; that of the region S. is about 68°. The warmest region is the lower Gila valley. Here the hottest temperature of the year hovers around 130°, the mean for the hottest month (July) is about 98°, and the mean for the year is from 68.9°-74.4° F. at different points. Some parts of the Santa Cruz valley are equally hot. In the hottest (western) portions of the true desert on the Mexican border the daily maximum temperature is about 110° F.; but owing to the rapid radiation in the dry, clear, cloudless air the temperature frequently falls 40-50° in the night. The coldest points on the high plateau have annual means as low as 45-48°, and a mean for the coldest month at times below 20° F. The range from high to low extreme on the plateau may be as great as 125°, but in the S.W. it is only about 70-80° F. The daily variation (not uncommonly 60° F.) is of course greatest in the most arid regions, where radiation is most rapid. And of all Arizona it should be said that owing to the extreme dryness of the air, evaporation from moist surfaces is very rapid,1 so that the high temperatures here are decidedly less oppressive than much lower temperatures in a humid atmosphere. The great difference between absolute and sensible temperature is a very important climatic characteristic of Arizona. Generally speaking, during two-thirds of the year the temperature is really delightful; the nights are cool, the mornings bracing, the days mild though splendid. Intense heat prevails in July, August and September. In lowness of humidity (mean annual relative humidity at Yuma about 39, at Phoenix 36.7, at Tucson 37.8) and clarity of atmosphere, southern Arizona rivals Upper Egypt and other famous arid health resorts.

Fauna and Flora.—Within the borders of Arizona are areas representative of every life zone save the humid tropical. From the summit of the San Francisco Mountains one may pass rapidly through all these down into the Painted Desert. The Boreal-Canadian, Transition and Upper Sonoran embrace the highlands. Coyotes are very common; wild cats and mountain lions are fairly plentiful. Deer and antelope are represented by various species. Prairie-dogs, jack-rabbits, crows and occasional ravens, quail, grouse, pheasants and wild turkeys are also noteworthy in a rather scant animal life. Characteristic forms of the Upper Sonoran zone are the burrowing owl, Nevada sage-thrush, sage-thrasher and special species of orioles, kangaroo rats, mice, rabbits and squirrels. The Lower Sonoran covers the greatest part of southern and western Arizona, as well as the immediate valleys of the Colorado and Little Colorado rivers. Its animal life is in the main distinguished in species only from that of the Upper Sonoran belt, including among birds, the desert sparrow, desert thrasher, mocking-bird, hooded oriole; and among mammals small nocturnal species of kangaroo rats, pocket mice, mice and bats. Jaguars occasionally stray into Arizona from Mexico. Lizards and toads are conspicuous in the more desert areas. Snakes are not numerous. The Gila-monster, tarantula, the scorpion and thelyphonus, scolopender and julus occur in some localities in the rainy season. The Arid-Tropical zone is represented by a narrow belt along the lower Colorado river, with a short arm extending into the valley of the Gila. The country is so arid that it supports only desert birds and mammals. Camels were very successfully employed as pack animals on the Tule desert in the palmy days of Virginia City, Nevada, before the advent of railways.

The general conditions of distribution of the fauna of Arizona are shown even more distinctly by the flora. There are firs and spruces on the mountains, characteristic of the Boreal zone; pines characteristic of the Transition zone; piñon juniper, greasewood and the universally conspicuous sage-brush, characteristic of the Upper Sonoran zone. In the Lower Sonoran belt, soapweed, acacias (Palo Verde or*Parkinsonia torreyana*), agaves, yuccas and dasylirions, the creosote bush and mesquite tree, candle wood, and about seventy-five species of cactuses—among them omnipresent opuntiae and great columnar "Chayas"—make up a striking vegetation, which in its colours of dull grey and olive harmonizes well with the rigidity and forbidding barrenness of the plains. It has exercised profound influence upon the industries, arts, faiths and general culture of

166

the Indians. In places the giant cactus grows in groves, attaining a height of 40 and even 50 ft. The mesquite varies in size from a tangled thorny shrub to a spreading tree as much as 3 ft. in diameter and 50 ft. high; it is normally perhaps half as high, and 6-8 in. in diameter. Enduring hardily great extremes of heat and moisture, it is throughout the arid South-west the most important, and in many localities the only important, native tree. From the great juicy, leafless, branchless stalk of the yucca, soap is prepared, and strong fibres useful in making paper, rope and fabrics. The fibre of the agave is also made into rope and its juice into pulque. The canaigre grows wild and is also cultivated. It is easy to exaggerate greatly the barrenness of an arid country. There are fine indigenous grasses that spring up over the mesas after the summer rains, furnishing range for live-stock; some are extraordinarily independent of the rainfall. In the most arid regions there is a small growth of green in the rainy season, and a rich display of small wild-flowers, as well as the enormous flower clusters of the yucca, and blooms in pink and orange, crimson, yellow and scarlet of the giant cactus and its fellows. Even in the Mexican border, desert oak, juniper and manzanita cover the mountains, and there is a vigorous though short-lived growth of grasses and flower from July to October. The cliff-dweller country supports a scant vegetation—a few cottonwood in the washes, a few cedars on the mesas.

Continuous forest areas are scant. A fair variety of trees—cottonwood, sycamore, ash, willow, walnut and cherry—grow in thickets in the canyons, and each mountain range is a forest area. Rainfall varying with the altitude, the lower timber line below which precipitation is insufficient to sustain a growth of trees is about 7000 ft., and the upper timber line about 11,500 ft. 546Oaks, juniper, piñon, cedars, yellow pine, fir and spruce grow on the mountains and over large areas of the plateau country.2 The Coconino forest is one of the largest unbroken pine forests (about 6000 sq. m.) in the United States. Since 1898 about 86% of the wooded lands have been made reservations, and work has been done also to preserve the forest areas in the mountains in the south-east, from which there are few streams of permanent flow to the enclosing arid valleys.

Soil.—The soils in the southern part of Arizona are mainly sandy loams, varying from light loam to heavy, close adobe; on the plateaus is what is known as "mesa" soil; and along the rivers are limited overflow plains of fine sediment—especially along the Colorado and the river Verde. These soils are in general rich, but deficient in nitrogen and somewhat in humus; and in limited areas white alkaline salts are injuriously in excess. Virgin soils are densely compact. By far the most useful crops are leguminous green manures, especially alfalfa, which grows four to seven cuttings in a year and as a soil flocculator and nitrogen-storer has proved of the greatest value. The greatest obstacle to agriculture is lack of water. Artesian wells are much used in the south-east. For the reservation of the water-partings—in the past considerably denuded by lumbermen and ranchmen—the increase of the forest areas, and the creation of reservoirs along the rivers, to control their erratic flow3 and impound their flood waste for purposes of irrigation, much has been done by the national government. The irrigated areas are only little spots along the permanent streams. In 1900 the farm area was only 2.7% of the total area of the state and only 0.31% was actually improved (including Indian reservations, 0.35%; in 1906, 0.92% was cultivated); of the land actually under crops, 88.5% was irrigated. The improved acreage more than quintupled from 1880 to 1900. The total irrigated area in 1900 was 185,000 acres and in 1902, 247,250 acres. The increase in land values by irrigation from 1890 to 1900 is estimated at $3,500,000. A reservoir was begun in 1904 just below the junction of the Tonto and the Salt with capacity to store 1,330,000 acre-ft. for irrigation, and develop also an electric power sufficient to pump underground water for an additional 50,000 acres at the lowest estimate4 of lands lying too high for supply by gravity. Another important undertaking begun about the same time was the throwing of an East Indian weir dam (the only one in the United States) across the Colorado near Yuma, and the confinement of both sides of the lower Gila and Colorado with levees.

Agriculture.—Strawberries and Sahara dates; alfalfa, wheat, barley, corn and sorghum; oranges, lemons, wine grapes, limes, olives, figs, dates, peanuts and sweet potatoes; yams and sugar beets, show the range of agricultural products. The date palm fruits well; figs grow luxuriantly, though requiring much irrigation; almonds do well if protected from spring frosts; sea-island cotton grows in the finest grades, but is not of commercial importance. The country about Yuma is particularly suited to subtropical fruits. Temperate fruits—peaches, pears, apples, apricots and small fruits—do excellently; as do all important vegetables. The fruit industry is becoming more and more important. Farming is very intensive, and crop follows crop in swift succession; in 1905 the yield of barley per acre, 44 bushels, was greater than in any other state or territory, as was the farm price per bushel on the 1st of December, 81 cents; the average yield per acre of hay was the highest in the Union in 1903, 3.46 tons, the general average being 1.54 tons, was fourth in 1904, 2.71 tons (Utah 3.54, Idaho 3.07, Nevada 3.04), the general average being 1.52 tons, and was highest in 1905, 3.75 tons, the general average for the country being 1.54 tons;

and in the same three years the average value per acre of hay was greater in Arizona than in any other state of the Union, being $35.78 in 1903, $40.22 in 1904, and $46.39 in 1905, the general averages for the country being $13.93, $13.23 and $13.11 respectively, for the three years. Of the total farm acreage of the state 97.6% were held in 1900 by the whites; and of these 80.2% owned in whole or in part the land they cultivated.

Stock-raising is a leading industry, but it has probably attained its full development. The over-stocking of the ranges has caused much loss in the past, and the almost total eradication of fine native grasses over extended areas. Of the neat cattle (7,042,635) almost 98%, and of the sheep (861,761) almost 100%, were in 1900 pastured wholly or in part upon the public domain. The extension of national forest reserves and the regulations enforced by the United States government for the preservation of the ranges have put limits to the industry. In 1900 the value of live-stock represented 15.7% of the capital invested in agriculture; the value of animals sold or slaughtered for food ($3,204,758) was half the total value of all farm products ($6,997,097). Ostrich farms have been successfully established in the Salt river valley since 1893; in 1907 there were six farms in the Salt river valley, on which there were about 1354 birds; the most successful food for the ostrich is alfalfa.

Minerals.—Mining is the leading industry of Arizona. Contrary to venerable traditions there is no evidence that mining was practised beyond the most inconsiderable extent by aborigines, Spanish*conquistadores*, or Jesuits. In 1738 an extraordinary deposit of silver nuggets, quickly exhausted (1741), was discovered at Arizonac. At the end of the 18th century the Mexicans considerably developed the mines in the south-east. The second half of the 19th century witnessed several great finds; first, of gold placers on the lower Gila and Colorado (1858-1869); later, of lodes at Tombstone, which flourished from 1879-1886, then decayed, but in 1905 had again become the centre of important mining interests; and still later the development of copper mines at Jerome and around Bisbee. Several of the Arizona copper mines are among the greatest of the world. The Copper Queen at Bisbee from 1880-1902 produced 378,047,210 ℔ of crude copper, which was practically the total output of the territory till after 1900, when other valuable mines were opened; the Globe, Morenci and Jerome districts are secondary to Bisbee. Important mines of gold and silver, considerable deposits of wolframite, valuable ores of molybdenum and vanadium, and quarries of onyx marble, are also worked. Low-grade coal deposits occur in the east central part of the state and near the junction of the Gila and San Pedro rivers. Some fine gems of peridot, garnet and turquoise have been found. The mineral products of Arizona for 1907 were valued at $56,753,650; of which $51,355,687 (more than that of any other state) was the value of copper; $2,664,000, gold; and $1,916,000, silver. In 1907 the legislature passed an elaborate act providing for the taxation of mines, its principal clause being that the basis of valuation for taxation in each year be one-fourth of the output of the mines in question for the next preceding year.

Manufactures.—The manufacturing industries are of relatively slight importance, though considerable promise attends the experiments with canaigre as a source of tannin. The Navaho and Moqui Indians make woollen blankets and rugs and the Pimas baskets. Onyx marbles of local source are polished at Phoenix. The capital invested in manufacturing industries increased from $9,517,573 in 1900 to $14,395,654 in 1905, or 51.3%, and the value of products from $20,438,987 in 1900 to $28,083,192 in 1905, or 37.4%. Of the total product in 1905 the product of the principal industry, the smelting and refining of copper ($22,761,981), represented 81.1%; it was 9.4% of all the smelting and refining of copper done in the United States in that year. The other manufactures were of much less importance, the principal ones being cars and general shop construction, including repairs by steam railway companies ($1,329,308), lumber and timber products ($960,778), and flour and grist mill products ($743,124).

Two transcontinental railway systems, the Southern Pacific and Santa Fe, were built across Arizona in 1878-1883. They are connected by one line, and a feeder runs S. into Sonora. The railway mileage of Arizona on the 1st of January 1908 was 1935.35 m.

Population.—The population of Arizona in 1880 was 40,440; in 1890, 59,620; in 1900, 122,931 (including 28,623 reservation Indians not counted before); in 1910, 204,354. The native population is of the most diverse origin; the foreign element is equally heterogeneous, but more than half (in 1900, 14,172 out of 24,283 foreign-born) are Mexicans, many of whom are not permanent residents; after 1900, immigrants were largely mine labourers, and included Slavonians and Italians. The largest towns in 1900 were Tucson, Phoenix, which is the capital, Prescott (pop. 3559), Jerome (pop. 1890, 250; in 1900, 2861); Winslow (pop. 1890, 363; in 1900, 1305), Nogales (pop. 1900, 1761), and Bisbee. The last was an insignificant mining camp in 1880, still unincorporated in 1900, but with an estimated population of 6000 in 1904. It is crowded picturesquely into several narrow confluent ravines. Railway connexion with El Paso was established in 1902. Douglas is another growing camp.

168

Over thirty Indian tribes are represented in the Indian schools of Arizona. The more important are the Hualapais or Apache-Yumas; the Mohaves; the Yavapais or Apache-Mohaves; the Yumas, whose lesser neighbours on the lower Colorado are the most primitive Indians of the United States in habits; the Maricopas; the Pimas and Papagoes, who figure much in early Arizona history, and who are superior in intelligence, adaptability, application and character; the Hopis or Moquis, possessed of the same good qualities and notably temperate and provident, famous for their prehistoric culture (Tusuyan); the Navaho, and the kindred Apaches, perhaps the most relentless and savage of Indian warriors. All the Indians of Arizona live on reservations save the few non-tribal Indians taxed and treated as active citizens. Even the Apaches after being whipped by relentless war into temporary submission have been bound by treaties which the gifts, vices and virtues of the reservation system have tempted them to observe. The Pimas and Papagoes were early converted by the Spaniards, and retain to-day a smattering of Christianity plentifully alloyed with paganism. Apaches, Pimas, Papagoes have been employed by the United States on great irrigation works, and have proved industrious and faithful labourers. In 1900 there were 1836 taxed Indians, 26,480 reservation Indians not taxed, and in addition many friendly Papagoes unenumerated.

In 1906 the Indian population was estimated as being 14% of the whole population of Arizona, and that they are singularly law-abiding is argued from the fact that in the same year the Indians furnished only 3% of the convicts in the territorial prison.

Government and Education.—Arizona became a territory of the first (or practically autonomous) class in 1863. Her organic law thereafter until 1910 consisted of various sections of the Revised Statutes of the United States. From the beginning she had a territorial legislature. Congress retained ultimately direct control of all government, administration being in the hands of resident officials appointed by the president and Senate. Special mention must be made of the secret police, the Arizona Rangers, organized in 1901 to police the cattle ranges; they are "fearless men, trained in riding, roping, trailing and shooting," a force whose *personnel* is not known to the general public. The legislature repealed the law licensing public gambling in 1907; enacted a law requiring the payment of $300 per annum as licence fee by retail liquor dealers; and provided for juvenile courts and probationary control of children. In 1907 the total tax valuation of property was $77,705,251; the net debt of the territory $1,022,972, and that of counties and towns $3,123,275. The receipts of the territorial treasury for the year ending on the 30th of June 1907 were $687,386, and the disbursements for the same period were $601,568. A homestead provision (1901) exempts from liability for debts (except mortgages or liens placed before the homestead claim) any homestead belonging to the head of a family, existing in one compact body and valued at not more than $2500; such a homestead a married man may not sell, lease or put a lien on without his wife's consent. Personal property to the value of $500 is exempt from the same liability. The public school system was established in 1871. A compulsory attendance law applies to children between 6 and 14 years of age, but it is not generally obeyed by the Mexican element of population. In 1907 there was an enrolment of 24,962 out of 33,167 children of school age; there were six high schools—three new in 1906; and the average number of school days was 128.4. In the fiscal year ending June 1907, the total receipts for schools were $697,762, and the expenditures were $701,102. Illiteracy is high, amounting in 1900 to 23.1% of native males, above 21 years of age, and 30.5% of foreign males, principally because of the large number of Indians, Chinese, Japanese and Mexicans in the state. There are two normal schools at Tempe (1886) and Flagstaff (1899), a university at Tucson with an agricultural experiment station that has done much for the industries of Arizona; there is a considerable number of Indian schools, the largest of which are maintained by the national government, and the funds of the university come largely from the same source. The first juvenile reform school, called the Territorial Industrial school, was opened in 1903 at Benson. The territorial prison, formerly at Yuma, was abandoned for a modern building at Florence, Pinal county; and a hospital for the insane is 3 m. from Phoenix.

History.—The history of the South-west is full of interest to the archaeologist. A prehistoric culture widely distributed has left abundant traces. Pueblo ruins are plentiful in the basins of the Gila and Colorado rivers and their tributaries. Geographical conditions and a hard struggle against nature fixed the character of this "aridian" culture, and determined its migrations; the onslaughts of nomad Indians determined the sedentary civilization of the cliff dwellers. A co-operative social economy is evidenced by the traces of great public works, such as canals many miles in length. The pueblos of the Gila valley are held to be older than those of the Colorado. Casa Grande, 15 m. S.E. of a railway station of the same name on the Southern Pacific railway, is the most remarkable of plain ruins in the South-west, the only one of its type in the United States. It resembles the Casa Grande ruin of Chihuahua, Mexico, with its walls of sun-dried puddled clay, and its area of rooms, courts and plazas, surrounded by a wall. It was already a ruin

169

when discovered in 1694 by the Jesuit father Kino. John Russel Bartlett described it in 1854, and in 1889 Congress voted that it be protected as a government reservation; in 1892 it was set apart by the government. Excavations were made there in 1906-1907 by Dr J. Walter Fewkes. Migration was northward. The valleys of the Salt river and its affluents, the Agua Fria, Verde and Tonto, are strewn with aboriginal remains; but especially important in migrations of culture was the Little Colorado. A very considerable population must have lived once in this valley. It is represented to-day by the still undeserted habitats of Zuñi (in New Mexico) and Tusayan; the Moquis, after the Zuñis, are in customs and traditions the best survival of the ancient civilization.

Arizona north of the Gila, save for a very limited and intermittent missionary effort and for scant exploring expeditions, was practically unknown to the whites until well after the beginning of American rule. The Santa Cruz valley, however, has much older annals of a past that charms by its picturesque contrasts with the present. Arizona history begins with the arrival in Sonora in 1536 of Alvar Nuñez Cabeza de Vaca, who, although he had not entered Arizona or New Mexico, had heard of them, and by his stories incited the Spaniards to explore the unknown north in hope of wealth. Marcos de Niza, a Franciscan friar to whom the first reconnaissance was entrusted, was the first Spaniard to enter the limits of Arizona. He crossed the south-eastern corner to Zuñi in 1539, passing through the Santa Cruz valley; and F.V. de Coronado (*q.v.*) was led by Fray Marcos over the same route in 1540; while Hernando Alarcon explored the Gulf of California and the lower Colorado river. Members of Coronado's expedition explored the Moqui country and reached the Grand Canyon, and after this a succession of remarkable and heroic explorations followed through the century; which however accomplished little for geography, further confusing 548and embellishing rather than clearing up its mysteries. All this has left traces in still living myths about the early history of the South-west. Early in the 17th century considerable progress had been made in Christianizing the Pimas, Papagoes and Moquis. Following 1680 came a great Indian revolt in New Mexico and Arizona, and thereafter the Moquis remained independent of Spanish and Christian domination, although visited fitfully by rival Jesuits and Franciscans. In 1732 (possibly in 1720) regular Jesuit missions were founded at Bac (known as an Indian rancheria since the 17th century) and at Guevavi. The region south of the Gila had already been repeatedly explored. In the second half of the century there was a presidio at Tubac (whose name first appears 1752) and some half-dozen pueblos de visita, including the Indian settlement of Tucson.

A few errors should be corrected and some credit given with reference to this early period. The Inquisition never had any jurisdiction whatever over the Indians; compulsory labour by the Indians was never legalized except on the missions, and the law was little violated; they were never compelled to work mines; of mining by the Indians for precious metals there is no evidence; nor by the Jesuits (expelled in 1767, after which their missions and other properties were held by the Franciscans), except to a small extent about the presidio of Tubac, although they did some prospecting. Persistent traditions have greatly exaggerated the former prosperity of the old South-west. The Spaniards probably provoked some inter-tribal intercourse among the Indians, and did something among some tribes for agriculture. Their own farms and settlements, save in the immediate vicinity of the presidio, were often plundered and abandoned, and such settlement as there was was confined to the Santa Cruz valley. From about 1790 to 1822 was a period of peace with the Apaches and of comparative prosperity for church and state. The fine Indian mission church at Bac, long abandoned and neglected, dates from the last decade of the 18th century. The establishment of a presidio at Tucson in 1776 marks its beginning as a Spanish settlement.

The decay of the military power of the presidios during the Mexican war of independence, the expulsion of loyal Spaniards—notably friars—and the renewal of Apache wars, led to the temporary abandonment of all settlements except Tubac and Tucson. The church practically forsook the field about 1828.

American traders and explorers first penetrated Arizona in the first quarter of the 19th century. As a result of the Mexican War, New Mexico, which then included all Arizona north of the Gila, was ceded to the United States. California gold discoveries drew particular attention to the country south of the Gila, which was wanted also for a transcontinental railway route. This strip, known as the "Gadsden Purchase" (see GADSDEN, JAMES), was bought in 1854 by the United States, which took possession in 1856. This portion was also added to New Mexico. The Mexicans, pressed by the Apaches, had, in 1848, abandoned even Tubac and Tamacácori, first a visita of Guevavi, and after 1784 a mission. The progress of American settlement was interrupted by the Civil War, which caused the withdrawal of the troops and was the occasion for the outbreak of prolonged Indian wars.

Meanwhile a convention at Tucson in 1856 sent a delegate to Congress and petitioned for independent territorial government. This movement and others that followed were ignored by

Congress owing to its division over the general slavery question, and especially the belief of northern members that the control of Arizona was an object of the pro-slavery party. A convention held in April 1860 at Tucson undertook to "ordain and establish," of its own motion, a provisional constitution until Congress should "organize a territorial government." This provisional territory constituted all New Mexico south of 34° 40′ N. Officials were appointed and New Mexican legislation for the Arizona counties ignored, but nothing further was done. In 1861 it was occupied by a Texan force, declared for the Confederacy, and sent a delegate (who was not admitted) to the Confederate congress. That body in January 1862 passed a formal act organizing the territory, including in it New Mexico, but in May 1862 the Texans were driven out by a Union force from California. By act of the 24th of February 1863 Congress organized Arizona territory as the country west of 109° W. long. In December an itinerant government sent out complete from Washington crossed the Arizona line and effected a formal organization. The territorial capital was first at Prescott (1863-1867), then at Tucson (1867-1877), again at Prescott (1877-1889), and finally at Phoenix (since 1889).

There have been boundary difficulties with every contiguous state or territory. The early period of American rule was extremely unsettled. The California gold discoveries and overland travel directed many prospecting adventurers to Arizona. For some years there was considerable sentiment favouring filibustering in Sonora. The Indian wars, breeding a habit of dependence on force, and the heterogeneous elements of cattle thieves, Sonoran cowboys, mine labourers and adventurers led to one of the worst periods of American border history. But since about 1880 there is nothing to chronicle but a continued growth in population and prosperity. Agitation for statehood became prominent in territorial politics for some years. In accordance with an act of Congress, approved on the 16th of June 1906, the inhabitants of Arizona and New Mexico voted on the 6th of November 1906 on the question of uniting the territories into a single state to be called Arizona; the vote of New Mexico was favourable to union and statehood, but these were defeated by the vote of Arizona (16,265 against, and 3141 for statehood). In June 1910 the President approved an enabling act providing for the admission of Arizona and New Mexico as separate states.

BIBLIOGRAPHY.—For the Colorado river and the Grand Canyon see those articles; for the Sonoran boundary region, *Report of the Boundary Commission upon the Boundaries between the United States and Mexico* (3 vols., Washington, 1898-1899, also as Senate Document No. 247, vols. 23-25, 55 Congress, 2 Session); for the petrified forest of the Painted Desert, L.F. Ward in *Smithsonian Institution* Annual Rep., 1899; for the rest of the area, various reports in the U.S. Geological Survey publications, bibliography in *Bulletin* Nos. 100, 177.—FAUNA and FLORA: U.S. Department of Agriculture, *North American Fauna*, No. 3 (1890), No. 7 (1893); *U.S. Biological Survey, Bulletin* No. 10 (1898); publications of the Desert Botanical Laboratory at Tucson; also titles under archaeology below, particularly Bandelier's "Final Report."—CLIMATE, SOIL, AGRICULTURE: U.S. Department of Agriculture, *Climate and Crop Service, Arizona,* monthly reports, annual summaries; Arizona Agricultural Experiment Station, *Bulletins.*—MINERAL INDUSTRIES: U.S. Geological Survey publications, consult bibliographies; *The Mineral Industry,* annual (New York and London).—GOVERNMENT: *Arizona Revised Statutes* (Phoenix, 1887); *Report of the Governor of Arizona Territory to the Secretary of the Interior,* annual.—ARCHAEOLOGY: An abundance of materials in the *Annual Report, U.S. Bureau of Ethnology* for different years; consult also especially A.F.A. Bandelier, "Contributions to the History of the South-western Portion of the United States," in *Archaeological Institute of America, Papers, American Series,* vol. 5 (Cambridge, 1890); "Final Report of Investigations among the Indians of the South-western United States," *ib.* vols. 3 and 4 (Cambridge, 1890-1892); other material may be found in Smithsonian Institution, *Annual Report,* 1896, 1897, &c., and many important papers by J.W. Fewkes, F.W. Hodge, C. Mendeleff and others in the *American Anthropologist* and *Journal of American Ethnology.*— HISTORY: H.H. Bancroft, *History of Arizona and New Mexico* (San Francisco, 1887); A.F.A. Bandelier, "Historical Introduction to Studies among the Sedentary Indians of New Mexico," in *Archaeological Institute of America, Papers, American Series,* vol. 1 (Boston, 1881); *The Gilded Man (El Dorado) and other Papers* (New York, 1893); G.P. Winship, "The Coronado Expedition," in *U.S. Bureau of Ethnology, 14th Annual Report* (1892-1893), pp. 339-613, with an abundant literature to which this may be the guide. The traditional errors respecting the early history of the Spanish South-west are fully exposed in the works of Bancroft and Bandelier, whose conclusions are supported by E. Coues, *On the Trail of a Spanish Pioneer, Francisco Garcés* (2 vols. New York, 1900).

1At Yuma, Phoenix and Tucson, the records of twenty-six, eighteen and fifteen years respectively show a rate of evaporation 35.2, 12.7, and 7.7 times as great as the mean annual rainfall, which was 2.84 in., 7.06 in. and 11.7 in. for the places named.

171

2The San Francisco yellow pine forest, with an area of some 4700 sq. m., is the finest forest of the arid south-west.

3The combined flow of the Salt and Verde varies from 100 to more than 10,000 cub. ft. per second.

4The dam locks a narrow canyon. The height is 284 ft., the water rising 230 ft. against it. The storage capacity is exceeded by probably but one reservoir in the world—the Wachusett reservoir near Boston.

ARJUNA, in Hindu mythology, a semi-divine hero of the *Mahabharata*. He was the third son of Pandu, son of Indra, His character as sketched in the great epic is of the noblest kind. He is the central figure of that portion of the epic known as the *Bhagwad-gita*, where he is represented as horrified at the impending slaughter of a battle and as being comforted by Krishna.

ARK (a word common to Teutonic languages, cf. Ger. *Arche*, adapted from the Lat. *arca*, chest, cf. *arcere*, to shut up, enclose), a chest, basket or box. The Hebrew word *tebah*, translated in the A.V. by "ark," is used in the Old Testament (1) of the box made of bulrushes in which Pharaoh's daughter found the infant Moses (Exodus ii. 3), and (2) of the great vessel or ship in which Noah took refuge during the flood (Genesis vi.-ix.).

Noah's Ark.—According to the story in Genesis, Noah's ark was large enough to contain his family and representatives of each kind of animal. Its dimensions are given as 300 cubits long, 50 cubits broad and 30 cubits high (cubit = 18-22 in.). It was made of "gopher" wood, which has been variously identified with cypress, pine and cedar. Before the days of the "higher criticism" and the rise of the modern scientific views as to the origin of species, there was much discussion among the learned, and many ingenious and curious theories were advanced, as to the number of the animals and the space necessary for their reception, with elaborate calculations as to the subdivisions of the ark and the quantities of food, &c., required to be stored. It may be interesting to recall the account given in the first edition of the *Encyclopaedia Britannica* (1771), which contained a summary of some of these various views (substantially repeated up to the publication of the eighth edition, 1853). "Some have thought the dimensions of the ark as given by Moses too scanty ... and hence an argument has been drawn against the authority of the relation. To solve this difficulty many of the ancient Fathers and the modern critics have been put to miserable shifts. But Buteo and Kircher have proved geometrically that, taking the cubit of a foot and a half, the ark was abundantly sufficient for all the animals supposed to be lodged in it. Snellius computes the ark to have been above half an acre in area ... and Dr Arbuthnot computes it to have been 81,062 tuns ... if we come to a calculation the number of species of animals will be found much less than is generally imagined, not amounting to a hundred species of quadrupeds, nor to two hundred of birds.... Zoologists usually reckon but an hundred and seventy species in all." The progress of the "higher criticism," and the gradual surrender of attempts to square scientific facts with a literal interpretation of the Bible, are indicated in the shorter account given in the eighth edition, which concludes as follows:—"the insuperable difficulties connected with the belief that all the existing species of animals were provided for in the ark, are obviated by adopting the suggestion of Bishop Stillingfleet, approved by Matthew Poole, Pye Smith, le Clerc, Rossenmüller and others, that the deluge did not extend beyond the region of the earth then inhabited, and that only the animals of that region were preserved in the ark." The first edition also gives an engraving of the ark (repeated in the editions up to the fifth), in shape like a long roofed box, floating on the waters; the animals are seen in separate stalls. By the time of the ninth edition (1875) precise details are no longer considered worthy of inclusion; and the age of scientific comparative mythology has been reached.

For a comparative study of the occurrence of the ark in the various deluge myths, in the present edition, see DELUGE;COSMOGONY; BABYLONIA AND ASSYRIA.

The *Ark of the Law*, in the Jewish synagogue, is a chest or cupboard containing the scrolls of the Torah (Pentateuch), and is placed against or in the wall in the direction of Jerusalem. It forms one of the most decorative features of the synagogue, and often takes an architectural design, with columns, arches and a dome. There is a fine example in the synagogue at Great St Helens, London.

(X.)

Ark of the Covenant, Ark of the Revelation, Ark of the Testimony, are the full names of the sacred chest of acacia wood overlaid with gold which the Israelites took with them on their journey into Palestine. The Biblical narratives reveal traces of a considerable development in the traditions regarding this sacred object, and those which furnish the most complete detail are of post-exilic date when the original ark had been lost. The fuller titles of the ark originate in the belief that it contained the "covenant" (bĕrīth) or "testimony" ('ēdūth), the technical terms for the Decalogue (q.v.); primarily, however, it would seem to have been called "the ark of Yahweh" (or "Elohim"), or simply "the ark." The word itself (ārōn) designates an ordinary chest (cp. Gen. i. 26; 2 Kings xii. 10), and the (late) description of its appearance represents it as an oblong box 2½ cubits long, 1½ cubits in breadth and height (roughly 1.2 by .75 metres). It was lined within and without with gold, and through four golden rings were placed staves of acacia wood, by means of which it was carried. A slab of the same metal (the so-called "mercy-seat," kappōreth, Gr. hilastērion) covered the top, and this was surmounted by two Cherubim (Ex. xxv. 10-22, xxxvii. 1-9). The latter, however, are not mentioned in earlier passages (Deut. x. 1, 3), and would naturally increase the weight of the ark, which, according to 2 Sam. xv. 29, could be carried by two men.

The ark was borne by the Levites (Deut. x. 8), and the latest narratives amplify the statement with a wealth of detail characteristic of the post-exilic interest in this order. (See LEVITES.) An interesting passage relating the commencement of an Israelite journey vividly illustrates the power of the sacred object. As the ark started, it was hailed with the cry,"Arise, Yahweh, let thine enemies be scattered, let them that hate thee flee from before thee," and when it came to rest, the cry again rang out,"Return, O Yahweh, to the myriads of families of Israel" (Num. x. 33-36). This saying appears to imply a settled life in Canaan, but both affirm the warlike significance of Yahweh and the ark. Thus it is the permanent pledge of Yahweh's gracious presence; it guides the people on their journey and leads them to victory. It is no mere receptacle, but a sacrosanct object as much to be feared as Yahweh himself. To presume to fight without it was to invite defeat, and on one notable occasion the Israelites attempted to attack their enemy north of Kadesh without its aid, and were defeated (Num. xiv. 44 sq.). There are many gaps in its history, and although at the crossing of the Jordan and at the fall of Jericho the ark figures prominently (Josh. iii. sq., vi. sq.), it is unaccountably missing in stories of greater national moment. Once it is found at Bethel (Judges xx. 27 sq.). It is met with again at Shiloh, where it is under the care of Eli and his sons, descendants of an ancient family of priests (1 Sam. ii. 28; cp. Josh. xviii. 1). After a great defeat of Israel by the Philistines it was brought into the field, but was captured by the enemy. The trophy was set up in the Philistine temple of Ashdod, but vindicated its superiority by overthrowing the god Dagon. A plague smote the city, and when it was removed to Ekron, pestilence followed in its wake. After taking counsel the Philistines placed the ark with a votive offering upon a new cart drawn by two cows. The beasts went of their own accord to Beth-shemesh, where it remained in the field of a certain Joshua. Again a disaster happened through some obscure cause, and seventy of the sons of Jeconiah were smitten (1 Sam. vi. 19, R.V., margin). Thence it was removed to the house of Abinadab of Kirjath-jearim, who consecrated his son to its service (1 Sam. iv.-vii. 1). For many years the ark remained untouched—apparently forgotten. Shiloh disappears from history; neither Saul nor even Samuel, whose youth had been spent with it, takes any further thought of it. After a remarkable period of obscurity, the ark enters suddenly into the history of David (2 Sam. vi.). Some time after the capture of Jerusalem the ark was brought from Baal-Judah, but at the threshing-floor of Nacon (an unintelligible name) Abinadab's son Uzzah laid hands upon it and was struck down for his impiety. On this account the place is said to have received the name Perez-Uzzah ("breach of Uzzah"). It was taken into the house of Obed-edom the Gittite (i.e. of Gath), and brought a blessing upon his house during the three months that it remained there. Finally the king had it conveyed to the city of David, where a tent was prepared to shelter it. Once at Jerusalem, it seems to have lost its unique value as the token of Yahweh's presence; its importance was apparently merged with that of the Temple which Solomon built. The foundation of the capital would pave the way for the belief that the national god had taken a permanent dwelling-place in the royal seat. The prophets themselves lay no weight upon the ark as the central point of Jerusalem's holiness. The real Deuteronomic code does not mention it, and to Jeremiah (iii. 16) it was a thing of no consequence. Later, in the age of the priestly schools, the ark received much attention, although it must obviously be very doubtful how far a true recollection of its history has survived. But nowhere is any light thrown upon its fate. The invasion of Shishak, the 550 capture of Jerusalem by Joash (2 Kings xiv. 13, 14), the troublous reign of Manasseh, the destruction of Jerusalem by Nebuchadrezzar, have found each its supporters. The wild legends of its preservation at the taking of Jerusalem (2 Macc. ii. and elsewhere) only show that the popular mind was unable to share the view that the ark was an obsolete relic. More poetical is the tradition that the ark was raised to heaven, there to remain till the coming of the Messiah, a thought which embodies the spiritual idea that a heavenly pledge of God's covenant and faithfulness had superseded the earthly symbol.1

A critical examination of the history of the Israelite ark renders it far from certain that the object was originally the peculiar possession of all Israel. Many different traditions have gathered around the story of the Exodus, and the ark was not the only divinely sent guide or forerunner which led the Israelites. Its presence at Shiloh, and its prominence in the life of Joshua, support the view that it was the palladium of the Joseph tribes, but the traditions in question conflict with others. The account of the commencement of the ark's journey associates it with Moses and his kin (Num. x. 29 sqq.)—that is, with the south Palestinian clans with which the term "Levites" appears to be closely connected. (See LEVITES.) A distinct movement direct into Judah is implied by certain old traditions (see CALEB), but this is subordinated to the more comprehensive account of the journey round by the east of the Jordan. (See EXODUS, THE.) The narratives in 1 Sam. iv.-vi. stand on a plane by themselves, and the gap between them and 2 Sam. vi. has not been satisfactorily fixed. But it is not certain that the two belong to the same cycle of tradition; Kirjath-jearim and Baal-Judah are identified only in later writings, and the behaviour of Saul's daughter (2 Sam. vi. 15 sqq.) may conceivably imply that the ark was an unknown object to Benjamites. It is of course possible that the ark was originally the sacred shrine of the clans which came direct to Judah, and that the traditions in 1 Sam. iv.-vi., Josh. iii. sqq. are of secondary origin, and are to be associated with its appearance at Shiloh, the fall of which place, although attributed to the time of Samuel, is apparently regarded by Jeremiah (xxvi. 6) as a recent event. Of these two divergent traditions, it would seem that the one which associates it with the kin of Moses and David may be traced farther in those late narratives which connect the ark closely with the Levites and even attribute its workmanship to Bezalel, a Calebite (Ex. xxxi. 2; 1 Chron. ii. 19 sqq.). The tradition in Psalms cxxxii. 6 of the search for the ark at Jaar (Kirjath-jearim) and Ephratah is not clear; but a comparison with 1 Chron. ii. 50 seems to show that it recognized the "Calebite" origin of the ark.

See, on this, S.A. Cook, *Critical Notes on 0. T. History* (*Index*s.v.), and, for other views, Kosters, *Theol. Tijd.* xxvii. 361 sqq.; Cheyne, *Encyc. Bib.* "Ark"; G. Westphal, *Yahwes Wohnstätten*, pp. 55 sqq., 85 sqq. (Giessen, 1908).

Whether the ark originally contained some symbol of Yahweh or not has been the subject of much discussion. Thus, it has been held that it contained stone fetishes (meteoric stones and the like) from Yahweh's original abode on Sinai or Horeb. As the palladium of the Joseph tribes, it has even been suggested that the bones of Joseph were treasured in the ark. Others have regarded it as an empty portable throne,[2] or as a receptacle for sacred serpents (analogies in Frazer,*Pausanias*, iv. pp. 292, 344). That it contained the tables of the law (Deut. x. 2; 1 Kings viii. 9) was the later Israelite view, and the subsequent development is illustrated in Heb. ix. 4. It is enough to decide that the ark represented in some way or other the presence of Yahweh and that the safety of his followers depended upon its security (analogies in Frazer, *Paus.* x. p. 283). The Semitic world affords many examples of the belief that a man's religion was part of his political connexion and that the change of nationality involved change of cult. He who leaves his land to enter another, leaves his god and is influenced by the religion of his new home (1 Sam. xxvi. 19; Ruth i. 16 sqq.), but strangers know not "the cult of the God of the land" (2 Kings xvii. 26). No nation willingly changes its god (Jer. ii. 11), and there are means whereby the follower of Yahweh may continue his worship even when outside Yahweh's land (2 Kings v. 17). When a people migrate they may take with them their god, and if they conceive him to be a spiritual being who cannot be represented by an image, they may desire a symbolical expression of or, rather, a substitute for his presence. Accordingly the conception of the ark must be based in the first instance upon the beliefs of the particular clans or tribes whose sacred object it was.

See further, W.R. Smith, *Religion of the Semites*, p. 37; Schwally, *Kriegsaltertümer*, i. p. 9; *Revue biblique* (1903), pp. 249 sqq.; and on the ark, generally, in addition to the literature already cited, Kautzsch, Hastings' *Dict. Bible*, v. p. 628; A.R.S. Kennedy,*Century Bible: Samuel* (*Appendix*); E. Meyer, *Die Israeliten, Index*s.v. *"Lade,"*; and R.H. Kennett, *Enc. of Rel. and Ethics*.

(S. A. C.)

1Cp. Rev. xi. 19, and W.R. Smith, *Old Test. in Jew. Church, Index*. For later traditional material, see Buxtorf, *De Arca Foederis*(Basel, 1659).

2But see Budde, *Expos. Times* (1898), pp. 398 sqq.; *Theolog. Stud. u. Krit.* (1906), pp. 489-507. The possibility must be conceded that there were several arks in the course of Hebrew history and that separate tribes or groups of tribes had their own sacred object.

ARKANSAS, a river of the United States of America, rising in the mountains of central Colorado, near Leadville, in lat. 39° 20′ N., long. 106° 15′ W., and emptying into the Mississippi, at Napoleon, Arkansas, in lat. 33° 40′ N. Its total length is about 2000 m., and its drainage basin (greater than that of the Upper Mississippi) about 185,000 sq. m. It is the greatest western affluent of the Missouri-Mississippi system. It rises in a pocket of lofty peaks at an altitude of 10,400 ft. on a sharply sloping plateau, down which it courses as a mountain torrent, dropping 4625 ft. in 120 m. At Canyon City it passes out of the Rockies through the Grand Canyon of the Arkansas; then turning eastward, and soon a turbid, shallow stream, depositing its mountain detritus, it flows with steadily lessening gradient and velocity in a broad, meandering bed across the prairies and lowlands of eastern Colorado, Kansas, Oklahoma and Arkansas, shifting its direction sharply to the south-east in central Kansas. The Arkansas ordinarily receives little water from its tributaries save in time of floods. In topography and characteristics and in the difficulties of its regulation the Arkansas is in many ways typical of the rivers in the arid regions of the western states. The gradient below the mountains averages 7.5 ft. per mile between Canyon City and Wichita, Kansas (543 m.), about 1.5 ft. between Wichita and Little Rock (659 m.), and 0.65 of a foot from Little Rock to the mouth (173 m.). The shores are sand, clay or loam throughout some 1300 m., with very rare rock ridges or rapids, and the banks rise low above ordinary water. The waters are constantly rising and falling, and almost never is the discharge at any point uniform. Every year there are, normally, two distinct periods of high water; one an early freshet due mainly to the heavy winter rainfall on the lower river, when the upper river is still frozen hard; the other in the late spring, due to the setting in of rains along the upper courses also, and to the melting of the snow in the mountains. The lowest waters are from August to December. In the summer there are sometimes violent floods due to cloud-bursts. Everywhere along the river there is a never-ending variation of velocity and discharge, and an equally ceaseless transformation of the river's bed and contour. These changes become revolutionary in times of flood. All these characteristics are accentuated below Little Rock. The depth of water at this point has been known to vary from 27 ft. to only half-a-foot, and the discharge to fall to 1170 cub. ft. per second. There is often no more than 1.5 ft. of water, and far below Little Rock a depth of 3 ft. on crossings is not infrequent. In many places there are different channels for high and low water, the latter being partly filled by each freshet, and recut after each subsidence; and the river meanders tortuously through the alluvial bottom in scores of great bends, loops and cut-offs. It is estimated that the eating and caving of the shore below Little Rock averages 7.64 acres per mile every year (as against 1.99 acres above Little Rock). By way of the White river cut-off the Arkansas finds an additional outlet through the valley of that river in times of high water, and the White, when the current in its natural channel is deadened by the backwaters of the Mississippi, finds an outlet by the same cut-off through the valley 551 of the Arkansas. This backwater, where it meets and checks the current of the Arkansas, occasions the precipitation of enormous alluvial deposits, and vast quantities of snags. The banks are disintegrated along this part of the river and built up again on the opposite side to their original height in the extraordinarily short time of two or three years, the channel remaining all the while narrow. At the mouth of the White, the Arkansas and the Mississippi the level of recurrent floods is 6 or 8 ft. above the timber-bearing soil along the banks, and all along the lower river the country is liable to overflow; and as the land backward from the stream slopes downward from the banks heaped up by successive flood-deposits, each overflow creates along the river a fringe of swamps. These features, although exaggerated in the portion of the river now in question, are qualitatively characteristic of its entire course below the mountains.

Up to the 30th of June 1907 the government of the United States expended $2,384,557 on improvements along the Arkansas. Almost half of this sum was required for snagging operations alone. There is a considerable traffic on the river within the borders of Arkansas in miscellaneous freights, and a slight passenger movement. The river is rarely navigable above Fort Smith, and during a considerable part of the year not above Pine Bluff. Steamer service is maintained the year round between this point and Memphis. Ordinarily there are some 400 m. of channel open to steamers part of the year, and in time of high flood considerably more. To the mouth of the Grand river (460 m.) the river is open about four months in a year for vessels of 4 ft. draft and about eight months for vessels of 2 ft. draft.

BIBLIOGRAPHY.—General descriptions of different portions of the river are indicated in the Index to the *Reports of the Chief of Engineers, U.S. Army* (many volumes, 1879-1900). See also H. Gannett, *Profiles of Rivers in the U.S.* (U.S. Geolog. Survey, 1901); Greenleaf, "Western Floods," in *Engin. Mag.* xii. 945-958; U.S. Geolog. Survey, *Bull.* 140; I.C. Russell, *Rivers of North America* (1898); T.J. Vivian, *Transportation, Rivers of the Miss. Valley* (U.S. Census, 1890, special Rp.).

ARKANSAS, one of the South Central states of the United States of America, situated between 89° 40' N. and 94° 42' W., bounded N. by Missouri, E. by the Mississippi river, separating it from Tennessee and Mississippi, and W. by Texas and Oklahoma. Its area is 53,335 sq. m., of which 810 are water surface.

Arkansas lies in the drainage basin of the lower Mississippi, and has a remarkable river system. The Arkansas bisects the state from W. to E.; along its valley lie the oldest and largest settlements of the state. Nine other considerable streams drain the state; of these, the Red, the Ouachita, the White and the St Francis are the most important. There are a number of swamps and bayous in the eastern part.

Physical Features.—The surface of Arkansas is the most diversified of that of any state in the central Mississippi valley. It rises, sloping upward toward the N.W., from an average elevation of less than 300 ft. in the south-east to heights of 2000 ft. and more in the north-western quarter. There are four physiographic regions: two of highlands; one of river valley plain separating the two highland areas; while the fourth is a region of hills, lowlands and scanty prairie. The last covers the E. half of the state, and is part of the Gulf or coastal plain province of the United States. If a line be drawn from the point where the Red river cuts the western boundary to where the Black cuts the northern, E. of it is the Gulf plain and W. of it are the highlands (over 500 ft.) and the mineral regions of the state. They are divided by the valley of the Arkansas river into two regions, which are also structurally different. South of the river are the Ouachita Mountains, and north of it are the Boston Mountains. The Ouachita Mountains are characterized by close folding and faulting. Their southern edge is covered with cretaceous deposits, and their eastern edge is covered as well with the tertiary deposits of the Gulf plains. The Arkansas valley is marked by wide and open folding. The Boston Mountains are substantially a continuation of the Ozark dome of Missouri. Their northern border is marked by an escarpment of 500 to 700 ft. in height. The trend is from E. to W. between Batesville and Wagoner, Oklahoma. In structure they are monoclinical, their rocks—sandstones and shales—being laid southward and blending on that side with the Arkansas valley region. The entire region is very much dissected by streams, and the topography is characteristically of a terrace and escarpment type. In the highlands N. of the Arkansas the country is very irregularly broken; S. of the river the hills lie less capriciously in short, high ranges, with low, fertile valleys between them. The Ouachitas extend 200 m., from within Oklahoma (near Atoka) to central Arkansas, near Little Rock. They are characterized by long, low ridges bearing generally W.-E., with wide, flat valleys. Near the western boundary of the state they attain a maximum altitude of 2900 ft. above the sea, and 2000 ft. above the valleys of the Arkansas and Red river; falling in elevation eastward (as westward) to 500-700 ft. at their eastern end. Five peaks rise above 2000 ft. Magazine Mountain, 2833 ft. above the sea-level and 2350 ft. above the surrounding country, is the highest point between the Alleghanies and the Rockies. Altitudes of 2250 ft. are attained in the Boston Mountains, which are the highest portion of the Ozark uplift, and the most picturesque. The streams are vigorous, and in their lower courses flow in deep-cut gorges, 500 to 1000 ft. deep, almost deserving the name of canyons. The main streams are tortuous, and their dendritic tributaries have cut the region into ridges. The mountains do not fill the N.W. quarter of the state, and are separated from a lower, greatly eroded highland region on their N. by a bold escarpment 500 to 1000 ft. in height. Along the upper course of the White river in the Bostons and in the country about Hot Springs in the Ouachitas is found the most beautiful scenery of the highlands; few regions are more beautiful. The valley region embraces the bottom-lands along the Mississippi, and up the Arkansas as far as Pine Bluff, and the cypress swamp country of the St Francis.

Climate.—The climate of the state is "southern," owing to the influence of the Gulf of Mexico. The mean temperatures for the different seasons are normally about 41.6°, 61.1°, 78.8° and 61.9° F. for winter, spring, summer and autumn respectively. The normal mean precipitations are about 11.7, 14.5, 10.5 and 10.2 in. for the same seasons. The extreme range of the monthly isotherms crossing the state is from about 35° in winter to 81° F. in summer, and the range of annual isotherms from about 54° to 60° F. That is, the variation of mean annual temperatures for different parts of the state is only 6° F. The variation of the mean annual temperature for the entire state is only 4° (from 59° to 63° F.). The variation of precipitation is as great as 30 in. (from 34 to 64 in.) according to locality. There is little snow, no severe winter cold, and no summer drought. Sheltered valleys in the interior produce spring crops three or four weeks earlier than is usual in Kansas. The climate is generally healthy.

Flora.—Arkansas lies in the humid, or Austroriparian, area of the Lower Austral life-zone, except the highlands of the Ozark uplift and Ouachita Mountains, which belong to the humid, or Carolinian, area of the Upper Austral. The state possesses a rich fauna and flora. From an economic standpoint its forests deserve special mention. The forest lands of the state include four-fifths of its area, and three-fourths are actually covered by standing timber. Valuable trees are of great variety: cottonwood, poplar, catalpa, red cedar, sweet-gum, birch-eye, sassafras, persimmon, ash, elm, sycamore, maple, a variety of pines, pecan, locust, dogwood, hickory, various oaks, beech, walnut and cypress are all abundant. There are one hundred and twenty-nine native species of trees. The yellow pine, the white oak and the cypress are the most valuable growths. The northern woods are mainly hard; the yellow pine is most characteristic of the heavy woods of the south central counties; and magnificent cypress abounds in the north-east. Hard woods grow even on the alluvial lands. "The hard-wood forests of the state are hardly surpassed in variety and richness, and contain inestimable bodies of the finest oak, walnut, hickory and ash timber" (U.S. Census, 1870 and 1900). The growth on the alluvial bottoms and the lower uplands in the E. is extraordinarily vigorous. The leading species of the Appalachian woodland maintain their 552full vigour of growth nearer to the margin of forest growth in this part of the Mississippi valley than in any other part of the United States; and some species, such as the holly, the osage orange and the pecan, attain their fullest growth in Arkansas (Shaler). There are two Federal forest reserves (4968 sq. m.).

Soil.—The soils of Arkansas are of peculiar variety. That of the highlands is mostly but a thin covering, and their larger portion is relatively poorly fitted for agriculture. The uplands are generally fertile. Their poor soils are distinctively sandy, those of the lowlands clayey; but these elements are usually found combined in rich loams characterized by the predominance of one or the other constituent. Finally the alluvial bottoms are of wonderful richness.

Agriculture.—This variety of soils, a considerable range of moderate altitudes and favourable factors of heat and moisture promote a rich diversity in agriculture. Arkansas is predominantly an agricultural state. The farm area of 1860 was only 28.2% of the whole area of the state, that of 1900 (16,636,719 acres) was 49%; and while only a fifth of this farm area was actually improved in 1860, two-fifths were improved in 1900; thus, the part of the state's area actually cultivated approximately quadrupled in four decades. The value of products in 1900 ($79.6 millions) was 44% of the total farm values ($181.4 millions). The rise in average value of farm lands since 1870 has not been a fifth of the increase of the aggregate value of all farm property.

The Civil War wrought a havoc from which a full recovery was hardly reached before 1890. The economic evolution of the state since Reconstruction has been in the main that common to all the old slave states developing from the plantation system of ante-bellum days, somewhat diversified and complicated by the special features of a young and border community. The farms of Arkansas increased in number 357.8%, in area 73.7% and in total true (as distinguished from tax) valuation about 53.8% between 1860 and 1900; the decade of most extraordinary growth being that of 1870-1880. Thus Arkansas has shared that fall in the average size of farms common to all sections of the Union (save the north central) since 1850, but especially marked since the Civil War in the "Cotton States," owing to the subdivision of large holdings with the introduction of the tenant system. The rapidity of the movement has not been exceptional in Arkansas, but the size of its average farm, less in 1850 than that of the other cotton states, was in 1900, 93.1 acres (108.8 for white farmers alone, 49.0 for blacks alone), which was even less than that of the North Atlantic states (96.5 acres, the smallest sectional unit of the Union). The percentage of farms worked by owners fell from 69.1% in 1880 to 54.6% in 1900; the difference of the balances or 14.5% indicates the increase of tenant holdings, two-thirds of these being for shares.

It is interesting to compare in this matter the whites and the negroes. In actual numbers the white farmers heavily predominate, whether as owners, tenants for cash or tenants on shares; but if we look at the numbers within each race holding by these respective tenures (65.0, 8.7 and 26.3% respectively for whites; 25.6, 33.7 and 40.7% for negroes, in 1900), we see the lesser independence of the negro farmer. The cotton counties, which are the counties of densest coloured habitancy, exemplify this fact with great clearness. The few negroes in the white counties of the uplands are much better off than those in the cotton lowlands; more than three times as large a part of them owners; the poorer element is segregated in the cotton region. In Arkansas, as elsewhere in the south, negro tenants, like white tenants, are more efficient than owners working their own lands. The black farmer is in bondage to cotton; for him still "Cotton is King." He gives it four-fifths of his land; while his white rival allows it only a quarter of his, less by half than the area he gives to live-stock, dairying, hay and grains. At Sunnyside, on the west bank of the Mississippi, negro tenant farmers have been practically forced out of business by Italians, who produced in 1899-1904 more than twice as much lint cotton per working hand, and 70% more per acre. The general place of the negro in agriculture is shown also by the fact that more than four-fifths of the farm acreage and farm values of the state are in the hands of the whites. The white farmer gives an outlay in labour and fertilizers on his farm greater by 61.4% than the black, gathers a produce greater by 22.5%, and possesses a farm of a value 53.5% greater (Census, 1900).

Cotton is the leading product. It absorbs about a third of the area under crops, and its returns ($28,000,000 in 1899) are about a half of the value of all crops. A part of the cotton lands of Arkansas are among the richest in the south. Other distinctively southern products (tobacco, &c.) are of no importance in Arkansas. Cereals are given more than twice as much acreage as cotton, but yield only a third as great aggregate returns, Indian corn being much the most remunerative; about three-fourths of the cereal acreage are given to its cultivation, and it ranks after cotton in value of harvest.1 For all the other staple agricultural products of the central states the showing of Arkansas is uniformly good, but not noteworthy. But its rank as a fruitgrowing country is exceptional. Plums, prunes, peaches, pears and grapes are cultivated very generally over the western half of the state (grapes in the east also), but with greatest success in the south-west; apples prosper best in the north-west. Small berries are a very important product. All fruits are of the finest quality. For apples the state makes probably a finer showing than that of any other state except Oregon. About ninety varieties are habitually entered in national competitions. The fruit industry generally has developed with extreme rapidity.

Manufactures.—Although Arkansas is rich in minerals and in forests, in 1900 only 2% of its population were engaged in manufacturing. But the development has been rapid; the value of products multiplied seven times, the wages paid nine, and the capital invested twelve, in the years 1880-1900; and the increase in the same categories from 1900-1905 was 35, 42.8 and 82.4% respectively.2 It must be noted as characteristic of the state that of the total manufactures in 1905, 80.3% were produced in rural districts (83.7 in 1900). About two-thirds of the increase between 1890 and 1900 was in the lumber industry which was of slight importance before the former year; it represented more than half the total value of the manufactures of the state in 1905 (output, 1905, $28,065,171 and of mill products $3,786,772 additional); in the value of lumber and timber products the state ranked sixth among the states of the United States in 1900, and seventh in 1905. After the lumber and timber industry ranked in 1905 the manufacture of cotton-seed oil and cake ($4,939,919) and flour and grist milling. Cotton ginning increased 739% from 1890 to 1900.

(Click to enlarge.)

Minerals.—The progress of coal-mining has been a striking feature of the state's economy since 1880. The field extends from Oklahoma eastward to central Arkansas, along both sides of the Arkansas river. A production of 5000 tons (short) in 1882 became 542,000 tons in 1891 and 2,229,172 tons in 1903—a maximum for the state up to 1905; in 1907 the yield was 2,670,438 tons, valued at $4,473,693; the value of the product increased more than eight-fold in 1886-1900. The United States Geological Survey estimates that three-fourths of the coal area (over 1700 sq. m.) can made commercially productive. Apart from coal the great and varied mineral wealth of the state has been only slightly utilized. The great zinc and lead area along the northern border in the plateau portion of the Ozark region has proved a disappointment in development; the iron areas have hardly been touched, and the product of the exceptionally promising deposits of manganese lost ground after 1890 before 55 the output of Virginia and Georgia. Among the products of the rich stone quarries of the state, only that of abrasive stones is important in the markets of the Union; the novaculites of Arkansas are among the finest whetstones in the world. Deposits of true chalk are utilized in the manufacture of Portland cement for local markets. The chalk region lies in the S.E. part of the state, S. of the Ouachita Mountains. Bauxite was discovered in the state in 1887, and the product increased from 5045 long tons in 1899 to 50,267 long tons in 1906, the production for the whole country in 1899 being 35,280 long tons and in 1906 75,332 long tons. The only other states in which bauxite was produced during the period were Alabama and Georgia, which in this respect have greatly declined in importance relatively to Arkansas. Extremely valuable and varied marls, kaolins and clays, fuller's earth, asphaltum and mineral waters show special promise in the state's industry. In 1906 diamonds were found in a peridotite dike in Pike county 2½ m. S.E. of Murfreesboro; this is the first place in North America where diamonds have been found *in situ*, and not in glacial deposit or in river gravel.

Communications.—The rivers afford for light craft (of not over 3 ft. draft) about 3000 m. of navigable waters, a river system unequalled in extent by that of any other state. The labours of the United States government have much extended and very greatly improved this navigation, materially lessening also the frequency and havoc of floods along the rich bottom-lands through which the rivers plough a tortuous way in the eastern and southern portions of the state. As a result of these improvements land and timber values have markedly risen, and great impetus has been given to traffic on the rivers, which carry a large part of the cotton, lumber, coal, stone, hay and miscellaneous freights of the state. The greatest of these internal improvements is the St Francis levee, from New Madrid, Missouri, to the mouth of the St Francis, 212 m. along the Mississippi; an area of 3500 sq. m., of exceptional fertility, is here reclaimed at a cost of about $1500 per sq. m. (as compared with $10,000 per sq. m. for the 2500 sq. m. reclaimed by the Nile works at Assuan and Assiut). Whether with regard to area or population, Arkansas is also relatively well supplied with railways (4,472.8 m. at the end of 1907). A state railway commission controls transportation rates, which are also somewhat checked by the competition of river freights. There is also a considerable passenger traffic on the Arkansas.

Population.—The population in 1910 was 1,574,449. The growth in 1880-1900 is shown by the following table:—

C	T	%	%	A	% Increase by

ensus Year.	otal Pop.	White Pop.	Negro Pop.	verage per sq. m.	decades		
					otal	hite	egro
1	80	7	2	15	6		7
880	2,525	3.7	6.3	.1	5.6	3.3	2.4
1	1,	7	2	21	3		4
890	128,211	2.6	7.4	.5	0.6	8.4	6.6
1	1,	7	2	25	1		1
900	311,561	2.0	8.0	.0	6.3	5.4	8.7

In 1900 the rank of the state in total population was twenty-fifth, and in negro population tenth. The proportion of the coloured element steadily rose from 11% in 1820 to 28% in 1900, at which time there were more than a dozen counties along the border of the Mississippi and lower Arkansas in which the negroes numbered 50 to 89% of the total. They have never been a large element in the highland counties; it was these counties which were most strongly Unionist at the time of the Civil War, and which to-day are the region of diversified industry. About a ninth of the state's population is gathered into towns of more than 2000 inhabitants. Fort Smith (pop. 11,587 in 1900), Little Rock, the state capital (38,307), and Pine Bluff (11,496) lie in the valley of the Arkansas. In 1900 a dozen other towns had a population exceeding 2500, the most important being Hot Springs (9973), Helena (5550), Texarkana (4914), Jonesboro (4508), Fayetteville (4061), Eureka Springs (3572), Mena (3423) and Paragould (3324). Foreign blood has only very slightly permeated the state; negroes and native whites of native parents make up more than 95% of its population. Immigration is almost entirely from other southern states. The strongest religious sects are the Methodists and Baptists.

Government.—The present constitution of the state dates from 1874 (with amendments). Few features mark it off from the usual type of such documents. The governor holds office for two years; he has the pardoning and veto power, but his veto may be overridden by a simple majority in each house of the whole number elected to that house (a provision unusual among the state constitutions of the Union). There is no lieutenant-governor. The legislature is bicameral, senators holding office for four years, representatives (about thrice as numerous) for two. The length of the regular biennial legislative sessions is limited to sixty days, but by a vote of two-thirds of the members elected to each house the length of any session may be extended. Special sessions may be called by the governor. A majority of the members elected to each of the two houses suffices to propose a constitutional amendment, which the people may then accept by a mere majority of all votes cast at an election for the legislature (an unusually democratic provision); no more than three amendments, however, can be proposed or submitted at the same time. The supreme court has five members, elected by the people for eight years; they are re-eligible. The population of the state entitles it to seven representatives in the national House of Representatives, and to nine votes in the Electoral College (census of 1900). Elections of members of the state legislature and of Congress are not held at the same time—a very unusual provision. Elections are by Australian ballot; the constitution prescribes that no law shall "be enacted whereby the right to vote at any election shall be made to depend upon any previous registration of the elector's name" (extremely unusual). The qualifications for suffrage include one year's residence in the state, six months in the county, and one month in the voting district, next before election; idiots, insane persons, convicts, Indians not taxed, minors and women are disqualified; aliens who have declared their intention to become citizens of the United States vote on the same terms as actual citizens. An amendment of 1893 requires the exhibition of a poll-tax receipt by every voter (except those "who make satisfactory proof that they have attained the age of twenty-one years since the time of assessing taxes next preceding" the election). There is nothing in the constitution or laws of Arkansas with any apparent tendency to disfranchise the negroes; there are statutory provisions (1866-1867) against intermarriage of the races and constitutional and statutory (1886-1887) provisions for separate schools, a "Jim Crow" law (1891) requires railways to provide separate cars for negroes, and a law (1893) provides for separate railway waiting-rooms for negroes. Giving or accepting a challenge to a duel bars from office, but this survival of the ante-bellum social life is to-day only reminiscent. Declared atheists are similarly disqualified. There is no constitutional provision for a census. Marriage is pronounced a civil contract. A law for compulsory education was passed in 1909.

Finance.—The constitution makes 1% on the assessed valuation of property a maximum limit of state taxation for ordinary expenses, but by an amendment of 1906 the legislature may levy three mills on the dollar per annum for common schools; and may "authorize school districts to levy by a vote of the qualified electors of such district a tax not to exceed seven mills on the dollar in any year for school purposes." The state debt in 1874 was $12,108,247, of which about $9,370,000 was incurred after the Civil War for internal improvement schemes. This new debt was practically repudiated in 1875 by a decision of the supreme court, and completely set aside in 1884 by constitutional amendment. Until 1900, when an adjustment of the matter was reached, there was also another disputed debt to the national government, owing to the collapse in 1839 of a so-called Real Estate Bank of Arkansas, in which the state had invested more than $500,000 paid to it by the United States in exchange for Arkansas bonds to be held as an investment for the Smithsonian Institution, on which bonds the state defaulted after 1839. If the unacknowledged debt be included (as it often is; and hence the necessity of reference to it), very few states—and those all western or southern—have a heavier burden per capita. But the acknowledged debt was in 1907 only $1,250,500, and this is 554 not a true debt, being a permanent school fund that is not to be paid off; of this total in 3% bonds, $1,134,500 is held by the common schools and $116,000 by the state university. In net combined state and local debt, Arkansas ranks very low among the states of the Union. The hired labourer suffers from the "truck" system, taking his pay in board and living, in goods, in trade on his employer's credit at the village store; the independent farmer suffers in his turn from unlimited credit at the same store, where he secures everything on the credit of his future crops; and if he is reduced to borrow money, he secures it by vesting the title to his property temporarily in his creditor. His legal protections under such "title bonds" are much slighter than under mortgages. Homesteads belonging to the head of a family and containing 80 to 160 acres (according to value) if in the country, or a lot of ¼ to one acre (according to value), if in town, village or city, are exempt from liability for debts, excepting liens for purchase money, improvements or taxes. A married man may not sell or mortgage a homestead without his wife's consent.

Education.—The legal beginnings of a public school system date from 1843; in 1867 the first tax was imposed for its support. Only white children were regarded by the laws before Reconstruction days. There are now separate race schools, with terms of equal length, and offering like facilities; the number of white and coloured teachers employed is approximately in the same proportion to the number of attending children of the respective races; in negro districts two out of three school directors are usually negroes. "The coloured race as a whole go to the schools as regularly and as numerously in proportion as do the whites" (Shinn). Of the current expenses of the common schools about three-fourths is borne by the localities; the state distributes its contribution annually among the counties. There is also a permanent school fund derived wholly from land grants from the national government. The total expenditure for the schools is creditable to the state; but before 1909 hardly half the school population attended; and in general the rural conditions of the state, the shortness of the school terms and the dependence of the schools primarily upon local funds and local supervision, make the schools of inadequate and quite varying excellence. The average expenditure in 1906 for tuition per child enrolled was $4.93, and the average length of the school term was only eighty-one days. In June 1906 there were 1102 school houses in the state valued at $100 or less. In 1905-1906 the Peabody Board gave $2000 to aid rural schools, and in general it has done much for the improvement of country public schools throughout the state. In 1906 an amendment to the state constitution, greatly increasing the tax resources available for educational work, was passed by a large popular vote. The University of Arkansas was opened at Fayetteville in 1872. The law and medical faculties are at Little Rock. A branch normal school, established 1873-1875 at Pine Bluff, provides for coloured students, who enjoy the same opportunities for work, and are accorded the same degrees, as the students at Fayetteville; they are about a fourth as numerous. In 1905-1906 there were 497 students in the college of liberal arts, sciences and engineering, 548 in the preparatory school and 26 in the conservatory of music and arts, all in Fayetteville; 171 in the medical school and 46 in the law school in Little Rock; and 240 in the branch normal college at Pine Bluff. The university and the normal school are supported by the Morrill Fund and by state appropriations. The state still suffered in 1906 from the lack of a separate and special training school for teachers; but in 1907 the legislature voted to establish a state normal school. Of the Morrill Fund (see MORRILL, JUSTIN SMITH), three-elevenths goes to the normal school. The agricultural experiment station of the university dates from 1887. The financial support of the university has been light, about three-fifths coming from the United States government. Besides the university there are about a score of denominational colleges or academies, of which half-a-dozen are for coloured students. Among the large denominational colleges are Philander Smith College, Little Rock (Methodist Episcopal, 1877); Ouachita College, Arkadelphia (Baptist, 1886); Hendrix College, Conway (Methodist Episcopal, South, 1884); and Arkansas College, Batesville (Presbyterian, 1872). There are few libraries in Arkansas. In this matter her showing has long been among the very poorest in the Union relatively to her population. Daily papers are few in number. The state charitable institutions—insane asylum, deaf-mute and blind institutes—and the penitentiary, are at Little Rock.

Local government is of the ordinary southern county type, without noteworthy variations. Municipal corporations rest upon a general state law, not upon individual charters. The liquor question is left by the state to county (*i.e.* including "local," or town) option, and prohibition is the most common county law, the alternative being high-licence.

History.—The first settlement by Europeans in Arkansas was made in 1686 by the French at Arkansas Post (later the residence of the French and Spanish governors, important as a trading post in the earlier days of the American occupation, and the first territorial capital, 1819-1820). In 1720 a grant on the Arkansas was made to John Law. In 1762 the territory passed to Spain, in 1780 back to France, and in 1803 to the United States as a part of the "Louisiana Purchase." Save in the beginnings of western frontier trade, and in a great mass of litigation left to the courts of later years by the curious and uncertain methods of land delimitation that prevailed among the French and Spanish colonists, the pre-American period of occupation has slight connexions with the later period, and scant historical importance.

From 1804 to 1812 what is now Arkansas was part of the district (and then the territory) of Louisiana, and from 1812 to 1819 of the territory of Missouri. Its earliest county organizations date from this time. It was erected successively into a territory of the first and second class by acts of Congress of the 2nd of March 1819 and the 21st of April 1820. By act of the 15th of June 1836 it was admitted into the Union as a slave state.

There is little of general interest in the history of ante-bellum days. Economic life centred in the slave plantation, and there was remarkable development up to the Civil War. The decade 1819-1829 saw the first newspaper (1819), the beginning of steamboating on Arkansas rivers, and the first weekly mail from the east. Trade was largely confined to the rivers and freighting for Sante Fé and Salt Lake before the war, but the first railway entered the state in 1853. Social life was sluggish in some ways and wild in others. An unhappy propensity to duelling, the origin in Arkansas of the bowie-knife,—from an alleged use of which Arkansas received the nickname, which it has always retained, of the "toothpick state,"—and other backwoods associations gave the state a reputation which to some extent has survived in spite of many years of sober history. The questions of the conduct of territorial affairs do not seem to have been contested systematically on national party lines until about 1825. The government of Arkansas before the Civil War was always in the hands of a few families closely intermarried. From the beginning the state has been unswervingly Democratic, save in the Reconstruction years, though often with heavy Whig or Republican minorities.

In February 1861 the people of Arkansas voted to hold a convention to consider the state of public affairs. The convention assembled on the 4th of March. Secession resolutions were defeated, and it was voted to submit to the people the question whether there should be "co-operation" through the Lincoln government, or "secession." The plan was endorsed of holding a convention of all the states to settle the slavery question, and delegates were chosen to the proposed Border State Convention that was to meet at Frankfort, Kentucky, on the 27th of May. Then came the fall of Fort Sumter and the proclamation of President Lincoln calling for troops to put down rebellion. The governor of Arkansas curtly refused its quota. A quick surge of ill-feeling, all the bitterer on account of the divided sentiments of the people, chilled loyalty to the Union. The convention reassembled on call of the governor, and on the 6th of May, with a single dissentient voice, passed an ordinance of secession. It then repealed its former vote submitting the question of secession 555to the people. On the 16th of May Arkansas became one of the Confederate States of America.

In the years of war that followed, a very large proportion of the able-bodied men of the state served in the armies of the Confederacy; several regiments, some of coloured troops, served the Union. Union sentiment was strongest in the north. In 1862-1863 various victories threw more than half the state, mainly the north and east, under the Federal arms. Accordingly, under a proclamation of the president, citizens within the conquered districts were authorized to renew allegiance to the Union, and a special election was ordered for March 1864, to reorganize the state government. But meanwhile, a convention of delegates chosen mainly at polls opened at the army posts, assembled in January 1864, abolished slavery, repudiated secession and the secession war debt, and revised in minor details the constitution of 1836, restricting the suffrage to whites. This new fundamental law was promptly adopted by the people, *i.e.* by its friends, who alone voted. But the representatives of Arkansas under this constitution were never admitted to Congress.

The Federal and Confederate forces controlled at this time different parts of the state; there was some ebb and flow of military fortune in 1864, and for a short time two rival governments. Chaotic conditions followed the war. The fifteenth legislature (April 1864 to April 1865) ratified the Thirteenth Amendment, and passed laws against "bush-whacking," a term used in the Civil War for guerilla warfare, especially as carried on by pretended neutrals. Local militia,

181

protecting none who refused to join in the common defence, and all serving "not as soldiers but as farmers mutually pledged to protect each other from the depredations of outlaws who infest the state," strove to secure such public order as was necessary to the gathering of crops, so as "to prevent the starvation of the citizens" (governor's circular, 1865). Struggling in these difficulties, the government of the state was upset by the first Reconstruction Act. The governor in these years (1865-1868) was a Republican, the caster of the single Union vote in the convention of 1861; but the sixteenth legislature (1866-1867) was largely Democratic. It undertook to determine the rights of persons of African descent, and regrettable conflicts followed. The first Reconstruction Act having declared that "no legal state government or adequate protection for life or property" existed in the "rebel states," Arkansas was included in one of the military districts established by Congress. A registration of voters, predominantly whites, was at once carried through, and delegates were chosen for another constitutional convention, which met at Little Rock in January 1868. The secessionist element was voluntarily or perforce excluded. This convention ratified the Fourteenth Amendment, and framed the third constitution of the state, which was adopted by a small majority at a popular election, marred by various irregularities, in March 1868. By its provisions negroes secured full political rights, and all whites who had been excluded from registration for the election of delegates to the convention were now practically stripped of political privileges. The organization of Arkansas being now acceptable to Congress, a bill admitting it to the Union was passed over President Johnson's veto, and on the 22nd of June 1868 the admission was consummated.

Arkansas now became for several years Republican, and suffered considerably from the rule of the "carpet-baggers." The debt of the state was increased about $9,375,000 from 1868 to 1874, largely for railroad and levee schemes; much of the money was misappropriated, and in a case involving the payment of railway aid bonds the action of the legislature in pledging the credit of the state was held nugatory by the state supreme court in 1875 on the ground that, contrary to the constitution, the bond issue had never been referred to popular vote. An amendment to the constitution approved by a popular vote in 1884 provided that the General Assembly should "have no power to levy any tax, or make any appropriation, to pay" any of the bonds issued by legislative action in 1868, 1869 and 1871. The current expenses of the state in the years of Reconstruction were also enormously increased. The climax of the Reconstruction period was the so-called Baxter-Brooks war.

Elisha Baxter (1827-1899) was the regular Republican candidate for governor in 1872. He was opposed by a disaffected Republican faction known as "brindletails," or as they called themselves, "reformers," led by Joseph Brooks (1821-1877), and supported by the Democrats. Baxter was irregularly elected. The election was contested, and his choice was confirmed by the legislature, the court of last resort in such cases. He soon showed a willingness to rule as a non-partisan, and favoured the re-enfranchisement of white citizens. This would have put the Democrats again in power, and they rallied to Baxter, while the Brooks party now assumed the name of "regulars," and received the support of the "carpet-bag" and negro elements. After Baxter had been a year in office Brooks received a judgment of *ouster* against him from a state circuit judge, and got possession of the public buildings (April 1874). The state flew to arms. The legislature called for Federal intervention (May 1874), and Federal troops maintained neutrality while investigations were conducted by a committee sent out by Congress. As a result, President Grant pronounced for Baxter, and the Brooks forces disbanded.

The chief result was another convention. In 1873 the article of the constitution which had disfranchised the whites was repealed, and the Democrats thus regained power. By an overwhelming majority the people now voted for another convention, which (July to October 1874) framed the present constitution. It removed all disfranchisement, and embraced equitable amnesty and exemption features. It also took away all patronage from the governor, reduced his term to two years, forbade him to proclaim martial law or suspend the writ of *habeas corpus*, and abolished all registration laws: all these provisions being reflections of Reconstruction struggles. The people ratified the new constitution on the 13th of October 1874. After Reconstruction the state again became Democratic, and the main interest of its history has been the progress of economic development.

The following is a list of the territorial and state governors of Arkansas:—

Territorial.

James Miller3	1819-1825
George Izard	1825-1828
John Pope4	1829-1835

State.

James S. Conway	1836-1840	Democrat
Archibald Yell5	1840-1844	"
Thomas S. Drew6	1844-1849	"
John S. Roane	1849-1852	"
Elias N. Conway	1852-1860	"
Henry M. Rector7	1860-1862	"
Harris Flannigan8	1862-1865	"
Isaac Murphy9	1864-1868	Republican
C.H. Smith10	1867-1868	"
Powell Clayton	1868-1871	"
Ozra A. Hadley11	1871-1873	"
Elisha Baxter	1873-1874	"
August H. Garland	1874-1877	Democrat
William R. Miller	1877-1881	"
Thomas J. Churchill	1881-1883	"
James H. Berry	1883-1885	"
Simon P. Hughes	1885-1889	"
James P. Eagle	1889-1893	"556
William M. Fishback	1893-1895	"
James P. Clarke	1895-1897	"
Daniel W. Jones	1897-1901	"
Jefferson Davis	1901-1907	"
John S. Little	1907-1908	"
X.O. Pindall, Acting Gov	1908	"
George W. Donaghey	1909	"

BIBLIOGRAPHY.—Information regarding the resources, climate, population and industries of Arkansas should be sought in the volumes of the United States Census, United States Department of Agriculture and the United States Geological Survey (for the last two there are various bibliographical guides); consult also the publications of the Arkansas (Agricultural) Experiment Station (at Fayetteville), the reports of the state horticulturist, the biennial reports of the state treasurer, of the auditor, and of the Bureau of Mines, Manufactures and Agriculture (all published at Little Rock).

The constitutional documents may best be consulted in the latest compiled *Statutes* of the state. See also J.H. Shinn, *Education in Arkansas* (U.S. Bur. of Education, 1900); W.F. Pope, *Early Days in Arkansas* (Little Rock, 1895); and F. Hempstead, *Pictorial History of Arkansas* (St Louis, 1890). Similar to the last in popular character, vast in bulk and loose in method, are a series of *Biographical and Pictorial Histories*, covering the different sections of the state (1 vol. by J. Hallum, Albany, 1887; four others compiled anonymously, Chicago, 1889-1891). For the Reconstruction period see especially the Poland Report in House Rp. No. 2, 43 Cong. 2 Sess., vol. i. (1874), and John M. Harrell's *The Brooks and Baxter War: A History of the Reconstruction Period in Arkansas* (St Louis, Missouri, 1893), which is frankly in favour of Baxter; also a paper by B.S. Johnson in vol. ii. (1908) of the *Publications of the Arkansas Historical Association.*

1For 1906 the *Yearbook* of the U.S. Department of Agriculture reported the following statistics for Arkansas:—Indian corn, 52,802,659 bu., valued at $24,817,207; oats 3,783,706 bu., valued at $1,589,157; wheat, 1,915,250 bu., valued at $1,436,438; rice, 131,440 bu., valued at $111,724; rye, 23,652 bu., valued at $19,631; potatoes, 1,666,960 bu., valued at $1,116,863; hay, 113,491 tons, valued at $1,123,561.

2The special census of the manufacturing industry for 1905 was concerned only with the establishment conducted under the so-called "factory system"; for purposes of comparison the figures for 1900 have been reduced to the same standard, and this fact should be borne in mind with regard to the percentages of increase given above.

3During this period Robert Crittenden, the secretary of the territory, was frequently the acting governor.

4Robert Crittenden was acting governor in 1828-1829.

5Samuel Adams was acting governor from the 29th of April to the 9th of November 1844.

6R.C. Byrd was acting governor from the 11th of January to the 19th of April 1849.

7Thomas Fletcher was acting governor from the 4th to the 15th of November 1862.

8Confederate governor.

9Union governor.

10United States military (sub) governor.

11Acting governor.

ARKANSAS CITY, a city of Cowley county, Kansas, U.S.A., situated near the S. boundary of the state, in the fork of the Arkansas and Walnut rivers. Pop. (1890) 8347; (1900) 6140, of whom 302 were negroes; (1905) 7634; (1910) 7508. The city is served by the Atchison, Topeka & Santa Fé, the Missouri Pacific, the St Louis & San Francisco, the Midland Valley and the Kansas South-Western railways. To the south is the Chilocco Indian school (in Key county, Oklahoma), established by the U.S. government in 1884. A canal joining the Arkansas and Walnut rivers furnishes good water power. The manufactures include flour mills, packing establishments, a creamery and a paint factory. The city is situated in the midst of a rich agricultural region and is a supply centre for southern Kansas and Oklahoma, with large jobbing interests. The municipality owns and operates the waterworks. Arkansas City, first known as Creswell, was settled in 1870, was chartered as a city under its present name in 1872 and was rechartered in 1880.

ARKLOW, a seaport and market town of Co. Wicklow, Ireland, in the east parliamentary division, 49 m. S. of Dublin, by the Dublin & South-Eastern railway. Pop. (1901) 4944. Sea-fisheries are prosecuted, and there are oyster-beds on the coast, but the produce requires to be freed from a peculiar flavour by the purer waters of the Welsh and English coast before it is fit for food. The produce of the copper and lead mines of the Vale of Avoca is shipped from the port. There are cordite and explosives works, established by Messrs Kynoch of Birmingham, England. In 1882 an act was passed providing for the improvement of the harbour and for the appointment of harbour commissioners. The town hall and the Protestant church (1899) were gifts of the earl of Carysfort, in whose property the town is situated. There are slight ruins of an ancient castle of the Ormondes, demolished in 1649 by Cromwell. On the 9th of June 1798 the Irish insurgents, attacking the town, were defeated by the royal troops near Arklow Bridge, and their leader, Father Michael Murphy, was killed.

ARKWRIGHT, SIR RICHARD (1732-1792), English inventor, was born at Preston in Lancashire, on the 23rd of December 1732, of parents in humble circumstances. He was the youngest of thirteen children, and received but a very indifferent education. After serving his apprenticeship in his native town, he established himself as a barber at Bolton about 1750, and later amassed a little property from dealing in human hair and dyeing it by a process of his own. This business he gave up about 1767 in order to devote himself to the construction of the spinning frame. The spinning jenny, which was patented by James Hargreaves (d. 1778), a carpenter of Blackburn, Lancashire, in 1770, though he had invented it some years earlier, gave the means of spinning twenty or thirty threads at once with no more labour than had previously been required to spin a single thread. The thread spun by the jenny could not, however, be used except as weft, being destitute of the firmness or hardness required in the longitudinal threads or warp. Arkwright supplied this deficiency by the invention of the spinning-frame, which spins a vast number of threads of any degree of fineness and hardness.

The precise date of the invention is not known; but in 1767 he employed John Kay, a watchmaker at Warrington, to assist him in the preparation of the parts of his machine, and he took out a patent for it in 1769. The first model was set up in the parlour of the house belonging to the free grammar school at Preston. This invention having been brought to a fairly advanced stage, he removed to Nottingham in 1768, accompanied by Kay and John Smalley of Preston, and there erected his first spinning mill, which was worked by horses. But his operations were at first greatly fettered by want of capital, until Jedediah Strutt (*q.v.*), having satisfied himself of the value of the machines, entered with his partner, Samuel Need, into partnership with him, and enabled him in 1771 to build a second factory, on a much larger scale, at Cromford in Derbyshire, the machinery of which was turned by a water-wheel. A fresh patent, taken out in 1775, covered several additional improvements in the processes of carding, roving and spinning.

As the value of his processes became known, he began to be troubled with infringements of his patents, and in 1781 he took action in the courts to vindicate his rights. In the first case, against Colonel Mordaunt, who was supported by a combination of manufacturers, the decision was unfavourable to him, on the sole ground that the description of the machinery in the specification was obscure and indistinct. In consequence he prepared a "case," which he at one time intended to lay before parliament, as the foundation of an application for an act for relief. But this intention was subsequently abandoned; and in a new trial (*Arkwright* v. *Nightingale*) in February 1785, the presiding judge having expressed himself favourably with respect to the sufficiency of the specification, a verdict was given for Arkwright. On this, as on the former trial, nothing was stated against the originality of the invention.

In consequence of these conflicting verdicts, the whole matter was brought, by a writ of *scire facias*, before the court of King's Bench, to have the validity of the patent finally settled, and it was not till this third trial, which took place in June 1785, that Arkwright's claim to the inventions which formed the subject of the patent was disputed. To support this new allegation, Arkwright's opponents brought forward, for the first time, Thomas Highs, or Hayes, a reed-maker at Bolton, who stated that he had invented a machine for spinning by rollers previously to 1768, and that he had employed the watchmaker Kay to make a model of that machine. Kay himself was produced to prove that he had communicated that model to Arkwright, and that this was the real source of all his pretended inventions. Having no idea that any attempt was to be made to overturn the patent on this new ground, Arkwright's counsel were not prepared with evidence to repel this statement, and the verdict went against him. On a motion for a new trial on the 10th of November of the same year it was stated that he was furnished with affidavits contradicting the evidence that had been given by Kay and others with respect to the originality of the invention; but the court refused to grant a new trial, on the ground that, whatever might be the fact as to the question of originality, the deficiency in the specification was enough to sustain the verdict, and the cancellation of the patents was ordered a few days afterwards. His fortunes, however, were not thereby seriously affected, for by this time his business capacity and organizing skill had enabled him to consolidate his position, in spite of the difficulties he had encountered not only from rival manufacturers but also from the working classes, who in 1779 displayed their antipathy to labour-saving appliances by destroying a large mill he had erected near Chorley.

Though a man of great personal strength, Arkwright never enjoyed good health, and throughout his career of invention and 557discovery he laboured under a severe asthmatic affection. A complication of disorders at length terminated his life on the 3rd of August 1792, at his works at Cromford. He was knighted in 1786 when he presented a congratulatory address from the wapentake of Wirksworth to George III., on his escape from the attempt on his life by Margaret Nicholson.

ARLES, a town of south-eastern France, capital of an arrondissement in the department of Bouches-du-Rhône, 54 m. N.W. of Marseilles by rail. Pop. (1906) 16,191. A canal unites Arles with the harbour of Bouc on the Mediterranean. Arles stands on the left bank of the Rhone, just below the point at which the river divides to form its delta. A tubular bridge unites it with the suburb of Trinquetaille on the opposite bank. The town is hemmed in on the east by the railway line from Lyons to Marseilles, on the south by the Canal de Craponne. Its streets are narrow and irregular, and, away from the promenades which border it on the south, there is little animation. In the centre of the town stand the Place de la République, a spacious square overlooked by the hôtel de ville, the museum, and the old cathedral of St Trophime, the finest Romanesque church in Provence. Founded in the 7th century, St Trophime has been several times rebuilt, and was restored in 1870. Its chief portal, which dates from the 12th century, is a masterpiece of graceful arrangement and rich carving. The interior, plain in itself, contains interesting sculpture. The choir opens into a beautiful cloister, the massive vaulting of which is supported on heavy piers adorned with statuary, between which intervene slender columns arranged in pairs and surmounted by delicately carved capitals. Two of the galleries are Romanesque, while two are Gothic. Arles has two other churches of the Romanesque period, and others of later date. The hôtel de ville, a building of the 17th century, contains the library. Its clock tower, surmounted by a statue of Mars, dates from the previous century. The museum, occupying an old Gothic church, is particularly rich in Roman remains and in early Christian sarcophagi; there is also a museum of Provençal curiosities. The tribunal of commerce and the communal college are the chief public institutions. Arles is not a busy town and its port is of little importance. There are, however, flour mills, oil and soap works, and the Paris-Lyon-Méditerranée Railway Company have large workshops. Sheep-breeding is a considerable industry in the vicinity. The women of Arles have long enjoyed a reputation for marked beauty, but the distinctive type is fast disappearing owing to their intermarriage with strangers who have immigrated to the town.

Arles still possesses many monuments of Roman architecture and art, the most remarkable being the ruins of an amphitheatre (the *Arénes*), capable of containing 25,000 spectators, which, in the 11th and 12th centuries, was flanked with massive towers, of which three are still standing. There are also a theatre, in which, besides the famous Venus of Arles, discovered in 1651, many other remains have been found; an ancient obelisk of a single block, 47 ft. high, standing since 1676 in the Place de la République; the ruins of the palace of Constantine, the forum, the thermae and the remains of the Roman ramparts and of aqueducts. There is, besides, a Roman cemetery known as the Aliscamps (*Elysii Campi*), consisting of a short avenue once bordered by tombs, of which a few still remain.

The ancient town, *Arelate*, was an important place at the time of the invasion of Julius Caesar, who made it a settlement for his veterans. It was pillaged in A.D. 270, but restored and embellished by Constantine, who made it his principal residence, and founded what is now the suburb of Trinquetaille. Under Honorius, it became the seat of the prefecture of the Gauls and one of the foremost cities in the western empire. Its bishopric founded by St Trophimus in the 1st century, was in the 5th century the primatial see of Gaul; it was suppressed in 1790. After the fall of the Roman empire the city passed into the power of the Visigoths, and rapidly declined. It was plundered in 730 by the Saracens, but in the 10th century became the capital of the kingdom of Arles (see below). In the 12th century it was a free city, governed by *apodesta* and *consuls* after the model of the Italian republics, which it also emulated in commerce and navigation. In 1251 it submitted to Charles I. of Anjou, and from that time onwards followed the fortunes of Provence. A number of ecclesiastical synods have been held at Arles, as in 314 (see below), 354, 452 and 475.

See V. Clair, *Monuments d'Arles* (1837); J.J. Estrangin, *Description de la ville d'Arles* (1845); F. Beissier, *Le Pays d'Arles* (1889); Roger Peyre, *Nîmes, Arles, Orange* (1903).

(R. Tr.)

Synod of Arles (314).—As negotiations held at Rome in October 313 had failed to settle the dispute between the Catholics and the Donatists, the emperor Constantine summoned the first general council of his western half of the empire to meet at Arles by the 1st of August following. The attempt of Seeck to date the synod 316 presupposes that the emperor was present in person, which is highly improbable. Thirty-three bishops are included in the most authentic list of signatures, among them three from Britain,—York, London and "Colonia Londinensium" (probably a corruption of Lindensium, or Lincoln, rather than of Legionensium or Caerleon-On-Usk). The twenty-two canons deal chiefly with the discipline of clergy and people. Husbands of adulterous wives are advised not to remarry during the lifetime of the guilty party. Reiteration of baptism in the name of the Trinity is forbidden. For the consecration of a bishop at least three bishops are required. It is noteworthy that British representatives assented to Canon I., providing that Easter be everywhere celebrated on the same day: the later divergence between Rome and the Celtic church is due to improvements in the *supputatio Romana* adopted at Rome in 343 and subsequently.

For the canons see Mansi ii. 471 ff.; Bruns ii. 107 ff.; Lauchert 26 ff. See also W. Smith and S. Cheetham, *Dictionary of Christian Antiquities* (Boston, 1875), i. 141 ff. (contains also notices of later synods at Arles); W. Bright, *Chapters of Early English Church History* (2nd edition, Oxford, 1888), 9 f.; Herzog-Hauck, *Realencyklopadie* (3rd edition), ii. 59, x. 238 ff.; W. Moller, *Kirchengeschichte* (2nd edition by H. von Schubert, Tubingen, 1902), i. 417. For full titles see Council.

(W. W. R.*)

ARLES, Kingdom of, the name given to the kingdom formed about 933 by the union of the old kingdoms of Provence (*q.v.*) or Cisjurane Burgundy, and Burgundy (*q.v.*) Transjurane, and bequeathed in 1032 by its last sovereign, Rudolph III., to the emperor Conrad II. It comprised the countship of Burgundy (*Franche-Comté*), part of which is now Switzerland (the dioceses of Geneva, Lausanne, Sion and part of that of Basel), the Lyonnais, and the whole of the territory bounded by the Alps, the Mediterranean and the Rhone; on the right bank of the Rhone it further included the Vivarais. It is only after the end of the 12th century that the name "kingdom of Arles" is applied to this district; formerly it was known generally as the kingdom of Burgundy, but under the Empire the name of Burgundy came to be limited more and more to the countship of Burgundy, and the districts lying beyond the Jura. The authority of Rudolph III. over the chief lords of the land, the count of Burgundy and the count of Maurienne, founder of the house of Savoy, was already merely nominal, and the Franconian emperors (1039-1125), whose visits to the country were rare and of short duration, did not establish their power any more firmly. During the first fifty years of their domination they could rely on the support of the ecclesiastical feudatories, who generally favoured their cause, but the investiture struggle, in which the prelates of the kingdom of Arles mostly sided with the pope, deprived the Germanic sovereigns even of this support. The emperors, on the other hand, realized early that their absence from the country was a grave source of weakness; in 1043 Henry III. conferred on Rudolph, count of Rheinfelden (afterwards duke of Swabia), the title of *dux et rector Burgundiae*, giving him authority over the barons of the northern part of the kingdom of Arles. Towards the middle of the 12th century Lothair II. revived this system, conferring the rectorate on Conrad of Zähringen, in whose family it remained hereditary up to the death of the last representative of the house, Berthold V., in 1218; and it was the lords of Zähringen who were foremost in defending the cause of the Empire against its chief adversaries, the counts of Burgundy. In the time of the Swabian emperors, the Germanic sovereignty in the kingdom of Arles was again, during almost the whole period, 558merely nominal, and it was only in consequence of fortuitous circumstances that certain of the heads of the Empire were able to exercise a real authority in these parts. Frederick I., by his marriage with Beatrix (1156), had become uncontested master of the countship of Burgundy; Frederick II., who was more powerful in Italy than his predecessors had been, and was extending his activities into the countries of the Levant, found Provence more accessible to his influence, thanks to the commercial relations existing between the great cities of this country and Italy and the East. Moreover, the heretics and enemies of the church, who were numerous in the south, upheld the emperor in his struggle against the pope. Henry VII. also, thanks to his good relations with the princes of Savoy, succeeded in exercising a certain influence over a part of the kingdom of Arles. The emperors further tried to make their power more effective by delegating it, first to a viceroy, William of Baux, prince of Orange (1215), then to an imperial vicar, William of Montferrat (1220), who was succeeded by Henry of Revello and William of Manupello. In spite of this, the history of the kingdom of Arles in the 13th century, and still more in the 14th, is distinguished particularly by the decline of the imperial authority and the progress of French influence in the country. In 1246 the marriage of Charles, the brother of Saint Louis, with Beatrice, the heiress to the countship of Provence, caused Provence to pass into the hands of the house of Anjou, and many plans were made to win the whole of the kingdom for a prince of this house. At the beginning of the 14th century the bishops of Lyons and Viviers recognized the suzerainty of the king of France, and in 1343 Humbert II., dauphin of Viennois, made a compact with the French king Philip VI. that on his death his inheritance should pass to a son or a grandson of the French king. Humbert, who was perhaps the most powerful noble in Arles, was induced to take this step as he had just lost his only son, and Philip had already cast covetous eyes on his lands. Then in 1349, being in want of money, he agreed to sell his possessions outright, and thus Viennois, or Dauphiné, passed into the hands of Philip's grandson, afterwards King Charles V. The emperor Charles IV. took an active part in the affairs of the kingdom, but without any consistent policy, and in 1378 he, in turn, ceded the imperial vicariate of the kingdom to the dauphin, afterwards King Charles VI. This date may be taken as marking the end of the history of the kingdom of Arles, considered as an independent territorial area.

See the monumental work of P. Fournier, *Le Royaume d'Arles et de Vienne* (Paris, 1890); Leroux, *Recherches critiques sur les relations politiques de la France avec l'Allemagne de 1292 à 1378*(Paris, 1882). For the early history of the kingdom, L. Jacob, *Le Royaume de Bourgogne sous les empereurs franconiens (1038-1129)*, (Paris, 1906). The question of the nature and extent of the rights of the Empire over the kingdom of Arles has given rise, ever since the 16th century, to numerous juridical polemics; the chief dissertations published on this subject are indicated in A. Leroux,*Bibliographie des conflits entre la France et l'Empire* (Paris, 1902).

(R. PO.)

ARLINGTON, HENRY BENNET, EARL OF (1618-1685), English statesman, son of Sir John Bennet of Dawley, Middlesex, and of Dorothy Crofts, was baptized at Little Saxham, Suffolk, in 1618, and was educated at Westminster school and Christ Church, Oxford. He gained some distinction as a scholar and a poet, and was originally destined for holy orders. In 1643 he was secretary to Lord Digby at Oxford, and was employed as a messenger between the queen and Ormonde in Ireland. Subsequently he took up arms for the king, and received a wound in the skirmish at Andover in 1644, the scar of which remained on his face through life.1 And after the defeat of the royal cause he travelled in France and Italy, joined the exiled royal family in 1650, and in 1654 became official secretary to James on Charles's recommendation, who had already been attracted by his "pleasant and agreeable humour."2 In March 1657 he was knighted, and the same year was sent as Charles's agent to Madrid, where he remained, endeavouring to obtain assistance for the royal cause, till after the Restoration. On his return to England in 1661 he was made keeper of the privy purse, and became the prime favourite. One of his duties was the procuring and management of the royal mistresses, in which his success gained him great credit. Allying himself with Lady Castlemaine, he encouraged Charles's increasing dislike to Clarendon; and he was made secretary of state in October 1662 in spite of the opposition of Clarendon, who had to find him a seat in parliament. He represented Callington from 1661 till 1665, but appears never to have taken part in debate. He served subsequently on the committees for explaining the Irish Act of Settlement and for Tangiers. In 1663 he obtained a peerage as Baron Arlington of Arlington, or Harlington, in Middlesex, and in 1667 was appointed one of the postmasters-general. The control of foreign affairs was entrusted to him, and he was chiefly responsible for the attack on the Smyrna fleet and for the first Dutch War. In 1665 he advised Charles to grant liberty of conscience, but this was merely a concession to gain money during the war; and he showed great activity later in oppressing the nonconformists. On the death of Southampton, whose administration he had attacked, his great ambition, the treasurership, was not satisfied; and on the fall of Clarendon, against whom he had intrigued, he did not, though becoming a member of the Cabal ministry, obtain the supreme influence which he had expected; for Buckingham first shared, and soon surpassed him, in the royal favour. With Buckingham a sharp rivalry sprang up, and they only combined forces when endeavouring to bring about some evil measure, such as the ruin of the great Ormonde, who was an opponent of their policy and their schemes. Another object of jealousy to Arlington was Sir William Temple, who achieved a great popular success in 1668 by the conclusion of the Triple Alliance; Arlington endeavoured to procure his removal to Madrid, and entered with alacrity into Charles's plans for destroying the whole policy embodied in the treaty, and for making terms with France. He refused a bribe from Louis XIV., but allowed his wife to accept a gift of 10,000 crowns;3 in 1670 he was the only minister besides the Roman Catholic Clifford to whom the first secret treaty of Dover (May 1670), one clause of which provided for Charles's declaration of his conversion to Romanism, was confided (seeCHARLES II.); and he was the chief actor in the deception practised upon the rest of the council.4 He supported several other pernicious measures—the scheme for rendering the king's power absolute by force of arms; the "stop of the exchequer," involving a repudiation of the state debt in 1672; and the declaration of indulgence the same year, "that we might keep all quiet at home whilst we are busy abroad."5 On the 22nd of April 1672 he was created an earl, and on the 13th of June obtained the Garter; the same month he proceeded with Buckingham on a mission, first to William at the Hague, and afterwards to Louis at Utrecht, endeavouring to force upon the Dutch terms of peace which were indignantly refused. But Arlington's support of the court policy was entirely subordinate to personal interests; and after the appointment of Clifford in November 1672 to the treasurership, his jealousy and mortification, together with his alarm at the violent opposition aroused in parliament, caused him to veer over to the other side. He advised Charles in March 1673 to submit the legality of the declaration of indulgence to the House of Lords, and supported the Test Act of the same year, which compelled Clifford to resign. He joined the Dutch party, and in order to make his peace with his new allies, disclosed the secret treaty of Dover to the staunch Protestants Ormonde and Shaftesbury.6 Arlington had, however, lost the confidence of all parties, and these efforts to procure support met with little success. On the 15th of January 1674 he was impeached by the Commons, the specific charges being "popery," corruption and the betrayal of his trust—Buckingham in his own defence having accused him the day before of being the chief instigator of the French and anti-Protestant policy, of the scheme of governing by 559the army, of responsibility for the Dutch War, and of embezzlement. But the motion for his removal, owing chiefly to the influence of his brother-in-law, the popular Lord Ossory, was rejected by 166 votes to 127. His escape could not, however, prevent his fall, and he resigned the secretaryship on the 11th of September 1674, being appointed lord chamberlain instead. In 1675 he made another attempt to gain favour with the parliament by supporting measures against France and against the Roman Catholics, and by joining in the pressure put upon Charles to remove James from the court. In November he went on a mission to the Hague, with the popular objects of effecting a peace and of concluding an alliance with William and James's daughter Mary. In this he entirely failed, and he returned home completely discredited. He had again been disappointed of the treasurership when Danby succeeded Clifford; Charles having declared "that he had too much kindness for him to let him have it, for he was not fit for the office."7His intrigues with discontented persons in parliament to stir up an opposition to his successful rival came to nothing. From this time, though lingering on at court, he possessed no influence, and was treated with scanty respect. It was safe to ridicule his person and behaviour, and it became a common jest for "some courtier to put a black patch upon his nose and strut about with a white staff in his hand in order to make the king merry at his expense."8 He was appointed a commissioner of the treasury in March 1679, was included in Sir William Temple's new modelled council the same year, and was a member of the inner cabinet which was almost immediately formed. In 1681 he was made lord lieutenant of Suffolk. He died on the 28th of July 1685, and was buried at Euston, where he had bought a large estate and had carried out extensive building operations. His residence in London was Goring House, on the site of which was built the present Arlington Street.

Arlington was a typical statesman of the Restoration, possessing outwardly an attractive personality, and according to Sir W. Temple "the greatest skill of court and the best turns of art in particular conversation,"[9] but thoroughly unscrupulous and self-seeking, without a spark of patriotism, faithless even to a bad cause, and regarding public office solely as a means of procuring pleasure and profit. His knowledge of foreign affairs and of foreign languages, gained during his residence abroad, was considerable, but long absence from England had also taught him a cosmopolitan indifference to constitutions and religions, and a careless disregard for English public opinion and the essential interests of the country. According to Clarendon, he "knew no more of the constitution and laws of England than he did of China, nor had he in truth a care or tenderness for church or state, but believed France was the best pattern in the world."[10] He was one of the chief promoters of the attempt to reintroduce into England arbitrary government after the French model, not because he imagined an absolute monarchy essential to the well-being and security of the state, but because under such an administration the favourites of a king enjoyed far greater privileges and profits than under a constitutional government. Of the same egotistical character was his religion, towards which his attitude was similar to that of Charles II. himself. He was credited with having inclined the king towards Romanism. Before the Restoration he had attended mass with the king abroad, and in opposition to Lord Bristol had urged Charles to declare publicly his conversion in order to obtain the long-expected succour from the foreign powers. But his religion sat lightly upon him as it did upon his master, and it was often convenient to disguise it. Like the king he continued to profess and practise Protestantism, and spent large sums in restoring the church at Euston; and, unlike Clifford, he took the Test in 1673 and remained in office, successfully concealing his faith till on his deathbed, when he declared himself an adherent of Roman Catholicism.[11]

He married Isabella of Beerwaert, daughter of Louis of Nassau, by whom he had one daughter, Isabella, who married Henry, duke of Grafton, the natural son of Charles II. and Lady Castlemaine.

AUTHORITIES.—In addition to those mentioned above, see *Biographia Britannica* (Kippis), accurate and careful, but too partial, and written without complete knowledge of Arlington's career; Wood's *Fasti Oxonienses* (Bliss), ii. 274; *Hist. of Great Britain* by J. Macpherson (1776), i. 132-133; *Lauderdale Papers*(Camden Soc. N.S., vols. 34, 36, 38), and MSS. in Brit. Mus.;*Original Letters of Sir R. Fanshaw* (1724); *Letters from the Secretaries of State to Francis Parry* (1817); *Add. MSS. Brit. Mus.*indexes; *Cat. of State Pap. Dom.*, and *Hist. MSS. Comm.—MSS. of Marquis of Ormonde, and Duke of Buccleugh at Montagu House*, ii. 49.

(P. C. Y.)

1See his portrait in the earl of Arlington's *Letters to Sir W. Temple*, by Tho. Babington (1701).

2Clarendon's *Life and Continuation*, 397.

3*Memoirs of Great Britain and Ireland*, by Sir John Dalrymple (1790), i. 125.

4*Ibid.* 114 et seq.

5Arlington to Sir B. Gascoyn, in J.T. Brown's *Miscellanea Aulica*(1702), 66.

6On the authority of Colbert, 20th November 1673; Dalrymple's*Memoirs*, i. 131.

7James's statement in Macpherson's *Orig. Pap.* i. 67.

8Eachard's *History of England* (1720), 911.

9*Memoirs of W. Temple*, ed. by T.P. Courtenay, ii. 27.

10*Life and Con.* 404.

11Cf. North's *Examen*, 26; Dalrymple's *Mem.* (1790) i. 40; Pepys's*Diary* (Feb. 17, 1663); *Cat. of Clarendon St. Pap.* iii. 295; T. Carte's *Life of the Duke of Ormonde* (1851), iv. 109.

ARLINGTON, a township of Middlesex county in E. Massachusetts, U.S.A. Pop. (1890) 5629; (1900) 8603, of whom 2387 were foreign-born; (1910 census) 11,187. Area, 5½ sq. m. It is served by the Boston & Maine railway. It has pleasant residential villages (Arlington, Arlington Heights, &c.) with attractive environs, and there is an excellent public library (the Robbins library). At Arlington Heights there are several well-known sanatoriums. Spy Pond (about 100 acres) is one of the prettiest bodies of water in the vicinity of Boston. Arlington is an important centre for market-gardening (in hot-houses), and along Mill Brook, in the township, are several factories, including chrome works, a large mill and a manufactory of pianoforte cases. In 1762 Arlington was made a "precinct" of Cambridge (of which it was a part from 1635 to 1807) under the name of Menotomy. In 1807 it became a separate township under the name (retained until 1867) of West Cambridge.

See B. and W.R. Cutter, *History of the Town of Arlington ... 1637-1879* (Boston, 1880); and C.S. Parker, *The Town of Arlington, Past and Present* (Arlington, 1907).

ARLON, the chief town of the Belgian province of Luxemburg, situated on a hill about 1240 ft. above the sea. Pop. (1904) 10,894. It is a very ancient town, and in the time of the Romans was called Orolaunum, being a station on the Antoninian way connecting Reims and Trèves. Authorities dispute as to the origin of the name, some tracing it to *Ara Lunae*, a temple of Diana having been erected here, while others more plausibly derive it from the Celtic words *ar* (mount) and *lun* (wooded). Nowadays the woods have disappeared, and Arlon is chiefly notable for the extensive views obtainable from the church of St Donat which crowns the peak. Arlon is no longer fortified. When Vauban by order of Louis XIV. turned it into a fortress in 1671 great damage was done to the old Roman wall, the foundations of which were practically intact. In the local museum are many Roman antiquities collected on the spot, including several large sculptural stones similar to the celebrated monument at Igel near Trèves. In the middle ages Arlon was the seat of a powerful countship (later marquisate), held after 1235 by the dukes of Luxemburg. As an important strategic position it was several times seized by the French,*e.g.* in 1647 and 1651.

ARM (a common Teutonic word; the Indo-European root is *ar*, to join or fit; cf. the Lat. *armus*, shoulder, and the plural word *arma*, weapons, Gr. ἁρμός, joint, and the reduplicated ἀραρίσκειν, to join), the human upper limb from the shoulder to the wrist, and the fore limb of an animal. (See ANATOMY: *Superficial and Artistic*, andSKELETON: *Appendicular*.) The word is also used of any projecting limb, as of a crane, or balance, of a branch of a tree, and so, in a transferred sense, of the branch of a river or a nerve. Through the Fr.*armes*, from the Lat. *arma*, and so in English usually in the plural "arms," comes the use of the word for weapons of offence and defence, and in many expressions such as "men-at-arms," "assault-at-arms," and the like, and for the various branches, artillery, cavalry, infantry, of which an army is composed, the "arms of the service." "Arms" or "armorial bearings" are the heraldic devices displayed by knights in battle on the defensive armour or embroidered on the surcoat worn over the armour and hence called "coats of arms." These became hereditary and thus are borne by families, and similar insignia are used by nations, cities, episcopal sees and corporations generally. (See HERALDRY.)

560

ARMADA, THE. The Spanish or Invincible Armada was the great fleet (in Spanish, *armada*) sent against England by Philip II. in 1588. The marquis of Santa Cruz, to whom the command had first been given, died on the 9th of February 1588 (according to the Gregorian calendar then used by Spain; on the 31st of January by the Julian calendar used in England; the other dates given in this article will be in Old Style, or Julian calendar). Santa Cruz was succeeded by Don Alonso Perez de Guzman, duke of Medina Sidonia, a noble of large estate, but of no experience or capacity, who took the command unwillingly, and only on the reiterated order of the king. The fleet was collected at Lisbon, after many delays, and sailed on the 20th of May 1588. Its nominal strength was 132 vessels, of 59,190 tons, carrying 21,621 soldiers and 8066 sailors. But from a third to a half of the vessels were transports, galleys or very small boats, and some of them never reached the Channel. The effective force was far below the paper strength. On the 10th of June, when the Armada had rounded Cape Finisterre, it was scattered by squalls. Some of the vessels went on to the appointed rendezvous at the Scilly Isles, but the majority anchored on the north coast of Spain. Medina Sidonia, who found many defects in his fleet, did not finally sail till the 12th of July. On the English side all the royal navy, and such armed merchant ships as could be obtained from the ports, had been collected under the command of the lord high admiral Howard of Effingham, who had with him Hawkins, Drake and Frobisher as subordinate admirals. The number of vessels is put at 197, but the majority were very small. It is impossible to state with confidence what were the relative numbers of guns carried by the two fleets. The Spaniards had more pieces, but their gunnery was inferior. The English fleet carried 16,000 or 17,000 men, of whom the large majority were sailors. About 100 of their ships were at Plymouth with the lord high admiral. The others were in the Downs with Lord Henry Seymour and Sir William Winter, to co-operate with a Dutch squadron under Justinus of Nassau in blockading the Flemish ports, then occupied by the Spanish army of the duke of Parma. The object was to prevent the proposed junction of the forces of Medina Sidonia and Parma. On the 20th of July the Armada was seen off the Lizard. It sailed past Plymouth, and was followed by the English fleet. The Spaniards, who were heavy sailers, and were hampered by the transports,

190

were much harassed by the more active English, and were defeated in all their attempts to board, which it was their wish to do in order to make use of their superior numbers of men. The flagship of the squadron of Andalucia, "Nuestra Señora del Rosario," commanded by Don Pedro de Valdes, was crippled, fell behind and had to surrender. On the 25th of July, when the fleets were near the Isle of Wight, a shift of the wind offered the Spaniards a chance of bringing on a close action, but it soon changed again. The English fleet, of which part had been in some danger, escaped uninjured, and the Spaniards stood on. They anchored on the 26th of July at Calais. The duke of Medina Sidonia now sent an officer to Parma, calling on him to come to sea and join in a landing on the shore of England. But Parma could not leave port in face of Justinus of Nassau's squadron. While these messages were going and coming, Lord Howard had been joined by Lord Henry Seymour and Sir William Winter from the Downs. A council of war was held, to decide on the measures to be taken to assail the Spaniards at Calais. The course taken was to send fireships among them. On the night of the 28th of July the fireships were sent in, and produced an utter panic in the Armada. Most of the Spanish vessels slipped their cables and ran to sea. Others weighed anchor, and escaped in a more orderly style. One great vessel ran ashore and was taken possession of by the English, who were however compelled to give her up by the French governor of Calais. On the 29th of July the scattered Spaniards, who were quite unable to restore order, were attacked by the English off Gravelines. The engagement was hot, and, though the English did not succeed in taking any of the Spaniards, they destroyed some of them, and their superiority in sailing force and gunnery was now so obvious that the duke of Medina Sidonia lost heart. His large vessels were indeed so helpless that only a timely shift of the wind saved many of them from drifting on to the banks of Flanders. Officers and men alike were completely discouraged. It was now recognized that an invasion of England could not be carried out in face of the more active English fleet and the proved impossibility of bringing about the proposed union with Parma's army. Suggestions were made that the Armada should sail to Hamburg, refit there, and renew the attack. But by this time the Spanish force was incapable of energetic action. Medina Sidonia and his council could think of nothing but of a return to Spain. As the wind was westerly, and the English fleet barred the way, it was impossible to sail down the Channel. The only alternative was to take the route between the north of Scotland and Norway. So the Armada sailed to the north. Lord Howard followed, after detaching Lord Henry Seymour to remain in the Downs. He watched the Spaniards to the Firth of Forth. The English had at that time little knowledge of the seas beyond the Firth, and they were beginning to run short of food and ammunition. On the 2nd of August, therefore, they gave up the pursuit. Medina Sidonia continued to the north, till his pilots told him that it was safe to turn to the west. Up to this time the loss of the Spaniards in ships had not been considerable. If the weather had been that of a normal summer, they would probably have reached home with no greater loss of men than was usually inflicted on all fleets of the age by scurvy and fever. But the summer of 1588 was marked by a succession of gales of unprecedented violence. The damaged and weakened Spanish ships, which were from the first greatly undermanned in sailors, were unable to contend with the storms. It is not possible to give the details of the disasters which overtook them. Nineteen of them are known to have been wrecked on the coasts of Scotland and Ireland. The crews who fell into the hands of the English officers in Ireland were put to the sword. Many more of them disappeared at sea. Of the total number of the vessels originally collected for the invasion of England one-half, if not more, perished, and the crews of those which escaped were terribly diminished by scurvy and starvation.

The failure of the Armada was mainly due to its own interior weakness, and as a military operation the English victory was less glorious than some other less renowned achievements of the British fleet. But the repulse of the great Spanish armament was an event of the first historical importance. It marked the final failure of King Philip II. of Spain to establish the supremacy of the Habsburg dynasty and of the Church of Rome, which he considered as being in a peculiar sense his charge, in Europe. From that time forward no serious attempt to invade England was, or could be, made. It became therefore the unconquerable supporter of that part of Europe which had thrown off the authority of the pope. The Armada had much of the character of a crusade. Though Philip II. had political reasons for hostility to Queen Elizabeth, they were so intimately bound up with the struggle between the Reformation and the Counter Reformation that the secular and the religious elements of the conflict cannot be separated from one another. The struggle was therefore not one between armed forces in national rivalry alone. It was a trial of strength between two widely different conceptions of life and of the state—between the medieval and the modern worlds. The volunteers of all ranks who came forward in large numbers on both sides were fighting for a religious cause as well as for the interests of their respective peoples.

AUTHORITIES.—The English side of the story of the Armada can best be studied in the *State Papers relating to the Defeat of the Spanish Armada*, edited by Sir J.K. Laughton, and printed for the Navy Records Society (London, 1894). The Spanish side will be found in *La Armada Invencible*, by Captain Cesareo Fernandez Duro (Madrid, 1884). Froude summarized the work of Captain Fernandez Duro in his brilliant *Spanish Story of the Armada*(London, 1892).

(D. H.)

ARMADILLO, the Spanish designation for the small mail-clad Central and South American mammals of the order Edentata, constituting the family *Dasypodidae*. The armature consists of a bony case, partly composed of solid buckler-like plates, and partly of movable transverse bands, the latter differing in number with 56 the species, and giving to the body a considerable degree of flexibility. The bony plates are overlain by horny scales. Armadillos are omnivorous, feeding on roots, insects, worms, reptiles and carrion, and are mostly, though not universally, nocturnal. They are harmless and inoffensive creatures, offering no resistance when caught; their principal means of escape being the extraordinary rapidity with which they burrow in the ground, and the tenacity with which they retain their hold in their subterranean retreats. Notwithstanding the shortness of their limbs they run with rapidity. Most of the species are esteemed good eating by the natives of the countries in which they live. They are all inhabitants of the open plains or the forests of the tropical and temperate parts of South America, with the exception of a few species which range as far north as Texas. The largest species is the giant armadillo (*Priodon gigas*), measuring nearly a yard long, from the forests of Surinam and Brazil; while one of the smallest is *Dasypus minutus*, a near ally of the larger *D. sexcinctus*. The peba (*Tatusia novemcincta*) represents a group with a large number of movable bands in the armour; while the apar (*Tolypeutes tricinctus*) and the other members of the same genus are remarkable for their power of rolling themselves up into balls. For the distinctive characters of these and the other genera see EDENTATA.

Peba Armadillo (*Tatusia novemcincta*).

ARMAGEDDON, a name occurring in the Authorized Version of the English Bible in Rev. xvi. 16. The Revised Version has Harmagedon. The form is commonly regarded as the Greek equivalent of the Hebrew *har megiddōn*, the mountain district of Megiddo. The writer is describing the place where the last decisive battle was to be fought at the Day of Judgment, and Harmagedon may have been chosen as the name because the district about Megiddo had been on several occasions the scene of great battles (cf. Judg. iv. 6 ff., v. 19). It has, however, been suggested in the *Zeitschrift für die Alttestamentliche Wissenschaft*, vii. 170 (1887), that the name is for *har migdo*, "his fruitful mountain"—the mountain land of Israel. Prof. Cheyne (*Encyc. Bibl.* s.v.) again, following suggestions of H. Gunkel, H. Zimmern and P. Jensen, compares the dragon of the Apocalypse with the Babylonian Tiãmat, thinks that some myth is referred to, and finds the μαγεδων of Άρμαγεδων in the divine name Ύεσεμμιγαδων, a Babylonian god of the underworld. The name of the place where Tiãmat was defeated by Marduk perhaps included that of a god of the underworld. (See ANTICHRIST.) From the application of the word Armageddon to the great battle of the End of Time comes the use of the phrase "an Armageddon" to express any great slaughter or final conflict.

ARMAGH, an inland county of Ireland, in the province of Ulster, bounded N. by Lough Neagh, E. by Co. Down, S. by Louth and W. by Monaghan and Tyrone. The area is 327,704 acres, or about 512 sq. m. The general surface of the county is gently undulating and pleasantly diversified; but in the northern extremity, on the borders of Lough Neagh, there is a considerable tract of low, marshy land, and the southern border of the county is occupied by a barren range of hills, the highest of which, Slieve Gullion, attains an elevation of 1893 ft. In the western portion of the county are the Few Mountains, a chain of abrupt hills mostly incapable of cultivation. The county is well watered by numerous streams. The principal are the Callan, the Tynan and the Tallwater, flowing into the Blackwater, which, after forming the boundary between this county and Tyrone, empties itself into the south-western angle of Lough Neagh. The Tara and Newtown-Hamilton, the Creggan and the Fleury, flow into the bay of Dundalk. The Cam or Camlin joins the Bann, which, crossing the north-western corner of the county, falls into Lough

Neagh to the east of the Blackwater. The Newry Canal, communicating with Carlingford Lough at Warrenpoint, 6 m. below Newry, proceeds northward through Co. Armagh for about 21 m., joining the Bann at Whitecoat. The Ulster Canal begins at Charlemont on the river Blackwater, near its junction with Lough Neagh, proceeding through the western border of the county, and passing thence to the south-west by Monaghan and Clones into Upper Lough Erne, after a course of 48 m. Part of Lough Neagh is in the county, and there are many small loughs, such as Gullion, Cam and Ross.

Geology.—The flat shore of Lough Neagh in the north is due to the thick deposit of pale-coloured clays with lignites, which are probably of Pliocene age, and indicate a reduction of the area of the lake in still later times. Between this lowland and Armagh city, the early Cainozoic basalts form slightly higher ground, while on the west a strip of Trias appears, overlying Carboniferous Limestone. A rough conglomerate containing blocks of this latter rock forms the hills on which Armagh itself is built; this outlier is probably Permian. The Carboniferous Limestone beneath it and around it is red-brown instead of grey, and is famous for its richness in fish remains. A hummocky irregular country spreads southward, where the Silurian axis is encountered, in continuation of the southern uplands of Scotland. Slates and fine-grained sandstones appear here freely through the glacial drift. In the south the granite core of this upland is revealed, and is quarried extensively about Bessbrook. It is penetrated by far younger intrusive masses at Slieve Gullion and Forkill. These rocks, which include some highly siliceous lavas, form part of the Eocene series that is so conspicuously displayed above Carlingford in Co. Louth. Lead-veins have been worked in various parts of the county from time to time.

Industries.—The soil of the northern portion of the county is a rich brown loam, on a substratum of clay or gravel. Towards Charlemont there is much reclaimable bog resting on a limestone substratum. The eastern portion of the county is generally of a light friable soil; the southern portion rocky and barren, with but little bog except in the neighbourhood of Newtown-Hamilton. The climate of Armagh is considered to be one of the most genial in Ireland, and less rain is supposed to fall in this than in any other county. Only about one-twentieth of the land is naturally barren, and Armagh offers a relatively large area of cultivable soil. Agriculture, however, is not far advanced, yet owing to the linen industry the inhabitants are generally in circumstances of comparative comfort. The principal crops are oats and potatoes, but all grain crops are decreasing, and flax, formerly grown to a considerable extent, is now practically neglected. The acreage under pasture slightly exceeds that of tillage. Cattle, sheep, pigs and poultry show a general increase in numbers. The principal manufacture, and that which has given a peculiar tone to the character of the population, is that of linen, though it has somewhat declined in modern times. It is not necessary to the promotion of this manufacture that the spinners and weavers should be congregated in large towns, or united in crowded and unwholesome factories. On the contrary, most of its branches can be carried on in the cottages of the peasantry. The men devote to the loom those hours which are not required for the cultivation of their little farms; the women spin and reel the yarn during the intervals of their other domestic occupations. Smooth lawns, pure springs and the open sky are necessary for perfecting the bleaching process. Hence the numerous bleachers dwell in the country with their assistants and machinery. Such is the effect 562of this combination of agricultural occupations with domestic manufactures that the farmers are more than competent to supply the resident population of the county with vegetable, though not with animal food; and some of the less crowded and less productive parts of Ulster receive from Armagh a considerable supply of oats, barley and flour. Apples are grown in such quantities as to entitle the county to the title applied to it, the orchard of Ireland.

Communications are monopolized by the Great Northern railway company, whose main line from Belfast divides at Portadown, sending off lines to Omagh, to Clones and to Dublin. A branch from Omagh joins the Dublin line to Goraghwood, and from this line there is a branch to Newry in Co. Down. An electric tram-way connects Bessbrook, a town with important linen manufactures and granite quarries, with Newry.

Population and Administration.—The population (72,286 in 1891; 65,619 in 1901) shows a heavy decrease, though emigration affects it less seriously than the majority of Irish counties. Of the total about 45% are Roman Catholics, 32% Protestant Episcopalians, and 16% Presbyterians, the Roman Catholic faith prevailing in the mountainous districts and the Protestant in the towns and lowlands. About 74% of the whole constitutes the rural population. The chief towns are Armagh (a city and the county town, pop. 7588), Lurgan (11,782), Portadown (10,092), Tanderagee (1427), Bessbrook (2977) and Keady (1466). Armagh is divided into eight baronies, and contains twenty-five parishes and parts of parishes, the greater number of which are in the Protestant and Roman Catholic dioceses of Armagh, and a few in the Roman Catholic diocese of Dromore. The constabulary has its headquarters at Armagh, the county being divided into five districts. Assizes are held at Armagh, and quarter sessions at Armagh, Ballybot, Lurgan,

Markethill and Newtown-Hamilton. The parliamentary divisions are three: mid, north and south, each returning one member.

History and Antiquities.—Armagh, together with Louth, Monaghan and some smaller districts, formed part of a territory called Orgial or Urial, which was long subject to the occasional incursions of the Danes. The county was made shire ground in 1586, and called Armagh after the city by Sir John Perrott. When James I. proceeded to plant with English and Scottish colonists the vast tracts escheated to the crown in Ulster, the whole of the arable and pasture land in Armagh, estimated at 77,800 acres, was to have been allotted in sixty-one portions. Nineteen of these, comprising 22,180 acres, were to have been allotted to the church, and forty-two, amounting to 55,620 acres, to English and Scottish colonists, servitors, native Irish and four corporate towns—the swordsmen to be dispersed throughout Connaught and Munster. This project was not strictly adhered to in Co. Armagh, nor were the Irish swordsmen or soldiers transplanted into Connaught and Munster from this and some other counties. The antiquities consist of cairns and tumuli; the remains of the fortress of Emain near the city of Armagh (*q.v.*), once the residence of the kings of Ulster; and Danes Cast, an extensive fortification in the south-east of the county, near Poyntzpass, extending into Co. Down. Spears, battle-axes, collars, rings, amulets, medals of gold, ornaments of silver, jet and amber, &c., have also been found in various places. The religious houses were at Armagh, Killevy, Kilmore, Stradhailloyse and Tahenny. Of military antiquities the most remarkable are Tyrone's ditches, near Poyntzpass; and the pass of Moyry, the entry into the county from the south, which was fiercely contested by the Irish in 1595 and 1600, is defended by a castle. The summit of Slieve Gullion is crowned by a large cairn, which forms the roof of a singular cavern of artificial construction, probably an early burial-place.

ARMAGH, a city and market town, and the county town of Co. Armagh, Ireland, in the mid parliamentary division, 89½ m. N.N.W. of Dublin by the Great Northern railway, at the junction of the Belfast-Clones line. Pop. (1901) 7588. It is said to derive its name of *Ard-macha*, the Hill of Macha, from Queen Macha of the Golden Hair, who flourished in the middle of the 4th century B.C. but earlier it was named from its situation on the sides of a steep hill called Drumsailech, or the Hill of Sallows, which rises in the midst of a fertile plain near the Callan stream. Of high antiquity, and, like many other Irish towns, claiming (with considerable probability) to have been founded by St Patrick in the 5th century, it long possessed the more important distinction of being the metropolis of Ireland; and, as the seat of a flourishing college, was greatly frequented by students from other lands, among whom the English and Scots were said to have been so numerous as to give the name of Trian-Sassanagh, or Saxon Street, to one of the quarters of the city. St Patrick's bell, long preserved at Armagh, the oldest Irish relic of its kind, is now, with its shrine of the year 1091, preserved in the museum of the Royal Irish Academy at Dublin. Of a synod that was held at Armagh as early as 448, there is an interesting memorial in the *Book of Armagh*, an Irish MS. dating about A.D. 800. Exposed to the successive calamities of the Danish incursions, the English conquest and the English wars, and at last deserted by its bishops, who retired to Drogheda, the venerable city sank into an insignificant collection of cabins, with a dilapidated cathedral. From this state of decay, however, it was raised, in the second half of the 18th century, by the unwearied exertions of Archbishop Richard Robinson, 1st Lord Rokeby (1709-1794), which, seconded by similar devotion on the part of succeeding archbishops of the Beresford family, notably Archbishop Lord John George Beresford (1773-1862), made of Armagh one of the best built and most respectable towns in the country. As the ecclesiastical metropolis and seat of an archbishop (Primate of all Ireland) in both the Protestant and Roman organizations, it possesses two cathedrals and two archiepiscopal palaces. As the county town Armagh has a court-house, a prison, a lunatic asylum and a county infirmary. Besides these there is a fever hospital, erected by Lord John George Beresford; a college, which Primate Robinson was anxious to raise to the rank of a university; a public library founded by him, an observatory, which has become famous from the efficiency of its astronomers; a number of churches and schools, and barracks. Almost all the buildings are built of the limestone of the district, but the Anglican cathedral is of red sandstone. It stands boldly on the top of the hill, a cruciform structure dating from the 13th, but practically rebuilt in the 18th century, in accordance with its original plan. The Roman Catholic cathedral is in the Decorated style, and was consecrated in 1873. Armagh was a parliamentary borough until 1885; and, having been incorporated in 1613, so remained until 1835. The administration is in the hands of an urban district council. Two miles W. of Armagh is Emain, Emania, or Navan Fort, with large entrenchments and mounds, the site of a royal palace of Ulster, founded by that Queen Macha who gave her name to the city. In A.D. 335 it was destroyed during the inroad on the defeat of the king of Ulster by the three brothers Colla, cousins of Muredach, king of Ireland. Armagh itself fell before the king Brian Boroime, who was buried here; and before Edward Bruce in 1315, while previous to the English war after the Reformation, it had witnessed the struggles of Shane O'Neill (1564).

ARMAGNAC, formerly a province of France and the most important fief of Gascony, now wholly comprised in the department of Gers (*q.v.*). In the 15th century, when it attained its greatest extent, it included, besides Armagnac, the neighbouring territories of Fezensac, Fezensaguet, Pardiac, Pays de Gaure, Rivière Basse, Eauzan and Lomagne, and stretched from the Garonne to the Adour. Armagnac is a region of hills ranging to a height of 1000 ft., watered by the river Gers and other rivers which descend fanwise from the plateau of Lannemezan. On the slope of its hills grow the grapes from which the famous Armagnac brandy is made. In Roman Gaul this territory formed part of the diocese of Auch (*civitas Ausciorum*), which corresponded roughly with the later duchy of Gascony (*q.v.*). About the end of the 9th century Fezensac (*comitatus Fedentiacus*), in circumstances of which no trustworthy record remains, was erected into an hereditary countship. This latter was in its turn divided, the south-western portion becoming, about 960, the countship of Armagnac (*pagus Armaniacus*). The domain of 563this countship, at first very limited in extent, continued steadily to increase in size, and about 1140 Count Gerald III. added the whole of Fezensac to his possessions. Under the English rule the counts of Armagnac were turbulent and untrustworthy vassals; and the administration of the Black Prince, tending to favour the towns of Aquitaine at the expense of the nobles, drove them to the side of France. The complaint against the English prince which Count John I., in defiance of the treaty of Brétigny, himself carried to Paris, was the principal cause of the resumption of hostilities of 1369, and of the incessant defeats sustained by the English until the accession of their king Henry V.

At that moment Count Bernard VII. was all-powerful at the French court; and Charles of Orleans, in order to be able to avenge his father, Louis of Orleans, who had been assassinated in 1407 by John the Fearless, duke of Burgundy, married Bonne, Bernard's daughter. This was the origin of the political party known as "the Armagnacs." With the object of combating the duke of Burgundy's preponderant influence, a league was formed at Gien, including the duke of Orleans and his father-in-law, the dukes of Berry, Bourbon and Brittany, the count of Alençon and all the other discontented nobles. Bernard VII. ravaged the environs of Paris; and the treaty of Bicêtre (November 2, 1410) only suspended hostilities for a few months, war breaking out afresh in the spring of 1411. Paris sided with the duke of Burgundy, and at his instigation Charles VII. collected an army to besiege the allies in Bourges. The peace of Bourges, confirmed at Auxerre on the 22nd of August, put an end to the war. Paris was dominated at that time by the party of the "butchers," or *Cabochiens*, which had been organized and armed by the count of Saint-Pol, brother-in-law of John the Fearless. But their excesses, and in particular the Cabochien ordinance of the 25th of May 1413, aroused public indignation; a reaction took place, and in the month of August the Armagnacs in their turn became masters of the government and of the king. The duke of Burgundy, besieged in Arras, only obtained peace (treaty of Arras, September 4, 1414), on condition of not returning to Paris.

Several months later Henry V. declared war against France; and when, in August 1415, the English landed in Normandy, the Armagnacs and Burgundians united against them, but were defeated in the battle of Agincourt (October 25, 1415). John the Fearless then began negotiations with the English, while Bernard VII., appointed constable in place of the count of Saint-Pol, who had been killed at Agincourt, returned to defend Paris. However, the excesses committed by the Armagnacs incensed the populace, and John the Fearless, who was ravaging the surrounding districts, re-entered the capital on the 29th of May 1418, in consequence of the treason of Perrinet Leclerc. On the 12th of June Bernard VII. and the members of his party were massacred. From this time onward the Armagnac party, with the dauphin, afterwards King Charles VII., at its head, was the national party, while the Burgundians united with the English. This division in France continued until the treaty of Arras, on the 21st of September 1435. The rivalry of the Burgundians and Armagnacs brought terrible disasters upon France, and for many years afterwards the name of "Armagnacs" was bestowed upon the bands of adventurers who were as much to be feared as the *Grandes Compagnies* of the preceding age.

In 1444-45 the emperor Frederick III. of Germany obtained from Charles VII. a large army of Armagnacs to enforce his claims in Switzerland, and the war which ensued took the name of the Armagnac war (*Armagnakenkrieg*). In Germany the name of the foreigners, who were completely defeated in the battle of St Jakob on the Birs, not far from Basel, was mockingly corrupted into *Arme Jacken*, Poor Jackets, or *Arme Gecken*, Poor Fools.

On the death of Charles of Armagnac, in 1497, the countship was united to the crown by King Charles VII., but was again bestowed on Charles, the nephew of that count, by Francis I., who at the same time gave him his sister Margaret in marriage. After the death of her husband, by whom she had no children, she married Henry of Albret, king of Navarre; and thus the countship of Armagnac came back to the French crown along with the other dominions of Henry IV. In 1645 Louis XIV. erected a countship of Armagnac in favour of Henry of Lorraine, count of Harcourt, in whose family it continued till the Revolution. James of Armagnac, grandson of Bernard VII., was made duke of Nemours in 1462, and was succeeded in the dukedom by his second son, John, who died without issue, and his third son, Louis, in whom the house of Armagnac became extinct in 1503.

In 1789 Armagnac was a province forming part of the *Gouvernement-général* of Guienne and Gascony; it was divided into two parts, High or White Armagnac, with Auch for capital, and Low or Black Armagnac. At the Revolution the whole of the original Armagnac was included in the department of Gers.

For authorities see U. Chevalier, *Répertoire des sources hist, du moyen âge*, s. Armagnac (Montbéliard, 1894). For the Armagnacs see Paul Dognon, "Les Armagnacs et les Bourguignons, le comte de Foix et le dauphin en Languedoc" (1416-1420) in *Annales du Midi* (1889); Rameau, "Guerre des Armagnacs dans le Mâconnais" (1418-1435) in the *Rév. soc. lit. de l'Ain* (1884); Berthold Zeller, *Les Armagnacs et les Bourguignons, la Commune de 1413*; E. Wulcker, *Urkunden und Schreiben betreffend den Zug der Armagnaken* (Frankfort, 1873); Witte, *Die Armagnaken im Elsass, 1439-1445* (Strassburg, 1889).

ARMATOLES (Gr. ἀρματωλός, a man-at-arms), the name given to some Greeks who discharged certain military and police functions under the Turkish government. When the Turks under Sultan Mahommed II. conquered Greece in the 15th century, many of the Greeks fled into the mountainous districts of Macedonia and northern Greece, and maintained a harassing warfare with the conquerors of their country. These men were called *Klephts* (modern Gr. κλέφτης, ancient κλέπτης, a thief, a brigand), and during the 16th century the Turkish pashas came to terms with some of them, and these men were allowed to retain their local customs, and were confirmed in the possession of certain districts, while in return they undertook some duties, such as the custody of the highroads. Those who accepted these terms were called *armatoles*, and the districts in which they lived *armatoliks*. Strengthened by a considerable number of Christian Albanians, they rendered good service in defending Greece, and to some extent repressed the ravages of the *Klephts*; but their power and independence were disliked by the Turks. After the peace of Belgrade in 1739 (between Austria and Turkey), the Turkish government sought to weaken the position of the *armatoles*. Their privileges were restricted, Mahommedan Albanians were introduced into the *armatoliks*, and towards the end of the 18th century their numbers were seriously reduced. Irritated by this policy the *armatoles* rendered considerable service to Ali Pasha of Iannina in his struggle with the Turks in 1820-22, and afforded valuable assistance to their countrymen during the Greek war of independence in 1830.

ARMATURE (from Lat. *armatura*, armour), a covering for defence. In zoology the word is used of the bony shell of the armadillo. In architecture it is applied to the iron stays by which the lead lights are secured in windows. (See STANCHION and SADDLE:*Saddle-Bars*.) In magnetism Dr William Gilbert applied the term to the piece of soft iron with which he "armed" or capped the lodestone in order to increase its power. It is also used for the "keeper" or piece of iron which is placed across the poles of a horse-shoe magnet, and held in place by magnetic attraction, in order to complete the magnetic circuit and preserve the magnetism of the steel; and hence, in dynamo-electric machinery, for the portion which is attracted by the electromagnet, as the moving part of an electric motor, or, by extension, the moving part of a dynamo (*q.v.*).

ARMAVIR, (1) The ruins of the old capital of Armenia, on the S.E. slope of the extinct volcano Ala-geuz, according to legend, built by Armais, a grandson of Haik, in 1980 B.C., and the capital of the Armenian kings till the 2nd century A.D. Now a small village, Tapadibi, occupies its seat. (2) A district town of Russia, northern Caucasia, province of Kuban, on Kuban river, and on the main line of the Caucasian railway, 40 m. by rail west of Stavropol, built in 1848 for the settlement of Armenian mountaineers, and now a well-built, growing town with 8000 inhabitants, the merchants of which carry on a lively trade.

564

ARMENIA (old Persian *Armina*, Armenian *Hayasdan*, or *Hayq*), the popular modern name of a district south of the Caucasus and Black Sea, which formed part of the ancient Armenian kingdom. The name, which first occurs in the cuneiform inscriptions of Darius Hystaspis, supplanted the earlier Urardhu, or Ararat, but its origin is unknown. In its widest extent Armenia stretched from 37° to 49° E. long., and from 37½° to 41½° N. lat.; but this area was never, or only for a brief period, united under one king. Armenia is now divided between Persia, Russia and Turkey, and the three boundaries have a common point on Little Ararat.

Geographically, Armenia is a continuation westward of the great Iranian plateau. On the north it descends abruptly to the Black Sea; on the south it breaks down in rugged terraces to the lowlands of Mesopotamia; and on the east and west it sinks more gradually to the lower plateaus of Persia and Asia Minor. Above the general level of the plateau, 6000 ft., rise bare ranges of mountains, which run from north-east to south-west at an altitude of 8000-12,000 ft., and culminate in Ararat, 17,000 ft. Between the ranges are broad elevated valleys, through which the rivers of the plateau flow before entering the rugged gorges that convey their waters to lower levels. Geologically, Armenia consists of archaic rocks upon which, towards the north, are superimposed Palaeozoic, and towards the south later sedimentary rocks. The last have been pierced by volcanic outbursts that extend southward to Lake Van. Amongst the higher mountains are the two Ararats; Ala-geuz Dagh, north of the Aras; Bingeul Dagh, south of Erzerum; and the peaks near Lake Van. The rivers are the Euphrates, Tigris, Aras, Churuk Su (Chorokh) and Kelkit Irmak, all rising on the plateau. The more important lakes are Van, 5100 ft., about twice the size of the Lake of Geneva, and Urmia, 4000 ft., both salt; Gokcha or Sevan, 5870 ft., discharging into the Aras; and Chaldir, into the Kars Chai. The aspect of the plateau is dreary and monotonous. The valleys are wide expanses of arable land, and the hills are for the most part grass-covered and treeless. But the gorges of the Euphrates and Tigris, and their tributaries, cannot be surpassed in wildness and grandeur. The climate is varied. In the higher districts the winter is long and the cold severe; whilst the summer is short, dry and hot. In Erzerum the temperature ranges from −22° to 84° F., and snow sometimes falls in June. In the valley of the Aras, and in the western and southern districts, the climate is more moderate. Most of the towns lie high, from 4000 to 6000 ft. The villages are usually built on gentle slopes, in which the houses are partially excavated as a protection against the severity of the weather. Many of the early towns were on or near the Araxes, and amongst their ruins are the remains of churches which throw light on the history of Christian architecture in the East. Armenia is rich in mineral wealth, and there are many hot and cold mineral springs. The vegetation varies according to the locality. Cereals and hardy fruits grow on the higher ground, whilst rice is cultivated in the hot, well-watered valley of the Araxes. The summer is so hot that the vine grows at much higher altitudes than it does in western Europe, and the cotton tree and all southern fruit trees are cultivated in the deeper valleys. On the fine pasture lands which now support the flocks of the Kurds, the horses and mules, so celebrated in ancient times, were reared. Trout are found in the rivers, and a small herring in Lake Van. The country abounds in romantic scenery; that of the district of Ararat especially has been celebrated by patriotic historians like Moses of Chorene and Lazarus of Pharb.

Population.—Accurate statistics cannot be obtained; but it is estimated that in the nine vilayets, which include Turkish Armenia, there are 925,000 Gregorian, Roman Catholic and Protestant Armenians, 645,000 other Christians, 100,000 Jews, Gypsies, &c., and 4,460,000 Moslems. The Armenians, taking the most favourable estimate, are in a majority in nine kazas or sub-districts only (seven near Van, and two near Mush) out of 159. In Russian Armenia there are 960,000 Armenians, and in Persian Armenia 130,000. According to an estimate made by General Zelenyi for the Caucasus Geographical Society (*Zapiski*, vol. xviii., Tiflis, 1896, with map), the population of the nine Turkish vilayets, Erzerum, Van, Bitlis, Kharput (Mamuret-el-Aziz). Diarbekr, Sivas, Aleppo, Adana and Trebizond, was 6,000,000 (Armenians, 913,875, or 15%; other Christians, 632,875, or 11%; and Moslems, 4,453,250, or 74%). In the first five vilayets which contain most of the Armenians, the population was 2,642,000 (Armenians, 633,250, or 24%; other Christians, 179,875, or 7%; and Moslems, 1,828,875, or 69%); and in the seven Armenian kazas the population was 282,375 (Armenians, 184,875, or 65%; other Christians, 1000, or 0.3%; and Moslems, 96,500, or 34.7%). In 1897 there were 970,656 Armenians in Russia, of whom 827,634 were in the provinces of Erivan, Elisavetpol and Tiflis.

The total number of Armenians is estimated at 2,900,000 (in Turkey, 1,500,000; Russia, 1,000,000; Persia, 150,000; Europe, America and East Indies, 250,000).

History.—The history of Armenia has been largely influenced by its physical features. The isolation of the valleys, especially in winter, encouraged a tendency to separation, which invariably showed itself when the central power was weak. The rugged mountains have always been the home of hardy mountaineers impatient of control, and the sanctuary to which the lowlanders fled for safety in times of invasion. The country stands as an open doorway between the East and the West. Through its long valleys run the roads that connect the Iranian plateau with the fertile lands and protected harbours of Asia Minor, and for its possession nations have contended from the remotest past.

197

The original inhabitants of Armenia are unknown, but, about the middle of the 9th century B.C., the mass of the people belonged to that great family of tribes which seems to have been spread over western Asia and to have had a common *Ethnology.*non-Aryan language. Mixed with these proto-Armenians, there was an important Semitic element of Assyrian and Hebrew origin. In the 7th century B.C., between 640 and 600, the country was conquered by an Aryan people, who imposed their language, and possibly their name, upon the vanquished, and formed a military aristocracy that was constantly recruited from Persia and Parthia. Politically the two races soon amalgamated, but, except in the towns, there was apparently little intermarriage, for the peasants in certain districts closely resemble the proto-Armenians, as depicted on their monuments. After the Arab and Seljuk invasions, there was a large emigration of Aryan and Semitic Armenians to Constantinople and Cilicia; and all that remained of the aristocracy was swept away by the Mongols and Tatars. This perhaps explains the diversity of type and characteristics amongst the modern Armenians. In the recesses of Mount Taurus the peasants are tall, handsome, though somewhat sharp-featured, agile and brave. In Armenia and Asia Minor they are robust, thick-set and coarse-featured, with straight black hair and large hooked noses. They are good cultivators of the soil, but are poor, superstitious, ignorant and unambitious, and they live in semi-subterranean houses as their ancestors did 800 years B.C. The townsmen, especially in the large towns, have more regular features—often of the Persian type. They are skilled artisans, bankers and merchants, and are remarkable for their industry, their quick intelligence, their aptitude for business, and for that enterprising spirit which led their ancestors, in Roman times, to trade with Scythia, China and India. The upper classes are polished and well educated, and many have occupied high positions in the public service in Turkey, Russia, Persia and Egypt. The Armenians are essentially an Oriental people, possessing, like the Jews, whom they resemble in their exclusiveness and widespread dispersion, a remarkable tenacity of race and faculty of adaptation to circumstances. They are frugal, sober, industrious and intelligent, and their sturdiness of character has enabled them to preserve their nationality and religion under the sorest trials. They are strongly attached to old manners and customs, but have also a real desire for progress which is full of promise. On the other hand they are greedy of gain, quarrelsome in small matters, self-seeking and wanting in stability; and they are gifted with a tendency to exaggeration and a love of intrigue which has had an unfortunate influence on their history. They are deeply separated by religious differences, and their mutual jealousies, their inordinate vanity 565their versatility and their cosmopolitan character must always be an obstacle to the realization of the dreams of the nationalists. The want of courage and self-reliance, the deficiency in truth and honesty sometimes noticed in connexion with them, are doubtless due to long servitude under an unsympathetic government.

The early history of Armenia, more or less mythical, is partly based on traditions of the Biainian kings (see ARARAT), and is interwoven with the Bible narrative, of which a knowledge was possibly obtained from captive Jews settled *Ancient kingdom.*in the country by Assyrian and Babylonian monarchs. The legendary kings are but faint echoes of the kings of Biainas; the story of Semiramis and Ara is but another form of the myth of Venus and Adonis; and tradition has clothed Tigranes, the reputed friend of Cyrus, with the transient glory of the opponent of Lucullus. The fall of the Biainian kingdom, perhaps overthrown by Cyaxares, was apparently soon followed by an immigration of Aryan (Medo-Persian) races, including the progenitors of the Armenians. But they spread slowly, for the "Ten Thousand," when crossing the plateau to Trebizond, 401-400 B.C., met no Armenians after leaving the villages four days' march beyond the Teleboas, now Kara Su. Under the Medes and Persians Armenia was a satrapy governed by a member of the reigning family; and after the battle of Arbela, 331 B.C., it was ruled by Persian governors appointed by Alexander and his successors. Ardvates, 317-284 B.C., freed himself from Seleucid control; and after the defeat of Antiochus the Great by the Romans, 190 B.C., Artaxias (Ardashes), and Zadriades, the governors of Armenia Major and Armenia Minor, became independent kings, with the concurrence of Rome. (See TIGRANES.) Artaxias established his capital at Artaxata on the Araxes, and his most celebrated successor was Tigranes (Dikran), 94-56 B.C., the son-in-law of Mithradates VI., the Great. Tigranes founded a new capital, Tigranocerta, in northern Mesopotamia, which he modelled on Nineveh and Babylon, and peopled with Greek and other captives. Here, and at Antioch, he played the part of "great king" in Asia until his refusal to surrender his father-in-law involved him in war with Rome. Defeated, 69 B.C., by Lucullus beneath the walls of his capital, he surrendered his conquests to Pompey, 66 B.C., who had driven Mithradates across the Phasis, and was permitted to hold Armenia as a vassal state of Rome.

The campaigns of Lucullus and Pompey brought Rome into delicate relations with Parthia. Armenia, although politically dependent upon Rome, was connected with Parthia by

198

geographical position, a common language and faith, *Under later Empire.*intermarriage and similarity of arms and dress. It had never been Hellenized, as the provinces of Asia Minor had been; the Roman provincial system was never applied to it; and the policy of Rome towards it was never consistent. The country became the field upon which the East and West contended for mastery, and the struggle ended for a time in the partition of Armenia, A.D. 387, between Rome and Persia. The Roman portion was soon added to the Diocesis Pontica. The Persian portion, Pers-Armenia, remained a vassal state under an Arsacid prince until 428. It was afterwards governed by Persian and Armenian noblemen selected by the "great king," and entitled *marzbans.* Before the partition, Tiridates, converted by St Gregory, "the Illuminator," had established Christianity as the religion of the state, and set an example followed later by Constantine. After the partition, the invention of the Armenian alphabet, and the translation of the Bible into the vernacular, 410, drew the Armenians together, and the discontinuance of 566Greek in the Holy Offices relaxed the ecclesiastical dependence on Constantinople, which ceased entirely when the Patriarch, 491, refused to accept the decrees of the council of Chalcedon. The rule of the *marzbans* was marked by relentless persecution of the Christians, forced conversions to Magism, frequent insurrections and the rise to importance of the great families founded by men of Assyrian, Parthian, Persian, Syrian and Jewish origin, and in some cases of royal blood, who had been governors of districts, or holders of fiefs under the Arsacids. Amongst the *marzbans* were Jewish Bagratids and Persian Mamegonians; and one of the latter family, Vartan, made himself independent (571-578), with Byzantine aid. In 632 the victories of Heraclius restored Armenia to the Byzantines; but the war that followed the Arab invasion, 636, left the country in the hands of the caliphs, who set over it Arab and Armenian governors (*ostikans*). One of the governors, the Bagratid Ashod I., was crowned king of Armenia by the caliph Motamid, 885, and founded a dynasty which ended with Kagig II. in 1079. A little later the Ardzrunian Kagig, governor of Vaspuragan or Van, was crowned king of that province by the caliph Moktadir, 908, and his descendants ruled at Van and Sivas until 1080. The Bagratids founded dynasties at Kars, 962-1080, and in Georgia, which they held until its absorption, 1801, by Russia. From 984 to 1085 the country from Diarbekr to Melasgerd was ruled under the suzerainty first of Arabs then of Byzantines and Seljuks, by the Mervanid dynasty of Kurds, called princes of Abahuni (Ἀπαχουνῆς). The Arab invasion drove many Armenian noblemen to Constantinople, where they intermarried with the old Roman families or became soldiers of fortune. Artavasdes, an Arsacid, usurped the Byzantine throne for two years; Leo V., an Ardzrunian, and John Zimisces, became emperors; whilst Manuel, the Mamegonian, and others were amongst the best generals of the empire. In 991, and again in 1021, Basil II. invaded Armenia, and in the latter year Senekherim, king of Vaspuragan, exchanged his kingdom for Sivas and its territory, where he settled down with many Armenian emigrants. Basil's policy was to make the great Armenian fortresses, garrisoned by imperial troops, the first line of defence on his eastern frontier; but it failed in the hands of his feeble successors, who thought more of converting heretical Armenia than of defending its frontier. The king of Ani, Kagig II., was compelled to exchange his kingdom for estates in Cappadocia. The country was raided by Seljuks and harried by Byzantine soldiers, and the miseries of the people were regarded as gain to the Orthodox church. After the defeat and capture of Romanus IV. by Alp Arslan, 1071, Armenia formed part of the Seljuk empire until it split up, 1157, into petty states, ruled by Arabs, Kurds and Seljuks, who were in turn swept away by the Mongol invasion, 1235. For more than three centuries after the appearance of the Seljuks, Armenia was traversed by a long*Medieval Partition.*succession of nomad tribes whose one aim was to secure good pasturage for their flocks on their way to the richer lands of Asia Minor. The cultivators were driven from the plains, agriculture was destroyed, and the country was seriously impoverished when its ruin was completed by the ravages and wholesale butcheries of Timur. Many Armenians fled to the mountains, where they embraced Islam, and intermarried with the Kurds, or purchased security by paying blackmail to Kurdish chiefs. Others migrated to Cappadocia or to Cilicia, where the Bagratid Rhupen had founded, 1080, a small principality which, gradually extending its limits, became the kingdom of Lesser Armenia. This Christian kingdom in the midst of Moslem states, hostile to the Byzantines, giving valuable support to the leaders of the crusades, and trading with the great commercial cities of Italy, had a stormy existence of about 300 years. Internal disorders, due to attempts by the later Lusignan kings to make their subjects conform to the Roman Church, facilitated its conquest by Egypt, 1375. The memory of Kiligia (Cilicia) is enshrined in a popular song, and at Zeitun, in the recesses of Mount Taurus, a small Armenian community has hitherto maintained almost complete independence. After the death of Timur, Armenia formed part of the territories of the Turkoman dynasties of Ak- and Kara-Kuyunli, and under their milder rule the seat of the Catholicus, which, during the Seljuk invasion, had been moved first to Sivas, and then to Lesser Armenia, was re-established, 1441, at Echmiadzin.

In 1514, the Persian campaign of Selim I. gave Armenia to the Osmanli Turks, and its reorganization was entrusted to Idris, the historian, who was a Kurd of Bitlis. Idris found the rich arable lands almost deserted, and the mountains *Under Turkey.* bristling with the castles of independent chieftains, of Kurd, Arab and Armenian descent, between whom there were long-standing feuds. He compelled the Kurds to settle on the vacant lands, and divided the country into small sanjaks which in the plains were governed by Turkish officials, and in the mountains by local chiefs. This policy gave rest to the country, but favoured the growth of Kurd influence and power, which by 1534 had spread westwards to Angora. Armenia was invaded by the Persians in 1575, and again in 1604, when Shah Abbas transplanted many thousand Armenians from Julfa to his new capital Isfahan. In 1639, the province of Erivan, which included Echmiadzin, was assigned by treaty to Persia, and it remained in her hands until it passed to Russia, 1828, under the treaty of Turkman-chai. The Turko-Russian War of 1828-29, which advanced the Russian frontier to the Arpa Chai, was followed by a large emigration of Armenians from Turkish to Russian territory, and a smaller exodus took place after the war of 1877-78, which gave Batum, Ardahan and Kars to Russia. In 1834 the independent power of the Kurds in Armenia was greatly curtailed; and risings under Bedr Khan Bey in 1843, and Sheik Obeidullah in 1880, were firmly suppressed.

After the capture of Constantinople, 1453, Mahommed II. organized his non-Moslem subjects in communities, or *millets*, under ecclesiastical chiefs to whom he gave absolute authority in civil and religious matters, and in criminal *Gregorian Armenians.* offences that did not come under the Moslem religious law. Under this system the Armenian bishop of Brusa, who was appointed patriarch of Constantinople by the sultan, became the civil, and practically the ecclesiastical head of his community (*Ermeni millet*), and a recognized officer of the imperial government with the rank of vizier. He was assisted by a council of bishops and clergy, and was represented in each province by a bishop. This *imperium in imperio* secured to the Armenians a recognized position before the law, the free enjoyment of their religion, the possession of their churches and monasteries, and the right to educate their children and manage their municipal affairs. It also encouraged the growth of a community life, which eventually gave birth to an intense longing for national life. On the other hand it degraded the priesthood. The priests became political leaders rather than spiritual guides, and sought promotion by bribery and intrigue. Education was neglected and discouraged, servility and treachery were developed, and in less than a century the people had become depraved and degraded to an almost incredible extent. After the issue, 1839, of the *hatt-i-skerif* of Gül-khaneh, the tradesmen and artisans of the capital freed themselves from clerical control. Under regulations, approved by the sultan in 1862, the patriarch remained the official representative of the community, but all real power passed into the hands of clerical and lay councils elected by a representative assembly of 140 members. The "community," which excluded Roman Catholics and Protestants, was soon called the "nation," "domestic" became "national" affairs, and the "representative" the "national" assembly.

The connexion of "Lesser Armenia" with the Western powers led to the formation, 1335, of an Armenian fraternity, "the Unionists," which adopted the dogmas of the Roman church, and at the council of Florence, 1439, was *Roman Catholics.* entitled the "United Armenian Church." Under the millet system the unionists were frequently persecuted by the patriarchs, but this ended in 1830, when, at the intervention of France, they were made a community (*Katoluk millet*), with their own ecclesiastical head. The Roman Catholics, through the works issued by the Mechitharists at Venice, have greatly promoted the progress of education and the development of Armenian literature. They are most numerous at Constantinople, Angora and Smyrna.

The Protestant movement, initiated at Constantinople by American missionaries in 1831, was opposed by the patriarchs and Russia. In 1846 the patriarch anathematized all Armenians with Protestant sympathies, and this led *Protestants.* to the formation of the "Evangelical Church of the Armenians," which was made, after much opposition from France and Russia, a community (*Protestant millet*), at the instance of the British ambassador. The missionaries afterwards founded colleges on the Bosporus, at Kharput, Marsivan and Aintab, to supply the needs of higher university education, and they opened good schools for both sexes at all their stations. Everywhere they supplied the people with pure, wholesome literature, and represented progress and religious liberty.

When Abd-ul-Hamid came to the throne of Turkey in 1876, the condition of the Armenians was better than it had ever been under the Osmanlis; but with the close of the war of 1877-78 came the "Armenian Question." By the treaty of San *Modern Armenian question.* Stefano, Turkey engaged to Russia to carry out reforms "in the provinces inhabited by the Armenians, and to guarantee their security against the Kurds and Circassians." By the treaty of Berlin, 13th of July 1878, a like engagement to the six signatory powers was substituted for that to Russia. By the Cyprus convention, 4th of June 1878, the sultan promised Great Britain to introduce necessary reforms "for the protection of the Christians and other subjects of the Porte" in the Turkish territories in Asia. The Berlin treaty encouraged the Armenians to look to the powers, and not to Russia for protection; and the convention, which did not mention the Armenians, was regarded as placing them under the special protection of Great Britain. This impression was strengthened by the action of England at Berlin in insisting that Russia should evacuate the occupied territory before reforms were introduced, and so removing the only security for their introduction. The presentation of identic and collective notes to the Porte by the powers, in 1880, produced no result, and in 1882 it was apparent that Turkey would only yield to compulsion. In 1881 a circular note from the British ministry to the five powers was evasively answered, and in 1883 Prince Bismarck intimated to the British government that Germany cared nothing about Armenian reforms and that the matter had better be allowed to drop. Russia had changed her policy towards the Armenians, and the other powers were indifferent. The so-called "Concert of Europe" was at an end, but British ministries continued to call the attention of the sultan to his obligations under the treaty of Berlin.

Russia began to interest herself in the Armenians when she acquired Georgia in 1801; but it was not until 1828-1829 that any appreciable number of them became her subjects. She found them necessary to the development of her *Russian policy.*new territories, and allowed them much freedom. They were permitted, within certain limits, to develop their national life; many became wealthy, and many rose to high positions in the military and civil service of the state. After the war of 1877-78 the Russian consuls in Turkey encouraged the formation of patriotic committees in Armenia, and a project was formed to create a separate state, under the supremacy of Russia, which was to include Russian, Persian and Turkish Armenia. The project was favoured by Loris-Melikov, then all-powerful in Russia, but in 1881 Alexander II. was assassinated, and shortly afterwards a strongly anti-Armenian policy was adopted. The schools were closed, the use of the Armenian language was discouraged, and attempts were made to Russify the Armenians and bring them within the pale of the Russian Church. All hope of practical self-government under Russian protection now ceased, and the Armenians of Tiflis turned their attention to Turkish Armenia. They had seen the success of the Slav committees in treating disturbances in the Balkans, and became the moving spirit in the attempts to produce similar troubles in Armenia. Russia made no real effort to check the action of her Armenian subjects, and after 1884 she steadily opposed any active interference by Great Britain in favour of the Turkish Armenians. When Echmiadzin passed to Russia, in 1828, the Catholicus began to claim spiritual jurisdiction over the whole Armenian Church, and the submission of the patriarch of Constantinople was obtained by Russia when she helped the sultan against Mehemet Ali. Subsequently Russia secured the submission of the independent catholicus of Sis, and thus acquired a power of interference in Armenian affairs in all parts of the world. During 1900 Russia showed renewed interest in Turkish Armenia by securing the right to construct all railways in it, and in the Armenians by pressing the Porte to restore order and introduce reforms.

The Berlin treaty was a disappointment to the Gregorian Armenians, who had hoped that Armenia and Cilicia would have been formed into an autonomous province administered by Christians. But the formation of such a province was impossible. The Gregorians were scattered over the empire, and, except in a few small districts, were nowhere in a majority. Nor were they bound together by any community of thought or sentiment. The Turkish-speaking Armenians of the south could scarcely converse with the Armenian-speaking people of the north; and the ignorant mountaineers of the east had nothing in common, *Revolutionary movement.*except religion, with the highly educated townsmen of Constantinople and Smyrna. After the change in Russian policy and the failure of the powers to secure reforms, the advanced party amongst the Armenians, some of whom had been educated in Europe and been deeply affected by the free thought and Nihilistic tendencies of the day, determined to secure their object by the production of disturbances such as those that had given birth to Bulgaria. Societies were formed at Tiflis and in several European capitals for the circulation of pamphlets and newspapers, and secret societies, such as the Huntchagist, were instituted for more revolutionary methods. An active propaganda was carried on in Turkish Armenia by emissaries, who tried to introduce arms and explosives, and represented the ordinary incidents of Turkish misrule to Europe as serious atrocities. The revolutionary movement was joined by some of the younger men, who formed local committees on the Nihilist plan, but it was strongly opposed by the Armenian clergy and the American missionaries, who saw the impossibility of success; and its irreligious tendency and the self-seeking ambition of its leaders made it unacceptable to the mass of the people. Exasperated at their failure, the emissaries organized attacks on individuals, wrote threatening letters, and at last posted revolutionary placards, 5th of January 1893, at Yuzgat, and on the walls of the American College at Marsivan. In the last case the object of the Huntchagists was to

201

compromise the missionaries, and in this they succeeded. The Americans were accused of issuing the placards; two Armenian professors were imprisoned; and the girls' school was burned down. Outbreaks, easily suppressed, followed at Kaisarieh and other places.

One of the revolutionary dreams was to make the ancient Daron the centre of a new Armenia. But the movement met with no encouragement, either amongst the prosperous peasants on the rich plain of Mush or in the mountain villages of Sasun. In the summer of 1893, an emissary was captured near Mush, and the governor, hoping to secure others, ordered the Kurdish Irregular Horse to raid the mountain district. The Armenians drove off the Kurds,1 and, when attacked in the spring of 1894, again held their own. The vali now called up regular troops from Erzingan; and the sultan issued a firman calling upon all loyal subjects to aid in suppressing the revolt. A massacre of a most brutal character, in which Turkish soldiers took part, followed; and aroused deep indignation in Europe. In November 1894 a Turkish commission of inquiry was sent to Armenia, and was accompanied by the consular delegates of Great Britain, France and Russia, who elicited the fact that there had been no attempt 568at revolt to justify the action of the authorities. Throughout 1894 the state of the country bordered upon anarchy, and during the winter of 1894-1895 the British government, with lukewarm support from France and Russia, pressed for administrative reforms in the vilayets of Erzerum, Van, Bitlis, Sivas, Memuret-el-Aziz (Kharput) and Diarbekr. The Porte made counter-proposals, and officials concerned in the Sasun massacres were decorated and rewarded. On the 11th of May 1895 the three powers presented to the sultan a complicated scheme of reforms which was more calculated than to lessen the difficulties connected with the government of Armenia; but it was the only one to which Russia would agree. The sultan delayed his answer. Great Britain was in favour of coercion, but Russia, when sounded, replied that she "would certainly not join in any coercive measures" and she was supported by France. At this moment, 21st of June 1895, Lord Rosebery's cabinet resigned, and when Lord Salisbury's government resumed the negotiations in August, the sultan appealed to France and Russia against England. During the negotiations the secret societies had not been inactive. Disturbances occurred at Tarsus; Armenians who did not espouse the "national" cause were murdered; the life of the patriarch was threatened; and a report was circulated that the British ambassador wished some Armenians killed to give him an excuse for bringing the fleet to Constantinople. On the 1st of October 1895 a number of Armenians, some armed, went in procession with a petition to the Porte and were ordered by the police to disperse. Shots were fired, and a riot occurred in which many Armenian and some Moslem lives were lost. The British ambassador now pressed the scheme of reforms upon the sultan, who accepted it on the 17th of October. Meanwhile there had been a massacre at Trebizond (October 8), in which armed men from Constantinople took part, and it had become evident that no united action on the part of the powers was to be feared. The sultan refused to publish the scheme of reforms, and massacre followed massacre in Armenia in quick succession until the 1st of January 1896. Nothing was done. Russia refused to agree to any measure of coercion, and declared (December 19) that she would take no action except such as was needed for the protection of foreigners. Great Britain was not prepared to act alone. In the summer of 1896 (June 14-22) there were massacres at Van, Egin, and Niksar; and on the 26th of August the Imperial Ottoman Bank at Constantinople was seized by revolutionists as a demonstration against the Christian powers who had left the Armenians to their fate. The project was known to the Porte, and the rabble, previously armed and instructed, were at once turned loose in the streets. Two days' massacre followed, during which from 6000 to 7000 Gregorian Armenians perished.

The massacres were apparently organized and carried out in accordance with a well-considered plan. They occurred, except in six places, in the vilayets to which the scheme of reforms was to apply. At Trebizond they took place *The massacres.*just before the sultan accepted that scheme, and after his acceptance of it they spread rapidly. They were confined to Gregorian and Protestant Armenians. The Roman Catholics were protected by France, the Greek Christians by Russia. The massacre of Syrians, Jacobites and Chaldees at Urfa and elsewhere formed no part of the original plan. Orders were given to protect foreigners, and in some cases guards were placed over their houses. The damage to the American buildings at Kharput was due to direct disobedience of orders. The attacks on the bazars were made without warning, during business hours, when the men were in their shops and the women in their houses. Explicit promises were given, in some instances, that there would be no danger to those who opened their shops, but they were deliberately broken. Nearly all those who, from their wealth, education and influence, would have had a share in the government under the scheme of reforms, were killed and their families ruined by the destruction of their property. Where any attempt at defence was made the slaughter was greatest. The only successful resistance was at Zeitun, where the people received honourable terms after three months' fighting. In some towns the troops and police took an active part in the massacres. At Kharput artillery was used. In some the slaughter

202

commenced and ended by bugle-call, and in a few instances the Armenians were disarmed beforehand. Wherever a superior official or army officer intervened the massacre at once ceased, and wherever a governor stood firm there was no disturbance. The actual perpetrators of the massacres were the local Moslems, aided by Lazis, Kurds and Circassians. A large majority of the Moslems disapproved of the massacres, and many Armenians were saved by Moslem friends. But the lower orders were excited by reports that the Armenians, supported by the European powers, were plotting the overthrow of the sultan; and their cupidity was aroused by the prospect of wiping out their heavy debts to Armenian pedlars and merchants. No one was punished for the massacres, and many of those implicated in them were rewarded. In some districts, especially in the Kharput vilayet, the cry of "Islam or death" was raised. Gregorian priests and Protestant pastors were tortured, but preferred death to apostasy. Men and women were killed in prison and in churches in cold blood. Churches, monasteries, schools and houses were plundered and destroyed. In some places there was evidence of the previous activity of secret societies, in others none. The number of those who perished, excluding Constantinople, was 20,000 to 25,000.2 Many were forced to embrace Islam, and numbers were reduced to poverty. The destruction of property was enormous, the hardest-working and best tax-paying element in the country was destroyed, or impoverished, and where the breadwinners were killed the women and children were left destitute. Efforts by Great Britain and the United States to alleviate the distress were opposed by the authorities, but met with some success. After the massacres the number of students in the American schools and colleges increased, and many Gregorian Armenians became Roman Catholics in order to obtain the protection of France.

The Armenian revolutionary societies continued their propaganda down to the granting of the Turkish constitution in 1908; and meanwhile further massacres occurred here and there, notably at Mush (1904) and Van (1908).

See Abich, *Geologie d. armenischen Hochlandes* (Wien, 1882); Bishop, *Journeys in Persia and Kurdistan* (Lond., 1891); Bliss, *Turkey and the Armenian Atrocities* (Lond., 1896); Bryce, *Transcaucasia and Ararat* (4th ed., Lond., 1896); De Coursous, *La Rébellion arménienne* (Paris, 1895); Lepsius, *Armenia and Europe* (Lond., 1897); Murray, *Handbook for Asia Minor* (Lond., 1895); Parly. Papers, *Turkey*, I. (1895); *Turkey*, I., II. (1896); Supan, "Die Verbreitung d. Armenier in der asiatischen Turkei, u. in Transkaukasien," in Pet. *Mitt.* vol. xlii. (1896); Tozer, *Turkish Armenia and Eastern Asia Minor* (Lond., 1881); Cholet, *Arménie, Kurdistan, et Mésopotamie* (1892); Lynch, *Armenia* (2 vols., 1901).

(C. W. W.)

1The Armenians and Kurds have lived together from the earliest times. The adoption of Islam by the latter, and by many Armenians, divided the people sharply into Christian and Moslem, and placed the Christian in a position of inferiority. But the relations between the two sects were not unfriendly previously to the Russian campaigns in Persia and Turkey. After 1829 the relations became less friendly; and later, when the Armenians attracted the sympathies of the European powers after the war of 1877-78, they became bitterly hostile.

2According to some estimates the number killed was 50,000 or more.

ARMENIAN CHURCH. No trustworthy account exists of the evangelization of Armenia, for the legend of King Abgar's correspondence with Christ, even if it contained any historical truth, only relates to Edessa and Syriac Christianity. That the Armenians appropriated from the Syrians this, as well as the stories of Bartholomew and Thaddeus (the Syriac *Addai*), was merely an avowal on their part that Edessa was the centre from which the faith radiated over their land. In the 4th century and later the liturgy was still read in Syriac in parts of Armenia, and the New Testament, the history of Eusebius, the homilies of Aphraates, the works of St Ephraem and many other early books were translated from Syriac, from which tongue most of their ecclesiological terms were derived. The earliest notice of an organized church in Armenia is in Eusebius, *H. E.* vi. 46, to the effect that Dionysius of Alexandria *c.* 250 sent a letter to Meruzanes, bishop of the brethren in Armenia. There were many Christians in Melitene at the time of the Decian persecution in A.D.250, and two bishops from Great Armenia were present at the council of Nice in 325. King Tiridates (*c.* A.D. 238-314) had already been baptized some time after 261 by Gregory the Illuminator. The latter was ordained priest and appointed *catholicus* or exarch of the church of Great Armenia by Leontius, bishop of Caesarea in Cappadocia. This one fact is certain amidst the fables which soon obscured the history of this great missionary. 569Thus the church of Great Armenia began as a province of the Cappadocian see. But there was a tradition of a line of bishops earlier than Gregory in Siuniq, a region east of Ararat along the Araxes (Aras), which in early times claimed to be independent of the catholicus. The Adoptianist bishop Archelaus, who opposed the entry of Mani into Armenia under Probus *c.*

277, was also perhaps a Syriac-speaking bishop of Pers-Armenia. Almost the earliest document revealing anything of the inner organization and condition of the Armenian church in the Nicene age is the epistle of Macarius, bishop of Jerusalem, to the Armenian bishop Verthanes, written between 325 and 335 and preserved in Armenian. Its genuineness has been unreasonably suspected. It insists on the erection of fonts; on distinction of grades among the ordained clergy; on not postponing baptism too long; on bishops and priests alone, and not deacons, being allowed to baptize and lay hands on or confirm the baptized; on avoiding communion with Arians; on the use of unleavened bread in the Sacrament, &c. We learn from it that the bishop of Basen and Bagrevand was an Arian at that time. By the year 450 these two districts already had separate bishops of their own. The letter of Macarius, therefore, if a forgery, must be a very early one.1 The Armenians must, like the Georgians a little later, have set store by the opinion of the bishop of Jerusalem, or they would not have sent to consult him. It was equally from Jerusalem that they subsequently adopted their lectionary and arrangement of the Christian year; and a 9th-century copy of this lectionary in the Paris library preserves to us precious details of the liturgical usages of Jerusalem in the 4th century. We can trace the presence of Armenian convents on the Mount of Olives as early as the 5th century.

Tradition represents the conversion of Great Armenia under Gregory and Tiridates as a sort of triumphant march, in which the temples of the demons and their records were destroyed wholesale, and their undefended sites instantly converted into Christian churches. The questions arise: how was the transition from old to new effected? and what was the type of teaching dominant in the new church? Armenian tradition, confirmed by nearly contemporary Greek sources, answers the first question. The old order went on, but under new names. The priestly families, we learn, hearing that the God preached by Gregory needed not sacrifice, sent to the king a deputation and asked how they were to live, if they became Christians; for until then the priests and their families had lived off the portions of the animal victims and other offerings reserved to them by pagan custom. Gregory replied that, if they would join the new religion, not only should the sacrifices continue, but they should have larger perquisites then ever. The priestly families then went over *en masse*. How far the older sacrificial rules resembled the levitical law we do not know, but in the canons of Sahak, *c.* 430, the priests already receive the levitical portions of the victims; and we find that animals are being sacrificed every Sunday, on the feast days which at first were few, in fulfilment of private vows, in expiation of the sins of the living, and still more of those of the dead. No one might kill his own meat and deprive the priest of his due; but this rule did not apply to the chase. The earliest Armenian rituals contain ample services for the conduct of an *agapē(q.v.)* or love feast held in the church off sacrificial meat. The victim was slaughtered by the priest in the church porch before the crucifix, after it had been ritually wreathed and given the holy salt, by licking which it appropriated a sacramental purity or efficacy previously conveyed into the salt by exorcisms and consecration. In the canons of Sahak the priest is represented as eating the sins of the people in these repasts.

It is easy to underrate the importance in religion of a change of names. The old sacrificial hymns were probably obscene and certainly nonsensical, and the substitution for them of the psalms, and of lections of the prophets and New Testament, was an enormous gain. We do not know precisely how the eucharistic rite was adjusted to these sacrificial meals; but, in the canons of Sahak, 1 Cor. xi. 17-34 is interpreted of these meals, which were known as the Dominical (suppers). The Eucharist was, therefore, long associated with the *matal*or animal victim, and only in the 8th century do we hear of an interval of time being left between the fleshly and the spiritual sacrifices, as the two rites were then called. The Basilian service of the Eucharist was used in the 5th century, but superseded later on by a Byzantine rite which will be found translated in F.E. Brightman's *Eastern Liturgies*. The Eucharist was no doubt the one important sacrifice in the minds of the clergy who had attended the schools of Constantinople and Alexandria; yet the heart of the people remained in their ancient blood-offerings, and as late as the 12th century they were prone to deny that the mass could expiate the sins of the dead unless accompanied by the sacrifice of an animal. Perhaps even to-day the worst fate that can befall a villager after death is to be deprived, not of commemoration in the mass, but of the victim slain for his sins. The keenest spiritual weapon of the Armenian priest was ever a threat not to offer the *matal*for a man when he died.

Another survival in the Armenian church was the hereditary priesthood. None but a scion of a priestly family could become a deacon, elder or bishop. Accordingly the primacy remained in the family of Gregory until about 374, when the king Pap or Bab murdered Nerses, who had been ordained by Eusebius of Caesarea (362-370) and was over-zealous in implanting in Armenia the canons about celibacy, marriage, fasting, hospices and monastic life which Basil had established in Cappadocia. It may be remarked that Gregory's own family was a cadet branch of the Arsacid kin which had occupied the thrones of Persia, Bactria, Armenia and Georgia. His primacy therefore was in itself a survival of an earlier age when king and priest were one. He was in fact a *rex sacrificulus*, and later on, when the Arsacid dynasty fell in Armenia *c.* A.D. 428, the Armenian catholicus became the symbol of national unity and the rallying-point of patriotism. The line of Gregory was restored in 390 in the person of Isaac or Sahak, son of Nerses, and his patriarchate was the golden age of Armenian literature. But by this time the autonomy of the Armenian church was thoroughly established. On the death of Nerses the right of saying grace at the royal meals, which was the essence of the catholicate, was transferred by the king, in despite of the Greeks, to the priestly family of Albianus, and thenceforth no Armenian catholicus went to Caesarea for ordination. The ties with Greek official Christendom were snapped for ever, and in subsequent ages the doctrinal preferences of the Armenians were usually determined more by antagonism to the Greeks than by reflection. If they accepted the council of Ephesus in 430 and joined in the condemnation of Nestorius, it was rather because the Sassanid kings of Persia, who thirsted for the reconquest of Armenia, favoured Nestorianism, a form of doctrine current in Persia and rejected in Byzantium. But later on, about 480, and throughout the following centuries, the Armenians rejected the decrees of Chalcedon and held that the assertion of two natures in Christ was a relapse into the heresy of Nestor. From the close of the 5th century the Armenians have remained monophysite, like the Copts and Abyssinians, and have only broken the record with occasional short interludes of orthodoxy, as when in 633 the emperor Heraclius forced reunion on them, under a catholicus named Esdras, at a council held in Erzerum. Even then all parties were careful not to mention Chalcedon. The march of Arab conquest kept the Armenians friendly to Byzantium for a few years; but in 718 the catholicus John of Odsun ascended the throne and at the council of Manazkert in 728 repeated and confirmed the anathemas against Chalcedon and the tome of Leo, that had been first pronounced by the catholicus Babken in 491 at a synod held in Valarshapat by the united Armenian, Georgian or Iberian, and Albanian churches. 570The Armenians marked their complete disruption with the Greeks by starting an era of their own at the synod of Dvin. The era began on the 11th of July 552, and their year is vague, that is to say, it does not intercalate a day in February every fourth year, like the Julian calendar.

The two churches of Iberia and Albania at first depended on the Armenian for ordination of their primates or *catholici,* and in large part owed their first constitution to Armenian missionaries sent by Gregory the Illuminator. The Iberians still reverence as saints the Armenian doctors of the 5th century, but as early as 552 they began to resent the dictatorial methods of the Armenians, as well might a proud race of mountaineers who never wholly lost their political independence; and they broke off their allegiance to the Armenian see very soon afterwards, accepted Chalcedon and joined the Byzantine church. The Albanians of the Caucasus were also converted in the age of Gregory, early in the 4th century, and were loyal to the Armenians in the great struggle against Mazdaism in the 5th; but broke away for a time towards 600, and chose a patriarch without sending him to Armenia for ordination. Eventually this interesting church was engulfed by the rising tide of Mahommedan conquest, but not before one of their bishops, named Israel, had converted (677-703) the Huns who lay to the north of the Caspian and had translated the Bible and liturgies into their language. If the Albanian and Hunnish versions could be found, they would be of the greatest linguistic importance.

The mother church of Armenia was established by Gregory at Ashtishat in the province of Taron, on the site of the great temple of Wahagn, whose festival on the seventh of the month Sahmi was reconsecrated to John the Baptist and Athenogenes, an Armenian martyr and Greek hymn writer. The first of Navasard, the Armenian new year's day, was the feast of a god Vanatur or Wanadur (who answered to Ζεὺς ξένιος) in the holy pilgrim city of Bagawan. His day was reconsecrated to the Baptist, whose relics were brought to Bagawan. The feast of Anahite, the Armenian Venus and spouse of the chief god Aramazd, was in the same way rededicated to the Virgin Mary, who for long was not very clearly distinguished by the Armenians from the virgin mother church. The old cult of sacred stones and trees by an easy transition became cross-worship, but a cross was not sacred until the Christ had been, by priestly prayer and invocation, transferred into it.

What was the earliest doctrine of the churches of Armenia? If we could believe the fathers of the 5th and succeeding centuries Nicene orthodoxy prevailed in their country from the first; and in the 5th century they certainly chose for translation the works of orthodox fathers alone, such as Chrysostom, Basil, Gregory of Nyssa and Gregory Nazianzen, Cyril of Jerusalem and Cyril of Alexandria, Athanasius, Julius of Rome, Hippolytus, Irenaeus, avoiding Origen and other fathers who were becoming suspect. However, we do hear of versions of Nestorian writers like Diodore of Tarsus being in circulation, and the *Disputation* of Archelaus proves that the current orthodoxy of eastern Armenia was Adoptianist, if not Ebionite in tone. The Persian Armenians as late as the 6th century had not heard of the faith of Nicaea, and only then received it from the

205

catholicus Babken. They sent a copy of their old creed to Babken, and it closely resembles the Adoptianist creed of Archelaus, the gist of which was that Jesus, until his thirtieth year, was a man mortal like other men; then, because he was righteous above all others, he was promoted to the honour and name of Son of God. He received the title by grace, but was not equal to God the Father. Because the Spirit worked with him, he was able to vanquish Satan and all desires, and because of his righteousness and good works he was made worthy of grace and became a Temple of God the Word, which came down from heaven in Jordan, dwelt in him and through him wrought miracles. From such a standpoint the baptism of Jesus was the moment of the divine incarnation. The man righteous above all others was then reborn of the Spirit, was illuminated, was spiritually anointed, became the Christ and Son of God. In effect the fathers of the Armenian church often fell back into such language, far removed as it is from orthodoxy; and they emphasized the importance of the baptismal feast of the Epiphany on the 6th of January by refusing to accept the feast of the physical birth of the 25th of December. As late as 1165 their patriarch Nerses defends the Armenian custom of keeping Christmas on the 6th of January on the express ground that as he was born after the flesh from the Virgin, *so he was born by way of baptism from the Jordan.* The custom from the first, he says, had been to feast on one and the same day the two births, much as they differed in sacramental import and in point of time. We see how deep the early Adoptianism had struck its roots, when a primate of the 12th century could still appeal to the baptismal regeneration of Jesus. The same Nerses held that the second Adam, Jesus Christ, received a new body and nature and the sevenfold grace of the Spirit *in the Jordan.* The Armenian doctors also taught that John by laying hands on Jesus and ordaining him at his baptism sacramentally transferred to him the three graces or *charismata* of kingship, prophecy and priesthood which had belonged to ancient Israel. After baptism, if not before, the flesh of Christ was incorruptible. It consisted of ethereal fire, and he was not subject to the ordinary phenomena of digestion, secretions and evacuations.

Monastic institutions were hardly introduced in Armenia before the 5th century, though Christian rest-houses had been erected along the high-roads long before and are mentioned in the *Disputation* of Archelaus. The Armenians called them *wanq,* and out of them grew the monasteries. The monks were, strictly speaking, penitents wearing the cowl, and not allowed to take a part in church government. This belonged to the elders. At first there was no separate episcopal ordination, and the one rite of elder or priest (Armen. *Qahanay,* Heb.*cohen*) sufficed. There were also deacons, half-deacons and readers. Besides these there was a class of *wardapets* or teachers, answering to the *didascalos* of the earliest church, whose province it was to guard the doctrine and for whom no rite of ordination is found in the older rituals.

A few other peculiarities of Armenian church usage or belief deserve notice. In baptism the rubric ordains that the baptized be plunged three times in the font in commemoration of the entombment during three days of the Lord. In the West trine immersion was generally held to be symbolic of the triune name of "Father, Son and Holy Ghost." This name the Armenians have used, at least since the year 700; before which date their fathers often speak of baptism into the death of Christ as the one essential. As late as about 1300 a traveller hostile to the Armenians reported to the pope that he had witnessed baptisms without any trinitarian invocation in as many as three hundred parish churches.

The paschal lamb is now eaten on Sunday, but until the 11th century, and even later, it was eaten with the Eucharist at a Lord's Supper celebrated on the evening of Maundy Thursday after the rite of *pedilavium* or washing of feet. On the morning of the same day the penitents were released from their fast.

The rite of extreme unction was introduced in the crusading epoch, although it was already usual to anoint the bodies of dead priests. The worship of images never seems to have taken root among Armenians; indeed they supplied the Greek world with iconoclast soldiers and emperors. The worship of crosses into which the Spirit or Christ had been inserted by the priest must have satisfied the religious needs of a people who, save in architecture, showed little artistic faculty. In their older rituals we find a rite for blessing a painted church, but no word of statues. Frescoes in their churches are rare, and mostly too high up for veneration to be paid to them.

On certain days the cross was washed, and the water in which it had been washed was a sovereign charm for curing sickness in men and animals and for bringing fertility to the land.

In the older rituals we find a rite of *exhomologesis,* for restoring those who had sinned after baptism. It was a medicine of sin that could only be used once and not a second time. In form it is a rehearsal of the first baptismal rite, but with omission of the water. It involved like the first rite open confession and repentance, and absolution by the church. In a later and less rigorous age this rite was abridged and adjusted to constant 571repetition, in such wise that a sinner could be restored to grace not once only, but as often as the clergy chose to accept his repentance and confession. Thus the whole development of the penitentiary system is traceable in the MSS.

The confession of a dying man might be taken by any layman present, and written down in order to be shown to the priest when he arrived. It then was the duty of the latter to supplicate for his forgiveness, and administer to him the Eucharist.

The clergy of all grades were originally married. The parish priests, or white clergy, are so still, except some of the Latinizing ones. But since the 12th century, or even earlier, the higher clergy, *i.e.* patriarchs and bishops, have taken monkish vows and worn the cowl.

There were abortive attempts to unite the Armenian church with the Byzantine in the 9th century under the patriarch Photius, and again late in the 12th under the emperor Manuel Comnenus, when a joint council met at Romkla, near Tarsus, but ended in nothing (A.D. 1179). Neither could the Armenians keep on good terms even with the Syriac monophysites. From the age of the crusades on, the Armenians of Cilicia, whose patriarch sat at Sis, improved their acquaintance with Rome; and more than one of their patriarchs adopted the Roman faith, at least in words. Dominican missions went to Armenia, and in 1328 under their auspices was formed a regular order called the United Brethren, the forerunners of the Uniats of the present day, who have convents at Venice and Vienna, a college in Rome and a numerous following in Turkey. They retain their Armenian liturgies and rites, pruned to suit the Vatican standards of orthodoxy, and they recognize the pope as head of the church.

The patriarchs of Great Armenia first resided at Ashtishat, on the Araxes. From 478 to 931 they occupied Dvin in the same neighbourhood, then Aghthamar, an island in the Lake of Van, 931-967, the city of Ani, 992-1054, where are still visible the magnificent ruins of their churches and palaces. Since 1441 the chief catholicus has sat at Echmiadzin, the convent of Valarshapat, now part of Russian Armenia. A rival catholicus, with a small following, still has his cathedral and see at Sis. The catholicus of Valarshapat is nominally chosen by all Armenians. A synod of bishops, monks and doctors meets regularly to transact under his eye the business of the convent and the oecumenical affairs of the church; but its decisions are subject to the veto of a Russian procurator. There are Armenian patriarchs, subject to the spiritual jurisdiction of Echmiadzin, in Constantinople and Jerusalem. In the latter place the Armenians occupy a convent on Mount Sion, and keep up in the churches of the Sepulchre and of Bethlehem their own distinct rites and feasts, the only ones there which at all resemble those of the 4th century.

The following list of councils was compiled by John, catholicus about the year 728, and read at the council of Manazkert, when the dogmatic and disciplinary attitude of the Armenian church was defined once and for all:—

1. In twentieth year of catholicate of Gregory and thirty-seventh of Trdat, the king, on return of Aristaces from council of Nice, bringing the Nicene creed and canons.

2. Council held by St Nerses on his return from the council of the 150 fathers at Constantinople against Macedonius.

3. Held by St Sahak and Mesrop on receipt of letters from Proclus and Cyril after the council of Ephesus, when the "Glory in the Highest" was adopted. Held against Nestorianism.

4. Held by Joseph, disciple of Mashdotz (Mesrop) and St Sahak, in Shahapiwan in the sixth year of King Yazkert (*i.e.* Yazdegerd) of Persia, for the regulation of the church. Forty bishops present. (The Massalians were anathematized.)

5. Held by Babken, catholicus, in the City-plain (*i.e.* Dvin), in the 18th year of King Kavat (*i.e.* Kavadh), against the heresy of Acacius and Barsuma (Bar-sauma), the friends of Nestorius. The true (Nicene) faith was sent to the Armenians of the farther East (shortly afterwards a slightly different creed was adopted, identical with a pseudo-Athanasian symbol used by Evagrius of Pontus and given in Greek in Patr. Gr. xxvi. Col. 1232).

6. At the beginning of the Armenian era, held by Nerses in Dvin, in the fourth year of his catholicate, in the fourteenth year of Chosroes' reign and in the fourteenth of Justinian Caesar. Held against Chalcedon, uniting the Baptism and Christmas feasts on the 6th of January (Epiphany), declaring for mono-physitism, and adopting in the *Trisagion* the words "who wast crucified for us." This settlement lasted for about seventy-four years.

7. After the retaking of Jerusalem and recovery of the Cross from the Persians in the eighteenth year of his reign, Heraclius called a mixed council at Karin (Theodosiopolis) of Greeks and Armenians under Ezr (Esdras), catholicus, at which the preceding council of Dvin was cursed, its reforms repudiated and the confession of Chalcedon adopted. This remained the official attitude of the Armenian church until the catholicate of Elias (703-717). John, catholicus, denies to Ezr's meeting the name of council, and so makes his own the seventh.

8. Under John, catholicus, in Manazkert, in the one hundred and seventieth year of the Armenian era (= A.D. 728) under the presidency of Gregory Asharuni Chorepiscopos (Gregory Asheruni). All the Armenian bishops attended, as also the metropolitan of Urhha (Edessa), Jacobite bishops of Gartman, of Nfrkert, Amasia, by command of the archbishop of Antioch. Chalcedon was repudiated afresh, union with the Jacobites instituted, use of water and leaven in

the Eucharist condemned, the five days' preliminary fast before Lent restored, Saturday as well as Sunday made a day of feasting and synaxis, any but the orthodox excluded from the Maundy Thursday Communion, the first communion of the new catechumens; union of the Baptismal and Christmas feasts was restored, and the faithful forbidden to fast on Fridays from Easter until Pentecost. In general these rules have been observed in the Armenian church ever since.

For list of authorities on the Armenian church see the works enumerated at the end of ARMENIAN LANGUAGE AND LITERATURE. For the relations of the Armenian church to the Persian kings see PERSIA: *Ancient History*, section viii. §§ 2 and 3.

(F. C. C.)

1If a forgery, why should this letter have been assigned to Macarius, a comparatively obscure person whose name is not even found in the menaea of the Eastern church? But convincing proof of its authenticity lies in Macarius' reference to himself as merely archbishop of Jerusalem, and his avowal that he was unwilling to advise the Armenians, "being oppressed by the weakness of the authority conceded him by the weighty usages of the church." Jerusalem was only allowed to rank as a patriarchate in 451, and the seventh canon of Nice subordinated the see to that of Caesarea in Palestine. To this decree Macarius somewhat bitterly alludes.

ARMENIAN LANGUAGE AND LITERATURE. The Armenian language belongs to the group called Indo-European, of which the Iranic and Indic tongues formed one branch, and Greek, Albanian, Italian, Celtic, Germanic and Baltic-Slavonic dialects the other great branch. Unlike *Language.* most of these, Armenian lost its genders long before the year A.D. 400, when the existing literature begins. Modern Persian similarly has lost gender; and in both cases the liberation must have been due to attrition of other tongues which had a different system of gender or none at all. So the Armenians were ever in contact on the north with the Iberians of the Caucasus who had none, and with the Semitic races on the south and east which had other ways of forming genders than the Indo-European tongues.

From the original Armenian stock can be readily distinguished a mass of Old and Middle Persian loan-words. These are so numerous that for a time Armenian was classed as an Iranian tongue. For more than a thousand years, say until A.D. 640, Armenia was an appanage of the realm of the Persians and Parthians. Until A.D. 428 the Armenian throne was occupied by a younger branch of the Arsacid dynasty that ruled in Persia until the advent of the Sassanids (*c.* A.D. 226), and the internal polity and court administration of Armenia were modelled on the Persian or Parthian. Accordingly over 200 proper and personal names in Armenia were Old Persian, as well as 700 names of things. If we count in the derivative forms of these words we get at least 2000 Old Persian words. Often the same Persian word was borrowed twice over in an earlier and later form at an interval of centuries, just as in English we inherit a word direct or have taken it from Latin, and have also assimilated from French a later form of the same. The Persian influence in Armenian was already strong as early as 400 B.C., when Xenophon used a Persian interpreter to converse. In some of the Armenian villages they answered him in Persian. The Persian loan-words already present in Armenian as early as A.D. 400 mirror the earlier political and social life of Armenia. Thus many of their kings and nobles had Persian names; Persian also were most 572 words used in connexion with horses and the chase, with war and army, with dress, trade and coinage, calendar, weights and measures, with court and political institutions, with music, medicine, school, education, literature and the arts. Many everyday words were of the same origin, *e.g.* the words for village, desert, building and build, need, rich or liberal, arm (of body), rod or goad, face, opposite, wicked, unfriendly, discontented, difficult, daughter, eulogy, a youth, wary, enjoy, unhappy, volition, voluntary, unwilling, blind, cautious, blood-kin, coquet with, slumber, humble, mad, grace or favour, memory or attention, grandfather, old woman, prepared, duty, necessary, end, endless, superior, confident, mistake, warmth, heat, glory. The language of their old religion was mainly Persian, but in the 4th century they derived numerous ecclesiological words from the Syrians, from whom by way of Edessa and Nisibis Christianity penetrated eastern Armenia. The language of the garden and the names of plants were also Persian. They had their own numerals, but the words for one thousand and for ten thousand are Persian.

Yet more indicative of the extent of the Persian influence is the adoption of the adjectival ending -*akan* and -*zan*, added to purely Armenian words; also of the preposition *ham*, answering to *con* in "conjoin," "conspire," added to purely Armenian words, as in *hambarnam*, I take away, and *hamboir*, a kiss, a word which, strange to say, the Iberians in turn borrowed from the Armenians. From Persia also the Armenians took their names for surrounding races, *e.g. Tatshik* or *Tajik*, first for Arab and then for Turk, *Ariq* for Persians, *Kapkoh* for Caucasus, *Hrazdan, Vaspuragan*, &c. The Armenians call themselves *Hay*, plural *Hayq*; their

208

country *Hayasdan*. The Iberians they called *Virq* or *Wirq* (where *q* marks the plural), the Medes *Marq*, the Cappadocians *Gamirq* (Cimmerians), the Greeks Yûnes or Ionians; Ararat they call *Masis*, the Euphrates the *Aradsan*, the Tigris *Teglath*, Erzerum is *Karin*, Edessa *Urhha*, Nisibis *Mdsbin*, Ctesiphon *Tizbon*, &c.

When the Persian and other loan-words are removed, a stock remains of native words and forms governed by other phonetic laws than those which govern the Aryan, *i.e.* Indian and Iranic, branch of the Indo-European tongues. Armenian appears to be a half-way dialect between the Aryan branch and Slavo-lettic. Much, however, in Armenian philology remains unexplained. For example the plural of nouns, pronouns and the first and second persons plural of verbs are all formed by adding a *q* or *k*, which has no parallel in any Indo-Germanic tongue. The genitive plural again is formed by adding a *tz* or *c*, and the same consonant characterizes the composite aorist and the conjunctive. In all three cases it is unexplained. In the verbs the termination *m* for the first singular at once explains itself, and the *n* of the third plural is the Indo-Germanic *nti*. But not so the second person singular ending in *s, e.g. berem*, I bear, *beres*, thou bearest. This has a superficial likeness to the I.-G. *esi* in *bheresi*, "thou bearest." Yet we should expect the *s* between vowels to vanish, and give us in Armenian *berē*. Perhaps, therefore, an old variant of *esi*, similar to theἐσσί, lies behind the Armenian *es*, thou art, and the *es* in *beres*, thou bearest. In any case it is clear that many of the oldest forms which Armenian shared with other Indo-Germanic dialects were lost and replaced by forms of which the origin is obscure. Perhaps a closer study of Mingrelian and Georgian will explain some of these peculiarities, for these and their cognate tongues must have had a wider range in the 7th and 8th centuries B.C. than they had later when clear history begins. The attempts made by S. Bugge to assimilate Old Armenian to Etruscan, and by P. Jensen to explain from it the Hittite inscriptions, appear to be fanciful. There is a large Semitic influence traceable in Armenian due to their early contact with the Syriac-speaking peoples to the south and east of them, and later to the Arab conquest. Much remains to be done in the way of collecting Armenian dialects, for which task there are written materials as far back as the 12th century over and above the work to be done by an intelligent traveller armed with a phonograph. Two main dialects of Armenian are distinguishable to-day, that of Ararat and Tiflis, and that of Stambul and the coast cities of Asia Minor. The latter is much overlaid with Tatar or Turkish words, and the Tatar order of words distinguishes the modern Armenian sentence from the ancient.

It remains to say that classical Armenian resembles rather the modern idiom of Van than of western Armenia. It was a plastic and noble language, capable of rendering faithfully, yet not servilely, the Greek Bible and Greek fathers. Often the Armenian translators, and especially after the 5th century, rendered word for word, preserving the order of the Greek. This literalness, though unpleasing from a literary standpoint, gives to many of their ancient versions the value almost of a Greek codex of the age in which the version was made. The same literalness also characterizes their translations from Syriac.

The Armenians had a temple literature of their own, which was destroyed in the 4th and 5th centuries by the Christian clergy, so thoroughly that barely twenty lines of it survive in the history of Moses of Khoren (Chorene). *Literature.* Their Christian literature begins about 400 with the invention of the Armenian alphabet by Mesrop. This was probably an older alphabet to which Mesrop merely added vowels; but, in order to pacify the Greek ecclesiastics and the emperor Theodosius the Less, the Armenians concocted a story that it had been divinely revealed. Once their alphabet perfected, the catholicus Sahak formed a school of translators who were sent to Edessa, Athens, Constantinople, Alexandria, Antioch, Caesarea in Cappadocia, and elsewhere, to procure codices both in Syriac and Greek and translate them. From Syriac were made the first version of the New Testament, the version of Eusebius' History and his Life of Constantine (unless this be from the original Greek), the homilies of Aphraates, the Acts of Gurias and Samuna, the works of Ephrem Syrus (partly published in four volumes by the Mechitharists of Venice). They include the commentaries on the *Diatessaron* and the Paulines, Laboubna and History of Addai, the Syriac canons of the Apostles.

From the original Greek were rendered in the 5th century the following authors and works. An asterisk is prefixed to those which have been printed:—*Eusebius' *Chronicon*; *Philo's lost commentaries on Genesis and Exodus, and his lost treatises on Providence and Animals, as well as a great number of his works still preserved in Greek; *the entire Bible (the New Testament is a recension after Antiochene Greek texts of an older version made from the oldest Syriac text); *the Alexander romance of the pseudo-Callisthenes; **Epistles* and *Acts* of Ignatius of Antioch; *many homilies of Gregory Thaumaturgus; *Athanasius (a large number of works, many of them wrongly attributed); Irenaeus, *Adversus Haereses* and *Ad Marcianum* (recently found); *Hippolytus' commentaries on the Song of Songs and Daniel, and many fragments; *Timotheus' life of Athanasius; Theophilus of Alexandria, various homilies; *Eusebius of Gabala or

Severianus, fifteen Homilies; *Cyril of Jerusalem, *Catecheses* and Letter to Constantine; *Wisdom of Ahikar*, *the *Apology* of Aristides; Gregory of Nazianzus, thirty-four Homilies; *Nonnus' work on Gregory (perhaps a version of 6th century); Basil of Caesarea, *Hexaëmeron*, fifteen Homilies on faith, epistle to Terentius, ascetic writings and canons, on the Holy Spirit, to Cledonius, &c. Helladius of Caesarea's life of Basil; Gregory of Nyssa's treatise on the Beatitudes, and many other homilies, Commentaries on Song of Songs, *On Human Nature (Nemesius), panegyrics on sundry Martyrs, and other works (but some of these versions belong to the beginning of the 8th century); Epiphanius of Salamis, Commentary on the Gospels, *On weights and measures*, *Physiologus*, canons and many homilies; Evagrius of Pontus, Homilies and Ascetic works, Letters to Melania, &c.; John Chrysostom, *Homilies and Prayers, in very beautiful language; *Proclus, patriarch of Constantinople, many homilies; *Nilus the Ascete, *On the Eight Spirits of Evil*; *Josephus, *On the Jewish War*; Dionysius of Alexandria, *Against Paul of Samosata* and other fragments; Acacius, bishop of Melitene, *Letters* to Sahak; Julius of Rome (fragments); Zenobius, Homilies (? from Syriac); the *History* of Julius Africanus was perhaps also translated in this century, but it is lost. To the 5th century belong the versions of the 5⁷³Nicene canons, of which the Armenian text as preserved is barely intelligible, of the eucharistic rites called of *Basil, *Chrysostom, *Ignatius and others; also the *Hours or Breviary, the *Rites of Ordination, Baptism, of the making and release of Penitents, of Epiphany, and perhaps the many rites of animal sacrifice, for these are partly originals, partly versions of lost Greek texts. A mass of martyrs' acts were also rendered in this century, including parts of the lost collection made by Eusebius. Among these the *Acts and Apology* of Apollonius restore a lost 2nd-century text. The *Canons* of Sahak also purport to be translated from a Greek original about the year 330.

The Armenians were so busy in this century translating Greek and Syriac fathers that they have left little that is original. Still a number of historical works survive: *Faustus of Byzantium relates the events of the period A.D. 344-392 in a work instinct with life and racy of the soil. It was perhaps first composed in Greek, but it gives a faithful picture of the court of the petty sovereigns of Armenia, of the political organization, of the blood feuds of the clans, of the planting of Christianity. Procopius preserves some fragments of the Greek.

The *History of Taron*, by Zenobius of Glak, is a somewhat legendary account of Gregory the Illuminator, and may have been written in Syriac in the 5th, though it was only Armenized in a later century.

*Elisaeus Wardapet wrote a history of Wardan (Vardan), and of the war waged for their faith by the Armenians against the Sassanids. He was an eye-witness of this struggle, and gives a good account of the contemporary Mazdaism which the Persians tried to force on the Armenians. *Lazar of Pharp wrote a history embracing the events of the 5th century up to the year 485, as a continuation of the work of Faustus.

*A history of St Gregory and of the conversion of Armenia by Agathangelus is preserved in Greek, Armenian and Arabic. The Arabic edited by Professor Marr of St Petersburg seems to be the oldest form of text. The Greek is a rendering of the Armenian. It is a compilation, and the second part which contains the *Acts* of Gregory and of St Rhipsima seems wholly legendary. The Greek and Armenian texts were edited together by Lagarde.

*The *History of Armenia* by Moses of Khoren (Chorene) relates events up to about the year 450. It is a compilation, devoid of historical method, value or veracity, from all sorts of previous authors, mostly from those which already existed in an Armenian dress. Some critics put down the date of composition as low as about 700, and it was certainly retouched in the late 6th century.

*A long volume of rhetorical exercises, based on Aphthonius, is also ascribed to Moses of Khoren, and appears to be of the 5th century. The *geography which passes under his name may belong to the 7th century. Various homilies of Moses survive, as also of Elisaeus.

Gorium wrote in this century a *Life of Mesrop*, and Eznik a *Refutation of the Sects*, based largely on antecedent Greek works. The sects in question are Paganism, Mazdaism, Greek Philosophy and Manicheism. A volume of *homilies under the name of Gregory the Illuminator, but not his, also belongs to this century, and a series of ascetic discourses attributed to John Mandakuni, who was patriarch 478-500.

Of the 6th and 7th centuries few works survive except anonymous versions of the *Acts of Thomas* (perhaps from the Syriac), of the *Acts of Peter and Paul*, *of John (pseudo-Prochorus), *of Bartholomew, and of other apostles; also of *the Acts of Paul and Thekla, *of Titus, *of the Protevangel, *of the Testaments of the patriarchs, of the *Gospel of Nicodemus*, or *Acts of Pilate*, of the *Book of Adam*, of the *Deaths of the Prophets*, of the *History of Baruch*, of the *Apocalypses of Paul and of the Virgin Mary, of the *Acts of Sylvester, and of an enormous number of other similar apocryphs. Some of these may be of the 5th century. Two volumes of these apocryphs of the Old and New Testaments have recently been published at Venice. To these centuries belong also the versions of the Acts of the council of Ephesus, of Gangra, Laodicea and of other councils. To the late 7th century belong the *calendarial works of Ananiah of Shirak, who also has left a *chronicon compiled from Eusebius, Andreas of Crete, Hippolytus and other sources. In the *Letter-book of the Patriarchs, lately printed at Tiflis, are to be found a number of controversial monophysite tracts of these and the succeeding three centuries, important for church history. It includes a mass of documents relative to the churches of Iberia and Albania. The chief literary monument of the 7th century is the history of the wars of Heraclius and of the early Mahommedan conquests in Asia Minor, by the bishop Sebeos, who was an eye-witness. The *history of the Albanians of the Caucasus, by Moses Kalankatuatzi, also belongs to the end of this century. To the middle of the 7th century also belong the translations of Aristotle's treatises *On the Categories, and *On Interpretation, and of *Porphyry's Isagoge, as well as of voluminous Greek commentaries on these books; the version of the *Grammar of Dionysius Thrax and an incomplete Euclid. The translator was one David called the Invincible, who also wrote monophysite tracts. At the end of this 7th century one Philo of Tirak is supposed to have made the version of the *History of Socrates, unless indeed it was made earlier. To this century also seems to belong the Armenian version of a *history of the Iberians, by Djuansher, a work full of valuable information.

The early 8th century was a time of great literary activity. Gregory Asheruni wrote an important *commentary on the Jerusalem Lectionary, and his friend *John the catholicus (717-728) commentaries on the other liturgical works of his church; he also collected all existing canon law, Greek or Armenian, respected in his church, wrote *against the Paulicians and Docetae, and composed many beautiful hymns. *Leoncius the priest has left a history of the first caliphs, and Stephanus, bishop of Siunik, translated the *controversial works of Cyril of Alexandria (whose Glaphyra and commentaries, however, seem to have been translated at an earlier period). He also translated the works of Dionysius the Areopagite, commented on the Armenian breviary and wrote hymns.

In the 9th century Zachariah, catholicus, the correspondent of Photius, wrote many eloquent homilies for the various church feasts. Shapuh Bagratuni wrote a history of his age, now lost. Mashtotz, catholicus, collected in one volume the Armenian rituals.

In the 10th century (c. 925) the catholicus John VI. issued his *history of Armenia, and Thomas Artsruni a *history of his clan carried up to the year 936. Ananias of Mok (943-965) wrote a great work against the Paulicians, unfortunately lost. Chosroes wrote a *commentary on the eucharistic rites and breviary, *Mesrop a history of Nerses the Great; *Stephen of Asolik wrote a history of the world, and a commentary on Jeremiah; *Gregory of Narek his famous meditations and hymns; Samuel Kamrdjtsoretzi a commentary on the Lectionary based on Gregory Asheruni.

In the 11th century the catholicus Gregory translated many Acts of Martyrs, and John Kozerhn wrote a history, now lost, as well as a work on the Armenian calendar; Stephen Asolik a *history of Armenia up to the year 1004; *Aristaces of Lastiverd a valuable history of the conquest of Armenia by the Seljuk caliphs. We may also mention a *monophysite work against the Greek doctor Theopistus by Paul of Taron; *letters and poems of Gregory Magistros, who also was the translator of the *Laws, Timaeus and other dialogues of Plato.

The 12th century saw many remarkable writers, mostly in Cilician Armenia, viz. Nerses the Graceful (d. 1165), author of an *Elegy on the taking of Edessa, of *voluminous hymns, of long *Pastoral Letters and Synodal orations of value for the historian of eastern churches. *Samuel of Ani composed a chronicle up to 1179. Nerses of Lambron, archbishop of Tarsus, left a *Synodal oration, a *Commentary on the liturgy, &c., and his contemporary Gregory of Tlay an *Elegy on the capture of Jerusalem, and various *dogmatic works. In this century the *history of Michael the Syrian was translated; Ignatius and Sargis composed *commentaries on Luke and *the catholic epistles, and *Matthew of Edessa a valuable history of the years 952-1136, 574 continued up to 1176 by Gregory the priest. Mechithar (Mekhitar) Kosh (d. 1207) wrote an elegant *Book of Fables, and compiled a *corpus of civil and canon law (partly from Byzantine codes).

In the 13th century the following works or authors are to be noticed:—*history of Kiriakos of Ganzak, which contains much about the Mongols, Georgians and Albanians; *Malakia the monk's history of the Tatars up to 1272; *Chronicle of Mechithar of Ani (fragmentary); *Vahram's rhymed chronicle of the kings of Lesser Armenia; *history of the world, by Vartan, up to 1269. In this century mostly falls the redaction of a large fable literature, recently edited in three volumes by Professor Marr of St Petersburg.

14th century: *history of Siunik, by Stephen Orbelian, archbishop of that province 1287-1304; *Sempat's chronicle of Lesser Armenia (952-1274), carried on by a continuator to 1331; *Mechithar of Airivanq, a chronography; *Hethoum's account of the Tatars, and chronography of the years 1076-1307. John of Orotn (d. 1388) compiled commentaries on John's gospel and the Paulines, and wrote homilies and monophysite works; his disciple Gregory of Dathev (b. 1340) compiled a *Summa theologiae called the Book of Questions, in the style of the Summa of Aquinas, which had been translated into Armenian c. 1330, as were a little later the *Summa of Albertus and works of other schoolmen.

15th century: *History of Tamerlane, by Thomas of Medsoph, carried up to 1447.

17th century, Araqel of Tabriz wrote a *history of the Persian invasions of Armenia in the years 1602-1661.

In the above list are not included a number of medical, astrological, calendarial and philological or lexicographic works, mostly written during or since the Cilician or crusading epoch. The hymns used in Armenian worship rarely go back to the 5th century; and they were still few in number and brief in length when Nerses the Graceful and his contemporaries more than doubled their number and bulk in the 12th century. Most Armenian poems embody acrostics, and their poets began to rhyme in the 8th century or thereabouts. Since the 15th century a certain number of profane poets have arisen, whose work is less jejune on the whole than that of the hymn and canticle writers of an earlier age. Gregory Magistros (d. 1058) abridged the whole of the Old and New Testaments in a *rhyming poem, and set a fashion to later writers. Such works as *Barlaam and Josaphat. the *History of the Seven Sages, the *Wisdom of Ahikar, the *Tale of the City of Bronze, were freely turned into verse in the 13th and following centuries.

It will be realized from the above enumeration of works written in each century that Armenian literature was purely monkish. There was no epic or romance literature; although this was not lacking in the contiguous country of Georgia, where there seem to have always been knights and ladies willing to read and keep alive a literature of poetry and narrative, not altogether suitable for monks, and more akin to Persian literature.

Other forms of faith than the orthodox had a hold in Armenia, particularly the Nestorian and the Manichean. Sundry works of Mani were translated in the year 588, but are lost. Perhaps certain works of Diodore of Tarsus survive, but the orthodox monks were so vigilant that there is little chance of finding any other monuments than those of the stereotyped orthodoxy.

The 16th century saw the first books printed in Armenian. A press was set up at Venice in 1565, and the psalms and breviary were printed. In 1584 the Roman propaganda began its issue of Armenian books with a Gregorian calendar. In the 17th century presses were working at Lembourg, Milan, Paris, Isfahan (where in 1640 a large folio of the Lives of the Fathers of the Desert appeared), in Leghorn, Amsterdam (where in 1664 the first edition of the Hymn-book, in 1666 the first Bible, and in 1667 the first Ritual were printed), Marseilles, Constantinople, Leipzig and Padua.

The press which has done most in printing Armenian authors is that of the Mechitharists of Venice. Here in 1836 was issued a magnificent thesaurus of the Armenian language, with the Latin and Greek equivalents of each word. At that time there was no dictionary of any language and literature to be compared with this for exhaustiveness and accuracy. There are now Armenian presses all over the world, reprinting old books or issuing new works, often translations of modern writers, English, French, Russian and German.

The chief collections of old Armenian MSS. are: at the convent of *Echmiadzin at Valarshapat; at Stambul in the library of the fathers of St Anthony; at Venice in the Mechitharist convent of San Lazaro; at the *Mechitharist convent in Vienna; in the *Royal library at Vienna; in the *Paris Bibliothèque Nationale; in the Vatican library; in the British Museum; in the *Bodleian; in the Rylands library; in the *Berlin and *Munich libraries; *in Tübingen; in St Petersburg, and in the *Lazarev institute at Moscow; at New Joulfa, the Armenian suburb of Isfahan. Private collections have been made by Mr Rendel Harris in Birmingham (presented to the university of Leiden); at Parham and elsewhere. A printed catalogue exists of those marked with an asterisk.

AUTHORITIES.—F. Combefis, Historia Monothelitarum (Paris, 1648); Arshak Ter Mikelian, Die armen. Kirche, iv. bis zum xiii. Jahrhundert (Leipzig, 1892); H. Gelzer, "Die Anfänge der armenischen Kirche" in the Berichte der Königlich. Sachsischen Gesellschaft der Wissenschaften: Historisch-philologische Classe(1895), p. 171; Gutschmid, Kleine Schriften (Leipzig, 1892), t. iii.; Langlois, Collection d'historiens arméniens (Paris, 1867) (the translations often careless); E.W. Brooks, The Syriac Chronicle known as Zachariah of Mitylene (London, 1899), p. 24; Dulaurier,Recherches sur la chronologie arménienne (Paris, 1859); Agop Manandian, Beiträge zur albanischen Geschichte (Leipzig, 1897); G. Owsepian, Die Entstehungsgeschichte des Monotheletismus(Leipzig, 1897); Cardinal Angelo Mai, Nova SS. patrum bibliotheca, 6 vols. (Rome, 1844-1871), vol. ii. contains Latin version of Armenian canons; Hergenrother, Photius (Regensburg, 1867); Tchamchian, History of Armenia (in Armenian at Venice and English abridged translation entitled M. Chamich by John Audall, Calcutta, 1827); Domini Joannis Onziensis, Opera Latine(Venice, 1834); Nersetis Clajensis, Opera omnia Latine (Venice, 1833); A. Papadopoulos-Kerameus in the Recueil de la société orthodoxe de Palestine (St Petersburg, 1892) (Armenian correspondence with Photius translated); Enthymius

Zigabenus,*Panoplia, Patrol. Gr.* vol. 130, col. 1173; E. Dulaurier, *Histoire de l'église armén.* (Paris, 1857); le Quien, *Oriens christianus;* Mansi,*Concilia,* vol. 25; Steph. Azarian, *Ecclesiae Armenae Traditio*(Rome, 1870); A. Balgy, *Historia doctrinae catholicae inter Armenos* (Vienna, 1878); Clemens Galanus, *Conciliatio Ecclesiae Armenae cum Romana* (Rome, 1690); L. Alishan, *Sissouan, contrée de l'Arménie* (Venice, 1893), in Armenian, but also in French translation; *Recueil d'actes relatifs aux Arméniens* (3 vols., Moscow, 1833); St Martin, *Mémoires historiques sur l'Arménie*(Paris, 1818); V. Langlois, *Voyage dans la Cilicie* (Paris, 1861); H.G.O. Dwight, *Christianity in Turkey* (London, 1854); De Damas,*Coup d'œil sur l'Arménie* (Lyon, 1887); H.F.B. Lynch, *Armenia* (2 vols., London, 1902); J. Issaverdens, *Armenia, Ecclesiastical History* (Venice, 1875); E. Dulaurier, *Historiens arméniens des Croisades* (Paris); Giovanni de Serpos, *Compendio Storico*(Venice, 1786); Garabed Chahnazarian, *Esquisse de l'histoire de l'Arménie* (Paris, 1856); Gelzer, "Armenien" in Herzog-Hauck,*Realencyklopadie für protestantische Theologie* (ed. 3, Leipzig, 1897); Hefele, *Hist. of Councils,* vols. 3 and 9; F. Néve, *L'Arménie chrétienne* (Paris); P. Hunanian, *Histoire des canciles d'Orient*(Vienna, 1847); Gr. Chalathianz, *Apocryphes* (Moscow, 1897), and other works; Brosset, *Collection d'historiens arméniens* (St Petersburg, 1874), and numerous other works by the same author; J. Catergian, *De fidei symbolo quo Armenii utuntur* (Vienna, 1893); Ricaut, *The present state of the Greek and Armenian Churches* (London, 1679); H. Denzinger, *Ritus orientalium*(Würzburg, 1863); Fred. C. Conybeare, *Rituale Armenorum*(Oxford, 1905); F.E. Brightman, *Eastern Liturgies* (Oxford, 1896); P. Vetter, *Chosroae magni explicatio missae* (Freiburg-im-Breisgau, 1880); L. Petit, articles on Armenian religious history, councils, literature, creed and discipline in *Diction. de théologie catholique,* cols. 1888-1968; F.C. Conybeare, "The Armenian canons of St Sahak" in the *American Journal of Theology*(Chicago, 1898), p. 828; C.F. Neumann, *Geschichte der armenischen Literatur* (Leipzig, 1836); Simon Weber, *Die katholische Kirche in Armenien* (Freiburg-im-Breisgau, 1903); Sukias Somal,*Quadro della Storia Letteraria di Armenia* (Venice, 1829); M.V. Ermoni, "L'Arménie" in *Revue de l'orient chrétien*(for year 1896); F. Tournebize, "Histoire de l'Arménie" (*ib.* 1902-3-4-5); R.P.D. Girard, "Les Madag" (*ib.* for year 1902); H. Hübschmann, *Armenische Studien* and *Grammatik* (Leipzig, 1883 and 1895). Grammars by Petermann (in *Porta Orientalium Linguarum* series), by Prof. Meillet of Paris, by Prof. N. Marr of St Petersburg (in Russian), by Joseph Karst (of the Cilician dialect). Texts of most of the Armenian fathers and historians have been printed by the Mechitharists of San Lazaro, Venice, and are readily procurable at their convent.

(F. C. C.)

ARMENTIÈRES, a town of northern France, in the department of Nord, on the Lys, 13 m. W.N.W. of Lille on the Northern railway from that city to Dunkirk. Pop. (1906) 25,408. The chief building is the hôtel de ville with a 17th-century belfry. There are communal colleges for girls and boys, a board of trade-arbitrators, a chamber of commerce and a national technical school. The town is an important centre for the spinning and weaving of flax and cotton; bleaching, dyeing and the manufacture of machinery are among the other industries. Its industrial prosperity dates from the middle ages, when, however, woollen, not cotton, goods were the staple product.

ARMET (diminutive of Fr. *arme*), a form of helmet, which was developed out of existing forms in the latter part of the 15th century. It was round in shape, and often had a narrow ridge or comb along the top. It had a pivoted or hinged vizor and nosepiece, and complete chin, neck and cheek protection, closely connected with the gorget. It is distinguished from the basinet by its roundness, and by the fact that it protects the neck and chin by strong plates, instead of a "camail" or loose collar of mail; from the salade and heaume by its close fit and skull-cap shape; and from the various forms of vizored burgonets by the absence of the projecting brim. It remained in use until the final abandonment of the complete closed head-piece.

ARMFELT, GUSTAF MAURITZ, COUNT (1757-1814), son of Charles II.'s general, Carl Gustaf Armfelt, was born in Finland on the 31st of March 1757. In 1774 he became an ensign in the guards, but his frivolity provoked the displeasure of Gustavus III. and he thought it prudent to go abroad. Subsequently, however, (1780) he met the king again at Spa and completely won the monarch's favour by his natural amiability, intelligence and brilliant social gifts. Henceforth his fortune was made. At first he was the *maître des plaisirs* of the Swedish court, but it was not long before more serious affairs were entrusted to him. He took part in the negotiations with Catherine II. (1783) and with the Danish government (1787), and during the Russian war of 1788-90 he was one of the king's most trusted and active counsellors. He also displayed great valour in the field. In 1788 when the Danes unexpectedly invaded Sweden and threatened

213

Gothenburg, it was Armfelt who under the king's directions organized the Dalecarlian levies and led them to victory. He remained absolutely faithful to Gustavus when nearly the whole of the nobility fell away from him; brilliantly distinguished himself in the later phases of the Russian war; and was the Swedish plenipotentiary at the conclusion of the peace of Verelä. During the last years of Gustavus III. his influence was paramount, though he protested against his master's headstrong championship of the Bourbons. On his deathbed Gustavus III. (1792) committed the care of his infant son to Armfelt and appointed him a member of the council of regency; but the anti-Gustavian duke-regent Charles sent Armfelt as Swedish ambassador to Naples to get rid of him. From Naples Armfelt communicated with Catherine II., urging her to bring about by means of a military demonstration a change in the Swedish government in favour of the Gustavians. The plot was discovered by the regent's spies, and Armfelt only escaped from the man-of-war sent to Naples to seize him, with the assistance of Queen Caroline. He now fled to Russia, where he was interned at Kaluga, while at home he was condemned to confiscation and death as a traitor, and his unjustly accused mistress Magdalena Rudenschöld was publicly whipped to gratify an old grudge of the regent's. When Gustavus IV. attained his majority, Armfelt was completely rehabilitated and sent as Swedish ambassador to Vienna (1802), but was obliged to quit that post two years later for sharply attacking the Austrian government's attitude towards Bonaparte. From 1805 to 1807 he was commander-in-chief of the Swedish forces in Pomerania, where he displayed great ability and retarded the conquest of the duchy as long as it was humanly possible. On his return home, he was appointed commander-in-chief on the Norwegian frontier, but could do nothing owing to the *ordres, contre-ordres et désordres* of his lunatic master. He would have nothing to say to the revolutionaries who in 1809 deposed Gustavus IV. and his whole family. Armfelt was the most courageous of the supporters of the crown prince Gustavus, and when Bernadotte was elected resolved to retire to Finland. His departure was accelerated by a decree of expulsion as a conspirator (1811). Over the impressionable Alexander I. of Russia, Armfelt exercised almost as great an influence as Czartoryski, especially as regards Finnish affairs. He contributed more than any one else to the erection of the grand-duchy into an autonomous state, and was its first and best governor-general. The plan of the Russian defensive campaigns is, with great probability, also attributed to him, and he gained Alexander over to the plan of uniting Norway with Sweden. He died at Tsarskoe Selo on the 19th of August 1814.

See Robert Nisbet Bain, *Gustavus III.* vol. ii. (London, 1895); Elof Tegner, *Gustaf Mauritz Armfelt* (Stockholm, 1883-1887).

(R. N. B.)

ARMIDALE, a town in Sandon county, New South Wales, Australia, 313 m. by rail N. of Sydney. Pop. (1901) 4249. It lies at an elevation of 3313 ft., in a picturesque mountainous district, for the most part pastoral and agricultural, though it contains some alluvial gold diggings. Antimony is found in large quantities near the town. Armidale is a cathedral town, being the seat of a Roman Catholic bishop and belonging to the joint Anglican diocese of Grafton; Armidale St Peter's, the Anglican cathedral, and St Mary's, the Roman Catholic, are both fine buildings. The town is the centre of great educational activity, its schools including the New England girls' school, St Patrick's college, the high school, the Ursuline convent and state schools. Armidale became a municipality in 1863.

ARMILLA, ARMIL or ARMILLARY SPHERE (from the Lat. *armilla*, a bracelet), an instrument used in astronomy. In its simplest form, consisting of a ring fixed in the plane of the equator, the *armilla* is one of the most ancient of astronomical instruments. Slightly developed, it was crossed by another ring fixed in the plane of the meridian. The first was an equinoctial, the second a solstitial armilla. Shadows were used as indices of the sun's position, in combination with angular divisions. When several rings or circles were combined representing the great circles of the heavens, the instrument became an armillary sphere. Armillae are said to have been in early use in China. Eratosthenes (276-196 B.C.) used most probably a solstitial armilla for measuring the obliquity of the ecliptic. Hipparchus (160-125 B.C.) probably used an armillary sphere of four rings. Ptolemy (*c.* A.D. 107-161) describes his instrument in the *Syntaxis* (book v. chap, i.), and it is of great interest as an example of the armillary sphere passing into the spherical astrolabe. It consisted of a graduated circle inside which another could slide, carrying two small tubes diametrically opposite, the instrument being kept vertical by a plumb-line.

From M. Blundeville's *Treatise of the first principles of Cosmography and specially of the Spheare.*

Armillary Sphere. A.D. 1636.

No material advance was made on Ptolemy's instrument until Tycho Brahe, whose elaborate armillary spheres passing into astrolabes are figured in his *Astronomiae Instauratae Mechanica.* 576The armillary sphere survives as useful for teaching, and may be described as a skeleton celestial globe, the series of rings representing the great circles of the heavens, and revolving on an axis within a horizon. With the earth as centre such a sphere is known as Ptolemaic; with the sun as centre, as Copernican.

The designer of the instrument shown no doubt thought that the north pole might suitably have the same ornament as was used to mark N. on the compass card, and so surmounted it with the *fleur-de-lys*, traditionally chosen for that purpose on the compass by Flavio Gioja in honour of Charles of Anjou, king of Sicily and Naples.

Armillary spheres occur in many old sculptures, paintings and engravings; and from these sources we know that they were made for suspension, for resting on the ground or on a table, for holding by a short handle, or either for holding or for resting on a stand.

AUTHORITIES.—Tycho Brahe, *Astronomiae Instauratae Mechanica*; M. Blundeville, *his Exercises*; N. Bion, *Traité des instrumens de mathématique*; also *L'Usage des globes célestes*; Sédillot, *Mémoire sur les instrumens*; J.B. Delambre, *Histoire de l'astronomie ancienne*; R. Grant, *History of Physical Astronomy*.

(M. L. H.)

ARMINIUS, the Latinized form of the name of HERMANN, or more probably ARMIN (17 B.C.-A.D. 21), the German national hero. He was a son of a certain Segimer, a prince of the tribe of the Cherusci, and in early life served with distinction as an officer in the Roman armies. Returning to his own people he found them chafing under the yoke of the Roman governor, Quintilius Varus; he entertained for them hopes of freedom, and cautiously inducing neighbouring tribes to join his standard he led the rebellion which broke out in the autumn of A.D. 9. Heavily laden with baggage the troops of Varus were decoyed into the fastnesses of the Teutoburger Wald, and there attacked, the completeness of the barbarian victory being attested by the virtual annihilation of three legions, by the voluntary death of Varus, and by the terror which reigned in Rome when the news of the defeat became known, a terror which found utterance in the emperor's despairing cry: "Varus, give me back my legions!" Then in A.D. 15 Germanicus Caesar led the Romans against Arminius, and captured his wife, Thusnelda. An indecisive battle was fought in the Teutoburger Wald, where Germanicus narrowly escaped the fate of Varus, and in the following year Arminius was defeated. The hero's later years were spent in fighting against Marbod, prince of the Marcomanni, and in disputes with his own people occasioned probably by his desire to found a powerful kingdom. He was murdered in A.D. 21.

In 1875 a great monument to Arminius was completed. This stands on the Grotenburg mountain near Detmold. Klopstock and other poets have used his exploits as material for dramas.

Much discussion has taken place with regard to the exact spot in the Teutoburger Wald where the great battle between Arminius and Varus was fought. There is an immense literature on this subject, and the following may be consulted:—T. Mommsen, *Die Ortlichkeit der Varusschlacht* (1885); E. Meyer, *Untersuchungen über die Schlacht im Teutoburger Walde* (1893); A. Wilms, *Die Schlacht im Teutoburger Walde* (1899); F. Knoke, *Das Schlachtfeld im Teutoburger Walde* (1899); E. Dünzelmann, *Der Schauplatz der Varusschlacht* (1889); and P. Höfer, *Die Varusschlacht* (1888). For more general accounts of Arminius see: Tacitus, *Annals,* edited by H. Furneaux (1884-1891); O. Kemmer, *Arminius* (1893); F.W. Fischer, *Armin und die Römer* (1893); W. Uhl, *Das Portrait des Arminius* (1898); and F. Knoke, *Die Kriegszüge des Germanicus in Deutschland* (1887).

ARMINIUS, JACOBUS (1560-1609), Dutch theologian, author of the modified reformed theology that receives its name of Arminian from him, was born at Oudewater, South Holland, on the 10th of October 1560. Arminius is a Latinized form of his patronymic Hermanns or Hermansen. His father, Hermann Jakobs, a cutler, died while he was an infant, leaving a widow and three children. Theodorus Aemilius, a priest, who had turned Protestant, adopting Jakob, sent him to school at Utrecht, but died when his charge was in his fifteenth year. Rudolf Snellius (Snel van Roijen, 1546-1613), the mathematician, a native of Oudewater, then a professor at Marburg, happening at the time to visit his early home, met the boy, saw promise in him and undertook his maintenance and education. But hardly was he settled at Marburg when the news came that the Spaniards had besieged and taken Oudewater, and murdered its inhabitants almost without exception. Arminius hurried home, but only to find all his relatives slain. In February the same year (1575), the university of Leiden had been founded, and thither, by the kindness of friends, Arminius was sent to study theology. The six years he remained in Leiden (1576-1582) were years of active and innovating thought in Holland. The War of Independence had started conflicting tendencies in men's minds. To some it seemed to illustrate the necessity of the state tolerating only one religion, but to others the necessity of the state tolerating all. Dirck Coornhert argued, in private conferences and public disputations, that it was wrong to punish heretics, and his great opponents were, as a rule, the ministers, who maintained that there was no room for more than one religion in a state. Caspar Koolhaes, the heroic minister of Leiden—its first lecturer, too, in divinity—pleaded against a too rigid uniformity, for such an agreement on "fundamentals" as had allowed Reformed, Lutherans and Anabaptists to unite. Leiden had been happy, too, in its first professors. There taught in theology Guillaume Feuguières or Feuguereius (d. 1613), a mild divine, who had written a treatise on persuasion in religion, urging that as to it "men could be led, not driven"; Lambert Danaeus, who deserves remembrance as the first to discuss Christian ethics scientifically, apart from dogmatics; Johannes Drusius, the Orientalist, one of the most enlightened and advanced scholars of his day, settled later at Franeker; Johann Kolmann the younger, best known by his saying that high Calvinism made God "both a tyrant and an executioner." Snellius, Arminius's old patron, now removed to Leiden, expounded the Ramist philosophy, and did his best to start his students on the search after truth, unimpeded by the authority of Aristotle. Under these men and influences, Arminius studied with signal success; and the promise he gave induced the merchants' gild of Amsterdam to bear the further expenses of his education. In 1582 he went to Geneva, studied there awhile under Theodore Beza, but had soon, owing to his active advocacy of the Ramist philosophy, to remove to Basel. After a short but brilliant career there he turned to Geneva, studied for three years, travelled, in 1586, in Italy, heard Giacomo Zarabella (1533-1589) lecture on philosophy in Padua, visited Rome, and, open-minded enough to see its good as well as its evil, was suspected by the stern Dutch Calvinists of "popish" leanings. Next year he was called to Amsterdam, and there, in 1588, was ordained. He soon acquired the reputation of being a good preacher and faithful pastor. He was commissioned to organize the educational system of the city, and is said to have done it well. He greatly distinguished himself by fidelity to duty during a plague that devastated Amsterdam in 1602. In 1603 he was called, in succession to Franz Junius, to a theological professorship at Leiden, which he held till his death on the 19th of October 1609.

Arminius is best known as the founder of the anti-Calvinistic school in Reformed theology, which created the Remonstrant Church in Holland (see REMONSTRANTS), and contributed to form the Arminian tendency or party in England. He was a man of mild and liberal spirit, broadened by varied culture, constitutionally averse from narrow views and enforced uniformity. He lived in a period of severe systematizing. The Reformed strengthened itself against the Roman Catholic theology by working itself, on the one hand, into vigorous logical consistency, and supporting itself, on the other, on the supreme authority of the Scriptures. Calvin's first principle, the absolute sovereignty of God, had been so applied as to make the divine decree determine alike the acts and the destinies of men; and his formal principle had been so construed as to invest his system with the authority of the source whence it professed to have been drawn. Calvinism had become, towards the close of the 16th century, supreme in Holland, but the very rigour of the uniformity it exacted provoked a reaction. Coornhert could not plead for the toleration of heretics without assailing the dominant Calvinism, and so he opposed a conditional to its unconditional predestination. The two ministers of Delft, who had debated the point with him, had, the better to turn his arguments, descended from the supralapsarian to the infralapsarian position, *i.e.* made the divine decree, instead of precede and determine, succeed the Fall. This seemed to the high Calvinists of Holland a grave heresy. Arminius, fresh from Geneva, familiar with the dialectics of Beza, appeared to many the man able to speak the needed word, and so, in 1589, he was simultaneously invited by the ecclesiastical court of Amsterdam to refute Coornhert, and by Martin Lydius, professor at Franeker, to combat the two infralapsarian ministers of Delft. Thus led to confront the questions of necessity and free will, his own views became unsettled, and the further he pursued his inquiries the more he was inclined to assert the freedom of man and limit the range of the unconditional decrees of God. This change became gradually more apparent in his preaching and in his conferences with his clerical associates, and occasioned much controversy in the ecclesiastical courts where, however, he successfully defended his position. The controversy was embittered and the differences sharpened by his appointment to the professorship at Leiden. He had as colleague Franz Gomarus, a strong supralapsarian, perfervid, irrepressible; and their collisions, personal, official, political, tended to develop and define their respective positions.

Arminius died, worn out by uncongenial controversy and ecclesiastical persecution, before his system had been elaborated into the logical consistency it attained in the hands of his celebrated successor, Simon Episcopius; but though inchoate in detail, it was in its principles clear and coherent enough. These may be thus stated:

1. The decree of God is, when it concerns His own actions, absolute, but when it concerns man's, conditional, *i.e.* the decree relative to the Saviour to be appointed and the salvation to be provided is absolute, but the decree relative to the persons saved or condemned is made to depend on the acts—belief and repentance in the one case, unbelief and impenitence in the other—of the persons themselves.

2. The providence or government of God, while sovereign, is exercised in harmony with the nature of the creatures governed, *i.e.* the sovereignty of God is so exercised as to be compatible with the freedom of man.

3. Man is by original nature, through the assistance of divine grace, free, able to will and perform the right; but is in his fallen state, of and by himself, unable to do so; he needs to be regenerated in all his powers before he can do what is good and pleasing to God.

4. Divine grace originates, maintains and perfects all the good in man, so much so that he cannot, though regenerate, conceive, will or do any good thing without it.

5. The saints possess, by the grace of the Holy Spirit, sufficient strength to persevere to the end in spite of sin and the flesh, but may so decline from sound doctrine as to cause divine grace to be ineffectual.

6. Every believer may be assured of his own salvation.

7. It is possible for a regenerate man to live without sin.

Arminius's works are mostly occasional treatises drawn from him by controversial emergencies, but they everywhere exhibit a calm, well-furnished, undogmatic and progressive mind. He was essentially an amiable man, who hated the zeal for an impossible orthodoxy that constrained "the church to institute a search after crimes which have not betrayed an existence, yea, and to drag into open contentions those who are meditating no evil." His friend Peter Bertius, who pronounced his funeral oration, closed it with these words: "There lived a man whom it was not possible for those who knew him sufficiently to esteem; those who entertained no esteem for him are such as never knew him well enough to appreciate his merits."

The works of Arminius (in Latin) were published in a single quarto volume at Leiden in 1629, at Frankfort in 1631 and 1635. Two volumes of an English translation, with copious notes, by James Nichols, were published at London, 1825-1828; three volumes (complete) at Buffalo, 1853. A life was written by Caspar Brandt, son of Gerard Brandt, the historian of the Dutch reformation, and published in 1724; republished and annotated by J.L. Mosheim in 1725; and translated into English by the Rev. John Guthrie, 1854. James Nichols also wrote a life (London, 1843).

ARMISTICE (from Lat. *arma*, arms, and *sistere*, to stop), a suspension of hostilities by mutual agreement between two nations at war, or their respective forces. An armistice may be either general or particular; in the first case there is a complete cessation of hostile operations in every part of the dominions of the belligerent powers; in the second there is merely a temporary truce between two contending armies, or between a besieged fortress and the force besieging it. Such a temporary truce, when for a very limited period and for a special purpose, *e.g.* the collection of the wounded and the burial of the dead, is termed a *suspension of arms*. A general armistice cannot be concluded by the commanders-in-chief unless special authority has been previously delegated to them by their respective governments; otherwise any arrangement entered into by them requires subsequent ratification by the supreme powers of the states. A partial truce may be concluded by the officers of the respective powers, without any special authority from their governments, wherever, from the nature and extent of the commands they exercise, their duties could not be efficiently discharged without their possession of such a power. The conduct of belligerent parties during an armistice is usually regulated in modern warfare by express agreement between the parties, but where this is not the case the following general conditions may be laid down. (1) Each party may do, within the limits prescribed by the truce, whatever he could have done in time of peace. For example, he can raise troops, collect stores, receive reinforcements and fortify places that are not actually in a state of siege. (2) Neither party can take advantage of the armistice to do what he could not have done had military operations continued. Thus he cannot throw provisions or reinforcements into a besieged town, and neither besiegers nor besieged are at liberty to repair their fortifications or erect new works. (3) All things contained in places the possession of which was contested, must remain in the state in which they were before the armistice began. Any infringement by either party of the conditions of the truce entitles the other to recommence hostile operations without previous intimation.

ARMOIRE, the French name (cf. ALMERY) given to a tall movable cupboard, or "wardrobe," with one or more doors. It has varied considerably in shape and size, and the decoration of its doors and sides has faithfully represented mutations of fashion and modifications of use. It was originally exceedingly massive and found its chief decoration in elaborate hinges and locks of beaten iron. The finer ecclesiastical armoires or aumbries which have come down to us—used in churches for the safe custody of vestments, eucharistic vessels, reliquaries and other precious objects—are usually painted, sometimes even upon the interior, with sacred subjects or with incidents from the lives of the saints. The cathedrals of Bayeux and Noyon contain famous examples; the most typical English one is in York minster. By the end of the 14th century, when the carpenter and the wood-carver had acquired a better mastery of their material, the taste for painted surfaces appears to have given place to the vogue of carving, and the simple rectangular panels gradually became sculptured with a simple motive, such as the linen-fold or parchment patterns. In the treasury of St Germain l'Auxerrois the ends of the 15th-century armoires are treated in this way. In that and the two following centuries the keys and the escutcheons of the locks became highly ornamental; usually in forged iron, they were occasionally made of more precious metals. By slow degrees the shape of this receptacle changed—from breadth was evolved height, and the tall form of armoire became characteristic. The Renaissance exercised a notable effect upon this, as upon so many other varieties of furniture. It became less obviously and aggressively a thing of utility; its proportions shrank from the massive to the elegant; its artistic effectiveness was vastly enhanced by its division into an upper and a lower part. Enriched with columns and pilasters, its panels carved with mythology, its canopied niches filled with sculptured statuettes, and terminating with a rich cornice and perhaps a broken pediment, it was widely removed in appearance, if not in purpose, from the uncompromising iron-mounted receptacle of earlier generations. During the 16th century, when the surging impulses of the Renaissance had died away, the armoire relapsed into plainness, its proportions increased, and it was again constructed in one piece. Ere long, however, it grew more sumptuous than ever. Boulle encrusted it with marqueterie from designs by Bérain; it glowed with *amorini*, with the torches and arrows of Cupid, with the garlands which he weaves for his captives, and when allusiveness left a corner vacant, it was filled with arabesques in ebony or ivory, in brass or white metal. While the royal palaces and the hôtels of the great nobility were filled with those costly splendours, the ordinary cabinetmaker continued to construct his modest pieces, and by the middle of the 18th century the armoire was found in every French house, ample in width and high in proportion to the lofty rooms of the period. It is not to be supposed that so useful a piece of furniture was confined to France. It was used, more or less, throughout a considerable part of Europe, but it was distinctively Gallic nevertheless, and never became thoroughly acclimatized elsewhere until about the beginning of the 19th century, when it developed into the glass-fronted wardrobe which is now an essential detail in the plenishing of the bed-chamber, not merely in France and England, but in many other countries. The *armoire à glace* was known and occasionally made in France as far back as the middle of the 18th century, and almost the earliest mention of it connects it with the scandalous relations of the Maréchal de Richelieu and the beautiful *fermière générale*, Mme de la Popelinière, who had one made to mask a secret door. In the conventional and not very attractive wardrobe of commerce it is difficult to descry the gracious characteristics of the armoire of the Renaissance or the 17th century, and it is not altogether surprising that Théodore de Banville should have condemned one of the most solidly useful of household necessaries as a "hideous monster."

ARMORICA (AREMORICA), the Roman name, derived from two Celtic words meaning the "seaside" (*ar*, on, and *mor*, sea), for the land of the Armorici, roughly the peninsula of Brittany. At the time of the Roman advance on Gaul there were five principal tribes in Armorica, the Namneti, the Veneti, the Osismii, the Curiosolitae and the Redones. It was subdued by Caesar, who entirely destroyed the seafaring tribe of its south coast, the Veneti. Under the Empire it formed part of the province of Gallia Lugudunensis (Lugdunensis). It contained hardly any towns, though many large country houses, and was perhaps less Romanized than the rest of Gaul. In and after the later part of the 5th century it received many Celtic immigrants from the British Isles, fleeing (it is said) from the Saxons; and the Celtic dialect which the Bretons still speak is thought to owe its origin to these immigrants. (See further BRITTANY.)

ARMOUR, PHILIP DANFORTH (1832-1901), American merchant and philanthropist, was born in Stockbridge, New York, on the 16th of May 1832. He was educated at Cazenovia Academy, Cazenovia, N.Y., worked for several years on his father's farm, and in 1852 with a small party went overland to California, a large part of the journey being made on foot. Here during the next four years he laid the foundations of his fortune. In 1856 he became associated with his friend, Frederick S. Miles, in a wholesale grocery and commission business at Milwaukee. In 1863 he became the head of the firm of Armour, Plankington & Co., pork packers, whose headquarters were at Milwaukee. He also obtained a large interest in the firm H.O. Armour & Co., which was founded by his brother, Herman Ossian Armour (1837-1901), and which, starting as a grain commission business, in 1868 established also a large pork-packing plant. Of this firm, the name of which was changed to Armour & Co. in 1870, he became the head in 1875, and thereafter the business made such rapid progress that in 1901 as many as 11,000 hands were employed. Besides contributing to many charitable enterprises, Armour founded the Armour Institute of Technology at Chicago in 1892 and the Armour Flats in Chicago, built for the purpose of supplying at a low rental good homes for working men and their families. He also contributed liberally to the Armour Mission in Chicago, which was founded in 1881 by his brother, Joseph Armour. At the time of his death, on the 6th of January 1901, Philip D. Armour's private fortune was supposed to exceed $50,000,000.

www.ingramcontent.com/pod-product-compliance
Lightning Source LLC
Chambersburg PA
CBHW070107290526
45789CB00005B/1958